THE MIDDLE STONE AGE OF ZAMBIA, SOUTH CENTRAL AFRICA

Lawrence Barham

With contributions by

Peter Andrews, Margaret Avery, Laura Bishop, Kathryn Cruz-Uribe, Paul Davies,
Nick Debenham, Mabs Gilmour, Andrew Goudie, Fred Grine, Emma Jenkins,
Richard Klein, Marco Madella, Osbjorn Pearson, Ana Pinto, Sally Reynolds,
Mike Simms, Stephen Stokes, Chris Stringer, and Tim Young

Published for CHERUB, the Centre for Human Evolutionary Research
at the University of Bristol
by the Western Academic & Specialist Press Limited

Published by Western Academic & Specialist Press Limited
Bristol, England
www.waspress.co.uk

ISBN 0 9535418 6 X

Typeset in Plantin Light by Exe Valley Dataset, Exeter
Printed and bound in the UK by Short Run Press Ltd, Bittern Road, Exeter

Contents

CONTENTS

Figures

Tables

Notes on contributors

Peter Andrews worked first in the forestry department in Kenya before studying Anthropology at Cambridge University. He worked with Louis Leakey in Kenya, first as his research assistant and then under his supervision on his PhD studying fossil apes from the early Miocene of Kenya. In 1974 he returned to England to take up a position at the Natural History Museum. He is Professor at University College, London, Erasmus Professor in Spain, former editor of the *Journal of Human Evolution* and Trustee of several anthropological trusts. His main fields of research are primate evolution, taphonomy and palaeoecology.

Margaret Avery is currently Head of the Division of Earth Sciences at the South African Museum in Cape Town, South Africa. Her research interest is in the application of environmental information from micro-mammals to a range of topics from human evolution to palaeoenvironmental and climate change to monitoring environmental degradation.

Larry Barham is Lecturer in Archaeology at the University of Bristol, England, and received his PhD from the University of Pennsylvania (1989). Since 1993 he has been directing excavations in Zambia at the sites of Mumbwa Caves and Twin Rivers. He is Director of the Centre for Human Evolutionary Research at the University of Bristol (CHERUB).

Laura Bishop is Senior Lecturer in Palaeoanthropology at Liverpool John Moores University. She received a PhD in Anthropology from Yale University in 1994. Her current research investigates hominid palaeoecology at African Pliocene and Pleistocene sites, particularly at Kanjera in western Kenya.

Kathryn Cruz-Uribe is Professor of Anthropology at Northern Arizona University. She has analysed numerous faunal samples from African archaeological sites.

Paul Davies is Senior Lecturer in Environmental Science at Bath Spa University College, England, and specialises in molluscan palaeoecology, being particularly interested in small-scale biogeography and the use of modern analogue studies in interpreting fossil assemblages. He has general interests in environmental archaeology, the archaeology of natural places and river and wetland histories.

Nick Debenham is a freelance scientific consultant specialising in archaeological and geological applications of thermoluminescence (TL) dating. He gained his doctorate in physics at Imperial College, London, and joined the Research Laboratory for Archaeology and History of Art in 1978 to work on the TL dating of stalagmitic calcite and sedimentary deposits. From 1985 he worked at the British Museum Department of Scientific Research, applying TL techniques to a variety of heated and unheated archaeological materials. He moved to Nottingham in 1993 to set up Quaternary TL Surveys.

Mabs Gilmour is an isotope geochemist in the Department of Earth Sciences at the Open University. Her current research includes u-series disequilibrium of carbonates in palaeoclimate and archaeological studies and molecular level carbon isotope studies of metabolites and photosymbiosis.

Andrew Goudie is Professor of Geography in the School of Geography and the Environment at the University of Oxford. He has worked extensively in Africa, the Middle East and India and his main interests are in geomorphology.

Fred Grine is Professor in the Departments of Anthropology and Anatomical Sciences at the State University of New York at Stony Brook. He earned his PhD from the University of the Witwatersrand in 1984. His research interests include dental anthropology in all phases of human evolution. His recent field projects include the excavation of the South African MSA site of Die Kelders.

Emma Jenkins is a PhD student at Cambridge University and is researching the use of microfaunal remains to reconstruct aspects of the natural and cultural environment at Neolithic sites in Turkey. She took part in the excavations at Mumbwa Caves in 1995.

Richard Klein lectures on human evolution at Stanford University. He is particularly interested in the co-evolution of human behaviour and human anatomy.

Marco Madella was awarded a MSc (Laurea) in Natural Sciences from the University of Milan (1989) and a PhD in Archaeobotany from the University of Cambridge in 2000. He is currently a senior research associate at the Macdonald Institute for Archaeological Research. Research interests include palaeoenvironments and palaeoeconomies in the Mediterranean and sub-tropics of the Old World.

Osbjorn Pearson received his PhD from the State University of New York at Stony Brook (1997) and is an Assistant Professor in the Department of Anthropology at the University of New Mexico. His research interests include the origin of modern humans and the functional adaptations of bones to habitual activity.

Ana C Pinto is a doctoral candidate at the Universidad de Oviedo (Asturias, Spain) and is currently working at the Natural History Museum, London, on palaeo-ecological research that involves taphonomic, dietary and pathological issues. Her interests include the surface alteration of bone and its interpretation.

Sally Reynolds is currently a PhD student at Liverpool John Moores University comparing taxa from east and southern African Plio-Pleistocene sites. Research interests include African palaeoenvironments, taphonomy, site formation and archaeology.

Mike Simms is Curator of Palaeontology at the Ulster Museum, Belfast. He read Geology with Zoology at Bristol University, with a PhD subsequently from Birmingham University, and has published on diverse subjects including fossil crinoids, Mesozoic palaeo-environments, and cave and karst geomorphology. His current research focus is the post-Palaeozoic evolution of the Irish landscape.

Stephen Stokes is Reader in Quaternary Environmental Change at the School of Geography and the Environment, University of Oxford. Research involves the development and application of luminescence dating methods as applied to low latitude environmental responses to Quaternary climatic cycles, aeolian sediment systems and to the Middle Palaeolithic archaeology of North Africa.

Chris Stringer is a Visiting Professor in the Department of Geography at Royal Holloway, and has worked in the Palaeontology Department of the Natural History Museum, London, for over 25 years. He is best known for his work on the "Out of Africa" theory concerning the global development of *Homo sapiens*. This has involved collaboration with archaeologists, dating specialists and geneticists in their attempts at reconstructing the evolution of modern humans. He has directed or co-directed excavations at sites in England, Wales and Turkey and currently leads the Gibraltar Caves Project, which is studying Neanderthal occupation of the region.

Tim Young is a geoarchaeological consultant on iron ores and slags, and part-time lecturer at Cardiff and Swansea Universities. His research interests include the geological origins of iron oxides (he served on the International Committee of IGCP Project 277 "Phanerozoic Oolitic Ironstones") and the development of ancient iron smelting technology.

Acknowledgement and dedication

L Barham

The LSB Leakey Foundation, the British Academy, the National Geographic Society, the Prehistoric Society and the Natural Environment Research Council (NERC) funded the research at Mumbwa Caves. The National Heritage Conservation Commission (NHCC) provided invaluable logistical support in the field in Zambia, along with the Livingstone Museum and the British Council (1995 season). Nicholoas Katanekwa and Donald Chikumbi of the NHCC deserve special thanks for their unflagging encouragement and practical guidance. Chief Mumba gave generously of his time and knowledge in helping to reconstruct the recent history of the caves. To the many student volunteers who took part in the excavations along with Zambian colleagues I owe you a debt of gratitude. Ken Bailey kindly identified the rocks and minerals from the Mumbwa region and Ed Pollard undertook the geological mapping. I am grateful to Sam Smith and Andy Clark not only for their diligent supervision of the excavations but also for their friendships. I thank Bristol University's Archaeology Department in the person of Richard Harrison for its ongoing support.

The LSB Leakey Foundation funded the excavations at Twin Rivers in 1999. Patrick and Stella Roberts unselfishly shared their farm and lives with us. Without them the excavations at Twin Rivers would not have been possible. Lake Patrick is named in their honour. Chris Hawkesworth was instrumental in arranging the uranium-series dating of the site.

My research has benefited greatly from the advice and encouragement of several key individuals. Desmond Clark has supported my efforts from the start for which I am grateful. He graciously gave unhindered access to the Twin Rivers collection curated in Berkeley and shared his deep knowledge of the Middle Stone Age. Hilary Deacon pointed me in the direction of Zambia in the first instance for which I will always be in his debt. Sally McBrearty, Alison Brooks and Patrick Quinney provided much valued intellectual stimulation. Peter Mitchell read a draft of this manuscript with great care and his comments have saved me from some embarrassment as well as improving the content. Thank you. Any factual errors, omissions and misreading of data are my responsibility.

The superb quality and clarity of the artwork is the work of Sue Grice and Joanna Richards. J Richards retains copyright on all images of flaked stone pieces in chapters 2, 10 and appendix 7. I am grateful to you both.

Finally, this book is dedicated to Mary who suffered the most from start to finish.

Foreword

Zambians have good reason to be proud of their heritage. It is one of the world's most ancient and one which has borne a long testimony to human development over millions of years. Thanks to the pioneering work of renowned archaeologists from the very beginnings of the last century and to some outstanding current work, we have now revealed a picture of world class importance. One milestone was the discovery in 1921 at Kabwe (Broken Hill) of the skull of *Homo rhodesiensis*, which established a likely link between premodern humans and the Middle Stone Age. Excavations in the 1920s and 1930s at Mumbwa Caves and around Victoria Falls demonstrated that there had been a long succession of prehistoric cultures in Zambia right to recent times. Six National Monuments ranging from the Early to Later Stone Age bear witness to this at the Victoria Falls World Heritage site. Key figures in this voyage of discovering Zambia's ancient heritage include Professor J Desmond Clark. His large scale excavations at Kalambo Falls and application of scientific analysis to resolving archaeological issues were not only ground breaking but created the foundations for Stone Age research in the region. Drs Laurel and David Phillipson extended the coverage of the Middle Stone Age to Western and Eastern Zambia respectively.

The renewed excavations at Mumbwa Caves and Twin Rivers by Larry Barham are the subjects of this book and the results give further and very revealing insights into this period of the Zambian past. Dr Barham's work builds on the legacy of the early pioneers and shows that Zambian prehistory still has much to tell. The broad range of specialists who have contributed to this volume reflects the close links that now exist between earth sciences and the study of mankind's development. One key feature of this new research has been to show how climate change has affected human prehistory. It certainly helps to learn how our ancestors responded to climate change and its impact on the landscape over 300,000 years ago. This information comes at a time when we must look at our contemporary climate and judge whether we must change our behaviour.

To scholars and Heritage Managers alike this book will prove very valuable. Our challenge now is to build on this emerging evidence by training new people to carry on the work and extend it into further corners of our large nation, as has happened with the archaeology of the Iron Age of Zambia. We would also encourage outside scholars to train local Zambians whilst contributing to international understanding of the story of human kind.

Finally, this work should not be the end of the story, but one more chapter in the richly woven tale that is the history of Zambia.

Nicholas M Katanekwa

Executive Director
National Heritage Conservation
Commission, Zambia

Preface and overview

L Barham

The nation state of Zambia lies at the geographical crossroads between southern, eastern and central Africa (fig. 0.1). Its fauna and flora contain elements of all three regions and together they offer a mosaic of opportunities for mobile human foragers to make a living. The modern mosaic has not been static. Orbital forcing of climate during the 400,000 years covered in this study has altered the biogeography of south central Africa with a periodicity linked to global glacial–interglacial cycles. As the distribution of plants and animals and the availability of surface water have changed, so have available resources for foragers. More than 20 years of palaeoecological research have demonstrated a firm link between global glacial periods and increased aridity in the African tropics. The geomorphological record of south central Africa preserves evidence of dramatic changes in the landscape with the expansion of the Mega Kalahari during glacials and stadials. The regularity of glacial cycles offers an analytical framework with which to assess long-term changes in the human capacity to respond to environmental stimuli. The responses may have been demographic, technological and social but they were also both behavioural and biological.

The phenotype is the interface between mind and body and produces the archaeological record. Anatomically modern humans had evolved by the outset of the Late Pleistocene (130 ka BP) in southern Africa. In Chapter 9, newly recovered hominid remains from Mumbwa Caves in central Zambia receive their first detailed examination and comparative assessment. Features of biological modernity were present in the Mumbwa material now dated to late in the Last Interglacial (~170 ka BP). The timing of the emergence of behavioural modernity is less clear, partly because the concept remains poorly defined or lacks consensus and partly because of gaps in the archaeological record of the Middle Pleistocene. In this study, behavioural modernity will remain undefined until the archaeological data has been reviewed (chapters 8,10,13). The separation of data from interpretation lends an air of objectivity that owes much to the scientific approach espoused by processual archaeologists of the 1960s. Convention plays a role too. Seeking objectivity is an ideal, and arguably a misguided one, but in striving to distinguish fact from imposed fiction personal biases emerge for the reader (and author) to assess.

Zambia is the geographical focus of this study but the scope of the analysis extends from southern Tanzania in the east to central Angola in the west and from northern Mozambique in the south to the southern third of the Democratic Republic of Congo (ex-Zaire) in the north. South central Africa as circumscribed here corresponds to the current distribution of deciduous woodland savannas on the high plateau that forms the watershed between the Congo and Zambezi rivers (fig. 0.1). The Zambezian ecozone incorporates the greatest diversity of plants and large mammals in southern Africa (chapter 12) and straddles the southern tropics from 5–17°S with an extension into the highlands of Zimbabwe. The linkage of the archaeological record with a modern biome serves two purposes. It gives the book a distinctive biogeographical focus, but more importantly provides an analytical tool for assessing the human response to habitat change over time. The rhythmic oscillation of glacials and interglacials has altered profoundly the distribution and structure of plant and animal communities across the region. Human foragers faced the sustained loss of woodland habitats with the glacial phase expansion of the Mega Kalahari north into the Congo basin and eastwards onto the Zambian plateau. The terrestrial, lacustrine and marine records for habitat change are reviewed in chapter 12. In the context of shifting resources, foragers made choices about where to live and how to organise their social lives. The technology for extracting energy and protein from the environment played a role in these decisions. Just how large a role is unknowable and this highlights the overriding frustration of Middle and Late Pleistocene research in the region.

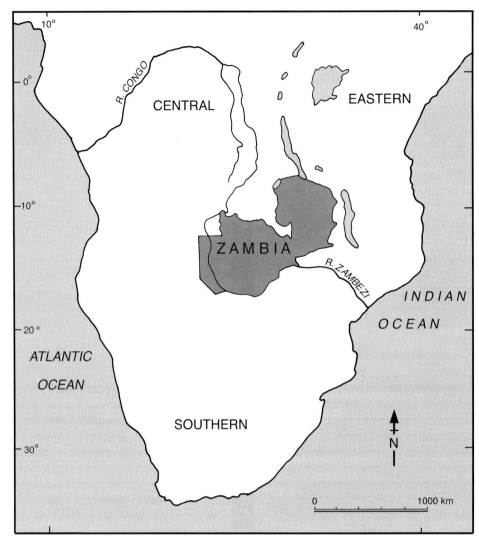

Figure 0.1 Location of Zambia in relation to eastern, central and southern Africa.

The limitations and gaps in the archaeological record of south central Africa are formidable from the perspective of the current research agendas that have proved so productive in the interpretation of later prehistoric periods (post 20,000 BP) in southern Africa. Issues of gender relations, acculturation and the primacy of image based belief systems (art) in the structuring of social lives have not been and probably can never be adequately addressed for much of the period discussed here. Fundamental problems remain with the database for south central Africa including inadequate chronological controls, limited intra and intersite spatial data, poor preservation of organic remains and simply too few archaeologists working in the region. The latter is discussed in chapter 1 in the context of the relatively long but sporadic history of research in the region. A basic techno-typological sequence based on a sound chronology is still to be constructed for the region and without that framework the more intellectually challenging issues about the internal dynamics of forager societies cannot begin to be addressed.

This study perforce resembles an extended site report placed in a broader regional context. The two Zambian sites that form the core of the data discussed, Mumbwa Caves and Twin Rivers, were most recently excavated between 1993 and 1996, and in 1999. The excavations were undertaken with the objective of building a culture-stratigraphic sequence for central Zambia that might be applied further afield. New dating techniques developed since the early 1980s enabled the archaeological record of these two sites to be extended beyond the radiocarbon barrier of 40 ka. The eight metres of deposit at Mumbwa Caves contained a sequence of intermittent occupation spanning the last 170 ka BP and Twin Rivers extended the Middle Pleistocene coverage with dates from 170 to greater than 400 ka BP (chapters 3,10). Together, the two sites provide a full archaeological sequence for central Zambia. The assumption is made that the general sequence of technological change seen at these two sites and elsewhere in Zambia is representative of south central Africa as a whole. The culture-stratigraphic sequence first developed for the region in the 1940s can now be expanded and fuller comparisons made with sequences south of the Zambezi and in east Africa (chapter 13).

The limestone caves of the central plateau of Zambia provide rare environments for the preservation of bone and other organic remains. Both Mumbwa Caves and Twin Rivers contain assemblages of fragmentary mammal remains (chapters 4,11) from which some inferences are drawn about local habitats and the role of meat in the diet of the human occupants. The assemblages of larger mammals are small, but provide the basis for future research involving isotopic methods of dietary and habitat analysis. An even smaller assemblage of human remains was found at Mumbwa Caves from which broader regional and continental comparisons are made (chapter 9). A single fragment of human bone was recovered from Twin Rivers and is described briefly in conjunction with the fauna from the site. The sample of microfauna recovered from the Mumbwa and Twin River sequences provides a nearly continuous record of changes in local habitats from the Middle Pleistocene to the historic present. Evidence for climate change at the regional scale emerges from this analysis and is integrated with other climatic indicators to show alternating wet and dry conditions linked to interglacial–glacial pulses. The microfaunal record from Zambia is unique for central Africa, as is the taphonomic analysis that accompanies the report (chapters 5, 6). Also a first for the region is the phytolith analysis from the Mumbwa sediments which is used in the reconstruction of the palaeoecology of the vicinity and of the plant species introduced by humans (chapter 7).

The new data emerging from Zambia shows that south central Africa has much to offer palaeoanthropology despite the limitations of the archaeological record. The excavations at Mumbwa and Twin Rivers will fuel ongoing debates about the role of sub-Saharan Africa in the evolution of anatomically and behaviourally modern humans. In particular, climate change is often invoked as the *deus ex machina* of speciation, innovation and dispersal without detailed consideration of the close links between plant, animal and human communities. A model is offered which ties together orbitally driven changes in biogeography with demographic and technological changes in the archaeological record of central Africa (chapter 12). The first regionally distinctive industry – the Lupemban – may have developed during the long interglacial of Stage 11 (423–362 ka BP) or at least by 270 ka BP (Stage 9) as conservatively dated at Twin Rivers. The Lupemban with its characteristic lanceolate bifaces is restricted in distribution to central Africa and arguably marks the development of identity conscious social groups with a common linguistic heritage (chapter 13). The Middle Stone Age of south central and central Africa thereafter retained an identity apart from regional trends seen elsewhere in sub-Saharan Africa. The roots of behavioural modernity appear to lie in the Middle Pleistocene with central Africa playing a formative role in the evolutionary process.

The hypotheses offered in this study will fall by the wayside in due course as new questions are asked of the existing record and as new data comes to light through fieldwork. If this volume has the effect of reviving research in the archaeology of south central Africa then the effort will have been well worthwhile.

1 Zambia in context

L Barham

Modern political boundaries have no meaning in the context of the early prehistory of Africa but they do affect the practice of archaeological field research on the ground. Research in Zambia, as in central Africa, has passed through a series of developmental stages from which the starting point was colonisation by Europeans in the nineteenth century. The division of the region by colonial powers left a legacy of differing intellectual approaches to archaeological research that has lingered into the present along with the international borders. Stone Age studies dominated the colonial era with the recent historic past largely marginalised for political purposes (Robertshaw 1990:4) and as a result of the European fascination with human origins. Zambia (northern Rhodesia) played an early and significant role in this period of research. On independence in the 1960s, the imbalance in research was redressed and the archaeology of indigenous farming communities came to the fore as new nations constructed new identities. Among prehistorians, interest in human origins continued to gather pace and the Later Stone Age, with its links to rock art and extant hunter-gatherers, attracted renewed interest. The Middle Stone Age as defined in the 1920s (Goodwin & van Riet Lowe 1929) was the neglected period in the Stone Age framework and remained so until the 1970s. Just as the Middle Stone Age began to receive international recognition as the temporal equivalent of the European Middle Palaeolithic (Clark 1975), research in Zambia was nearing an end (DW Phillipson 1976; L Phillipson 1978). A long interval followed, for reasons described below, until the resumption of excavations at Mumbwa Caves in 1993. In the intervening years, the Middle Stone Age emerged as the testing ground for the theory of a recent African origin for behaviourally modern humans (Stringer & Andrews 1988; Deacon 1992).

Archaeological research in central and southern Africa began in the late nineteenth century at a time when Palaeolithic archaeologists were formulating typologies and relative chronologies. The still new theories of biological and social evolution drove the intellectual exercise of collecting and ordering stone tools into developmental sequences. In colonial Africa, collections of stone artefacts were made initially by engineers,

administrators, geologists and other interested amateurs associated with the consolidation of the colonial infra-structure. At the outset of this pioneer phase (Clark 1990), the recent African past was assumed to have little time depth, a matter of a few hundreds of years at best for farming communities but longer for the preceding Stone Ages. The identification of the African Stone Age as a separate entity from the recent prehistory of indigenous farmers and pastoralists enabled early colonial administrators and settlers effectively to ignore or denigrate the history of those they had conquered (Robertshaw 1990:4). A notable exception was the recognition in the Belgian Congo that the complexity of iron working by indigenous peoples indicated some antiquity for this craft (De Maret 1990:113). In the absence of stratigraphic excavations and direct means of dating, the time depth of the African past was left to speculation. The Stone Age could be placed in existing evolutionary frameworks that gave Europe primacy and put Africa in the passive role of the recipient of innovations by diffusion. The existence of hunter-gatherers in the Congo basin and in the interior of southern Africa was used to support nineteenth-century ideas of social evolution that placed Europeans at the pinnacle of progress (Trigger 1990).

After the First World War, south central Africa was divided between Britain (Northern Rhodesia, Nyasaland), Portugal (Angola, Mozambique), Belgium (Belgian Congo) and France (French Equatorial Africa). Belgium with its single colony invested proportionally more effort in unravelling the prehistory of the region than the other colonial powers (De Maret 1990). The result was an early synthesis of the Stone Age sequence based on systematic excavations. Colette's (1935) excavations at Kalina Point, Léopoldville (Kinshasa) in the mid-1920s established a culture-stratigraphic sequence for the southern Congo basin and one that employed a local terminology rather than transplanted European Palaeolithic labels. The sequence, deposited in deep Kalahari sands, contained from base to surface recognisable aggregates of artefacts, each distinguished from its predecessor by a progressive refinement in technology. The sequence of named phases – Kalinian, Djokocian, and Ndolian – persisted through the 1970s when the site was re-excavated and the integrity of the aggregates was questioned on taphonomic grounds (Cahen & Moeyersons 1977). In the interim, sub-phases were recognised and the scheme was greatly expanded, in particular by Breuil (1944) who defined a Lupemban phase of the Djokocian. The Lupemban was and remains a distinctive industry of the Middle Stone Age of central Africa with a blend of small flake and blade tools and large finely flaked bifacial lanceolates (chapters 10,13). The southern Congo basin sequence as a whole is largely post-Acheulian in age.

In South Africa, an early synthesis of the Stone Age by Péringuey (1911), an entomologist, combined European and local names to create a mixed terminology. The result was a synthesis based on style or typology rather than stratigraphy. The arrival in the 1920s of the first academically trained archaeologist, AJ Goodwin, introduced much needed rigour to the ordering of the Stone Age. Goodwin, South African by birth and Cambridge trained (Deacon 1990), worked closely with C van Riet Lowe, a civil engineer with archaeological experience. Together, they produced a new classification scheme for the region based on typological comparisons and the then rare evidence from excavated sequences. The result was a tripartite division of the Stone Age into an Earlier, Middle and Later Stone Age (Goodwin & van Riet Lowe 1929). The terminology owed nothing to the European Palaeolithic other than the concept of progressive stages. Regional

variants were added and named after type localities. In keeping with the diffusionist thinking of the time, Goodwin and van Riet Lowe attributed changes in the Stone Age sequence to outside influences, in particular to migrations from Europe. Africa was the recipient and not the innovator.

The basic divisions recognised by Goodwin and van Riet Lowe are still used, though as a general descriptive shorthand rather than as clearly demarcated chronostratigraphic stages. The Middle Stone Age was defined by the absence of large cutting tools, cleavers and handaxes, the use of prepared core technology and tools made on flakes. This basic technological definition is retained here, but with the recognition that prepared core and even blade technology was already an established component of the Early Stone Age. The primary difference between the two stages lies in a shift in emphasis toward the greater use of composite or hafted tool technology (Clark 1992). The loss of large cutting tools reflects that shift.

BROKEN HILL AND MUMBWA CAVES

Goodwin returned to South Africa soon after the discovery in 1921 of a hominid skull and other human remains in a cave exposed during zinc mining at Broken Hill (Kabwe), northern Rhodesia (Zambia) (fig. 1.1). The Broken Hill skull attracted considerable attention because of its combination of a large, modern-sized brain (1280 cc) with heavy archaic browridges (Pycraft et al

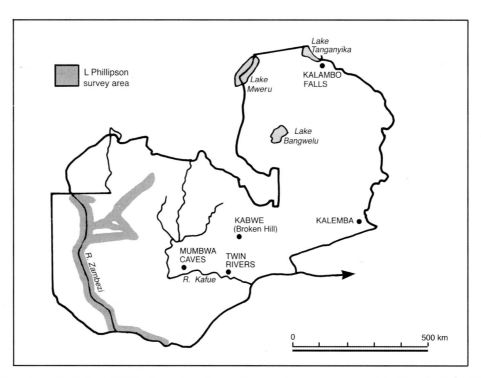

Figure 1.1 Location of principal Middle Stone Age sites and research areas investigated in Zambia from 1926 to 1999.

1928). The mining operation exposed a cave system containing well preserved large and small fauna of extant species. A modern fauna in association with an archaic hominid, *Homo rhodesiensis*, fuelled preconceptions that human evolution in Africa lagged behind that in Europe. This frankly racist view could still be found in texts of the 1950s:

Indeed, it seems that *Homo rhodesiensis* reveals to us the persistence in Africa of a human type, long since become fossil in France. . . . We are thus led to think that he must have survived for a long time in the Dark Continent, as the last representative of a very ancient human form, now obsolete, in the midst of modern black races, several of whom are themselves archaic in type and on the point of extermination.

(Boule & Vallois 1957:455)

Stone and possible bone tools were also found at Broken Hill and have been variously attributed to the late Acheulian or an early Middle Stone Age variant called the Sangoan (Clark et al 1947; Howell & Clark 1963).

The discovery of Broken Hill brought northern Rhodesia to the attention of the archaeological world. The first controlled excavations were undertaken in 1925 by FB Macrae, a District Commissioner in the colonial administration who had been given a brief background in archaeology by Miles Burkitt at Cambridge before being posted to Africa (Clark 1994:5). Macrae (1926) investigated a large dolomite outcrop near the township of Mumbwa, about 130 miles (217 km) west of Broken Hill, that contained sediment-filled cave passages. An entrance was explored with a trench that reached a depth of 10 feet (3 m). Microlithic tools were found in the first foot (30 cm) and Macrae compared them to the Azilian of the Pyrenees. Beneath were found Solutrean-like laurel leaf points and lower down large heavy tools comparable to the *coup-de-poings* of the Acheulian. The use of European terminology to describe the Mumbwa Caves sequence reflected the still pioneering stage of African archaeology in the 1920s.

The apparent discovery of an African Acheulian phase at Mumbwa attracted the attention of an international team led by Commander A Gatti. The team benefited from the surveying skills of N del Grande and the anatomical expertise of R Dart, who in 1924 had announced the discovery of a distant human ancestor in *Australopithecus africanus* to an incredulous scientific establishment. The Italian Scientific Expedition approached the excavation of Mumbwa with the objective of establishing the true parentage of the Acheulian and its successors (Dart & Del Grande 1931:27–8). Were they ultimately of European or African origin? The terraces of the Vaal river in South Africa were already known for their handaxes found in stratigraphic contexts that were comparable to the terrace sequences of the Thames, the Seine and other rivers in northern Europe. Mumbwa Caves offered a rare stratified context with

which to explore the full succession of palaeolithic cultures from the Acheulian onwards. The extent of European influence on the Stone Ages of Africa could now be examined.

Two entrances were selected for investigation, the largest of which was extensively excavated with a deep trench that struck bedrock 25 feet (8 m) below the entrance surface. A sequence of seven culture-stratigraphic units was defined with a basal 'Old Palaeolithic' stratum overlain by sterile red clay and then a 'Mousterian' unit separated by a stone line from the 'Furnace Stratum' and 'Solid Ash' layer that was succeeded by a 'Pure Stone Culture'. An 'Iron Arrowheads' stratum topped the sequence. Fragmented animal bone was found throughout the sequence but only three disc cores or choppers and eight scrapers were recovered from the Old Palaeolithic stratum. The excavators were aware of Goodwin and van Riet Lowe's three age system, but chose not to apply the scheme. The Pure Stone Culture contained both Middle and Later Stone Age material (Dart & Del Grande 1931:388).

An unexpected discovery was made in the Furnace Stratum. Two beehive shaped stone enclosures had been built against the cave wall and on excavation contained fragmentary human remains. The tombs were and remain unique in the archaeological record of southern Africa. A lingering uncertainty still exists about the contemporaneity of the burials with the deposit. An intrusive origin from later periods of occupation cannot be dismissed (Clark 1992) (see chapter 8). In all, the remains of 16 individuals were recovered from the five main strata including the Furnace Stratum. Dart and Del Grande (1931: 390) believed that the cave itself with its natural through-draft from east to west had been used as a furnace for smelting iron. Large blocks of apparently burnt refuse containing stone, ash and clay lay outside the cave entrance. Oval features within the cave defined by burnt limestone blocks were recognised as individual smelting areas. It seemed that Later Stone Age peoples had learned the craft of smelting from incoming iron-workers. Diffusionism once again underlay culture change.

JD Clark was the first professionally trained archaeologist to be resident in northern Rhodesia. Clark arrived from England in 1937 to be curator of the newly founded David Livingstone Memorial Museum and secretary for the Rhodes-Livingstone Institute for Social Anthropology (Clark 1994). Between 1937 and 1960, when he left for the University of California at Berkeley, Clark transformed the archaeology of this colony. He knitted together a culture-stratigraphic framework for the Stone Age based on meticulous excavations combined with an encyclopaedic knowledge of sites and sequences. Clark also introduced an ecological approach to explaining cultural variability and change and integrated the natural sciences (and scientists) into his excavations and reports. Mumbwa Caves was his first project as a newly arrived and inexperienced archaeologist. The report on Mumbwa bore the hallmarks of an integrated approach to archaeology in which Clark treated archaeology as an historical science with particularly close links to the biological and earth sciences. In a contribution on the geology of the site, F Zeuner (in Clark 1942:149–153) demonstrated convincingly that the 'furnace slag' reported in 1930 was in fact the natural dolomite of the cave that had simply weathered. Zeuner also produced an outline of the climatic sequence at Mumbwa, with the sterile red clay attributed to dry aeolian conditions and the overlying Middle Stone Age occupation to a seasonally wet and dry climate similar to today. The most recent excavations at Mumbwa have since confirmed his climatic inferences.

Clark approached Mumbwa with the objective of reclassifying the upper Stone Age assemblages using the current terminology of Goodwin and van Riet Lowe (Clark 1942:138). He had seen in the collection deposited by Dart and Del Grande at the Livingstone Museum evidence for regional facies of the Middle and Later Stone Ages. This now well known cave site warranted a thorough re-examination. Clark placed trenches near the two entrances previously investigated in 1925 and 1930. A single season of excavation in 1939 provided sufficient data to make Mumbwa Caves the type site for the Northern Rhodesian Wilton industry of the Later Stone Age and to link definitively the Middle Stone Age assemblage with the Rhodesian Stillbay. The latter was recognised by bifacially flaked points and the predominance of flakes from prepared cores. A small percentage of the Rhodesian Stillbay retouched tool category comprised crescent shaped backed blades and flakes. The discovery of the latter at Mumbwa Caves strengthened the cultural connection with Rhodesia. The large size of the Stillbay crescents distinguished them from the small, refined Later Stone Age counterparts. These and other basic differences led Clark to propose an intermediate archaeological culture as the origin of the Wilton because no real continuity could be demonstrated between the Stillbay and Wilton. The parent source was located to the north in the Wilton culture of Kenya (ibid:193) from which a gradual southward migration of 'an incoming small race of Bush stock' led to technological and presumably biological hybridisation with indigenous populations. The result was a new industry, the Magosian, which combined prepared core technology with microlithic technology. Strangely, the Magosian was absent from Mumbwa so the Wilton here was interpreted as an early stage in the southward migration and not fully expressed. In an appendix to the article, Clark reports that after having seen Kenya and Somali Wilton material first-hand during military service in East Africa, he was now of the opinion that this was simply a local variant of a culture that originated in North Africa and then spread southwards as well as into Europe.

Through the 1950s, explanations of culture change continued to be framed in terms of migrations of people, usually from north to south, and featured in the first synthesis of the Northern Rhodesian Stone Age (Clark 1950). A later overview of the prehistory of southern Africa (Clark 1959) retained diffusionism but introduced the foundations of ecologically based explanations of change that would prevail from the 1960s onwards. The widespread application of radiocarbon dating combined with changes in theoretical and methodological approaches linked to the New Archaeology would hasten the decline of the diffusionist paradigm.

INDEPENDENCE, DATING AND ENVIRONMENTAL CHANGE

The 20 years before 1980 brought profound political changes to sub-Saharan Africa with the independence of most states from colonial rule and the onset of long guerilla wars in Angola, southwest Africa (Namibia), Mozambique and Rhodesia. With independence came a redressing of the balance in archaeological research with the prehistory of farming and iron-using communities coming to the fore in south central Africa (De Maret 1990) and in southern Africa (Hall 1990). Archaeology as a discipline expanded during a brief period of economic prosperity in the 1960s with new appointments in academic and research institutions across southern Africa (Deacon 1990). New blood meant new ideas and new excavations. Much of the expansion came in the study of recent prehistory but Stone Age research benefited despite its taint by association with the old colonial agenda. A revolution in dating techniques made the Stone Age relevant to some emerging African nations. The advent of isotopic dating techniques pushed the Early Stone Age in east Africa to the limits of the Pleistocene, and subsequently into the Pliocene, and gave Africa pride of place in human evolution.

Middle Stone Age research also underwent a revolution in dating. In the *Prehistory of Africa* (Clark 1970: fig. 1), the Middle Stone Age of Zambia, like that elsewhere in sub-Saharan Africa, was considered to be no more than 35 ka BP and to have ended 15 ka BP with the Magosian transitional phase to the Later Stone Age. Modern humans, *Homo sapiens*, were the makers of the Middle Stone Age and they had replaced *Homo erectus*, who was equated with the Acheulian of the Early Stone Age. The replacement was perceived as relatively sudden 'which suggests that modern man evolved in some other part of the world' (ibid:120), probably the Near East. By comparison with Europe, the Middle Palaeolithic came

4

to an end just as the Middle Stone Age began. Africa was still out of step with Europe and oddly so with effectively the same technology made by Neanderthals now being produced in Africa by modern humans.

Shortly after this summary, new radiocarbon dates were reported from South Africa (Beaumont & Vogel 1972) for the end of the Middle Stone Age as found in deeply stratified cave sequences. The dates of 40–30 ka BP altered radically the time depth of the Middle Stone Age by placing it apparently beyond the range of radiocarbon dating. Chronological parity had now been achieved with the European Middle Palaeolithic (Clark 1975). The Later Stone Age became the chronological if not the technological equivalent of the Upper Palaeolithic and the product of anatomically modern humans. The hominid associated with the Middle Stone Age was now no longer a certainty. At the other end of the chronological spectrum, potassium-argon dates of 180 ka BP from central Ethiopia pushed the Middle Stone Age into the Middle Pleistocene (Wendorf et al 1975). Similar dates were emerging for the European sequence making the transition from Acheulian to prepared core technology nearly synchronous on the two continents.

The dating revolution transformed perceptions of the African Stone Age. From recipient of innovations, Africa was now the originator in the case of the Early Stone Age and an equal partner with Europe in the Middle Palaeolithic/Middle Stone Age transition. Since the 1970s, the accumulated weight of new dating evidence has highlighted the disparities rather than similarities between the two continents. The Middle Stone Age is now arguably older (chapter 13) and technologically more diverse than the Middle Palaeolithic (McBrearty 1999), and across much of sub-Saharan Africa flake and blade assemblages persist until almost 20 ka BP (Thackeray 1992). The Middle/Upper Palaeolithic transition of Europe has no direct parallels in sub-Saharan Africa. Behavioural and biological continuity characterise the sub-Saharan record and reflect a distinctly different evolutionary history from that of Europe. Goodwin and van Riet Lowe recognised the importance of assessing the African Stone Age as an independent entity. The development of isotopic dating techniques has revealed the extent to which Eurocentric biases have governed interpretations of the African archaeological record.

As radiocarbon dating made its impact felt in southern Africa, diffusionist models of cultural change came under scrutiny and were gradually abandoned. The rise of the New Archaeology in the 1960s hastened the process. The prevailing culture-historical approach of ordering cultures in space and time was challenged as static and ultimately unscientific in its empiricism. Greater methodological rigour was espoused as archaeology emulated the natural sciences by adopting deductive models of hypothesis testing in search of general laws of human behaviour. The effects were felt in Stone Age studies as a new generation of archaeologists refined the ecological approach to explaining variability and change that had emerged in Britain in the 1950s (Deacon 1990). The new rigour extended to excavation techniques, the quantification of data, spatial analyses, the use of ethnographic analogy and to the study of site formation processes (eg, Isaac 1972). This period of intellectual ferment produced lasting changes in the methodology and role of theory in Stone Age studies.

The integration of palaeoecology into African archaeology was already a well established part of the research agenda of Early Stone Age studies before the 1960s. Climatic and faunal correlations played an integral role in the relative dating of hominid sites in eastern and southern Africa (Cooke 1952). The long-held correlation between wetter (pluvial) conditions in Africa and glacial periods in Europe (Wayland 1929) unravelled under the weight of new geological, faunal and dating evidence. By the early 1960s, the revolution in absolute dating techniques had made its impact felt on climatic studies. In 1961, at a Wenner-Gren conference on African Ecology and Human Evolution (Howell & Bourlière 1963), De Heinzelin (1963: 287–89) integrated into the existing African database the recently reported marine core record of oxygen isotope stages and the Milankovitch model of orbitally governed cycles of climate change. An uneasy fit resulted, partly because of the limitations of the existing terrestrial record for the tropics and partly because of the legacy of the pluvial theory. The conference highlighted the need for greater integration between natural scientists and archaeologists and for more basic research on African biogeography, present and past.

As the New Archaeology emerged as an intellectual force in Anglo-American archaeology, the terminological scheme of Goodwin and van Riet Lowe came under critical scrutiny by Africanists. By the mid-1950s, the scheme had been expanded to include two transitional stages, the First and Second Intermediate, that bridged the Early/Middle Stone Age and the Middle/Later Stone Age. The creation of the intermediate stages recognised formally the widespread practice of applying the term Fauresmith to presumed late Acheulian assemblages with small handaxes and the term Magosian to assemblages with both Middle and Later Stone Age elements. Both terms originated from type sites, Fauresmith in South Africa and Magosi in Uganda, but gradually became shorthand descriptors used across sub-Saharan Africa. The Third Pan-African Congress in 1955 adopted the spatially neutral terminology of First and Second Intermediate (Clark & Cole 1957). These changes aside, the diffusionist culture-historical paradigm remained intact.

Ten years later further correctives were needed to restrict the continued uncritical application of terms far beyond type areas. At the 1965 Wenner-Gren conference on the Background to Evolution in Africa, the recommendation was made that regional correlations should be based on local sequences derived from individual sites and their deposits (Kleindienst 1967). A classification system was proposed that integrated archaeological data into a hierarchy of increasing abstraction from the minimal unit of stratigraphic significance within a site to industrial complexes on a regional scale (Clark et al 1966). Industrial complexes, it was argued, were the highest level of abstraction that should be used as the Stone Ages could no longer be considered clearly constrained periods of time or content. The concept of intermediate transitional phases was also challenged. The re-excavation of the Magosian type site (Cole 1967) confirmed growing suspicions (Hole 1959) that the assemblage was the product of mixed Middle and Later Stone Age deposits and not a meaningful entity. The First and Second Intermediate stages were abandoned in the absence of stratified, dated deposits. The concept of transitional stages also contained implicit assumptions about the process of technological change that had yet to be demonstrated.

The Wenner-Gren meeting took place at a time of growing awareness of the shortcomings of the culture-historical approach as an analytical framework (Trigger 1994). The intention of the participants was to improve the methodology rather than discard it, but in making changes to the classificatory scheme they exposed the weaknesses of the underlying theory. A willingness to consider change at the methodological level enabled some ideas of the New Archaeology to take hold with relative ease. Interdisciplinary research teams became the norm for tackling specific issues or regions. Palaeo-ecological reconstructions were recognised as the framework on which to mount questions of behavioural and biological change. The now commonplace intertwining of the natural and social sciences had its early practitioners in south central Africa.

KALAMBO FALLS

Two decades before the emergence of an explicitly scientific archaeology, researchers in sub-Saharan Africa had pioneered a new approach to excavation that emphasised the careful spatial recording of large horizontal exposures of artefacts. The excavation of 'living floors' had been developed in the 1940s by Mary and Louis Leakey at the Acheulian site of Olorgesailie (Kenya) (Isaac 1977) and then refined at Olduvai Gorge (Leakey 1971). This approach was first applied in south central Africa by Clark (1969, 1974) at the site of Kalambo Falls. The Kalambo river flows into Lake Tanganyika on the border with Tanzania and Zambia

(fig. 1.1) after dropping 220 m over the Rift escarpment. Above the falls, the Kalambo river had been blocked at various times in the past forming a small lake in the valley. The lake attracted humans who lived on its margins and waterlogged sediments have preserved evidence for the use of wood, bark and the availability of edible seeds, fruits and nuts for the Acheulian occupants. No bone survived. Large-scale horizontal excavations were undertaken between 1956 and 1966 and revealed undisturbed surfaces strewn with Acheulian artefacts and perhaps the foundations of a windbreak. Two separate hollows containing grass may have been used as sleeping areas. The shaped wooden tools, perhaps a digging and throwing stick and the end of a spear, are unique for this period in Africa.

The innovation of excavating living floors was combined with the more traditional concern with defining a technological sequence. Kalambo Falls produced a succession of assemblages from Acheulian to Iron Age that remains a rarity in south central Africa (see chapter 13). The sequence is not continuous, as there is a stratigraphic break between the Acheulian and the overlying Sangoan. The duration of the interval is unknown in the absence of reliable dates from the site (Sheppard & Kleindienst 1996). The Sangoan marks the replacement of the bifacial tools of the Acheulian (handaxes and cleavers) by different forms of large tools (picks and core-axes) and a greater variety of flake tools. The Sangoan represents the first post-Acheulian assemblage at Kalambo and across central Africa generally. Above the Sangoan was a Lupemban assemblage and the earliest clearly Middle Stone Age technology at the site with an emphasis on flakes produced from prepared cores accompanied by finely worked lanceolate bifaces. Clark (1974:250) discussed the changes in the sequence in terms of adaptation rather than replacement by diffusion: 'we now believe there to be valid reasons for suggesting that the technological innovations we have been considering may be the direct outcome of independent experiment by the exponents of the individual African regional traditions.' The theoretical and methodological tenets of processual archaeology had made a profound impact on Stone Age research.

EASTERN AND WESTERN ZAMBIA

As the excavations at Kalambo Falls neared an end, two new research programmes started in Zambia that together extended the geographical coverage of the Middle Stone Age to much of the country (fig. 1.1). In eastern Zambia, the later phases of the Middle Stone Age came to light in the excavation of Kalemba Rock Shelter in 1970–1971 (DW Phillipson 1976). Two lithic assemblages were recognised, the older radiocarbon dated to >37 ka BP and the younger to 27–24 ka BP. Both contained unifacial points and scrapers and faunal remains of zebra and large bovids. A gradual transition over six thousand years was observed between the latest Middle Stone Age and the earliest fully microlithic assemblages dated to ~17 ka BP. The Kalemba sequence demonstrated continuity rather than replacement (ibid:193) and in doing so supported the still new idea of independent development linked to environmental change.

Phillipson also made a methodological contribution in his efforts to resolve some of the issues raised in 1965 about the classification of the Stone Age. He applied JGD Clark's (1969) scheme of five modes of lithic technology to the eastern Zambian sequence. The flake based Middle Stone Age was equated with Mode 3 and the microlithic Later Stone Age with Mode 5. An Upper Palaeolithic equivalent of a blade based Mode 4 had no Zambian counterpart. The Mode concept freed researchers from the chronological connotations of the three age scheme and it made no assumptions about rates or sequences of technological change. What was gained by the apparent objectivity of the scheme was lost in its inflexibility. The co-existence of differing modes in one assemblage, such as choppers (1), flakes (3) and blades (4), could not be readily communicated, neither could temporal or spatial differences be expressed within a single mode. The latter limitation emerged in the following study.

In western Zambia, a programme of extensive survey and excavation was carried out between 1967 and 1969 within the drainage basin of the upper Zambezi from Livingstone in the south to the Angola and Zaire borders in the north (L Phillipson 1978). The project produced a much needed culture-stratigraphic sequence for a large but little known region that lacked caves and shelters. Mode 3 or Middle Stone Age assemblages were recognised and showed considerable variability in percentage frequencies of large tools, such as picks and choppers, small flake tools, unifacial and bifacial points, prepared cores and backed microliths. A general developmental trend emerged from large to smaller tools culminating in Mode 5 assemblages. Earlier and later Mode 3 assemblages were recognised, but cultural labels were eschewed in favour of a 'dynamic model of considerable inter-site variability within broadly defined parameters. . .' (ibid:107). The archaeological record of the Zaire basin provided the closest typological parallels with the Mode 3 to 5 Lupemban-Tshitolian tradition (chapter 13).

Radiocarbon dates were obtained from the site of Kandanda in the southern reaches of the Zambezi valley. The river terrace location provided a sequence of occupation from Mode 3 to Mode 5 with Mode 2 (Acheulian) on the surface. Near the base of the two metre sequence of Kalahari sands lay an assemblage of scrapers, large core tools, prepared core flakes, blades, backed blades,

radial and other core types attributed to Mode 3 but radiocarbon dated to ~3500 BP (ibid:69). Such a late date for an early looking assemblage was explained in the context of late dates for similar material in the Zaire basin. The use of mode terminology in this instance freed the analyst from the developmental assumptions of traditional culture-historical frameworks.

TWIN RIVERS HILL

This hilltop site in central Zambia (fig. 1.1) was excavated in 1954 and in 1956 (Clark & Brown in press) but the first published analysis of the data was framed in the context of interpretative issues raised in the 1960s (Clark 1971). Twin Rivers Kopje, as it was then known, provided faunal remains in association with typologically early Middle Stone Age artefacts interstratified with speleothem. Radiocarbon dates on the speleothem ranged from 23 to >33 ka BP and were in keeping with assumptions that the Middle Stone Age post-dated its European equivalent. Twin Rivers formed part of a wide ranging assessment of the effects of ecological variability on the composition of assemblages at four sites of similar age but from differing ecozones in central and southern Africa (ibid:1212). This analysis of assemblage variability typified contemporary concerns of the New Archaeology with the disentangling of cultural and non-cultural sources of patterning in the archaeological record (eg, Binford 1965; White 1968). Clark's (1969, 1974) excavations of Acheulian living floors at Kalambo Falls and of a possible Sangoan elephant butchery site in Malawi (Clark & Haynes 1970) contributed a spatial dimension to the issue of variability

MUMBWA CAVES REVISITED

Further excavations took place at Mumbwa Caves in 1973 as part of a doctoral research project on the Later Stone Age of Zambia (Savage 1983). A previously unexplored extension was investigated because of extensive damage to the main site caused by the collapse of sections and illicit digging. The cave deposits here were shallow and partially mixed by solutional weathering of the dolomite cave floor. A small sample of Middle Stone Age artefacts was found at the base of the sequence that included bifacial points and core-axes. The overlying deposits proved to be Holocene in age but no radiocarbon dates were obtained for the basal assemblage.

APARTHEID, THE COLD WAR AND ECONOMIC DECLINE

After 1973, active fieldwork on the Middle Stone Age of Zambia ceased. Research interests shifted toward later periods (eg, Musonda 1984), but the greatest impact on fieldwork in the country would be political and economic rather than academic. The growing regional and international resistance to apartheid in South Africa and the fight against white minority rule in Rhodesia affected Zambia directly. Zambia became a 'frontline' state for both conflicts and the African National Congress (ANC) in exile made its headquarters in the capital Lusaka. A regional coalition of southern African states was formed to put economic pressure on South Africa to hasten the end of apartheid and to give Namibia its independence. Zambia joined Tanzania, Malawi, Botswana and the newly independent states of Mozambique, Angola and Zimbabwe in the Southern African Development Community to implement trade and other sanctions against the regime in Pretoria. The resulting diminished trade and contact with South Africa contributed to the decline in Zambia's economy, in particular to the nationalised copper industry that relied on South African markets, materials and expertise.

Further economic disruption followed, as the newly formed Marxist governments of Mozambique and Angola became embroiled in an extension of the Cold War. South Africa and the United States supported anti-government forces in Angola where the government was receiving Soviet and Cuban military aid. Mozambique appealed to Western states to put pressure on South Africa to end its involvement with insurgent guerilias (Clapham 1996:140). Zambia, in addition to harbouring the ANC, allowed anti-South African guerillas to operate from bases in western Zambia and assisted the Mozambique government in its fight against South African surrogates. In reprisal, South Africa launched military attacks against Zambia in the late 1980s. Railway links to the ports of Benguela and Beira were cut in the course of the conflicts with the consequence that Zambia's export of copper had to be re-routed through Tanzania to the smaller port of Dar-es-Salaam.

After independence in 1964, Zambia gradually loosened its economic ties with Britain and chose a path of non-alignment which had the effect of deterring Western commercial investment in the country (ibid: 65). China proved a useful ally with its involvement in the development of Zambia's transport and water supply infrastructure. Following the Rhodesian unilateral declaration of independence in 1965, China built the TanZam railway that linked Zambia with Dar-es-Salaam to enable these countries to by-pass white minority controlled transport routes (ibid:144). In 1971 blasting to produce gravel for a new Chinese-built road system destroyed a large area of the western outcrop at Mumbwa Caves. The area destroyed had not been explored and displaced remnants of red cave earth with Middle Stone Age artefacts can still be found in the gravel. The road to Mumbwa was literally paved with the past. Economic stagnation spread across the region starting early in the 1970s with the rise in world oil prices and accelerated in the cases of Zambia and Zaire

with the collapse in the price of copper in 1975.

Economic decline continued through the 1980s, exacerbated by drought, the fight against South Africa and an inefficient parastatal sector. Requests for foreign aid became linked to World Bank demands for structural adjustment of the Zambian economy which in turn led to public unrest as austerity measures took hold (ibid:177). The government responded by relaxing its implementation of economic reforms and in turn aid was cut. The see-saw between donor and recipient ultimately forced multiparty elections which brought a change of government after 27 years of one-party rule. Under these difficult conditions, archaeological research was not a priority. The Livingstone Museum, the former Rhodes-Livingstone Institute, ceased to be an active organisation in the field. The University of Zambia, a creation of the newly independent state, did not offer archaeology as a subject for study. In the late 1970s and early 1980s the only active archaeological research was a doctoral project on the Later Stone Age of central Zambia (Musonda 1983). The Middle Stone Age as a subject of study faded from the research agenda just as the period achieved international recognition with the rise of the 'Out of Africa' model of modern human origins.

A RECENT AFRICAN ORIGIN

During the late 1970s and through the 1980s the southern African Middle Stone Age came to the forefront of academic debate as a result of new excavations combined with human fossil discoveries, the application of new dating techniques and the sequencing of human mitochondrial DNA (mtDNA). In South Africa, the excavation of cave sites with deeply stratified deposits provided new data with which to build technological and environmental sequences. These combined with the advent of new dating techniques to extend the archaeological record into the Last Interglacial (130–115 ka BP) and beyond. The remains of anatomically modern humans were also discovered from Last Interglacial deposits and forced a reconsideration of the link between behavioural and anatomical modernity. Finally, the development of mitochondrial DNA sequencing of living populations placed the origin of *Homo sapiens* in Africa between 200 and 100 ka BP. The Middle Stone Age was now at the centre of a contentious and highly publicised debate over the evolution of modern humans.

The site of Border Cave on the South Africa/ Swaziland frontier had been known since the 1930s for its Stone Age deposits with hominid remains (Cooke et al 1945). Excavations in the 1970s (Butzer et al 1978) and in 1987 (Miller & Beaumont 1989) increased the hominid sample and provided charcoal for radiocarbon dating and animal teeth for the application of the newly developed dating technique of electron spin resonance

(ESR). ESR and amino acid racemisation (AAR) dating of ostrich eggshell has since extended the sequence beyond the 40 ka limit of the radiocarbon method and into the Middle Pleistocene (~220 ka BP) (Miller et al 1999). Anatomically modern human remains were recovered from Middle Stone Age contexts in 1941 (infant skeleton, Border Cave 3), in 1975 (a lower jaw, Border Cave 5) and from uncontrolled guano mining in 1940 (an incomplete cranial vault and partial mandible, Border Cave 1 and 2). The provenance and age of the hominid material has been disputed (Sillen & Morris 1996) with counter arguments put forward that retain a Middle Stone Age association dating between 70 and 220 ka BP (Grün & Beaumont in press).

Secure evidence for anatomically modern humans in association with Middle Stone Age technology came from excavations at the cave and shelter near Klasies River Mouth on the eastern Cape coast. The excavations were undertaken in 1967–1968 but published in 1982 (Singer & Wymer 1982) by which time the Middle Stone Age was already known to be at least 40,000 years old (Clark 1975). A sequence of four Middle Stone Age assemblages, numbered MSA I–MSA IV from base to top, was recognised based on differing proportions of cores, flake-blades, retouched points and retouched flakes. Overlying MSA II and covered by MSA III assemblages, a fifth entity was recognised, the Howieson's Poort industry. The Howieson's Poort, named after a rockshelter in the eastern Cape, was characterised by blades and flakes retouched to form crescent shaped inserts for composite tools. At Klasies River Mouth, imported fine grained raw materials were used to make the blades. The crescents are of standardised size and shape, like those of the microlithic Later Stone Age, but larger. In Europe, the backing of blades into standardised inserts was thought to be associated with the Upper Palaeolithic and modern humans after 40 ka BP, but in the Klasies assemblage the Howiesons Poort developed significantly earlier.

Radiocarbon dates showed the Middle Stone Age sequence to be effectively beyond the range of the technique (Singer & Wymer 1982:192). The marine shells found throughout the Klasies main sequence provided an alternative means of dating the Middle Stone Age (MSA). Carbonates in the shells retained the oxygen isotope ratios in seawater at the time of shell formation. The ratios were correlated with the deep-sea core isotope record to give an approximate date for the occupation of the site. On the basis of two hundred samples, MSA I was correlated with the Last Interglacial (130–120 ka BP), MSA II to about 100 ka BP or 80 ka BP and the Howieson's Poort to 50 ka or 30 ka BP (Shackelton 1982:199). The age estimates of MSA I and II have since been independently supported by other dating techniques and the Howieson's Poort at Klasies appears to be about 70 ka years old (Deacon 1992; Miller et al 1999). At other long sequence sites such as Border Cave, Apollo 11 Cave (Namibia) and Boomplaas Cave (southern Cape) the Howiesons Poort fell in the time range of 59–80 ka BP with a median of 67 ka BP (Miller et al 1999). The crescent shaped backed blades formed a distinctive technological horizon in the Middle Stone Age south of the Limpopo River (Thackeray 1992). The Late Pleistocene archaeological record to the north remained undated and largely unknown.

The bulk of the human remains from Klasies was associated with the lower two strata which contained MSA I and II assemblages. A sample representing about 10 robust but anatomically modern humans was now convincingly linked with both a Middle Palaeolithic-like technology (MSA I, II, III) and an Upper Palaeolithic-like technology (Howiesons Poort) that predated the European sequence by 40 ka. By the late 1980s, the new sequences and dates had distinguished the southern African record of technological development from its contemporaries in the Old World. The Howiesons Poort stood apart but remained puzzling because of its discontinuity (Klein 1992). If these were the tools of behaviourally modern humans then why did they not build on this achievement and develop a fully blade-based technology from 70 ka BP onwards? Ideas of what constituted modern behaviour were still based on eurocentric comparisons with the Upper Palaeolithic. The ability of the Klasies moderns to hunt large dangerous game, as would be expected of behaviourally modern humans, also became, and remains, a contentious issue (Binford 1984; Ambrose & Lorenz 1990; Deacon 1992; Milo 1998; Klein 2000).

The contribution that DNA analyses would make to the development of a recent African origin model for modern humans (Stringer & Andrews 1988) took place after the Middle Stone Age had emerged as the temporal equivalent of the Middle Palaeolithic. The extended age range of the southern African archaeological record remained largely unknown outside the community of specialists working in the region. By the mid-1980s, the technology of DNA analysis had advanced beyond the study of the products of DNA (eg, blood proteins) to the analysis of the DNA itself. Mitochondrial DNA achieved fame and notoriety as the biological evidence for an African source of all mtDNA in living humans (Cann et al 1987). The source was traced to a single female ancestor who lived only 200 ka BP based on estimated rates of mutation in a portion of the mtDNA genome. Outside Africa, all mtDNA sequences were younger and indicative of a recent replacement. The molecular evidence accorded well with the fossil record for the evolution of anatomically modern humans in Africa and the hybridisation of the two data sets resulted in the 'Out of Africa' model (Stringer & Andrews 1988).

Subsequent analyses of the original mtDNA data revealed statistical flaws that undermined the argument for an African root (Templeton 1992). More recent analyses of mtDNA and nuclear DNA, including the male Y chromosome DNA reaffirmed the original conclusion of an African origin in the late Middle Pleistocene (Kittles & Keita 1999 for overview).

The Middle Stone Age by default became the behavioural record of anatomically modern humans in Africa. The 'Out of Africa' theory focused attention on the South African archaeological record after years of relative academic obscurity. The Middle Stone Age was now the testing ground for the most radical theory to emerge in palaeoanthropology in the late twentieth century. Did the development of modern behaviours precede, coincide with or post-date the evolution of the modern form? To frame an answer to this question some consensus needed to be reached about what constituted modern behaviour. That consensus eluded archaeologists and continues to do so (cf McBrearty & Brooks 2000; Klein 2000). Since 1988, the South African archaeological record – and its Near Eastern counterpart – has provided the primary data for the debate. New data from other regions of Africa has been slow to emerge, partly because of political and economic obstacles. The study presented here began in 1993 with the aim of contributing to the 'Out of Africa' debate by providing new archaeological, environmental and, with luck, fossil human data from a neglected region of south central Africa.

2 Mumbwa Caves 1993–1996

L Barham

BACKGROUND

By the mid-1970s this once well known site had slipped into academic obscurity. The early investigations in 1925, 1930 and 1939 established the value of the main cave as a source of deep deposits containing stone tools, fauna and human remains. The Middle and Later Stone Age were represented, as were more recent iron using farming communities. Dart and Del Grandes' (1931) basal 'Old Palaeolithic' stratum held the promise of an Early Stone Age occupation. These features of the Mumbwa sequence had been largely forgotten in the wake of the successful cave excavations in South Africa during the 1970s and 1980s. In Zambia, the political and economic turmoil of the post-independence years, combined with the lack of academic support within the country, contributed to the neglect of this promising site.

By the early 1990s, developments in science-based dating techniques along with the rapidly improving political climate in the region made the re-excavation of the Mumbwa sequence an attractive proposition. The reports of animal teeth throughout the deposit raised the possibility that ESR dating could be applied to enamel in conjunction with the thermoluminescence dating (TL) of burnt stone. The furnaces or hearths encountered in 1930, if genuine, meant that burnt quartz – the most common raw material used at the site – could provide the basis for a chronology. In Clark's report (1942:152), the red clay stratum underlying the Middle Stone Age (Stillbay) stratum was thought by Zeuner to be of aeolian origin and indicative of dry climatic conditions. A variant of TL dating called optically stimulated luminescence (OSL) was being applied in the early 1990s to sun bleached quartz grains found in sand dunes (eg, Stokes 1993). The aeolian red clay stratum might be suitable for dating by OSL and provision was made to include this technique in the first season of excavation. Charcoal had also been reported by Dart and Del Grande throughout the sequence and would be useful for dating as well as for palaeoecological analysis.

Research by geomorphologists in neighbouring Botswana, Zimbabwe and Namibia had established the correlation between the expansion of the Kalahari and glacial (dry) phases of the Late Pleistocene (Thomas & Goudie 1984). Palaeoecological and archaeological data emerging from South Africa showed a direct link between climate change and human population distributions during the Late Pleistocene and Holocene (Deacon & Thackeray 1984). The southern African interior was effectively abandoned during dry phases and re-occupied during interglacials. Demographic responses aside, the human capacity to adapt to the repeated restructuring of habitats provides a gauge of cognitive abilities (Mithen 1990). In the case of Mumbwa Caves, its location 120 km east of the margins of the Mega Kalahari meant that the site and its occupants would have been exposed to significant fluctuations in climate in the past. The response of behaviourally and anatomically modern Later Stone Age peoples to climate change could in theory be contrasted with that of the Middle Stone Age occupants whose behavioural modernity was in question. If Middle Stone Age hominids were cognitively more modern than their Neanderthal contemporaries then the differences should be visible in the context of environmental stress. This was the theoretical aim of the planned re-investigation of the site. A more specific objective involved the construction of a basic culture-stratigraphic and palaeoecological framework for the site that could be used more broadly for regional comparisons. The lack of a well dated Late Pleistocene technological and environmental sequence from south central Africa gave added impetus to the project.

THE SITE

Mumbwa Caves (15°01'S; 26°59'E) earns the plural in its name from the multiple cave entrances that open into a free standing outcrop of dolomite that sits in a shallow closed basin or *dambo* (fig. 2.1). The outcrop forms part of an extended distribution of Late Precambrian meta-carbonates of the Katanga System, Lower Kundulungu Series, that underlie large areas of central and north-western Zambia (Kaiser et al 1998). Cave formation at Mumbwa began below the water table with solutional weathering (phreatic) of the dolomite along joints and fractures (Simms 1994). The passages were then exposed to atmospheric (vadose) weathering with the lowering of the surrounding landscape. Today the outcrop rises abruptly above the valley bottom reaching

Figure 2.1 The main dolomite outcrop of Mumbwa Caves as viewed from the dambo.

a height of 21 metres with cave openings at ground level at the southeastern end and up to two metres above the dambo level on the western side (fig. 2.2). The largest opening or main cave was accessible to humans at least 170 ka BP which gives a minimum age for the exposure of the outcrop. Three other entrances are known (fig. 2.2), two of which have been excavated but neither has reached the depth of the main cave. A fifth opening existed on the eastern face at some time in the past but is now effectively blocked by roof fall.

The outcrop follows a northwest–southeast trend and extends approximately 60 metres to the southeast and reaches a maximum width of 36 m at the northern end and a minimum width of 11 m at roughly its midpoint. A horizontal shelf or platform extends 24 m along the western side with a maximum width of 12 m. Blocks of artefact-bearing breccia lie on the platform outside the two cave entrances and suggest that these openings once extended further but have since collapsed or weathered away. The breccias are the surviving remnants of former cave deposits. Radial cores, flakes, bone and burnt stone are visible in the breccia with the cores indicative of a Middle Stone Age occupation. To the southeast, the dolomite extends for another 100 m as less pronounced and discontinuous outcrops. Excavations were undertaken along the eastern face in 1973 (Savage 1983) and blasting in 1971 destroyed the westernmost outcrop. The dolomite exposure as a whole provides a boundary for the seasonally flooded dambo.

The physical features of the outcrop deserve some further comment because they would have affected living conditions for the human occupants as well as governing the deposition of sediments within the cave system. A plan of the outcrop (fig. 2.2) shows that the four openings are linked by two passages that follow the northwest–southeast trend of the structure. The longer and narrower passage formed along a fault line that runs from the main cave to the southeastern entrance. This corridor acts as a funnel for the daytime winter easterlies that blow from May to August. The main cave receives the worst of the draught and without protection would have been dusty during the day. Windchill aside, table 2.1 shows that the cave offers a more equable environment in which to live compared with the surrounding landscape. In the early morning, between 5 and 6 am, the cave was on average 5°C warmer than the dambo surface. The cave retained its warmth into the evening being on average 4°C warmer than the dambo between 9 and 11 pm. During the hottest part of the day the cave was cooler than the surrounding landscape. In the heat of summer the pattern is reversed with the cave being cooler at night and throughout the day. The advantages of living in the main chamber in summer or winter would presumably have been the same regardless of the climate. Local oral history recounts small bands of hunter-gatherers (bushmen) camping against the outcrop in the late nineteenth and early twentieth century, in areas similar to that excavated in 1973 on the southern extension (Savage 1983). The cave at this time was filled with sediment and not accessible for habitation but the outcrop would have provided some warmth and protection from winds.

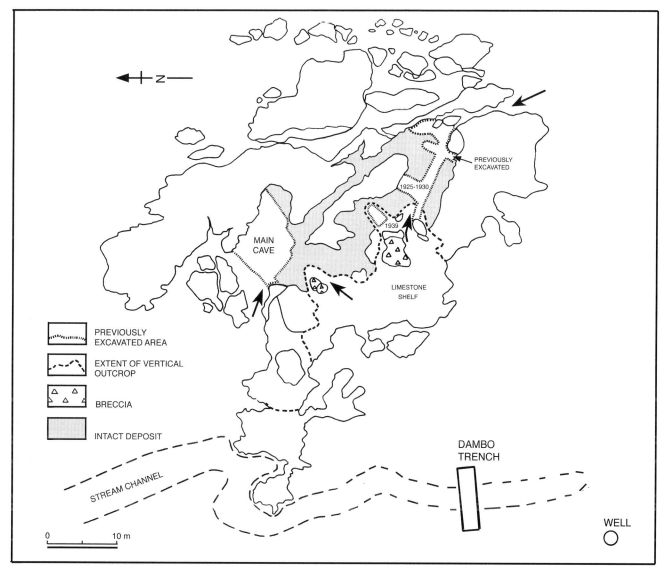

Figure 2.2 Plan of the main outcrop of Mumbwa Caves showing entrances, areas of previous excavation, the internal passages and the location of the excavation on the dambo margin.

During the coldest nights of July 1994, when temperatures on the dambo regularly fell below freezing, the main cave emitted a deep low frequency hum. This may have been a feature of the cooling dolomite or a sound produced by the large colonies of bees that nest inside vents and avens. The bees provide a much valued source of honey today. Other inhabitants of the outcrop include at least two dozen barn owls that use the site as a roost, bats, a colony of hyrax, a porcupine, a side striped jackal living in the main cave, and a cane rat. The many crevices and fallen blocks of dolomite provided homes to a variety of poisonous snakes including a black mamba, black and Egyptian cobra, and a puff adder that lived beneath a boulder at the entrance of the main cave.

The nocturnal non-human occupants have contributed to local beliefs about the site as a place inhabited by

spirits. Witches are said to inhabit the cave and take the form of owls and jackals but unfortunately the fear of the supernatural has not prevented the continuing vandalism to the site. The Kaonde, who settled in the area from Angola or northwestern Zambia in 1890, treat the cave as a shrine where offerings in the form of chickens and beer are made to placate the spirits of ancestors and to celebrate the arrival of the Kaonde. A female initiation ceremony is also to be reinstated at Mumbwa by the Kaonde and this involves initiates spending time in the caves. The renewed traditional respect for the site may spare it from further damage.

Two features of the outcrop that do not directly affect the quality of life at Mumbwa but that deserve mention are its acoustic and visual properties. The northern end of the outcrop in which the main entrance is situated

Table 2.1 Temperatures (°C) recorded in the main cave and on the dambo margin in the morning (5–6 am) and evening (9–11 pm)

Date	Cave–AM	Dambo–AM	Cave–PM	Dambo–PM
18 Jul 95	2	4	16	10
19 Jul	12	5	15	11
20 Jul	14	5	15	12
21 Jul	12	6	15	11
22 Jul	12	6	16	12
23 Jul	13	8	16	13
24 Jul	16	12	18	18
25 Jul	12	6	17	12
26 Jul	12	6	16	11
27 Jul	11	5	16	11
28 Jul	12	7	17	13
29 Jul	15	9	17	17
30 Jul	14	8	17	12
31 Jul	14	8	17	14
1 Aug	13	6	17	13
2 Aug	14	8	16	12
3 Aug	13	7	16	11
4 Aug	14	8	17	14
5 Aug	14	14	19	18
6 Aug	18	13	–	–
Average	12	7	16	12

forms a natural amphitheatre (figs 2.2 and 2.3). To assess the acoustics of the site, an informal experiment was devised that involved one person standing at the cave entrance and another 15 m away at the edge of the outcrop. The latter person made single sharp handclaps that were repeated at 5 m intervals across the opening of the amphitheatre. For both observers, the claps were amplified and echoed, and from the position of the entrance the shifting source of the sound did not diminish in resonance. As a general observation, human and animal noises from the surrounding landscape are amplified on the western side of the outcrop that faces the dambo. The outcrop surrounding the main cave also provides a backdrop for casting shadows from fires lit on the cave apron. These acoustic and visual properties make the site a natural stage. There is no direct archaeological or oral evidence that the site was used as a communal ritual centre by foragers, but its inherent suitability for such performances may have made the site a focal point in the social landscape.

The morphology of the outcrop with its linked tunnels and east-facing openings provided the opportunity for sediment to enter the caves. Figure 2.4 shows a vertically exaggerated cross-section of the cave in relation to the valley side to the east and the dambo to the west. The pediment slope has a gradient averaging 3–5° and is mantled with colluvial sediments of varying depths. Colluvium fills all the cave passages and must have entered the outcrop through openings on the east side (fig. 2.2). On the west side, roof falls or some other form of blockage at the cave entrances acted as barriers that allowed sediment to accumulate in the passages. Dart and Del Grande (1931) reported that the caves were filled with deposit nearly to the roof leaving only crawl spaces. Colluviation as a geomorphological process is not occurring on the surrounding vegetated slopes today and the climatological implications of the cave sediments (eg, MF Thomas 1999) are discussed in appendix 2.

Figure 2.3 A view of the entrance to the main cave (centre bottom) from the dambo. The outcrop forms a natural amphitheatre around the entrance.

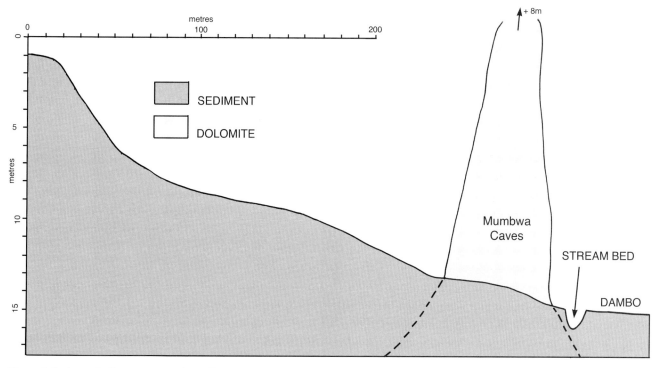

Figure 2.4 A vertically exaggerated profile (10:1) of the valley showing the position of the outcrop in relation to hillslope to the east and the dambo to the west. The hill would have been the source of the colluvium that filled the main cave.

THE SETTING

The Mumbwa Caves site forms part of a gently undulating landscape that typifies the south central African plateau between 7 and 17°S. The plateau ranges in altitude between 1000 and 1500 m above mean sea level and Mumbwa township stands at 1350 m. Rainfall at Mumbwa averages 1400 mm per annum and falls mostly between the summer months of late October to March followed by a prolonged winter dry season from April to October. The monsoonal rainfall supports a deciduous woodland savanna with vegetation well adapted to drought and tolerant of early dry season bush fires (Werger 1978). Species of *Brachystegia* and *Julbernardia* dominate (White 1983) and form a distinctive open canopy characterised by trees of medium height, with feathery leaves and gnarled boles (fig. 2.5) that collectively are known as *miombo* woodland. The biogeography of miombo woodland is discussed in chapter 12 but in brief it offers wood for fuel and tools, bark for making clothing, twine and trays as well as edible but seasonally available fruits, nuts, seeds and geophytes. The open canopy enables a grass layer to grow which supports the greatest diversity of large mammal species in sub-Saharan Africa (Klein 1984b) but in low densities. Miombo game animals tend to be highly selective grazers that occur in small numbers and only elephant, buffalo and hippopotamus are widespread (East 1984). Rainfall and soil nutrients are limiting factors on the plant and animal biomass and so affect human population densities (Barnes & Lahm 1997), but the availability of surface water, especially in the dry season, has the most immediate impact on the distribution of human foragers.

The dambo on which Mumbwa Caves abuts has formed between two sandstone ridges that are part of a series of parallel hills that extend westwards. The hills and slopes are covered with miombo but the dambo and its margins are open grassland. Dambos are closed basins that form at the headwaters of drainage systems and become waterlogged during the summer wet season and retain a water table beneath the surface during the winter months (Mäckel 1974:332). They are an essential source of surface water for animals during the wet season, and by digging wells, humans can survive on the plateau through the long dry season. According to local sources, until the 1980s the dambo to the front of Mumbwa Caves attracted large game, in particular elephant, zebra, and buffalo to the area during the wet season, drawing animals away from the Kafue river valley 60 km to the west. Dambo soils are relatively rich in nutrients compared with the surrounding hills. The grass cover is often lush and at Mumbwa reaches heights of 3 m. The reports of hunter-gatherers at the caves as recently as 1900 reflect the continuing value of the site as a wet season habitat. Until tsetse fly were brought under control in the 1950s, the area around Mumbwa was marginal grazing land for domesticated animals (Trapnell & Clothier 1996:18). During the rains, a small

Figure 2.5   Miombo woodland 3 km west of Mumbwa Caves.

ephemeral stream flows past Mumbwa Caves before disappearing into the dambo. The availability of standing water would have been critical to the use of the caves by humans and would have been a determining factor in the seasonality of occupation. A dambo or stream must have been accessible from the cave during the Middle and Late Pleistocene episodes of occupation otherwise the site would have been uninhabitable.

Dambos as a geomorphological feature of the Zambian plateau provide uninterrupted tracts of grassland for grazers but they also create natural avenues of communication for humans in the dry season. Footpaths linking villages often follow dambo margins before crossing hills. About a third of the landscape around Mumbwa today is open dambo grassland. Farming and late season burning of the landscape may have extended the natural distribution of grassland, nevertheless, dambos should be considered a feature of interglacial landscapes on the plateau.

LITHIC RAW MATERIALS

Mumbwa is situated on the southern margins of the plateau before it drops 300 m to the seasonally flooded grasslands of the Kafue River (fig. 10.1). More immediately to the south of Mumbwa lies a range of prominent hills composed of crystalline iron oxide (specularite). The Nambala hills, 18 km from the caves, dominate the near distant landscape and are visible from the top of the outcrop and from the surrounding sandstone ridges. The Nambala hills are a likely source of the specularite brought to Mumbwa to produce a pigment. This material and other sources of colourants are reviewed in chapter 8, but they highlight the extent to which the Late Pleistocene occupants travelled to collect minerals.

The lithic resource most used throughout the Mumbwa sequence was vein quartz and, in contrast to specularite, it was available locally. Veins of milky quartz up to 30 cm thick occur within 300 m of the main cave, to the northeast, and provide a ready source of stone for knapping (fig. 2.6). Radial cores and flakes found on the surface around the veins show the attraction of this material. Clear crystalline quartz was used by the Middle Stone Age occupants of Mumbwa, but a local source could not be identified in the modern landscape. A granite batholith that is exposed 50 km to the west of Mumbwa and known as the Hook Granite Massif (Thieme & Johnson 1981) is a possible source. The Kafue river flows around the batholith and the gravels contain crystalline quartz pebbles, but this seems an unusually long distance to travel for a basic raw material. Vein quartz cobbles were also knapped at Mumbwa. A 10 km radius survey of the landscape around the site failed to locate a source of river cobbles. The local streams carry a light sediment load that is free of cobbles >20 mm. A quartz gravel exists in the sediment profile of the dambo as seen in the nearby wells but at a depth of 4 m below the ground surface. The use of cobbles by the Middle Stone Age inhabitants of Mumbwa suggests that exposures of some raw materials available during the Mid-Late Pleistocene are no longer accessible. Colluviation may have buried stream channels as well as outcrops of other rocks and minerals. Pale amethyst artefacts occur occasionally in the Mumbwa sequence, but the source could not be located.

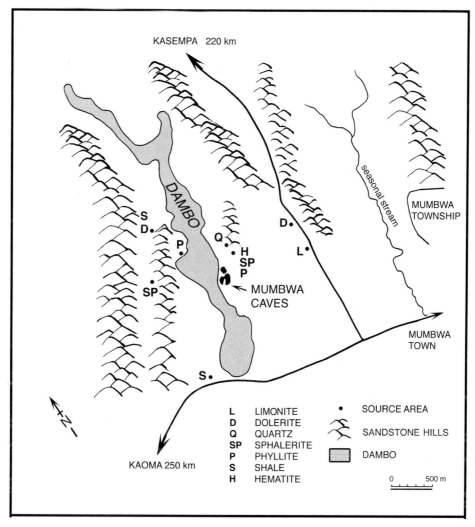

Figure 2.6 Location map of stone resources within 2 km of Mumbwa Caves.

Other siliceous materials used for tools include a fine-grained brown quartzite and a coarser ferruginous quartzite. Quartzite ridges outcrop more than 10 km west of Mumbwa but neither the brown nor red variants were found in these hills. Also eluding detection was the source of a fine black chert that was knapped at the site. A single pale chert core was found on a ridge near the Mumbwa to Kaoma road about seven kilometres to the southwest of the cave. Cherts are also known to occur 25 km to the northwest (Cikin & Drysdall 1971), but the source was not visited in the course of the study. Degraded artefacts of dolerite are found in the Middle and Late Peistocene assemblages and are often difficult to recognise as struck flakes. A yellow-brown weathering rind often permeates to the centre of the piece and diagnostic percussion features are often too eroded to be easily identified. When fresh, dolerite can be readily flaked and produces a durable cutting edge. A dolerite dyke swarm is located 2 km to the north of Mumbwa Caves (fig. 2.6). Two bifacially flaked shale

artefacts were found in the Last Interglacial (130–115 ka BP) deposits and are described in chapter 8. Various sources of shale occur within a 2 km radius of the site (fig. 2.6).

A single triangular (Levallois) flake of a pale igneous material with phenocrysts of sanidine feldspar (fig. 2.7) was also found in the Last Interglacial assemblage amongst an arc-shaped feature interpreted as a wind-break (chapter 8). The flake has been identified as either Luapula porphyry or Kafue rhyodacite (K Bailey pers comm). Neither material is local to the Mumbwa area nor could they have been deposited locally by natural processes. Kafue rhyodacite is found 200 km to the southeast and the Kafue rivers flows eastward toward the Zambezi and away from Mumbwa. Luapula porphyry is found 450 km to the north-northeast along the Congo river watershed. The geochemical makeup of the pheno-crysts in the Kafue rhyodacite does not match that of the flake from Mumbwa (E Pollard pers comm), but without a petrographic analysis a definitive identification of the

Figure 2.7 Triangular flake (Levallois) of Luapula porphyry from Area I (H7) windbreak feature.

source cannot be made. Regardless of the origin, long distance transport is involved and the behavioural implications are discussed in chapter 13.

Phyllite and sandstone were also imported to the cave but from local sources. Both are found as blocks around hearths along with dolomite, quartz and hematite. The sandstone and quartz in particular retain heat long after the fire has died down and may have been selected for this property. Phyllite outcrops on the western edge of the dambo 300 m from the cave. Sandstone is available on the nearest ridge 500 m to the west (fig. 2.6), and as well as being used as a hearthstone smaller pieces are found among knapping debris and may have been used as abraders.

From the perspective of hunter-gatherers living at Mumbwa Caves during an interglacial, the site and its environs offered shelter, warmth, food, water – in the wet season but potentially year round – and the raw materials for making tools and pigments. The acoustic and visual properties of the outcrop are less tangible attractions, but potentially important features for framing the social context in which pigments may have been used at the site. The drier climate associated with glacial and stadial phases would have altered the biogeography of the Zambian plateau and with it the food and water resources available to foragers (chapter 12). Vein quartz for making tools would have remained a constant in the equation of changing opportunities and new constraints. The excavations that began in 1993 would demonstrate a correlation between the human occupation of the site and interglacial or interstadial

conditions. The availability of surface water appears to have been a limiting factor from the Holocene to the Middle Pleistocene.

THE 1993 EXCAVATIONS

The initial three week season of investigation began with the objective of assessing the extent and content of intact Middle Stone Age deposits in the main cave (Barham 1993). In 1930, Dart and Del Grande removed 462 tons of sediment from the two largest entrances at Mumbwa. The main cave (fig. 2.2) provided the deepest sequence and the only sample of an 'Old Palaeolithic' assemblage that could be either Early or Middle Stone Age using Goodwin and Van Riet Lowe's terminology. This basal assemblage underlay an artefactually sterile 'red clay' deposit. To reach the sterile clay, the Italian Expedition removed the overlying sediments across an area 21 ft (6.4 m) long by a maximum of 24 ft (7.3 m) wide to a depth of 16 ft (4.8 m). At this depth they left intact an oval feature of burnt dolomite blocks. This 'furnace' remained a visible feature in the cave when I visited in March 1993 but by June 1993 it had been vandalised and the dolomite blocks removed and scattered. Dart and Del Grande sank a 'central pit' into the sterile clay and excavated until hitting bedrock a further 12 ft (3.6 m) down. The pit measured roughly 6 ft (1.8 m) wide by 8 ft (2.4 m) long before stepping in to a length of 6ft (1.8m). A series of steps was cut into the deposit to enable the spoil to be removed from the pit. In all, 250 tons of sediment were excavated from the main cave in 20 cm spits (Dart & Del Grande 1931:384).

Between 1930 and 1993, the 21 ft long main section, orientated along the northwest–southeast axis of the cave, had collapsed and the central pit was filled with displaced sediment. The back wall of the excavation, however, survived largely intact and this was used in 1993 to lay out a grid system that approximated the original geometry of the 1930 excavation (fig. 2.8). A site datum was etched onto a dolomite block lying in the cave entrance and given the arbitrary height of 00.00 m (all measurements are in centimetres below datum). The datum stone was one of three large blocks of fallen dolomite left from a roof collapse (fig. 2.8). The collapse covers a Later Stone Age deposit of largely Holocene age so must have happened relatively recently, perhaps in the last two thousand years. The roof fall has reduced the dimensions of the living area of the cave by

approximately 1.5–2.0 m and brought the seasonal drip line further into the entrance.

The surface of the site was cleared of loose sediment down to intact surfaces and three one metre square units were laid out for excavation. Squares H6 and G4 were placed beneath the overhang where Dart and Del Grande had uncovered two stone built structures containing human bone. Their excavation had ceased in the sterile red clay deposit and in intervening years illicit digging in this area had left the surface disturbed and strewn with dolomite blocks, a human vertebra and a large (12×6 cm) discoidal core of vein quartz (fig. 2.9). The core closely resembled a *coup-de-poing* illustrated by Dart and Del Grande (1931: fig. 8) from the 'furnace stratum' in which the stone tombs were found. The possible Early Stone Age (Old Palaeolithic) stratum was

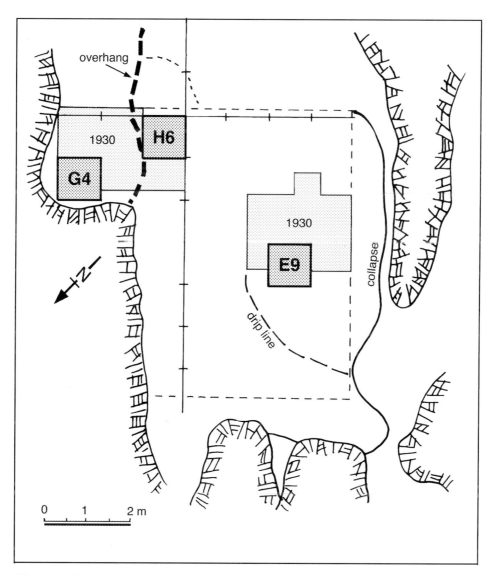

Figure 2.8 Plan of 1993 excavations in the main cave showing the location of the central pit and northern extension of the 1930 excavations. The central pit marks the deepest deposits in the site.

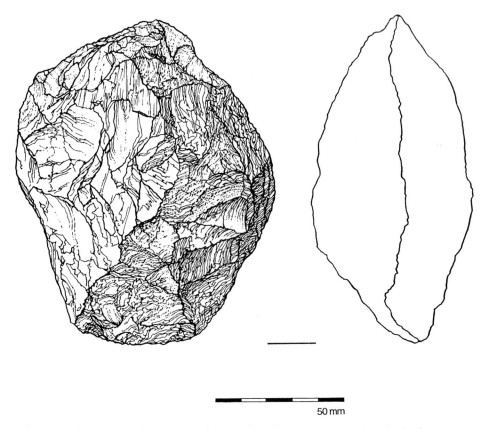

50 mm

Figure 2.9 Vein quartz discoidal core found in 1993 from disturbed deposits in G4.

originally found beneath the red clay in the centre of the site and the excavation of H6 and G4 was intended to trace the horizontal extent of the deposit. Both squares were excavated to bedrock and only in H6 was any artefactual material found and at approximately the same depth as the Dart and Del Grande's basal stratum. Manganese-stained bone and a radial quartz core were found at a depth of 5.8 m below datum (fig. 2.10). Only two fragments of charcoal were found in G4 and came from near the top of the sequence. Accelerator mass spectrometry (AMS) radiocarbon dates showed them to be modern and intrusive (chapter 3).

The third square-metre unit to be excavated, E9, was placed on the western edge of the central pit (figs. 2.8, 2.11). E9 extended 50 cm into intact deposit and the remainder was the pit fill. The two deposits were readily distinguished and the pit fill was removed to expose the section face of E9, which was then used as a stratigraphic guide to excavation (fig. 2.12). Quartz flakes and cores and bone were found in the first 50 cm (156 and 205 cm) of intact deposit which was excavated in 5 cm spits following the slight eastward slope of the deposit. All sediment was passed through a 0.5 mm sieve. Between 205 and 225 cm below datum fewer artefacts were found with almost no finds below 225 cm. From this point onwards, 10 cm and then 20 cm spits were

used as time and funds were running short. An artefactually sterile layer of colluvium persisted from 225 to 359 cm below datum and matched the description of the red clay stratum of Dart and Del Grande. Beneath this, bone and quartz artefacts reappeared but in lower concentrations than above the colluvium. The Old Palaeolithic stratum had been rediscovered but was typologically Middle Stone Age (Barham 1993). Late on the afternoon of the final day, two human radius fragments were found at a depth of 540 cm below datum (see chapter 9) and at 600 cm the area of intact E9 gave way to pit fill and the excavation was stopped. Throughout the final metre of the excavation the area of intact deposit progressively lessened until a 10 cm band remained, the other 90 cm being infill (fig. 2.12). The articulated and relatively fresh looking skeleton of a hyrax was found at the base of the fill along with the intact skull of a bat. Both had fallen into the pit and were buried rapidly, perhaps by the collapse of the main section or by slumping of the central pit section itself.

Square E8 was opened as part of the search for the lower stratum, but only the western third of E8 was intact and excavated from 166 to 212 cm below datum before stopping for the season. Dripline runoff had cut a channel into the remainder of the square which had filled with redeposited sediment.

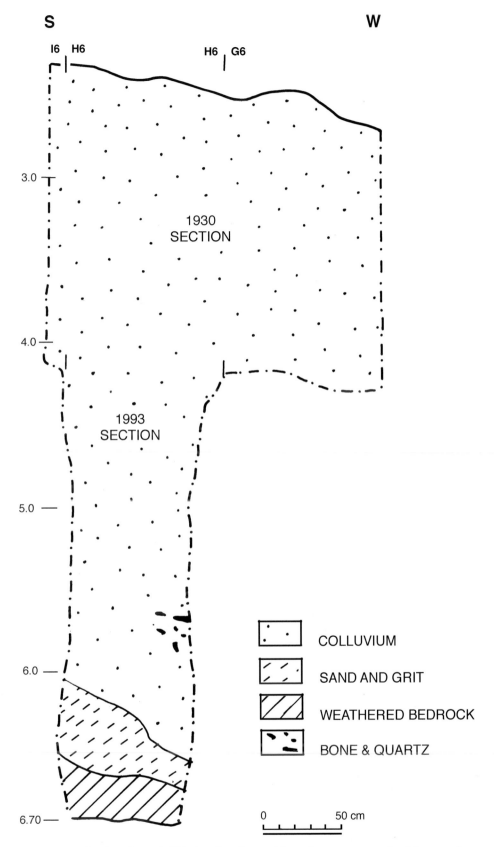

Figure 2.10 Section through H6 showing the position of manganese stained bone and quartz artefacts near the base of the deposit.

Figure 2.11   The excavation of E9 on the margins of the 1930 central pit.

The short 1993 season re-established the existence and location of the early material found in 1930. Fragmentary bone of large mammals was found above and below the colluvium along with the jaws and teeth of small mammals, mostly rodents. The presence of microfauna raised the possibility that an environmental sequence could be reconstructed for the local habitat. Burnt quartz and tooth enamel were noted from the perspective of TL and ESR dating potential. Three samples for OSL dating were collected from the intact section that formed the Y-coordinate of the grid system and from H6. *In situ* dosimetry readings were taken, including a sample from the supposed aeolian deposits of the red clay. The results are described in chapter 3, but in brief, the quartz sand fraction from all the samples was saturated and gave uninformative dates of >100 ka BP. Either the sediments were actually this age and older or the quartz grains had been incompletely reset by sunlight. The colluvial origin of the sediments made the latter option the more likely. A systematic

sampling of the sediment profile was made at 10 cm intervals down the surviving 1930 section and through the H6 sequence to bedrock (appendix 2). Appendix 1 lists the individual excavation units by square and depths for all four seasons at Mumbwa.

THE 1994 EXCAVATIONS

The baseline established in 1993 had been removed in our absence and illicit digging had taken place in the surviving 1930 section and evidence was found of digging around the three 1993 test pits. A cairn of dolomite blocks had been erected inside the entrance for no obvious purpose. The baseline was re-established using two buried nails, but the resulting grid system was 5 cm out of alignment with the 1993 grid. The nails appeared to have shifted in the soft sediment as a result of trampling.

The primary objective of this season (20 June to 3 August) was to establish the extent of intact deposits either side of the central pit and then to excavate these horizontally with three-dimensional plotting of all material larger than 20 mm. The Iron Age and Later Stone Age sequence excavated near the entrance in 1939 (Clark 1942) had not been dated and this area was targeted for stratigraphic excavation to build a radiocarbon chronology and to recover comparative environmental and technological data. Three excavation areas were defined and the irregular topography of the cave floor was mapped (fig. 2.13). Area I incorporated a block of intact Middle Stone Age deposits with the boundaries defined by the central pit and Dart and Del Grande's extension beneath the overhang to the north. The resulting rectangular platform of deposit measured 2×3 m and was contained in squares G7, H7, G8, H8, G9 and H9. Area II incorporated intact deposits along the western edge of the central pit with squares E8, E9, D8, D9 and D10. Area III sampled the standing remnant of the 1930 main section nearest the entrance that contained Iron and Later Stone Age deposits. The Area III sequence would also provide a stratigraphic link between the Later and Middle Stone Age and give a full sequence through the site when combined with Area II. The squares that defined Area III included D11, D12 and C12.

The excavation methodology included the erection of a suspended grid system anchored to the cave roof to provide permanent square boundary markers. Corner stakes shifted in the relatively soft sediments in Areas II and III making constant reference points a necessity. All sediment excavated was sieved through a 0.5 mm synthetic mesh to recover small mammal remains and other microfauna. Flotation was attempted, but abandoned on ethical and practical grounds. Water had to be collected from a well in the dambo which held a rapidly dwindling supply that was shared by a widely dispersed

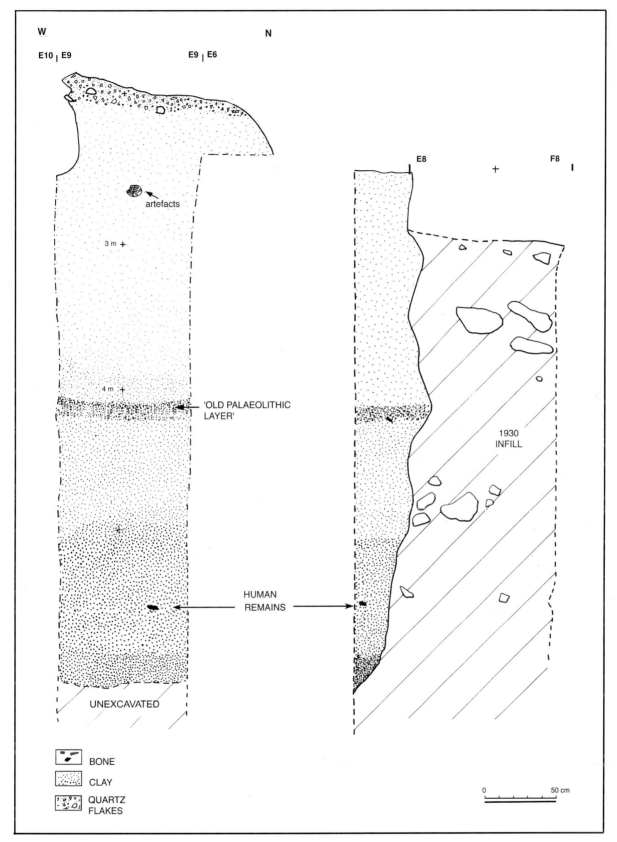

Figure 2.12 Section through E9 showing an artefact concentration near the top of the sequence that overlies artefactually sterile colluvium. A darkening of the deposit at the base of the colluvium marks the appearance of Dart and Del Grande's Old Palaeolithic stratum. Fragmentary human remains were recovered in 1993 at a depth of 540 cm below datum.

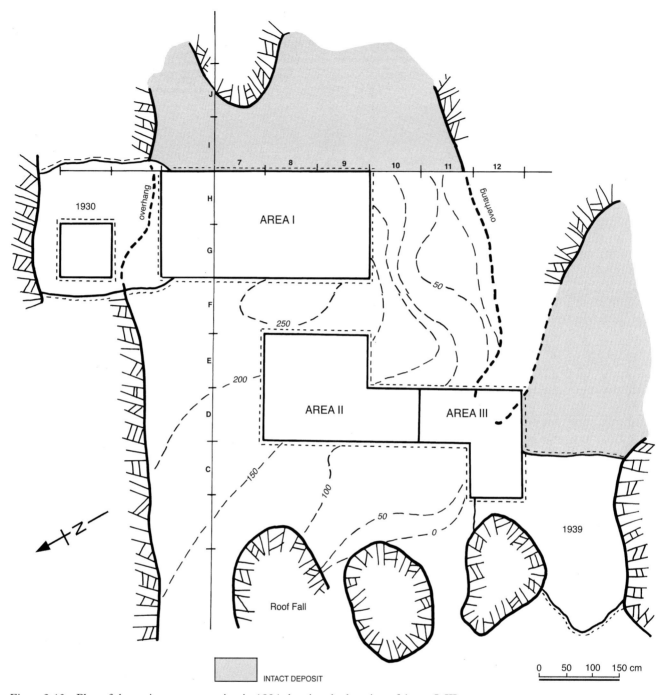

Figure 2.13 Plan of the main cave excavation in 1994 showing the location of Areas I–III.

community of farmers. Our need for the well water was not justifiable. The flotation system also attracted swarms of bees from the outcrop which limited the safe washing of sediments to the cool of the early morning and evening when the bees were inactive. The final obstacle to flotation was the destruction of the drying rack on which the skimmed float was stored. Termites ate through the tent floor and devoured the rack, collapsing a week's work into a single pile.

Area I

Intact deposit was found at a depth of 177 cm below datum and excavation began with the planning and removal of the base of the furnace feature left *in situ* in 1930. Excavation took place in 1–5 cm spits. Evidence of burning in the form of a concentration of ash, calcined bone, degraded dolomite and hardened, reddened sediment was found within an oblong area 150× 100 cm and 10 cm thick (fig. 2.14). The feature has

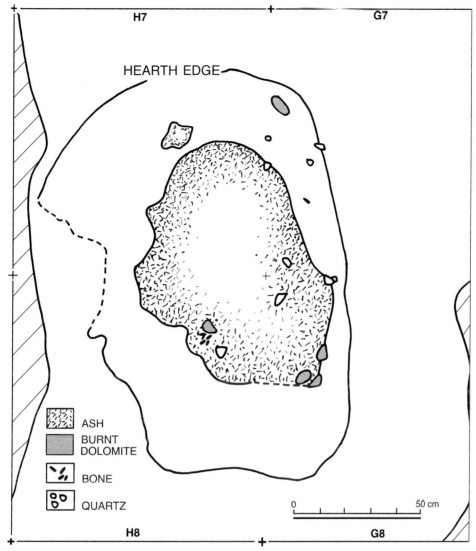

Figure 2.14   Plan of the 'furnace' feature or hearth excavated in Area I. Large stones originally lined the perimeter of the ash spread.

been interpreted as a hearth (Barham 1996) and a photograph from 1930 (Dart & Del Grande 1931:plate XXXI) shows that the feature had been surrounded by stone blocks and was at least 20 cm thick.

Beneath the hearth at a depth of 202–8 cm, an arc shaped concentration of artefacts, bone, ash, and hardened sediment emerged across squares H7, H8 and into G8 with the opening of the arc facing east towards the opening of the cave (fig. 2.15). Excavation proceeded with the removal of sediment surrounding the arc with the result that the arc broadened at its base to the depth of 254 cm. Near the base of the arc, three circular features ranging in diameter from 7 to 12 cm were found inside the arc and resembled post and stake holes. The arc and postholes taken together were seen as evidence for a windbreak built to shelter the occupants from wind funnelled through the eastern opening of the

outcrop (Barham 1996:197). Samples of ash from the feature were collected for phytolith analysis to identify the kinds of vegetation used in building the structure. Evidence for two additional windbreaks was found at lower levels across Area I and is discussed in detail in chapter 8. Excavation in Area I stopped with a portion of a possible windbreak remaining in H9–G9. The lithic debitage found among the concentrations was technologically Middle Stone Age (chapter 8) and included evidence for techniques of prepared core flaking. Teeth and burnt quartz were collected for dating.

Area II

The surface of the deposits had been disturbed by a combination of drip line erosion, root penetration and slumping along the edges of the 1930 excavation. Dart and Del Grande had cut a series of steps into the deposit

Figure 2.15 View from the eastern passage of the excavation of the windbreak feature in Area I. The excavator is standing in H6.

and these remained as a series of uneven levels across the area. Intact sediments lay just beneath the disturbed surfaces of D9 and D10. The first 100 cm of deposit contained a concentration of multiple and intercutting areas of burning. Ash lenses with associated stones, discoloured sediments and burnt bone were interpreted as hearths built over a period of time near the entrance of the cave. The average size of the hearths was difficult to estimate because the area was truncated by the previous excavation and the hearths overlapped with stones being re-used or discarded (fig. 2.16a,b). Discrete ash concentrations, where intact, were similar in size to the concentration associated with the large hearth in Area I. An unusual basin-shaped feature in D10 had 15 cm thick ash walls that extended 30 cm in depth. A burnt piece of quartz was recovered from the base of this oven-like structure and submitted for TL dating (chapter 3, fig. 3.1). The stone artefacts among the hearths were Middle Stone Age in technology, and burnt pieces were set aside for dating. The excavation continued to a depth of 190 cm by which point artefacts had decreased in number.

Square D8 had been excavated in 1930 as part of the stairway to the central pit and the pick marks of the excavators were still visible. What was now D8 had filled with redeposited sediment to a depth of 184 cm and was cleared and set aside for later excavation. A small area of E9 (10×100 cm) became available for excavation at 150 cm as a result of the slight shift in the grid system between seasons. This shelf was excavated in concert with D9.

Area III

Clark (1942) excavated a rectangular area originally 9×5 ft (2.7×1.5 m), then extended to 10×7 ft (3.0×2.1 m), beneath the overhanging entrance to the main cave with the trench abutting the cave wall (fig. 2.2). The archaeological sequence extended from the Iron Age in the first 12 inches (30 cm) to a Later Stone Age assemblage which reached a depth of roughly 24 inches (60 cm) preceded by Middle Stone Age deposits that could not be fully excavated because of time constraints.

The Area III excavations focused on D11 and D12 where the deposit extended under the overhang and was intact (fig. 2.17). Differences in colour, texture and content of the sediments were obvious compared with the generally homogeneous colluvial deposits in Areas I and II. The excavation followed the natural stratigraphy with spits of 1–5 cm. Charcoal was also abundant, again in contrast to the lower deposits. A culture-stratigraphic sequence emerged that closely resembled that seen by Clark. The upper 28 cm contained plain sherds and an iron bead. Microlithic debitage was found amongst the Iron Age deposits and dominated the artefact content between 28 and 91 cm. Other items of material culture that can be attributed to the Later Stone Age included a fragment of bored stone made of specularite, ostrich eggshell beads, a shell bead, bone tools including points and an incised bone with hematite staining. This element of the Mumbwa sequence will be analysed and published separately.

From a depth of 40 cm downward, the southern half of D12 was filled with a hard pinkish-white deposit that

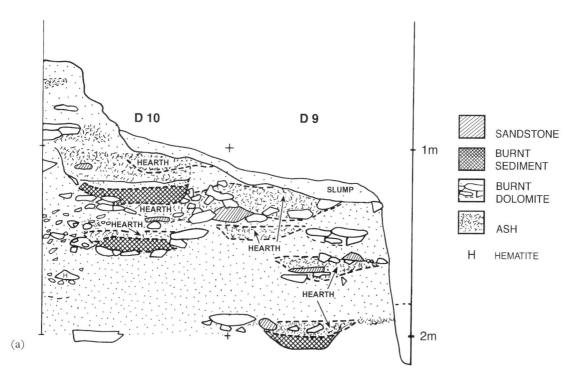

(a)

(b)

Figure 2.16 (a) Composite section of D9/D10 (Area II) showing the concentration of hearths in the deposit
from 96–200 cm below datum. (b) View of Areas
II and III in relation to the cave entrance. The
Area II hearths occur beneath the black plastic
bags protecting the section.

obscured the stratigraphy (fig. 2.17). Clark had observed
a similar feature and analysis by Zeuner (in Clark
1942:151–152) led to the conclusion that this material
originated as a dripline feature that had undergone
solution weathering which removed much of the calcium
leaving a phosphate rich deposit. Dart and Del Grande
had exposed a similar band of white material at the back
of the cave that they interpreted as solidified ash. Their
surviving section was sampled in H8 (fig. 2.18) and the
white deposit analysed and found to be phosphate rich
and probably bat guano in origin (appendix 2). The
deposit in D12 may also be guano and occupies a similar
stratigraphic position that underlies the Later Stone Age
and sits above colluvium.

From a depth of about 90 cm the whole of D11 was
filled with signs of combustion – ash, burnt bone and
stone – and large stones forming a rough circle and dipping toward the centre of the square (fig. 2.19). The
stones included dolomite, sandstone, phyllite and quartz.
Smaller pieces of hematite were found amongst them.
This hearth extended into C12 at which point the
square was excavated. C11 was only briefly sampled and
found to be too disturbed by erosion and trampling
along the entrance path to warrant further excavation.

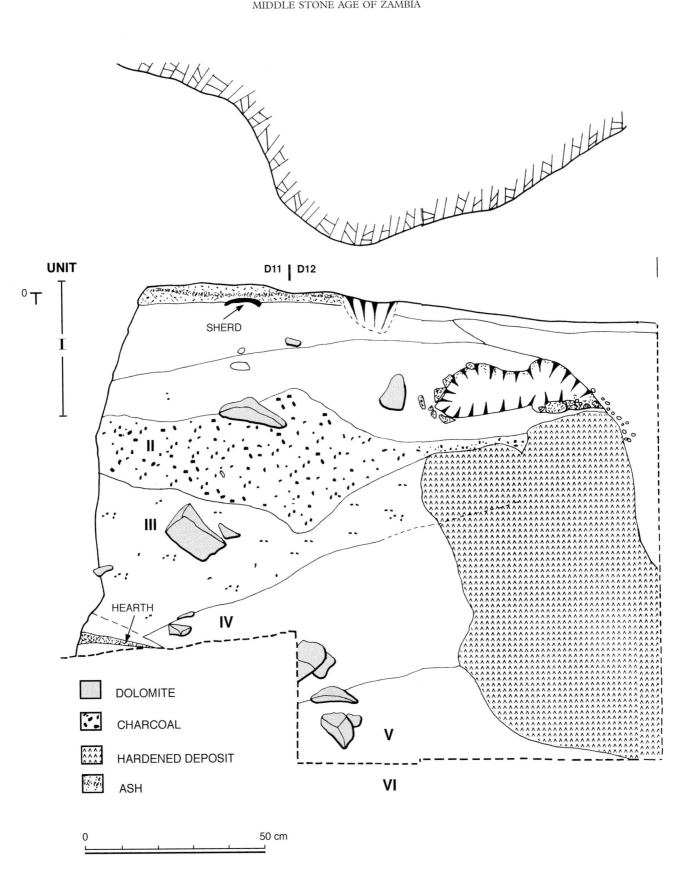

Figure 2.17 Section through D11/D12 showing the stratigraphic sequence in Area III.

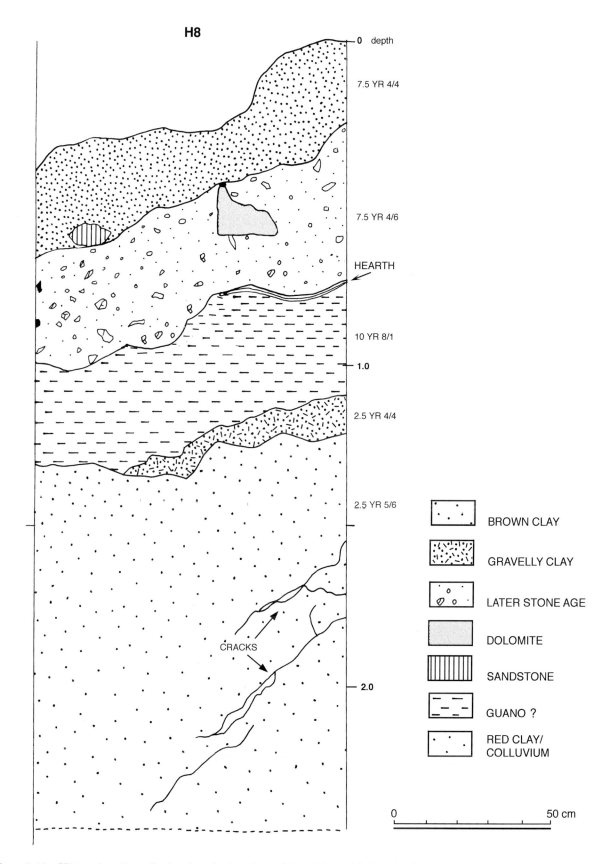

H8

0   depth

7.5 YR 4/4

7.5 YR 4/6

HEARTH

10 YR 8/1

1.0

2.5 YR 4/4

2.5 YR 5/6

CRACKS

2.0

BROWN CLAY

GRAVELLY CLAY

LATER STONE AGE

DOLOMITE

SANDSTONE

GUANO ?

RED CLAY/
COLLUVIUM

0   50 cm

Figure 2.18   H8 section (Area I) showing the location of the white 'ash' deposit of 1930 that may be bat guano. A small Later Stone Age hearth is exposed in the upper right part of the section.

Figure 2.19   Stone-lined hearth in D11 (Area III) at the top of the Middle Stone Age sequence. 10 cm scale.

At the north end of D11, the hearth marked a boundary between microlithic and non-microlithic or Middle Stone Age lithics, but the interface was higher up the sequence in D12 (60 cm) where the deposit dips steeply to the north (fig. 2.17). Some mixing of sediments has occurred along this interface in D12 and what appears to be a guano deposit has obscured the interface further. The excavation of D11 stopped at a depth of 96 cm with much of the hearth left intact to avoid debris from D11 falling into Area II (D10). In D12 the deposit was excavated below the hearth to a depth of 126.5 cm and stopped as the quantity of artefacts declined.

The 1994 season demonstrated that where intact deposit survived to any extent, a spatial approach to excavation proved highly rewarding. A relatively gentle process of sedimentation had preserved areas of patterned behaviours, such as the placement of hearths near the entrance and windbreaks further in. The sediments removed in 1930 presumably contained similar spatial data but it would be unfair to judge the objectives of Dart and Del Grande by current archaeological practice. That said, the need to build a basic culture-stratigraphic sequence for the site has remained unchanged.

THE 1995 SEASON

In the intervening year the elevated grid system on the main cave ceiling had been removed along with the baseline and the protective sandbags used to retain the exposed sections in all three areas. As a consequence, D11 and the hearth feature had collapsed and sediments had washed over Area II and into Area I from beneath

the collapsed roof fall blocks at the cave entrance. A baseline was re-established once again using two surviving pins but the grid system was again slightly out of alignment with that of 1994. No attempt was made to re-erect the vertical grid. The four-week-long season (9 July to 8 August) began with the limited objective of continuing the spatial recording of artefact concentrations in Areas I and II and excavating these areas to the sterile colluvium. No work was done in Area III.

Three more bands of concentrated debitage, ash, bone and hardened sediments were recorded in Area I at depths from 240 to 254 cm. These were less clearly defined in outline and no postholes, with one possible exception in G8, were found (fig. 2.20). In G9, a roughly linear spread of artefacts, dolomite blocks, bone and ash (fig. 2.21) continued to a depth of 272 cm below which the deposit became hard and artefactually sterile. The extra depth of this concentration in comparison with the other features in G7–G8 matches Dart and Del Grande's (1930:388) description of an undulating line of 'boulders of fractured quartz, quartzite, sandstones, and ironstone' that underlay the stratum containing the large hearth. Beneath this zone of concentrated occupation debris lies the artefactually sterile colluvium. The transition takes place gradually across Area I at depths between 250 and 270 cm (fig. 2.22). Two possible bone points were found in the G9 concentration and are described in chapter 8.

In Area II, the excavation of E9, D9 and D10 began at a depth of 175–180 cm, the same level as the large hearth in Area I. As the excavation continued in 1–5 cm spits, further evidence of burning (fig. 2.16a and b) was

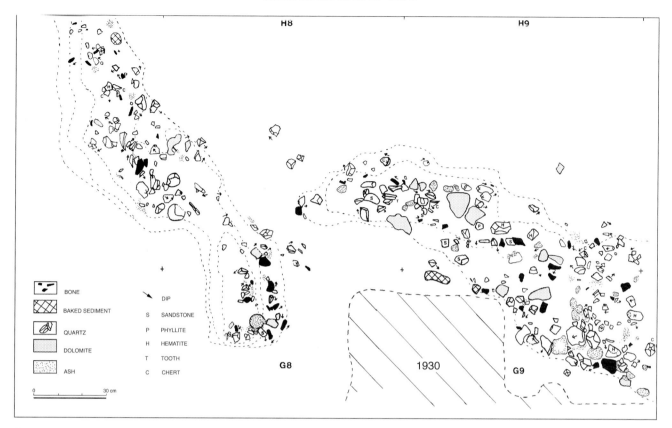

Figure 2.20   Plan of artefact and debris spread across H7, H8, H9, G7 and G8 at a depth of 240–244 cm below datum.

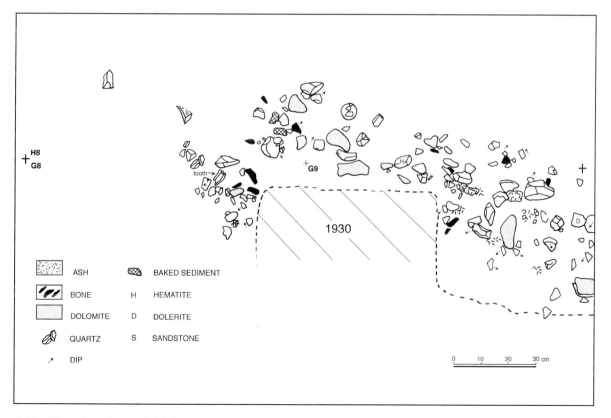

Figure 2.21   Plan of artefact and debris spread across G8, G9, H8 and H9 at a depth of 250–255 cm below datum.

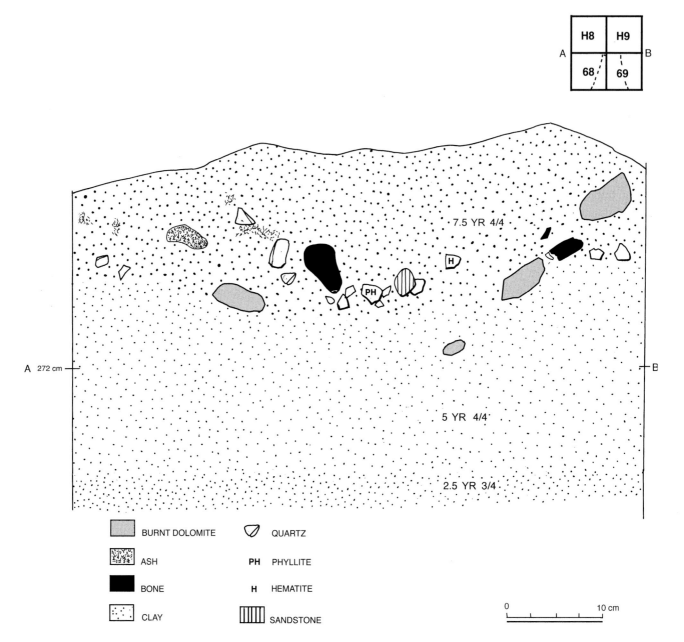

Figure 2.22   Section in G9 at the edge of Dart's central pit showing the gradual transition to artefactually sterile colluvium in Area I at depth of 250–270 cm below datum.

found associated with largely quartz debitage of Middle Stone Age affinity. The density of occupation debris decreased with depth and horizontally from west to east. A section along the D10/D11 boundary (fig. 2.23) shows the eastward dip of the deposit. The homogeneity of the sediment matrix made the dip difficult to detect and to retain in individual spits. A discrete area of burning – a hearth – was found near the bottom of the artefact concentration in D9 between 190 and 210 cm below datum. From a depth of 220 cm and below, almost no artefacts were found and this was interpreted as the top of the sterile colluvium. A crescent-shaped backed blade

was found in D10 at a depth of 215 cm and resembled in size and shape the backed blades dated to 59–80 ka BP in the southern Cape and attributed to the Howiesons Poort industry (Deacon 1992). A similar artefact was found in E9 at a depth of 212 cm and beneath the main artefact concentration. Late in the season, E10 was opened as a narrow triangular extension (26×82 cm) of intact deposit from D10 and another crescentic backed blade was found.

The excavation of the partial squares D8 and E8 resumed at 184 cm. A concentration of quartz artefacts and evidence of burning was found which gave way to

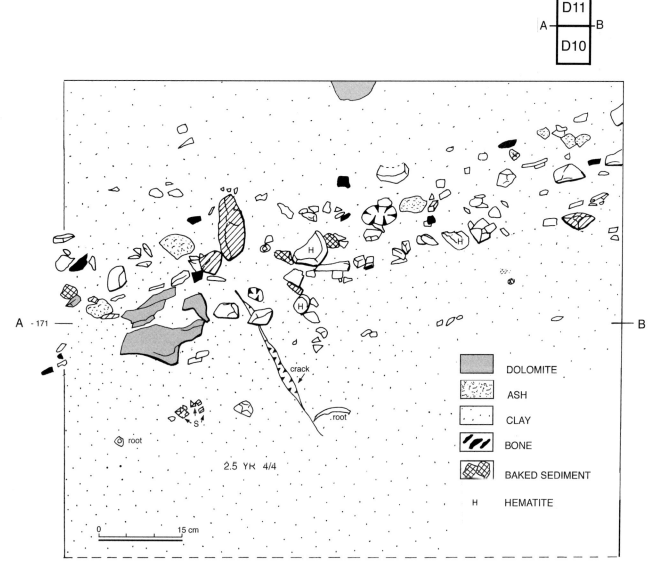

Figure 2.23   D10/D11 section showing the eastward dip of the deposit toward the interior of the cave (Area II).

artefactually sterile deposits at 220 cm. An arc of braided pale sediment bent across the two squares (fig. 2.24) and was initially thought to be the top of another structure despite opening inwards toward the direction of the winter wind. The pale deposit was thin (from 217 to 225 cm below datum) and contained no artefacts, ash, burnt stone, etc. The ceiling immediately above is coated with a calcium crust that roughly matches the shape of the feature in D8. This putative arc was probably a drip line formation.

The 1995 season ended with deposits in Areas I and II all excavated into the hard red colluvium that was effectively lacking evidence of human occupation. The recovery of backed blades gave a guide to the potential age of the Middle Stone Age deposits and raised the

possibility that Howiesons Poort-like technology was more widespread than thought. The archaeological record of the Late Pleistocene north of the Zambezi was too poorly known to be certain that backed blades were a feature of the Middle Stone Age (Volman 1984), though they had been reported from Mumbwa Caves (Clark 1942). The sterile colluvium, if it was deposited during glacial or stadial conditions, could be either Stage 4 (64–74 ka BP) or Stage 6 (186–130 ka BP) in origin. The backed blades were found above the colluvium making this technology either younger than 64 ka BP or Last Interglacial in age. If the latter, then the Mumbwa Caves segments represented an unexpectedly early expression of backed tool technology. The TL dating of burnt quartz from Areas I and II resolved this issue (chapter 3).

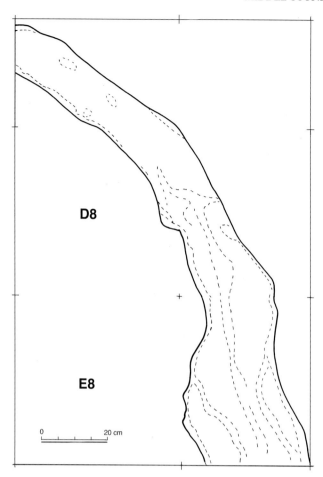

Figure 2.24 Plan of drip line deposit of calcium carbonate in D8/E8 at a depth of 225 cm. The deposit formed near the top of the artefactually sterile colluvium (unit VIII).

The artefact concentrations in Area I appeared to show the repeated use of this portion of the cave as a living area. Alternatively, the features formed as part of the process of sedimentation in which deposits were concentrated by debris flows from the entrance or side passages into a low lying area. The main Middle Stone Age occupation above the sterile colluvium dips eastwards into the cave. The extent of the dip can be measured by comparing the height of the top of the colluvium in D9 (220 cm) with that of H9 (270 cm) and H7 (250 cm). The 30–50 cm drop takes place across 500cm and gives a gradient of 6–10 per cent. Would this slope be sufficient for dripline runoff to transport the blocks of dolomite and quartz found and then arrange them into arc-shaped fans? Postholes are another matter altogether. Regardless of the formation processes operating in Area I, the Middle Stone Age archaeological assemblage here and in Area II was deposited after a period of little or no occupation of the cave. The assemblages from both areas were considered to be approximately contemporaneous.

THE 1996 SEASON

The now familiar discovery that the site had been vandalised in the off season was repeated in 1996. Further erosion of the sections had occurred following the theft of protective sandbagging and the removal of stone used as backfill. Graffiti had been painted onto the 1930 section and was trowelled away with no harm to the deposit. The baseline pins had been well concealed and the grid system was intact.

The primary objective of this final season (9 July to 19 August) was to sample the deposits underlying the sterile colluvium. Given the limited time and the expected depth to bedrock of about five metres, the excavations were concentrated on Area II where Dart's Old Palaeolithic stratum had been found in 1993. The intact edge of the central pit was located, infill removed and excavation begun in D10, E10, D9 and E9. On clearing the infill from beneath E10, a broken biface (handaxe) was found (fig. 2.25). The biface was made on a quartzite flake and the edges were slightly abraded. The object may have come from lower deposits in which case the basal assemblage may be Acheulian in origin. Alternatively, it could have been introduced by the Middle Stone Age occupants and used as a hearthstone or curated for other less practical purposes. Macrae (1926) had found a biface in his excavations in the other western entrance.

In the off season, sediment had slumped across the surface of E10 and in removing this material a large backed blade was found. Also from this same deposit came a human molar. In the course of straightening the E11/E10 section an incomplete femur emerged (see chapter 9). Some uncertainty must remain about the stratigraphic context of these two finds. The molar was in loose sediment and the femur came from deposits that may have slumped from above.

Each square was excavated in 10 cm spits through the hard sterile colluvium. At a depth of about 350 cm below datum, a subtle change took place in the sediment colour and texture. The colluvium from 220 to 350 cm had been uniformly dark reddish brown (2.5YR 3/4), but became less red changing to a paler hue of dark reddish brown (5YR 3/4) to reddish brown (5YR 4/4) and then to dark brown (7.5 YR 3/4) by 360 cm. The texture now included an element of coarse grit bands within the colluvial clay. The grit appeared to be degraded limestone and reacted to dilute acetic acid. Across Area II, this combined colour and texture change was recognised as an interface zone between the colluvium and the surface of the underlying deposits. The surface was irregular with an erosional channel in D10 dipping to the east. Several intact long bones of bovids lay on this interface surface (fig. 2.26). The presence of complete bones was most unusual as the fauna was almost all fragmented (chapter 4) in the sediments above

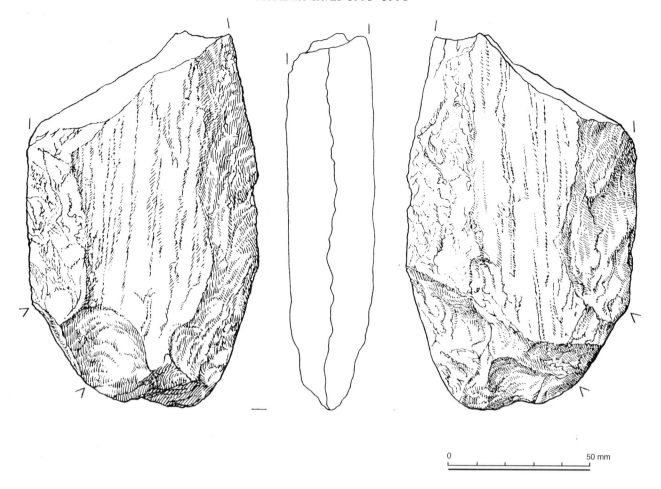

Figure 2.25   Broken quartzite handaxe from the infill of Dart's central pit.

and below the interface. The bone here had not been trampled or chewed or otherwise damaged. The interface surface looked as though it had been gently buried and the site not re-occupied for some time.

In all the deposits below the interface the traces of human occupation were scattered. The contrast was stark between the large hearths and abundant occupation debris above the colluvium and the discrete clusters of artefacts (fig. 2.27) with patches of burnt sediment and sandstone found below the colluvium. A pattern of ephemeral occupation characterised the early use of the cave.

The soil colour darkened below the interface as manganese concretions became more common and formed large discontinuous nodules at 510 cm and 630 cm. Small (<10 mm) manganese nodules were present throughout and some may have been mistaken for charcoal in 1930 (as they were in Barham 1993) because no charcoal was found at this depth. The movement of water through the sediment and saturation conditions above bedrock led to the precipitation of manganese in solution. Manganese-stained bone had been found in H6 at similar depths in 1993.

At a depth of 480 cm the excavation of D10 stopped as time ran short (fig. 2.28). The effort to reach bedrock was now focused on D9/E9. No additional human remains were found at the level where radius fragments were recovered in 1993 (540 cm below datum). Though disappointing, the lack of bone was in part offset by the similarity of the texture and composition (>3 mm grit or yellow pisoliths) of the sediments at this depth to that seen three years earlier. Any doubt that the human material had not come from intact deposits (Barham 1993) was now dismissed. Bone preservation was also particularly good at this depth. The sediment gradually turned to a dark brown (10YR 2/2) from 550 cm to 630 cm and then to strong brown (7.5YR 4/6). A gravelly layer of dark yellowish brown decayed bedrock persisted from 760–790 cm when bedrock itself was reached on the final day. Twenty-centimetre thick excavation levels had to be used from 630 cm onwards to finish the project.

The rarity of retouched tools in the lower deposits, and the few cores found, made it difficult to determine conclusively whether the occupation represented either Acheulian or Middle Stone Age technologies or both.

Figure 2.26 Intact bovid metapodial lying on the surface of the interface (unit IX) between the base of the colluvium (unit VIII) and the top of unit X in D10.

Figure 2.27 A vein quartz radial core and flake found as a discrete cluster at a depth of 417 cm below datum in D10 (unit X).

Figure 2.28 The excavation of Area II in 1996 with the base of D10 forming a platform to the left of the excavator in D9.

Blade and radial cores were found but neither type is exclusive to one tradition.

DAMBO DIG

In conjunction with the main cave excavations in 1996, a rectangular trench 9×2 m was opened on the edge of the dambo and near the caves where the seasonal stream cuts a shallow channel (fig. 2.29). The objective of sampling these deposits was to test the proposition that the absence of Middle Stone Age sites in the surrounding landscape was a geomorphologically controlled phenomenon. Surface surveys undertaken each season since 1993 had failed to locate unambiguous evidence of Middle Stone Age living sites. Cores had been found at an outcrop of quartz 300 m to the northeast of the cave, but no other traces of occupation were found. Later periods were well represented by scatters of microlithic debitage and ceramics. The absence of prepared core technology and associated debitage was at odds with the

discovery of Middle Stone Age surface sites on the plateau of western Tanzania (Willoughby 1993) and along the Zambezi (L Phillipson 1978). In the case of the Mumbwa area, the mantle of colluvium that blankets the valley slopes and fills the dambos may have covered or redeposited open sites from earlier periods.

The dambo was excavated to a depth of 120 cm below an arbitrary datum across the length of the trench and then stepped down in the last 3 m of the trench to a depth of 220 cm with a final step inwards spanning 2 m that reached dolomite bedrock at 240–260 cm (fig. 2.30). No bone survived in these acidic sediments. The upper 50–60 cm consisted of a relatively soft and dark grey (5YR 4/1) organic sand-clay horizon which contained potsherds. The grey sediment was thickest in the stream channel. Beneath this deposit and to either side of the channel were found 10–40 cm thick lenses of brown (10YR 5/3) sand-clay which gave way to a light yellowish brown coarse sand and clay (2.5YR 6/4). This sediment was indurated and could only be excavated with picks despite the dense concentration of artefactual material, much of which was damaged in the process. A selected sample of artefacts >20 mm in length was retained because of the density of quartz debitage and because of time constraints.

At a depth of 120 cm, a lens of quartz, dolerite and hematite artefacts was encountered that was approximately 4–50 cm thick. The lens extended for 3.7 m and approximated the shape of the stream channel but offset to the west of the current channel (fig. 2.30). Unworked pebbles and gravel among the debitage indicated that the material had been redeposited. The artefacts were slightly abraded and had not been transported far, perhaps from living areas outside the caves. Technologically and typologically the material was Middle Stone Age (chapter 8) as typified by vein quartz bifacial points, faceted flakes and radial cores. At a depth of 170–200 cm the assemblage changed with an increased use of quartz cobbles (>40 mm) as cores and greater use of bipolar flaking. The cobbles deserve further comment. Their presence suggests that a ready source existed either in the stream or nearby and could account for the cobbles found in the main cave sequence. The stream bed today carries only fine sediment with neither cobbles nor angular fragments of quartz. A much more aggressive flow regime would have had to exist in the past for the quartz to be transported and to be rounded. Other components of this assemblage include blade cores, flake blades and an odd multifaceted hematite ball (see chapter 8).

Between 200 and 220 cm, the quantity of manuports of hematite, specularite, laterite, sandstone and phyllite increased. If phyllite was for hearthstones as was the case in the main cave, then its presence suggests that the open air living site was near what is now the dambo

Figure 2.29   The dambo trench at the start of the excavation with the main outcrop in the background.

margin. Two quartzite hammerstones were also found. Informally flaked cores are more common and resemble those found beneath the colluvium in the main cave. From 220 cm to bedrock, the artefacts are larger than above and burnt blocks of sandstone were recovered. The material from 220 cm and below, if contemporaneous with the lower deposits in the main cave, could account for the scarcity of artefacts in the cave. Perhaps the main living area was outside the cave. Burnt quartz from the dambo sequence was submitted for TL, but no reliable signals were generated.

In eastern Zambia, the landscape has undergone a relatively recent (Late Glacial/early Holocene) transformation with landslides and extensive colluviation transporting large sediment lodes (Thomas 1999). The rapid movement of sediments is thought to have originated with the reduced vegetative cover across the region during the dry conditions of the Last Glacial Maximum (21 ka Cal BP). Weathered parent material on exposed slopes gave way with the onset of increased rainfall at the Late Glacial/Holocene transition. If a similar erosional/depositional process took place along the sandstone hills surrounding Mumbwa Caves, then Middle Stone Age surface sites would now be redeposited and buried.

The prospects are bleak for a landscape-based archaeology of the Late Pleistocene in this area and for much of the south central African plateau. Surface sites may exist on hilltops, but their distribution would reflect geomorphological biases rather than human behaviour.

THE MUMBWA SEQUENCE

The nearly eight metres of deposit can now be partitioned into a manageable sequence of descriptive units for analysis. Appendix 3 details the culture-stratigraphic groupings and the associated excavation levels by square. Details of the dating of the sequence are discussed in chapter 3. Fourteen units are recognised, with the potential for further subdivision and consolidation at a later stage. The units are partly chronological, sedimentological and technological and where appropriate they are correlated with marine isotope stages. The dating of the units is discussed in chapter 3. The radiocarbon calendar calibrations are calculated using INCAL98 and based on the Pretoria Calibration Procedure (Talma & Vogel 1993). The artefact content of each unit is described in chapter 8. Units I–VII are found in Area III, units IV–XIV are represented in Area II and deposits of units VII–VIII occur in Area I (fig. 2.13).

Unit I – Late Holocene: present–2000 BP (Later Stone Age and Iron Age)

A sequence of eight AMS and extended radiocarbon dates on charcoal from D11 brackets the top 33 cm between 330 Cal BP and 2330 Cal BP. The deposit contains pottery and microlithic debitage and is treated as a single unit in this study.

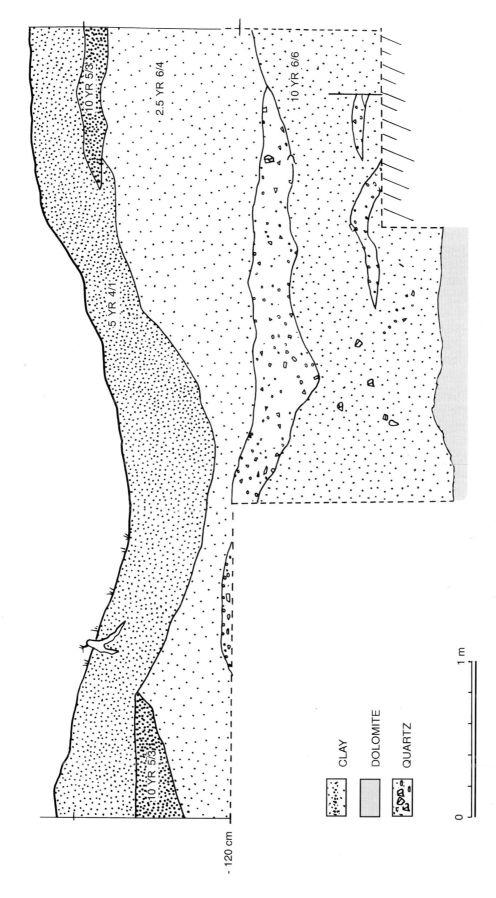

Figure 2.30 Section of the main trench across the dambo showing the Middle Stone Age artefact concentrations (120–260 cm) formed by stream action.

CLAY

DOLOMITE

QUARTZ

10 YR 5/3

2.5 YR 6/4

10 YR 6/6

5 YR 4/1

10 YR 5/3

- 120 cm

0   1 m

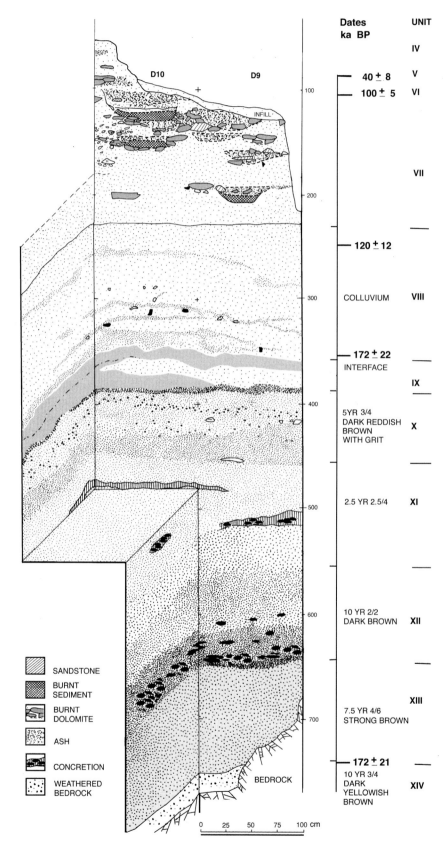

Figure 2.31 Main section through Area II (D10/D9) from 55 to 790 cm below datum
(bedrock) shows depth of stratigraphic units and associated dates.

40

Mid-Holocene: absent

Unit II – Early Holocene: 6600–8100 Cal BP (Later Stone Age)

Radiocarbon dates for the deposit between 33 and 62 cm span part of the early Holocene and are associated with a microlithic assemblage featuring backed flakes and bladelets and small scrapers (<20 mm).

Unit III – Late Glacial/early Holocene: 9–15,000 BP (Later Stone Age)

Two ESR dates on enamel from deposits between 62 and 83 cm range in age from 9–12,000 BP and are associated with a microlithic assemblage similar to that from Unit II. Charcoal is largely absent below this depth, with the notable exception of a single fragment found at a depth of 132 cm in D10. This gave a date range of 15,835–15,540 Cal BP and is associated with Middle Stone Age deposits and is considered intrusive (see chapter 3), but it is suggestive of a human presence at Mumbwa Caves during the Late Glacial.

Unit IV – Stage 2? (Later Stone Age/Middle Stone Age interface: age uncertain)

The deposit between 82 and 91 cm in D11 is undated and represents the base of the microlithic Later Stone Age sequence in this square. In D12, the Later/Middle Stone Age interface is located higher up the section and less well defined as a result of the formation of the hardened deposit. Considerable mixing has occurred at this interface, perhaps because of a long interval of exposure of the top of the Middle Stone Age sequence.

Unit V – Stage 3: 40,000 BP (top of Middle Stone Age)

The large D11 hearth produced a TL of 39±7 ka BP at a depth of 96cm and marks the top of the Middle Stone Age sequence. This is a chronological entity with little depth (5–10 cm) and poorly represented in terms of artefacts, but warranting distinction from units below on the basis of chronology alone.

Unit VI – hiatus: 40–100,000 BP?

A thin lens of microfauna without artefacts near the base of D12/C12 may represent a break in the occupation or depositional sequence.

Unit VII – Stage 5: 107–120,000+ BP (Middle Stone Age)

A sedimentological as well as an archaeological unit spanning 1.7 m of deposit from 100 cm in D10 to a depth of 270 cm in G9. The sediment is largely of colluvial origin with the addition of human occupation debris and varies slightly in colour from reddish brown (2.5YR 4/4) to dark reddish brown (2.5YR 2.5/4). The deposit includes areas of burning (hearths) and curvilinear and linear concentrations of artefacts and occupation debris (windbreaks?) associated with prepared core technology, bifacial and unifacial points, awls, borers, scrapers and rare backed blades all attributed to the Middle Stone Age. One windbreak feature is dated by TL on burnt quartz to 120±13 ka BP and another by OSL on burnt sediment to 130±6 ka BP. Crescentic backed blades occur between 174 and 220 cm and must be at least as old as the minimum date of 107±11 ka BP for the top of the deposit.

Unit VIII – Stage 6 colluvium: 170–130,000 BP

A 1.3 m thick deposit of dark reddish brown (2.5YR 3/4) clay rich colluvium spanned a depth of 220–350 cm. The low frequencies of artefacts suggest a period of infrequent human occupation. Bracketed in time by TL dates above and below.

Unit IX – Stage 7/6 interface: 170,000 BP (uncertain typological affinity) (fig. 2.32)

A band of sediment 10–30 cm thick (350–380 cm below datum) marked by a change in colour, texture and an increase in artefact content, including well preserved bone. Colour varies from dark brown (7.5 YR 3/4) to dark reddish brown (2.5 YR 3/4). Lenses of degraded limestone grit are intercalated with colluvium. An irregular undulating surface that looks eroded and on which complete bovid longbones were found. Represents exposed surface of the deposit before it was buried by colluvium. A single TL date of 172±22 ka BP on burnt quartz is associated with this unit.

Unit X – Stage 7, dark reddish brown sediment: 170,000+

Sedimentological unit from 380 to 460 cm distinguished by colour (5YR 3/4), gritty texture and some manganese nodules and pale mottling. Not directly dated and assumed to be greater than 170 ka BP.

Unit XI – Stage 7, dark reddish brown sediment: 170,000+

Sedimentological unit from 460 to 560/580 cm with slight colour change (2.5YR 2.5/4) and reduction in grit content. Human radius fragments found at 540 cm. Not directly dated.

Unit XII – Stage 7, very dark brown sediment: 170,000+

Sedimentological unit from 560 to 650 cm defined by colour (10YR 2/2) and comparatively soft texture. Manganese nodules increasingly common toward the bottom of the unit where they coalesce into blocks. Not directly dated.

Figure 2.32 The D10/D9 section at the end of the 1996 season. The pale band of sediment beneath the string is the Stage 6/7 interface (unit IX). The sediment above is Stage 6 colluvium (unit VIII). The colluvium and the interface are the two most distinctive stratigraphic markers across the site.

Unit XIII – Stage 7, strong brown sediment: 170,000+

Sedimentological unit between 650 and 750 cm defined by colour (7.5YR 4/6). Undated.

Unit XIV – Stage 7, dark yellowish brown: 170,000+

Sedimentological and archaeological unit from 750 to 790 cm that ends with dolomite bedrock. The sediment is defined by its colour (10YR 3/4) and gritty texture that results from weathered bedrock. Probably a lag deposit of informal quartz cobble cores and flakes. Abundant microfauna. Dated to 172 ± 21 ka BP, which is assumed to be a minimum age.

Aspects of the sediment chemistry, mineralogy and granulometry are described in appendix 2. The analyses confirm a colluvial origin for the deposit as a whole. The combined evidence of shifts in carbonate content, magnetic susceptibility and grain size ratios reflect two major stratigraphic boundaries in the sequence at 100 cm and approximately 300 cm below datum. The first corresponds with a depositional hiatus between 96 and 103 cm (unit VI) that separates the occupation of unit V (40 ka BP) and the main Middle Stone Age occupation dated to the Last Interglacial (see next chapter). The second boundary at 300 cm occurs in the middle of unit VIII (260–365 cm) which is dated to Stage 6. This artefactually poor deposit represents a long interval of little or no occupation of the cave. The sedimentological signatures may be recording an interval of maximum aridity and cold. Below 500 cm, cave spall makes a larger contribution to the sediment matrix than previously. The infrequent and ephemeral human presence in the lower units may account for the increased proportions of autochthonous sediments.

3　Mumbwa Caves chronology

L Barham and N Debenham

Before the renewed excavations at Mumbwa Caves in 1993, the only radiometric dates published for the Middle Stone Age of Zambia came from Kalemba Rock Shelter (DW Phillipson 1976), Twin Rivers (Clark 1971) and Kalambo Falls (Clark 1969, 1974). At Kalemba, the radiocarbon samples dated the later phases of the technological tradition (~27–23 ka BP, see chapter 13) with an underlying phase associated with an infinite date (>37 ka BP). At both Twin Rivers and Kalambo Falls, the assemblages attributed to the first phases of the Middle Stone Age (Sangoan–Lupemban) are now considered to be beyond the range of the radiocarbon technique (Clark 1988; Barham & Smart 1996; Sheppard & Kleindienst 1996). As a consequence, most of the Middle Stone Age in Zambia is effectively undated. A similar situation prevails in Zimbabwe where assemblages thought to be older than 40 ka BP have not been dated by techniques other than radiocarbon (Walker 1995). Further afield in central Africa, the only TL and ESR dates from the region have come from the controversial site of Katanda 9, former Zaire (Brooks et al 1995); otherwise the Middle Stone Age sequence is bracketed by radiocarbon dates (van Noten 1982). The most comprehensively dated sequences come from cave sites in South Africa (eg, Klasies River Mouth, Border Cave, Die Kelders) where two or more independent techniques have been used to extend sequences beyond the limitations of the radiocarbon technique. The southern African model of dating the Middle Stone Age provided a stimulus for the renewed excavation of Mumbwa Caves.

A range of techniques has been applied to the Mumbwa sequence including radiocarbon (charcoal), thermoluminescence (burnt quartz and calcite), optically stimulated luminescence (sediment) and electron spin resonance (tooth enamel). Amino acid racemisation as a dating technique was not attempted given the absence of ostrich eggshell in the pre-Holocene units. Charcoal was also scarce below a depth of 60 cm in Area III and where found in Areas I and II it proved to be intrusive (see below). The most effective technique to date has been TL on burnt quartz and calcite. These two materials, recovered from hearths or areas with other signs of burning, provided the basis for building the chronological framework.

THERMOLUMINESCENCE

Thirty-five samples of burnt quartz and calcite were submitted for TL analysis to Quaternary TL Surveys (QTLS). The samples represented the full main cave sequence and three were submitted from the dambo excavation. Quartz samples were identified *in situ* as heated if they exhibited cracking and discoloration that might include a dull white crust. An informal experiment was carried out at Mumbwa using the campfire and local vein quartz to develop guidelines for recognising burnt quartz in the deposits. Flakes and cores were placed at roughly 10 cm intervals across the fire and heated overnight. In the morning, when removed from the ashes the quartz retained considerable heat. Large blocks such as those found in the Area II and III hearths would have made natural radiators for use in the cave. The flakes nearest the centre of the fire were, unsurprisingly, most affected by the heat. Cracks were extensive and the surface texture had altered from waxy to matt and developed an uneven white crust. The density of the quartz changed too with the most heavily burnt pieces becoming friable and powdery. Samples near the edge of the fire showed little visible evidence of heating. A gradient of decreasing cracking and surface alteration could be traced from the centre to periphery of the hearth. TL sensitivity is affected by overheating and underheating of quartz and can make the samples unsuitable for palaeodose measurement. Quartz suitable for TL dating need not bear visible signs of heat damage, but in the case of Mumbwa only those pieces that showed some signs of heating were collected. The practical difficulties of transporting large numbers of samples for analysis and the potential costs meant the collection strategy had to be tightly focused.

To be dateable by TL quartz must be heated to at least 450°C as is the case for flint (Valladas 1992). The experiment at Mumbwa did not include temperature readings of the camp fire or control over the kinds and quantity of woods burned. The size of the quartz samples and the duration of exposure were not controlled either, but the exercise provided some basic visual clues for the excavators to use in deciding whether to retain samples for dating. The context in which the samples were found was also weighed in the balance. Discoloured and cracked quartz that was not directly associated with an area of burning was not usually submitted for analysis. In practice, the overlapping of hearths in the top metre of D9/D10 (fig. 2.16a) will have resulted in the mixing and reheating of earlier samples by later fires. The exception in Area II was the thick ash feature (fig. 3.1) which was a discrete feature. A single piece of quartz was incorporated into the baked sediment at the base of the feature and was submitted for dating. The large hearth in D11 (Area III) (fig. 2.19) contained burnt quartz and was also a well-defined feature with no evidence of re-use. A sediment sample was taken from a 30 cm radius around each quartz and calcite piece for laboratory measurement of the background radiation in the burial environment.

Palaeodose evaluation

The TL dating procedure involves two measurements. The first is an evaluation of the total radiation dose received by the sample since it was heated in antiquity. This quantity of radiation, which is referred to as the palaeodose, is determined by observing the TL emissions of the material. The second phase of the date measurement is an assessment of the rate at which the palaeodose was received by the sample from naturally occurring radioactive sources both within and around

the buried object. By combining these two measurements, the length of time over which the palaeodose accumulated can be calculated. Of the thirty-five samples submitted, all but six had TL signals in saturation and could not be used for palaeodose measurement. This poor result can be explained in part by the low saturation dose for quartz in general, and more specifically by the high radiation levels in the cave combined with the potential age of the site.

The evaluation of the palaeodose received by the Mumbwa specimens began with the removal of the outer 3 mm of the stones. This surface layer had been exposed to light and to beta radiation from the surrounding sediment. The interior part was crushed and sieved to select grains 75–125 μm in size. These grains were deposited onto a set of stainless steel discs for TL examination.

TL observations were performed to measure the natural TL intensity induced by the palaeodose. Approximately half of the sample discs were irradiated with different beta doses, while the rest were left unirradiated. The unirradiated discs yielded the natural TL intensity, while observations of the irradiated discs showed the growth of TL intensity with increasing beta dose. The palaeodose was evaluated by extrapolating the TL

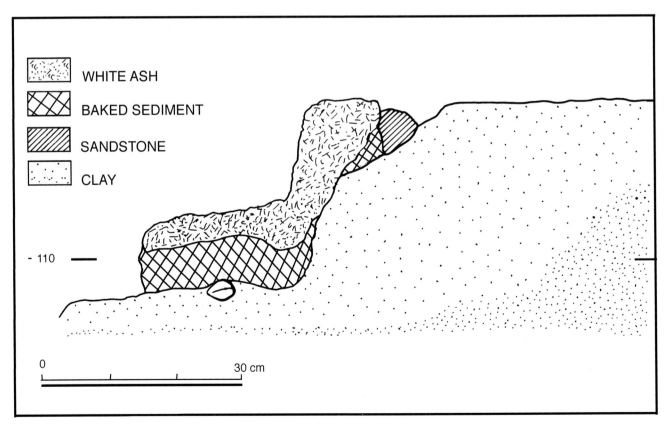

WHITE ASH

BAKED SEDIMENT

SANDSTONE

CLAY

- 110

0   30 cm

Figure 3.1 Section through an ash filled pit in D10 (Area II) showing the location of a quartz core at the base of the area of burning. The sample is dated by TL to 113±13 ka BP.

growth to its initial state of zero intensity. The form of the curve of TL growth versus dose used for this extrapolation is generally non-linear, and was obtained from a second set of observations. The measured values of the palaeodoses are given in table 3.1.

Because a small part of the palaeodose is contributed by alpha rays, it is necessary to measure the TL response of the samples to alpha irradiation. These measurements were performed on fine grains of approximately 2–10 μm size, which were deposited onto a set of aluminium discs. The growth of TL in these discs under alpha irradiation was measured and compared with that induced by beta radiation.

Dose rate assessments

During burial the Mumbwa stones were exposed to alpha and beta radiation originating from naturally occurring radioactive elements within the samples, to gamma rays from the surrounding sediment and also to cosmic rays. The radiation dose rates resulting from the alpha and beta components were measured by means of alpha counting and potassium analysis of the stones. The gamma dose rates were assessed by applying the same techniques to representative samples of the sediments and rock found close to the TL samples. Strong spatial variations in gamma flux would have occurred near the cave walls, but only one specimen recovered near bedrock (D9–13–2) was subjected to this source of variation. In this case, three-dimensional computer modelling was used to aid the dose rate evaluations. Cosmic dose rates were estimated from the overburden

of material that had covered the TL samples. The various dose rate assessments are summarised in table 3.2. These assessments take account of the present water contents of the sediments and of the uncertainties in the past water contents. The effective alpha dose is calculated using the measured alpha responses of the fine grains discs.

The total dose rate, being the sum of the alpha, beta, gamma and cosmic contributions, gives the rate at which the palaeodose accumulated. The TL age is obtained as the ratio of the palaeodose to the total dose rate, and gives the date of the last heating of the stone to temperatures in excess of 400°C. The results of the date measurements are shown below. The error limits include both random and systematic uncertainties and represent the 68 per cent confidence level.

There is no measurable age difference between the Area II samples from a hearth (D10–2–8, 103 cm) and the ash feature (D10–2–11, 115 cm) and the Area I artefact concentration interpreted as a windbreak (G8–9–1, base of feature at 254–259 cm). All effectively date to the Last Interglacial. The TL dates for the top of the interface (Unit IX, square E10–1–19, 350–366 cm) and for the base of the deposit (Unit XIV, square D9–13–2, 770–790 cm) are also statistically identical. They are both attributable to either the end of interglacial Stage 7 or to early glacial Stage 6. The samples dated from the windbreak and from the basal deposit were heated calcite which was datable by virtue of its high saturation dose.

The sample from the large hearth in Area I (D11–8–1,

Table 3.1 Palaeodoses, total dose rates and TL dates

Square	Depth/Unit (cm)	Palaeodose (Gy)	Total dose rate (Gy/ka)	TL age (ka BP)
D11–8–1	96/V	36.4±6.1	0.919±0.086	39.6±7.6
D10–2–8	103/VII	100.2±5.3	0.890±0.087	113±13
D10–2–11	115/VII	99.2±4.6	0.930±0.078	107±11
G8–9–1	254–9/VII	175±11	1.461±0.106	120±12
E10–1–19	348–66/IX	238±21	1.388±0.124	172±22
D9–13–2	770–90/XIV	473±21	2.746±0.323	172±21

Palaeodoses are expressed in Grays (Gy) and total dose rates are given in Grays per millennium (Gy/ka).

Table 3.2 Alpha, beta, gamma and cosmic dose rate assessments

Square	Effective alpha (Gy/ka)	Beta (Gy/ka)	Gamma (Gy/ka)	Cosmic dose rate (Gy/ka)
D11–8–1	0.003	0.002	0.885	0.028
D10–2–8	0.008	0.009	0.845	0.028
D10–2–11	0.027	0.060	0.816	0.028
G8–9–1	0.082	0.095	1.259	0.025
E10–1–19	0.002	0.012	1.350	0.023
D9–13–2	0.014	0.015	2.698	0.019

Dose rate are given in Grays per millennium (Gy/ka).

96 cm) at 40±7.6 ka BP was considerably younger than all the others, but only separated by seven to nine centimetres from the underlying D10 dates of 107–113 ka BP. Such a large chronological lacuna suggests either an erosional episode that has removed 60,000 years of deposit or a period of minimal human occupation and sedimentation.

TL on sediments – optically stimulated luminescence (OSL)

As part of the 1993 investigation of the feasibility of dating the Mumbwa sequence, three sediment samples were collected for optically stimulated TL dating. The dating of sediments by TL relies on the exposure of sediment grains (quartz in the case of Mumbwa) to sunlight at the time of deposition. Sunlight bleaches the TL signal and is the starting point for the accumulation of TL caused by ionising radiation from the surroundings. Depending on the intensity of the sunlight, the length of exposure needed to reset individual grains varies from one day to a week. The current TL intensity of the sediments reflects the combined effects of the environmental dose of radiation and time since deposition and is the basis for calculating a date (Aitken 1998). Sediments that have received prolonged exposure to sunlight are most suitable and these include aeolian sediments and low energy fluvial and lacustrine deposits. The maximum age range of the technique is 100–150,000 years.

In his analysis of the sterile red clay deposit, Unit VIII in this study, Zeuner (in Clark 1942:152) identified an aeolian origin for the clay particles. The possibility that TL could now date this stratum was integrated into the 1993 excavation strategy. Three sediment samples were collected and *in situ* readings of environmental radiation were taken with a portable gamma spectrometer. The samples were collected from above and below the colluvium as well as from the red clay deposit itself. S Stokes undertook the analysis at the School of Geography, University of Oxford. The results were equivocal. The quartz sand fraction was small and discoloured but a fine-grained (4–11 μm) quartz fraction was extracted (S Stokes pers comm). Initial measurements on the sand

fraction showed a high degree of scatter and no signal growth consistent with samples in saturation and undatable. Saturation resulted from either the samples being older than the maximum age of quartz dosimetry (>100 ka) or the sand grains having not been fully exposed to sunlight at deposition and so not being completely reset. In light of the TL results on burnt quartz from units VII and IX, the colluvium is indeed too old for this technique as are the lower sediments. The deposits above the colluvium may also be too old. Equally, the colluvial origin of unit VIII and for almost all of the Mumbwa deposit (appendix 2) meant that full exposure to sunlight was unlikely. The fine-grained fraction was not analysed because it also would have been in saturation.

The disappointing results of the analyses were partially offset by an OSL date on burnt sediment collected from Area I. The sample was collected from beneath the large hearth in H7 and just above the arc-shaped concentration of occupation debris. M D Bateman undertook the analysis at the Sheffield Centre for International Drylands Research (SCIDR). An age estimate of 130±6 ka BP was based on a single aliquot approach (because of a high degree of scatter) and an average palaeomoisture of 1%±1% derived from non-cave sediments from Zambia (MD Bateman pers comm). The possibility of partial resetting could not be ruled out. The analytical data is presented in table 3.3. The date is consistent with the Last Interglacial results obtained by TL on heated calcite from Area I and on burnt quartz from Area II.

ELECTRON SPIN RESONANCE (ESR) DATING

Seven teeth and associated sediments from a 30 cm radius were submitted to L Zhou at the Godwin Laboratory for ESR dating. The theory and practice of the technique is described elsewhere (Aitken 1998; Schwarcz in press) and need not be reviewed except to note that with enamel the dose rate is greatly affected by the absorption of uranium from the burial environment. The burial environment of the Mumbwa samples proved to be a factor in the limited success of this technique. Samples were submitted for analysis from the Area I

Table 3.3 Analytical data for sediment sample from H7–2–8 (195–202 cm), Area I

ED evaluation

Method	TL/IRSL/OSL	Maximum dose	ED ±	Type	Age
additive dose	OSL	350 Gy	467.82±16.54	single aliquot	130.0±6.2

Dosimetry ICP method

Uranium	Thorium	Potassium	Cosmic dose	Moisture	Total dose
(ppm)	(ppm)	(%)	(μGy/a)	(%)	(μGy/a)
3.70±0.17	14.80±0.75	1.37±0.07	176.73±8.84	1±1	3599±115

windbreak features (H9), the main Middle Stone Age occupation deposits in Area II (D9, D10) and the lower portion of the Later Stone Age in Area III from 56–78 cm (D12–2–6 and D12–2–10). The Area II enamel samples were too altered by mineralisation to be datable and the analysis of the single Area I sample has yet to be completed. Preliminary dates from Area III indicate a Late Glacial to early Holocene age between 12 and 9 ka BP. This range is based on five sub-samples that behave consistently with a high dose rate. The full analytical data for these samples will be published separately (L Zhou pers comm). Sample D12–2–6 with an age of 9 ka BP comes from approximately the same depth as a radiocarbon sample (D11–6–3) with a calibrated age of approximately 7.6 ka BP (table 3.4). The discrepancy may not be significant depending on the final analytical report that will incorporate the effects of estimated water content on the ESR age.

RADIOCARBON DATING

Charcoal was reported by Dart and Del Grande to be a feature of the Mumbwa sequence from top to bottom. Excavations in 1993 of the lower deposits beneath unit VIII recovered only sparse traces of charcoal that proved to be intrusive or part of the infill of the central pit. The abundant manganese nodules throughout the lower deposits may have been mistaken for charcoal in 1930 as they were initially in 1993 (Barham 1993). The only two charcoal fragments found in the colluvium of G4 were submitted for AMS analysis and the essentially modern dates show them to have been intrusive (Barham 1996, 192). No other charcoal was found in Area I. A single piece was found in Area II at a depth of 130 cm below datum among the intercalated hearths. AMS analysis of this piece produced a conventional radiocarbon age of 13,040±130 BP with a two sigma calibrated range of 15,985 to 15,420 Cal BP (Beta–126843) and a C13/C12 ratio of −26.0‰. This Late Glacial age conflicts with the TL dates of 107 ka and 113 ka BP from the overlying

hearths in Area II. The charcoal also comes from a depth that is 50 cm below the ESR sample dated to 12 ka BP from Area III. The difference between the two results should be greater than 3 ka even given variable rates of sedimentation. The radiocarbon age is too young to be explained by contamination with modern carbon (N Debenham pers comm) so displacement seems the likely process involved. This area had been disturbed by the steps cut in 1930, as well as by root penetration from vegetation at the entrance and termite activity. A piece of charcoal from the first layer of D9 (106 cm) also proved to be intrusive (1280±50, −24.4‰, 1295–1075 Cal BP, Beta–126842).

Charcoal was found in Area III in the first 60 cm of deposit and 12 samples were submitted in 1999 to Beta Analytic for AMS or extended count analysis. Four samples were submitted to the University of Cambridge Radiocarbon Dating Research Group in 1994 and the results have yet to be reported. The dated samples represent a nearly continuous sequence of 2–5 cm thick excavation levels in D11. The Beta Analytic results are in table 3.4.

The dates for the first 34 cm show a progressive increase in age from the historic present to about 2000 BP. The first occurrence of pottery in the sequence is associated with a date of 1080±80 BP (D11–5–1). A period of approximately 4–5000 years separates the late Holocene sequence from the underlying dates. The separation takes place across a depth of only 5cm between 34 and 39 cm below datum and reflects either a period of minimal human occupation or a depositional/ erosional lacuna. Of the five dates from 34 to 62 cm, three (D11–5–4, 5–5 and 6–3) show a stratigraphic progression in age, one is intrusive (D11–6–1) and the other is inverted in the sequence (D11–5–3). The intrusive sample notwithstanding, the dates form an early Holocene cluster.

Beneath 60 cm, the frequency of charcoal in the deposit declines noticeably and from the rare samples

Table 3.4 Radiocarbon analyses on charcoal from Area III, Mumbwa Caves

Square locus/level	Depth cm	C13/C12 ratio	Conventional	Cal BP C14 age BP	Lab no. 2 sigma
D11–1–1	2–8	−24.7‰	440±50	360–330	Beta–126838
D11–1–2	8–14	−26.2‰	150±60	305–0	Beta–126839
D11–2–1	14–17	−25.0‰	440±70	550–315	Beta–126840
D11–3–1	17–20	−26.0‰	1140±50	1175–945	Beta–126841
D11–4–1	20–22	−25.0‰	1040±90	1165–755	Beta–126844
D11–5–1	22–28	−25.0‰	1080±80	865–800	Beta–126845
D11–5–2	28–34	−25.0‰	2080±100	2330–1830	Beta–126846
D11–5–3	34–39	−26.8‰	7300±80	8220–7955	Beta–126847
D11–5–4	39–44	−25.7‰	5700±80	6670–6305	Beta–126848
D11–5–5	44–48	−26.3‰	6400±70	7415–7260	Beta–126849
D11–6–1	48–56	−25.6‰	390±50	525–310	Beta–126850
D11–6–3	58–62	−24.0‰	6700±80	7680–7435	Beta–126851

found and dated in Areas I and II the occurrence of charcoal below this depth is almost always the result of displacement. A range of taphonomic factors could have contributed to the vertical movement of charcoal. Erosion of the exposed deposits has been extensive since the first excavation in 1930 and has accelerated in recent years with the current project. Section faces are degrading and collapsing with some mixing of deposit occurring as a result, especially along the drip line. The steps cut down through the deposit in 1930 have contributed to the contamination of the Area II sediments with more recent material. Excavators and other vandals aside, biological agents continue to affect the integrity of the site. Termites are active in the upper 150 cm of deposit especially where roots are most common. The termites create voids where roots have been digested and these voids then fill with overlying sediments or simply collapse. Wasps have burrowed into all the standing sections and in doing so have transformed these surfaces into a sponge like structure. The intersecting burrows not only weaken section faces but also contribute to the vertical movement of sediment. The mammals living in the cave, in particular, a cane rat, side striped jackal and porcupine are all active burrowers.

DATING OVERVIEW

A pattern of intermittent occupation emerges from the still inadequately dated Mumbwa sequence. The site was not continuously occupied over the past 170+ ka: five phases of use are separated by four periods of abandonment or by depositional lacunae (fig. 3.2). These are equated with the global sequence of isotope stages to form a tentative analytical framework with which to view human demographic responses to climate change (chapter 12). The linking of global stages to phases in an incomplete cave sequence involves assumptions of correspondence based on chronology alone. Chapters 4–7 will provide additional palaeoecological data with which to assess these assumptions.

Units XIV–IX represent the earliest phase of occupation and the top of unit IX coincides with the onset of Stage 6 (186–130 ka BP) glacial conditions. The TL date of 172±21 ka BP from unit XIV can be considered a minimum age. The true age range of the earliest occupation may extend to 255 ka BP (Stage 7.4) based on the micromammal content reported in chapter 6. Full glacial conditions are reached during the deposition of unit VIII (colluvium) and the site is effectively abandoned between 170 and 130 ka BP. The longest phase of occupation occurs during the Last Interglacial (Stage 5.5) between 130 and 115 ka BP and perhaps through 105 ka BP (Stage 5.3). The deposits within this time range are treated as a single analytical entity (unit VII) because of the lack of clear stratigraphic separation and limited chronological control. A few centimetres (unit

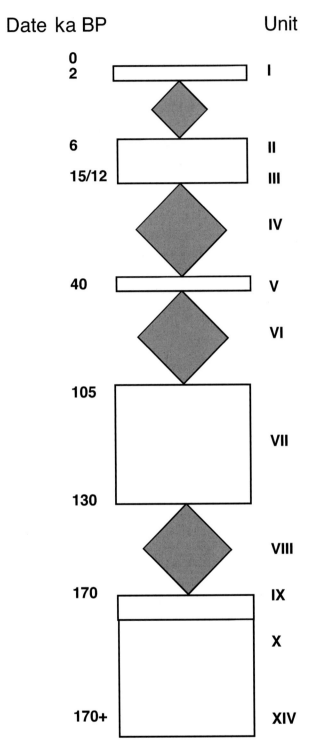

Figure 3.2 Schematic diagram of periods of occupation (open rectangles) and non-occupation (black diamonds) at Mumbwa Caves and associated stratigraphic units.

VI) separate unit VII and unit V, but the chronological hiatus spans 60 ka. This portion of the sequence is poorly preserved in Area II and the inferred gap in occupation is a working hypothesis. This caveat aside, the period from 100–40 ka BP spans the climatic downturn of Stage 4 (74–59 ka BP) and ends with the onset of the Stage 3 Hengelo interstadial (~39 ka BP). Mumbwa Caves was probably occupied during other interstadials of Stage 5 and 3, but without additional dates for the sequence this remains an unsupported assumption. Another chronological gap occurs between units V and III, from 40 to 15/12 ka BP. Thirteen centimetres of undated deposit separate the two in Area I (unit IV), and this deposit can be correlated, in part, with the Last Glacial Maximum (21 ka Cal BP) and the preceding climatic downturn. Unit IV also marks the latest occupation of the site by foragers who made Middle Stone Age tools and may date to about 23 ka BP by correlation with dated deposits at Kalemba Rock Shelter in eastern Zambia (DW Phillipson 1976) and Leopard's Hill Cave near Lusaka (Miller 1969). Unit III represents a Late Glacial to early Holocene occupation from 15–9 ka BP and unit II is strictly early Holocene in age (9–6.6 ka BP). Only 5 cm of deposit marks the mid-Holocene gap (6–2 ka BP) that separates the early and later Holocene in Area I. This lacuna is neatly bracketed by radiocarbon dates and coincides with a period of active dune formation in western Zambia (O'Connor & Thomas 1999).

The chronological framework for the Mumbwa Caves sequence clearly needs refining to substantiate the proposed pattern of intermittent occupation governed by climate change. In the interim, two periods of abandonment appear to be relatively well dated, unit VIII (170–130 ka BP) and the mid-Holocene gap (6–2 ka BP). Both periods are associated with increased aridity on a regional scale and provide the link between the Mumbwa Caves sequence and climatically driven changes in biogeography (see chapter 12).

4 Macromammals and reptiles

RG Klein and K Cruz-Uribe

The 1993–1996 excavations at Mumbwa Caves produced 687 macromammal bones that we could identify to skeletal part and taxon. We define macromammals as species in which adults weigh at least 0.75 kg, which excludes tiny rodents, insectivores, and other micromammals that owls commonly collect. Mumbwa has provided a large micromammal sample that is described in chapters 5 and 6. Along with the macromammal bones there were three bones of tortoise and nine of monitor lizard which are also listed here.

In our analysis, we recorded the field excavation unit for each bone, but the individual field units generally contained fewer than five identifiable bones, and we therefore summarise the fauna according to the seven major culture-stratigraphic units established as outlined on pages 38, 41 and 42. From top to bottom, these are: Iron Age/LSA (unit I), Early Holocene LSA (unit II), Late Glacial LSA (unit III), LSA/MSA Interface (unit IV), Upper MSA (unit V), Middle or main MSA occupation (unit VII), and Lower MSA (units VIII–XIV) We have specifically ignored 10 bones that could not be un-equivocally assigned to one of these units.

Our study revealed essentially the same macro-mammal taxa that Broom and Cooke reported from prior excavations (Clark 1942; Cooke 1950). Table 4.1 presents the Number of Identified Specimens (NISP) and the Minimum Number of Individuals (MNI) by which each taxon is represented in each 1993–1996 culture-stratigraphic unit. Klein and Cruz-Uribe (1984) explain the logic behind the MNI calculations. The MNIs were computed on the premise that the same individuals could be represented in any excavation sub-unit within a more comprehensive culture-stratigraphic unit. Since the culture-stratigraphic units often span thousands or tens of thousands of years, this is clearly a very conservative assumption, and the actual number of individuals in any cultural unit may lie closer to the NISP. The MNIs tend to be very small, and figure 4.1 therefore employs the NISPs to illustrate the relative abundance of the principal mammalian taxa or taxonomic groups in each cultural unit.

Table 4.1 and figure 4.1 show that bovids dominate heavily, but their bones are mainly small fragments that we could not identify to species. We therefore assigned them to four successive size categories: small, small-medium, large-medium, and large. Other analysts (including, for example, Bartram and Marean (1999), Brain (1981), Plug (1985), and Voigt (1983)) routinely use the same categories, although they often label them 1 to 4, from smallest to largest. With regard to bovid species represented by teeth at Mumbwa Caves, small species include oribi and grysbok/steenbok, small-medium species are antilopini and grey duiker, large-medium species include kudu, roan and sable antelope, southern reedbuck, blue wildebeest, and other possible alcela-phines, and large species are only eland. Antilopini are represented by two teeth whose morphology suggests springbok (*Antidorcas marsupialis*) as opposed to a like-sized gazelle (*Gazella thomsoni*), but a firm identification would require additional specimens. Three teeth that appeared too small for blue wildebeest, but that we could not identify more precisely represent 'Other possible alcelaphines'. From an historic perspective, the most likely species are Lichtenstein's hartebeest (*Alcelaphus lichtensteini*) and tsessebe (*Damaliscus lunatus*).

Table 4.2 provides the number of bones in each culture-stratigraphic unit on which we observed burning (charring) and other kinds of damage. Table 4.3 lists the NISP and MNI per skeletal part for each bovid size group in the pure Stone Age units below the composite Iron Age/LSA unit I. We excluded the Iron Age/LSA bones because they are much less heavily leached, and this alone would probably produce a difference in skeletal part representation. The data in the tables and figure inform mainly on the identity of the bone collector and on the environment(s) in which the bones accumulated.

THE BONE COLLECTOR

The abundance of artefacts at Mumbwa and the repeated occurrence of hearths clearly indicate that people accumulated many of the bones, but seven coprolites (one from the Early Holocene LSA (unit II), two from the Late Glacial LSA (unit III), one from the LSA/MSA Interface (unit IV) and three from the Middle MSA (unit VII)) show that hyaenas may also have contributed. In sub-Saharan caves, it is always possible that porcupines also played a role. As we sorted, we examined the

Table 4.1 The Number of Identifiable Specimens (NISP) and the Minimum Number of Individuals (MNI) by which large mammals are represented in the main culture-stratigraphic units at Mumbwa Cave. The NISPs and MNIs for individual hyrax, suid, and bovid species are based on teeth alone. The NISPs and MNIs for the general hyrax and suid categories and for the bovid size categories are based on all identifiable elements. For definitions of the bovid size categories, see the text

Linnaean name	Vernacular name	Iron age and LSA NISPs	MNIs	Early Holocene LSA NISPs	MNIs	Late Glacial LSA NISPs	MNIs	LSA/MSA Interface NISPs	MNIs	Upper MSA NISPs	MNIs	Middle MSA NISPs	MNIs	Lower MSA NISPs	MNIs
Leporidae gen. et sp. indet.	hare(s)	0	0	6	1	2	1	0	0	0	0	10	2	0	0
Thryonomys swinderianus	larger cane rat	1	1	4	1	0	0	0	0	0	0	3	1	1	0
Hystrix africaeaustralis	porcupine	1	1	3	1	2	1	0	0	0	0	5	1	0	0
Phataginus temminicki	Cape pangolin	0	0	1	1	1	1	0	0	0	0	1	1	0	0
Papio ursinus	chacma baboon	0	0	1	1	0	0	0	0	0	0	1	1	0	0
Canis sp.	dog and/or jackal	0	0	1	1	0	0	0	0	0	0	1	0	2	1
Lycaon pictus	Cape hunting dog	0	0	0	0	0	0	0	0	0	0	2	1	0	0
Vulpes chama	Cape fox	0	0	0	0	0	0	0	0	0	0	0	0	0	0
Herpestes ichneumon	Egyptian mongoose	0	0	2	1	0	0	0	0	0	0	0	0	0	0
Suricata suricatta	suricate	0	0	0	0	0	0	0	0	0	0	0	0	0	0
Hyaenidae gen. et sp. indet.	hyaena	0	0	1	1	3	1	1	1	0	0	3	1	0	0
Felis libyca	wildcat	0	0	2	1	1	1	0	0	0	0	1	1	0	0
Panthera pardus	leopard	0	0	0	0	0	0	1	1	0	0	0	0	0	0
Viverridae gen. et sp. Indet.	Egyptian mongoose-size viverrid	2	1	1	1	0	0	0	0	0	0	0	0	0	0
Carnivora gen. et sp. Indet.	wildcat-size carnivore	0	0	1	1	0	0	0	0	0	0	1	1	0	0
Carnivora gen. et sp. Indet.	leopard-size carnivore	0	0	1	1	0	0	0	0	0	0	0	0	0	0
Orycteropus afer	aardvark	0	0	2	1	1	1	0	0	0	0	2	0	0	0
Procavia capensis	rock hyrax	6	2	4	1	2	1	0	0	0	0	2	0	2	0
Dendrohyrax arboreus	tree hyrax	2	1	0	0	0	0	0	0	0	0	0	0	0	0
Hyracoidea – general	hyraxes (independent of species)	14	2	10	1	4	1	1	1	0	0	5	1	0	0
Equus burchelli	plains zebra	3	1	10	2	7	1	0	0	4	1	8	1	0	0
Rhinocerotidae gen. et sp. indet.	indeterminate rhinoceros	0	0	0	0	0	0	0	0	0	0	1	1	0	0
Potamochoerus porcus	bushpig	1	1	0	0	0	0	0	0	0	0	0	0	0	0
Phacochoerus aethiopicus	warthog	1	1	10	1	1	1	0	0	0	0	10	1	1	1
Suidae – general	pigs (independent of species)	5	1	38	2	19	2	1	1	0	0	21	1	1	1
Taurotragus oryx	eland	0	0	0	0	0	0	0	0	0	0	1	1	1	1
Tragelaphus strepsiceros	greater kudu	0	0	0	0	0	0	0	0	0	0	0	0	1	1
Hippotragus sp.	roan or sable antelope	0	0	3	1	1	1	0	0	0	0	0	0	1	1
Redunca arundinum	southern reedbuck	1	1	2	1	2	1	0	0	3	1	3	1	2	1
Connochaetes taurinus	blue wildebeest	1	1	11	3	2	1	1	1	1	1	11	3	1	1
Alcelaphini – general	wildebeest and possible hartebeest	1	1	12	3	2	1	1	1	1	1	12	3	2	1
Antilopini gen.et sp. Indet.	springbok or gazelle	0	0	0	0	0	0	0	0	0	0	0	0	2	1
Sylvicapra grimmia	gray duiker	1	1	0	0	0	0	0	0	0	0	1	1	2	1
Ourebia ourebi	oribi	1	1	0	0	0	0	0	0	0	0	1	1	0	0
Raphicerus sp(p.)	grysbok and/or steenbok	0	0	2	1	0	0	0	0	0	0	0	0	0	0
	small bovid(s)	7	1	28	1	8	1	3	1	0	0	7	1	1	1
	small-medium bovid(s)	4	1	26	2	15	1	2	1	0	0	14	1	4	1
	large-medium bovid(s)	15	1	95	3	62	3	9	1	3	1	50	3	10	1
	large bovid(s)	3	1	33	2	34	2	6	1	2	1	11	1	3	0
Varanus sp.	monitor lizard	3	1	4	1	1	1	1	0	0	0	1	1	1	0
Chelonia gen. et sp. Indet.	unidentified tortoise	0	0	3	1	0	0	0	0	0	0	0	0	0	0

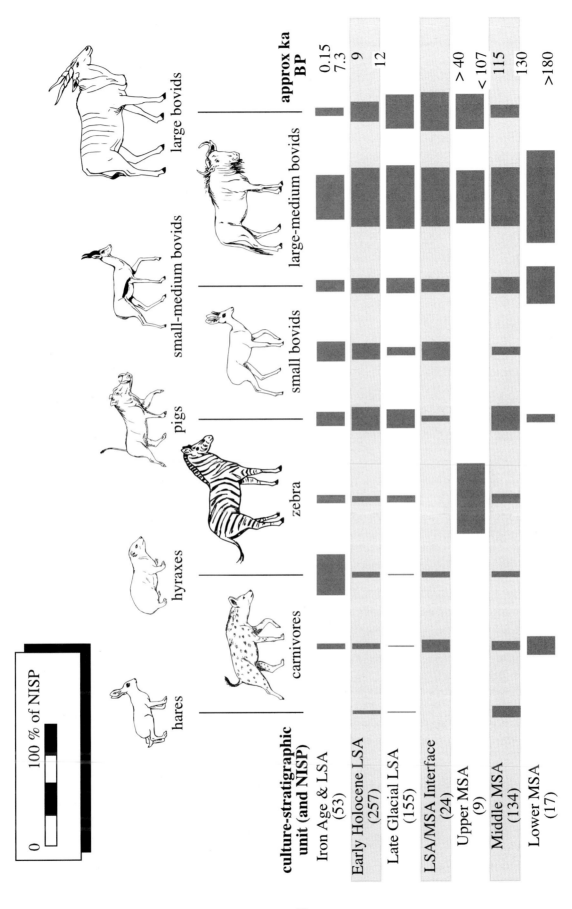

Figure 4.1 The relative abundance of the principal mammalian taxa or taxonomic groups in each unit based on Number of Identifiable Specimens (NISP).

Table 4.2 The number of identified bones with macroscopically conspicuous damage in the principal culture-stratigraphic units of Mumbwa Caves

Units	Burned	Carnivore-chewed	Cut	Acid-etched	Porcupine-gnawed	Total
Iron Age and LSA – I	0	0	0	0	1	55
Early Holocene LSA – II	23	0	1	1	2	268
Late Glacial LSA – III	12	0	0	0	1	159
LSA/MSA interface – IV	3	0	0	0	0	24
Upper MSA- V	1	0	0	0	0	9
Middle MSA- VII	7	0	0	0	0	145
Lower MSA – VIII – XIV	0	0	0	0	0	17

bones for telltale damage that might reveal the relative roles of people, hyaenas, and porcupines. Porcupine gnaw marks are particularly conspicuous and durable, and table 4.2 shows that we found them on only four bones. Since porcupines tend to gnaw more than 60 per cent of the bones they collect (Brain 1981), a significant porcupine contribution can probably be ruled out.

Damage is less helpful in separating the roles of people and hyaenas. Table 4.2 shows that burned bones are relatively common and, like the artefacts, they suggest an important human contribution. However, the table also shows that we observed only one stone tool cut mark and no carnivore tooth marks, although we did find one bone that may have been etched (or 'reduced') by hyaena gastric acids. Microscopic examination might increase the number of chewed or cut specimens, but the increase would probably be insubstantial, because table 4.3 shows that the fauna comprises relatively few of the meat and marrow-rich upper limb bones (humeri, radioulnae, femora, and tibiae) that people and hyaenas tend to damage most heavily. Instead, it is dominated by isolated teeth, podials, sesamoids, and fragmentary phalanges that have little or no food value and that are therefore less likely to exhibit cut or chew marks.

In theory, the pattern of skeletal part representation might itself be used to identify the collector. However, in this instance it is ambiguous, since it could have been created by either people or hyaenas, if they mainly scavenged carcasses from which other predators had already deleted the meatiest parts (upper limb bones) (Binford 1981, 1984). There is also the possibility that skeletal part representation in the Mumbwa Caves Stone Age units says less about collector behaviour than about post-depositional profile compaction and leaching. The Mumbwa bones are heavily leached and fragmented, and an indeterminate number of upper limb bones may have been rendered unidentifiable after burial or may have disappeared altogether. The Mumbwa pattern in which small, hard, readily identifiable bones prevail tends to dominate most fossil assemblages that have experienced equally intensive leaching and fragmentation (Klein 1980b).

In sum, based on bone damage, skeletal part representation, and associated items (artefacts and coprolites), people, hyaenas, or both could have contributed to the Mumbwa bone assemblage, and only the abundance of artefacts and burned bones implies that people were more important. A larger role for people may also be implied by the rarity of carnivores, since carnivore bones commonly make up more than 20 per cent of the total in fossil assemblages where abundant coprolites and a lack of stone artefacts unequivocally identify hyaenas as the principal collectors (Klein et al 1991).

THE PALAEOENVIRONMENT

Mumbwa Caves is situated in the heart of a vast stretch of wooded grassland that ecologists often call 'miombo woodland' and that Devred (in De Vos 1975) has designated the Zambezian Ecozone. In modern political terms, this zone includes southern Tanzania, southern Congo (ex-Zaire), most of Angola, Zambia, Malawi, northern Mozambique, and northern Zimbabwe.

Within the Zambezian Zone, the vegetation on relatively well-drained ridges, hills, or interfluves tends to comprise tall grass interspersed with trees that lose their leaves in the long dry season. In river valleys and along drainage lines, trees, consisting mainly of *Acacia*, are rarer, and tall grasses predominate. Mumbwa lies on the boundary between deciduous woodland to the north and acacia grassland to the south (Clark 1942). The Mumbwa people could also have exploited the seasonally flooded grassy flats along the Kafue River yet further south.

The mammalian fauna of the Zambezian Zone was highly diverse (Smithers 1966). Grazers dominated overall, but browsers including bushpig, bushbuck (*Tragelaphus scriptus*), steenbok (*Raphicerus campestris*), Sharpe's grysbok (*Raphicerus sharpei*), and grey duiker were locally numerous. (We provide Linnaean names only when these were not given previously and are not listed in table 4.1.) The principal grazers were plains (or Burchell's) zebra, warthog, blue wildebeest, Lichtenstein's hartebeest, tsessebe, and oribi. In more wooded settings, these species were joined by sable antelope (*Hippotragus*

Table 4.3 The Number of Identifiable Specimens (NISP) and the Minimum Number of Individuals (MNI) per skeletal part for bovids in the Stone Age culture-stratigraphic units at Mumbwa Caves. For definitions of the bovid size categories, see the text

	small bovids		small-medium bovids		large-medium bovids		large bovids	
	NISPs	**MNIs**	*NISPs*	**MNIs**	*NISPs*	**MNIs**	*NISPs*	**MNIs**
frontlet	0	**0**	0	**0**	0	**0**	0	**0**
occipital condyle	0	**0**	0	**0**	0	**0**	0	**0**
auditory bulla	0	**0**	0	**0**	0	**0**	0	**0**
premaxilla	0	**0**	1	**1**	0	**0**	0	**0**
maxillary dentition	3	**1**	4	**2**	21	**5**	1	**1**
mandibular dentition	3	**1**	10	**2**	19	**3**	2	**1**
hyoid	0	**0**	0	**0**	1	**1**	0	**0**
atlas	0	**0**	0	**0**	0	**0**	0	**0**
axis	0	**0**	0	**0**	0	**0**	0	**0**
cervical vertebrae 3-7	0	**0**	1	**1**	1	**1**	0	**0**
thoracic vertebrae	1	**1**	1	**1**	4	**2**	0	**0**
lumbar vertebrae	0	**0**	1	**1**	0	**0**	1	**1**
sacrum	0	**0**	0	**0**	1	**1**	0	**0**
caudal vertebrae	0	**0**	0	**0**	1	**1**	1	**1**
sternebrae	0	**0**	0	**0**	0	**0**	0	**0**
ribs	6	**1**	2	**1**	7	**2**	2	**1**
scapula	0	**0**	0	**0**	0	**0**	0	**0**
proximal humerus	0	**0**	0	**0**	0	**0**	0	**0**
distal humerus	0	**0**	0	**0**	1	**1**	0	**0**
proximal radius	0	**0**	0	**0**	2	**1**	3	**2**
distal radius	0	**0**	1	**1**	0	**0**	1	**1**
proximal ulna	2	**1**	0	**0**	1	**1**	2	**1**
distal ulna	1	**1**	0	**0**	0	**0**	0	**0**
carpals	0	**0**	2	**1**	13	**3**	5	**2**
proximal metacarpal	1	**1**	1	**1**	5	**1**	3	**1**
distal metacarpal	2	**2**	2	**2**	7	**3**	3	**1**
first phalange	11	**1**	12	**2**	30	**2**	15	**2**
second phalange	3	**1**	3	**1**	21	**3**	10	**2**
third phalange	4	**1**	4	**1**	7	**1**	1	**1**
pelvis	2	**1**	0	**0**	1	**1**	0	**0**
proximal femur	0	**0**	0	**0**	1	**1**	0	**0**
distal femur	0	**0**	1	**1**	0	**0**	0	**0**
patella	0	**0**	0	**0**	1	**1**	0	**0**
proximal tibia	0	**0**	1	**1**	0	**0**	0	**0**
distal tibia	0	**0**	1	**1**	2	**2**	3	**2**
distal fibula	0	**0**	0	**0**	4	**3**	0	**0**
calcaneum	1	**1**	2	**2**	5	**2**	1	**1**
astragalus	2	**2**	3	**2**	6	**3**	2	**1**
naviculo-cuboid	2	**2**	1	**1**	5	**3**	1	**1**
cuneiform tarsals	0	**0**	1	**1**	5	**4**	4	**3**
proximal metatarsal	0	**0**	2	**1**	8	**1**	0	**0**
distal metatarsal	2	**1**	0	**0**	6	**2**	3	**1**
proximal sesamoids	0	**0**	2	**1**	29	**1**	20	**1**
distal sesamoids	0	**0**	2	**1**	14	**2**	2	**1**
TOTALS FOR BONES	40	**2**	47	**2**	189	**4**	83	**3**
TOTALS FOR TEETH	6	**1**	14	**2**	40	**5**	3	**1**
GRAND TOTALS	46	**2**	61	**2**	229	**5**	86	**3**

niger), roan antelope (*Hippotragus equinus*), and impala (*Aepyceros melampus*). Southern reedbuck, waterbuck (*Kobus ellipsiprymnus*), puku (*Kobus vardoni*), sitatunga (*Tragelaphus spekei*), and especially lechwe (*Kobus lechwe*) and buffalo (*Syncerus caffer*) occupied floodplains and floodplain margins. Eland, giraffe (*Giraffa camelopardalis*), elephant (*Loxodonta africana*), and black rhinoceros (*Diceros bicornis*) occurred sporadically throughout. White rhinoceros (*Ceratotherium simum*) were locally common, and hippopotamus (*Hippopotamus amphibius*) inhabited all the large rivers. Among the smaller mammals, vervet monkey (*Cercopithecus aethiops*), chacma baboon, hares, porcupine, larger cane rat, and springhare (*Pedetes capensis*) were all abundant, as were a wide range of carnivores, including all the top predators found elsewhere in Africa.

Table 4.1 shows that the Mumbwa fauna comprises a subset of the historic Zambezian aggregate. Small sample size could explain the absence of many historic species, particularly large ones like giraffe, elephant, and hippopotamus that are rare even in much larger samples from cave sites in other parts of Africa (Klein 1980a). The Mumbwa fauna is dominated by precisely those grazing ungulates – plains zebra, warthog, and blue wildebeest – that probably dominated nearby historically, and their prominence more or less throughout suggests that the bones accumulated mostly under historic or near-historic conditions. Only the presence of an antilopine (springbok or gazelle) in the Lower MSA hints at a possibly changed setting. Historically, there were no antilopines in the Zambezian Zone, and their former occurrence might reflect somewhat drier, less wooded conditions. However, gazelle has been reported in a mid-Holocene (LSA) level at Kalemba Rock Shelter in eastern Zambia (Phillipson 1976), in a late Holocene (LSA) deposit at Chencherere Rock Shelter in central Malawi (Crader 1984), and provisionally at late Holocene (Iron Age) sites in southern Malawi (Voigt 1973). In addition, gazelle and springbok commonly accompany blue wildebeest and plains zebra in ecozones to the northeast and south respectively, and they have no obvious ecological vicar within the Zambezian Zone.

The sum suggests that they may have disappeared from the zone only recently, perhaps due to unsuccessful competition with Iron Age sheep and goats or to vegetational change initiated by Iron Age farmers after 2000 years ago (Klein 1984).

The absence of discernible faunal change at Mumbwa is noteworthy, because the bones accumulated over a very long interval in the middle and late Quaternary, when global glacial and interglacial fluctuations were remarkable. The apparent faunal continuity may be due to small sample size or it may reflect a tendency for bone accumulators to abandon Mumbwa whenever conditions differed sharply from historic ones. However, other regional faunas, such as those from the Gwisho A, B, and C spring mounds (Fagan & van Noten 1971; Gabel 1965), Twin Rivers Kopje (Clark 1971 and Bishop this volume), Leopard's Hill Cave (Klein 1984), and the Makwe, Thandwe, and Kalemba shelters (DW Phillipson 1976), also fail to suggest conspicuous vegetational differences between glacial and interglacial times, and there is a stark contrast with the Cape Ecozone at the southwestern tip of Africa, where even small samples often reveal radical environmental shifts. The implication may be that Quaternary climatic fluctuations had more limited impact on African macromammal communities that existed closer to the Equator.

5 The taphonomy of the small mammal faunas

P Andrews and E Jenkins

INTRODUCTION

Small mammals are found throughout the Mumbwa sequence. It is our purpose here to describe these remains and to try to identify the taphonomic agents responsible for their accumulation. Taxonomic identifications have been made by Margaret Avery (chapter 6) and will not be considered here other than at an ordinal level. Taphonomic processes under consideration here mainly relate to predation and the effects of breakage and digestion on the small mammal remains. Post-depositional damage is extremely extensive, which has led us to limit analysis to the most robust skeletal elements, which are the only ones to survive this damage, namely mandibles, incisors and molars, femora and humeri. Other cranial and postcranial elements are almost totally lacking in the Mumbwa assemblages: for example, only a single rodent maxilla was found compared with 129 rodent mandibles. The taphonomic processes and the modifications they produce follow the definitions and convention laid out in Andrews (1990).

The Mumbwa Caves stratigraphy is described in detail in chapter 2. Since we are concerned with taphonomic change throughout the sequence, we selected the single most complete record available from the 1994–1996 excavations, which is that in square D9. The sequence sampled is restricted to the Middle Stone Age and encompasses unit VII at the top (Stage 5) to unit XII at a depth of 684 cm below datum. Of the 78 levels excavated in D9, we sampled 55 with small mammals, providing a total of 5703 identified bones. In levels of microfaunal richness, we investigated 50 per cent samples. In addition, a sample of 5045 identifiable elements was analysed from the 1994 collection, mostly from the Later Stone Age and the Iron Age in the Mumbwa sequence. These came from the Area III squares D12–1–1, D12–1–2, D11–2–1 and D11–1–1 (unit I, Iron Age) and square D11–5–5, D11–6–1 to 8, D11–7–1, D11–8–1 (unit II, early Holocene Later Stone Age).

Avery (1996) has identified 27 small mammal species from the Mumbwa sequence, consisting of four insectivores, two bats and 21 rodents. Without considering possible taphonomic alteration of species composition, Avery concluded that the environment during the Middle Stone Age was grassy dambos (low-lying flooded edaphic grasslands) with woodland on the higher ground with savanna away from the dambos. During the Later Stone Age there was riverine vegetation and savanna woodland, replaced by savanna grassland in the Iron Age. The environment today is similar to these reconstructions, with the limestone massif in which the caves were formed rising out of a grassland dambo with low scrubby woodland on the slopes away from the dambo. The woodland is greatly altered by human activity, however, and with the presence of isolated larger trees of *Ficus*, *Schlerocarya* and *Albizia*, all in the immediate vicinity of the cave, the indications are that the woodlands were much denser in the past before human clearances and human-induced fire.

TAPHONOMIC MODIFICATIONS

Preliminary observations in the field during the 1995 field season led us to believe there was some taphonomic variability in the Mumbwa sequence. Differences in degrees of digestion were observed in the D9–9 levels, with some having next to no digested bones and others having greater degrees of digestion, and this led to the hypothesis that different predators may have occupied the cave at different times. In this event, the faunal analysis would need to take these differences into account, for predators with different hunting habits produce different faunal composition in their prey assemblages even when hunting in the same area. The detailed analysis that follows is designed to test this hypothesis.

Breakage

The bones from all levels at Mumbwa are extremely broken, with great loss of elements. This is attributed to post-depositional damage because it is similar at all levels. Similarly, the majority of bones are either heavily stained or show considerable all-over surface corrosion, both of which are also attributed to post-depositional processes. As a result, bone breakage and the all-over corrosion of the bone surfaces are not primary indicators of mode of accumulation at Mumbwa, since any pattern resulting from initial accumulation has been destroyed by the later, post-depositional, breakage. As a result of this, most skeletal elements are either not preserved at all, or, if present, are usually less than 1 per cent of the expected number calculated from the estimated number of individuals. Only the femur and humerus for the postcranial skeleton are preserved in any numbers, and the mandible and incisors (rodent only) for cranial remains.

The femur is the most abundant element in all levels, with 686 specimens for the whole Middle Stone Age sequence in square D9 (table 5.1). Of these, 94.8 per cent consist of just the proximal end, usually with a small portion of the shaft. Mid-shaft diaphyses are the next most abundant, and distal ends are rare, only 14 specimens or 2.1 per cent. Complete specimens, where parts of proximal and distal ends are preserved with the diaphysis, make up 3.1 per cent of the sample (diaphyses were not counted separately). Similar figures were found for Iron Age and Later Stone Age levels, although the number of distal ends was slightly higher than in the Middle Stone Age. The only other common limb element in the Middle Stone Age levels was the humerus. There were 512 specimens of which 95.7 per cent had just the distal end with part of the shaft, 3.7 per cent complete and 0.9 per cent proximal ends. In the case of the humerus, proximal ends were considerably more common relative to distal ends in the Later Stone Age and especially in the Iron Age compared with the Middle Stone Age (table 5.1), suggesting a slightly lower degree of breakage at these levels. The only other limb element at all common in the Middle Stone Age was the tibia, but these were not separately recorded. They were relatively more abundant in the Iron Age and Later Stone Age, with 253 and 96 specimens respectively, and at all levels the distal end makes up around 50 per cent of the sample with almost no complete elements.

The minimum number of individuals indicated by these specimens is 343 in the Middle Stone Age based on the femur, taking into account lefts and rights but not size differences or species identifications. In the Later Stone Age, the MNI is 62 and for the Iron Age it is 174, based on the humerus in both cases. Both the humerus and femur occur in greater numbers than the mandible in most levels. In the Middle Stone Age, only 176 mandibles were found, 129 rodents and 47 insectivores, more than from other levels, and they were more broken than in either the Iron Age or the Later Stone Age deposits (table 5.1). This is similar to the pattern seen for the femur and humerus. The mandibles are extremely fragmentary in all the deposits, with few retaining any part of the ascending ramus and most with broken inferior borders and missing incisors. In this particular instance, the Middle Stone Age breakage is slightly less than in other levels. The lower numbers of mandibles is interesting, and if this is a true reflection of the original faunal composition, it suggests that there may have been a bias against cranial elements in the Mumbwa Caves faunas (but see below).

Rodent incisors are by far the most abundant skeletal element, with 4093 specimens recorded from the Middle Stone Age in the D9 section. The Iron Age count is lower, 1220 specimens, and the Later Stone Age is the lowest with only 230 specimens. These numbers are misleading as indicators of abundance, however, for all incisors were broken. From a small subset of 100 rodent incisors, it is estimated that on average the rodent incisors in the Middle Stone Age were broken into 3.4 fragments per individual. The MNI based on rodent incisors therefore is 1043 for the Middle Stone Age based on left/right and upper/lower, and this is reduced to 307 taking breakage into account. This number is marginally fewer than the MNI based on the femur, but it is greater than that indicated by the humerus (N=512, MNI=256). The estimated MNIs for incisors in the Iron Age deposits is 90 and for the Later Stone Age is only 17, both being considerably below the numbers of postcranial elements (table 5.1). This supports the suggestion above that there was a bias against cranial elements in the two upper levels, but in the Middle Stone Age the number of incisors is similar to those for humeri and femora and the evidence is equivocal. Molars are much less common, 53 only from the whole Middle Stone Age sequence and 85 from the Iron Age. The marked disparity in numbers could reflect a sampling error caused during excavation, but a 0.5 mm fabric mesh was used for screening all sediments in Areas II and III.

It is hard to account for the shortfall in mandible numbers compared with numbers of isolated incisors. This is all the more so since about 22 per cent of the rodent mandibles still had their incisors present in the jaw. Even more dramatic is the near absence of maxillae, with only 19 rodent maxillae being found in the Mumbwa

Table 5.1 Breakage of skeletal elements in the Mumbwa Caves sequence

Skeletal element	Iron Age	Late Stone Age	Middle Stone Age
femur N	233	117	686
proximal	164	86	651
distal	33	16	14
complete	36	15	21
humerus N	348	123	512
proximal	106	17	4
distal	205	77	490
complete	37	29	18
mandible N	270	54	176
complete	9	4	4
no ramus	62	9	92
inferior bdr broken	180	34	80

sequence. These are more prone to destruction than mandibles, and the conclusion must be that post-depositional destruction was so great that approximately 80 per cent of mandibles and 97 per cent of maxillae were so totally destroyed that no evidence of their existence remained in the Mumbwa deposits except the broken remains of their incisor teeth.

Digestion

Small proportions of rodent teeth and postcrania show signs of digestion throughout the Mumbwa sequence (see figs 5.1, 5.2 and 5.3). This is seen particularly in the rodent incisors. Only one molar was observed showing digestion (from level D9–7–9 in unit VIII). Six proximal femora also showed signs of digestion, always when digestion is also present on the rodent incisors from the same level. Of the 4093 rodent incisors, 158 showed signs of digestion, which comes to just under 4 per cent. Most of these had a very slight degree of digestion, defined as category 1 digestion in Andrews (1990). Ten of the 55 fossiliferous levels that we examined had rodents with no evidence of digestion, but many of these had rather small samples (table 5.2) and it is possible that larger samples would have shown evidence of some degree of digestion. Twenty-five levels having rodent incisors with digestion had levels of digestion less than 5 per cent and only three levels had the percentage occurrence of digestion greater than 20 per cent. For example, levels D9–1–4 and D9–1–5 both have high proportions of digestion, and they both have at least some teeth digested to a greater degree, but the sample sizes are small, 16 and 23 rodent incisors respectively, and the significance of this is uncertain. Level D9–9–3 is the only other level with a high proportion of digestion, but in this case it is all category 1.

The majority of levels in the D9 sequence have samples of incisors sufficient in size to give a reliable estimate of the presence or absence of digestion. It would appear, therefore, that most levels show rodent remains with only low proportions and low degrees of digestion, and the most likely predator to produce these is the barn owl (*Tyto alba*). The evidence of higher digestion in three levels could indicate a different predator in this stage of the sediment accumulation, but the evidence is not convincing, either because sample sizes are too small or because the degree of digestion is no greater than at other levels. What might be indicated at these levels is that the same predator was present, but that at these stages it was nesting. It has been demonstrated (Andrews 1990) that nesting barn owls produce small mammal samples with a higher degree of digestion than roosting adult individuals, because the pellets produced by nestlings contain more digested bones than do pellets from adults.

The data for the Later Stone Age and Iron Age levels

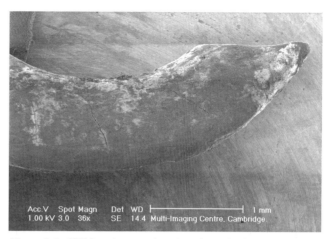

Figure 5.1 SEM micrograph of rodent incisor with light digestion on the tip. This gradual corrosion of the enamel tip is a very distinctive form of digestion.

Figure 5.2 SEM micrograph of rodent incisor with moderate digestion on the enamel tip, and also further along in the middle of the incisor.

Figure 5.3 SEM micrograph showing rodent incisor with moderate digestion. This image illustrates clearly the intermittent corrosion that can occur along the incisor leaving islands of enamel.

Table 5.2 Distribution of digested bones in the D9 sequence at Mumbwa Caves. The context is based on square, locus, level designations from appendix 1; N is the number of rodents incisors; Cat. 1 etc refers to the category of digestion (Andrews 1990); total I is the total number of rodent incisors in the Mumbwa sequence divided by 3.4 (see text)

Context no	N	Cat. 1	Cat. 2	Cat. 3	Cat. 4	Total I	Cat1/N	Cats. 1–4/N	Cats. 1–4/1203
D9–1–1	23	2	1			1203	8.7	13.0	0.25
D9–1–2	26					1203	0.0	0.0	0.00
D9–1–3	4					1203	0.0	0.0	0.00
D9–1–4	16	3		1	1	1203	18.8	31.3	0.42
D9–1–5	23	3	1	1		1203	13.0	21.7	0.42
D9–2–1	2					1203	0.0	0.0	0.00
D9–2–2	2					1203	0.0	0.0	0.00
D9–2–3	28		1	1		1203	0.0	4.2	0.17
D9–4–4	96	4		1		1203	4.2	5.2	0.42
D9–4–7	215	1				1203	0.5	0.5	0.08
D9–4–8	106					1203	0.0	0.0	0.00
D9–6–1	44					1203	0.0	0.0	0.00
D9–7–1	24					1203	0.0	0.0	0.00
D9–7–2	43					1203	0.0	0.0	0.00
D9–7–3	196	3				1203	1.5	1.5	0.25
D9–7–4	21					1203	0.0	0.0	0.00
D9–7–5	45					1203	0.0	0.0	0.00
D9–7–7	232	2				1203	0.9	0.9	0.17
D9–7–8	160	3				1203	1.9	1.9	0.25
D9–7–9	84	3				1203	3.6	3.6	0.25
D9–7–10	54	4				1203	7.4	7.4	0.33
D9–7–11	44	1				1203	2.3	2.3	0.08
D9–7–12	141	2				1203	1.4	1.4	0.17
D9–7–13	116	3				1203	2.6	2.6	0.25
D9–7–14	57	1				1203	1.8	1.8	0.08
D9–7–15	42	2				1203	4.8	4.8	0.17
D9–7–16	34	3				1203	8.8	8.8	0.25
D9–7–17	43	2				1203	4.7	4.7	0.17
D9–7–18	56	1				1203	1.8	1.8	0.08
D9–7–19	73	2				1203	2.7	2.7	0.17
D9–7–20	56	2				1203	3.6	3.6	0.17
D9–9–1	113	4				1203	3.5	3.5	0.33
D9–9–3	45	9				1203	20.0	20.0	0.75
D9–9–4	144	6		2		1203	4.2	5.6	0.67
D9–9–5	121	6		3		1203	5.0	7.4	0.75
D9–9–6	98	2				1203	2.0	2.0	0.17
D9–9–7	80	5				1203	6.3	6.3	0.42
D9–9–8	76	2				1203	2.6	2.6	0.17
D9–9–9	52	1				1203	1.9	1.9	0.08
D9–10–1	78	4				1203	5.1	5.1	0.33
D9–10–2	66	2				1203	3.0	3.0	0.17
D9–10–3	59	1	1			1203	1.7	3.4	0.17
D9–10–5	136	5				1203	3.7	3.7	0.42
D9–10–6	92	4	2	2		1203	4.3	8.7	0.67
D9–10–7	120	4				1203	3.3	3.3	0.33
D9–10–8	101	5		4		1203	5.0	8.9	0.75
D9–10–9	98	3				1203	3.1	3.1	0.25
D9–11–2	120	3				1203	2.5	2.5	0.25
D9–11–4	64	4				1203	6.3	6.3	0.33
D9–12–3	51	3		2		1203	5.9	9.8	0.42
D9–12–5	120	6		1		1203	5.0	5.8	0.58
D9–13–2	133	7				1203	5.3	5.3	0.58
Totals	4093	133	6	18	1	1203	3.25	3.86	13.13

Table 5.3 Distribution of digested bones in the three stages represented in the Mumbwa Caves sequence. Abbreviations as in table 5.1

Context	N	Cat. 1	Cat. 2	Cat. 3	Cat. 4	Cat. 5	% digestion
Iron Age	1220	40	0	11	16	3	5.7
LSA	189	9	0	1	3	0	6.9
MSA (table 1)	4093	133	6	18	1	0	3.9

are similar to those for the Middle Stone Age just described. What we show in table 5.3, therefore, is a summation of digestion proportions by these three stages. The Later Stone Age and Iron Age have slightly higher degrees of digestion, but the difference is small and throughout the Mumbwa sequence it appears that the barn owl is the predator accumulating small mammal remains.

DISCUSSION

Two main taphonomic processes have been identified in the Mumbwa sequence. These are post-depositional breakage and corrosion, and digestion by the predator accumulating the assemblage. Some of the breakage could have been caused by the predator, but so great has been the later breakage that this could not be identified. The barn owl is considered to be the only likely predator accumulating the small mammal remains in the cave, and variations in digestion in some levels is attributed more to changes in behaviour of the owl, nesting as opposed to roosting, than to a different predator being involved. There may still be a change in the food items owls bring to their nestlings, although there is little evidence that this occurs, but the principal bias in the accumulation of the small mammal fauna at Mumbwa is that introduced by the barn owl. This makes the ecological interpretation relatively straightforward, and it justifies the conclusions of Avery (1996b), although there are still issues to be addressed in the behaviour patterns of the barn owl.

The barn owl is a small to medium-sized owl that feeds mainly on mammals, taking the most abundant prey in its habitat. Many insectivores are included in its diet as well as rodents, but few birds are eaten, although it must be said that some individual barn owls may specialise on particular prey (Andrews 1990:29). This is the exception, however, and in general barn owls take a representative sample of prey in relation to their hunting territory, but they select their prey within a relatively narrow size range. Both larger and smaller rodents are under-represented in the owl's prey assemblage, and very small animals such as insects or other invertebrates are much less common than their actual abundance in the habitat. In addition, barn owls hunt generally by slow flight over relatively open ground, and their prey assemblages reflect this, sampling open country species to a greater extent than closed country ones. Indeed, species that may be common in thick woodland within the hunting area of a barn owl may be greatly under-represented because they are only rarely taken as the owl flies along the edges of the woodland. All these are limiting factors to barn owl behaviour that introduce elements of selectivity to its prey assemblages. On the other hand, barn owl activity patterns are broader than those of many other predators, for they are not as strictly nocturnal as most other owls and so are not limited only to prey with nocturnal habits.

Given the biases to the Mumbwa faunas introduced by the common predator, the barn owl, some doubt remains about the ecological conclusions of Avery (1996b). The general conclusions about open habitats such as grassland and savanna may be correct when one considers the preferred hunting habits of the owl, since these are the habitats barn owls like to hunt in, but it leaves open the question as to what other kind of habitats may have been present that the owl did not hunt in because they are not suited to its method of hunting. Avery's (1996b) conclusion about Iron Age habitats at Mumbwa was that the most likely environment was savanna grassland, and at earlier levels her conclusions were similar, but given the nature of barn owl hunting methods these conclusions may not be the whole story. It is likely that the barn owls living at Mumbwa today would provide similar indications, but the present-day area is woodland with dambos, much altered by human activity, and it is certain that sampling current barn owl prey assemblages would not be representative of the range of habitats present. Neither would they have been in the past. These issues are addressed in chapter 6.

6 Past and present ecological and environmental information from micromammals

D M Avery

INTRODUCTION

Mumbwa Caves (15°01'S; 26°59'E) is located in a limestone outcrop that rises approximately 25 m above the surrounding countryside, on the edge of a dambo. This seasonally waterlogged depression is currently planted with maize at the appropriate time of the year. The natural vegetation of the area is open *Brachystegia* woodland (Surveyor-General 1988) but the area is today widely farmed. According to Clark (1942), however, scarce settlement was located along the Kafue River, while in 1930 the area was 'a wonderful big game territory covered with luxuriant grass, 8 to 10 ft high, and scattered brush, forming rolling parklands – an environment ideally conceived by nature as a home for early mankind' (Dart & Del Grande 1931:381). The general rainfall pattern for Zambia is strongly seasonal, with the main rains in December to February and a lack of rain in June to August (Surveyor-General 1988). At Kabwe and Lusaka, the nearest data available, mean annual rainfall is 930 mm and 840 mm respectively. Mean annual temperature ranges between about 24.5°C in September and 16.5°C in June (Surveyor-General 1988).

A preliminary list and interpretation of the micro-mammals from the 1994 excavation have been published (Avery 1996a and b). The present account provides an update of these papers, which includes all available samples from 1993 to 1996. A sample from modern barn owl (*Tyto alba*) pellets collected from a roost some 25 m from the archaeological site is also included for comparative purposes. (These pellets, and others from nearby roosts, were collected in 1994 for another study that will be published in due course.) The taphonomic study of the fossil samples has shown that they appear to have been collected by barn owls (Andrews & Jenkins, this volume) so that it is appropriate to compare the modern material with that from the archaeological deposits.

METHODS

The material was identified and counted using the upper and lower jaws. Minimum numbers were calculated for each basic excavation level. The scores were then added to provide a total for each stratigraphic unit, as listed in table 6.1. In turn, units III–VI were lumped together because of small sample size. Where possible, the ecological corre-

Table 6.1 List of stratigraphic groupings employed in the analyses. Information based on chapter 3 except generalised dates (★) from Martinson et al (1987)

Unit	Period	Dates	Notes
I	Late Holocene	150±60 BP–2080±100 BP	Iron Age/Later Stone Age
II	Early Holocene	5700±80 BP–7300±80 BP	Later Stone Age
III	Late Glacial	12 ka BP	Later Stone Age
IV			Later Stone Age/ Middle Stone Age interface
V	? Stage 3	39.6±7.6 ka BP	upper Middle Stone Age
VI			? hiatus
VII	Stage 5	107±11 ka BP–130±6.2 ka BP	main Middle Stone Age occupation
VIII	Stage 6	172±22 ka BP	colluvium
IX	Stage 6/7 interface	±189 ka BP★	360–380 cm below datum
X	Stage 7	±220 ka BP★	dark reddish brown with grit (380–460 cm)
XI	Stage 7	±230 ka BP★	dark reddish brown with clay, grit and manganese concretions (460–580 cm)
XII	Stage 7	±240 ka BP★	dark brown with manganese concretions (580–650 cm)
XIII	? Stage 8	±245 ka BP★	basal stratum – strong brown (650–750 cm)
XIV	? Stage 8	172±19 ka BP±255 ka BP★	weathered bedrock - dark yellowish red (750–790 cm)

Table 6.2 Ecological correlates of species represented in Mumbwa Caves archaeological site and modern barn owl pellets

Species	Feeding[1]	Vegetation[2]	Locomotion[3]	Location[4]	Flexibility[5]	Mean mass[6]
C. fuscomurina	I	W	T	F		5
C. cf. hirta	I	GW	T	FR	CO	15
C. mariquensis	I	GW	T	R		10
C. olivieri	I	GS	T			
S. infinitesimus	I	W	T	F	O	5
S. campestris	IW	W	B	F	O	45
D. melanotis	IW	GW	C	FR		5
S. pratensis		GW	B	F	C	25
G. cf. paeba	IW	GW	B	F		25
T. leucogaster	GW	GW	B	F	O	70
A. spinosissimus	W	G	T	H		25
A. chrysophilus	IW	G	T	F	O	70
A. kaiseri		GW	T	F	C	
A. niloticus		GW	T	F	C	
D. incomtus	GW	GS	T	R		130
G. dolichurus	GW	W	C			30
M. natalensis	IW	GSW	BT	F	CO	50
M. minutoides	IW	GW	BT	F	CO	5
M. triton	I	GSW	T	R		10
P. fallax	GW	GS	T	FR	C	125
R. pumilio	GW	GW	BT	F	O	45
? Z. hildegardeae	GW	GSW	T	F	C	
T. paedulcus	GW	W	C	R		60
O. angoniensis	GW	GS	T	FR		100
G. microtus		W	C		C	
C. hottentotus	W	GW	F	F	C	125
E. brachyrhynchus	I	W	B	F		45

[1]Feeding: G=Herbivorous (green plant matter); I=Insectivorous and carnivorous; W=Herbivorous (white plant matter).
[2]Vegetation: G=Grassland, S=Swamp, W=Woodlands and Forest (after Ansell 1978).
[3]Locomotion: B=Burrowing and fossorial; C=Climbing, T=Terrestrial.
[4]Location: F=Flats, H=Hillsides, R=Riparian.
[5]Flexibility: C=Commensal & cultivated land, O=Opportunistic and catholic.
[6]Mean mass to the nearest 5 g.

lates of each species were ascertained (table 6.2). The main source of information is Skinner and Smithers (1990), with supplementary data from Ansell (1978). Feeding information and mean mass were unavailable for species that do not occur in southern Africa. Three feeding categories were recognised: insectivorous (including carnivorous for this purpose) and herbivorous, subdivided into green and white plant matter. The vegetational associations of the species were grouped into woodland (including forest for this purpose), grassland and swamp, based on finer categories given by Ansell (1978). Locomotion categories comprise burrowing (including fossorial), climbing and terrestrial. Landscape, divided into flats, hillsides and riparian, is useful for more precise allocation of vegetation to different parts of the countryside. Flexibility, which is the ability of species to take advantage of human activity (labelled commensal) and/or general disturbance (opportunistic and catholic), can provide some indication of general climatic conditions. These are also indicated by scores of the Shannon index of diversity in which the number and equality of representation of species in a sample is reflected in the equation $H = \Sigma(n_i/N) \star LN(n_i/N) \star -1$. Here n_i is the number of individuals assigned to each species and N is the total number of individuals in the sample. Mean individual mass of a sample was calculated using the equation $G = \Sigma(n_i g)/Nx$ where g is the mean individual mass of each species (to the nearest 5 g) and Nx is the total number of individuals in the sample, omitting those species whose mean mass is unknown. Mean mass may provide information on general climatic conditions and openness of the vegetation. The latter is based on the concept that it will only be profitable to hunt very small species if the vegetation is sufficiently open for them to be easily seen.

Assessment of the relative proportions of the various categories represented was based on the presence of each species rather than minimum numbers of individuals (table 6.3). This has the effect of reducing the importance of the best-represented species, which might otherwise overwhelm the calculations. At the same time it increases the relative importance of poorly represented species. It could, however, perhaps be argued that the potential information content of a species is the same

Table 6.3 Percentage representation of micromammalian species in Mumbwa Caves modern barn owl (AI) and archaeological (I–XIV) samples based on presence/absence of species, and general diversity and mean individual mass based on minimum numbers of individuals

	AI	I	II	III	VII	VIII	IX	X	XI	XII	XIII	XIV
Grassland	35.9	38.1	39.2	50.0	39.1	45.4	47.2	42.5	44.4	44.4	47.8	48.5
Swamp	9.0	10.3	9.8	4.5	10.9	9.3	5.6	10.0	7.8	11.1	11.1	7.6
Woodland and Forest	55.1	51.6	51.0	45.5	50.0	45.4	47.2	47.5	47.8	44.4	41.1	43.9
Riparian	11.5	28.6	32.4	18.2	26.1	25.0	25.0	22.5	20.0	33.3	26.7	9.1
Insectivorous and Carnivorous	61.5	35.7	44.1	43.3	34.8	41.7	41.7	37.5	46.7	43.3	40.0	36.4
Herbivorous (Green veg)	3.8	14.3	11.8	10.0	13.0	8.3	8.3	10.0	6.7	10.0	10.0	9.1
Herbivorous (White veg)	19.2	31.0	26.5	26.7	34.8	33.3	25.0	32.5	33.3	33.3	30.0	36.4
Burrowing and Fossorial	46.2	28.6	35.3	45.5	30.4	33.3	33.3	30.0	33.3	20.0	33.3	45.5
Climbing	0.0	19.0	11.8	0.0	13.0	11.1	8.3	10.0	6.7	13.3	0.0	0.0
Terrestrial	53.8	52.4	52.9	54.5	56.5	55.6	58.3	60.0	60.0	66.7	66.7	54.5
General diversity	1.10	2.63	2.52	2.30	2.45	2.59	2.37	2.59	2.37	2.49	2.47	2.15
Commensal and Opportunistic	69.2	57.1	52.9	63.6	56.5	55.6	58.3	60.0	60.0	46.7	60.0	72.7
Mean mass	45.2	34.2	37.7	38.9	26.4	28.9	15.8	25.9	27.8	42.6	31.9	38.9

however well or poorly it is represented. Certainly, using presence/absence data has the effect of reducing predator bias, the extent of which is essentially unknowable but is almost certainly variable, depending on the information being examined. Another argument in favour of using presence/absence is the difficulty of identifying some of the specimens, because of the presence of very similar forms compounded by the fact that much of the material is broken and covered with concretion. A cluster analysis (fig. 6.8) was performed using all the categories shown in figures 6.1–7 based on data given in table 6.4.

IDENTIFICATIONS

Several species identifications have been revised since previous publications (Avery 1996a and b), mainly due to the acquisition of the modern samples. It appears that the species of gerbil represented is the bushveld gerbil *Tatera leucogaster* rather than *T. valida* as previously suggested. The modern dormouse material confirms the likelihood that the species presented is the savanna dormouse *Graphiurus microtus* rather than the woodland dormouse *Graphiurus murinus*. The single-striped mouse *Lemniscomys rosalia* has been removed from the list and the material reassigned. Approximately

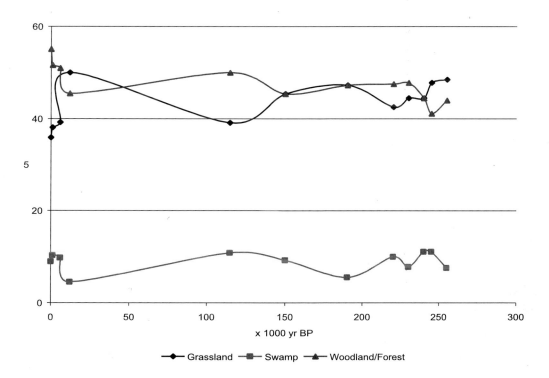

Figure 6.1 Percentage representation of vegetation categories based on data given in table 6.3.

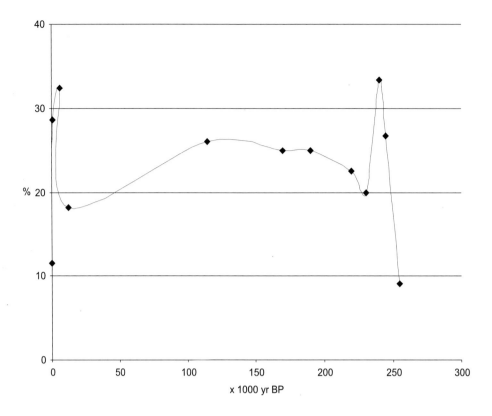

Figure 6.2 Percentage representation of the riparian element based on data in table 6.3.

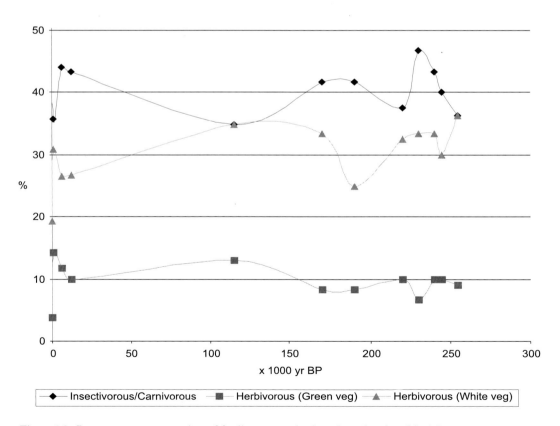

Figure 6.3 Percentage representation of feeding categories based on data in table 6.3.

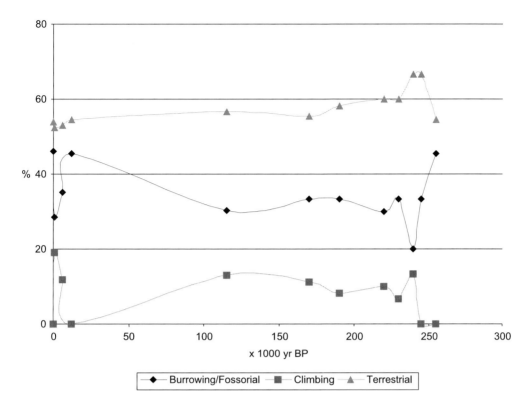

Figure 6.4 Percentage representation of locomotor categories based on data in table 6.3.

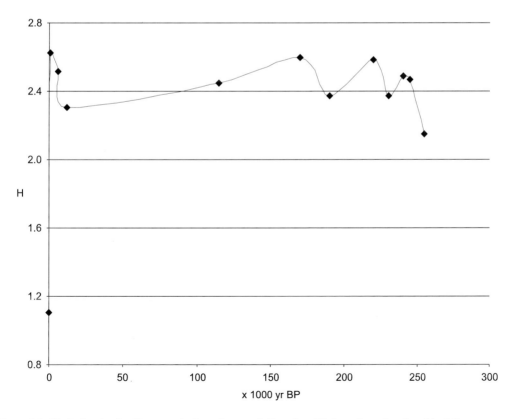

Figure 6.5 Variation in the Shannon index of general diversity (H) based on data in table 6.3.

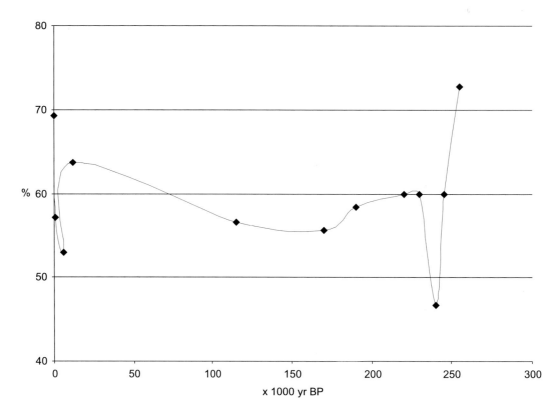

Figure 6.6 Percentage representation of commensal and opportunistic species based on data in table 6.3.

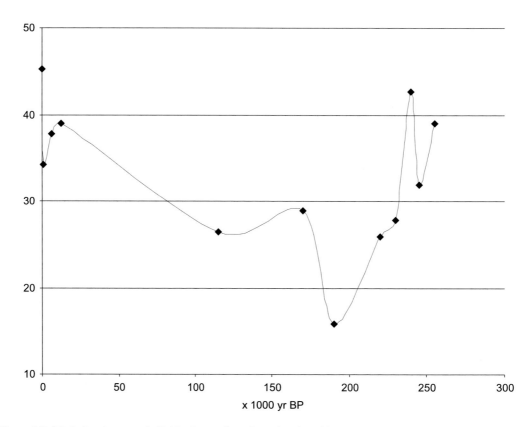

Figure 6.7 Variation in mean individual mass based on data in table 6.3.

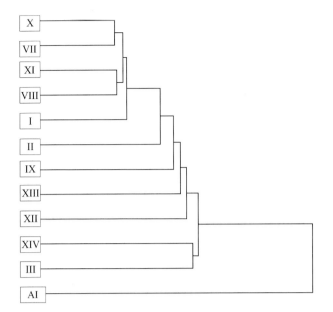

Figure 6.8 Clustering of samples from Mumbwa Caves based on all categories used in figures 6.1–6.7 and data in table 6.4. See table 6.1 for details of samples.

half of the species recovered from the archaeological samples are not represented in the modern sample (table 6.5). One notable example is the hairy-footed gerbil *Gerbillurus* cf. *paeba*, which is represented by one mandible in the Stage 5 sample (unit VII). There are currently no small gerbils in Zambia, which lies in a broad trans-African zone that separates the northern *Gerbillus* spp. from the southern *Gerbillurus* spp. Another, previously mentioned (Avery 1996a) is a mandible of the four-striped grass mouse *Rhabdomys pumilio*, which Ansell (1978) considered now to be confined to the eastern highland area bordering Malawi. There are, conversely, two species of shrew represented in the modern sample that have not been found in the fossil samples. One is the giant musk shrew *Crocidura olivieri* (listed by Ansell (1978) as *C. flavescens*), which is not unexpected in the Mumbwa area. The other is the least dwarf shrew *Suncus infinitesimus*, which has not previously been recorded from Zambia, although Ansell (1978:13) thought it might be found in due course since it occurs to the north and the south of Zambia.

Table 6.4 Percentage representation of micromammalian species in Mumbwa Caves modern barn owl (AI) and archaeological (I–XIV) samples based on minimum numbers of individuals. Bold numbers indicate best represented species: underlining indicates second-best represented species

	AI	I	II	III	VII	VIII	IX	X	XI	XII	XIII	XIV
C. fuscomurina	0.6	4.8	3.1		8.3	4.0	9.1	2.0	4.0	2.2		
C. cf. *hirta*	5.0	<u>12.5</u>	9.4	6.7	<u>20.5</u>	6.9	4.5	14.9	4.0	8.7	8.3	6.3
C. mariquensis		12.2	<u>12.5</u>	**20.0**	23.2	6.4	9.1	9.5	<u>17.6</u>	<u>13.0</u>	**16.7**	
C. olivieri	0.6											
S. infinitesimus	0.6											
S. campestris	<u>5.0</u>	5.6	5.2	6.7	1.1	1.7		0.7	1.6		2.1	6.3
D. melanotis		5.3	3.1		1.9	5.8	4.5	4.1				
S. pratensis	<u>5.0</u>	6.6	8.3	<u>13.3</u>	1.3	5.2	<u>13.6</u>	1.4			2.1	3.1
G. cf. *paeba*					0.2							
T. leucogaster	1.9	4.0	10.4	<u>13.3</u>	5.2	<u>10.4</u>	4.5	2.0	5.6		4.2	9.4
A. spinosissimus					0.8	4.0	9.1	1.4	5.6	2.2	2.1	12.5
A. chrysophilus	0.6	7.2	3.1	6.7	1.7	2.3		4.7	1.6	<u>13.0</u>	4.2	3.1
A. kaiseri		2.9	8.3	6.7	3.0	6.9	9.1	**14.9**	21.6	15.2	<u>12.5</u>	**28.1**
A. niloticus	1.9	1.3	1.0		1.1	1.2	4.5	3.4	2.4	2.2	4.2	
D. incomtus		1.3	2.1		0.5	0.6		0.7		2.2	4.2	
G. dolichurus		0.3										
M. natalensis	**75.0**	**18.8**	**20.8**		7.4	4.6		4.1	4.8	6.5	6.3	6.3
M. minutoides	1.3	5.6	3.1	6.7	3.8	**22.5**	**18.2**	10.8	11.2	8.7	**16.7**	<u>15.6</u>
M. triton	1.9	4.5	3.1		7.2	6.4	9.1	13.5	7.2	6.5	6.3	
P. fallax		0.5			0.6							
R. pumilio				6.7								
? Z. hildegardeae					1.3		4.5	0.7				
T. paedulcus		0.5	2.1		0.3					2.2		
O. angoniensis		1.3	1.0	6.7	3.6	2.3		3.4	2.4	8.7	2.1	6.3
G. microtus		0.8			0.3			2.7				
C. hottentotus		1.1			0.3	1.7		0.7	0.8	2.2		
E. brachyrhynchus	0.6	2.9	3.1	6.7	6.6	6.9		4.7	9.6	6.5	8.3	3.1
SAMPLE SIZE	160	377	96	15	638	173	22	148	125	46	48	32

Table 6.5 List of micromammalian species represented in samples from Mumbwa Caves archaeological site (A) and modern barn owl pellets (M)

Family	Genus and species	Common name	Archaeological/Modern
Insectivora	*Crocidura fuscomurina*	tiny musk shrew	A M
	Crocidura cf. *hirta*	lesser red musk shrew	A M
	Crocidura mariquensis	swamp musk shrew	A
	Crocidura olivieri	giant musk shrew	M
	Suncus infinitesimus	least dwarf shrew	M
Rodentia	*Saccostomus campestris*	pouched mouse	A M
	Dendromus melanotis	grey climbing mouse	A
	Steatomys pratensis	common fat mouse	A M
	Gerbillurus cf. *paeba*	hairy-footed gerbil	A
	Tatera leucogaster	bushveld gerbil	A M
	Acomys spinosissimus	common spiny mouse	A
	Aethomys chrysophilus	red veld rat	A M
	Aethomys kaiseri	bush rat	A
	Arvicanthis niloticus	unstriped grass mouse	A M
	Dasymys incomtus	African marsh rat	A
	Grammomys dolichurus	woodland mouse	A
	Mastomys natalensis sensu lato	multimammate mouse	A M
	Mus minutoides	pygmy mouse	A M
	Mus triton	grey-bellied pygmy mouse	A M
	Pelomys fallax	creek rat	A
	Rhabdomys pumilio	four-striped grass mouse	A
	Zelotomys hildegardeae	broad-headed mouse	A
	Thallomys paedulcus	acacia rat	A
	Otomys angoniensis	Angoni vlei rat	A
	Graphiurus microtus	savanna dormouse	A
	Cryptomys hottentotus	Cape molerat	A
	Elephantulus brachyrhynchus	short-snouted elephant shrew	A M

RESULTS

Proportional representations of micromammalian species based on minimum numbers of individuals are given in table 6.4. The figures for units IV, V and VI are too small to be significant (samples sizes are three, three and two respectively) and have been omitted from consideration. The modern and two Holocene samples are distinguished by having the multimammate mouse *Mastomys natalensis sensu lato* most prominent. The bush rat *Aethomys kaiseri* is very well represented in the earliest five samples and shows a general decline thereafter. The mice *Mus* spp. are also prominent in the lower half of the sequence while the two shrews, *Crocidura* cf. *hirta* and *C. mariquensis*, occur in reasonably high proportions throughout except in the modern sample.

Based on the presence of micromammalian species grass was most prominent in the Late Glacial (unit III) but was better represented at all times before the late Holocene (unit I) (fig. 6.1). Swamp vegetation, on the other hand, tends to be less well represented than in the late Holocene. Swamp vegetation is particularly ill represented in the Late Glacial and at the Stage 7/6 boundary (unit IX). Interestingly, woodland is better represented in the modern sample than it is in all the archaeological samples, which, in turn, contain a smaller woodland

element than does the late Holocene. The great majority of the species occur on the flats (table 6.2), with only the common spiny mouse *Acomys spinosissimus* preferring hillsides and four other species being more or less restricted to riparian environments. The riparian element is particularly poorly represented in the earliest sample (unit XIV) and in the modern sample (A1); it is best represented in early Stage 7 (unit XII) and again in the early Holocene (unit II) (fig. 6.2). Insectivores are best represented in the modern sample and secondarily in middle Stage 7 (unit XI), and least in Stage 5 (unit VII) (fig. 6.3). Green herbivores, on the other hand, reached a peak in the late Holocene, as did climbing species (fig. 6.4). Burrowing species were prominent in the earliest sample and again in the Late Glacial and modern samples. Diversity was highest in the late Holocene and is very much lower in the modern sample than in any of the archaeological samples (fig. 6.5). Opportunist species tend to vary inversely with diversity and the highest proportions occur in the modern, Late Glacial and earliest samples, and the lowest in early Stage 7 (unit XII) (fig. 6.6). Mean individual mass was lowest during the period from mid Stage 7 (unit XI) to Stage 5 (unit VII) (fig. 6.7). The cluster analysis (fig. 6.8) shows that the Late Glacial (unit III) and earliest sample (unit

XIV) are closest to each other and to the modern sample (A1) although the latter is well separated from all archaeological samples.

DISCUSSION

If the cluster analysis is examined in the light of the various figures it becomes clear that the modern sample is distinguished from the archaeological groups of samples by a combination of low diversity, high proportions of burrowing and opportunistic species and high mean individual mass. The nearest archaeological samples are the oldest (unit XIV) and the Late Glacial (unit III, 15–12 ka BP), which also contain high proportions of burrowing species and high proportions of grass. In addition, the oldest sample has low diversity, high individual mean mass and a high proportion of catholic species. This suggests that all three samples indicate harsh conditions. It must be assumed, however, that the causes were different in the earlier times than they are at present. Whereas the modern micromammal community is heavily influenced by farming and other human activity, the high proportions of opportunist species and relatively low diversity in the early samples must have resulted from natural conditions, almost certainly extreme or variable climate. It was previously suggested (Avery 1996b) that the apparently surprising coincidence of lower diversity and greater emphasis on swamp vegetation probably indicated the increased importance of the wetter vegetation during times of general dryness. The present evidence does not generally indicate that there was an important damp refuge for micromammals, which predators targeted in times of generally harsh conditions. Indeed, both the modern and oldest samples show that very little hunting took place in the riparian part of the landscape. There is, however, a relatively high proportion of swamp vegetation represented in the modern sample as well as the other two Holocene samples. This may suggest one way in which it is possible to distinguish between climatic harshness (ie, drought) and other adverse conditions, in this case human activities. The combination of factors makes it likely that the Late Glacial and unit XIV climate was relatively or seasonally dry. Conversely, the climate during the period represented by units XII and XIII (Stage 7) was perhaps wetter since there is a combination of high swamp vegetation and the riparian element is well represented in the later of the two samples. High mean individual mass in this sample also indicates relatively dense vegetation. It is not immediately clear what conditions the unit IX sample (Stage 7/6 boundary) represents. The extremely low mean individual mass suggests open vegetation, which was apparently savanna grassland.

The two closest pairs in the cluster analysis are VII (Stage 5) with X (Stage 7), and VIII (Stage 6) and XI (Stage 7). Units X and VIII are both characterised by

high diversity while all four groups have high or relatively high proportions of woodland. In unit VII the emphasis is on herbivores whereas insectivores dominate in unit XI, as they do in unit II (early Holocene). Unit VIII (Stage 6) has high diversity, which is not what would be expected of a glacial environment. However, the date of ±173 ka BP indicates that the group of samples was accumulated during a relatively warm phase of Stage 6 (Martinson et al 1987). In fact, it is noticeable that none of the samples seems to have been accumulated during full glacial conditions. Either the deposits have been removed, perhaps by wash-outs, or the site was not occupied during periods of possibly extreme drought. This remains to be considered further.

In view of the fact that the various Stage 7 units (X–XII) have not yet been dated it may be useful to suggest indirect dates. Given that unit X is similar to unit VII, which is dated to Stage 5, it is possible that unit X accumulated during substage 7.3 with a date of about 220 ka BP (Martinson et al 1987). By the same process, unit XI, which is similar to unit VIII, may represent substage 7.4, dated to about 230 ka BP. Unit XIV, which appears to represent quite extreme conditions, may date to around 255 ka BP in substage 8.1. This leaves unit XII at substage 7.5 (±240 ka BP) and unit XIII at substage 8.0 (±245 ka BP). All dates are from Martinson et al 1987. This does not agree with the TL date of 172±21 ka BP for unit XIV. However, this date is at odds with the other information provided for units VIII–XII (table 6.1) and can reasonably be set aside for the present.

It is unfortunate that the late Holocene group of samples (unit I) cannot be subdivided or, failing that, that no dates are available for the largest micromammal samples from this group. The period represented by this group of samples must cover much of the time from when farmers first moved into the region, on the basis of what is known about the arrival of farmers in South Africa (Hall 1987). It would be of great interest to be able to compare the young samples (±150 BP) with the older ones (±2000 BP) and with the modern samples. One might expect some evidence of human activity fairly soon after the advent of farming. However, since there appears not to have been major disturbance of the vegetation as late as this century, as noted above, it may well be that Iron Age people did not practise intensive farming. Certainly the micromammal evidence would suggest this was the case since the modern sample is very different from the late Holocene *sensu lato*, which, in turn, is much more like the early Holocene and, indeed, other earlier samples. The major difference between the modern sample and those preceding it is the extreme emphasis on the multimammate mouse *Mastomys natalensis sensu lato*, which is the common commensal mouse of most of the savanna regions. High proportions of this species, or species group, are characteristic of savanna environments where people and farming are common. A rapid increase in this mouse has been documented in South Africa with the arrival of Iron Age farmers (Avery 1987, 1997). In the present instance, however, it is interesting to note that *M. natalensis* was already the major prey item from the early Holocene onwards but was not represented in the Late Glacial (table 6.4). One other point to note about the modern sample is that it was collected in August and it is therefore likely that the cold dry months of June to August are represented. Other bulk samples have yet to be analysed but it will be interesting to discover whether there is any significant difference in prey composition when other seasons are included.

Previously (Avery 1996b) it was noted that the earlier samples were separated from the later ones by a change in dominance from *Crocidura* spp. shrews to *Mastomys natalensis sensu lato*. The enlarged samples confirm this broad pattern but also show other groupings (table 6.4) that blur the clear dichotomy between earlier and later samples that was noticed before. The bush rat *Aethomys kaiseri* is prominent in the early part of the sequence to the end of Stage 7, to be replaced first by the pygmy mouse *Mus minutoides* in Stage 6 and then by *Crocidura mariquensis* in Stage 5 and in the Late Glacial (Stage 2/1 boundary). The prominence of *M. natalensis sensu lato* is a Holocene (Stage 1) phenomenon, as has been noted above. It is difficult to identify the specific reasons for change from one main prey species to another.

Andrews and Jenkins (chapter 5) discuss some of the possible biases associated with the barn owl as a predator although they concede that this bird tends to take a representative selection of appropriate prey in its hunting range. There are, however, a few comments that can be made. First, small prey size is not necessarily an obstacle (pers obs). This can be seen in the present samples where, as has been pointed out, the very small *Mus minutoides* is the best represented species in Stage 6. While under-representation of closed vegetation may conceivably cause distortion in the interpretation, a possibly greater problem concerns the over-representation of the riparian element of the landscape. It has been demonstrated for the early Pleistocene environments of Sterkfontein and Swartkrans that presence/absence data appear to cause less bias and not to reduce the information content appreciably (Avery in press). It seems likely therefore that the present interpretations contain less chance of being biased in this manner.

It is undoubtedly true that there are many complications that have yet to be addressed and, probably, recognised. It is clear, for instance, that precisely because barn owls are so successful in many different habitats, it is unwise to make broad generalisations about their behaviour. An extension of this fact is the difficulty of determining which of a possible range of reasons explains an observed pattern. For instance, the present modern sample shows little indication that the owls hunted the riparian part of the landscape. This may be either because the hunting took place during the dry season or because the abundance of *Mastomys natalensis sensu lato* made it unnecessary to hunt this area. It would also be difficult to determine whether dry conditions reflected the season of collection or overall drought conditions. Some of these problems may be unsolvable, but merely by acknowledging their existence one may attempt more sophisticated interpretations that should be closer to reality than are other possibly more elegant but less realistic pictures of past conditions.

7 The analysis of phytoliths from Mumbwa Caves

M Madella

INTRODUCTION

The analysis of phytoliths from geological and archaeological sediments is a well-established technique for investigating past environment and ancient economies (Madella 2000; Pearsall 2000; Piperno 1988). This methodology in Africa has been applied to the investigation of the biogeochemical cycle of silicon in tropical soils (Alexandre, Colin & Meunier 1994; Alexandre et al 1997) and palaeoenvironmental reconstruction in both intertropical and tropical areas (Alexandre et al 1997). East African plants and soils have been extensively studied by Runge with the intent to create a reference collection of modern analogues for the humid and semi-arid zones of east Africa (Runge 1995, 1996; Runge & Runge 1997). Phytolith studies on modern soils in southern central Africa are not available.

The vegetation of Zambia is a complex mosaic affected by rainfall, altitude, drainage pattern and soils. The two main forest types are the miombo and mopane woodlands (White 1983). Miombo woodland is defined as any woodland which is dominated by species of three genera of the Leguminosae family: *Brachystegia*, *Julbernardia* and *Isoberlinia*. This type of vegetation is also rich in herbs and shrubs and subjected to fires. The area of Mumbwa Caves is today characterised by a miombo woodland. Mopane woodlands are mainly associated with hot, dry valleys but are also common in the southern plateau on alkaline, salty soils. These woodlands are dominated by *Colophospermum mopane*. The climatic conditions of this woodland are generally unfavourable to the growth of most of other species of trees. The particular mopane superficial root system is also able to suppress the growth of perennial grasses.

Prehistoric cave deposits, the like of Mumbwa Caves, can be important archives for investigating ancient economies and changes in the environment. The formation of phytolith assemblages in a prehistoric cave is caused by several processes (Madella & Power-Jones 1998). *In situ* deposition of phytoliths from growing plants is generally insignificant as the presence of plants is mainly controlled by paucity of light in the cave. Silica bodies that enter the cave mainly originate from the local zone or from the regional zone. The plants from the local zone are not directly influenced by the presence of the cave but they might reflect the micro-habitat to which the cave is related (eg, a gorge – Madella & Power-Jones 1998). Plants from the regional zone are controlled by the general climate and the soil, and sometimes influenced by biotic and human population (ibid 1998). Phytoliths can enter the cave by airborne, waterborne and animal-borne transport and, in anthropic deposits, by human transport. The phytoliths actively brought into the cave by human action can be an important fraction of the assemblage when the cave has been utilised as a living or resting area. The silica bodies originate from plants that may reflect a choice in respect to food and utility, building purposes and movements of soil. Once phytoliths are deposited in the cave they can undergo several processes which affect their preservation. There are two categories of processes: physical and chemical (Madella and Power-Jones 1998). Both of these agents of destruction can act individually or in co-operation as soon as the phytoliths are deposited (Madella 2000) and their action is related to climate, water regime, rate of sedimentation, bioturbation, temperature, pH, etc.

METHODOLOGICAL APPROACH

Sediment samples were collected from sections in Area III (D11) and Area II (D9) during 1996. These two sections together span the full depositional sequence of the main cave. Of the 90 samples collected, 37 were selected for phytolith analysis. These represent the Middle Pleistocene (units VIII–XIV), Late Glacial (unit III) and Holocene (units II and I) occupation of the main cave. The Last Interglacial deposits (unit VII) will be analysed and published separately.

Three grams of sediment were processed for each sample and phytoliths were extracted using the Madella, Power-Jones and Jones (1998) technique. This is an extraction method that eliminates carbonates with HCl and organic matter by chemical digestion with H_2O_2. The phytoliths are then separated from the remaining insoluble residue by heavy liquid flotation of the siliceous fraction. Clays are separated from the other fractions during the various steps of the extraction by low speed centrifugation.

The final siliceous residue was mounted on microscopy slides and viewed at a magnification of 400×. The slides were scanned to count a minimum of 250 phytoliths, logging all the encountered morphotypes. For the assemblages from the Late Pleistocene/Holocene sequence (Section D11) an additional count of 200 short cells from grasses was also performed.

The Middle Pleistocene sediments (D9) – units VIII–XIV

The samples analysed from the D9 section range in age from approximately 172 ka BP at the base of unit VIII (Stage 6), to the Stage 6/7 transition (unit IX) c 189 ka BP, through Stage 7 (units X–XII) and into Stage 8 (units XIII–XIV). The dating of the lower beyond 172 ka BP is based on the results of the analysis of microfauna reported by Avery (this volume) and is treated as provisional. The uppermost seven samples are very poor in phytoliths, almost sterile. It was not possible to perform a total count of 250 and therefore a 'time catch' approach (Madella 2000) was carried out, counting the silica bodies encountered in a three-hour count. Sample 14 (430–440 cm, unit X) to sample 42 (720–730 cm, unit XIII; see table 7.1), covering Stage 7 and possibly part of Stage 8, have uniform assemblages and do not show important differences in composition. The samples have an even representation of both grass and arboreal phytoliths without any noticeable variability between or within these two categories. The irregulars are highly represented, probably as a result of heavy chemical and mechanical weathering. Mechanical weathering is possibly related to transport. Occupation of the cave during the Middle Pleistocene was minimal and *in situ* deposition by human transport is probably non-existent.

Late Glacial – Holocene Sequence (section D11): units III–I

A total of 15 samples were analysed, spanning from about 150 years BP to about 12,000–15,000 years BP. The sedimentary sequence shows a mid-Holocene gap in the radiocarbon dates (table 7.2) between sample 6 (dated at 2080±100 BP) and sample 7 (dated at 7300± 80 BP) (see also chapter 3). The lacuna may reflect a regional change in climate.

It is possible in this sequence to identify a group of samples where phytoliths from trees and shrubs are more common. These assemblages are characteristic of the units that span the Holocene (I and II) between about 150 and 7000 yr BP (samples 1–12). The samples have a high presence of phytoliths from arboreal dicotyledonous plants (eg, Mimosaceae and tracheids morphotypes; Mercader et al 2000) and spherical morphotypes, probably from leaf venation (eg, sphericals; Runge & Runge 1997). In general the phytolith assemblages are also rich in compact bodies (Runge & Runge 1997) and variable (irregular) morphologies (Albert et al; Madella et al in press). Phytoliths from grasses are present but in lower frequencies than in the pre-Holocene samples (table 7.2 and fig 7.1). However, bulliforms (fig 7.2) from grass leaves are well represented. Articulated phytoliths (silica skeletons) have been encountered only in the uppermost sediments, dated from 1080±80 BP.

A second group of samples (table 7.2) is constituted only by the three lowermost layers of the sequence (samples 13 to 15) and corresponds to the Late Glacial (unit III) sediments. Grass phytoliths are most frequent in this group. Arboreal phytoliths are still present but with definitively lower frequencies. The only exception is the tracheids with ring-shaped surface, attributed to the Mimosacae (Leguminosae) and possibly representing input from *Acacia* sp. or related genera.

For the Late Glacial/early Holocene samples a 200 grass short cell scan was performed to investigate possible changes in the type of grass plants. Short cell phytoliths are characteristic at the sub-family level (Twiss 1992; Fredlund & Tieszen 1994) and they can positively identify the grass vegetation composition in terms of photosynthesis pathway (C_3 or C_4). C_3 plants are better adapted to cooler climates while C_4 are normally the most common elements in warm or arid climates. The Panicoid and Chloridoid C_4 types in the Mumbwa Caves sediments are consistently the most common (fig. 7.1). Pooideae short cells from C_3 grasses gain in frequency in the Late Glacial deposits. Bulliform types in the Late Glacial assemblages are also more varied in comparison with the Holocene assemblages, with a greater variety of different shapes.

DISCUSSION

The Middle Pleistocene deposits investigated for their phytolith content span from 300 cm (unit VII) to 730 cm (unit XIII) in depth. The first part of the sequence, from 300 cm to about 350 cm, is colluvium deposited during Stage 6. The underlying sediments from 350 cm to the bedrock are Stage 6/7, Stage 7 and perhaps Stage 8 glacial deposits. There is little evidence of a human presence in the cave during this period, and phytoliths should be considered as deposited by colluvial influx from water entering the cave and other non-anthropic means of transport like wind and animal droppings. These assemblages should reflect a phytolith rain from local and regional habitats.

The sediments for Stage 6 (samples 0 to 6), the interface 6/7 (sample 8) and the first two samples from Stage 7 (samples 10 and 12) are almost sterile. The lack of phytoliths in these sediments could be attributed to pre-depositional (outside the cave) and post-depositional (inside the cave) weathering processes or to a low

Table 7.1 Phytolith assemblages expressed in absolute numbers on a total count of 250 morphotypes for the Middle Pleistocene sequence of Section D9

Section D9

Depth (cm)	Sample	Square/Level	Monocots Poaceae Dendritics	Long cells	Short cells	Bulliforms	Hairs	Palmae	Annonaceae	Leguminosae Mimosaceae	Dicots Hairs	Tracheids	Faceted polyhedrals	Faceted elongates	Opaque perf. plat.	Sphericals	Ovals	3-D irregulars	2-D irregulars	Stomata	Not ident.	Starch	Total counted
290-300	0	D9-7-13	0	12	3	0	1	0	0	0	0	0	0	0	0	0	0	0	2	0	5	0	23
310-320	2	D9-7-15	0	7	2	1	0	0	0	0	1	0	0	0	0	0	0	3	0	0	7	0	23
330-340	4	D9-7-17	0	9	5	0	0	0	0	0	0	1	0	0	0	2	1	3	2	0	4	0	25
350-360	6	D9-7-19	0	5	3	2	0	0	0	0	1	2	0	0	0	3	0	2	3	0	12	0	33
370-380	8	D9-8-2/9-1	0	10	2	0	1	0	0	0	0	0	0	0	0	0	0	2	0	0	9	0	24
390-400	10	D9-9-3	0	4	1	1	0	0	0	0	0	1	0	0	0	0	1	0	1	0	6	0	15
410-420	12	D9-9-5	0	2	3	0	0	0	0	0	0	0	0	0	0	0	1	2	1	0	13	0	22
430-440	14	D9-9-7	1	93	16	42	10	0	0	0	1	9	7	2	0	2	1	29	14	0	23	0	250
450-460	16	D9-9-9	0	79	20	37	27	0	0	0	1	8	3	4	1	4	2	11	19	0	34	0	250
470-480	18	D9-10-2	0	102	18	27	21	0	0	0	2	4	5	4	0	2	0	19	21	0	27	0	250
490-500	20	D9-10-4	1	105	21	38	10	0	0	0	1	6	9	7	2	1	0	16	13	0	20	0	250
510-520	22	D9-10-6	0	99	28	22	11	0	0	0	3	6	3	6	2	3	1	15	13	0	38	0	250
530-540	24	D9-10-8	0	88	19	43	22	0	0	0	0	3	6	4	0	6	0	18	16	0	25	0	250
550-560	26	D9-10-10	0	108	23	34	10	0	0	0	4	6	3	4	0	0	0	12	17	0	29	0	250
570-580	28	D9-11-1	0	111	27	26	7	0	0	0	1	7	3	8	0	4	2	11	11	0	32	0	250
590-600	30	D9-11-3	0	95	23	33	12	0	0	0	2	9	5	3	1	2	0	19	18	0	28	0	250
610-620	32	D9-11-5	0	103	24	29	4	0	0	0	6	7	2	5	0	0	0	13	18	0	39	0	250
630-640	34	D9-11-7	1	108	24	32	8	0	0	0	2	3	1	3	1	0	4	17	13	0	33	0	250
650-660	36	D9-12-1	0	98	16	25	4	0	0	0	5	6	1	9	0	1	0	15	17	0	53	0	250
670-680	38	D9-12-2	0	97	22	27	12	0	0	0	2	4	6	2	1	0	1	17	11	0	48	0	250
690-700	40	D9-12-3	0	118	23	24	2	0	0	0	5	5	3	1	1	1	1	12	19	0	35	0	250
720-730	42	D9-12-4	0	114	11	28	4	0	0	0	5	5	4	9	0	0	1	13	18	0	38	0	250
			3	1567	334	471	166	0	0	0	42	92	61	69	9	31	16	249	247	0	558	0	3915

75

Table 7.2 Phytolith assemblages expressed in absolute numbers on a total count of 250 morphotypes for the Late Glacial to Holocene sedimentary sequence of Section D11

Section D11				Monocots							Palmae	Annonaceae	Leguminosae	Dicots												
				Poaceae									Mimosaceae	Dicotyledonous arboreal												
Depth (cm)	Sample	Square/Level	DATE (BP)	Dendritics	Long cells	S.c. pooideae	S.c. Panicoideae	S.c. Chloidoideae	Bulliforms	Hairs				Hairs	Tracheids	Faceted polyhedrals	Faceted elongates	Opaque perf. plat.	Sphericals	Ovals	3-D irregulars	2-D irregulars	Stomata	Not ident.	Starch	Total counted
5	1	D11-1-1	440±50	4	54	5	9	2	32	24	0	0	2	0	3	28	0	1	6	4	57	11	0	8	5	250
10	2	D11-1-2	150±60	5	71	6	11	1	25	13	0	1	7	5	8	19	2	0	3	3	52	16	0	2	5	250
15	3	D11-2-1	440±70	3	57	7	12	2	22	19	0	0	6	11	4	16	9	1	4	2	56	14	1	4	5	250
20	4	D11-4-1	1040±90	1	45	6	9	2	4	20	0	1	5	4	12	14	4	2	18	1	85	17	0	0	3	250
25	5	D11-5-1	1080±80	2	32	2	11	4	18	15	0	0	7	6	9	13	4	1	14	6	64	42	0	0	6	250
30	6	D11-5-2	2080±100	1	47	3	13	1	21	16	0	0	9	9	12	22	5	0	9	3	58	16	1	3	5	250
35	7	D11-5-3	7300±80	1	55	3	9	2	27	18	0	0	4	8	11	27	9	0	12	9	32	16	7	0	0	250
40	8	D11-5-4	5700±80	0	0	0	0	0	0	0	0	2	0	0	0	0	0	0	0	0	0	0	0	0	1	250
45	9	D11-5-5	6400±70	0	44	5	8	1	20	16	2	0	5	9	12	13	6	4	20	7	42	19	0	15	0	250
50	10	D11-6-1		1	65	7	10	1	12	10	0	0	8	3	3	31	4	0	2	5	52	29	4	3	0	250
55	11	D11-6-2		3	16	6	9	2	17	18	0	0	6	3	9	23	2	0	4	9	45	18	3	12	0	250
60	12	D11-6-3	6400±70	1	59	8	15	2	16	18	0	0	5	7	2	18	6	1	8	8	51	15	0	0	0	250
65	13	D11-6-4	9000 ESR	4	78	20	11	13	41	13	0	0	12	5	7	4	3	0	8	5	17	9	0	0	0	250
70	14	D11-6-5		2	72	28	15	16	34	21	0	0	16	4	3	5	4	1	4	6	13	2	1	4	0	250
75	15	D11-6-6	c12000BP	1	58	23	18	15	39	12	0	0	13	7	2	7	2	0	5	5	19	9	4	11	0	250
				29	797	129	150	64	338	233	2	4	105	81	97	240	60	12	117	73	643	233	21	62	27	3500

76

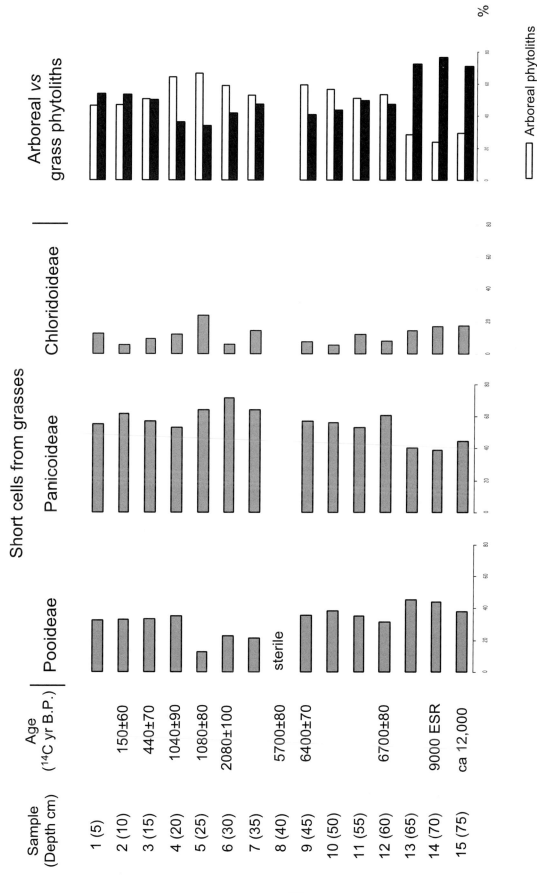

Figure 7.1 Section D11 – Late Glacial to Holocene. Frequency of arboreal and grass phytoliths (last column on right) as a percentage of the total 250 phytolith count and frequencies of grass short cells as a percentage of the 200 short cell morphotypes count.

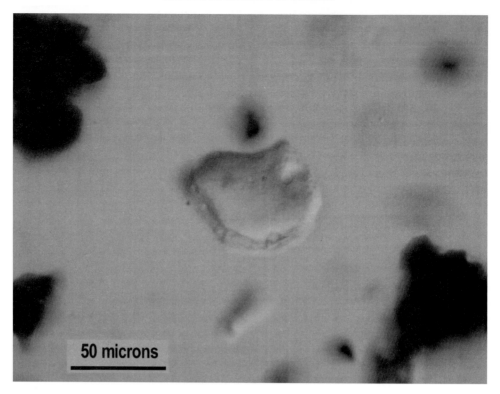

Figure 7.2 A bulliform cell phytolith from section D11 sample 2 (150±60 BP) from grass leaves.

opal silica production by the vegetation. Samples from 14 and below (Stage 7 and earlier) have assemblages dominated by grass morphotypes and indeterminable opal silica bodies. The important presence of indeterminable phytolith morphotypes also testifies to the strong action of both chemical and mechanical weathering in the cave during this period. The high frequency of grass phytoliths suggests a grassland environment with a small presence of arboreal species. The Stage 7 sample does not reflect the same mix of vegetation seen during the Holocene interglacial, but the low frequency of arboreal species may be a consequence of taphonomic biases.

Late Glacial Pleistocene/Holocene assemblages

The records of phytoliths and microfauna (Avery this volume) from the sedimentary sequence of Mumbwa Caves suggest that the Last Glacial, between *c* 12–15 ka BP, was dry and cool. Similar climatic conditions seem to have prevailed in tropical west Africa between 22 and 10.5 ka BP as based on phytolith and pollen sequences (Mercader et al 2000; Talbot & Johannessen 1992). Where the environment was drier the forest retreated and became intermixed with open environments, savannas, or montane elements (Maley & Brenac 1998; Elenga et al 1994; Runge 1995; Brook et al 1990). In other cases, cool and humid environments possibly sustained forested landscapes (Mercader et al 2000;

Jahns et al 1998). As for the Late Glacial to early Holocene phytolith assemblages from Mumbwa Caves, the woodland appears to have given way to, or become intermixed with open environments where the grass element became more important or predominant in the vegetation structure. Panicoid and Chloridoid C_4 grasses (dumbbells – see fig. 7.3, crosses, polylobates and saddles) always dominate the short cell morphotype group in the sequence. However, the Late Glacial sediments recorded a noticeably higher frequency of the Pooid type phytoliths and these reflect more C_3 grasses and a cooler climate. The drier and cooler climate, however, was apparently not enough to eliminate completely the arboreal presence from the landscape, as indicated by the occurrence of phytoliths from woody plants in the Late Glacial sediments.

The variability in the Holocene phytolith assemblages may, on the contrary, reflect highly varied use of plant resources by the human groups who frequented the cave. This normally would have involved changes in food gathering and processing at the cave, but might also be related to transformation in the distribution and abundance of such resources. Plant material of anthropogenic origin could also have been brought into the cave for bedding and thatching and as medicinal or ritual plants. Similar taxa variability has been observed in the phytolith assemblages from modern soils and sediments from tropical African forests (Runge & Runge 1997;

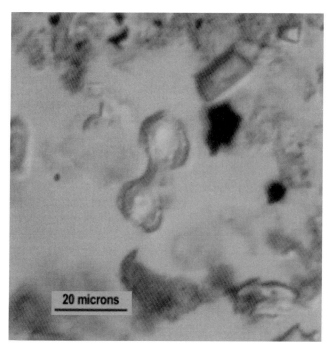

Figure 7.3 A dumbbell morphotype from section D11 sample 6 (2080±100 BP) originating from the epidermis of a Panicoid (C_4) grass.

Mercader et al 2000). This evidence corroborates the reconstruction of a wooded and diverse environment in the area of Mumbwa Caves during the Holocene (fig. 7.4, faceted elongate morphotype from an arboreal taxa).

There is no evidence for any drastic change in plant exploitation in the Late Holocene (unit I) when the cave could have been used by Iron Age agriculturalists. Articulated phytoliths from the inflorescence portion of grass crops were not present and dendritic morphotypes from inflorescence have low frequencies. This might suggest that activities related to crop-processing were not carried out in or near the cave, or that the groups frequenting the cave relied on wild resources during both the Stone Age and the Iron Age periods. If this second hypothesis is true, it could be explained by the utilisation of the cave by forager groups during the Iron Age (cf Musonda 1984), or to a specific use of the cave by agriculturalists. The microfaunal record (chapter 6) for the late Holocene (unit I) shows no impact of farmers on the local habitat until very recently, and according to local oral history Bushmen used the caves until 1900 (chapter 2). Farmers and foragers appear to have coexisted in the area. The site might have been frequented by both groups for religious practices or for the exploitation of particular products of the woodland, and only on a seasonal basis. The very low frequency in the whole sequence of dendritic phytoliths, typical of the grass inflorescence, may indeed imply that the cave has been occupied seasonally in all periods when the grasses did not have mature spikelets (Handreck & Jones 1968; Hutton & Norrish 1974). A spring and early summer occupation would coincide with available surface water in the dambo. On the other hand, it is possible that the

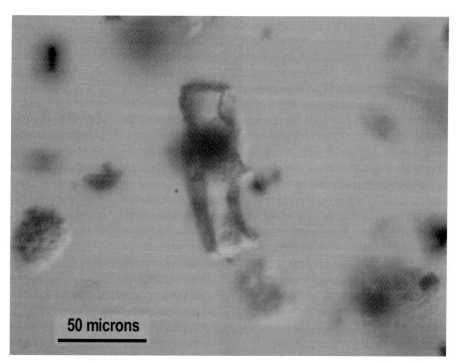

Figure 7.4 A faceted elongate morphotype from an arboreal plant, section D11 sample 9 (6400±70 BP).

79

plant material brought into the cave was mainly the vegetative portions of the grasses.

In samples 1 to 6 (between *c* 150 and 2080 BP) some starch grains have been identified, but in low numbers. However, the presence of starch indicates the possible use in the cave of starchy plant parts such as grains, fruits and tubers or the consumption of some kind of food or beverage derived from the processing of these starchy organs. The current use of the site by the Kaonde as a place for making offerings to ancestors (see chapter 2) may have a long history.

CONCLUSIONS

The analysis of phytoliths from Mumbwa Caves suggests that during the Middle Pleistocene, the habitat around the site was characterised by open grasslands during Stage 6 and late Stage 7 and by grasslands with an arboreal element in Stage 7 and possibly Stage 8. Mechanical and chemical weathering have affected the composition of the phytolith assemblages from the lower units (VIII–XIII). A woodland environment was established from the beginning of the Holocene as the result of a more humid and warmer climate.

The human occupants of the cave from the Middle Stone Age seem to have relied on the exploitation of varied plant products, from leaves to fruits and wood, probably collected in the local zone, several kilometres around the cave. There is no evidence of the use in the cave of cultivated grasses during the Iron Age. This could be due to a continuous use of the cave by hunter-gatherers. Alternatively, use of the cave by agriculturalists might have been related to religious performances and not for habitation. The presence of starch during the Iron Age implies the use of starchy plant organs or food/beverages processed from these plant parts.

8 The Mumbwa Caves behavioural record

L Barham, AC Pinto and P Andrews

INTRODUCTION

The primary source of behavioural information about the occupants of the cave comes from the tens of thousands of fragments of stone left from making and using tools. The tools themselves are rare, but the processes revealed by the stages involved in their manufacture reflect the cognitive abilities of the makers to plan and execute strategies in stone. In this chapter, the analysis of the abundant lithic record will be used to build a typological sequence for the site and for wider comparisons, but also to assess changing patterns of tool production in search of signatures of modern behaviours. Modern human societies are founded on our ability to express complex thoughts through systems of shared symbols or language (Goodenough 1990). Societies based on syntactic language structure the worlds in which they live in symbolic and material ways (Mithen 1996b). The material signatures of modernity include innovation and relatively rapid change as well as distinctive styles recognised as spatially and temporally restricted ways of making or doing things (Hodder 1990). The material record from Mumbwa, and Twin Rivers, will be analysed from the dual perspective of identifying technological changes as chronological markers and of detecting patterns of stylistic development that may reflect the emergence of socially constructed boundaries.

The process of collecting raw materials and of transforming them into tools for extracting energy and protein from the environment involves a series of decisions made by both tool maker and user. The decisions are based, in part, on an understanding of the physical properties of the raw materials and of the demands of the tasks to be performed. Other factors include time constraints, needs for portability, flexibility and reliability in use as well as the distribution and availability of lithic resources (Torrence 1989; Nelson 1991; Hayden et al 1996). The perceived options and the decisions taken are the product of individual experience tempered by social convention. Conventions are learned by enculturation and become inextricably bound into the form and function of tools (Sackett 1990). Among modern small-scale societies, standards of tool making are typically conservative and constrain the behaviour of artisans (Wynn 1994:339). The range of technological solutions deemed appropriate by a community, usually unconsciously, reflects the group's identity and becomes an index or signal of the community (ibid:402). Tool styles are also used actively to promote the identity of groups and individuals (eg, Wiessner 1985) but in the broad time span of the Middle Stone Age the resolution of the archaeological record is poor and active style will be obscured by the weight of passive tradition. Recognising past social boundaries in the absence of adequate contextual data is difficult and this is the case in south central Africa. The Mumbwa assemblages are scrutinised for indexical behaviours in the form of production patterns that may reflect socially derived conventions. On a practical level, the lithic analysis was designed to be carried out relatively rapidly in the field with a minimum of attributes recorded and without need for special equipment.

There is more to the Mumbwa behavioural record than patterns of tool manufacture. In chapter 2, the excavation was described of features interpreted as hearths and windbreaks. These features are analysed in greater detail and implications drawn about the manipulation of space within the cave, the potential number of occupants and changes in settlement strategies. The collection of raw materials from local and distant sources reflects a high degree of planning related to stone tool manufacture but also for unrelated activities such as building hearths and making pigments. Dart and Del Grande (1931) excavated three features they described as tombs from what is now known to be the main occupation unit of the Last Interglacial. The dating and cultural attribution is reviewed of these potentially unique examples of Middle Stone Age mortuary behaviour. The identification of possible bone tools is described and their significance assessed in the context of current knowledge of Middle Stone Age bone working. All the various strands of behavioural data are drawn together in an overview of the Mumbwa sequence in chapter 13.

LITHIC TYPOLOGY

The classification scheme used in the analysis of the Mumbwa and Twin Rivers assemblages is one widely applied to the Later Stone Age of southern Africa

(J Deacon 1982) but also adapted to earlier assemblages (Thackeray & Kelly 1988). J Deacon (1984:226) has argued that a separate typology should be applied to the Middle Stone Age, in particular to the range of retouched tools. In this study, the use of a single typology is preferred because it emphasises underlying continuities in flaking strategies rather than highlighting differences in one category of artefacts (cf Mitchell 1994:22; Clark 1997:119). The scheme used here incorporates the concept of the *chaîne opératoire* (Inizan et al 1992) or reduction sequence of stone tool production. A series of decisions is made in the process of transforming a raw material into a finished tool, including its use and eventual discard. Each link in the chain leaves physical signatures that can be read by the analyst familiar with techniques of stone working. Each individual object is assessed for diagnostic clues to its place in the reduction sequence. The first step involves the observation of surface conditions and determination of the raw material, then the identification of the type of blank and whether it is flaked or not. If flaked, then the techniques and methods used are described followed by examination for signs of use or edge damage. Specialised techniques of production are identified at this stage such as use of the burin and tranchet blow. Intentionally shaped blanks are ascribed to a tool type and the techniques of shaping described. Signs of use damage and evidence of repairs are noted.

For each square and level the artefacts are assigned to one of the following categories: manuports, debitage (flakes, cores, core by-products), used/edge damaged and retouched tools. The categories, their subdivisions and code numbers are outlined in appendix 4. The attributes measured are listed in appendix 3. Basic descriptive statistical assessments are calculated for artefact types within each category and comparisons made between stratigraphic units. The units amalgamate occupation debris from periods of varying duration and intensity of use of the site and as such they are imperfect comparative devices. The history of the excavation of the main cave also distorts the contents of the units. A large portion of the centre of the site was removed in 1930 and the material is not available as a coherent assemblage for analysis. The material retained from the 1939 excavation is a selected sample and is not included in this analysis. Further distortions in the sample size are introduced by the unequal size of the areas excavated in the 1990s. Appendix 1 lists the squares and levels attributed to each unit. The upper 40 ka years of occupation (units I–VI) are represented only in five squares (D11, D12, C11, C12, D10) compared to the Last Interglacial Middle Stone Age (unit VII) which is covered by eight full metre squares (D9, D10, H7, H8, H9, G7, G8, G9) and three partial squares (D8, E9, E10). The underlying colluvium (unit VIII) was sampled in Area I, but exposed largely in Area

II. Area II is also the source of most of the data for the basal sequence (units IX–XIII) and is represented in two full squares (D9, D10) and two partial squares (E9, E10). Units XII–XIII are only exposed in one square (D9–E9) in Area II. The disparity in exposures does affect the analysis: comparisons based on artefact frequencies alone will be skewed by the absolute abundance of unit VII material. Comparisons based on percentage frequency data are used to equalise the disparities in sample size. In cases where the sample size is too small for meaningful frequency data (n<30), the sample is either described in qualitative terms or amalgamated with those from overlying or underlying units.

A pattern of occupation emerges with units II and VII representing the most intensive use of the site. The rarity of artefacts from unit VIII and below appears to be a genuine reflection of the pattern of occupation of this *part* of the site. What cannot be known without further excavation is whether the focus of the early occupation (pre-130 ka BP) was further forward toward the current entrance. Weathering has undoubtedly altered the shape of the cave and reduced the habitable area as demonstrated by the roof fall blocks that cap Holocene deposits in the entrance today.

Manuports

This category encompasses all lithic material brought to the site that is not knapped and shows no signs of modification from use. Included in this category are rocks found among areas of burning and interpreted as hearthstones. Materials that may have been a source of pigment are also included, even though they may show evidence of alteration by heating, rubbing and scraping.

Table 8.1 shows the frequency and percentage of manuports by raw material for each unit. As expected from the density of occupation debris in unit VII, this Last Interglacial deposit contains the largest number and greatest diversity of materials (n=475) transported to the site. The lowest frequencies of manuports occur in units that are known from relatively small volumes of excavated material (I, IV, V, IX) and should not be considered to be representative of the respective periods. Unit VIII is an exception. This colluvial deposit is 1.3 m thick and the artefact sample comes from Areas I and II. The relatively low number of manuports (n=47) reflects the intermittent use of the cave in contrast to the intensity of occupation seen in the overlying unit. The total weight of manuports for each unit (table 8.2) confirms the marked differences between units VIII (210 g) and VII (36,867g).

A more general pattern of raw material use distinguishes the Holocene (units I and II) deposits from all preceding periods. Iron oxides (hematite and specularite) are the most common import in the Holocene levels in contrast to the predominance of sandstone and phyllite in

Table 8.1 Raw material frequencies and percentage frequencies by stratigraphic units

Raw material					Raw material (*continued*)				
Unit		Frequency	Per cent	Cumulative per cent	Unit		Frequency	Per cent	Cumulative per cent
I	Other	2	16.7	16.7		Quartzite	7	1.5	84.3
	Crystal	1	8.3	25.0		Granular quartz	14	2.9	87.2
	Vein quartz	1	8.3	33.3		Chalcedony	1	0.2	87.4
	Hematite	3	25.0	58.3		Green quartz	2	0.4	87.8
	Specularite	4	33.3	91.7		Dolerite	10	2.1	89.9
	Sandstone	1	8.3	100.0		Diorite	1	0.2	90.1
	Total	12	100.0			Shale	22	4.6	94.7
						Talc	6	1.3	96.0
II	Crystal	1	2.4	2.4		Galena	1	0.2	96.2
	Vein quartz	1	2.4	4.9		Limonite	17	3.6	99.8
	Hematite	13	31.7	36.6		Other	1	0.2	100.0
	Specularite	13	31.7	68.3		Total	475	100.0	
	Sandstone	11	26.8	95.1					
	Magnetite	1	2.4	97.5	VIII	Crystal	1	2.1	2.1
	Phyllite	1	2.4	100.0		Vein quartz	9	19.1	21.2
	Total	41	100.0			Specularite	1	2.1	23.3
						Sandstone	23	48.9	72.2
III	Crystal	4	15.4	19.2		Phyllite	9	19.1	91.3
	Vein quartz	2	7.7	23.1		Dolerite	1	2.1	93.4
	Hematite	1	3.8	26.9		Shale	2	4.3	97.7
	Specularite	4	15.4	42.3		Talc	1	2.1	100.0
	Sandstone	9	34.6	76.9		Total	47	100.0	
	Magnetite	2	7.7	84.6					
	Phyllite	2	7.7	92.3	IX	Vein quartz	3	18.8	18.8
	Amethyst	1	3.8	96.1		Sandstone	8	50.0	68.8
	Dolomite	1	3.8	100.0		Phyllite	5	31.3	100.0
	Total	26	100.0			Total	16	100.0	
IV	Crystal	1	11.1	11.1	X	Vein quartz	15	26.3	26.3
	Hematite	3	33.3	44.4		Sandstone	34	59.6	85.9
	Sandstone	3	33.3	77.7		Phyllite	6	10.5	96.4
	Quartzite	3	33.3	100.0		Specularite	1	1.8	98.2
	Total	9	100.0			Chert	1	1.8	100.0
						Total	57	100.0	
V	Vein quartz	2	16.7	16.7					
	Hematite	4	33.3	50.0	XI	Vein quartz	3	12.5	12.5
	Specularite	1	8.3	58.3		Sandstone	15	62.5	75.0
	Sandstone	5	41.7	100.0		Magnetite	1	4.2	79.2
	Total	12	100.0			Phyllite	4	16.7	95.9
						Talc	1	4.2	100.0
VII	Other	3	0.6	0.6		Total	24	100.0	
	Crystal	5	1.1	1.7					
	Vein quartz	35	7.4	9.1	XII	Vein quartz	5	12.2	12.2
	Hematite	59	12.4	21.5		Sandstone	26	63.4	75.6
	Specularite	11	2.3	23.8		Phyllite	7	17.1	92.7
	Sandstone	210	44.2	68.0		Quartzite	1	2.4	95.1
	Magnetite	6	1.3	69.3		Limonite	2	4.9	100.0
	Phyllite	63	13.3	82.6		Total	41	100.0	
	Dolomite	1	0.2	82.8					
					XIII	Vein quartz	1	100.0	100.0

units III–XII. The distinction is mirrored in the distribution of raw materials by weight in units II and VII (fig. 8.1a,b). The association of sandstone and phyllite blocks with hearths explains the pattern. Both materials are consistently found among areas of burning in the earlier deposits, whereas Holocene ash lenses are free of stones. The pre-Holocene hearths also differ in the greater extent and depth of ash and these features are discussed in detail below. Sandstone and phyllite outcrop within 300–500 m of the main cave today and would have been available locally in the Middle and Later Pleistocene. Their transport to the cave and use around hearths reflects a degree of planning not required by the more informal hearths made by the Holocene occupants.

Table 8.2   Total manuport weights in grams by stratigraphic units

Unit	Weight (g)
I	671
II	595
III	3538
IV	885
V	5943
VII	36867
VIII	210
IX	260
X	1428
XI	4946
XI	878
XIII	16

Iron oxides (hematite, n=59 and specularite, n=11) and iron hydroxides (limonite, n=17) are the next most common manuports in units III–VIII. Among this sample, only four pieces (4.6 per cent) bear evidence of use in the form of facetted surfaces formed by rubbing (fig. 8.2) or as incised lines or grooves (fig. 8.3). Macroscopic inspection (×10) of the incisions shows them to vary in profile from V to U shape and range in width from 1 to 3 mm. The grooves appear to have been cut by both sharp and blunt-edged tools, such as a flake, scraper or awl. The used pieces all come from the main Last Interglacial (unit VII). The intentional rubbing and scraping of iron oxides would have produced a coloured powder. Powdered hematite derived from local laterites ranges in colour from deep red (10R 5/8–4/8, Munsell) to brown red (10R 6/6). Specularite from lateritic sources and from the Nambala hills to the south produces a reddish purple streak (10R 4–3/3–3) that sparkles in sunlight. The local lateritic limonite creates a bright yellow powder (2.5Y 8/8). In addition to iron minerals, potential sources of pigments occur in the form of ferruginous sandstone and yellow sandstone. The red sandstone, as a powder or when soaked in water (P Vandiver pers comm), releases a pinkish red colour similar to soft hematite. The local sandstone is largely grey in colour, but grades naturally into red in some places or can be transformed by heating into red. Yellow sandstone outcrops within 1 km of the cave and it provides a bright powder similar in colour to limonite. Neither shade of sandstone has the natural staining properties of the iron minerals. The latter adhere easily to dry skin and penetrate porous rock surfaces without further preparation.

Found in Area I, in association with the artefact concentrations described below, was a thumb-shaped stick of baked clay that produces a red streak (fig. 8.4a). A flat-based groove is cut perpendicular to the axis of the piece and near the tip. Another stick of baked clayey sediment was found in Area II in unit VII, but with flat grooves parallel to length of the piece (fig. 8.4b). The clay sticks appear to be intentional forms and heated (K Bailey pers comm). These are not included in the manuport category but can be considered as possible sources of reddish brown colour in crayon form.

The frequency of potential pigments declines markedly below unit VII. Hematite is absent from the sample and only two small pieces of limonite occur along with four blocks of yellow sandstone. Manganese dioxide is represented by one piece but it may have formed *in situ* as a concretion and as such may not be a genuine manuport. Manganese dioxide as a source of grey-black pigment was not widely used. Magnetite is available locally and produces a grey streak (7.5R N4/), but there is no evidence that this material was used as a pigment. The few pieces of iron minerals found in the lower units reflect the generally low frequency of manuports in these earliest occupation phases. Among the category as a whole, sandstone and phyllite are the predominant materials and are indicative of either sporadic occupation of the cave in the Middle Pleistocene or its use by small groups for whom pigments were not needed.

Because manuports are transported items, their presence in the cave is an indicator of the occupants' use of the landscape, of planning and their awareness of the properties of various raw materials. All the material found in the Mumbwa sequence occurs within a 15 km radius of the cave with the exception of some specularite. A grey, heavy and densely crystalline form outcrops as the Nambala hills 18 km to the south of Mumbwa and produces a sparkling reddish purple streak. Other sources of specularite exist nearby but in laterite deposits and in quartz veins. These local sources offer platy crystals of laterite and a massive form, both of which produce sparkling purple powder similar to the Nambala material. The latter differs in its greater silica content that allows it to be knapped or to be used as hammerstones. Nambala specularite is uncommon in the manuport assemblage (n=2). The Later Pleistocene and Holocene occupants of the cave made use of a similar range of local resources, with little apparent difference in distances travelled or degree of planning with the exception of the use of sandstone and phyllite. The higher frequencies of these two rocks in the pre-Holocene deposits suggest a deliberate selection of these materials for their specific properties and a differing pattern of occupation in the cave. The use of stone around the early hearths is discussed in detail below.

Debitage

The term applies to the activity of blank production and its products. Whole flakes are analysed using attributes that reflect the method of debitage (Dibble & Whittaker

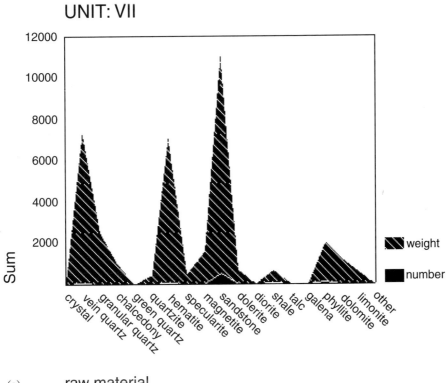

(a)   raw material

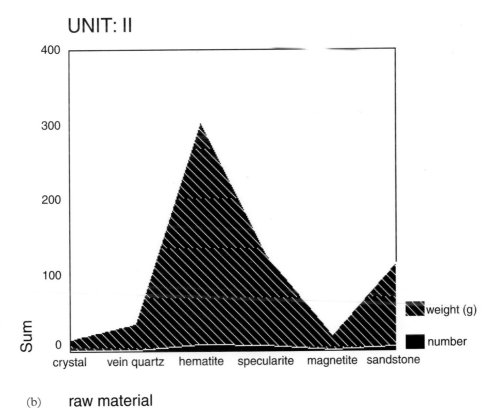

(b)   raw material

Fig. 8.1   Manuport weights (grams) by raw material in units VII (a) and II (b).

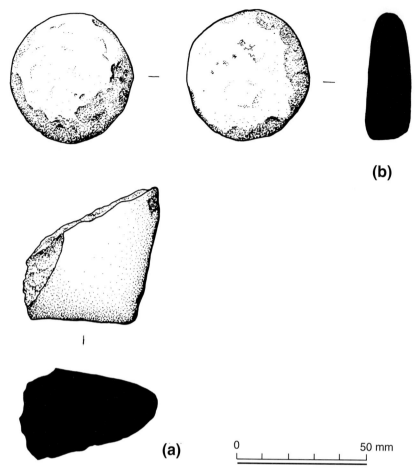

Figure 8.2 Hematite from unit VII shaped by rubbing (a) and pecking or rubbing (b).

Figure 8.3 Specularite with incised v-shaped grooves from unit VII, Area II (E8–1–1).

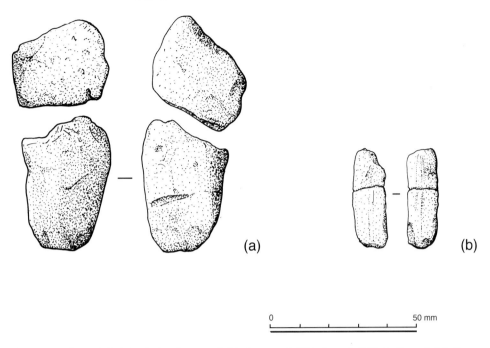

0   50 mm

Figure 8.4 Iron-rich baked clay 'crayons' (a) from unit VII, Area I (H8–9–1) and (b) from unit VII, Area II (E10–10–2).

1981; Dibble 1997). These include platform preparation, dorsal surface scar pattern and the morphology of the flake. The presence of cortex on the dorsal surface is noted as evidence of an early stage in the reduction process (Bradbury & Carr 1995), but also as an indicator of the source of the raw material (eg, river cobble). Technological attributes such as flake termination profiles, edge angles and breakage patterns (eg, Thackeray 1989) are not included because of time constraints. All measurements were taken in the field. The flake class is subdivided into blades and bladelets with method of debitage noted (eg, bipolar, prepared core). Broken or incomplete flakes are included in the debitage category, against strict use of the term (Inizan et al 1992:45) and analysed simply by raw material and size class. Size and morphology further divide the shatter or waste resulting from knapping with a separate class for angular chunks as distinguished from flake waste. Vein quartz was the primary material used at both Mumbwa and Twin Rivers and this brittle material produces abundant shatter, much of it less than 10 mm in size. The presence of fine shatter, especially in large quantities, indicates that primary knapping took place on site and that the deposits have not been reworked and winnowed by taphonomic processes such as running water (eg, Sheppard & Kleindienst 1996). The refitting of flakes to cores is another indicator of the vertical and horizontal integrity of deposits, but is an impractical approach with quartz-based assemblages. Bulbs of percussion and other classic markers of the application of

force to stone are muted in quartz (Knight 1991) and this, combined with its proclivity to shatter, makes refitting an exercise in futility. Refitting was attempted with non-quartz materials.

Cores as a class of debitage preserve the scars of the last blank removals in a sequence. As such, earlier stages are usually removed or obscured, which limits the value of cores as indicators of the intentions of the knapper. Despite this limitation, cores do reflect general methods or strategies of blank production. A prepared core represents a more considered sequence of removals than a simple chunk with two or three flake scars. The typology of cores distinguishes between methods of debitage (radial, discoidal, Levallois, blade, bladelet, bipolar). Centripetal flaking was a common approach to blank production used by the inhabitants of Mumbwa and distinctions made in the typology between radial and discoidal (disc) cores are somewhat arbitrary. Both core forms bear the scars of flake removals from around the periphery towards the core centre. The radial core in profile is biconical and the disc core has a flattened surface, but the latter can be produced from a radial core in the course of reduction. The resulting flakes are identical in morphology with intersecting surface scars and a tendency toward pentagonal and triangular shapes. The Levallois core also involves centripetal flaking in its shaping but differs in having two asymmetrical convex surfaces and consistent use of a proximal striking platform in relation to the long axis of the core (van Peer 1992:113). The resulting flakes are not always easily distinguished from other centripetal reduction methods with the exception of flakes with faceted butts. Facetting produces broad thin flakes (ibid:39), but not all Levallois flakes are faceted. Flakes with simple facets are created by centripetal reduction methods so the distinction is made between multiple and minimally faceted butts to separate Levallois from non-Levallois methods.

More informal methods of blank production are recognised in cores with one or more platforms, not including blade cores. The geometry of these unspecialised forms is often used to create classes of cores based on the number and location of platforms in relation to each other (eg, Clark & Kleindienst 1974:81). In this study, a few basic forms are recognised including single platform, opposed platforms, two platforms at right angles and three or more platforms. Multiple platform cores appear to be opportunistic approaches to available angles on the raw material.

The category of core by-products encompasses broken cores and the results of efforts to extend the working life of cores. Among the class of core rejuvenation flakes is an odd peaked form called a 'topknot' flake (Barham 1995). The shape results from the clearance of the intersection of flake scars at the apex of a radial core. The presence of topknot flakes suggests that not all quartz was equal in terms of flaking quality. Vein quartz varies widely in its internal homogeneity, even within a single source. The knappers at Mumbwa recognised when a core responded in a predictable way and was worthy of prolonged use. Topknot flakes were themselves used as cores with the broad ventral surface often centripetally flaked or fashioned into small Levallois cores.

Bipolar flaking produces its own characteristic set of debitage including flakes and cores but also a split core (fig. 8.5) that resembles a segment of an orange (Barham 1987). Bipolar segments are included in the by-products category and in the Mumbwa sequence they are invariably associated with the reduction of cobbles (>30mm) and pebbles (<30mm). The frequency of bipolar debitage is used as a proxy indicator of the selection of stream-worn materials from the landscape. The absence of cobbles and pebbles from the local area today makes the presence of bipolar flaking an indirect indicator of more active flow regimes in the past or a willingness to travel long distances (>50km) to the Kafue river gravels.

The extensive list of artefacts considered as debitage reflects the importance of this category as a source of data about the techniques and methods of artefact production and also the abundance of this material in comparison to retouched tools. The choice of primary reduction technique makes a large contribution to variability in any lithic assemblage (Dibble & Lenoir 1995). Other influences include raw material availability, subsistence practices, local vegetation and climate as well

Figure 8.5 Bipolar reduction technique applied to quartz pebble with resulting bladelet. The technique creates a characteristic segment and pillow shaped cores with damage to both ends (Barham 1987).

social conventions. The effect of raw material selection on assemblage variability is a relative constant in the case of Mumbwa (and Twin Rivers) given the predominance of vein quartz in all reduction categories. The other sources of variation are less readily accommodated because of the lack of data, especially for subsistence behaviours (see chapter 4). The effects of changes in biogeography on assemblage variability and the elucidation of social conventions from the patterns of debitage will be discussed in chapter 13. In the interim, a culture-stratigraphic sequence is constructed based on shifting trends in flaking technology combined with patterns of retouched tool production.

The lithic assemblages also are examined for evidence reflecting the changing use of the cave. Each reduction category indicates a stage in the process of making tools from introducing raw materials to the discard of debitage and shaped tools. The percentage frequencies of artefacts at each stage in the reduction sequence are a measure of the intensity and types of activities within the cave. This behavioural data could in theory be used to distinguish between the use of the cave by residential groups as opposed to short-term special purpose task groups. In reality, the deposits are too fragmented by previous excavations and mixed by taphonomic processes to support this kind of spatial analysis. Regardless, some basic behavioural information is contained in the range of reduction categories represented.

Analysis

CORES

Table 8.3 outlines the frequency and percentage frequencies of core types by stratigraphic unit. The largest numbers are found in units II (n=132), III (n=71) and

Table 8.3 Frequency and percentage frequency of core types by stratigraphic unit

Type				
Unit		Frequency	Per cent	Cumulative per cent
I	Radial	1	3.6	3.6
	Single platform	4	14.3	17.9
	Multiple platforms	10	35.7	53.6
	Bladelet	5	17.9	71.4
	Bipolar	1	3.6	75.0
	Chunk	7	25.0	100.0
II	Radial	9	6.8	6.8
	Single platform	51	38.6	45.5
	Multiple platforms	34	25.8	71.2
	Bladelet	7	5.3	76.5
	Chunk	30	22.7	99.2
	On flake	1	0.8	100.0
	Total	132	100.0	
III	Radial	6	8.5	8.5
	Single platform	29	40.8	49.3
	Multiple platforms	7	9.9	59.2
	Bladelet	15	21.1	80.3
	Chunk	14	19.7	100.0
IV	Radial	3	11.5	11.5
	Single platform	6	23.1	34.6
	Multiple platforms	4	15.4	50.0
	Bladelet	2	7.7	57.7
	Bipolar	1	3.8	61.5
	Chunk	10	38.5	100.0
	Total	26	100.0	
V	Radial	2	7.7	7.7
	Single platform	10	38.5	46.2
	Multiple platforms	2	7.7	53.8
	Bladelet	3	11.5	65.4
	Chunk	9	34.6	100.0
	Total	26	100.0	
VII	Radial	127	18.7	18.7
	Single platform	140	20.6	39.3
	Multiple platforms	108	15.9	55.2
	Bladelet	6	0.9	56.1
	Bipolar	16	2.4	58.5
	Chunk	189	27.8	86.3
	On flake	9	1.3	87.6
	2-platform, right	2	0.3	87.9
	Prepared	40	5.9	93.8

Type (*continued*)				
Unit		Frequency	Per cent	Cumulative per cent
	Blade	24	3.5	97.3
	On core	6	0.9	98.2
	Opposed platform	3	0.4	98.6
	Disc	10	1.5	100.0
	Total	680	100.0	
VIII	Radial	3	23.1	23.1
	Single platform	1	7.7	30.8
	Multiple platforms	1	7.7	38.5
	Bipolar	1	7.7	46.2
	Chunk	5	38.5	84.6
	On flake	1	7.7	92.3
	Disc	1	7.7	100.0
	Total	13	100.0	
IX	Radial	3	100.0	100.0
X	Radial	1	4.5	4.5
	Single platform	1	4.5	9.1
	Multiple platforms	3	13.6	22.7
	Bipolar	2	9.1	31.8
	Chunk	6	27.3	59.1
	Prepared	1	4.5	63.6
	Opposed platform	1	4.5	68.1
	Disc	7	31.8	100.0
	Total	22	100.0	
XI	Radial	3	17.6	17.6
	Single platform	3	17.6	35.3
	Multiple platforms	4	23.5	58.8
	Bipolar	1	5.9	64.7
	Chunk	1	5.9	70.6
	Blade	3	17.6	88.2
	Disc	2	11.8	100.0
	Total	17	100.0	
XII	Radial	2	14.3	14.3
	Single platform	3	21.4	35.7
	Multiple platforms	1	7.1	42.9
	Bipolar	4	28.6	71.6
	Chunk	1	7.1	78.6
	Prepared	1	7.1	85.7
	Blade	1	7.1	92.8
	On core	1	7.1	100.0
	Total	14	100.0	

VII (n=682). Below unit VII, the numbers of cores assigned to individual units fall below a minimum threshold (n=30) for comparative statistical analysis. The frequencies for unit XII are in fact a combined number for units XII–XIV. Scrutiny of basic percentages does provide some guide to patterns of blank production. Equally, the sample sizes in units I, IV and V are too small for comparative analysis, but the percentages reveal changing trends in flaking.

Looking at the percentages from the bottom of the sequence upwards, three trends emerge in the tech-

niques of flake production. First is the prevalence of centripetal methods of flaking (radial, disc, prepared) in units XII to VII (~20–30 per cent of cores). Among these types, radial flaking is the most common technique (figs 8.6 and 8.7). The percentage declines to single figures in unit III (Late Glacial) reaching a low of 3.6 per cent in unit I. The changing percentages show continuity in centripetal flaking throughout the sequence but the sharp decline between unit VII and V–VI marks a shift in techniques of flake production between the Last Interglacial and the last 40 ka. The second trend is the

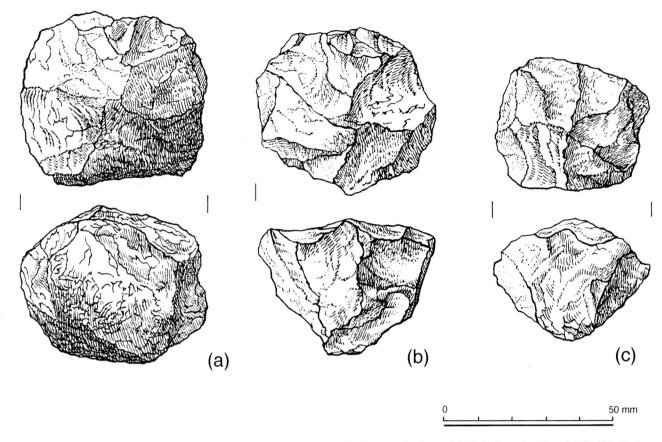

(a)　　　　　(b)　　　　　(c)

0 _____ 50 mm

Figure 8.6　Vein quartz radial cores from Mumbwa Caves: (a) unit X (E9–3–24); (b) unit VII (D9–1–4); (c) unit VII (E9–2–4).

replacement of blade cores in units VII–XII by bladelet cores from unit V onwards. For comparative purposes, units VIII–XII are amalgamated (table 8.4) below into a single pre-130 ka block to show the combined frequencies and percentages of cores. Blade cores account for 5.8 per cent of this artificial assemblage and 3.5 per cent of unit VII cores. Blades are produced from opposed platforms with the resulting cores having flattened rather than pyramidal profiles (fig. 8.8). The cores from the combined lower units tend to be more rectangular and would have produced wider blades than those made during the Last Interglacial. A combining of the low frequencies of units V and IV into a single analytical block (table 8.5) shows more clearly the shift toward bladelet making and the retention of centripetal flaking as a diminished technological inheritance.

The shift in percentage frequencies of centripetal and lamellar flaking methods is mirrored by a gradual shift towards smaller cores of both types. Table 8.6 shows mean values for radial core length, width and thickness using the combined unit data in XII and IV. The largest radial cores, as measured across all three dimensions, occur in the lowest units (XII and VII) and the size range decreases through the sequence.

Blade and bladelet cores follow a similar trajectory from larger to smaller through the sequence. The longest blade cores occur in the combined unit XII and none is found above unit VII (table 8.7). The bladelet cores in unit VII are wider than those made in later units.

Bladelet cores occur in unit VII and are larger than those in unit IV but closer in dimensions to those in unit II (table 8.8). Size variation is less pronounced than among radial cores, as would be expected from a class in part defined by its dimensions. The presence of blade and bladelet cores in the Last Interglacial deposits deserves further comment as this is the main Middle Stone Age occupation layer and these flaking strategies are producing low frequencies of blanks (next section) that are transformed into crescentic backed blades – a typologically significant tool type.

Across all units, vein quartz is the primary material used to produce flakes and blades (table 8.9). Quartz crystals or clear quartz often produce distinct conchoidal fractures and tend to be more homogeneous than milky vein quartz. Crystalline quartz can be used to produce fine blades, particularly when struck with a soft hammer (Knight 1991). In the Mumbwa sequence, some preference is given to quartz crystal for bladelet

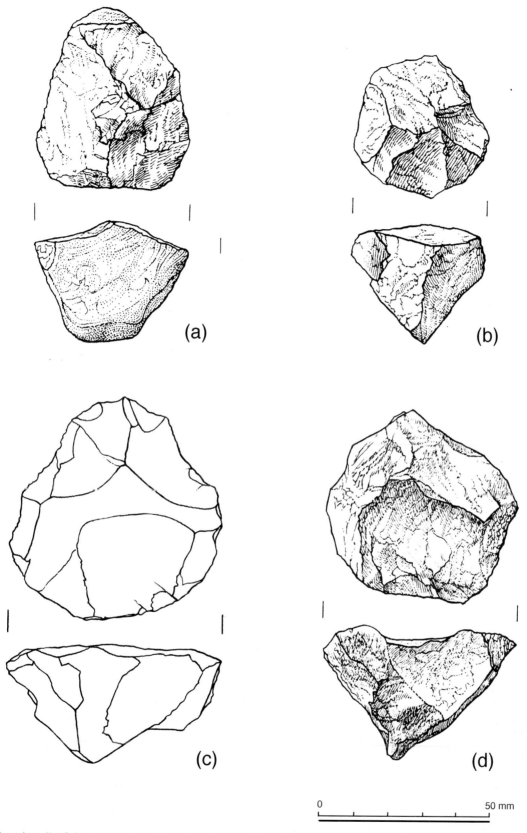

Figure 8.7 Centripetally flaked cores from Mumbwa Caves: (a) radial core on a quartz cobble, unit VII (D10–2–15); (b) vein quartz radial core, unit VII (G8–3–1); (c) discoidal chert core, unit VII (G9–1–2); (d) vein quartz radial/Levallois core on a topknot flake, unit VII (H7–4–1).

Table 8.4 Combined core type frequency and percentage data for units VIII–XII

Type

	Frequency	Per cent	Cumulative per cent
Radial	12	17.4	17.4
Single platform	8	11.6	29.0
Multiple platforms	9	13.0	42.0
Prepared	2	2.9	44.9
Blade	4	5.8	50.7
Bipolar	8	11.6	62.3
Chunk	13	18.8	81.2
On flake	1	1.4	82.6
On core	1	1.4	84.1
Opposed platform	1	1.4	85.5
Disc	10	14.5	100.0
Total	69	100.0	

production (table 8.10), but vein quartz is the material of choice for the larger blade cores found in units XII–VII. In these same units, a range of coloured quartz is used including blue, green and a yellow granular form. These sources of quartz were not exploited in later periods, or perhaps were no longer available because of changes in the geomorphology of the surrounding landscape. Nambala specularite was flaked in unit VII along with a dark siliceous magnetite of unknown origin. A fine-grained sandstone was also occasionally used by the Last Interglacial occupants and chert was used in all periods if infrequently.

The third trend to emerge from the core frequency data in table 8.3 is the decreasing use of the bipolar technique through the sequence. In the combined unit XII data (table 8.4), 11.6 per cent of cores are bipolar, in

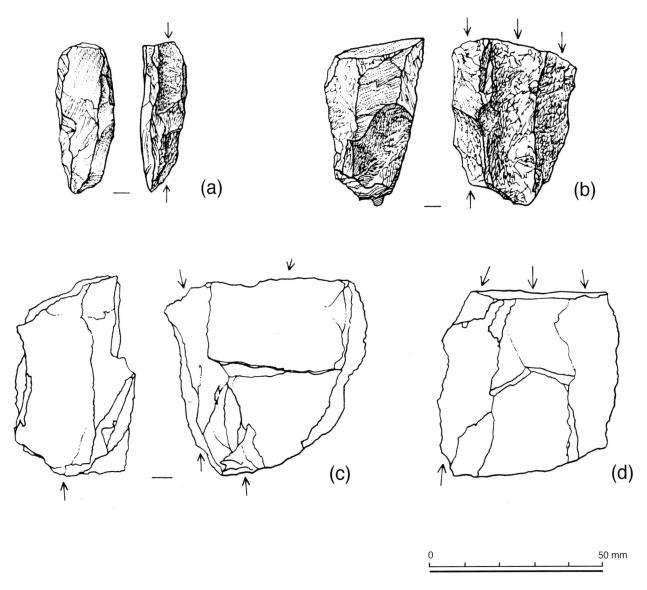

Figure 8.8 Vein quartz, opposed platform blade cores from Mumbwa Caves: (a) unit VII (D10–4–4); (b) unit VII (G8–4–3); (c) blade and flake core, unit VII (D9–1–1); (d) unit XI (E10–4–1).

Table 8.5 Combined core type frequency and percentage data for units V–IV

Type

	Frequency	Per cent	Cumulative per cent
Radial	5	9.6	9.6
Single platform	16	30.8	40.4
Multiple platforms	6	11.5	51.9
Blade	5	9.6	61.5
Bipolar	1	1.9	63.5
Chunk	19	36.5	100.0
Total	52	100.0	

unit VII 2.3 per cent and in combined unit IV 1.9 per cent of cores are produced on an anvil from river cobbles. The technique was not used in units III and II (Late Glacial to early Holocene). Although the frequencies of bipolar cores are low they are nonetheless significant in reflecting either changing availabilities of raw materials or changes in perceptions of which raw materials are suitable for knapping. The former explanation seems most likely given the geomorphological and palaeoecological evidence for greater variablity in local environmental conditions during the Mid-Later Pleistocene. Essentially modern hydrological conditions existed by the early Holocene and presumably the low

Table 8.6 Mean radial core length, width and thickness (mm) by stratigraphic unit. Units IV and XII are amalgamations of data from adjacent units (see text)

Descriptive statistics

Unit		N	Minimum	Maximum	Mean	Std deviation
I	Length	1	24	24	24.00	.
	Width	1	23	23	23.00	.
	Thickness	1	14	14	14.00	
II	Length	9	24	48	32.00	7.68
	Width	9	25	39	31.00	4.18
	Thickness	9	13	30	19.89	5.80
III	Length	6	15	36	25.83	8.42
	Width	6	17	33	24.17	6.43
	Thickness	6	13	23	17.83	3.60
IV	Length	5	22	35	29.80	4.87
	Width	5	25	40	33.20	5.81
	Thickness	5	20	30	24.40	4.04
VII	Length	127	19	94	40.97	11.73
	Width	127	4	348	49.96	41.33
	Thickness	127	11	53	28.24	8.62
XII	Length	12	30	91	56.42	16.22
	Width	12	30	62	49.17	11.46
	Thickness	12	18	53	35.08	10.97

Table 8.7 Mean dimensions (mm) for blade cores from units XII and VII. Unit XII results are an amalgamation of data from units VIII–XIV

Descriptive statistics

Unit		N	Minimum	Maximum	Mean	Std deviation
VII	Length	24	16	58	42.08	11.76
	Width	24	14	142	42.71	31.44
	Thickness	24	18	73	36.00	16.82
XII	Length	4	30	68	49.50	16.05
	Width	4	21	44	34.75	9.78
	Thickness	4	18	48	30.75	13.30

Table 8.8 Mean length, width and thickness (mm) of bladelet cores by stratigraphic unit

Descriptive statistics

Unit		N	Minimum	Maximum	Mean	Std deviation
I	Length	5	21	34	25.80	4.97
	Width	5	11	21	16.80	3.90
	Thickness	5	10	20	15.80	3.96
II	Length	7	15	27	20.71	3.82
	Width	7	10	20	14.29	4.42
	Thickness	7	8	32	15.29	8.44
III	Length	15	8	30	18.73	5.06
	Width	15	7	25	14.93	4.92
	Thickness	15	14	33	22.07	5.52
IV	Length	4	3	14	10.00	4.97
	Width	4	9	13	10.75	2.06
	Thickness	4	15	23	20.50	3.79
VII	Length	6	10	26	18.50	6.28
	Width	6	7	31	18.17	9.37
	Thickness	6	11	20	15.67	3.78

Table 8.9 Raw material frequencies and percentages of cores in each stratigraphic unit

Raw material

Unit		Frequency	Per cent	Cumulative per cent
I	Quartz crystal	2	7.1	7.1
	Vein quartz	25	89.3	96.4
	Chalcedony	1	3.6	100.0
II	Quartz crystal	15	11.4	11.4
	Vein quartz	115	87.1	98.5
	Chert	2	1.5	100.0
	Total	132	100.0	
III	Quartz crystal	8	11.3	11.3
	Vein quartz	60	84.5	95.8
	Chert	3	4.2	100.0
	Total	71	100.0	
IV	Quartz crystal	2	3,8	3,8
	Vein quartz	47	90.4	94.2
	Chalcedony	1	1,9	96.2
	Chert	1	1.9	98.1
	Other	1	1.9	100.0
	Total	52	100.0	

Raw material (*continued*)

Unit		Frequency	Per cent	Cumulative per cent
VII	Quartz crystal	22	3.2	3.2
	Vein quartz	605	89.0	92.2
	Chert	15	2.2	94.4
	Other	1	0.1	94.5
	Amethyst	3	0.4	94.9
	Blue quartz	4	0.6	95.5
	Granular quartz	2	0.3	95.8
	Green quartz	10	1.5	97.3
	Quartzite	11	1.6	98.9
	Specularite	1	0.1	99.0
	Magnetite	4	0.6	99.6
	Shale	2	0.3	99.9
	Total	680	100.0	
XII	Quartz crystal	2	2.9	2.9
	Vein quartz	58	84.1	87.0
	Chert	1	1.4	88.4
	Blue quartz	4	5.8	94.2
	Green quartz	2	2.9	97.1
	Quartzite	1	1.4	98.5
	Magnetite	1	1.4	100.0
	Total	69	100	

energy seasonal streams found in the area today were also present in some form. As a consequence, cobbles and pebbles would not have been available locally.

Among the other core types, single and multiple platform cores are common throughout all the units. They represent a practical and less formal approach to flaking angular blocks of quartz. Cores on chunks show no patterning of flake removal and reflect opportunistic flaking.

Prepared or Levallois cores account for 5.9 per cent of the unit VII assemblage and 2.9 per cent of the combined unit VIII–XII assemblage and are not found in any of the later units. The low percentage frequencies reflect the dominance of radial flaking as a means of rapidly producing thin flakes. The fact that the core preparation took place indicates a need for the specific products of this form of flaking, in particular thin but wide convergent flakes. Among the prepared cores

Table 8.10 Raw material frequencies and percentages for bladelet cores by stratigraphic unit

Unit	Raw material	Frequency	Per cent	Cumulative per cent
I	Quartz crystal	1	20.0	20.0
	Vein quartz	4	80.0	100.0
	Total	5	100.0	
II	Quartz crystal	3	42.9	42.9
	Vein quartz	4	57.1	100.0
	Total	7	100.0	
III	Quartz crystal	3	20.0	20.0
	Vein quartz	11	73.3	93.3
	Chert	1	6.7	100.0
	Total	15	100.0	

Unit	Raw material (continued)	Frequency	Per cent	Cumulative per cent
IV	Quartz crystal	2	40.0	40.0
	Vein quartz	2	40.0	80.0
	Chalcedony	1	20.0	100.0
	Total	5	100.0	
VII	Quartz crystal	3	50.0	50.0
	Vein quartz	2	33.3	83.3
	Amethyst	1	16.7	100.0
	Total	6	100.0	

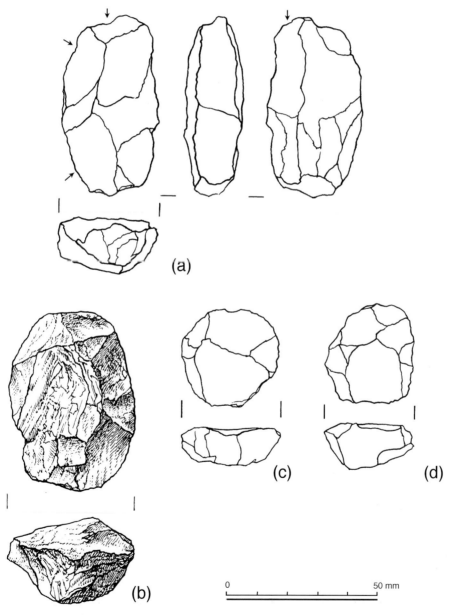

Figure 8.9 Vein quartz prepared cores from Mumbwa Caves: (a) flake/blade core, unit VII (D9–4–7); (b) unit X (E9–3–18); (c) and (d) small flat cores, unit VII (H7–7–1).

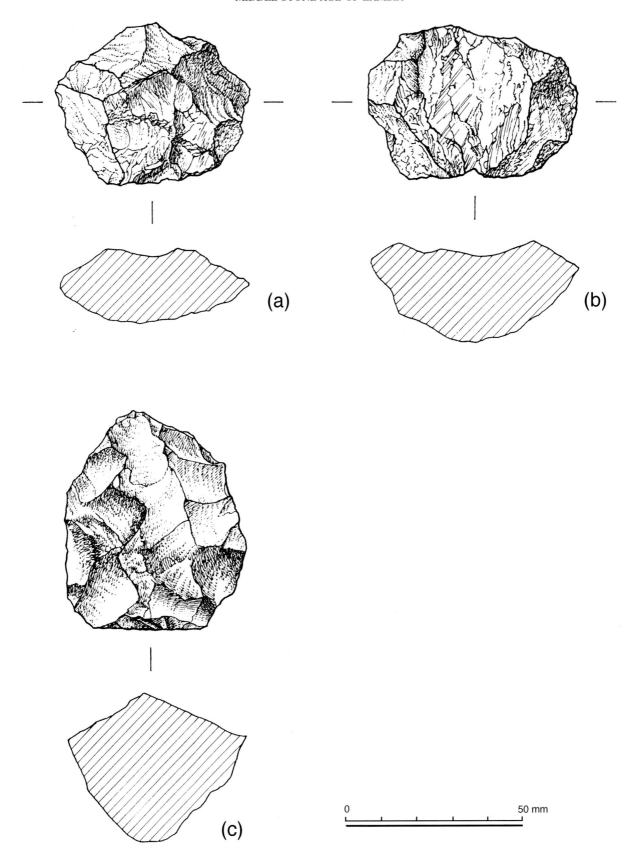

Figure 8.10 Prepared cores from Mumbwa Caves: (a) vein quartz, unit VII (H7–2–10); (b) vein quartz, unit VII (D10–4–3); (c) chert, unit VII (E9–1–7).

Table 8.11 Mean length, width and thickness (mm) of prepared cores by stratigraphic unit

Descriptive statistics

Unit		N	Minimum	Maximum	Mean	Std deviation
VII	Length	40	25	77	41.55	9.81
	Width	40	8	78	39.20	17.05
	Thickness	40	8	34	18.65	5.92
X	Length	1	60	60	60.00	.
	Width	1	43	43	43.00	.
	Thickness	1	29	29	29.00	.
XII	Length	1	57	57	57.00	.
	Width	1	42	42	42.00	.
	Thickness	1	21	21	21.00	.

(figures 8.9 and 8.10) in unit VII, the majority are small (30–40 mm in length) (table 8.11) and of these some are made on topknot flakes (fig. 8.7d). The dorsal surface of the topknot provides a ready-made convex undercarriage. The flakes produced from these cores would also be small and presumably were hafted. The absence of prepared cores in the uppermost Middle Stone Age deposit (unit V) may be a factor of the small area excavated or a reflection of a genuine shift in techniques of flaking as seen in the diminished use of centripetal methods of flaking in this and later units.

CORE BY-PRODUCTS

This category of artefacts reflects purposeful behaviours applied to the extension of the productive life of cores (rejuvenation flakes) as well as to the discard of exhausted and broken cores. Bipolar cores reach a stage at which no further flakes can be removed from the wedge shape mass and are considered to be exhausted at this point. Quartz cores can shatter or split because of the application of too much force or because of internal flaws. These artefacts are evidence for the later stages of the reduction sequence taking place in the cave. Bipolar cores at Mumbwa are all made on cobbles and as a consequence they provide evidence for access to this form of raw material.

Table 8.12 shows the frequency of the types of core by-products in each unit. Only unit VII has a sample large enough (n=201) for statistical analysis but some general observations can be made about the full sequence. Artefacts of bipolar flaking occur in units I–III and VII, which suggests that cobbles were available as a resource to the occupants during the Holocene, as well as during the Later Pleistocene. No local source has been found under modern conditions and this implies either a change in local stream flow regimes in the recent past or the long-distance collection of cobbles. Topknot flakes as a form of radial core rejuvenation flake are restricted to

Table 8.12 Core by-product frequencies by type and stratigraphic unit

Type

Unit		Frequency	Per cent	Cumulative per cent
I	Exhausted bipolar	1	14.3	14.3
	Bipolar split segment	5	71.4	85.7
	Core fragment	1	14.3	100.0
	Total	7	100.0	
II	Bipolar split segment	5	18.5	18.5
	Core fragment	11	40.7	59.2
	Rejuvenation flake	10	37.0	96.2
	Split radial core	1	3.7	99.9
	Total	27	100.0	
III	Bipolar split segment	2	40.0	40.0
	Core fragment	2	40.0	80.0
	Rejuvenation flake	1	20.0	100.0
	Total	5	100.0	
IV	Core fragment	2	66.7	66.7
	Rejuvenation flake	1	33.3	100.0
	Total	3	100.0	
VII	Exhausted bipolar	2	1.0	1.0
	Bipolar split segment	12	6.0	7.0
	Core fragment	55	27.4	34.4
	Rejuvenation flake	14	7.0	41.4
	Split radial core	76	37.8	79.2
	Topknot flake	36	17.9	97.0
	Split prepared core	3	1.5	98.5
	Blade core fragment	3	1.5	100.0
	Total	201	100.0	
VIII	Split radial core	1	100.0	100.0
X	Split radial core	1	100.0	100.0
XII	Split radial core	1	100.0	100.0

unit VII which also has a high percentage (37.8 per cent) of split radial cores. Fragments of blade and prepared cores occur in low frequencies in common with the low frequencies of whole blade and prepared cores. The presence of split radial cores in units VIII, X and XII reflects the sparse record of human habitation during the Middle Pleistocene.

The raw material frequencies show the overwhelming predominance of vein quartz in all units (table 8.13). Unit VII has the greatest variety of materials used including a shade of blue quartz that is unique to this period.

FLAKES AND BLADES

The attributes assessed in this class of artefacts include raw materials used, aspects of size (length, width, thickness), method of production (butt preparation, dorsal surface scars) and stage in the reduction sequence (cortex). Only complete flakes were included in the analysis. Unit IX had only three flakes and unit XI just one and these four flakes have been added to the unit XII total. Despite the amalgamation of the lower units, the resulting total of 12 flakes is insufficient for comparative statistical analysis. The three flakes from unit VI have been added to the unit V total. No unbroken flakes were

Table 8.13 Raw material frequencies of core by-products by stratigraphic unit

Raw material

Unit		Frequency	Per cent	Cumulative per cent
I	Vein quartz	6	85.7	85.7
	Hematite	1	14.3	100.0
	Total	7	100.0	
II	Vein quartz	26	96.3	96.3
	Hematite	1	3.7	100.0
	Total	27	100.0	
III	Vein quartz	4	80.0	80.0
	Hematite	1	20.0	100.0
	Total	5	100.0	
IV	Vein quartz	2	66.7	66.7
	Hematite	1	33.3	100.0
	Total	3	100.0	
VII	Vein quartz	192	95.5	95.5
	Crystal	3	1.5	97.0
	Amethyst	1	0.5	97.5
	Blue quartz	2	1.0	98.5
	Quartzite	1	0.5	99.0
	Chert	1	0.5	99.5
	Shale	1	0.5	100.0
	Total	201	100.0	
VIII	Vein quartz	1	100.0	100.0
X	Vein quartz	1	100.0	100.0
XII	Vein quartz	1	100.0	100.0

found in unit VIII. Table 8.14 shows the frequencies and percentages of raw materials used in each unit. Unit VII contains the largest number of whole flakes (n=942), followed by unit II (n=315), unit I (n=156) and unit III (n=56). Units IV and V contain 32 and 31 flakes respectively and are marginally suitable for statistical analysis.

Vein quartz dominates the percentages in each unit and ranges from 83–92 per cent of all flakes. The units with the greatest variety of raw materials used are those with the largest samples, but these are also the units linked to interglacial conditions (VII, II–I). What seems to be a promising correlation between climate, variety of materials used and intensity of occupation is partly confounded by the problems of sample size associated with transitional phases as outlined at the outset of this chapter. The near absence of human occupation of the cave during the deposit of unit VIII (Stage 6) is supported by the lack of whole flakes. In this case, a link can be made between climate and intensity of occupation.

No strong trends are apparent in the raw material data, with the exception of the increasing use of quartz crystal from the Late Glacial (unit IV) into the Holocene (units II–I) as compared to the Stage 3 Middle Stone Age (unit V). This shift coincides with the increased production of bladelets in these same units. The general pattern of raw material use during the Last Interglacial does differ slightly from that of later periods in the variety of materials selected. A greater range of quartz colours was used in unit VII (blue, green, yellow or granular). These flakes are presumably from the cores of the same colour that were also recovered from unit VII. A fine-grained dark brown quartzite was used exclusively in unit VII and in similar frequencies to chert. Two conjoining flakes of quartzite were found in Area I within an ash spread associated with the structure interpreted as a windbreak (page 135). The flakes were separated by 5 cm. Other rare materials used include Nambala specularite (listed as hematite, n=2) and a heavy siliceous mafic material (listed as magnetite, n=7). The most unusual material that was found in unit VII was a single convergent flake of Luapula porphyry. As discussed in chapter 2, the porphyry was transported a minimum distance of 200 km and came from either the eastern edge of the Kafue basin or from northeastern Zambia. The flake was associated with the windbreak structure in Area I. No evidence of long-distance transport of materials was found in the Holocene units.

The techniques used to manufacture flakes are reflected in the preparation and dimensions of the butts or platforms. The presence and type of faceting indicates the extent of core preparation with simple facets formed in the course of centripetal flaking and multiple facets a feature of the greater platform preparation associated with Levallois cores. Plain and cortical platforms are linked to more informal flaking

Table 8.14 Raw material used for flaking in each stratigraphic unit

Raw material Unit			Frequency	Per cent	Valid per cent	Cumulative per cent
I	Valid	Quartz crystal	13	8.3	8.6	8.6
		Vein quartz	126	80.8	83.4	92.1
		Blue quartz	2	1.3	1.3	93.4
		Chalcedony	1	0.6	0.7	94.0
		Green quartz	1	0.6	0.7	94.7
		Quartzite	1	0.6	0.7	95.4
		Chert	3	1.9	2.0	97.4
		Hematite	1	0.6	0.7	98.0
		Magnetite	1	0.6	0.7	98.7
		Sandstone	1	0.6	0.7	99.3
		Dolomite	1	0.6	0.7	100.0
		Total	151	96.8	100.0	
	Missing		5	3.2		
	Total		156	100.0		
II		Quartz crystal	21	6.7	6.7	6.7
		Vein quartz	265	84.1	84.1	90.8
		Chalcedony	1	0.3	0.3	91.1
		Quartzite	2	0.6	0.6	91.7
		Chert	8	2.5	2.5	94.3
		Hematite	5	1.6	1.6	95.9
		Magnetite	3	1.0	1.0	96.8
		Sandstone	1	0.3	0.3	97.1
		Dolomite	1	0.3	0.3	97.4
		Dolerite	6	1.9	1.9	99.3
		Diorite	1	0.3	0.3	99.6
		Other	1	0.3	0.3	100.0
		Total	315	100.0	100.0	
III		Quartz crystal	4	7.1	7.1	7.1
		Vein quartz	42	75.0	75.0	82.1
		Chert	5	8.9	8.9	91.0
		Sandstone	1	1.8	1.8	92.8
		Dolerite	3	5.4	5.4	98.2
		Amethyst	1	1.8	1.8	100.0
		Total	56	100.0	100.0	
IV		Quartz crystal	2	6.3	6.3	6.3
		Vein quartz	25	78.1	78.1	84.4
		Chalcedony	1	3.1	3.1	87.5
		Chert	1	3.1	3.1	90.6
		Hematite	1	3.1	3.1	93.7
		Sandstone	1	3.1	3.1	96.9
		Amethyst	1	3.1	3.1	100.0
		Total	32	100.0	100.0	
V		Quartz crystal	1	3.2	3.2	3.2
		Vein quartz	28	90.3	90.3	93.5
		Chert	2	6.5	6.5	100.0
		Total	31	100.0	100.0	
VII		Quartz crystal	25	2.7	2.7	2.7
		Vein quartz	776	82.4	83.0	85.7
		Blue quartz	12	1.3	1.3	87.0
		Chalcedony	8	0.8	0.9	87.9
		Green quartz	1	0.1	0.1	88.0
		Quartzite	45	4.8	4.8	92.8
		Chert	41	4.4	4.4	97.2
		Hematite	2	0.2	0.2	97.4
		Magnetite	6	0.6	0.6	98.0
		Sandstone	3	0.3	0.3	98.3
		Dolerite	7	0.7	0.7	99.0
		Diorite	1	0.1	0.1	99.1
		Amethyst	3	0.3	0.3	99.4
		Granular quartz	2	0.2	0.2	99.6
		Shale	3	0.3	0.3	100.0
		Total	935	99.3	100.0	
	Missing		7	0.7		
	Total		942	100.0		
XII	Valid	Vein quartz	10	83.3	83.3	83.3
		Blue quartz	1	8.3	8.3	91.6
		Dolerite	1	8.3	8.3	100.0
		Total	12	100.0	100.0	

methods as seen in single and multiple platform cores and to the early stages in the reduction sequence. Shattered and point platforms are indicators of the method of the application of force. Quartz is brittle and platforms often shatter with the use of hard hammers, especially in the case of clear quartz (Knight 1991). Shattered platforms are also a feature of bipolar flaking.

Point platforms are indicative of the use of a punch, but lipping, which is a feature of the punch technique (Crabtree 1972), does not appear to form on quartz.

The two most common butt forms are plain and simple facets (table 8.15) and together they account for between 70 and 80 per cent of the sample through the sequence. Plain butts are the most common type in units

Table 8.15 Frequencies and percentages of butt types by stratigraphic unit

Butt preparation

Unit			Frequency	Per cent	Valid percent	Cumulative per cent
I		Plain	82	52.6	55.8	55.8
		Simple facet	29	18.6	19.7	75.5
		Shattered	24	15.4	16.3	91.8
		Cortical	6	3.8	4.1	95.9
		Point	6	3.8	4.1	100.0
		Total	147	94.2	100.0	
	Missing		9	5.8		
	Total		156	100.0		
II		Plain	176	55.9	59.1	59.1
		Simple facet	55	17.5	18.5	77.5
		Shattered	34	10.8	11.4	88.9
		Cortical	30	9.5	10.1	99.0
		Point	2	0.6	0.7	99.7
		Multifaceted	1	0.3	0.3	100.0
		Total	298	94.6	100.0	
	Missing		17	5.4		
	Total		315	100.0		
III		Plain	26	46.4	47.3	47.3
		Simple facet	13	23.2	23.6	70.9
		Shattered	11	19.6	20.0	90.9
		Cortical	2	3.6	3.6	94.5
		Multifaceted	3	5.4	5.5	100.0
		Total	55	98.2	100.0	
	Missing		1	1.8		
	Total		56	100.0		
IV		Plain	16	50.0	55.2	55.2
		Simple facet	6	18.8	20.7	75.9
		Shattered	4	12.5	13.8	89.7
		Cortical	2	6.3	6.9	96.6
		Point	1	3.1	3.4	100.0
		Total	29	90.6	100.0	
	Missing		3	9.4		
	Total		32	100.0		
V		Plain	18	58.1	58.1	58.1
		Simple facet	7	22.6	22.6	80.6
		Shattered	4	12.9	12.9	93.5
		Cortical	2	6.5	6.5	100.0
		Total	31	100.0		
VII		Plain	342	36.3	37.2	37.2
		Simple facet	399	42.4	43.4	80.6
		Shattered	91	9.7	9.9	90.5
		Cortical	60	6.4	6.5	99.5
		Point	5	0.5	0.5	100.0
		Total	919	97.6	100.0	
	Missing		23	2.4		
	Total		942	100.0		
XII		Plain	4	33.3	33.3	33.3
		Simple facet	3	25.0	25.0	58.3
		Shattered	5	41.7	41.7	100.0
		Total	12	100.0	100.0	

V–I and in unit XII, but the sample size is too small in the latter case to be meaningful. The pattern is reversed in unit VII with simple faceted butts the most common form. This reflects the predominant role of centripetal flaking during the Last Interglacial occupation. In all units, shattered butts are the third most common form and are an expected outcome of the use of quartz. Cortex is found on butts in all the units and averages about 6.5 per cent in the Later Pleistocene units (VII–IV) and increases to 10.1 per cent of butts in the early Holocene (II). The first stages of knapping took place in the cave during each phase of occupation and the inhabitants had access to river cobbles through the early Holocene. Bipolar flaking was not a feature of the early Holocene but cobbles were used to produce bladelets using a single platform technique. The use of a punch as reflected by point form butts is not a consistently significant feature of any period in the sequence, though it is more common in the late Holocene than previously. Multifaceted butts are restricted to units VII and III and occur in low frequencies. In unit VII the percentage of flakes with multifaceted butts (2.4 per cent) is less than half the percentage frequency of prepared cores (5.9 per cent) from the same unit. The discrepancy suggests that these flakes were used and discarded elsewhere. The relative rarity of prepared core flaking supports the interpretation that flakes were made for specific and limited purposes.

An examination of the mean values of butt width and thickness by units (table 8.16) shows a gradual diminution in both dimensions over time. These features of the butt are correlated with the knapper's control of

flake length, width and thickness (Dibble & Whittaker 1981). Table 8.17 and figure 8.11 show that flake length and width are greatest in unit VII and decrease progressively through the stratigraphic sequence. Thickness is the least variable of the dimensions.

A statistically significant correlation exists between butt width and flake length in unit VII alone (Pearson Correlation 0.214; 2-tailed sig=0.01). Butt thickness appears to be a better predictor of flake length given the significant Pearson correlations between these two variables in units II (0.233; 2-tailed sig=0.01), III (0.340; 2-tailed sig=0.05), IV (0.407; 2-tailed sig=0.05) and VII (0.309; 2-tailed sig=0.01). The unique correlation link between butt width and length in unit VII, as seen in the scatterplot (fig. 8.12), can be partly accounted for by the prevalence of centripetal flaking methods which produce flakes with relatively wide butts in relation to length. Flake morphology and size was being controlled by the knappers at Mumbwa, in particular during the Last Interglacial when an emphasis was placed on the creation of relatively wide flakes. The shift toward relatively narrower flakes from the Late Glacial onwards marks a break in the prevailing convention. This shift is also reflected in the patterns of flake production preserved on the dorsal surfaces of the whole flake sample.

Scarring on the dorsal surface of flakes reflects previous flake removals and is used as an indirect indicator of the technique of flake production. A radial pattern (fig. 8.13) indicates centripetal flaking. Two forms of convergent scarring are recognised: convergence from one direction and from two directions. The latter is

Table 8.16 Mean values (mm) of butt width and thickness by stratigraphic unit

Descriptive statistics

Unit		N	Minimum	Maximum	Mean	Std deviation
I	Butt width	125	1	177	13.87	15.90
	Butt thickness	123	1	55	5.18	5.34
II	Butt width	264	2	119	13.81	9.30
	Butt thickness	259	1	21	5.51	3.19
III	Butt width	46	5	42	16.63	9.09
	Butt thickness	46	1	27	6.93	4.48
IV	Butt width	27	5	33	15.33	5.92
	Butt thickness	25	1	13	6.20	3.04
V	Butt width	29	6	35	16.72	8.59
	Butt thickness	29	1	16	7.17	4.12
VII	Butt width	840	3	65	20.30	9.12
	Butt thickness	829	0	24	8.11	3.88
XII	Butt width	11	3	30	14.36	9.05
	Butt thickness	10	1	12	5.90	3.48

Table 8.17 Mean whole flake length, width and thickness (mm) by stratigraphic unit

Descriptive statistics

Unit		N	Minimum	Maximum	Mean	Std deviation
I	Length	152	10	51	26.83	6.63
	Width	152	5	34	20.49	7.10
	Thickness	151	2	125	7.62	10.05
II	Length	311	13	229	31.34	17.35
	Width	309	4	118	23.57	10.33
	Thickness	309	0	21	7.82	3.67
III	Length	56	10	49	33.39	8.59
	Width	56	11	50	27.43	7.79
	Thickness	55	4	27	9.42	4.22
IV	Length	32	22	55	32.31	8.28
	Width	31	10	43	26.06	7.89
	Thickness	30	3	18	9.27	3.62
V	Length	31	21	55	32.52	7.82
	Width	31	13	48	28.13	7.85
	Thickness	31	3	20	10.06	4.43
VII	Length	941	13	89	37.54	9.96
	Width	941	4	83	31.39	9.78
	Thickness	937	1	41	10.49	4.44
XII	Length	12	20	62	34.75	12.41
	Width	12	18	41	28.00	8.21
	Thickness	12	4	20	10.58	4.44

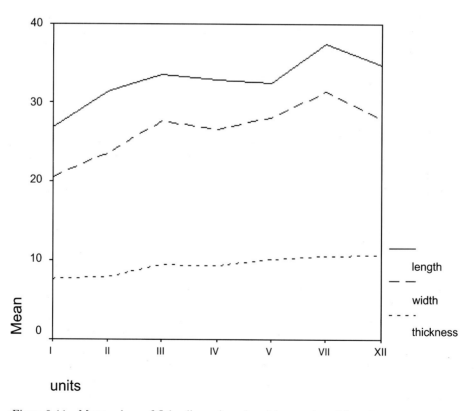

Figure 8.11   Mean values of flake dimensions (mm) by stratigraphic unit.

UNIT: VII

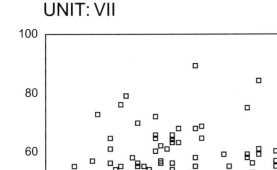

Figure 8.12   Scatterplot showing the correlation between butt width and flake length in unit VII.

linked to the production of triangular flakes by the prepared core or classic Levallois technique (Van Peer 1992). The other patterns are less indicative of particular flaking techniques. An irregular pattern of scarring with flakes removed from two or more directions is labelled 2D (table 8.18). A distinction is also made between scars opposed to the butt only and those opposed from both distal and proximal ends. The distinction was made as an indicator of the intensity of the reduction of a core and this applies to irregular flakes as well. Flakes with more than 50 per cent cortex are evidence of early stages in the reduction sequence. Table 8.18 shows the percentages of dorsal types and figure 8.14 illustrates the changing frequencies of types by unit.

A prominent trend in the scar data is the gradually declining percentage of radial flaking from the Last Interglacial (unit VII=28.8 per cent) to the Late Glacial (III=10.9 per cent). The percentage in the early Holocene (unit II) is half that in the Late Glacial and the technique has effectively disappeared by the late Holocene. The percentage frequency of convergent scarring also follows a pattern with consistent levels of 12 per cent in units VII to IV followed by a continuing decline from 7.3 per cent in the Late Glacial to 1.3 per cent in the late Holocene. A reversed pattern of increasing frequencies is seen in flakes with scars parallel to the flaking axis. These flakes are made from single and multiple platform cores. The percentage of parallel scars varies from 22 to 34 per cent in units XII–IV and increases to 49 per cent in the Late Glacial reaching a maximum of 59 per cent in the late Holocene. The contrasting decline in radial flaking and rise in the use of single and multiple platform cores constitutes a fundamental shift in the techniques of flaking that distinguishes the Middle from the Later Stone Age at Mumbwa Caves. The chronological and depositional gaps in the sequence make the process of change difficult to characterise as either gradual or rapid. The most marked change takes place between units IV (40 ka BP) and III (15–12 ka BP), but the sequence of occupation is discontinuous.

Dorsal surfaces with cortex occur in all units. Flakes derived from cobbles can be distinguished by the rough texture and rounded shape of the cortex as compared with those derived from veins. Cobble surfaces are indicators of riverine sources of quartz that are not currently available locally. In unit VII, 31 per cent (n=18) of cortex flakes are of cobble origin. The single flake with cortex recorded from unit IV has a cobble surface. No cobble surfaces are recorded for units V and III whereas in the unit II (early Holocene) assemblage 51 per cent (n=18) of flakes are struck from cobbles. In unit I, 21 per cent (n=3) of cortex-covered flakes are of cobble origin. Bipolar flaking is a feature of units XII–VII and is

103

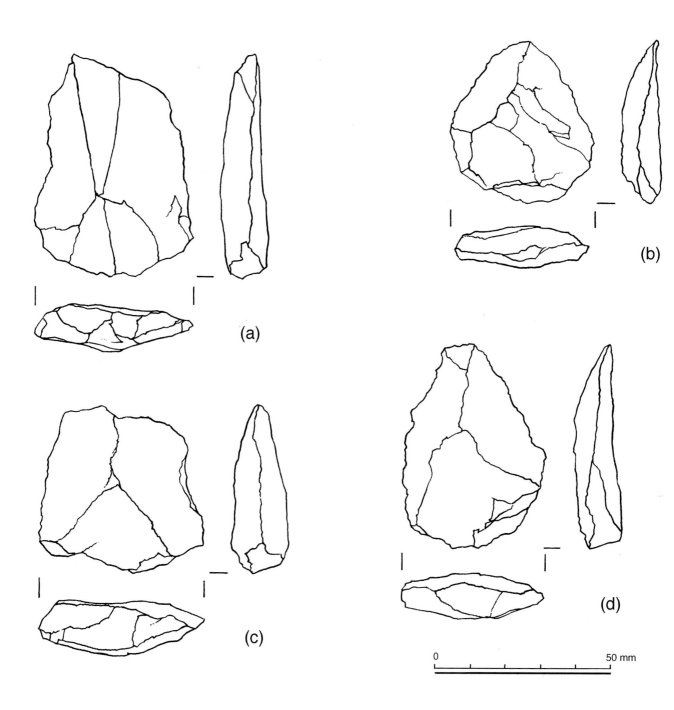

Figure 8.13 Dorsal scar pattern and butt types represented on flakes from unit VII: (a) radial pattern, multifaceted; (b) radial, plain; (c) convergent, multifaceted; (d) radial, simple facets; (e) convergent, simple facets.

Table 8.18 Frequencies and percentages of dorsal scar patterns on whole flakes for each stratigraphic unit

Dorsal surface					
Unit		Frequency	Per cent	Valid per cent	Cumulative per cent
I	Cortex	14	9.0	10.1	10.1
	Parallel	81	51.9	58.7	68.8
	Convergent	2	1.3	1.4	70.3
	Irregular	7	4.5	5.1	75.4
	Opposed	14	9.0	10.1	85.5
	Radial	1	0.6	0.7	86.2
	Irregular-2D	19	12.2	13.8	100.0
	Total	138	88.5	100.0	
	Missing	18	11.5		
	Total	156	100.0		
II	Cortex	35	11.1	11.9	11.9
	Parallel	139	44.1	47.3	59.2
	Convergent	13	4.1	4.4	63.6
	Irregular	17	5.4	5.8	69.4
	Opposed	37	11.7	12.6	82.0
	Radial	15	4.8	5.1	87.1
	Irregular-2D	38	12.1	12.9	100.0
	Total	294	93.3	100.0	
	Missing	21	6.7		
	Total	315	100.0		
III	Cortex	6	10.7	10.9	10.9
	Parallel	274	8.2	49.1	60.0
	Convergent	4	7.1	7.3	67.3
	Irregular	3	5.4	5.5	72.7
	Opposed	4	7.1	7.3	81.8
	Radial	6	10.7	10.9	92.7
	Irregular-2D	4	7.1	7.3	100.0
	Total	55	98.2	100.0	
	Missing	1	1.8		
	Total	56	100.0		
IV	Cortex	1	3.1	3.4	3.4
	Parallel	10	31.3	34.5	37.9
	Convergent	4	12.5	13.8	51.7
	Irregular	1	3.1	3.4	55.2
	Radial	5	15.6	17.2	72.4
	Irregular-2D	8	25.0	27.6	100.0
	Total	29	90.6	100.0	
	Missing	3	9.4		
	Total	32	100.0		
V	Cortex	3	9.7	9.7	9.7
	Parallel	7	22.6	22.6	32.3
	Convergent	4	12.9	12.9	45.2
	Irregular	1	3.2	3.2	48.4
	Opposed	3	9.7	9.7	58.1
	Radial	7	22.6	22.6	80.6
	Irregular-2D	6	19.4	19.4	100.0
	Total	31	100.0		
VII	Cortex	58	6.2	6.3	6.3
	Parallel	281	29.8	30.3	36.6
	Convergent	114	12.1	12.3	48.9
	Irregular	29	3.1	3.1	52.1
	Opposed	88	9.3	9.5	61.6
	Radial	267	28.3	28.8	90.4
	Irregular-2D	85	9.0	9.2	99.6
	Opposed-butt	3	0.3	0.3	99.9
	Convergent-2D	1	0.1	0.1	100.0
	Total	926	98.3	100.0	
	Missing	16	1.7		
	Total	942	100.0		

Table 8.18 (continued)   Frequencies and percentages of dorsal scar patterns on whole flakes for each stratigraphic unit

Dorsal surface *(continued)*

Unit		Frequency	Per cent	Valid *per cent*	Cumulative *per cent*
XII	Cortex	1	8.3	8.3	8.3
	Parallel	4	33.3	33.3	41.7
	Convergent	1	8.3	8.3	50.0
	Irregular	1	8.3	8.3	58.3
	Opposed	3	25.0	25.0	83.3
	Radial	1	8,3	8.3	91.7
	Irregular-2D	1	8.3	8.3	100.0
	Total	12	100.0	100.0	

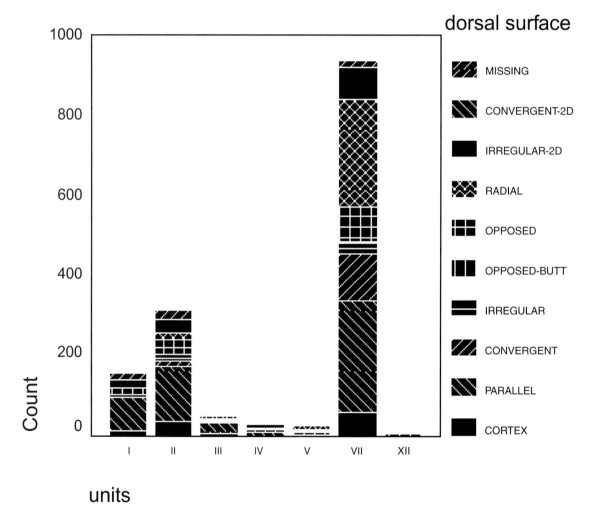

Figure 8.14   Frequencies of dorsal scar patterns by stratigraphic unit.

a simple method of reducing cobbles along the long axis to produce flakes. The technique used in the early Holocene differs in intention with the cobbles split perpendicular to the long axis to produce flat striking platforms for the controlled removal of small flakes and bladelets. The evidence for access to riverine derived sources of quartz in the early Holocene suggests that the current flow regime of the dambo and its tributaries is a relatively recent phenomenon.

Flake morphology is recorded in the typological scheme derived from that of Deacon (1982) in which flake form and butt attributes are combined. The scheme has been adapted for use with the Mumbwa and Twin Rivers assemblages with the addition of pentagonal flake forms as produced by radial and discoidal flaking techniques and by the inclusion of bipolar debitage and burin spalls. The type codes and names are listed in appendix 4. The type frequencies by stratigraphic unit are included in appendix 9. Quadrilateral and irregular forms account for 50 per cent or more of all types in each unit. These can be considered the basic or background shapes against which temporal patterning can be assessed. Two underlying trends are evident in the sequence with convergent and pentagonal forms comprising 14.7 per cent and 9.1 per cent respectively of the unit VII sample. Pentagonal flakes as products of centripetal flaking cease to be made after the Last Interglacial. The percentage of convergent forms decreases in unit III to 10.7 per cent of the assemblage and continues to decline to 5.1 per cent in the late Holocene. Convergent flakes with faceted butts are found only in unit VII and constitute a small percentage (1.5 per cent) of the assemblage. The relative rarity of flakes from prepared cores corresponds with the relative paucity of the cores themselves, though there are comparatively fewer flakes than cores and the implications have been discussed above.

Whole blades (fig. 8.15) as a component of the full sequence never account for more than 8 per cent of an assemblage with the exception of unit XII (41.7 per cent) but the sample of 12 flakes is too small to be statistically viable. In the Last Interglacial deposits of unit VII, blades and broken blades together comprise 4.4 per cent of the assemblage and this includes a crested blade indicative of the initial stage of blade production. No blades were found in units VI and V. In unit IV blades account for 6.3 per cent of the assemblage and for 7.3 per cent (broken and whole) of the unit III assemblage. The percentage frequency increases in the early Holocene to 10.9 per cent (includes broken blades) with a similar combined figure of 9.0 per cent in the late Holocene. Bladelets are a neglible component of the Last Interglacial assemblage (0.8 per cent) as are bladelet cores (0.9 per cent). No bladelets were found in unit III and two broken bladelets were found in unit IV. The frequency increases in the early Holocene (unit II) to 4.1 per cent (including broken bladelets) and accounts for 10.3 per cent of the late Holocene (including broken bladelets).

The flake morphology data supports the pattern seen in the dorsal scar and core typologies of a technological threshold being crossed between 40 ka and the Late Glacial. A shift takes place away from centripetal flaking techniques towards single and multiple platform cores. The blanks produced by these two broad groups of techniques differ in geometry with radial flakes being relatively short and wide and flat platform (quadrilateral) flakes longer and narrower. These differences are evident in comparisons of ratios of flake width : length by flake type. Among convergent flakes with plain platforms, those from unit VII are wider than those from unit II (table 8.19). (The sample sizes from the other units are

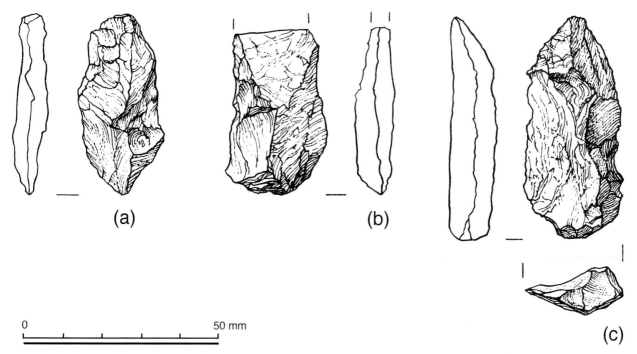

Figure 8.15   Vein quartz blades from unit VII, Mumbwa Caves; (a) from opposed platform core, with point butt (D10–4–5); (b) snapped broad blade, unit VII (D9–4–3); (c) flake/blade with simple faceted butt, unit VII (E10–1–0).

Table 8.19 Ratio values of mean flake width : length (mm) for convergent flakes with plain platforms by stratigraphic unit

Unit	N	Minimum	Maximum	Mean	Std Deviation
I	8	0.54	0.89	0.6934	0.1432
II	23	0.48	1.11	0.7075	0.1370
III	6	0.58	1.25	0.8698	0.2442
IV	5	0.65	0.83	0.7510	0.1830
V	4	0.67	1.00	0.8829	0.1495
VII	103	0.41	1.41	0.8075	0.1857

Table 8.20 Ratio values of mean flake width : length (mm) for quadrilateral flakes by stratigraphic unit

Unit	N	Minimum	Maximum	Mean	Std Deviation
I	54	0.55	1.73	0.8408	0.2411
II	108	0.10	4.92	0.8548	0.4483
III	18	0.54	1.14	0.8066	0.1860
IV	9	0.53	1.22	0.8774	0.2554
V	11	0.52	1.40	0.9784	0.3151
VII	300	0.51	2.31	0.8855	0.2327
XII	1	1.40	1.40	1.4000	

Table 8.21 Ratio value of mean flake width : length (mm) for pentagonal flakes in unit VII

Unit	N	Minimum	Maximum	Mean	Std Deviation
VII	82	0.08	1.45	0.9386	0.2158

too small for comparison.) Among quadrilateral flakes (table 8.20), those from unit VII are somewhat wider than those from units II and I. The sample numbers from the remaining units are too small for meaningful comparison. Pentagonal flakes (table 8.21) are restricted to unit VII and the width : length ratio shows that radial flaking produces flakes that are wider than comparably sized samples of convergent and quadrilateral flakes.

Two remaining classes of debitage remain to be considered: chunks and broken flakes. Chunks are angular fragments of cores and flakes that are created in the course of flaking. As a class, these artefacts are largely unused but occasionally they are flaked informally (chunk cores) or retouched into steep angled scrapers. The frequency and weight of this material are treated as indicators of the relative intensity of flaking and duration of occupation averaged across each unit. Table 8.22 and figure 8.16 illustrate the total number and weight of chunks by unit. The largest number and greatest weight are found in the main phases of occupation represented by units VII, II and III. The units preceding the Last Interglacial (VIII–XII) are characterised by low frequencies and weights of chunks and this pattern is interpreted as indicative of intermittent and short-term periods of occupation.

Vein quartz is the predominant material used in all units (fig. 8.17) with relatively little variation between units. Chert is more common in the Holocene (II–I) and

Table 8.22 Frequency and weight (g) of chunks >20 mm in size, by stratigraphic unit

Unit		N	Sum
I	Number	16	238
	Weight	11	1995
II	Number	31	790
	Weight	9	6730
III	Number	14	286
	Weight	8	3255
IV	Number	6	78
	Weight	4	940
V	Number	9	100
	Weight	6	1180
VI	Number	2	8
	Weight	2	97
VII	Number	219	2278
	Weight	194	22812
VIII	Number	14	21
	Weight	13	140
IX	Number	4	8
	Weight	3	24
X	Number	4	7
	Weight	4	58
XI	Number	5	7
	Weight	5	38
XII	Number	10	21
	Weight	10	162

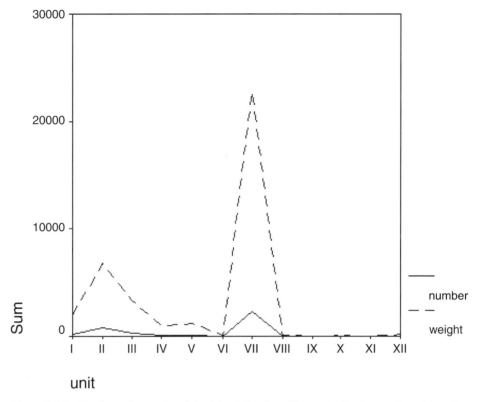

Figure 8.16 Total number and weight (g) of chunks >20 mm in size by stratigraphic unit.

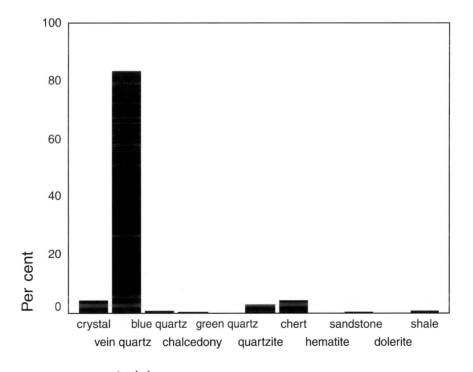

Figure 8.17 Percentage frequencies of chunks by raw material for all stratigraphic units combined.

coloured quartz is associated with the Last Interglacial occupation. These subtle variations coincide with raw material patterns seen among cores and flakes.

Table 8.23 and figure 8.18 display the numbers and weights of broken flakes by stratigraphic unit. As with chunks, the largest sample of broken flakes comes from the Last Interglacial occupation (n=6824) followed by the early Holocene (n=1172) and Late Glacial units (n=517). The Middle Pleistocene units (VIII–XII) together are represented by 92 pieces (table 8.23). This low number is consistent with a pattern of short-lived occupation by small groups of foragers.

A distribution of broken flake frequencies by size class (fig. 8.19) shows the preponderance of small flakes (20–30 mm) in all units and the presence in unit VII of the largest numbers of flakes greater than 40 mm. This pattern corresponds with the whole flake size distribution (table 8.17). Vein quartz is the predominant raw material in all units (fig. 8.20) with chert and quartz crystal more common in the Holocene units and fine-grained quartzite and coloured quartz more common in the Last Interglacial. These slight variations through the sequence mirror those seen among the chunks, whole flakes and cores.

The final class of artefacts in the flake debitage category encompasses all material less than 20 mm in size

Table 8.23 Frequency and weight (g) of broken flakes by stratigraphic unit

Unit		Sum
I	Number	374
	Weight	1921
II	Number	1172
	Weight	6036
III	Number	517
	Weight	3237
IV	Number	137
	Weight	713
V	Number	209
	Weight	1092
VI	Number	21
	Weight	75
VII	Number	6924
	Weight	36032
VIII	Number	26
	Weight	78
IX	Number	3
	Weight	13
X	Number	1
	Weight	4
XI	Number	6
	Weight	24
XII	Number	56
	Weight	98

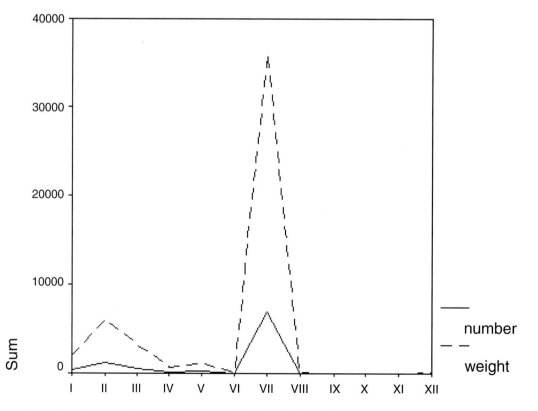

Figure 8.18   The numbers and weights of broken flakes by unit.

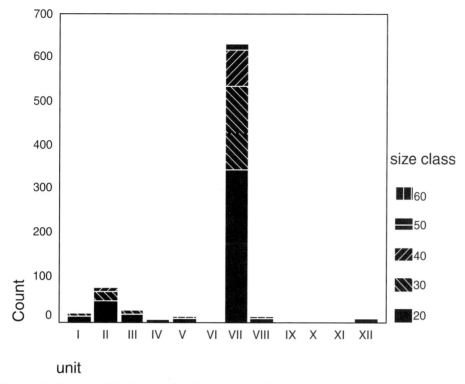

Figure 8.19 Broken flake frequencies by size class (20–30 mm; 30–40 mm; 40–50 mm; 50–60 mm and >60 mm) and stratigraphic unit.

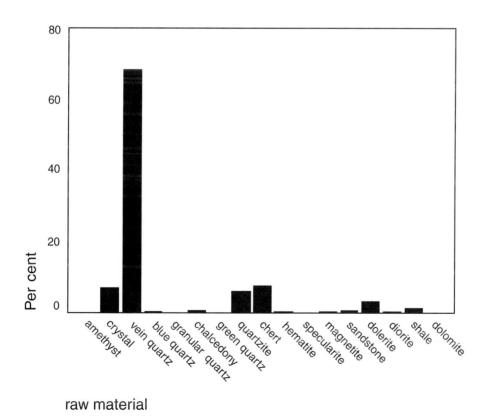

Figure 8.20 Raw material percentages for broken flakes from all units combined.

Table 8.24 Frequency and weight (g) of small flaking debris (<20) by stratigraphic unit

Unit		Sum
I	Number	3800
	Weight	2715
II	Number	10589
	Weight	8616
III	Number	4209
	Weight	4215
IV	Number	615
	Weight	590
V	Number	1008
	Weight	1220
VI	Number	161
	Weight	120
VII	Number	42497
	Weight	34904
VIII	Number	1117
	Weight	582
IX	Number	140
	Weight	78
X	Number	245
	Weight	124
XI	Number	207
	Weight	101
XII	Number	425
	Weight	337
XIII	Number	27
	Weight	28

including chips, chunks and flakes and broken flakes. The quantity and weight of small flaking debris is an additional indicator of the intensity of stone working and indirectly a measure of primary reduction of raw materials in the cave itself. Quartz produces greater amounts of small debris than other raw materials because of its brittle qualities, but given the predominance of quartz in all units the quantity of small flaking debris can be used as a measure of the activities taking place on site.

Table 8.24 and figure 8.21 together show the amount of debris by stratigraphic unit. The results repeat the pattern seen above for other forms of debitage with the Last Interglacial contributing the largest number and greatest weight followed by the early Holocene occupation and the Late Glacial unit. The presence of 1117 pieces of debitage in unit VIII demonstrates a human presence during the deposition of the colluvium and the activity of making or maintaining tools by the occupants. In each unit, the number of pieces is greater than the total weight in grams. This ratio is evident in figure 8.21, which demonstrates the small size of the debitage.

The cumbersome category of utilised and edge-damaged flakes reflects the real difficulty of distinguishing between edge damage on flakes caused by use and that arising from taphonomic processes such as trampling and sediment compaction. Use-wear analysis can

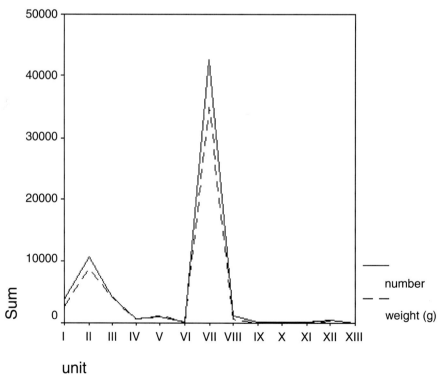

Figure 8.21 The frequency and weight (g) of small flaking debris (<20 mm) by stratigraphic unit.

discriminate between potential sources of damage, but use-wear itself is subject to alteration by post-depositional processes (Levi Scala 1996) as well as being enormously time consuming and difficult to apply to quartz. No use-wear analyses were undertaken on the Mumbwa or Twin Rivers assemblages. This reduction category also includes manuports and other natural pieces that bear traces of use, such as hammerstones and abraders. A distinction is made between *pièces esquillées* as used flakes and exhausted bipolar cores. The latter have a distinctive lenticular profile (Barham 1987). Flakes with edge damage are classified according to a modified version of Deacon (1982) that includes spheroids, abraders and the additional flake forms included in the whole flake analysis (see appendix 4).

The percentage frequency of utilisation among the whole flake assemblage decreases gradually from the bottom to the top of the sequence: unit XII=60.0 per cent; VII=9.5 per cent; V=9.8 per cent; IV=8.6 per cent; III=5.0 per cent; II=1.6 per cent; I=5.4 per cent (table 8.31). The uniformity of the trend suggests that length of exposure to taphonomic processes governs the frequency of edge damage. The older the deposit the greater the likelihood of unintentional damage. For this reason, detailed analysis of the frequency and location of edge damage offers only limited behavioural potential and is more likely to reflect the acuteness of edge angles, the brittle character of quartz and the general frequency of whole flake forms. The latter is the case in unit VII. Of the 94 edge-damaged flakes, 43 per cent are on quadrilateral forms which corresponds with the figure of 39 per cent for quadrilateral flakes among the whole flake assemblage. No further analysis of this category has been attempted.

HAMMERSTONES, ABRADERS AND SPHEROIDS

Among the manuports with use damage, some behavioural information can be derived from the occurrence of tools used in the flaking process, such as hammerstones, abraders and spheroids. The latter form is currently considered a type of hammerstone (eg, Willoughby 1985) and this interpretation is used here, though with reservations as explained below. The presence of flaking tools supports inferences drawn from other categories of behavioural data that the main cave was a living site in which a range of activities was undertaken including the making of tools. Grindstones are also indicative of the processing of materials and their presence is noted.

Table 8.25 shows the frequency of utilised or modified natural objects. Unit VII contains the largest collection of these artefacts. Hammerstones are identified by the presence of pitting at one or both ends of what tend to be oblong objects, and this is the most common artefact type. Spheroids are round or nearly so as the

name suggests and apparently the product of prolonged use of hammerstones. Abraders are recognised by the presence of a groove or grooves and by raw material. Sandstone was used in the three objects identified as abraders. Grindstones have one or more flattened surface created by abrasion and quartzite was the raw material used at Mumbwa.

The sample of hammerstones is small (n=20), and concentrated in unit VII, but it does support the evidence from the cores, cortex on flakes and the small flaking debris that the inhabitants made flake tools in the cave. Primary reduction of stone took place during the main Middle and Later Stone Age phases of occupation. Table 8.26 gives the mean dimensions and preferred raw materials for use as hammerstones. All the materials used were collected as cobbles including specularite and a heavy dark material listed as magnetite. The source of

Table 8.25 Type and number of utilised, non-flake, tools by stratigraphic unit

Type

Unit		Frequency	Per cent	Cumulative per cent
II	Hammerstone	2	66.7	66.7
	Grindstone	1	33.3	100.0
	Total	3	100.0	
VII	Hammerstone	16	53.3	53.3
	Grindstone	3	10.0	63.3
	Spheroid	8	26.7	90.0
	Abrader	3	10.0	100.0
	Total	30	100.0	
XI	Hammerstone	1	100.0	100.0

Table 8.26 Dimensions (a) (mm) and raw material frequencies (b) for hammerstones

Descriptive statistics

	N	Minimum	Maximum	Mean	Std deviation
Length	20	42	103	60.90	13.99
Width	20	32	70	48.15	10.10
Thickness	20	26	53	38.55	7.98
Weight	15	54	540	214.13	129.97

(a)

Raw material

Unit	Frequency	Per cent	Cumulative per cent
Vein quartz	11	55.0	55.0
Quartzite	3	15.0	70.0
Specularite	5	25.0	95.0
Magnetite	1	5.0	100.0
Total	20	100.0	

(b)

these cobbles is unknown, but presumably they came from active rivers no longer visible or were transported from the Kafue river to the west.

The raw materials and dimensions of spheroids as a class are shown in table 8.27. A wide range of raw materials was selected for use including a siliceous form of limonite that is presumably of lateritic origin. If these non-quartz materials were indeed used as hammerstones then they could be considered as soft hammers. Soft hammers are an advantage when knapping brittle quartz because they produce fewer incipient cones and reduce the likelihood of flakes splitting (Knight 1991). Non-quartz hammers would presumably have been especially in demand and sources of suitable materials were well known to the inhabitants. The nearest outcrop of granite, 18 km to the south at Nambala, is also a source of a heavy siliceous specularite. The rounded to sub-rounded shape is less desirable for delicate knapping or even primary reduction. The shape offers less control on the location of the blow on the platform than the oblong form of the hammerstone, as based on personal observation. The Mumbwa spheroids are also heavier than the hammerstones, though the sample is small and unreliable for comparison.

Table 8.27 Raw material frequencies (a) and dimensions (b) (mm) of spheroids from unit VII

Raw material

	Frequency	Per cent	Cumulative per cent
Vein quartz	4	50.0	50.0
Quartzite	1	12.5	62.5
Sandstone	1	12.5	75.0
Granite	1	12.5	87.5
Limonite	1	12.5	100.0
Total	8	100.0	

(a)

Descriptive statistics

	N	Minimum	Maximum	Mean	Std deviation
Length	7	60	80	69.86	8.32
Width	7	55	75	64.29	8.04
Thickness	7	50	65	56.57	5.65
Weight	4	190	370	254.00	79.65

(b)

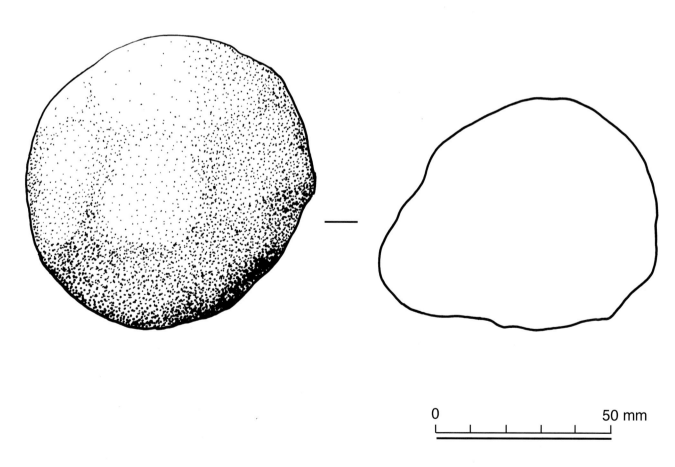

0   50 mm

Figure 8.22   Granite sub-spheroid, unit VII (E9–1–3).

RETOUCHED TOOLS

The objects in this category are almost all made on flakes with the rare exceptions of cores retouched as scrapers, large bifaces and chunks with retouch. The classes of tools in the category follow conventional usage that mixes presumed function with morphology: scrapers, backed tools, step-flaked tools, pointed tools, points, and tranchet edged tools. Tool types identified in the earlier Middle Stone Age assemblages at Kalambo Falls (Clark & Kleindienst 1974) have been incorporated into the analysis to extend the typological range of the scheme (appendix 4).

Table 8.28 shows the frequency of retouched tools by raw material and unit. Vein quartz is the material of choice for shaping into tools in all periods. The sample of tools is too small in units III, IV, V, VIII, X and XI for statistical comparison but vein quartz is the dominant material in these units. The greatest variety of materials is used in unit VII, but still nearly 88 per cent of the assemblage is made on vein quartz.

Tool frequencies by type are shown in table 8.29 and the type labels are found in appendix 4. The trends that emerge from this category reinforce those observed among the classes of debitage. A broad distinction can be drawn between units III–I and the preceding units based on frequencies of backed tools made on bladelets and small flakes. In unit I, small segments (<25mm) comprise 42.9 per cent of the assemblage and large segments (>25mm) 8.6 per cent. Backed bladelets account for 8.6 per cent. The combined percentage of backed artefacts is 60.1 per cent of the total with scrapers accounting for 20 per cent of the retouched category. The predominance of backed tools over scrapers continues in unit II. Small segments account for 36.1 per cent of the assemblage, large segments 33.1 per cent and backed bladelets 4.8 per cent. *Petits tranchets* or trapezes account for 3.6 per cent and the combined total of backed pieces is 74 per cent of the retouched category. Scrapers account for 14.4 per cent of the assemblage. The number of artefacts in units III–V is too low for meaningful comparison, except to note that two segments occur in unit III, but none in units IV or V. Awls and scrapers occur in all three units; one obliquely truncated blade was found in IV and one in unit V.

The proportions of backed to other retouched tool types differs markedly in the Last Interglacial sample. In unit VII, backed tools exist as a small but diverse proportion of the assemblage (7.5 per cent). Large segments (fig. 8.23) account for 2.2 per cent (n=4) of the total, obliquely truncated blades for 1.6 per cent, straight backed blades for 1.1 per cent, backed flakes for 1.6 per cent, obliquely truncated flakes 0.5 per cent and a tranchet (trapeze) flake for 0.5 per cent. The sample of

Table 8.28 Raw material frequencies and percentages for retouched tools by stratigraphic unit

Raw material				
Unit		Frequency	Per cent	Cumulative per cent
I	Other	2	5.7	5.7
	Amethyst	1	2.9	8.6
	Crystal	3	8.6	17.1
	Vein quartz	28	80.0	97.1
	Chert	1	2.9	100.0
	Total	35	100.0	
II	Crystal	6	7.2	7.2
	Vein quartz	75	90.4	97.6
	Chert	2	2.4	100.0
	Total	83	100.0	
III	Vein quartz	5	71.4	71.4
	Chert	2	28.6	100.0
	Total	7	100.0	
IV	Vein quartz	5	83.3	83.3
	Chert	1	16.7	100.0
	Total	6	100.0	
V	Vein quartz	5	100.0	100.0
VII	Amethyst	1	0.5	0.5
	Crystal	8	4.3	4.9
	Vein quartz	161	87.5	92.4
	Chert	7	3.8	96.2
	Blue quartz	2	1.1	97.3
	Chalcedony	1	0.5	97.8
	Quartzite	3	1.6	99.4
	Shale	1	0.5	100.0
	Total	184	100.0	
VIII	Vein quartz	2	100.0	100.0
X	Vein quartz	6	100.0	100.0
XI	Vein quartz	2	100.0	100.0

segments is too small for comparative analysis, but the mean dimensions of this group are larger than the means for units II and I (table 8.30)

The variety of backed types exceeds that found in the Holocene units, but the emphasis on tool making lies elsewhere. Awls, borers and scrapers dominate the retouched category with 15.2 per cent, 16.3 per cent and 26 per cent of artefacts respectively. The distinction between the two types is often arbitrary with the degree of retouch that makes the tip of an artefact a borer or an awl being a matter of judgement. The most common technique used to make awls involved creating two intersecting flake scars to form a broad point (fig. 8.24a). Alternatively, striking a burin blow opposite a flake scar (fig. 8.24b) formed a finer tip.

Among the class of pointed tools, the artefacts traditionally attributed to 'points' and considered diagnostic of Middle Stone Age technology account for 7.6 per cent of the unit VII assemblage. Of the three bifacially flaked objects (1.5 per cent) one is large (fig.

Table 8.29 Frequencies of retouched tool types (coded) by stratigraphic unit

Type Unit		Frequency	Per cent	Cumulative per cent	Type (continued) Unit		Frequency	Per cent	Cumulative per cent
I	03112	1	29	2.9	VII	03112	24	13.0	13.0
	03130	2	5.7	8.6		03211	4	2.2	15.2
	03131	1	2.9	11.4		03212	2	1.1	16.3
	03132	2	5.7	17.1		03213	3	1.6	17.9
	03134	1	2.9	20.0		03214	1	0.5	18.4
	03211	3	8.6	28.6		03430	30	16.3	34.7
	03212	1	2.9	31.4		03720	3	1.6	36.3
	03213	1	2.9	34.3		03115	14	7.6	43.9
	03214	1	2.9	37.1		03321	11	6.0	49.9
	03221	15	42.9	80.0		03600	2	1.1	51.0
	03222	3	8.6	88.6		03111	6	3.3	54.3
	03225	2	5.7	94.3		03120	1	0.5	54.8
	03430	1	2.9	97.1		03121	1	0.5	55.3
	03720	1	2.9	100.0		03125	2	1.1	56.4
	Total	35	100.0			03216	3	1.6	58.0
II	03112	2	2.4	2.4		03217	1	0.5	58.5
	03130	1	1.2	3.6		03230	1	0.5	59.0
	03131	1	1.2	4.8		03233	1	0.5	59.5
	03211	28	33.7	38.5		03250	1	0.5	60.0
	03213	1	12	39.7		03310	1	0.5	60.5
	03221	30	36.1	75.8		03312	2	1.1	61.6
	03222	4	4.8	80.6		03320	1	0.5	62.1
	03225	2	2.4	83.0		03322	1	0.5	62.6
	03110	1	1.2	84.2		03323	2	1.1	63.7
	03113	1	1.2	85.4		03330	1	0.5	64.2
	03115	1	1.2	86.6		03420	28	15.2	79.4
	03122	4	4.8	91.4		03500	1	0.5	79.9
	03133	1	1.2	92.6		03510	4	2.2	82.1
	03223	3	3.6	96.2		03511	6	3.3	85.4
	03221	1	1.2	97.4		03512	2	1.1	86.5
	03520	1	1.2	98.6		03521	1	0.5	87.0
	03600	1	1.2	99.8		03700	12	6.5	93.5
	Total	83	100.0			03701	1	0.5	94.0
III	03112	3	42.9	42.9		03702	1	0.5	94.5
	03221	2	28.6	71.5		03710	1	0.5	95.0
	03430	1	14.3	85.8		03730	7	3.8	98.8
	03115	1	14.3	100.0		03740	1	0.5	100.0
	Total	7	100.0			Total	184	100.0	
IV	03213	1	16.7	16.7	VIII	03115	2	100.0	100.0
	03430	2	33.3	50.0					
	03122	2	33.3	83.3	X	03115	1	16.7	16.7
	03111	1	16.7	100.0		03321	1	16.7	33.4
	Total	6	100.0			03111	2	33.3	66.7
V	03213	1	20.0	20.0		03420	2	33.3	100.0
	93430	1	20.0	40.0		Total	6	100.0	
	03115	1	20.0	60.0					
	03600	1	20.0	80.0	XI	03111	1	50.0	50.0
	03111	1	20.0	100.0		03323	1	50.0	100.0
	Total	5	100.0			Total	2	100.0	

8.25c) and resembles a small handaxe made on vein quartz. Its tip is broken, as is one lateral edge, and the base shows crushing damage. This piece can be considered to be a discard and an example of the end of the reduction chain. The two other bifacially flaked pieces are also heavily damaged (fig. 8.26) and, un-usually, are made of mudstone or shale. Both pieces bear a single deep hinged flake scar that originated from the distal end, and in one case the piece snapped as a result of the blow. The cutting edges are not sharp nor is the raw material durable. As a purely speculative interpret-ation, these appear to be practice pieces used for

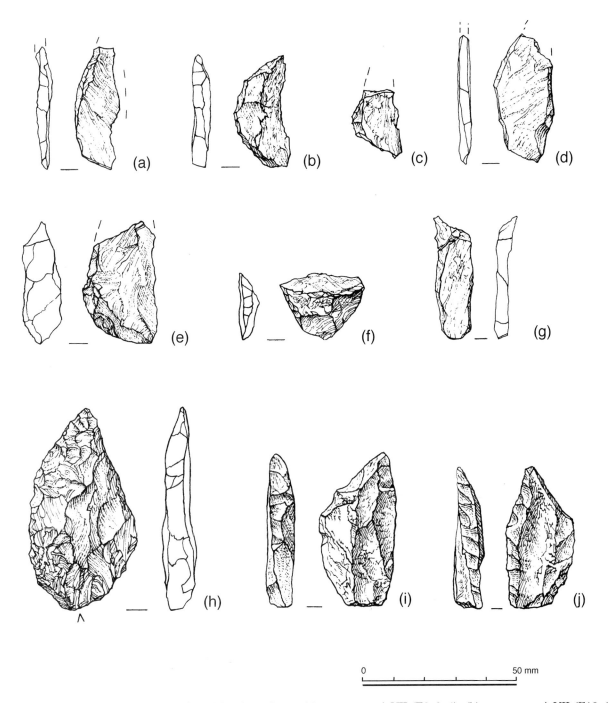

0   50 mm

Figure 8.23   Vein quartz backed pieces from Mumbwa Caves: (a) segment, unit VII (E9–3–4); (b) segment, unit VII (E10–1–2);
(c) broken segment, unit VII (E10–1–2); (d) broken segment, unit VII (D10–4–5); (e) broken thick segment, unit VII
(D10–2–11); (f) *tranchet* or trapeze, unit VII (H7–4–1); (g) backed blade, unit VII (D10–4–5); (h) backed flake with
retouched cutting edge (knife), unit VII (E10–1–1); (i) obliquely backed flake, unit VII (D10–2–7); (j) backed and
truncated flake/blade, unit VII (E9–2–4).

teaching the steps in bifacial flaking on a non-brittle
material.

A fully bifacial point made on vein quartz was found
in unit II (fig. 8.25b) in square D12 at a depth of 66 cm
in what appeared to be a stratigraphically mixed level
that included microlithic debitage. The point closely

resembles those illustrated by Clark (1942) from the
'Stillbay' Middle Stone Age levels excavated near the
entrance of the main cave and from a similar depth
below the ground surface.

Among the miscellaneous retouched pieces, a partially
bifacially shaped quartz flake from unit VII stands apart

Table 8.30 Mean length, width and thickness of segments >25 mm in length in units I, II and VII

Descriptive statistics

Unit		N	Minimum	Maximum	Mean	Std deviation
I	Length	3	20	27	24.00	3.61
	Width	3	10	15	12.33	2.52
	Thickness	3	3	8	5.00	2.65
II	Length	27	17	46	26.48	6.20
	Width	28	8	26	13.96	4.15
	Thickness	28	3	12	5.75	1.90
VII	Length	4	25	41	32.75	6.85
	Width	4	14	17	15.25	1.26
	Thickness	4	4	7	5.50	1.29

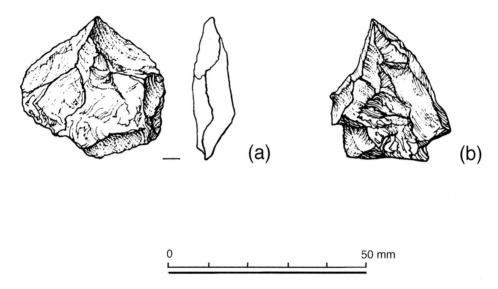

(a) (b)

0   50 mm

Figure 8.24 Quartz awls made by intersecting flake scars (a), unit X (E9–3–19) and by burin blow opposite a flake scar (b), dambo (Level IV).

for its apparent symmetry and cutting surfaces (fig. 8.27). On its long axis, not the flaking axis, intersecting scars on both surfaces form a shouldered triangular tool with steeply angled edges that form a continuous acute cutting edge. The base is thinned by a single flake removal as if designed for hafting. This artefact is unique at Mumbwa, but has a parallel at Twin Rivers (chapter 10).

Among the class of scrapers, two features distinguish the Holocene assemblages from earlier ones: size and edge shape. The majority of Holocene scrapers fall in the small to medium size ranges <20–30 mm maximum dimension. In unit I, 14.3 per cent of retouched tools are scrapers <20 mm and 2.9 per cent are scrapers >30 mm. In unit II, small to medium sized scrapers account for 8.4 per cent of tools and scrapers >30 mm for 6.0 per cent of retouched artefacts. Scraper frequencies are low

in each unit (I=7; II=12) and the percentages may not be representative, but they are similar to those reported for Holocene assemblages elsewhere in Zambia (Miller 1969). The scraper sample from unit VII is appreciably larger (n=48). Among these, none fall in the <20 mm range. Large scrapers comprise 20.6 per cent of tools and medium size (20–30 mm) account for 2.1 per cent. As well as having larger scrapers, the Last Interglacial sample is also notable for the frequency of concave-edged scrapers. This type is distinguished from spoke-shaves that also have concave edges, but these are formed by notching rather than by continuous retouch for scrapers. Among the retouched category, concave scrapers account for 7.6 per cent of tools (n=14) and spokeshaves for 8.1 per cent (n=15). By contrast, neither type occurs in unit I. In unit II, 1.2 per cent (n=1) of scrapers are concave and 1.2 per cent of tools are spoke-

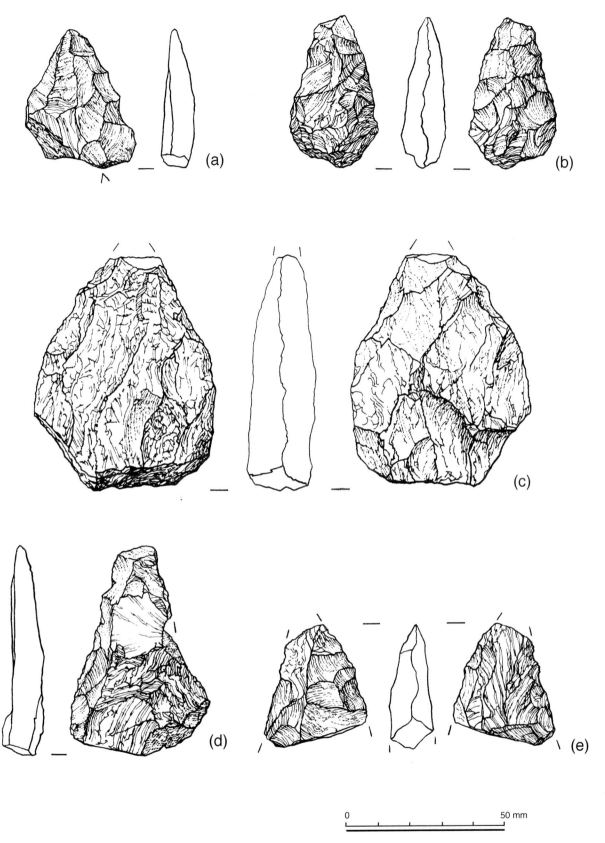

0   50 mm

Figure 8.25 Quartz unifacial and bifacial pieces from Mumbwa Caves: (a) unifacial point, unit VII (D9–4–6); (b) bifacial point, unit II (D12–2–6); (c) biface with snapped tip and heavy damage to both laterals, unit VII (D10–2–17); (d) unifacial point on triangular faceted flake, dambo (Level 4); (e) broken bifacial point, unit VII (E10–1–6).

119

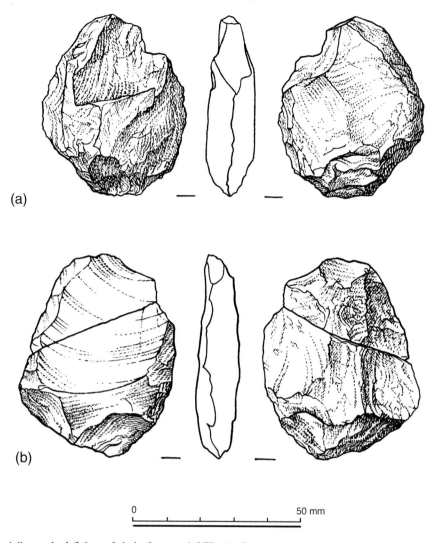

Figure 8.26 Bifacially worked flakes of shale from unit VII; (a) G9–2–2; (b) E10–1–2. Both pieces bear a prominent single scar with a hinge fracture struck from the distal end.

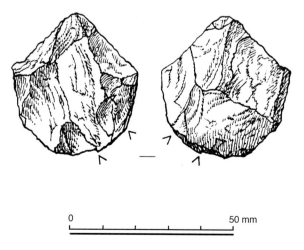

Figure 8.27 Shouldered, bifacially shaped quartz flake with intersecting burin blows forming a thin tip, unit VII (D9–1–4). Basal thinning indicates that this was a hafted piece.

shaves (n=1). Concave scraping and cutting edges have been shown experimentally to be effective for whittling and wedging wood and shaping bone (Keeley 1980). The Last Interglacial occupants of Mumbwa, by extension, could have been engaged in working organic materials, which is not surprising given that shaped wooden artefacts have been recovered from a late Acheulian context at Kalambo Falls (Clark 1969). Evidence for the intentional shaping of bone at Mumbwa is assessed below.

A numerical summary of the lithic artefacts from the main cave (table 8.31) confirms the dominance of the Last Interglacial phase of occupation in all categories. This is as might be expected given the length of the period (~20 ka) and the extent of the deposit excavated in relation to the other units. The underlying colluvium does represent an even longer period (~50 ka) and the deposit was well sampled in Areas I and II and in theory it should be as rich in artefacts as unit VII but it clearly is not. Mumbwa Caves appears to have been largely deserted during the period from 130 to 170 ka BP. The basal units also show evidence of sparse use of the cave with the lithic artefacts largely concentrated among manuports and small flaking debris.

The categories of debitage when taken as a whole form a picture of shifting methods or strategies of flake production. A methodological threshold is crossed between 40 ka and 15 ka BP. In this interval, the strategy applied by the mid-Later Pleistocene occupants changed from one that emphasised the making of relatively short triangular flakes using centripetal techniques to a strategy that emphasised relatively longer and narrower flakes made from single and multiple platform cores. The shift in methods was built on existing techniques of flake and blade making. A technological and cognitive continuum existed as no new techniques of flaking were developed between the Last Interglacial and the early

Holocene. Only the shift in emphasis was new. A similar pattern of continuity and gradual change is reported from south of the Limpopo at the deeply stratified site of Rose Cottage Cave, South Africa (Clark 1997, 1999).

The category of retouched tools represents a fraction of any one unit but the deliberate shaping of blanks into tools provides an indirect guide to shifting social conventions that governed the transformation of raw materials to meet specific needs. As with the core and flake debitage, no techniques of tool making were employed in the Holocene that did not exist during the Last Interglacial. The segments and scrapers characteristic of the early Holocene were made before, but in differing percentages and to differing templates of size. The Late Glacial and Holocene range of tools was in fact narrower than that of the Last Interglacial. Backed blade and bladelet-based tools had become a specialisation of these later populations. The Last Interglacial occupants had their own specialisations that included the production of awls, borers and a variety of scrapers.

In terms of the traditional classification of Goodwin and Van Riet Lowe, units VII–IV can be attributed to the Middle Stone Age and units III–I to the Later Stone Age. The Middle Pleistocene phases of occupation are less easily assigned to the Middle Stone Age on the basis of retouched tools alone, but the approach to flaking resembles that of the Last Interglacial with its emphasis on radial cores and some blade making.

Dambo dig

The archaeological sequence recovered from the dambo has not been analysed because the material could not be excavated to the same standard as the main cave. Full recovery of all debitage was not possible because of the hardness of the clay deposit. Comparative analyses between the sites would be misleading, but some similarities exist with the Mumbwa Middle Stone Age

Table 8.31 A numerical summary of the lithic artefacts from the main cave and percentages by reduction category per unit

Unit	Manuports N	%	Cores N	%	Core by-products N	%	Whole flakes N	%	Broken flakes N	%	Chunks N	%	Small flaking debris N	%	Edge damaged N	%	Utilised non-flake N	%	Retouched N	%	Totals
I	12	0.3	28	0.6	7	0.1	156	3.3	374	8.0	238	5.1	3800	81.6	9	0.2	0	0.0	35	0.8	4659
II	41	0.3	132	1.0	27	0.2	315	2.4	1172	8.9	790	6.0	10589	80.5	5	0.04	2	0.02	83	0.6	13156
III	26	0.5	71	1.4	5	0.1	56	1.0	517	10.0	286	5.5	4209	81.3	3	0.06	0	0.0	7	0.1	5180
IV	9	1.0	26	2.9	3	0.3	32	3.5	137	15.1	78	8.6	615	67.6	3	0.3	0	0.0	6	0.7	909
V	12	0.9	26	1.9	0	0.0	28	2.0	209	15.0	100	7.2	1008	72.4	3	0.2	2	0.1	5	0.3	1393
VI	0	0.0	0	0.0	0	0.0	3	1.6	21	10.9	8	4.1	161	83.4	0	0.0	0	0.0	0	0.0	193
VII	834	1.5	682	1.2	201	0.4	942	1.7	6824	12.5	2278	4.2	42497	77.9	99	0.2	30	0.05	184	0.3	54571
VIII	174	12.8	14	1.0	1	0.1	0	0.0	26	2.0	21	1.5	1117	82.4	0	0.0	0	0.0	2	0.1	1355
IX	144	47.8	3	1.0	0	0.0	3	1.0	3	1.0	8	2.6	140	46.5	0	0.0	0	0.0	0	0.0	301
X	378	57.2	23	3.5	1	0.1	0	0.0	1	0.1	7	1.1	245	37.1	0	0.0	0	0.0	6	0.9	661
XI	33	12.0	17	6.2	0	0.0	1	0.4	6	2.2	7	2.5	207	75.5	0	0.0	1	0.4	2	0.8	274
XII	125	18.8	15	2.3	1	0.1	8	1.2	56	8.5	21	3.2	425	64.1	12	1.8	0	0.0	0	0.0	663
XIII	7	20.6	0	0.0	0	0.0	0	0.0	0	0.0	0	0.0	27	79.4	0	0.0	0	0.0	0	0.0	34
Totals	1795	2.1	1037	1.2	246	0.3	1544	1.8	9346	11.2	3842	4.7	65040	78.0	134	0.2	35	0.04	330	0.4	83349

sequence. Among the small sample of retouched tools, bifacial points (n=2) were found only in Level 1 and a single unifacial point (fig. 8.25d) was found at the base of the sequence. A borer and concave scraper were found in the middle of the sequence. Among the larger but still small sample of cores (table 8.32) in Level 1 (60–120 cm), radial, single, multiple platform and cores on topknot flakes are evenly represented. In Level 2 (120–180 cm), the frequencies of radial, single and multiple platform cores are similar, but bipolar cores on cobbles are the most common type. Blade cores are also well represented. In Level 3 (180–220 cm), bipolar cores are also the most numerous followed by radial cores. No complete cores were found in Level 4 (220–240 cm).

The overall tool and core sequence is, at a qualitative level, Middle Stone Age in technology and typology and resembles the Middle Stone Age sequence in the main cave (units VII–V). Levels 2 and 3 can be equated with unit VII and Level 1 with unit V in technology and perhaps in chronology. No backed tools were found and there was no evidence of a Later Stone Age occupation of the dambo margin. Specularite occurred in all four levels with little hematite or limonite in the assemblage. An intentionally faceted specularite object (fig. 8.28)

Table 8.32 Core frequencies and percentages by type and excavation level in the dambo

Type

Unit		Frequency	Per cent	Cumulative per cent
1	Radial	3	18.8	18.8
	Single platform	3	18.8	37.5
	Multiple platform	4	25.0	62.5
	Blade	1	6.3	68.8
	Chunk	2	12.5	81.3
	Core on flake	3	18.8	100.0
	Total	16	100.0	
2	Radial	3	14.3	14.3
	Single platform	3	14.3	28.6
	Multiple platform	3	14.3	42.9
	Blade	4	19.0	61.9
	Core on flake	1	4.8	66.7
	Prepared	1	4.8	71.5
	Bipolar	6	28.6	100.0
	Total	21	100.0	
3	Radial	5	20.0	20.0
	Single platform	2	8.0	28.0
	Multiple platform	3	12.0	40.0
	Blade	1	4.0	44.0
	Chunk	1	4.0	48.0
	Core on flake	3	12.0	60.0
	Prepared	3	12.0	72.0
	Bipolar	7	28.0	100.0
	Total	25	100.0	

appears to be a spheroid in the making. The presence of a Middle Stone Age sequence so near to Mumbwa Caves is a salutary reminder that much of the contemporary landscape lies buried, as does the evidence for its use by humans.

BONE TOOLS
AC Pinto, P Andrews and L Barham

Five pointed bone objects were recovered from unit VII (Areas I and II) and examined for signs of intentional shaping and use. A well-crafted bone point from the Late Glacial occupation (Area III) provides a comparative sample with which to assess the putative points. The specimens are numbered as follows:

1. unit III;   D11–6–6   (fig. 8.29)
2. unit VII;   D9–7–3   (fig. 8.30)
3. unit VII;   G9–1–2   (fig. 8.31)
4. unit VII;   G9–1–2(a) (fig. 8.32)
5. unit VII;   H9–3–2   (fig. 8.33)
6. unit VII;   H8–4–3   (fig. 8.34)

All six objects are pointed and rounded and in some cases polished. At the blunt end (ie, the non-pointed end), specimens 1, 2 and 5 have transverse fractures with sharp edges. Specimens 3 and 4 appear quite rounded at both ends, and the rounding in specimen 3 seems contemporary with all the other features of this object. The broken end on specimen 4 appears rounded as if it had been broken when the bone was fairly fresh. Both 3 and 4 were found together amongst a concentration of occupation debris. Specimen 6 has what looks like small toothmarks, and also some small notches associated with the distal breakage. The breakage could be the result of carnivore activity.

Descriptions

1. D11–6–6

This is a finely-pointed bone that is undoubtedly a humanly produced tool (fig. 8.29a) made by the same process used for making bone points and needles at Gwisho Springs on the Kafue Flats (Fagan & van Noten 1971). It measures 50 mm long with a maximum width of 7.1 mm. The marks on this object are not visible using a binocular lens, but are very apparent under scanning electron microscopy (SEM). The surface shows the markings similar to an Upper Palaeolithic bone point (Olsen 1984), and there can be little doubt that this is an intentionally-shaped tool. Regular parallel polishing lines uniformly cover the surface along the main axis (fig. 8.29b,c,d). Two stages were involved in the production of this artefact; the first involving the rough configuration of the shape and the second the polishing of the surface. The polishing marks on the surface were

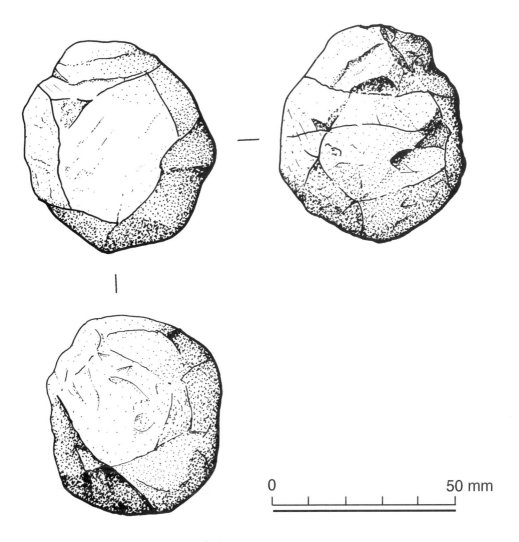

Figure 8.28 Faceted specularite ball, dambo (Level 3).

produced in this second stage and they have obliterated the first stage marks.

2. D9–7–3

This is a split-shaft fragment with rounded edges except at the broken end. This broken area has a flat, somewhat pointed shape (fig. 8.30a). It measures 31 mm long, 3 mm thick at its thinnest part and 11.2 mm wide at its maximum width. The outer bone layer is damaged (fig. 8.30b) and there are what appear to be manganese deposits that further obscure the surface. Faint parallel striations have been picked out on one edge, suggesting possible workmanship, but the evidence is inconclusive. One side of the bone is slightly concave, and on this surface there are diagonal striations that because of their position are unlikely to have been caused by trampling or by any other post-depositional process. It is likely that these were produced during the initial shaping of the bone point. Although this evidence is suggestive, it is

difficult to come to a decisive conclusion that the object shows human workmanship.

3. G9–1–2

This specimen has the shape of a pointed bullet (fig. 8.31a). It measures 33.5 mm long and 8 mm in diameter at its widest point. The outer bone surface looks intact, and there are consistent marks that could be produced by human action (fig. 8.31b,c). No vertical polishing comparable to that of specimen 1 is visible, but then only well-polished tools show that particular form of modification. 'Chiselled-out' features or chattermarks are visible on all the bone surfaces (fig. 8.31d) and these can be the result of manufacture or of use. Experimental replication of Natufian bone tools has shown that chattermarks are created in the course of carving with flaked stone (Newcomer 1974). Carving is the first stage in the process of shaping bone, and if the tool is not polished before use the marks will remain intact.

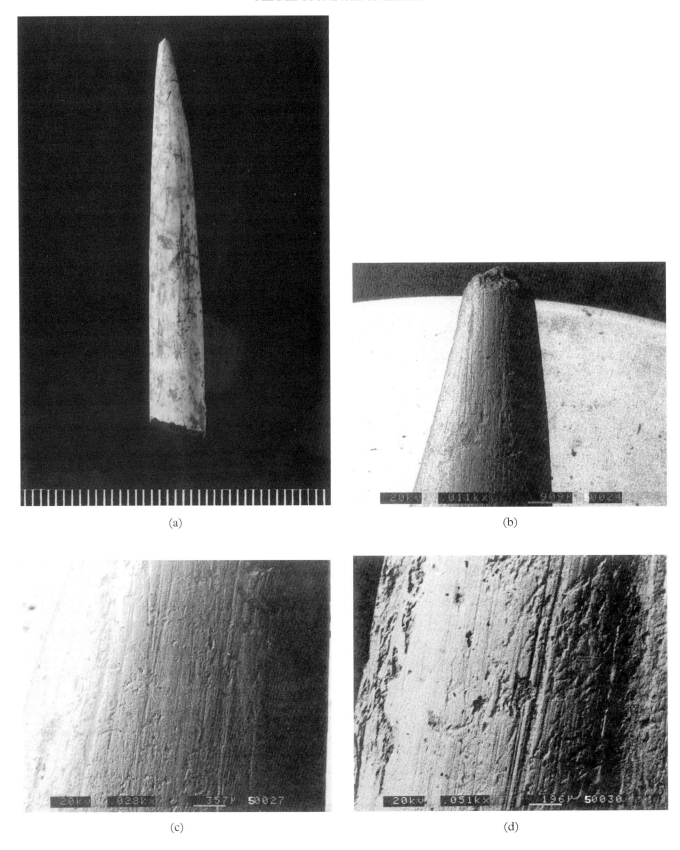

Figure 8.29 Specimen 1, unit III (D11–6–6): (a) plan view of the artefact, scale in mm; (b) the pointed tip showing vertical polishing lines spread uniformly over the surface; (c) detail of polishing lines on the tip; (d) detail of polishing lines overlying first stage shaping marks.

(a)

(b)

Figure 8.30 Specimen 2, unit VII (D9–7–3): (a) general view of the object, scale in mm; (b) detail of the tip showing the deteriorated surface.

4. G9–1–2(a)

This specimen is also pointed and bullet shaped (fig. 8.32a), but it is smaller than specimen 3. The object measures 20 mm in length and 5.3 mm in diameter. Areas of the surface appear to be quite polished (fig. 8.32b). As with specimen 3, the bone surface is well preserved, and chisel-like extractions extend from the point downwards (fig. 8.32c). It can be argued that this is a humanly produced and used artefact, although again no vertical polishing comparable to that of specimen 1 is visible. The evidence for human working is inconclusive because the polishing could occur naturally, but the chattermarks are suggestive of human agency.

5. H9–3–2

A wedge-shaped object with a well-rounded point (fig. 8.33a) that measures 19 mm in length with a maximum width of 10 mm. The bone surface is altered and has manganese deposits that obscure any detail, but where the surface is visible faint striations can just be seen (fig. 8.33b,c), particularly to the top left in figure 8.33c. As

with specimen 4, the marks could be the result of human activity, but they could also be produced by post-depositional processes such as trampling. The altered surface prevents further analysis of the morphology of the striations.

6. H8–4–3

This is a small fragment of pointed bone with a shape similar to that of specimen 2. It is 13 mm long, 8.2 mm wide and 4 mm thick (all maximum measurements). On some areas the surface of the bone is well polished (fig. 8.34a), and at the tip there are a series of small radiating striations that appear to be the result of the use of the implement to penetrate an object harder than the bone itself (fig. 8.34c). There also appear to be tiny tooth-marks on the edge of the bone, apparently made before polishing since the depressed areas of the toothmarks are polished to the same degree as the areas outside the marks (fig. 8.34b,d). The specimen has the same chisel-like extractions as described for specimens 3 and 4 and the bone surface seems to be in good condition

(a)

(b)

(c)

(d)

Figure 8.31 Specimen 3, unit VII (G9–1–2): (a) plan view of the object, scale in mm; (b) view of the tip showing smooth featureless polishing as the dominant feature; (c) detail of the tip showing vertical parallel features as well as triangular 'chiselled out ' marks; (d) closer detail of the triangular marks in c.

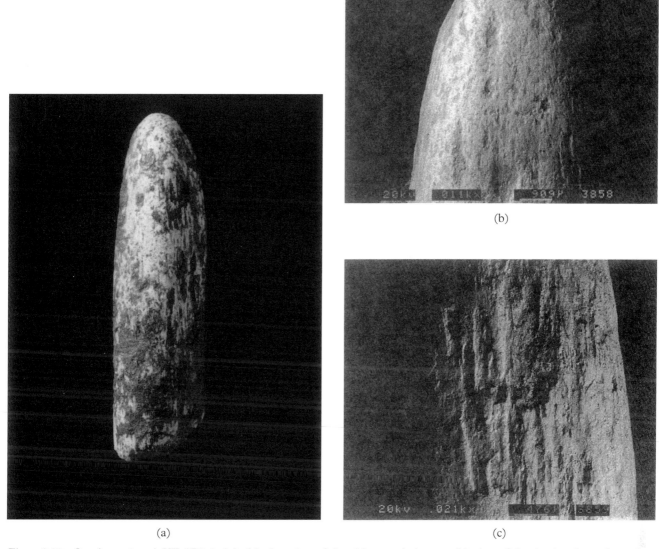

(a)

(b)

(c)

Figure 8.32 Specimen 4, unit VII (G9–1–2a): (a) plan view of the object, scale in mm; (b) view of the tip showing a featureless polished surface; (c) detail of the 'chiselled out' features.

(fig. 8.34e). It could be argued that this is a humanly-produced and used artefact.

Discussion

Strong evidence exists for the presence of a single bone point in the Later Stone Age of unit III. The specimen from D11–6–6 has all the attributes of a bone tool and there is little doubt about its attribution. One specimen from unit VII (H8–4–3) may also be a bone tool. It has polished surfaces with pointed ends that have been well rounded. The surface of the bone has striations running longitudinally and partly obliquely along the length of the shaft, together with chisel-like extractions probably made in the initial stages of shaping. It is possible for

these marks to occur naturally, but the combination of features makes this a likely product of human action. Two other specimens (2 and 4) may be worked by humans, but the evidence is ambiguous. These and the remaining bones are superficially similar to humanly-worked bone points in that they are polished and have pointed ends that have been partly rounded, but they lack any of the distinctive features indicative of human action. On the contrary, they are similar to rounded bones from hyaena dens (fig. 6 in Andrews 1997) which also have rounded and pointed ends with considerable polishing. It is not possible with the level of resolution available to identify the agent of formation of these three specimens with any certainty, and so long as doubt

Figure 8.33 Specimen 5, unit VII (H9–3–2): (a) general view of the object, scale in mm; (b) view of the object's point; (c) detail of the surface showing faintly visible parallel lines.

remains it is wise to take the conservative option of rejecting them as artefacts. The one likely tool from unit VII (Last Interglacial) joins a small but growing catalogue of bone tools associated with Middle Stone Age contexts (Henshilwood & Sealy 1997; Yellen 1998). The behavioural implications of the Mumbwa Caves specimen are discussed in chapter 13.

SPATIAL DATA

The excavation of features interpreted as windbreaks in Area I has been described in chapter 2. This section provides details of the form of the features and outlines the behavioural interpretation based on shape, internal structure and content. The first and most intact of the three concentrations of ash, baked sediment, stone and bone forms a partial arc that extends 175 cm from G8 into G7 and H7 (fig. 8.35). Either end of the arc has been truncated by the excavation in 1930 of the central pit (G8) and by the northern extension (G7). The exposed sections have weathered and termites have tunnelled beneath the arc in parts of G8. The band of concentrated occupation debris has a variable width of 30–40 cm and thickness of 20–25 cm that builds to a peak at the centre of the arc. A 1–2 cm thick spread of ash and debris into H7 interrupts the sweep of the feature.

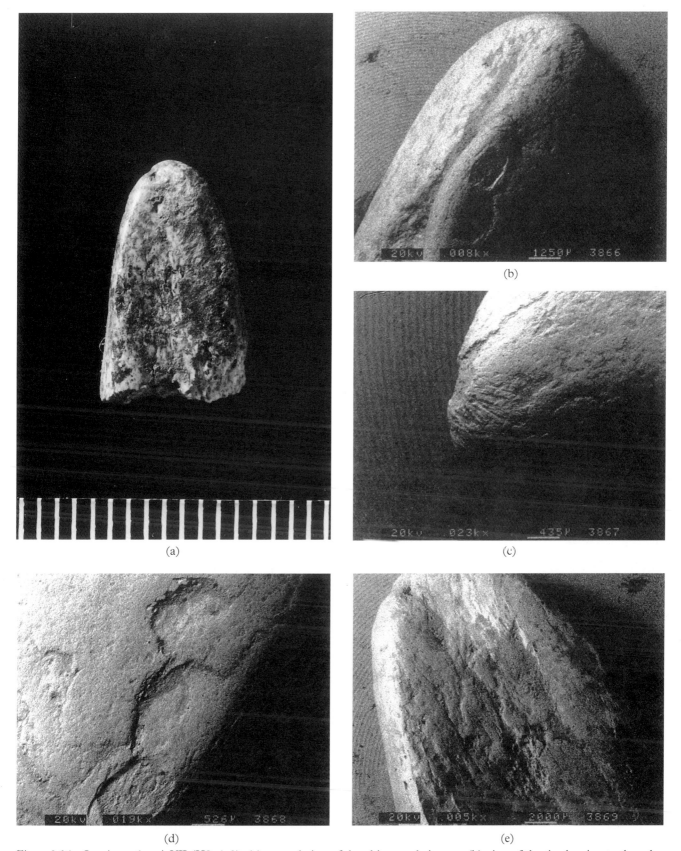

Figure 8.34 Specimen 6, unit VII (H8–4–3): (a) general view of the object, scale in mm; (b) view of the tip showing teethmarks; (c) view of the tip showing possible use-wear; (d) teethmarks on bone edge; (e) obverse side showing good condition of bone and deep vertical grooves.

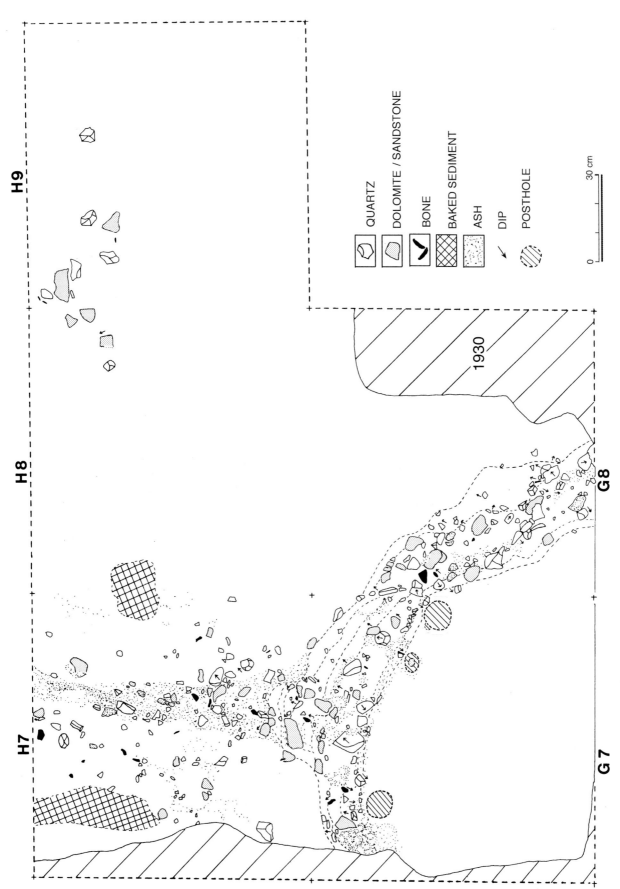

Figure 8.35 Plan view of a partial arc of concentrated lithic and bone debris mixed with ash and baked sediment in Area I, depth 202–239 cm below datum. Three postholes occur on the inside bend of the arc which is free of debris. The feature is interpreted as the base of windbreak (see text). The ends of the feature are truncated by excavations in 1930.

Figure 8.36 shows a contour plan of the arc with the increasing height of the feature illustrated in 5 cm intervals. An apparent symmetry emerges in the distribution of debris either side of the central peak or plateau, but the deposit rises more steeply against the inner face of the arc and then tapers towards the east (H7, H8). The dip of artefacts within the concentration illustrates the difference in slope between the inner to outer bends (fig. 8.35). The majority of pieces are found on the backslopes and dip southeastwards between 30 and 45°. Two sections through the feature (fig. 8.37a,b) in G8 reveal a consistent pattern in the internal structure of the arc. The steeper inner face contains few artefacts and is composed of pale sediments identified as ash (fig. 8.38). A concentration of debris sits on the ash bank and slopes southeastwards in discrete bands (fig. 8.37a,b). The whole structure rests on the red colluvial deposit of unit VIII.

A distinct pattern occurs in the distribution of artefacts and other occupation debris to either side of

the feature. The area defined by the inner bend contains few artefacts whereas bone, ash, hardened sediment and stone artefacts are spread across H7 and into H8 beyond the outer bend of the feature (fig. 8.35). Streaks of pale sediment, possibly ash, lead up to the inner face of the arc and as shown in section (fig. 8.37b) the ash is banked steeply against the inside of the arc.

Pit and postholes?

Three roughly circular features occur at the base of the inner face of the arc in G7 (fig. 8.35). Dark brown sediment (10 YR 3/3) distinguishes the features from the mottled matrix of the surrounding sediment (5YR 4/4) and from the arc (fig. 8.39). The middle feature is oblong and the smallest of the three, measuring 7.5 cm across by 5 cm wide and 4 cm deep. It contains a further circular feature (2–3 cm) of white powdery sediment (2.5 YR N8) that resembles ash. A section (fig. 8.40a) shows the internal structure.

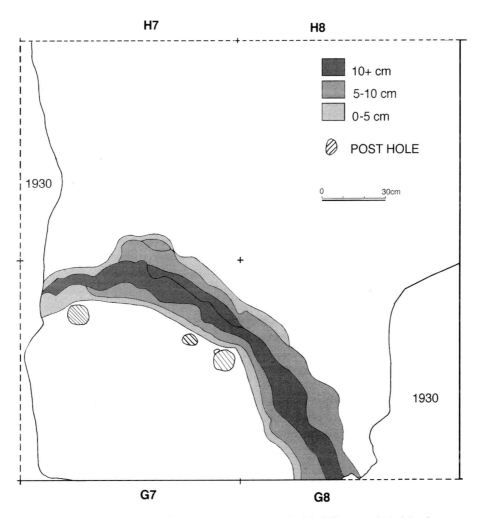

Figure 8.36   A contour plan of the arc feature in Area I with differences in height shown as
5 cm intervals from the base of the feature upwards.

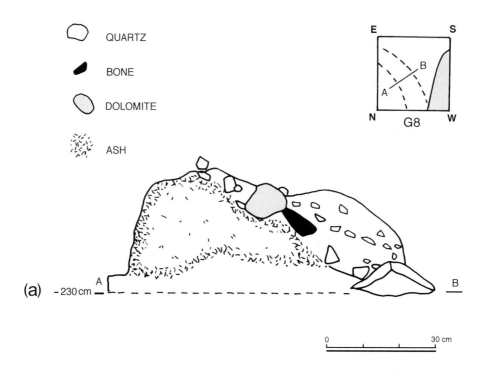

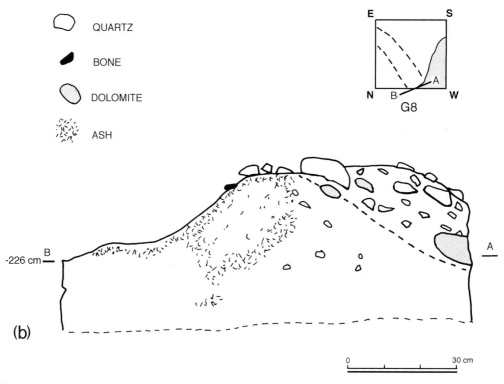

Figure 8.37 Two sections through the arc feature in Area I, G8, showing the uneven distribution of ash on the inner face of the arc and the dip of stone and bone debris down the outer bend.

Figure 8.38　Photograph of the section illustrated in figure 8.37b showing the ash core of the feature and dipping deposit on the backslope (5 cm scale).

Figure 8.39　Photograph of the largest posthole associated with the arc feature in G7, Area I. An inner and outer ring are discernible as colour differences (5 cm scale).

A larger circular feature located 15 cm to the southwest has a diameter of 10–12 cm, a depth of 9 cm, and is surrounded by brown sediment (10YR 3/3). The core of the feature (fig. 8.40b) is compacted sediment that tapers slightly to a flat base. The surrounding fill also tapers to a truncated base. Termite tunnels underlie part of the feature and appear to have cut into the base. Only the bottom of the third circle, located near the northern

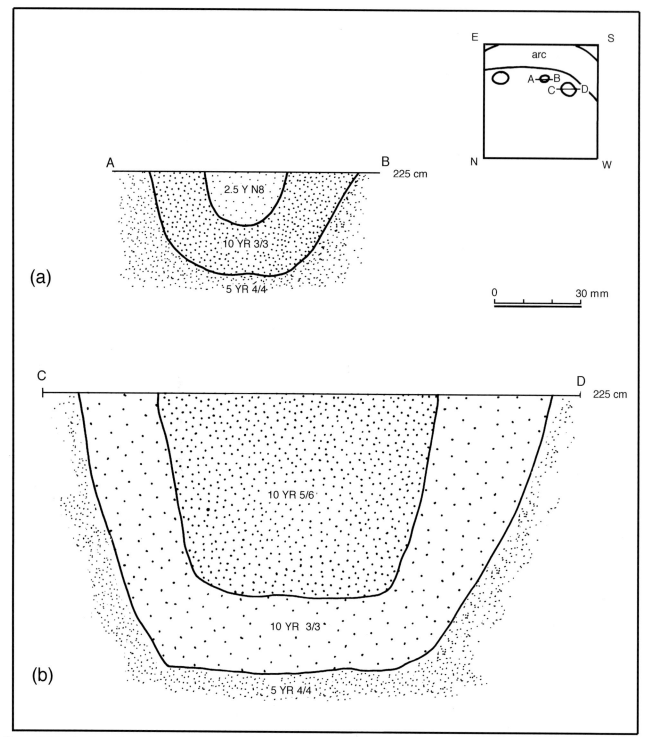

Figure 8.40 Sections through two of three circular features on the inner bend of the arc feature, G7, Area I: (a) the smallest feature contains an inner core of white powdery sediment (ash) surrounded by a darker fill; (b) the largest of features contains an inner core set within deposit that differs in colour from the surrounding matrix. These features are interpreted as postholes (see text).

end of the arc, was planned and had a depth of only 2–3 cm. It contained a similar brown sediment fill (10YR 3/3) to the other features.

These three features have been interpreted as post-

holes (Barham 1996:197) based on their structure and location. They exhibit typical cut and fill profiles associated with pit and postholes (Barker 1993). Pit holes encompass postholes and are often distinguished by differences in sediment colour and texture. Two of the circular features contain an outer darker fill with paler inner cores that may mark the position of a former stake and post in the small and large circle respectively. The stake appears to have disintegrated into ash and the post transformed into a hard granular deposit. The presence of old termite tunnels beneath this feature may account for the unusual texture of the deposit. Termites are known to reduce a tree to a soft shell and then to solidify the cast (Josens 1983). The location of the circles on the inner face of the banked feature suggests a deliberate placement indicative of a human origin.

A windbreak

The placement of the arc in relation to the structure of the main cave and its linking passages contributes to a behavioural interpretation of the feature. During the winter months of June–September the daytime winds come from the east-southeast and enter the cave system on the eastern and southern face. They flow up the narrow passage and enter the cave with some force. At night a cold easterly breeze descends on the dambo. The passage at the time of the occupation of Area I would have been wider with less of a funnelling effect, but the main cave would still have been draughty. A windbreak would have kept the occupants warm as well as preventing ash from blowing across the living area.

The opening of the arc-shaped feature faces away from the prevailing wind toward the northwest. By treating the arc as a portion of a full circle, the diameter of the structure would have been about 2.8 m. This is large by comparison with the huts and windbreaks built today by the !Kung-speaking Ju/'hoansi of northern Botswana (Dobe area) and the G/wi (or /Gui) of central Botswana. Wet season huts among the Ju/'hoansi are circular thatched structures 2 m high and 2 m wide with a hearth out to the front (Yellen 1976:63). Among the G/wi, the more substantial wet season hut is replaced in the dry season by informal semicircular windbreaks oriented away from the prevailing wind with some facing north to minimise exposure from bitter southerlies (Silberbauer 1981:230). Relatively recent archaeological examples of huts show similarities in structure and layout. At Gwisho hot springs on the Kafue floodplain to the south of Mumbwa, peat deposits preserved the organic remains of at least one and perhaps two huts or windbreaks facing away from the prevailing wind (Fagan & Van Noten 1971:25–6). The bases of three wooden posts were found associated with a rough semicircle of stones and inter-mixed with grass. One post with a pointed base had a diameter of 3 cm, which matches the width of the possible stake hole in G7. The Gwisho settlement is dated to about 4300 BP. A cluster of eight semicircles of stone has been excavated at the site of Orangia 1 on the Orange River and interpreted as a set of windbreaks (Sampson 1968).

The openings of the windbreaks face to the northwest away from the prevailing wind and range in diameter from 1.5 to 2.0 m. The site was originally reported to be a Middle Stone Age camp but has since been re-assessed as a Holocene occupation on earlier deposits (Sampson pers comm). A possible early example of a windbreak comes from Kalambo Falls where a rough 2 m semicircle of stone cobbles was excavated from a late Acheulian context (Clark 1969).

The treatment of space within and around wind-breaks by the Ju/'hoansi and G/wi has relevance for the interpretation of the Mumbwa arc feature. Among the Ju/'hoansi, few activities take place inside a hut other than sleeping and storage of objects. The hearths located to the front of the huts are the focal points for cooking and tool making (Yellen 1976:65). At long-lived winter camps, the fires are kept burning through the night and the resulting ash is dumped behind the huts (ibid). Among the G/wi, Silberbauer (1981:230) records that 'Shelters and their forecourts are swept several times a day. A ridge of detritus soon forms a perimeter of the forecourt and this remains to mark the site long after the thatch and wooden frameworks have decayed to dust.' The area 'inside' the Mumbwa arc is nearly free of debris in marked contrast to the back of the feature.

The combined evidence of the shape of the arc, its orientation, content and the presence of postholes together support the original interpretation (Barham 1996) that this was a structure and most likely a wind-break. A reconstruction is shown in figure 8.41 that is based on the dimensions of the three postholes and the shape of the arc extended into the 1930 excavation area. Grass bundles are tied with bark strips into the framework of sticks and posts.

During the 1996 season at Mumbwa, an experiment in 'living archaeology' was undertaken involving the construction of a replica windbreak based on the above image. The structure was used at lunch times for shade and in the evening for card games and received an occasional sweeping with debris pushed back against the grass walls. The windbreak was to be set alight at the end of the season and the distribution of ash recorded and a section excavated through the debris bank. An uncon-trolled bush fire swept through the camp mid-way through the season and destroyed the windbreak before the experiment could be completed. Despite this set-back, the burnt windbreak provided useful spatial information. The small posts in the framework caught fire and burnt through to ash and collapsed as linear features onto the charred mass of grass that accumulated to the outside of the structure (fig. 8.42). The area inside the windbreak was largely clear of debris. Parallels can be drawn with the distribution of ash and occupation debris at the back of the arc in Area I (fig. 8.35). The narrow ash spread that begins at the break closely

135

0   10   20   30   40   50 cm

Figure 8.41   A reconstruction of the windbreak in Area I based on the dimensions of the
feature and the placement of the postholes.

resembles a fallen pole in the burnt replica. Perhaps the windbreak collapsed after a similar conflagration in the Last Interglacial.

If the site was occupied during climatic conditions similar to those of today, then the windbreak suggests use during the winter months. Surface water is scarce during the winter today with the dambo becoming dry. The only water available locally comes from wells dug up to six metres deep into the dambo clay. Either the Middle Stone Age occupants did the same or the dambo behaved differently and retained some surface water. The river cobbles used at Mumbwa for making tools indicate a stronger river flow regime than at present, which means that current interglacial conditions are not the appropriate climatic analogue. Alternatively, the windbreak feature reflects occupation during cooler stadial events in the Last Interglacial or perhaps the use

of the cave at the Stage 6/5 boundary. Wind speeds would have been higher in the tropics during glacial (and stadial) phases because of the increased temperature gradient between the equator and the poles (Flohn 1984:5). The alignment of fossil linear dune systems in western Zambia reflects an intensified easterly or anticyclonic flow of air during glacial periods (Thomas & Goudie 1984; O'Connor & Thomas 1999). Mumbwa Caves would have offered shelter during these cool dry phases – with the aid of windbreaks – but the availability of surface water would have remained a limiting factor. The dating of the Area I occupation and that of the main Middle Stone Age deposit (unit VII) is too coarse grained to resolve the issue of the seasonality or phases of occupation. Chronology and climate aside, the presence of a possible windbreak implies awareness on behalf of the occupants of their immediate living conditions and

Figure 8.42   Burnt remains of the experimental windbreak constructed to the front of the cave. Charred grass fell within the outline of the arc and small branches used as supports fell across the grass and burnt to ash. The pattern of burning resembles the debris and ash spread of the archaeological feature.

the intellectual ability to alter the interior landscape of the cave to solve a particular problem.

Other features in Area I

The windbreak spanned a depth of deposit from 202 to 230 cm below datum. Two additional concentrations of sediment, ash and artefacts emerged from lower levels (235–254 cm) adjacent to the windbreak. Both of these features lacked the consistent definition and internal structure that made the arc so distinctive. Figure 8.43 shows the outline of the windbreak in relation to the underlying concentration of occupation debris in G8 and H7. In G8, the feature resembles its successor in structure with dipping artefacts and an inner ash content, but dissolves into an amorphous spread in H7. A fourth pit and posthole feature occurs here and two additional circular patches of hardened sediment (fig. 8.43 and 8.44) follow the inside curve of the feature. These may represent the bases of pit holes that were destroyed in the later construction of the windbreak. The G8/H7 feature as a whole looks to have suffered from the reuse of the site.

The top of another feature emerges in H8 (fig. 8.43) at a depth of 235 cm and is fully exposed at a depth of 250 cm (fig. 8.44). This too is a concentration of baked sediment, stone, bone, and dolomite blocks with some internal structure of dipping artefacts. The feature is vaguely linear in form as it stretches across H9 and disappears into the section face. Whether this was a

windbreak, a dumping zone or some other behavioural feature is difficult to determine. No postholes were found and the excavation of the central pit in 1930 truncated a spread of artefacts around the feature.

An unusually shaped piece of burnt and now soft dolomite was recovered from the artefact concentration in H8/H9 and merits a brief description. The object resembles a human form with two legs formed by a linear division that stops along a vein of quartz (fig. 8.45a,b). Above the vein the object narrows to a waist. The piece as a human form is headless and with one projection that could be construed as an arm. The 'Venus of Mumbwa' is put forward with no claim that this is an intentional construction but merely that the dolomite has some human-like features, especially to eyes familiar with modern art. Whether it was recognised as a human image by the occupants is unknowable, but the association with the artefact concentration makes it likely that the object would have been seen if it existed in its current form. The possibility remains that the dolomite weathered into a human shape long after the area had been abandoned. Further analysis of the surface and in particular of an apparent incision that formed the legs is needed to clarify the formation of the piece.

Hearths

The intellectually neutral term of 'combustion zone' should be applied to the features interpreted as hearths

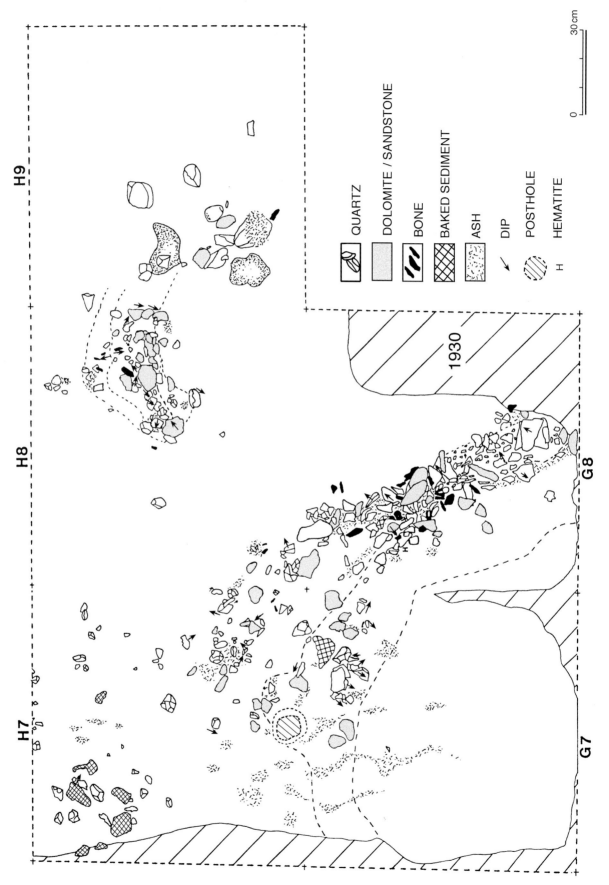

Figure 8.43 Plan view of the distribution of stone, bone, ash and burnt sediment immediately beneath the windbreak in G8 and H7, Area I. A posthole feature in H7 marks an earlier phase of windbreak building in roughly the same area.

QUARTZ

DOLOMITE / SANDSTONE

BONE

BAKED SEDIMENT

ASH

DIP

POSTHOLE

HEMATITE

30 cm

0

1930

H9

H8

H7

G8

G7

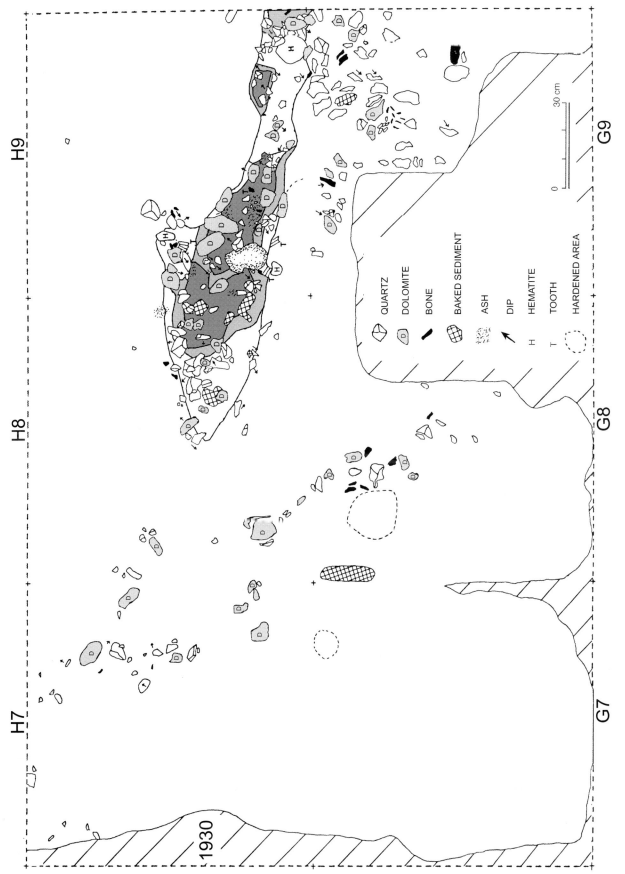

Legend:

QUARTZ
DOLOMITE
BONE
BAKED SEDIMENT
ASH
DIP
HEMATITE
TOOTH
HARDENED AREA

Figure 8.44 Plan view of a concentration of stone and bone debris associated with ash and burnt sediment at a depth of 250 cm in Area I.

(a)

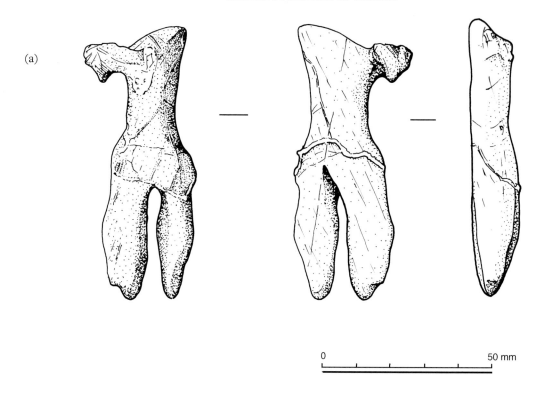

0   50 mm

(b)

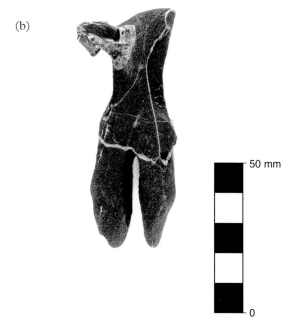

50 mm

0

Figure 8.45 An illustration (a) and photograph (b) of a piece of burnt dolomite with a human-like form, minus head and complete arms, found in association with the debris concentration illustrated in figure 8.43.

in Areas I–III (Stringer et al 1999), but the more emotive term is retained for reasons developed below. Dart and Del Grande preferred 'furnace' to describe the large areas of burning surrounded by stone that they mistakenly believed were used for smelting iron. Hearths are a feature of the main cave deposits and they serve as culture-stratigraphic markers as well as behavioural features. In the lower deposits (units IV–IX, >170 ka BP), the evidence for burning is restricted to discrete

patches of reddened and hardened clay that range in diameter from 40 to 60 cm by 10 cm in depth (fig. 8.46) and associated with fragments of burnt sandstone, bone and occasional flecks of charcoal. Single blocks of sandstone and quartz often accompany these early features and may have been used as surrounds to retain ash and heat, but no intact arrangement of stones was found around a hearth. Single blocks of stone are found around the hearths of the Ju/'hoansi (Yellen 1976:65) where they are used as anvils and work surfaces. Hearths similar in size to those from the basal units occur in the Holocene deposits with discrete lenses of burnt sediment with ash and charcoal still visible in Dart and Del Grande's section that forms the main axis of the grid system. An example is recorded in the section of H8 (fig. 2.18) and is 40 cm in diameter and 5 cm thick. These small hearths from the very earliest and latest occupation of the main cave give the impression of ephemeral use of the cave. A fire was lit on the surface of Area I before our arrival in 1996 and this modern feature had a diameter of 50 cm and depth of ash of only 3 cm. (The excav-

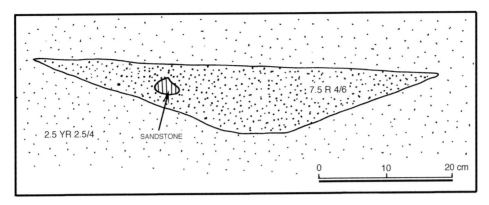

Figure 8.46   Section of hearth in unit X, D10–7–4.

ation had been backfilled at the end of 1995 and the fire did not affect the intact deposit.) The main cave is now used for the isolation of girls as part of initiation rituals when they reside at the site for a few days. The hearth may have been left after one of these short-lived episodes.

In the Last Interglacial occupation layer (unit VII), the areas of burning range in diameter from 90 to 150 cm. The largest was the Area I hearth left by Dart and Del Grande and which was excavated in 1994. This feature (fig. 8.47a,b) had a central core of ash 100×82 cm wide that was 9 cm thick. The effects of burning as seen in hardened and discoloured sediment extended across an oval-shaped area 150×100 cm wide and 10 cm deep. A few fragmentary blocks of burnt dolomite and quartz were found in and around the ash. The feature had been left as a stone surrounded hearth in 1930 and survived largely intact until just before the start of the 1993 season. A photograph (Dart & Del Grande 1931: photo 5) shows large stone blocks (~20–30 cm estimated length) enclosing the full extent of the feature, not just the ashy core.

The size, structure and depth of the hearth all indicate that this was a permanent fixture in the living area of the main cave and used over relatively long periods. If the Last Interglacial occupants of Mumbwa used the hearth in ways similar to those observed among the Ju/'hoansi (Yellen 1976:68–9), then this structure would have been the focal point not just for cooking and warmth but of the manufacture and maintenance of tools. 'One other characteristic of all [Dobe] camps is debris scatter generally confined to the area immediately surrounding each hearth' (ibid:64). If the analogy holds, then the Mumbwa hearth should also be the centre of a concentration of food remains and debitage. The previous excavation of the immediately surrounding deposits makes this an untestable proposition.

In Area II, at least five hearths were excavated (fig. 2.16a) of which four were inter-cutting. The original

dimensions of the features have been partially obscured by the re-use of the area and by the excavation of steps in 1930 through this deposit and its subsequent erosion. Blocks of dolomite, sandstone and quartz were found in association with the hearths but not in consistent arrangements. Re-use of stone may account for the irregular distribution. Figure 8.48 illustrates a relatively intact hearth from D10/D9 (193–198 cm). A core area of ash has a diameter of 50 cm within which ghosts of calcined bone were found. With increasing distance from the ash the surrounding bone was less burnt, as might be expected. The effects of the heat of the fire extended approximately 80 cm around the ash core and to a depth of 15 cm. A burnt dolomite block approximately 20 cm in length bordered the ash and was itself surrounded by burnt bone. A larger fire-cracked boulder lay 50 cm to the south. Quartz debitage, sandstone fragments, hematite, as well as bone and teeth comprised the occupation debris associated with the hearth.

Assuming contemporaneity across this assemblage, the accumulation corresponds with the ethnographic model of the hearth as the centre of domestic activities. The ethnographic data can be stretched further to explain the differences in the size of hearths between the lower units and the main Middle Stone Age occupation of unit VII. Among the Ju/'hoansi and G/wi, the length of occupation and number of occupants of a camp is reflected in the quantity of debris left behind. Areas that offer favourable combinations of water, plant and animal foods and firewood will be used longer and by more people. A single dry season waterhole attracts the Dobe residents for long periods of up to six months (Yellen 1976:65) and the G/wi, who live in an area without permanent water supplies, congregate during the wet season around seasonal pools (Silberbauer 1981). In both areas, these periods of maximum population density are associated with more permanent hut structures, greater quantities and varieties of occupation debris and larger hearths. The latter develop simply from the

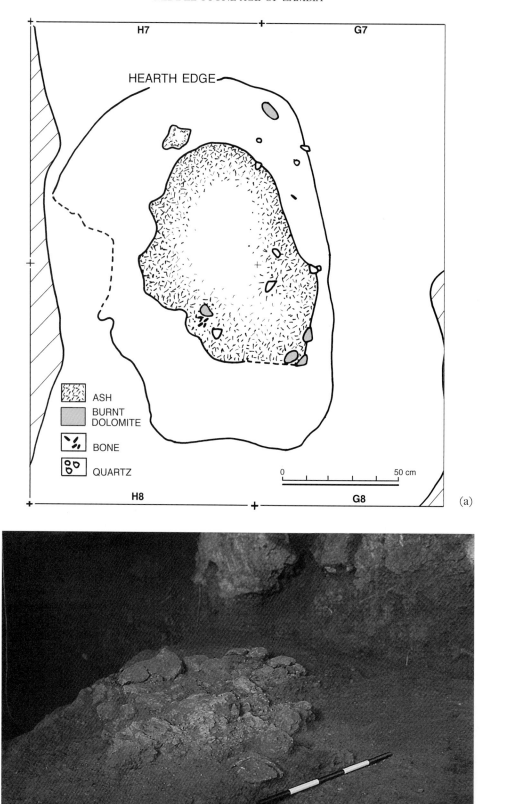

Figure 8.47   (a, b) Remnant of hearth ('furnace') in Area I, 177–186 cm, showing the consolidated ash core. 10 cm scale.

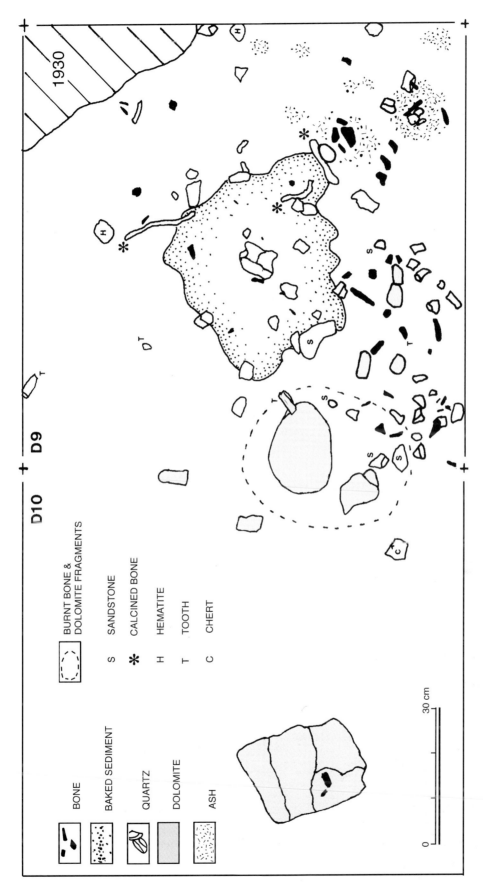

BONE

BAKED SEDIMENT

QUARTZ

DOLOMITE

ASH

BURNT BONE &
DOLOMITE FRAGMENTS

S   SANDSTONE

*   CALCINED BONE

H   HEMATITE

T   TOOTH

C   CHERT

1930

D10   D9

30 cm

Figure 8.48   Hearth and associated debris in unit VII, Area II (D10/D9).

143

prolonged use of individual hearths. The depth of the hearth increases from the use of sticks to rake coals and extract food from the ashes (Yellen 1976:64). By contrast, wet season camps in the Dobe area are short-lived and used by smaller social groups that are dispersed among temporary waterholes and nutgroves. During the dry winter months, the G/wi disperse into individual family units. These dispersal phase camps for both groups of Kalahari foragers leave a comparatively impoverished material signature including smaller, thinner hearths.

The ethnographically observed link between seasonal scheduling of resource use and settlement size can be extended to the main cave hearth features. Below the colluvium (unit VIII), small areas of burning and associated patches of bone, stone and artefacts reflect short-lived occupations, perhaps only a few days in duration, by small numbers of people. This archaeological pattern parallels the G/wi dry winter season strategy of separating into individual family units until the rains return. The more substantial hearths of the Last Interglacial occupation (unit VII) reflect the structured use of space in the cave by larger social groups or by a small group staying for a longer period of time. The main cave could have held four families, each with a windbreak and hearth, based on the hut and hearth distribution recorded at a nutgrove in the Dobe region (Yellen 1976:fig. 2.3). At Dobe, the four families and a lone male, 15 people in total, occupied a space approximately 9×8 m with a central communal open

area. Without the communal space, an additional two families could have squeezed into the cave but with the loss of some privacy. The shared communal space that is used for rituals involving dancing and for the distribution of meat (ibid:68) may have had its counterpart on the platform outside the cave entrance.

The final feature in Area II to be described is a truncated ash-lined pit in D10 (fig. 8.49). Approximately 50 per cent of the pit was cut away with the creation of steps down into the cave in 1930. In section, the J-shaped pit (fig. 3.1) is lined with ash to a depth of 25 cm and 12 cm thick. The sediment beneath the ash is reddened (10R 4/6) to a depth of a further 10 cm. This baked deposit supplied a piece of burnt quartz with a TL date of 113±ka BP (see chapter 3). In plan view (fig. 8.50), the diameter of the feature can be estimated to have been at least 70 cm. It differs from the hearths in its depth and heavy ash content. Blocks of dolomite, phyllite and sandstone occur on the pit edge and nearby, but the subsequent use of the area for hearths has disturbed any patterning to the west. The feature is interpreted as a cooking pit for which there are ethnographic parallels again among the Ju/'hoansi (Yellen 1976:64). These are often associated with special activities such as feasting and dancing to celebrate a successful kill of a large animal (Lee 1979).

In Area III, the large hearth that marks the latest Middle Stone Age occupation at ~40 ka BP has been described in chapter 2 (fig. 2.19). This feature warrants further consideration because it represents a relatively

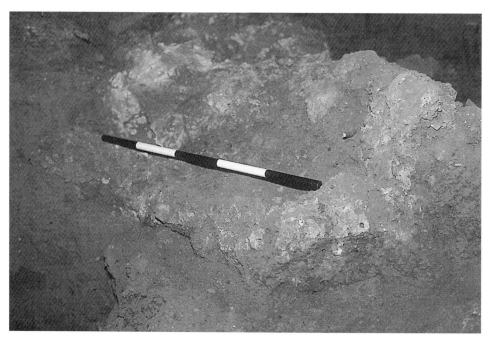

Figure 8.49   Photograph of ash filled pit in Area II (D10) with TL date of 113 ka BP. The pit was truncated during the 1930 excavation. 10 cm scale.

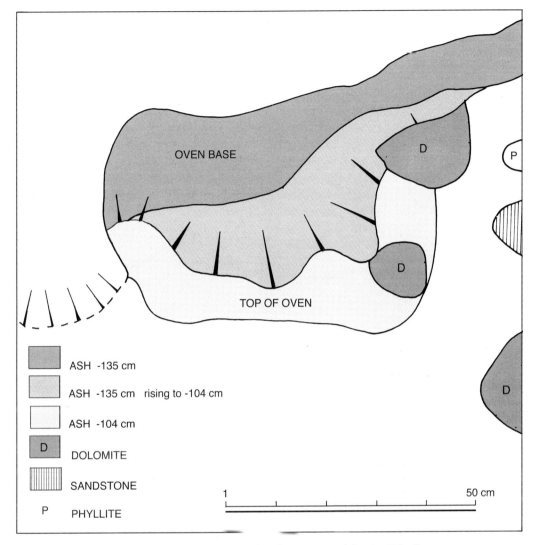

Figure 8.50 Plan of the ash pit in Area II showing the extent and depth of the feature.

undisturbed example of a hearth that incorporates blocks of stone (fig. 8.51). The northeast edge has partially collapsed but the remainder of the feature is intact. Ash underlies most of the arrangement of stone that is roughly circular and dipping inwards toward the centre of the square. The majority of the stone blocks >10 cm in length are dolomite (n=21) with sandstone the next most numerous (n=7) followed by quartz (n=3) and phyllite (n=1). Three pieces of hematite were found in association with the larger stones (fig. 8.51). None of the stone, with the exception of dolomite, occurs naturally in the cave and must have been transported across distances of 300–500 m. The selection of sandstone, quartz and phyllite for use as hearthstones has a practical basis in that they all retain heat longer than dolomite. The stones act as natural radiators and this property has some value in the cool of winter mornings. Informal experiments carried out around the

campfire at Mumbwa in 1994 demonstrated the thermal properties of these crystalline materials. They also showed that dolomite loses its physical integrity with exposure to heat as it degrades to a grey powder. The earliest inhabitants of Mumbwa may have been aware of the heat-retaining properties of differing types of stone. A few blocks, but mostly fragments, of sandstone were found in the early units (XIV–IX) in association with patches of burning and low frequencies of lithic debitage.

No hearths were excavated in the overlying Later Stone Age deposits but the small ash lenses associated with the Holocene sections do not appear to have hearthstones. In this respect they resemble campfires made by Ju/'hoansi and G/wi foragers. Hearthstones are not necessary for cave living, but they would be useful during the cool windy months of winter to contain ash and provide added warmth.

D11 HEARTH

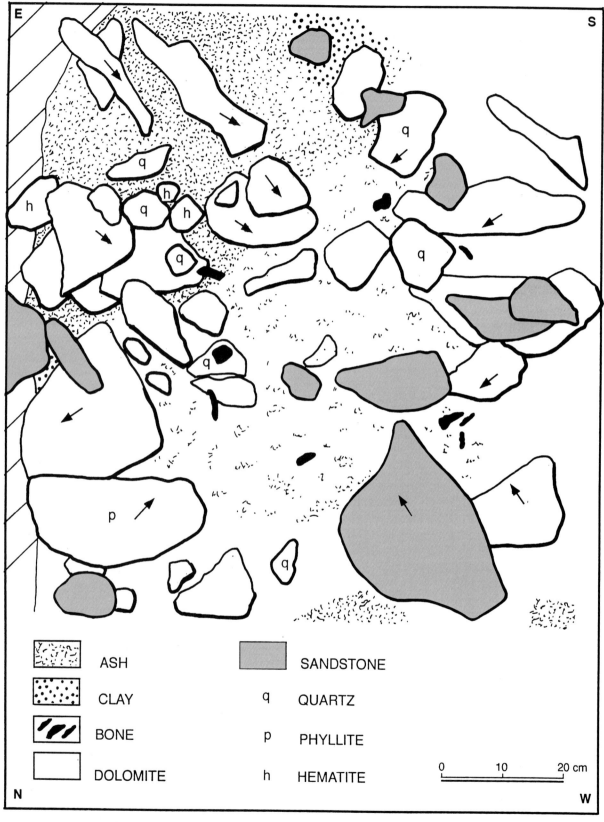

ASH

CLAY

BONE

DOLOMITE

SANDSTONE

q QUARTZ

p PHYLLITE

h HEMATITE

0   10   20 cm

Figure 8.51 Large stone lined hearth in unit V, Area III, (D11) with associated TL date of 40 ka BP. This feature marks the top of the Middle Stone Age deposit.

Burials

Dart and Del Grande (1931) recovered the fragmentary remains of 16 individuals from contexts now attributable to the Iron Age, Later Stone Age and the main Middle Stone Age occupation above the sterile colluvium (unit VIII). Three stone-built features were found to contain human bone and all came from deposits associated with the Middle Stone Age. Two structures, called tombs A and B, were built against the overhanging wall of the northern extension at a depth of 18 inches (46 cm) below the large hearth ('furnace'). The Area I hearth as excavated in 1994 was exposed between 175 and 186 cm below datum which places the tombs of 1930 at depths of 220 cm and lower. These levels correlate with the windbreaks and other concentrations of occupation debris found in Area I. The structures are described as beehive-shaped enclosures constructed of stacked dolomite blocks with the cave wall used as a fourth side (fig. 8.52). The dimensions, as estimated from the published plans (ibid: figs 3 and 7), are approximately 100–110 cm long by 60 cm wide and about 60 cm in height. Large tree roots with associated termites had fixed onto the structures 'and together these factors had played great havoc with the human remains' (ibid:390).

The fragmentary cranial and postcranial elements found in tombs A and B were attributed on morphological grounds to modern Bushmen (ibid:426; Jones 1940:318). Evidence of a deliberate burial is recorded in one tomb: 'it appeared, from the general size and form of the structure and the positions of calvaria found, that the body had been cramped into the foetal position so as to assume the minimum space, and in a sitting position' (Dart & Del Grande 1931:390). A third tomb was found in the northern extension at a depth of 70 cm below the first two and that places this structure at a minimum of 290 cm below the current datum and into the sterile colluvium (unit VIII). Only a single piece of bone was recovered, that of a humerus.

The non-human contents associated with the first two tombs include: '22 quartz flakes, 5 pieces of shell-nacre, hundreds of small pieces of bone, some of which have been trimmed or hollowed or smoothed, single teeth of at least 6 different species of antelope, 1 wart hog molar, and a lion's canine' (ibid:426). The flakes are not described in sufficient detail to make a technological attribution of either Later or Middle Stone Age, but the presence of mother of pearl (nacre) is suggestive of a later origin. In the most recent excavations, shell survives to a depth of only 75 cm (Area III, D11–6–6), which is dated to the early Holocene. Clark (1942:179) argues that the burials are intrusive from the Later Stone Age on the basis of the physical types found but also from analogy with burial practices among the Namib and Narib Bushmen who dig deep burials and use stone.

The third tomb contained '1 rostro-carinate, 1 detaching hammer, 1 chisel, 2 snubbed points, and 9 wrought flakes' (Dart & Del Grande 1931:426). By current typological standards, the objects classified and illustrated (ibid:fig. 17) as detaching hammers and chisels would be described as disc and radial cores and attributed to the Middle Stone Age. Similarly, the points are also Middle Stone Age forms. The position of the structure within the top of the colluvium suggests that

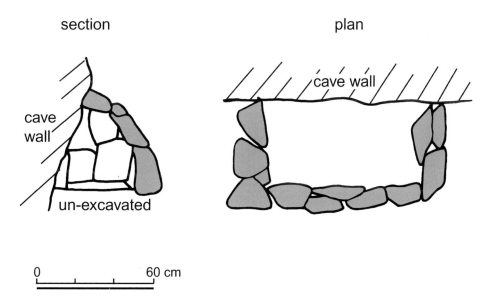

section   plan

cave wall

un-excavated

cave wall

0   60 cm

Figure 8.52   Section and plan of a stone built tomb or enclosure built against the wall of the northern extension (fig. 2.8) at an estimated depth of 290 cm (after Dart & Del Grande 1931). Human remains were found inside and outside the tomb.

the artefacts are either deliberate additions or inadvertent fill.

The attribution of the tombs and their contents to particular physical types (cf Jones 1940; Gabel 1963) and to cultural periods remains inconsistent (cf Clark 1942; Protsch 1977; Clark 1989). Dart and Del Grande assigned separate labels to the artefact sequence and to the human remains without making clear the links between the two. Some loss of specimens has added to the confusion (Rightmire 1984:166) as has the use of differing numbering systems when describing the specimens (eg, Gabel 1963). In the mid-1970s, a single radiocarbon date on bone collagen from the lower tomb seemed to demonstrate conclusively that the structure and its content were Middle Stone Age in origin (Protsch 1977). The date of 19,780±130 BP (UCLA–1750C) and the conclusion reached by Protsch were both problematical. The sample dated 'consisted of several fragments of bone, one of which, the fibula, made up the main portion of the material used for dating' (ibid:6). Dart and Del Grande (1931:393,426) stated clearly that only one fragment of bone was present in the tomb and it was from a humerus. They did find fragmentary human bone, including fibulae, in the deposits around the tomb but not in the tomb itself. The discrepancy undermines confidence in the stratigraphic attribution of the samples.

Since the 1970s, as pretreatment techniques have improved for the extraction of modern carbon contamination from bone collagen, the reliability of earlier dates has come under question (P Pettitt pers comm). A more cautious reappraisal of the Mumbwa date would be that it represents a minimum age. The date also seems too young by current knowledge for attribution to the Middle Stone Age (see chapter 1). At the time Protsch (1977:6) was writing, the Middle Stone Age of east Africa was still considered to be relatively recent having ended only 10,000 years ago. The date of 20,000 BP, if accurate, would now be viewed as neither clearly Middle nor Later Stone Age but something in the continuum that marks the gradual shift in technologies between the two (Thackeray 1992; Wadley 1993).

The development of the 'Out of Africa' theory of modern human origins in the late 1980s brought a reassessment of potential evidence for the early emergence of complex, symbol-based behaviours. In this context, the Mumbwa tombs were cited as a rare example of possible care for the dead in the Middle Stone Age (Clark 1989:577). Given the continuing uncertainty about the age and the shifting cultural attribution of the tombs, an attempt was made to resolve the chronology of the burials by the application of AMS dating. The technique requires only minute amounts of bone (200 mg) and so minimises the loss to the curated sample. Material from the stratigraphically earliest tomb and from tomb A ('furnace stratum', 220 cm below current datum) was sent from the Raymond Dart Collection held at the University of Witwatersrand Medical School to the Research Laboratory for Archaeology and the History of Art at Oxford University. The Witwatersrand accession number for the earliest bone (A–345, M1) indicates that it came from the same collection dated by Protsch, in other words from outside the tomb. The sample of unidentifiable fragments was mineralised in contrast to the section of fresh looking humerus submitted from tomb A (A–340). The original description of the human remains found in tomb A did not include a humerus, but humeri were found in tomb B (Dart & Del Grande 1931:426). This discrepancy in provenance raises the possibility that some mixing of the samples has occurred in the past.

The earlier sample (A–345) contained low amounts of collagen and insufficient carbon for dating, despite three attempts at extraction (P Pettitt pers comm). The tomb A/B sample gave a result of 1060±35 BP, with a 2 sigma range of 890–1030 AD (INTCAL 98), d13C=−8.3 (OxA–8879).

The results fail to resolve the outstanding issues of chronology or cultural affiliation but they do clarify the ongoing debate. The lack of collagen in the Oxford sample suggests that Protsch's date of 19,780±130 BP may have indeed been the product of contamination and should be treated with caution. The human remains come from a context that has been dated independently to the Last Interglacial (chapter 3), and unless they are intrusive the bones should be considered of equivalent age. The tomb itself and its content of one bone has not been dated, but it seems unlikely that it is Last Interglacial in age given the result from tomb A/B. The late Holocene age of the bone accords with the reported association with shell in the tomb. Shell is only found in the Holocene deposits at Mumbwa as based on the findings from the current excavations. Clark's (1942) original attribution of the tombs to Later Stone Age hunter-gatherers seems highly plausible in retrospect. The stratigraphically earlier tomb should also be considered a later intrusion. The Middle Stone Age occupants of the main cave did leave their dead behind (see chapter 9), but not in stone built tombs.

9 Human remains from the Middle and Later Stone Age of Mumbwa Caves

O Pearson, F Grine, L Barham, and C Stringer

INTRODUCTION

The renewed excavations of Mumbwa Caves from 1993 to 1996 produced a modest sample of human remains comprising six isolated teeth or tooth fragments, two fragmentary femoral shafts, two radius fragments, and a proximal pedal phalanx. Some of these remains derive from the Middle Stone Age levels with certainty, others came from uncertain contexts and may be of Later Stone Age rather than Middle Stone Age antiquity. One femoral fragment described below derived from the Later Stone Age levels and is described here principally for comparative purposes and for its taphonomic interest. Given the fact that the fossil evidence suggests modern humans most likely evolved in Africa during the Middle Stone Age (Bräuer 1984; Rightmire 1984; Rightmire and Deacon 1991; Stringer et al 1984; Kennedy 1984; Stringer 1994; Day & Stringer 1991; Day et al 1991; Vermeersch et al 1998; Klein 1999) and the general scarcity of human remains from the period, new Middle Stone Age human fossils are important for the potential they offer to shed new light on the origin of modern humans.

Comparative samples for the Mumbwa postcranial remains include penecontemporaneous remains such as Middle Stone Age or inferred Middle Stone Age hominin fossils from Klasies River Mouth, Omo Kibish, Cave of Hearths, Koobi Fora Chari or Galana Boi Formation (KNM–ER 999), early modern (or 'near-modern' (Klein 1999)) humans from Skhul and Qafzeh, Neanderthals (pooled European and Near Eastern specimens), *Homo heidelbergensis* or primitive *H. neanderthalensis* specimens from the *c* 300 ka-old site of Sima de los Huesos in Atapuerca, and the *c* 800 ka-old specimens from the Gran Dolina site in Atapuerca. Additional comparisons with recent Aboriginal Australian and sub-Saharan African populations are also presented. The limitation of comparisons to these recent human samples is done to control as much as possible for the effects of ecogeographical variation. Modern humans from warm climates such as much of sub-Saharan Africa and Australia tend to have long bones that have slender shafts and epiphyses relative to their lengths (Pearson 2000), narrow hips (Ruff 1994), and elongated limbs, especially the distal limb segments (Trinkaus 1981; Ruff 1994; Holliday 1997a, b). Similar ecogeographical patterns characterised fossil hominins (Ruff 1994; Holliday 1997a, b). Restriction of the recent comparative samples to groups from warm climates helps to partially eliminate one source of variation. Each of the fragments is described below, with details on their stratigraphic position and morphological comparisons to fossil hominins and recent humans. The term hominin is used in preference to hominid (cf Wood 1992; Potts 1998).

PART I: HUMAN DENTAL REMAINS FROM MUMBWA CAVES

The 1994 and 1996 excavation seasons at Mumbwa Caves resulted in the recovery of six isolated human teeth or tooth fragments. The specimens (table 9.1) include one that derives from *in situ* Later Stone Age, all definitely Holocene deposits, and two that were recovered during surface cleaning and therefore cannot be attributed to either the Later Stone Age or the Middle Stone Age with certainty. A fourth tooth that was recovered in association with quartz debitage during section cleaning can be attributed to the Middle Stone Age with some degree of certainty. The final two specimens are undoubtedly attributable to the Middle Stone Age.

These six teeth are described below. They are illustrated in figure 9.1, and their principal crown diameters are recorded in table 9.2. The specimens are described according to the grid square from which they derive.

Table 9.1 Human dental remains from Mumbwa Caves

Attribution	Element	Grid coordinate
Later Stone Age	R$\bar{C}$	D11–6–1
Uncertain	RI$_2$	H9–1–0
	RM$_2$	H9–1–0
Probable Middle Stone Age	LM$_2$	E10–1–0
Middle Stone Age	RM?	D9–9–4
	M frag.	D9–9–4

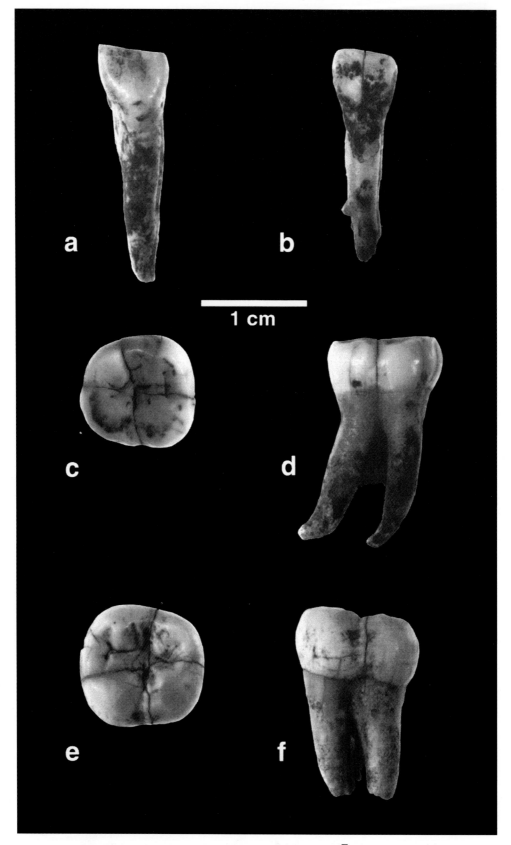

Figure 9.1 Human dental remains from Mumbwa Caves: (a) R$\overline{\text{C}}$ (D11–6–1), lingual view; (b) RI$_2$ (H9–1–0), lingual view; (c) RM$_2$ (H9–1–0), occlusal view; (d) RM$_2$ (H9–1–0), buccal view; (e) LM$_2$ (E10–1–0), occlusal view; (f) LM$_2$ (E10–1–0), buccal view.

Table 9.2 Principal crown dimensions of Mumbwa human teeth (mm)

Element	Grid Coordinate	MD meas.	MD est.	BL trig.	BL tal.	BL max.
I_2	H9–1–0	6.5	6.5			6.0
$\bar{C}$	D11–6–1	7.2	7.3			7.7
M_2	H9–1–0	11.6	11.8	11.0	10.5	11.0
M_2	E10–1–0	12.5	12.5	11.9	11.1	11.9

Later Stone Age attribution

D11–6–1 (unit II). $R\bar{C}$. (figure 9.1a)

This specimen was recovered at a depth of 55 cm below datum. It comprises a moderately worn, albeit complete crown and root of a mandibular right canine. Apical wear has exposed a small dentine island in the centre of a flat facet with a strong distal bevel. There is a moderate mesial interproximal contact facet (ICF) and a small distal ICF. Lingually, the crown has a small cervical eminence that gives rise to very narrow mesial and distal marginal ridges; there is no lingual tubercle, and no shovelling. There are several faint hypoplastic bands in the middle of the labial face.

The root is straight and its labial and lingual edges taper apically; there is a moderate mesial longitudinal furrow. The root is 15.2 mm long. The apex is complete, which suggests an ontogenetic age of beyond 10.5 years by recent human standards (Smith 1991).

Uncertain attribution

H9–1–0 (unit VII). RI_2, RM_2. (figure 9.1b, c)

These teeth were recovered at a depth of between 162 and 178 cm below datum. They were found during surface cleaning and cannot, therefore, be attributed to either the Later Stone Age or Middle Stone Age with any degree of certainty.

RI_2. (fig. 9.1b). The mandibular right lateral incisor is minimally worn, with a faint enamel facet on the incisal margin. The crown and root are complete. The crown has a triangular outline with a slight lingual cervical eminence. The mesial and distal marginal ridges are barely perceptible; there is no lingual tubercle, and no shovelling. The labial face is unremarkable. Calculus is preserved along the mesiolingual extent of the cervical margin.

The root has a slight distal curve over its apical fifth, and the labial and lingual margins taper. There is a moderate distal longitudinal furrow. The root is 12.5 mm long. The apex is complete, which suggests an onto-genetic age beyond 8.5 years by recent human standards (Smith 1991).

RM_2. (fig. 9.1c, d). The mandibular right molar is interpreted as a second rather than a first because of the reduced hypoconulid, which is very infrequent among first permanent molars (Grine 1981; Irish 1997). Occlusal wear is slight: buccal cusp height is reduced, enamel facets are present on all cusps, and dentine is not exposed. There is a moderate mesial ICF, and a very small distal ICF, which indicates that the M_3 had recently erupted (ie, an ontogenetic age of approximately 18 years). The crown and root are complete. The crown has four well-developed cusps and the hypo-conulid was evidently greatly reduced in size. There is no indication of either a C6 or a C7. The buccal aspect of the protoconid is worn, but there is no indication of a protostylid, and the metaconid crest does not appear to have taken the form of a deflecting wrinkle. There is no accessory distal trigonid crest. The metaconid and hypoconid are in contact, resulting in a Y occlusal pattern. There is no buccal enamel extension.

The root has a moderately (c 4.6 mm) tall neck, suggestive of hypotaurodontism. The mesial root plate is vertical for most of its length, with a strong distal curvature over its apical fifth; its buccal and lingual edges are strongly tapered apically. The distal root plate is narrower and has a slight distal tilt; its apical end is also curved distally. The mesial and distal roots are about 15.2 mm long. Their apices are closed, which suggests an ontogenetic age in excess of 13.5 years (Smith 1991).

Probable Middle Stone Age attribution

E10–1–0 (unit VII). LM_2. (figure 9.1e, f)

This tooth was recovered at a depth of 174 cm below datum. It was found during section cleaning in association with quartz debitage, and may be attributed to the Middle Stone Age with some degree of certainty.

This is a slightly worn crown and complete root of a mandibular left second molar. It is interpreted as a second rather than a first molar because it lacks a hypoconulid. Four-cusped first mandibular molars are very infrequent, especially among sub-Saharan African populations (Grine 1981; Irish 1997). The crown is cracked, with transverse and longitudinal cracks meeting in the approximate centre of the talonid basin. Occlusal wear has produced small, flattened enamel facets on the buccal cusps. There is a tiny mesial ICF, and no distal ICF. The crown has four cusps; the protoconid is dominant, and the hypoconid is slightly larger than the entoconid. The protostylid, C6, C7, and distal trigonid crest are all absent, and there is no deflecting wrinkle. The protoconid contacts the entoconid by a narrow extension of its principal crest, producing an X occlusal pattern.

The root has a moderate (*c* 14.0 mm) neck, suggestive of cynodontism or perhaps hypotaurodontism. The mesial and distal roots are incompletely formed; they have a slight distal tilt and their buccal and lingual edges taper. Radicular formation is estimated to have reached just over 3/4 at time of death, which suggests an ontogenetic age of between about 11 and 12 years according to recent human standards (Smith 1991).

Middle Stone Age attribution

D9–9–4 (unit X). RM? frag., M frag. (no illustration)
These fragments were recovered at a depth of between 400 and 410 cm below datum. They were found in direct association with burnt quartz and other occupation debris. They are, therefore, certainly attributable to the Middle Stone Age and date to >170 ka BP.

RM?.
This fragment preserves part of a very heavily worn crown, most of the mesial root, and a small segment of the distal root of a permanent right mandibular molar. The crown is represented by a large, concave dentine exposure together with a small piece of enamel on the buccal side that surrounds the groove between the protoconid and hypoconid. The mesial root plate extends vertically for about 13.5 mm, and its buccal and lingual edges are strongly tapered apically. The root apex is closed. The root neck appears to have been very short (*c* 4 mm), suggestive of cynodontism.

M frag. (?RM₃).

M frag. (?RM_3).
This fragment preserves a tiny part of the crown and almost half of the root of what is possibly a third permanent molar. The root comprises three fused segments that combine to form a single, closed apical canal. The pulp chamber is exposed, and it has a 'C-shaped' transverse cross-section. The crown is represented by a small bit of enamel that surrounds a lateral fissure. The fragment is possibly from a mandibular right third molar. If this is so, then the preserved part of the crown would conform to the buccal groove between the protoconid and hypoconid. The fissure extends to the cervical margin without interruption, and there is a slight enamel extension over the root neck. The mesial root plate has a subdivided appearance with slender radicular columns separated by a narrow furrow. The distal root plate is single, and incompletely separated from the mesial by a deep furrow. The deepest furrow is along the buccal aspect of the root between the mesial and distal radicular columns. The root is some 10.8 mm long.

Discussion

The crown morphologies displayed by the Later Stone Age mandibular canine and the mandibular lateral incisor of uncertain provenance are like those that characterise recent sub-Saharan African populations (Irish 1997; Scott & Turner 1997). Thus, for example, the lingual marginal ridges are weakly developed and there is no shovelling, and the lingual tubercle is faint. Furthermore, the MD and BL diameters of these crowns (table 9.2) fall comfortably within the ranges observed for recent southern African populations, and the Mumbwa canine and incisor values are very close to the South African means recorded by Jacobson (1982).

The mandibular second molars are not unusual among recent African homologues in the considerable reduction or loss of the hypoconulid, with between 52 per cent of South African and 81 per cent of east African M₂s being 4-cusped (Chagula 1960; Grine 1981). They are also comparable to the vast majority of sub-Saharan African homologues in lacking the C6, C7, deflecting wrinkle, and distal trigonid crest (Grine 1981). While the molar of uncertain provenance (H9–1–0) is comparable to the majority of recent African homologues in possessing a Y occlusal pattern, the other crown (E10–1–0) is unusual in presenting an X pattern. The latter occurs in about 2 per cent of modern San and 9 per cent of modern South African blacks (Grine 1981).

The crown diameters of the Mumbwa mandibular second molars are larger than the averages recorded for modern South African blacks, but these dimensions fall within the ranges observed for recent samples (Jacobson 1982). In particular, the BL (11.9 mm) and especially the MD (12.5 mm) diameters of the M₂ from E10–1–0 are comparatively large by recent standards. Jacobson (1982) reported male and female BL means of 10.7 and 10.5 mm respectively, and corresponding MD means of 11.1 and 10.8 mm, and the MD diameter of the Mumbwa crown exceeds the upper limit of the recent South African female observed range (12.0 mm) recorded by Jacobson (1982). If the molar from E10–1–0 is indeed in a Middle Stone Age context, its comparably large crown is not surprising in light of the generally comparatively large sizes of other teeth that have been reported from the Middle Stone Age of sub-Saharan Africa (Grine 2000).

Table 9.3 Human postcranial remains from Mumbwa Caves

Attribution	Element	Grid Coordinate
Later Stone Age	femoral diaphysis	D12-2-8
	proximal pedal phalanx	D12-2-9
Probable Middle Stone Age	femoral diaphysis	E10-1-0
Middle Stone Age	1 proximal and 1 distal fragment of radial diaphyses	E9-3-24

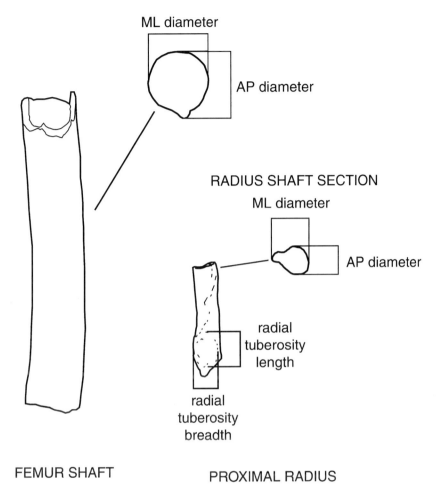

Figure 9.2 Measurements of the femora and radius.

PART II: POSTCRANIAL REMAINS

The 1993–1996 excavations at Mumbwa Caves uncovered a small sample of human postcranial remains
comprising two femoral diaphyses, a proximal pedal
phalanx, and two fragments of radial diaphyses (table
9.3). Figure 9.2 shows the principal measurements of
the femoral and radial diaphyses that were made for
descriptive and comparative purposes. The descriptions
of the remains follow below, starting with those from the
Later Stone Age and ending with the radial fragments,
which are undoubtedly from Middle Stone Age strata.

Later Stone Age attribution

D12–2–8 (unit II). Femur (figure 9.3, table 9.4)
The D12–2–8 femur was recovered from a depth of
68–73 cm below datum. This archaeological level belongs

to the Later Stone Age and dates from the early
Holocene (*c* 9 ka BP).

The specimen consists of a 126 mm-long segment of
a right femoral diaphysis from the region around and
distal to midshaft (fig. 9.3). The periosteal surface of the
bone is stained a light yellowish brown from burial in the
sediments. Fresh fractures on the lateral side of the
proximal end and the lateral quarter of the distal end
reveal white cortical bone. The nutrient foramen opens
from the shaft near the distal edge of the posterior side
of the shaft. The lateral side of the shaft shows a greater
degree of concavity anterior to the linea aspera than
does the medial side. Gnawing by rodents, as revealed by
numerous characteristic, paired grooves made by their
incisors, has destroyed extensive areas of the periosteal
surface and cortex on both sides of the linea aspera. The

Table 9.4 Measurements of the E10–1–0 and D12–2–8 femora with midshaft diameters and pilastric indices of comparative samples. The statistics reported for the comparative groups are the mean±1 standard deviation

	sex	n	AP diameter	ML diameter	AP/ML index
E10-1-0 proximal end		1	28.4	24.8	114.5
E10-1-0 distal end		1	30.1	28.5	105.6
E10-1-0 middle★		1	28.4	25.8	110.1
D12-2-8 proximal end		1	29.0	23.7	122.4
D12-2-8 distal end		1	(29.5)	23.5	(125.5)
D12-2-8 middle★		1	30.0	23.4	128.2
H. heidelbergensis and early H. sapiens					
Kabwe E 690		1	25.9	25.3	102.4
KNM-ER 999		1	37.5	34.4	109.0
Berg Aukas (distal break)		1	35.9	31.5	114.0
Neanderthal	F	3	26.8±2.8	27.8±1.5	96.4±9.6
Neanderthal	M	8	32.6±2.4	30.5±2.4	109.3±10.4
Skhul-Qafzeh	F	2			102.2 - 130.1
Skhul-Qafzeh	M	4	36.9±3.1	28.5±2.3	129.5±10.5
Gravettian	F	3	28.0±2.2	27.9±0.3	100.3±6.9
Gravettian	M	5	31.6±5.7	27.4±3.6	116.7±10.2
Khoisan	F	23	25.3±2.1	21.9±1.7	115.3±8.3
Jebel Sahaba	F	12	27.0±2.1	25.0±1.5	108.4±7.1
Zulu	F	31	27.5±2.4	24.3±1.5	113.6±10.9
African American	F	31	27.6±1.5	24.8±2.0	112.0±12.0
Aboriginal Australians	F	6	24.9±2.1	22.6±2.7	110.9±9.5
Khoisan	M	31	28.9±2.7	22.9±1.7	126.2±9.6
Jebel Sahaba	M	18	31.2±2.5	26.4±2.2	118.1±8.7
Zulu	M	31	29.7±2.5	26.8±2.0	111.0±8.3
African American	M	41	29.4±2.8	28.1±2.5	105.4±13.7
Aboriginal Australians	M	18	29.0±2.6	24.9±1.9	116.7±10.2

★ The level most likely to approximate midshaft.

femur bears a well-developed pilaster, the relief of which has been accentuated by the rodent-gnawing. The rodent-gnawing appears to be ancient in origin: all of the tooth marks have the same patina and coloration as the external surface of the bone.

Despite the presence of the rodent-gnawing, which accentuates the linea aspera, it is apparent that the D12–2–8 femur had a strongly developed pilaster, which contrasts sharply with the slight development of this feature in the E10–1–0 femur, which most likely derives from unit VII (see below). The pilastric index (a ratio calculated as 100*AP/ML diameter at midshaft) calculated at the middle (which approximates midshaft) of the D12–2–8 femur equals 128.2, which falls very close to the mean pilastric index of a sample of Khoisan males and over one standard deviation above the means of the other recent samples (table 9.4). Similarly strong development of a femoral pilaster is common among the early modern humans from Skhul and Qafzeh. In terms of its AP and ML midshaft dimensions, the D12–2–8 femur also closely approximates the means for Khoisan males, but comparable midshaft dimensions could be encountered in many of the recent comparative samples.

The D12–2–8 specimen has slightly thicker cortical bone than the E10–1–0 specimen (fig. 9.3). At its distal end, which falls close to the level of the nutrient foramen, the cortical bone of the D12–2–8 fragment measures 5.0 mm anteriorly (the measurement is somewhat diminished by abrasion of the anterior surface), 9.0 mm posteriorly, 6.6 mm medially, and 6.5 mm laterally. The same measurements at approximately the level of the nutrient foramen in the E10–1–0 femur are 5.8 mm, 8.1 mm, 7.0 mm, and 6.0 mm, respectively.

In sum, the morphology of the Mumbwa D12–2–8 femur resembles that of highly mobile recent hunter-gatherers. It bears an especially close resemblance to Khoisan males, hunter-gatherers and pastoralists from the later Holocene of the southwestern Cape of South Africa.

D12–2–9 (unit II) Proximal Pedal Phalanx (figure 9.3, table 9.5)

The D12–2–9 toe bone was recovered from early Holocene deposits containing a Later Stone Age industry. The specimen consists of a human proximal pedal phalanx of digit II–V. Most likely it belongs to digit II–IV

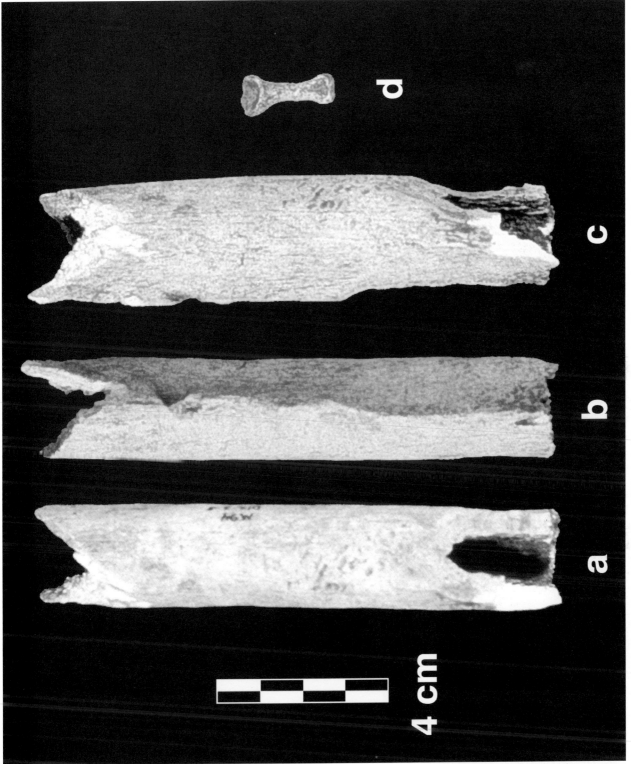

Figure 9.3 Later Stone Age postcranial remains: (a) D12–2–8 femur, anterior view; (b) posterior view; (c) lateral view; (d) D12–2–9 proximal pedal phalanx, dorsal view.

155

Table 9.5 Measurements of the D12–2–9 proximal pedal phalanx and comparative proximal pedal phalanges

Specimen	Maximum length	Proximal end: max. width	Proximal end: max. height	Distal end: max. width	Distal end: max. height	Midshaft ML diameter	Midshaft dorso-plantar diameter
Mumbwa D12–2–9	22.7	9.9	8.9	7.3	4.4	4.2	4.6
San males (n=19)[2], digit II (range of values):	26.3 (21.0– 30.0)	–	–	–	–	5.5 (4.0–7.0)	5.6 (4.0–7.0)
San males (n=12)[2], digit III (range of values):	22.6 (20.0–27.0)	–	–	–	–	5.2 (3.0–7.0)	5.2 (4.0–6.0)
San males (n=14)[2], digit IV (range of values):	21.8 (17.0–25.0)	–	–	–	–	4.9 (3.0–6.5)	4.8 (3.0–6.5)
San males (n=6)[2], digit V (range of values):	20.4 (16.0–25.0)	–	–	–	–	4.8 (3.0 -6.0)	4.5 (3.5–5.5)
San females (n=6)[2], digit II (range of values):	23.8 (18.0–28.0)	–	–	–	–	5.0 (4.5–6.0)	5.0 (4.0–7.0)
San females (n=5)[2], digit III (range of values):	21.3 (17.0–26.5)	–	–	–	–	4.6 (4.0–5.5)	4.7 (4.0–5.5)
San females (n=3)[2], digit IV (range of values):	19.1 (15.0–23.5)	–	–	–	–	4.2 (3.5–5.0)	4.5 (4.0–5.0)
San females (n=1)[2], digit V (range of values):	17.8 (13.0–21.0)	–	–	–	–	4.7 (4.0–6.0)	4.5 (4.0–5.0)
Skhul IV, digit II (left)[1]	32.0	15.0	13.0	11.0	7.0	7.5	8.0
Skhul IV, digit III (left)[1]	30.0	13.2	12.0	10.0	7.0	8.0	7.0
Skhul IV, digit IV (left)[1]	28.0	13.0	11.5	9.0	6.0	7.0	6.2
Qafzeh 6, digit II (right)[3]	25.7	–	–	–	–	–	–
Qafzeh 8, digit II (right)[3]	28.8	–	–	–	–	–	–
Qafzeh 8, digit III (right)[3]	26.3	–	–	–	–	–	–
Qafzeh 8, digit IV (right)[3]	25.2	–	–	–	–	–	–
Qafzeh 8, digit V (right)[3]	23.4	–	–	–	–	–	–
Qafzeh 9, digit II (right)[3]	28.3	–	–	–	–	–	–
Qafzeh 9, digit III (right)[3]	25.6	–	–	–	–	–	–
Qafzeh 9, digit IV (right)[3]	24.0	–	–	–	–	–	–
Tabun I, digit II (right)[1]	22.5	12.0	11.2	9.0	6.0	6.5	6.0
Tabun I, digit III (right)[1]	20.0	12.0	10.5	10.0	7.0	7.0	6.0
Tabun I, digit IV (right)[1]	(16.5)	–	10.5	(10.0)	–	6.0	5.0
Shanidar 3, digit II (right)[4]	(26.5)	15.3	14.3	–	–	9.3	7.6
Shanidar 4, digit II (left)[4]	25.0	15.4	13.2	11.0	7.0	8.7	8.1
Shanidar 4, digit III (right)[4]	23.2	12.7	11.0	10.7	8.4	8.6	8.5
Shanidar 4, digit IV (right)[4]	22.5	14.0	12.4	10.3	7.5	8.2	7.6
Shanidar 4, digit V (right)[4]	17.6	13.1	10.9	9.9	7.5	8.0	6.4
Shanidar 8, digit II (right)[4]	23.0	12.9	11.3	9.9	5.9	8.1	6.6
Shanidar 8, digit III (left)[4]	21.1	11.2	9.9	–	–	8.1	6.6
Shanidar 8, digit V (right)[4]	17.2	12.4	9.8	8.9	6.1	6.0	5.4

[1] from McCown and Keith 1939.
[2] from Kaufmann 1941.
[3] from Vandermeersch 1981.
[4] from Trinkaus 1983.

because the fifth proximal phalanx tends to be more robust and exhibits a degree of medial torsion of the shaft relative to digits II–IV. The fossil consists of a perfectly preserved bone, evenly stained reddish-brown in colour, and quite slender and gracile in overall appearance. The phalanx has a maximum length of 22.7 mm and an articular length, measured from the centre of the proximal articular surface to the middle of the distal articular surface, of 19.7 mm. Table 9.5 presents the principal measurements of the phalanx and comparative data from recent San and fossil hominins.

As the measurements in table 9.5 show, the D12–2–9 proximal pedal phalanx is a very small bone. The Mumbwa toe approximates most closely the size of San male or female proximal pedal phalanges II–IV. Its length also resembles that of small female Neanderthals such as Tabun I and Shanidar 8, but it has much smaller proximal and distal epiphyses and a far smaller midshaft transverse diameter, which are notably elevated in Neanderthals (Trinkaus & Hilton 1996). The Mumbwa and San proximal phalanges are far shorter and smaller in every other respect than the toes of the early modern humans from Qafzeh and Skhul, which reinforces the impression that the Mumbwa toe belonged to a small, Khoisan-sized individual.

Probable Middle Stone Age attribution

E10–1–0 (unit VII). Femur (figures 9.4 and 9.5, table 9.4)
A fragment of a human femoral diaphysis was recovered from square E10–1–0 at a depth of 164–174 cm below datum. The femur lay in a horizontal position on top of intact Middle Stone Age sediment. The femur and Middle Stone Age sediments were covered by section wall collapse from the adjacent section of E11. The bones in the loose sediment from the collapse lay at odd angles compared to the horizontal orientation of the femur, which suggests that the femur lay on the compact Middle Stone Age surface before the collapse piled 10 cm of sediment on top of square E10. A human left second lower molar described earlier came from the same sediment and was found during the same wall straightening exercise. It is possible that the femur and molar derive from Later Stone Age or Iron Age sediments in square E11. However, as explained in detail below, the morphology of the E10–1–0 femur differs sharply from that of the undoubted Later Stone Age femur (from D12–2–8) and in many respects resembles archaic human femora.

The E10–1–0 femur consists of a 196.4 mm long fragment of a left femoral diaphysis. The specimen was reassembled from a 160.0 mm long fragment which conjoins three additional fragments from the proximal portion of shaft (figs 9.4 and 9.5). The three small fragments may be refitted to the main fragment to make a fragment 196.4 mm in length (fig. 9.5). The breaks

between the proximal femoral fragments have off-white, cream-coloured bone exposed at each break. In contrast, the old proximal end and the lateral half of the distal end as well as periosteal and endosteal surfaces are stained reddish brown from contact with the sediment.

The shaft bears a moderately rugose linea aspera, 4.8 mm in width, but the shaft does not have a well-developed pilaster. The shaft is slightly bowed laterally, with a concave medial border and a faintly convex lateral border. The cross-section of the diaphysis is roughly circular in shape with slightly higher antero-posterior (AP) than medio-lateral (ML) diameters throughout its length. At the proximal end of the fragment, the shaft exhibits a pronounced lateral flare for a third trochanter at the attachment site of the *gluteus maximus*. The anterior surface of the most proximal 40 mm of the shaft is transversely flattened and has a shallow vertical sulcus that separates the lateral swelling for the third trochanter from the rest of the shaft. The nutrient foramen may be observed within the posterior cortex at the level of the proximal break. The external opening for the nutrient foramen lies 48.3 mm from the most proximal point on the fragment. The cortical bone thickness at the proximal end of the main fragment measures 5.8 mm anteriorly, 8.1 mm posteriorly, 7.0 mm medially, and 6.0 mm laterally. The cortex thins considerably from proximal to distal, so that at the distal end of the main, 160 mm long fragment of the shaft, it measures 3.4 mm anteriorly, 5.3 mm posteriorly, 4.6 mm medially, and 4.3 mm laterally. Table 9.4 lists the antero-posterior (AP) and medio-lateral (ML) dimensions of the femur at its middle, proximal, and distal ends.

Radiographs show that the cortical thickness of the E10–1–0 femur is considerably lower than that of the D12–2–8 Later Stone Age (fig. 9.3). If the E10–1–0 femur derives from the Middle Stone Age, the observation that it has relatively thin cortical bone is rather anomalous: the other known Early Stone Age and Middle Stone Age postcranial remains from southern Africa have notably thick cortical bone (Kennedy 1984; Stringer 1986; Grine et al 1995; Churchill et al 1996; Pearson and Grine 1996, 1997).

FUNCTIONAL AND PHYLOGENETIC ASSESSMENT

Phylogenetic and functional assessments of the femoral diaphysis must centre around the shape of diaphyseal cross-section. The cross-sectional shape of a femoral diaphysis provides clues regarding phylogenetic affinities, but these hints should be viewed with caution because the shape of a femoral cross-section is highly plastic with regard to activity. Trinkaus (1976), building upon earlier observations by Boule (1911–1913), Weidenreich (1941), Day (1971), and other authors, described the general pattern of the evolution of the shape of the femoral diaphysis within the genus *Homo*.

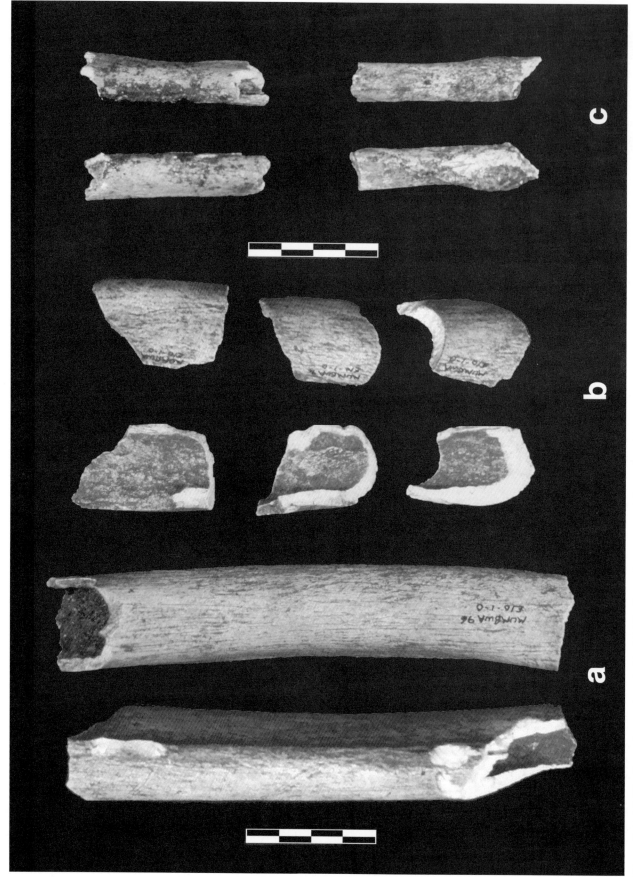

Figure 9.4 Middle Stone Age and probable Middle Stone Age postcranial remains: (a) main fragment of the E10–1–0 femur, posterior and anterior views; (b) additional fragments of the E10–1–0 femur, endosteal and periosteal views; (c) E9–3–24 radius fragments, anterior (left) and posterior (right) views.

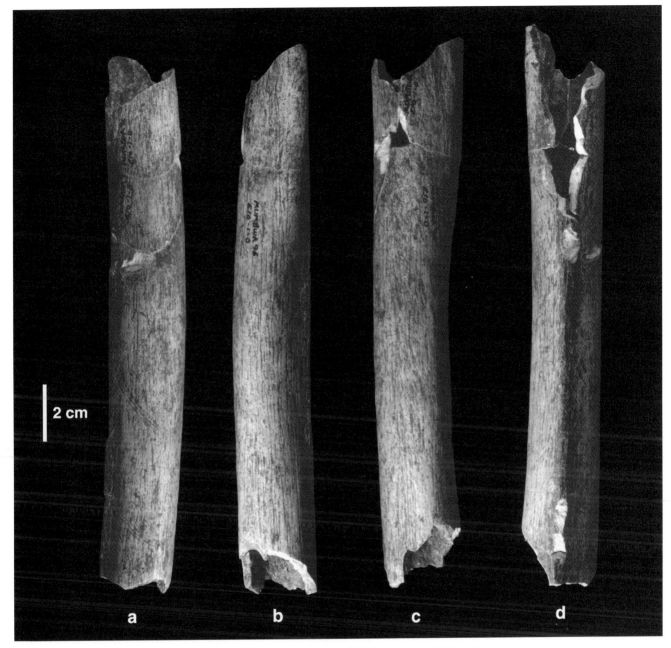

Figure 9.5 The E10–1–0 femur: (a) medial view; (b) lateral view; (c) anterior view; (d) posterior view.

Early examples of the taxon such as the *Homo ergaster* and *Homo erectus* femora from East Africa, China, and Java tend to have an elliptical midshaft section that has its long axis aligned medio-laterally (ML) so that the ML diameter of the shaft is longer than the antero-posterior (AP) diameter and lack the development of a femoral pilaster. Neanderthals and other archaic hominins from the Middle-Later Pleistocene of Europe and Africa tend to have approximately equal AP and ML midshaft diameters but lack a distinct femoral pilaster. Only with the advent of early modern humans, especially those from the sites of Skhul and Qafzeh, do hominins appear

that have a well-developed pilaster and an AP midshaft diameter greatly exceeding the ML diameter (Trinkaus 1976, 1992). Early Upper Palaeolithic femora resemble the Skhul–Qafzeh hominins in having a high ratio of midshaft AP relative to ML diameter (ie, they share an elevated pilastric index). However, recent humans have quite variable values for the pilastric index.

There is considerable evidence that the variation in the pilastric index among groups of recent humans corresponds to differences in habitual activity. Ruff (1987) noted that, among modern humans, the pilastric index tends to be sexually dimorphic in hunter-gatherer and horticultural populations but not in industrialised populations. In particular, Ruff documented that hunter-gatherers have an exaggerated AP relative to ML midshaft diameter, and that this tends to be more pronounced in males than females. In industrialised populations, on the other hand, males and females both tend to have almost equal AP and ML midshaft diameters. Ruff (1987) explained these differences in the shape of femoral midshaft sections as a consequence of differences in mobility and the need to add AP reinforcement to the femoral shaft to compensate for greater AP stresses applied to the shaft during the more active locomotor activities of hunter-gatherers. Applying Ruff's observation to earlier Pleistocene hominins entails greater difficulties because the shaft shapes of these hominins often do not correspond to the morphology observed in recent hunter-gatherers.

Most authorities agree that *Homo ergaster, Homo erectus,* Neanderthals, and other Middle Pleistocene hominins led active and probably highly mobile lives, so the observation that they have pilastric indices that resemble those of the most sedentary modern humans has proved difficult to explain. Certainly the cortical thickness and second moments of area of the femoral shafts of early *Homo* are greatly elevated in comparison to modern, sedentary *Homo sapiens* (Ruff et al 1993). The best working hypothesis for the apparent contradiction is that Neanderthals may have required greater ML reinforcement of the femoral midshaft shaft to compensate for added ML bending moments applied to their femora by their wide hips and heavy bodies (Ruff 1995; Trinkaus & Ruff 1999). Ruff (1995) proposed that the striking medial buttressing of *H. ergaster* and *H. erectus* femoral shafts stemmed from a different mechanical configuration of the hip that imposed greater ML bending moments upon the femur. Ruff (1995) proposed that expansion of neonatal brain size and birth canal diameters among the Middle Pleistocene hominins began gradually to alter the mechanical configuration inherited from *H. erectus,* and that these alterations diminished the ML bending moments acting on the femoral midshaft. Alternatively, the difference in midshaft cross-sectional shapes between Neanderthals and early modern humans such as the fossils from Qafzeh and Skhul could have stemmed directly from differences in habitual activities or a combination of differences in activities (eg, Lieberman 1993, 1998; Lieberman and Shea 1994) and body proportions including pelvic breadth (Trinkaus & Ruff 1999).

The recent descriptions (Trinkaus et al 1998, 1999) of the right proximal femur from the Saint Césaire Neanderthal, associated with an Upper Palaeolithic (Châtelperronian) industry, challenge the notion that body proportions alone may account for the low pilastric indices of Neanderthals. Saint-Césaire's femur, while lacking a true pilaster, has an elevated ratio of AP to ML second moment of area at midshaft (as well as its ratio of AP to ML midshaft diameters) in comparison to other Neanderthals but not relative to Upper Palaeolithic modern humans (Trinkaus et al 1998, 1999). Trinkaus and colleagues (1998, 1999) argue that the specimen's femoral morphology resulted from an increased level of mobility that resembled that of Upper Palaeolithic modern humans rather than earlier Neanderthals. Such an interpretation would require that earlier Neanderthals were, in fact, not very mobile, which would be surprising.

Regardless of the controversy surrounding the causal factors underlying the development of the cross-sectional shape of Neanderthal femora, it remains true that, at least until the Neolithic, femoral cross-sectional shapes of *Homo* roughly correspond to phylogenetic groups. Within this context, the shape of the Mumbwa E10–1–0 femoral shaft is quite interesting. At the middle of the fragment, the level that most closely approximates midshaft, the ratio of the AP to ML diameter is 110.1 (table 9.4). This ratio falls above that of most of the Neanderthals listed by Trinkaus (1976) and approximates a more modern condition. Specifically, the pilastric index of the Mumbwa E10–1–0 femur closely resembles that of KNM-ER 999, a massive specimen from the Chari or Galana Boi Member of the Koobi Fora Formation, Kenya (Day and Leakey 1974; Trinkaus 1993). Bräuer et al (1997) report a direct gamma-ray spectrometry U-Th date for the KNM-ER 999 femur of 272 (+∞, –113) ka BP and a U–Pa age of >180 ka BP. The KNM-ER 999 femur, therefore, falls within roughly the same period as, or slightly before, the Mumbwa Middle Stone Age human remains from unit VII.

KNM-ER 999 resembles early modern femora in its moderately elevated pilastric index and high neck-shaft angle (Trinkaus, 1993) as well as the fact that its point of minimum circumference falls proximally on its shaft rather than distally as in *H. erectus* (Day and Leakey, 1974). Although the KNM-ER 999 and Mumbwa E10–1–0 femora have very similar pilastric indices, the Mumbwa femur has much smaller midshaft dimensions than KNM-ER 999 (table 9.4), and clearly derived from a smaller individual.

SCRATCH MARKS

A striking and unusual feature of the E10–1–0 femur is the presence of two clearly visible scratches running down the shaft (posterior and superior to anterior and inferior) along the medial side of the shaft (fig 9.6). Each mark consists of a very shallow depression measuring 2.9 mm in width with a slightly more deeply incised groove running down the centre. The superior mark starts at the linea aspera and runs to the ridge defining the medial buttress of the shaft. The superior mark measures 28.1 mm in length. The lower mark also starts at the linea

Figure 9.6 Scratch marks on the E10–1–0 femur.

aspera and runs to the medial buttress, but measures only 19.8 mm in length. The scratch marks bear the same patina from contact with the soil as the rest of the external surface of the bone and appear to be ancient in origin. The marks follow an approximately parallel course, but appear to diverge slightly proximally. They are separated by a perpendicular distance of 34 mm.

The shapes of the scratch marks do not correspond either to the usual morphology of carnivore tooth-marks or to the scratches commonly made by stone tools (Andrews pers comm; Potts & Shipman 1981). The origin of the marks, therefore, remains a mystery. They do not appear to have been made by a sharp stone tool and their orientation, which would run transversely through the bellies of the *vastus lateralis* and *vastus intermedius*, is poorly suited to fillet a large amount of muscle from the bone. Thus the marks do not provide evidence of the sort of intentional defleshing or butchering by other humans that White (1987) described for many of the Klasies River Mouth remains.

Middle Stone Age attribution

E9–3–24 (unit XII). Radius fragments (figure 9.4, table 9.6)
The E9–3–24 radius fragments were found at a depth of 540 cm below datum. The base of the relatively sterile red clay occurs 363 cm below datum and is dated to 177±22 ka BP. The radius fragments lay approximately 187 cm below the base of the red clay and are therefore dated between *c* 177 and 240 ka BP (see page 71), the approximate earliest date for occupation of the site. The equivalent layer excavated in 1996 in square E9 (E9–4–3) and D9 (D9–10–7/8) contained discrete clusters of quartz artefacts and patches of burnt stone. Two human radial fragments were recovered from the E9–3–24 level approximately 20 cm from the edge of Dart's pit. Thus the radius fragments and human teeth clearly derive from the early part of the Middle Stone Age.

Both radial fragments are lightly mineralised and have off-white, cream coloured cortical bone wherever the cortex is exposed by fresh breaks or other recent damage to their surface. The periosteal and endosteal surfaces of the bones are stained a light reddish-brown and bear dark grey to black stained patches. The dark patches are particularly frequent on the lateral aspect of the distal fragment and the proximal part of the dorsal side of the shaft of the proximal fragment. Manganese staining of bone is common in the lower units. On the proximal radial fragment, the proximal break appears to be fresh and lacks any stain imparted from contact with sediment whereas the distal break appears to be old. Both breaks on the distal fragment appear to be recent in origin.

The first specimen consists of a proximal fragment of a right radius. The radius is broken proximally at the junction between the neck and the radial tuberosity and

Table 9.6 Measurements of the Mumbwa radial fragments and midshaft dimensions of comparative samples. The mean±one standard deviation is given for samples of three or larger, the range is presented for samples of two. A number in parentheses following the standard deviation or range indicates the sample size if it differs from the sample size indicated on the left

Specimen	ML diameter	AP diameter	AP/ML index	Radial tuberosity length	Radial tuberosity breadth	Maximum radius length
Mumbwa proximal fragment, distal break	12.7	10.7	84.3	(22.0)	(14.0)	–
Mumbwa distal fragment, distal end	14.9	11.5	77.2	–	–	–
Mumbwa distal fragment, middle	13.7	11.8	86.1	–	–	–
Mumbwa distal fragment, proximal end*	14.1	12.2	86.5	–	–	–
Cave of Hearths[†1,2]	15.1	11.3	74.8	25.3	12.7	–
Omo 1 (cast, left side)[2]	14.0	12.4	88.6	23.5	15.3	–
KRM 27889[1]	–	–	–	21.5	14.2	–
Skhul II (right side)[2]	–	–	–	22.1	13.0	–
Skhul IV (left side)[2]	15.1	13.1	86.8	(30.0)	–	(272.5)
Skhul V (right side)[2]	13.8	11.7	84.8	25.1	17.5	(257)
Skhul VII (left side)[2]	10.2	9.3	91.2	26.2	10.8	–
Qafzeh 9 (right side)[2]	15.1	11.5	76.2	22.3	(14.3)	254
Atapuerca ATD6-43 (left side)[3]	13.0	12.6	96.9	–	–	(257.0)
Atapuerca SH (n=3)[3]	13.0±1.1	11.0±1.7	84.3±5.8	–	–	233.3±7.5
Neanderthal females (n=4)[2]	13.1±1.7	9.4±0.4	72.3±7.5	22.6±3.4	12.1±1.4	215.5–222.0 (2)
Neanderthal males (n=9)[2]	15.0±1.0	11.1±0.8	74.4±3.8	26.7±5.6 (8)	14.7±1.7	239.9±11.2 (6)
Khoisan females (n=21)	11.9±1.0	9.0±0.8	76.0±6.0	19.5±2.4	10.2±1.3	217.0±10.5
Zulu females (n=30)	13.5±1.2	10.4±0.6	77.2±4.4	21.7±2.1	12.3±1.5	233.4±10.3
African American females (n=31)	15.0±1.5	10.6±0.7	71.3±7.0	23.3±2.2	13.0±1.4	240.1±10.2
Australian females (n=7)	12.8±1.3	9.5±0.8	74.8±8.7	18.6±0.9	12.6±0.8	232.0±13.8
Khoisan males (n=25)	12.6±1.7	9.9±1.1	79.4±6.5	20.1±2.1	10.9±1.5	228.3±13.6
Zulu males (n=31)	15.9±1.8	12.2±1.1	77.7±7.8	23.4±2.3	14.0±1.6	258.1±15.3
African American males (n=41)	17.0±2.1	12.5±1.0	74.0±6.5	23.6±2.3	14.2±2.0	260.4±16.5
Australian males (n=17)	16.0±1.8	11.6±0.7	73.2±5.4	22.6±2.1	15.9±1.6	250.0±14.7

* Closest to the midshaft level.

[†] 'Midshaft' measurements are of the distal end of the fragment which is proximal to midshaft.

[1] Data from Pearson and Grine 1997.

[2] Data from Pearson 1997.

[3] Data from Carretero et al 1999. SH=Sima de los Huesos.

distally approximately 26 mm inferior to the radial tuberosity. The fragment measures 58.6 mm in length. The radial tuberosity is badly abraded by a series of irregularly shaped pits, especially along its medial side. The abrasion and breakage preclude accurate measurement of the radial tuberosity, but its approximate dimensions are 22 mm in length and 14 mm in breadth. In its preserved portions, the proximal radial fragment is comparable in size to the Klasies River Mouth (KRM) 27889 left proximal radius (Singer & Wymer 1982;

Pearson & Grine 1997) with the exception that the distal end of the neck may be somewhat thicker in the KRM specimen. Singer and Wymer (1982:146) stated that the KRM radius 'is suggestive of a small, lightly built individual.' The same appears to be true of the Mumbwa E9–3–24 proximal radial fragment.

The distal end of the radial tuberosity gives rise to a weakly developed anterior oblique line. A rounded buttress projects from the shaft medially in the distal third of the fragment, indicating the position of the interosseous margin. The damaged radial tuberosity faces antero-medially relative to the interosseous border. Trinkaus and Churchill (1988) observed that the orientation of the radial tuberosity tends to distinguish Neanderthals from modern humans. Most Neanderthals have a more medially orientated radial tuberosity than modern humans and the Mumbwa E9–3–24 proximal radial fragment. However, Trinkaus and Churchill (1988) found that 11.7 per cent (2 of 17) of Neanderthals had an antero-medially facing radial tubersoity like the Mumbwa radius and the majority of modern humans and that between 8.0 per cent and 11.2 per cent of recent humans had a medially facing radial tuberosity like the majority of Neanderthals. The feature, therefore, has taxonomic valence, but it should be assessed in terms of frequencies, which renders taxonomic assessments based on single specimens difficult. Nevertheless, the Cave of Hearths radius, which derives from either the Acheulian or the Middle Stone Age (Tobias 1971), also has an antero-medially facing radial tuberosity (Pearson & Grine 1997). Given the shared radial tuberosity orientation of the Mumbwa and Cave of Hearths radii, it is possible that this was the common form of the trait among African hominins in the late Acheulian and early Middle Stone Age and that this morphology was conserved in modern humans.

Such an interpretation does not settle the issue of whether the prevalence of medially-orientated radial tuberosity among Neanderthals represents the primitive condition for the common ancestor of Neanderthals and modern humans or if the Neanderthal condition is the derived one. Trinkaus and Churchill (1988) examined the proximal radii of fossil hominins and found that AL 288–1, KNM-ER 1500, and OH 62 all had a medially-orientated tuberosity. Thus, they reasoned the primitive hominin condition was probably a medial orientation and that most Neanderthals conserved this morphology. However, Carretero et al (1999) report that in the three radii from the c 300 ka-old hominins from Atapuerca Sima de los Huesos in which the orientation of the radial tubersoity can be observed, it faces antero-medially. In addition, Carretero et al (1999) note that the ATD6–43 radius from the c 800 ka-old Gran Dolina site at Atapuerca also has an antero–medially facing radial tuberosity. Given this prevalence of antero–medially facing radial tuberosities in potential ancestors of the Neanderthals (especially the Sima de los Huesos sample), it is possible that the common ancestor of Neanderthals and modern humans (a species commonly called *Homo heidelbergensis* (Rightmire 1996)) most often had an antero–medially facing radial tuberosity and that the Neanderthal condition represents a reversal (Carretero et al 1999).

Clearly, more discoveries of fossil radii will be needed to resolve the polarity of radial tuberosity orientation,

but at a minimum, the antero-medial orientation of the Mumbwa E9–3–24 radial tuberosity distinguishes it from the great majority of Neanderthals. Whether the orientation is a shared, derived trait that links the Mumbwa radius with modern humans is more debatable given the possibility that this may be the plesiomorphic condition characteristic of *H. heidelbergensis*.

The distal radial fragment appears to be approximately around the level just distal to mid-shaft and has a teardrop shaped cross-section throughout its length. It is difficult to determine from which side the fragment derives. Radial shafts tend to be gently convex dorsally and ventrally flat or slightly concave, with a slight sulcus separating the main part of the shaft from the interosseous crest. The Mumbwa distal radial fragment does not display a marked difference in the curvature of its dorsal and ventral sides. One side has a slight concavity, which suggests that it is ventral. If this interpretation is correct, the fragment comes from a left radius and cannot be part of the same bone as the proximal radial fragment. Both fragments agree in terms of size, however, and it is conceivable that they derived from a single individual. The distal radial fragment measures 58.5 mm in length.

The proximal end of the fragment lies closer to the midshaft level because the cortical bone thins considerably in the distal portion of the fragment. At the level of the proximal break, the thickness of the cortical bone measures 3.3 mm anteriorly, 4.4 mm posteriorly (the fractured edge is recessed posteriorly and difficult to measure), 5.6 mm medially, and 3.4 mm laterally. At the distal break, the cortical bone measures 1.9 mm anteriorly, 2.8 mm posteriorly, 2.2 mm medially, and 2.4 mm laterally. Measurements of the AP and ML dimensions of the shaft are presented in table 9.6. There is no trace of a muscle impression for the insertion of the *pronator teres*, which should fall approximately at mid-shaft on the lateral aspect of the diaphysis.

DISCUSSION AND CONCLUSIONS

The human fossil remains from the 1993–1996 excavations of Mumbwa Caves provide new information regarding hominin morphology in the Middle Stone Age of southern Africa and document the presence of Khoisan-sized individuals in central Zambia in association with Later Stone Age industries.

The teeth that derive from or possibly derive from (ie, the E10–1–0 LM₂) the Middle Stone Age levels of Mumbwa Caves display moderately enlarged crowns relative to recent southern African populations. In addition, their crown morphology resembles the dentitions of recent sub-Saharan Africans (Irish 1997; Scott & Turner 1997) with the exception of the X occlusal pattern of the E10–1–0 molar. Human teeth from other Middle Stone Age sites often present a similar combination of moderately enlarged bucco-lingual and mesio-distal diameters, with most crown morphology similar to recent sub-Saharan Africans (which, however, is the plesiomorphic condition for modern humans (Grine 2000)), and a few crown variants that are rare in recent sub-Saharan populations (Grine & Klein 1985; Grine et al 1991; McCrossin 1992; Grine 2000). Some Middle Stone Age teeth such as the second molars from Mumba Cave, Tanzania (Bräuer and Mehlman 1988) and the teeth of the KRM 16425 mandible (Singer & Wymer 1982; Rightmire & Deacon 1991) depart from this general pattern, however, in having diminutive crown dimensions – smaller than the teeth of most recent sub-Saharan Africans.

In both size and morphology, the postcranial remains from the early Holocene Later Stone Age strata of Mumbwa Caves resemble the bones of Khoisan hunter gatherers and pastoralists of the western Cape of South Africa. The well-developed pilaster of the Later Stone Age femur (D12–2–8) clearly aligns the specimen with the Khoisan, especially Khoisan males, and contrasts with the much less pronounced pilaster of the E10–1–0 femur, which probably derives from the Middle Stone Age.

The postcranial remains from Mumbwa attributed to, or probably attributable to, the Middle Stone Age present several interesting features. The probable Middle Stone Age E10–1–0 femoral shaft has a moderate degree of enlargement of its midshaft AP diameter relative to ML diameter. The resulting moderately elevated pilastric index resembles those of the Middle Pleistocene Kabwe and KNM-ER 999 femora and serves to distinguish all of these femora from those attributed to *H. erectus* (Day 1971). However, the Mumbwa E10–1–0 femur derives from a much smaller individual than the KNM-ER 999 or Kabwe specimens.

The E9–3–24 Middle Stone Age radial fragments from Mumbwa also have moderate to small dimensions which suggest a fairly small individual by modern standards. The proximal fragment's radial tuberosity faces antero-medially, an orientation that it shares with most modern humans (Trinkaus & Churchill 1988), the Early Stone Age or Middle Stone Age Cave of Hearths radius (Pearson & Grine 1997), and the *H. antecessor* and *H. heidelbergensis* or early *H. neanderthalensis* radii from Atapuerca (Carretero et al 1999). Neanderthals and australopithecines differ from this morphology in most commonly possessing a medially-facing radial tuberosity. Given the new evidence from Mumbwa and Atapuerca, it now seems probable that the common ancestors of modern humans and Neanderthals had developed a high frequency of antero-medially facing radial tuberosities and that most modern humans retained this morphology while most Neanderthals reverted to the plesiomorphic condition.

ACKNOWLEDGEMENTS

Thanks to Andy Griner, University of New Mexico (UNM) Hospital for making the radiographs, Tom Estenson (UNM) for arranging the use of hospital facilities, Bob Leonard (UNM) for digital photographs of scratch marks, Alison Brooks (George Washington University) for advice, and Luci Betti (SUNY Stony Brook) for composing figure 9.1. Peter Andrews graciously examined the unusual scratch marks on the E10–1–0 femur in figure 9.6 and reported that they did not appear to him to be cut or tooth marks. Julie Angel took the photographs in figure 9.5.

10 Twin Rivers, excavation and behavioural record

L Barham, MJ Simms, M Gilmour and N Debenham

The hilltop site at Twin Rivers farm (15°31′S; 28°11′E) lies 150 km to the southeast of Mumbwa Caves (fig. 10.1). The site was extensively excavated in the mid-1950s and a typologically early Middle Stone Age assemblage was reported in association with faunal remains preserved in breccia (Clark 1971). Radiocarbon dates on the breccia placed the assemblage in a time range between 23 and >33 ka BP. In the context of the time, the date for Twin Rivers fell within the accepted chronology of the Midde Stone Age. By the early 1980s however, the site appeared to be too young against the background of emerging dates for a Last Interglacial age of the earliest phases of the Middle Stone Age in southern Africa (Volman 1984:185). The dating revolution of the 1970s-1980s (chapter 2) had broken the radiocarbon barrier and previously reported finite dates were now considered to be beyond the range of the technique. The site was revisited in the course of the Mumbwa Caves project in 1995 and samples of speleothem (travertine) were collected from exposed sections for uranium-series dating. The results placed the site in the late Middle Pleistocene at approximately 230,000 BP

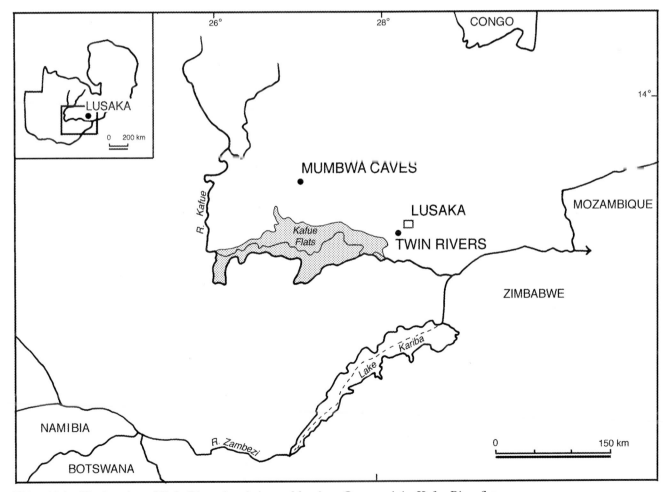

Figure 10.1   The location of Twin Rivers in relation to Mumbwa Caves and the Kafue River flats.

(Barham & Smart 1996). The analysis of speleothem collected in 1996 confirmed the great antiquity of the site and samples of pigment were also reported (Barham 1998). This combination of new behavioural data with the known preservation of bone in now datable contexts prompted the re-excavation of the site in 1999. The excavation was an opportunity to extend the Middle Stone Age sequence beyond the age range of the Mumbwa sequence and to provide another set of data for comparison. The results of the archaeological and geological analyses are reported here and the faunal remains are discussed separately in chapter 11.

HISTORY OF EXCAVATION

The pre- and post-World War II discoveries in South Africa of early hominid remains preserved in limestone breccias (Gowlett 1990) brought renewed interest in the site of Twin Rivers. A long breccia-filled fissure had been noted near the top of the hill in 1939, and in 1953 KP Oakley of the British Museum and JD Clark undertook a preliminary assessment of the potential of the deposit as a source of more early hominid material (Oakley 1954). Bone had been observed in breccia exposed in a sinkhole and further up the hill. Two breccias were recognised, one thought to be Early Pleistocene in age with pebble tools and the other somewhat later with Middle Stone Age artefacts. Teilhard de Chardin visited the site later that year and confirmed the consensus that extensive excavation could yield important fossil material and stone artefacts.

Excavation began in 1954 (April–June) with the selection of five breccia-bearing areas for testing. The areas, labelled A–E Blocks, ran from below the top of the hill and down the western flank along the course of the main fissure. A sixth area, F Block, was excavated on the top of the hill in 1956. Controlled blasting was necessary in all but one area given the hardness of the breccia. In brief, the two-phase theory of breccia formation was abandoned, as it became clear that a single industry and faunal assemblage was represented in all the deposits. F Block provided the largest collection of artefacts and the clearest evidence that the assemblage was typologically early in the Middle Stone Age sequence. A Block, the area that would be the focus of the 1999 excavation, contained few diagnostic artefacts. The assemblage as a whole was largely characterised by quartz flake tools but also by a small but typologically significant proportion of heavy-duty tools that included picks, core axes, spheroids, grindstones and spear-shaped bifaces or lanceolates. In the first published description of the Twin Rivers material (Clark 1971), typological comparisons were made with the Lupemban industry represented at Kalambo Falls in northern Zambia.

That link has since been strengthened with the publication of a full report and interpretation of the site

(Clark & Brown in press). The contents of the individual excavation areas are described in detail and the Lupemban attribution explained. The labelling of two of the excavation units has changed in the most recent report with A and C Blocks now transposed in contrast with the designations in Clark 1971:fig. 2. In the discussions that follow, the original locations are retained for the sake of consistency because they were used in the field in 1995–6, in 1999 and they appear in subsequent publications (Barham & Smart 1996; Barham 1998).

A brief trip to Twin Rivers from Mumbwa in 1995 took place with the express purpose of locating *in situ* speleothem for dating. Uranium-series as a technique of dating carbonates and other materials had developed since the 1970s and the original report illustrated lenses of speleothem interstratified with the breccia in F Block (Clark 1971:fig. 3). Remnants of breccia and speleothem were attached to the large dolomite boulders that framed the 1956 trench and a sample was taken from near the top to give a minimum age for the deposits. The resulting uranium series date of $230\pm35/28$ ka BP ($^{230}Th/^{234}U$) transformed the significance of the site (Barham & Smart 1996). Twin Rivers became one of only a handful of Middle Stone Age assemblages isotopically dated to the Middle Pleistocene (cf McBrearty et al 1996) and it now provided a reference date for the Lupemban at Kalambo Falls and for central Africa as a whole.

Given the apparent importance of the site, confirmation of the age was needed and in 1996 another collection of speleothem was made in F Block and from A Block located just below the crest of the hill (fig. 10.2). The resulting mass spectrometric date on the F Block speleothem was slightly younger at 195 ± 19 ka BP (2 sigma), but within the error margin of the conventional U-series age (Barham 1998). A weathered and detritally contaminated piece of speleothem from the top of A Block gave an unexpectedly early age of >350 ka BP. If correct, the date indicated that the deposits excavated here in 1954 were close to the age limits of the dating technique. This seemed to be too early an age for the flake technology characteristic of the Middle Stone Age. The Early to Middle Stone Age transition was not thought to have taken place much before 200 ka BP (Clark 1988). Further excavation and dating of the A Block deposits was now necessary to resolve this issue. Also in need of resolution was the extent of pigment use at Twin Rivers. Three rounded pieces of hematite had been found in a pocket of partially dissolved breccia in A Block with large quartz flakes and cores. More pieces were visible in the surviving sections. A weathered lump of limonite was recovered from beneath the basal stalagmite layer in F Block in association with a quartzite spheroid. The presence of what appeared to be pigment came as a surprise given the early age of both deposits. A sample of four was too small to conclude that pigment

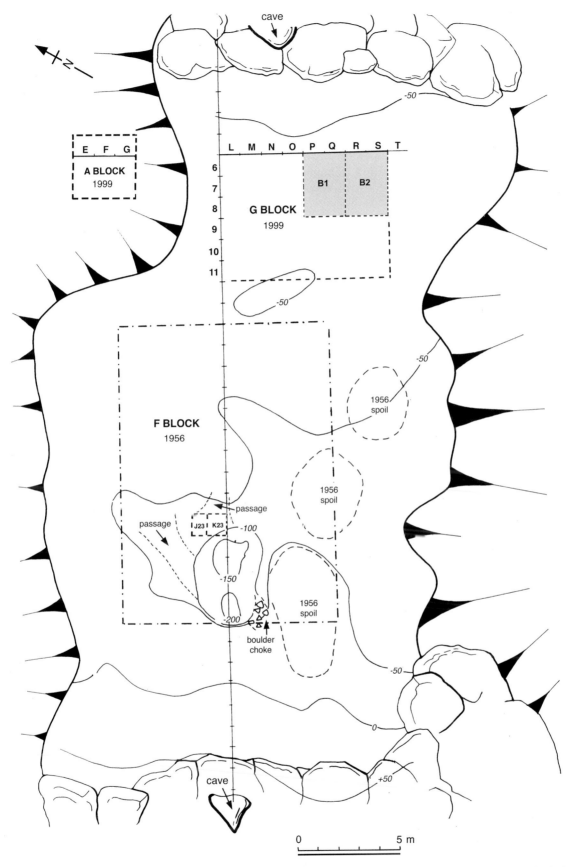

Figure 10.2   Site plan of Twin Rivers showing the location of A, F and G Blocks and the topography of the central platform.

use was a consistent element of the behavioural record at Twin Rivers.

Further excavation was planned for Twin Rivers in 1999 with the objectives of collecting more speleothem for dating, especially from A Block, and of enlarging the artefact sample from A Block to determine its typological affinity. The recovery of more pigment was anticipated, as was the recovery of faunal remains. A geological survey of the site and the surrounding landscape was also planned with the aims of reconstructing the formation of the caves and of locating potential sources of lithic raw materials accessible to the occupants of Twin Rivers.

THE 1999 EXCAVATIONS

Excavations began on 10 July with a team of four archaeologists, one geologist and one environmental archaeologist. The site was cleared of vegetation and a grid system of 1 m squares was established which extended across the flat hilltop to incorporate F Block and down the western side to encompass A Block. An area of undisturbed surface deposits was located north of F Block and designated G Block (fig. 10.2).

In F Block, a small area of intact cave sediments (1.5×1×0.30 m) was found inside a narrow cave passage with grid co-ordinates J23 and K23 (fig. 10.3). Approximately 0.45 cubic metres of sediment were

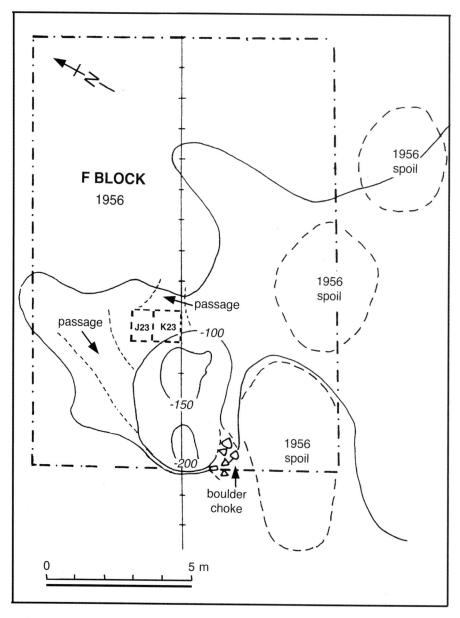

Figure 10.3   Plan of F Block showing the 1999 excavations (J23, K23) in relation to the former cave passages.

excavated. The surviving intact deposits in A Block were restricted to the irregular margins of the 1954 excavation and accorded with grid squares E4, E5, E6, E7, F4, F5, G4 and G5. In G Block, an area 4×3 m (squares P6–S6) was subdivided into two rectangles 2×3 m each and labelled B1 and B2. The excavations in all three blocks took place in arbitrary 10 cm levels in the absence of natural stratigraphic units.

In F Block, the yellowish red (5YR 4/6) sandy deposit had a maximum depth of 30 cm in J23 and minimum depth of 15 cm in K23 above bedrock (fig. 10.4a,b). A 5–8 cm thick layer of ferro-manganese concretion sealed the lower 8–10 cm of sediment and contributed to the preservation of bone, in particular microfauna.

The A Block deposits comprised two archaeological units: pink breccia and reddish brown (5YR 4/4) sandy sediment. The sediment would be the focus of the excavation (fig. 10.5). It reached a depth of 60 cm, a width of 30 cm and a maximum continuous length of 480 cm all contained within a wedge-shaped cavity formed by the dolomite cave walls (to the west and north) and by an inner rim of breccia (fig. 10.6). Approximately 0.58 cubic metres of loose sediment were excavated which effectively removed all remaining deposit from A Block.

In G Block, the dark reddish brown (5YR 3/4) sandy sediment reached a maximum depth of 80 cm. At approximately 40–70 cm below datum, the area of deposit in B1 and B2 was confined within a near linear grike (fissure formed by solution) that extended across both units and which reached a minimum width of 20 cm near bedrock (fig. 10.7a,b). No breccia was found in G Block in contrast to the results of the 1956 excavation in adjacent F Block.

The excavation strategy of A Block initially included the controlled removal of blocks of breccia for gradual dissolution in dilute hydrochloric acid. In practice, the use of acid baths proved impractical and the breccia was left largely intact. Samples of breccia were subjected to increasing strengths of acid (4–10 per cent) in an attempt to dissolve the matrix and remove the encased bone and stone artefacts. All visible bone was coated with a paraloid and acetone solution to minimise the corrosive effects of the acid. The breccia resisted even the highest concentrations of acid which were applied at maximum intervals of eight hours over a period of four weeks. The 10 per cent acid concentration also degraded the surface of quartz artefacts and the decision was made to abandon acid baths in the field. Controlled laboratory conditions will be needed if the remaining breccia in A Block is to be dissolved systematically.

All excavated sediment in A Block was sieved through a 2 mm mesh and in squares J23 and K23 a 0.5 mm fabric mesh was used to maximise the recovery of micro-

fauna. A preliminary washing and sorting of artefacts took place at the base camp.

Site formation

MJ Simms and L Barham

The hilltop at Twin Rivers (fig. 10.8) overlooks the floodplain of the Kafue River to the south and east and the Lusaka dolomite plateau to the west and north. The hill itself is an extension of the plateau and straddles the ecotone between the plateau woodlands and the edaphic grasslands of the floodplain (Clark 1971). Karst features have developed on the crest and sides of the hill (Kaiser et al 1998) including the known fissures and cave passages. The main area of archaeological interest is the central platform on the summit and its northwestern slopes where unroofed sections of cave passages have been previously excavated (F and A Blocks respectively). Exposed on the slopes to the north and east of the summit are truncated phreatic cave passages that formed under hydrological conditions very different from the present. The water table must have been significantly higher and the regional land surface is estimated to have been at least 100 m above that of today. Several millions of years of denudation are needed to account for the change in relief. The lowering of the surface of the hill by dissolution of the dolomite will have concentrated sediment and artefacts into solutional fissures as is the case with G Block (B1 and B2 grike).

The cave passages in F and A Blocks are phreatic in origin. F Block preserves a T-shaped fragment of a cave network with the stem of the 'T' descending as a dip tube eastwards from a horizontal north–south cross passage (fig. 10.9). The excavations in J23–K23 sampled the dip tube deposits. The passage is blocked at its southern end by a boulder choke cemented into a breccia. Flowstone (speleothem) and a coarse breccia containing quartz artefacts and bone, line parts of the cross passage that is largely filled with remnant blocks of dolomite from the collapse of the roof. Much of the artefact-bearing breccia excavated in 1956 came from this passage. The roof collapse occurred as a consequence of the gradual lowering of the hill surface by solutional weathering.

The dip tube excavated in J23/K23 contains unconsolidated sediment protected by the intact phreatic passage. Debris from roof collapse at the 'T' junction may have acted as a sieve for sediment moving down the dip tube restricting larger material from entering the tube (Simms 1994). This area produced the greatest volume of debitage <10 mm from any part of the site. An 80–100 mm thick manganese crust near the base of J23/K23 (fig. 10.4b) formed as a result of standing water in this part of the cave, probably with much rotting vegetation.

The boulder choke at the southern end of F Block contains a stratified sequence of quartz artefacts show-

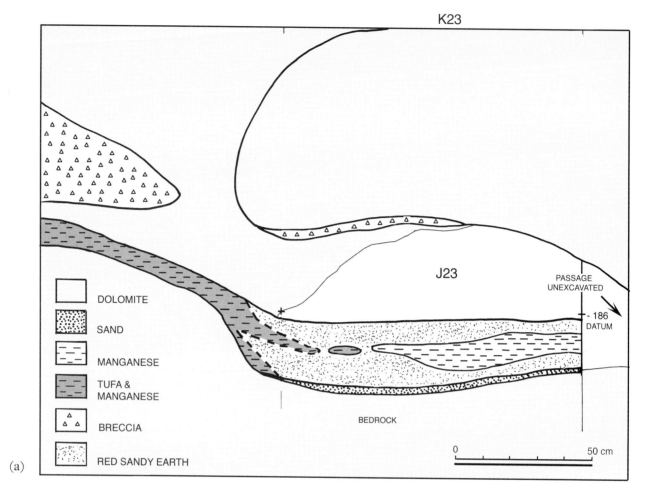

(a)

DOLOMITE

SAND

MANGANESE

TUFA &
MANGANESE

BRECCIA

RED SANDY EARTH

K23

J23

PASSAGE
UNEXCAVATED

- 186
DATUM

BEDROCK

0   50 cm

(b)

Figure 10.4   (a) Section drawing of the deposits in K23/J23 (F Block) showing the location of
the passage entrance and the continuous band of manganese concretion that filled
much of the deposit; (b) the view into K23/J23.

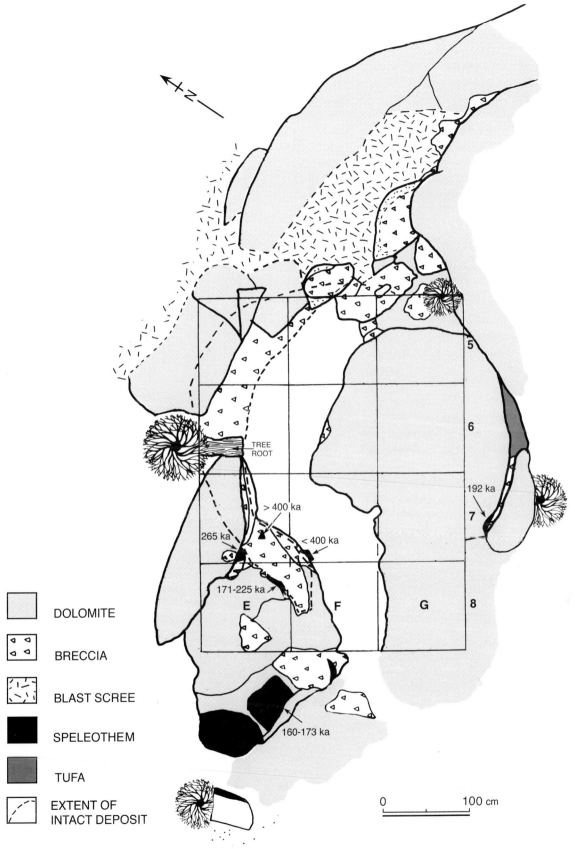

DOLOMITE

BRECCIA

BLAST SCREE

SPELEOTHEM

TUFA

EXTENT OF
INTACT DEPOSIT

TREE
ROOT

> 400 ka

265 ka

< 400 ka

171-225 ka

192 ka

160-173 ka

5

6

7

8

E   F   G

0   100 cm

Figure 10.5   Plan of the A Block deposits excavated in 1999. The sediments filled a cavity between the cave walls and the rim of
intact breccia. Speleothem (black) are shown with associated uranium–thorium dates.

below the northern knoll (figs 10.10 and 10.11). The passage rises 1 m onto a ledge which forms a narrow phreatic tube that is exposed in the current cliff face. The slope of the passage and constricted area of the A Block cavity lead to the conclusion that the main occupation was near or at the entrance, as was the case in F Block.

A thin layer of flowstone coats the floor of A Block (see dating) and is immediately overlain by fine to coarse breccia that contains abundant artefactual material and some bone. Little or no sediment accumulation took place in the cave before the first human occupation. Speleothem probably formed from water percolating through fractures in the cave roof and then spread across the sediment fill. Lenses of speleothem separate the breccia into discrete units but there is no obvious difference in the matrix of the breccia from the base to the top of the sequence. The absence of evidence of any reworking of the top of each breccia unit suggests that the passage was protected from storm runoff. The quartz artefacts in the breccia have pristine edges, and this evidence combined with the unsorted breccia matrix indicates that the A Block deposits originated as gentle slurry flows, perhaps as single short lived events. In support of this interpretation, a large flake of quartzite attached to the breccia (fig. 10.12a) in E6 was refitted to a core in the loose sediment fill in the same square and at the same depth (fig. 10.12b). The horizontal distance between the two objects was 15 cm.

Dating

M Gilmour, N Debenham and L Barham
Speleothem samples were dated from A and F Blocks using thermal ionisation mass spectrometry (TIMS) uranium-series (table 10.1). Of the six samples dated in A Block, two can be directly related to the archaeological deposits excavated in 1999. The remainder date individual periods of flowstone formation and provide maximum and minimum ages for the existence of the cave. A single TL date was calculated on a piece of calcite recovered from the loose sediment fill in A Block. In F Block, a flowstone formation from near the base of the sequence was sampled for TIMS uranium-series analysis. These new dates from F Block complement those that have been previously reported for the top of the sequence (Barham & Smart 1996; Barham 1998). Thermoluminescence was used to date the basal deposits in G Block. AMS radiocarbon dating of bone was also attempted for the upper part of G Block but with limited results.

Uranium-series procedures and results
The ^{230}Th/^{234}U method of dating can be used to date carbonates from a few hundred years to 400 ka BP, with an error of about 1 per cent on the age. The ease of

Figure 10.6 The interior of A Block showing the irregular passage floor, the remaining walls of the former cave and the area excavated in 1999 beneath the seated figure.

ing changing conditions of deposition from freely flowing water to a more gradual slurry flow at the top which is capped by speleothem. This is the speleothem dated to ~200 ka BP (Barham 1998).

The original size and height of the cave cannot be reconstructed because of the extensive lowering of the hill surface. Occupation may have taken place in or near the cave mouth with the debris entering the passage as slurry. Two small cave openings survive today in the rocky knolls at either end of the central platform (fig. 10.2) and provide analogues for the now unroofed passages. The openings offer some shelter, in particular from the prevailing winter winds, but the floors are irregular and slope inwards.

A Block formed as an irregular phreatic passage with fairly abrupt changes in dimensions. The original entrance may have been level with the central platform with the passage descending steeply to the area of the current excavations on the western slope of the hill and

(a)

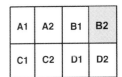

B2 LEVEL 4

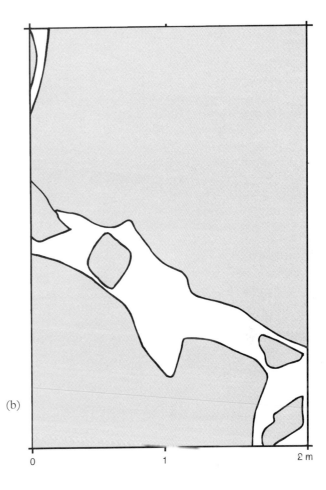

(b)

0   1   2 m

Figure 10.7 (a) The linear grike in G Block (B2); (b) the
grike in plan view (B1).

dating a carbonate depends on the uranium content of the sample and obviously its age. Old carbonates that are uranium rich are easy to analyse. The limiting factor for getting an actual age estimation is the abundance of ^{230}Th. One ppm of ^{238}U in a sample of 1 g weight, that is 10 ka, means that there will be circa 200 counts per second of ^{230}Th to analyse by TIMS, over a 30 min run. The dating of calcite hangs on the decay scheme of ^{238}U and ^{234}U to ^{230}Th. An assumption is made that calcite is precipitated with associated U but essentially no Th, a function of the mobility of U and Th in aqueous solution: U is mobile, Th is not.

An atomic ratio for ^{230}Th/^{232}Th of $>20 \times 5.381 \times 10^{-6}$ is a typical value for carbonates, if the value is less than this, the sample is considered to be detritally contaminated. Assuming the carbonate is free of Th at the time of deposition, all ^{230}Th found in the calcite has to have originated from the decay of ^{238}U and ^{234}U. Thus, in

clean calcite samples, the (^{230}Th/^{234}U) activity ratio is initially zero, and this increases with time with the in-growth of ^{230}Th to reach a value of unity after about 400 ka, after which time the ratio remains the same. Activity ratios are a measure of the decay rate of U-series isotopes and are a leftover concept from the days of alpha spectrometry, a technique which uses tens of grams of sample, 50 g is typical. The advantage of solid source mass spectrometry is that one can analyse much smaller samples. So, by measuring the ratio of ^{230}Th/^{234}U we are essentially measuring the age of the sample. However, we also have to make an allowance for the fact that ^{234}U is produced from the decay of ^{238}U.

Three potential problems need to be considered:

1 This technique only holds in a closed system, so there has to be no exchange between the sample and another source. For example, because of the porous

173

Figure 10.8 The hilltop of Twin Rivers as viewed from the south. The central platform lies between the two rocky promontories.

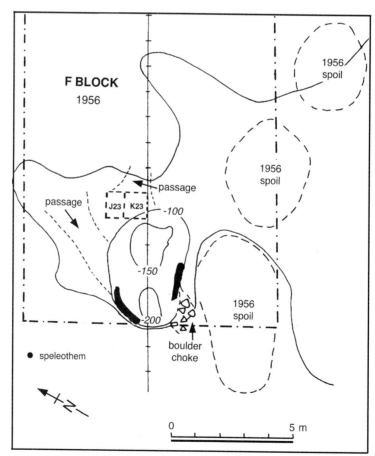

Figure 10.9 A plan view of the cave passages in F Block showing the location of K23/J23 in the dip tube and the boulder choke at the southern end of the system.

Figure 10.10 View of A Block showing the upward slope of the passage towards the central platform. The standing figure marks the estimated location of the cave mouth.

nature of bone the U is quite likely to exchange with any aqueous solutions able to permeate into the sample, so the direct dating of bone samples is problematic. No bone was dated from Twin Rivers.

2   The presence of any silicate or organic material trapped into the calcite during its formation can introduce extra Th isotopes. This problem can give older ages than are expected because there is extra ^{230}Th. The presence of these so-called detrital components can be quite obvious in the form of dirty bands in the calcite and these can be removed when possible. However when mechanical removal is impracticable it is easy to detect the presence of detrital Th during analysis because of the existence of ^{232}Th. The correction for such detrital contamination is problematic, but possible given several assumptions about the character of the detrital component. To check whether there is detrital Th

present, we measure the ^{230}Th/^{232}Th in the sample and calculate the activity ratio (^{230}Th/^{232}Th) – a calcite is regarded as uncontaminated if the ratio is >20, really clean calcites give (^{230}Th/^{232}Th) activity ratios of >500.

3   Some carbonate samples are so contaminated with detrital Th that it is virtually impossible to date the calcite component. In this case it is often better to go for an isochron method. This involves either stepped leachates and dissolutions of a sample or total dissolution of different size fractions of the sample.

Age calculation thus requires the concentrations of ^{234}U, ^{238}U and ^{230}Th in the sample using standard isotope dilution techniques. In addition, to assess the detrital Th component the concentration of ^{232}Th is measured.

Nine samples in total were submitted for analysis including six from A Block, one from F Block and two samples of tufa from the Casavera stream bed to the northwest of Twin Rivers. The A Block samples, in descending stratigraphic order below datum, are labelled TRA5A (220 cm), TRA4A (243 cm), TRA3A (320 cm), TRAA1 (340 cm), TRA14A (383 cm) and TRA2A (390 cm). Samples TRA3A and TRA4A were sub-sampled as two distinct layers where visible and these are labelled layer 1 and layer 2. The F Block sample, labelled TRF2 (163cm), was collected from a 20 cm thick band of flowstone and was also subdivided. TRF2 was subdivided into layers 1 and 2. Two additional samples were collected from tufa cascades deposited above a stratified series of lacustrine and terrestrial deposits (see appendix 7). Small samples of calcite were cut from the speleothem and the calcite pieces washed with ultra pure water and a quick leach in dilute HCl to wash off any surface contaminants prior to weighing for analysis. Any obvious silicate material is usually hand picked out (under a microscope) from a coarse crushing of the sample. It is lab policy to totally dissolve all samples rather than leach them with HNO$_3$. The reasons for this are:

1   In leaching speleothems/flowstones, with even small amounts of detrital material, it is very difficult to dissolve the calcite totally, without leaching any detrital Th from any silicate material that may be in the speleothem. The dating technique is based on the fact that uranium is mobile in aqueous solutions and that Th is not. As the dating technique relies on the decay of deposited uranium to ^{230}Th any additional ^{230}Th will yield an age which is older than actuality. Extra Th from a detrital silicate source however pushes up the amount of ^{230}Th that is measured to give an older age than actuality. (Although natural Th is mainly ^{232}Th, a very small proportion is also present as ^{230}Th.) It is possible to correct for this detrital component provided several assumptions are

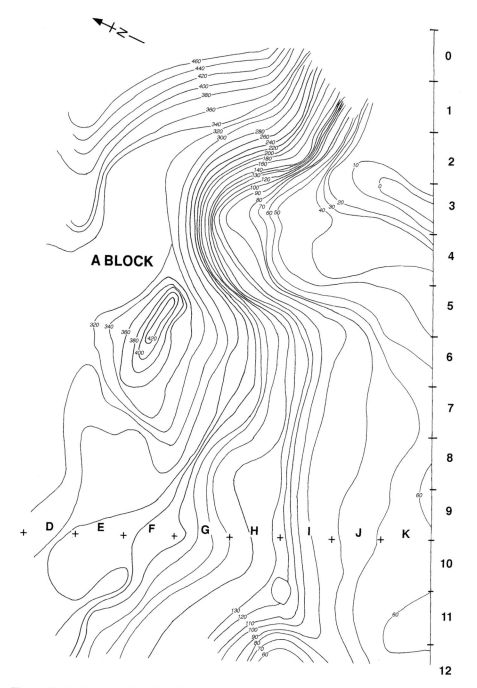

Figure 10.11 Contour plan of A Block showing the steep drop from the central platform and the depth of the base of the cave passage.

made, which are outlined below.

2   It is necessary to keep the acidity of the leaching acid high, so that Th is kept in solution. Unfortunately, the higher acidities mean that leaching of detrital Th is more likely. If the acidity is reduced, to minimise or stop detrital component leaching, the Th falls out of solution back onto the detrital residue. In order to ensure all Th is in solution, total dissolutions are undertaken.

Speleothem samples (typically 1–3 g) were totally dissolved and spiked with a mixed $^{229}Th/^{236}U$ spike. TRA4A layer 1 required HNO_3 dissolution only. All other samples required the use of a small quantity of HF plus HNO_3 and HCl to provide total dissolution for analysis. Uranium and thorium fractions were separated on 2 ml anion exchange columns using standard techniques (Edwards et al 1986). Uranium and thorium fractions were loaded onto graphite coated Re filaments and

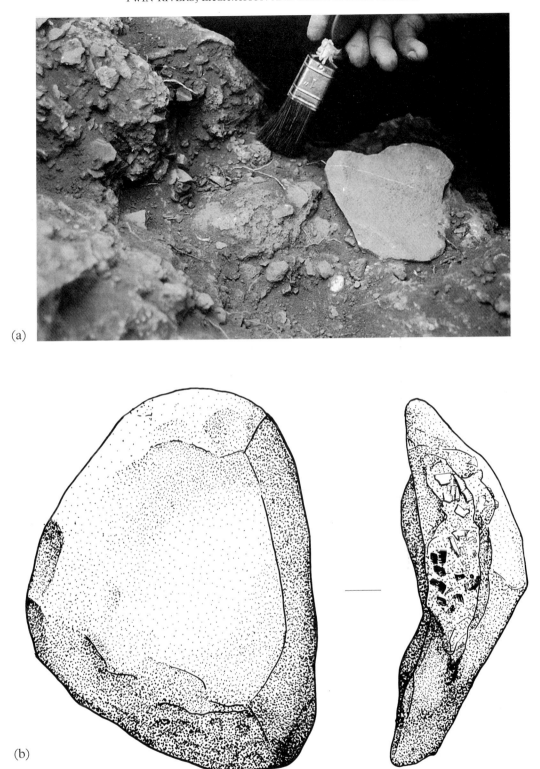

Figure 10.12 (a) The excavation of a large quartzite flake cemented into the breccia in E6; (b) the flake refitted to a core from the loose sediment fill of E6. The flake and core came from the same depth (365 cm below datum).

177

analyses carried out using a Finnigan MAT262 mass spectrometer equipped with a retarding potential quadrapole and secondary electron multiplier (described by van Calsteren and Schwieters 1995). A dynamic peak switching routine was employed measuring $^{234}U/^{236}U$ and $^{235}U/^{236}U$ (a proxy for ^{238}U, assuming a $^{238}U/^{235}U$ natural ratio of 137.88) and $^{230}Th/^{229}Th$ and $^{232}Th/^{229}Th$. Although ^{232}Th abundance is not required for the age calculation it is always measured so that we can monitor detrital Th input and consequently correct for its presence.

All the isotope ratios given in table 10.1 are raw data and uncorrected for detrital input unless indicated. Both raw uncorrected and corrected ages are given. The detrital calculation used in this study corrects for both uranium and thorium detrital contribution to the sample. It is assumed that the detrital component is in secular equilibrium and that all the ^{232}Th is of detrital origin. A value is assumed for the $^{232}Th/^{238}U$ molecular ratio in the detritus and in this case a value of 5.3 has been used. This value was derived from the analysis of clays incorporated within the flowstones TRA2A and TRA14A, speleothem samples that had particularly low $(^{230}Th/^{232}Th)$ activity ratios. The clays were removed from the flowstone by washing the total sample with a dilute acid to remove the carbonate material. After washing with pure water and drying, the clays were then totally dissolved and subsequently analysed for the U and Th contents. The analysed clays provide a Th/U value which falls within the Th/U range of average crustal silicate rocks and is the best estimate for the detrital component at this time.

Since the $(^{230}Th/^{232}Th)$ activity ratios for both TRA3A layer 1 and TRA4A layer 1 were both >200 they can essentially be viewed as having negligible detrital input, hence the detrital correction on these samples is very small. All other samples had $(^{230}Th/^{232}Th)$ ratios that ranged from 2.3 to 15.5 and have significant detrital Th contamination. All of the samples are corrected for the presence of detrital Th for consistency, including those samples with $(^{230}Th/^{232}Th)$ ratios of >200. Ages were calculated using the standard equation and the decay constants used for ^{234}U, ^{238}U, ^{230}Th and ^{232}Th were 2.835×10^{-6}, 1.55125×10^{-10}, 9.1952×10^{-6} and 4.9475×10^{-11} yr^{-1} respectively. Total procedure blanks for ^{238}U and ^{232}Th averaged 33 pg and 96 pg respectively for total dissolutions involving HF and for nitric acid only dissolution blanks are generally lower at around 20–40 pg.

Three in-house standards are also used to assess external reproducibilities.

1   A natural uranium standard spiked with ^{236}U single spike. This standard (lab code 'U456 std2') had a reproducibility of 0.2 per cent and 0.4 per cent for

$^{235}U/^{236}U$ and $^{234}U/^{236}U$ measurements respectively over the analysis period, and gave a 1 standard deviation error of 0.4 per cent for the $(^{234}U/^{238}U)$ activity ratio calculated from the measured ratios.

2   A thorium standard (lab code 'CP230/229') which is a mix of ^{230}Th and ^{229}Th spikes with a $^{230}Th/^{229}Th$ ratio which mimics that of a young carbonate sample. A reproducibility of 0.4 per cent was achieved for this sample over the analysis period.

3   A carbonate solution standard prepared from Iceland spar calcite. Reproducibilities were 0.2 per cent and 0.3 per cent for calculated $(^{234}U/^{238}U)$ and $(^{230}Th/^{234}U)$ activity ratios respectively (n=17, 1 standard deviation). Measurement of the powder for this standard provided reproducibilities of 0.2 per cent and 0.49 per cent for $(^{234}U/^{238}U)$ and $(^{230}Th/^{234}U)$ respectively (n=12, 1 standard deviation).

Based on the external reproducibilities of the calcite standard the one standard deviation errors on calculated ages are realistically unlikely to be better than 1.0 per cent on any age determination.

Of the A Block samples, TRAA1 (266 ka BP) and TRA14A (>400 ka BP) (figs. 10.13, 10.14) can be related directly to the deposits excavated in 1999. TRAA1 forms part of a breccia wedge between two dolomite blocks. The breccia degrades into a continuous lens of a loose red sandy sediment that extends from E7 northwards. The age of the speleothem is considered to be an approximate date for the majority of the deposits excavated in 1999. Sample TRA14 is a triangular fragment of speleothem that was incorporated into the breccia that abuts E7 (fig. 10.5). Its age is not necessarily a guide to the age of the enclosing breccia. A nearby flowstone (fig. 10.5) deposited on the cave floor (TRA2A) is also dated to >400 ka BP and may have been the source of the speleothem in the breccia. A later slurry flow could have incorporated fragments of the early flowstone. The dates of >400 ka BP provide a maximum age for the overlying deposits, but a hiatus of unknown duration separates the formation of the speleothem and the deposition of the slurry flow.

The remaining dates from A Block with the exception of TRA5A come from a concentration of speleothem on the western edge of cave that lies above the deposits excavated in 1999. This portion of the site represents a remnant of either a parallel passage now destroyed by cliff retreat or a 'gull' fissure which developed under the influence of gravity and vegetation (M Simms pers comm). The passage or fissure existed during the interval from 160/173 ka BP (TRA4A) to 225 ka BP (TRA3A). The latter sample lies upslope of TRAA1 (266ka BP) at a depth of 320 cm and together they form part of a chronological progression in A Block from 160– >400 ka BP. Sample TRA5A (192 ka BP) comes

Table 10.1 Analytical data for $^{230}Th/^{234}U$ dating of speleothem from Twir, Rivers, A & F Blocks and for Casavera stream tufa cascades. All ratios in parenthesis in the table are activity ratios with 1 standard deviation errors. The errors are propagated from the in-run precision errors. In-run precision errors averaged 0.1 per cent, 0.4 per cent and 0.5 per cent (1 stdev) for $^{235}U/^{236}U$, $^{234}U/^{23}U$ and $^{230}Th/^{229}Th$ measured ratios respectively

From site datum	A BLOCK 220cm	A BLOCK 390cm	A BLOCK 340cm	A BLOCK 320cm	A BLOCK 320cm	A BLOCK 383cm	A BLOCK 243cm	A BLOCK 243cm	TUFA DOWN STREAM	TUFA UP STREAM	F BLOCK 163cm	F BLOCK 163cm
Sample no	TRA5A	TRA2A	TRAA1	TRA3A LAYER 1	TRA3A LAYER 2	TRA14A	TRA4A LAYER 1	TRA4A LAYER 2			TRF2 LAYER 1	TRF2 LAYER 2
U (238U ppm)	0.03958	0.02454	0.03301	0.03709	0.09601	0.02086	0.03973	0.10646	0.21901	0.26040	0.02729	0.01490
err on ppm	0.00006	0.00003	0.00002	0.00004	0.00011	0.00002	0.00007	0.00022	0.00026	0.00033	0.00003	0.00002
(234U/238U)	2.1626	1.0337	1.0959	1.2424	1.3624	1.0584	1.2506	1.4617	1.5450	1.1674	1.1308	1.1862
err on activity ratio	0.0062	0.0042	0.0019	0.0051	0.0039	0.0032	0.0088	0.0074	0.0033	0.0035	0.0044	0.0065
234 (ppm)	4.61E-06	1.36E-06	1.95E-06	2.48E-06	7.04E-06	1.19E-06	2.67E-06	8.37E-06	1.82E-05	1.64E-05	1.66E-06	9.51E-07
err on ppm	1.35E-08	5.98E-09	3.50E-09	1.07E-08	2.07E-08	4.05E-09	1.96E-08	4.32E-08	3.89E-08	4.95E-08	7.34E-09	6.05E-09
230(ppb)	0.001323	0.000412	0.000557	0.000690	0.001820	0.000374	0.000673	0.002118	0.005092	0.005030	0.000419	0.000216
err on ppm	0.000006	0.000002	0.000002	0.000002	0.000005	0.000003	0.000002	0.000014	0.000023	0.000023	0.000005	0.0C0001
232 (ppb)	42.319	31.542	17.508	0.533	47.942	31.931	0.476	52.240	142.744	131.954	5.406	2.818
err on ppm	0.095	0.061	0.014	0.001	0.069	0.093	0.002	0.145	0.502	0.337	0.008	0.002
(230/232)	5.93	2.53	6.06	248.32	7.19	2.28	269.45	7.65	6.71	7.18	15.32	15.46
err on activity ratio	0.03	0.02	0.02	0.89	0.02	0.02	1.31	0.05	0.04	0.04	0.17	0.07
(230/234)	0.9480	0.9963	0.9443	0.9186	0.8534	1.0396	0.8305	0.8350	0.9232	1.0150	0.8319	0.7493
err on activity ratio	0.0049	0.0073	0.0041	0.0049	0.0034	0.0085	0.0067	0.0069	0.0047	0.0055	0.0099	0.0059
AGE in years	199835	>400Ka	275138	225576	178770	>400Ka	173262	166655	206498	>400Ka	181374	141914
plus error	2502		5797	4273	1840		3695	3213	2854		5792	2452
minus error	2453		5500	4108	1807		3559	3122	2787		5491	2390
Detrital correction Assuming Th/U of detritus=5.3 (using clays from samples)												
(234U/238U)corrd	2.4660	1.0449	1.1069	1.2431	1.4011	1.0829	1.2511	1.5101	1.6237	1.1856	1.1360	1.1933
err on activity ratio	0.0070	0.0042	0.0019	0.0051	0.0040	0.0033	0.0088	0.0077	0.0035	0.0035	0.0045	0.0066
(230/234)corrd	0.9424	0.9951	0.9386	0.9185	0.8422	1.0550	0.8302	0.8235	0.9163	1.0164	0.8260	0.7413
err on activity ratio	0.0048	0.0073	0.0041	0.0045	0.0034	0.0086	0.0067	0.0068	0.0047	0.0055	0.0098	0.0058
Corrected AGE (years)	192135	>400Ka	265550	225370	171976	>400Ka	173088	160624	199295	>400Ka	177893	138748

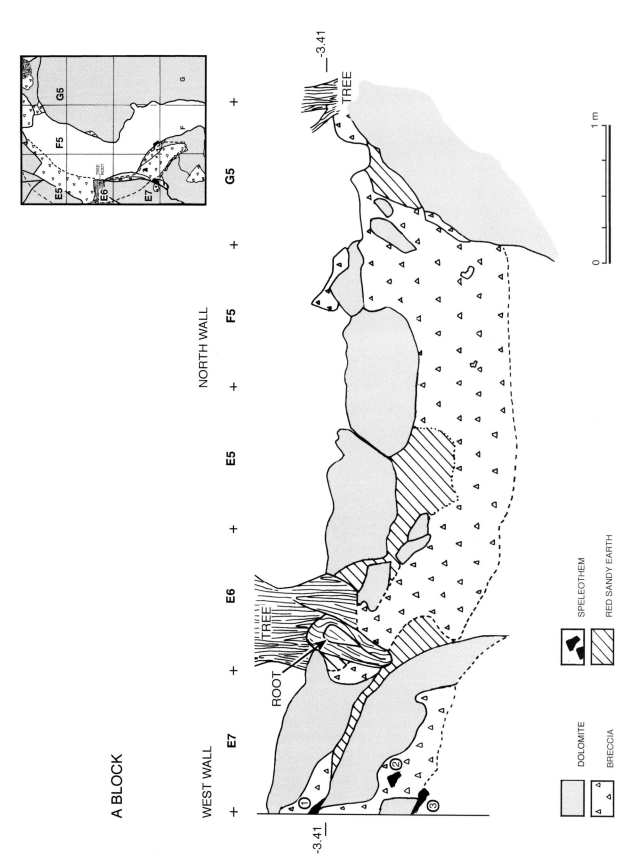

Figure 10.13 Section of A Block (west wall) showing the location of dated speleothem in relation to breccia and loose sediment. Sample 1=266 ka BP, sample=>400 ka BP, sample 3=>400 ka BP.

Figure 10.14 The location of speleothem sample TRA14A (>400 ka BP) within breccia.

from the eastern side of A Block and had been dated to >300 ka BP (Barham 1998). A second sample was collected in 1999 and the analysis presented above has reduced the age to 192 ka BP. The reduction resulted from the application of a detrital correction factor based on the clays incorporated in samples TRA2A and TRA14A. Sample TRA5A could not be directly correlated with the deposits excavated in 1999, but it comes from the highest intact breccias in the main area of A Block (fig. 10.5).

The age of the top of A Block corresponds closely with a uranium–thorium date of 195±19 ka BP for a speleothem at the top of F Block (Barham 1998). The two former cave passages appear to have been open at approximately the same time. Younger dates of 139 and 178 ka BP are reported above from a lower speleothem in F Block (TRF2) that dips across the deposit (fig. 10.15). The flowstone extends upwards towards the cross passage and continues to the top of the deposit. The irregular morphology of the cave passages has

made the stratification of speleothem in F Block more complex than in A Block. A Block is the older of the two passages with flowstone forming more than 400 ka BP and the deposition of sediment following at some point afterwards. Given the uncertainty about the length of the interval between formation of the basal flowstone and the first slurry flow, the age range of the archaeological deposits in A Block is conservatively estimated to be between ~266 and 170 ka BP. The deposits could in theory be as old as the 400 ka BP speleothem, but this cannot be demonstrated directly. The F Block deposits are placed later in the time range from ~200 to 170/140 ka BP.

Thermoluminescence and AMS dates
A single TL date on a calcite fragment from E5/E6 (408–423 cm) gave an age of 132±31 ka BP, which is significantly younger than the uranium-thorium dates. The analytical data are in table 10.2

The gamma dose rate included estimates of the effects of the dolomite cave walls and the breccia, both of which lay within a 10 cm radius of the sample. Three dimensional computer modelling was used to aid the dose rate evaluations. Cosmic dose rates were estimated from the overburden that had covered the sample. No sediment directly associated with the sample was available for the dose rate assessment and in its place sediment from higher up the sequence was used. The age estimate reflects the length of burial of the calcite since its formation.

For G Block, four TL samples of burnt quartz were analysed and the results (tables 10.3 and 10.4) show the effects of the mixing of the deposit caused by the formation of the grike. Two samples from the basal level in B2 (130–140 cm) and one from the same depth in B1 give Last Interglacial (Stage 5.3) (101±16 ka BP) and Late Glacial ages (17±3.1 and 12.7±1.5 ka BP). Mixing is also evident in the overlying level (B2-7, 116–130 cm) with dates of 56.5±8.3 ka BP and 15.8±2.4 ka BP.

The two earliest dates for B2 record Middle Stone Age occupations about 100 ka BP and at about 57 ka BP with an overlay of occupation during the Late Glacial (17–13 ka BP). The latter three dates are of particular interest because they are not well represented in the Mumbwa Caves sequence. The mixing of the lower deposits in G Block appears to be extensive based on the TL dates. In contrast, the archaeological content of these two lower levels shows no obvious microlithic component that would be indicative of Later Stone Age technology. At some point during the Last Glacial Maximum or early in the Late Glacial the surface of the central platform had been used again as a living site and the exposed Middle Stone Age deposits were subjected to trampling and other taphonomic processes including

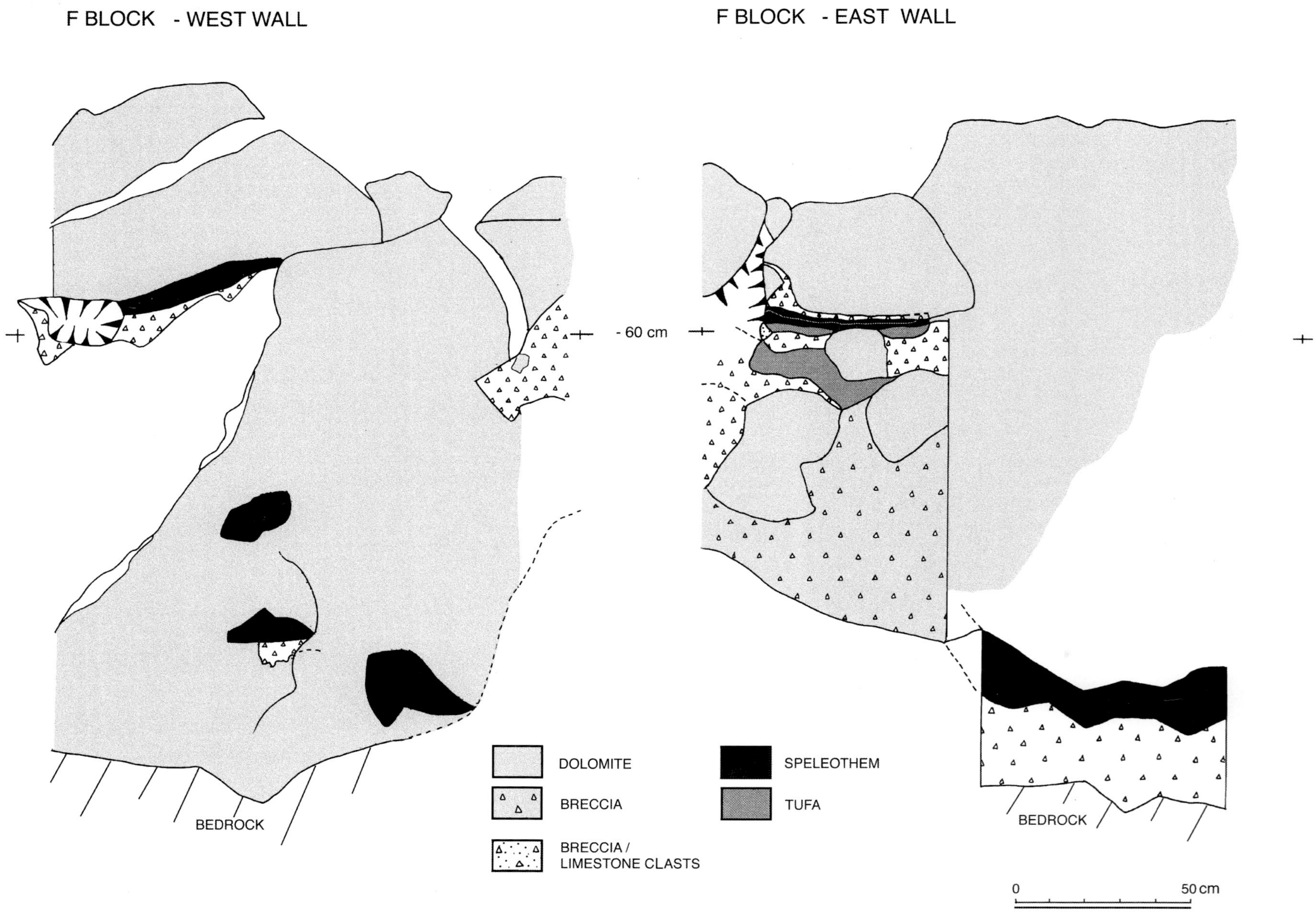

F BLOCK - EAST WALL

F BLOCK - WEST WALL

- 60 cm

50 cm

0

BEDROCK

BEDROCK

SPELEOTHEM

TUFA

DOLOMITE

BRECCIA

BRECCIA /
LIMESTONE CLASTS

Figure 10.15 F Block sections (east and west walls) showing the location of dated speleothem samples.

182

Table 10.2 A Block TL date on calcite from E5/E6 (408–423cm). Dose rates are given in Grays per millennium (Gy/ka)

Alpha dose rate	Beta dose rate	Gamma dose rate	Cosmic dose rate	Palaeodose (Gy)	Total dose rate
0.125	0.069	0.723	0.140	135±27	1.057±0.124

Table 10.3 G Block: palaeodoses, total dose rates and TL dates

Sample	Depth (cm)	Palaeodose (gy)	Total dose rate (gy/ka)	TL age (ka BP)
B2–7	116–130	70.4±6.7	1.247±0.141	56.5±8.3
B2–7	116–130	15.5±0.8	0.984±0.137	15.8±2.4
B2–8	130–140	57.6.5	0.569±0.074	101±16
B2–8	130–140	9.0±0.5	0.714±0.075	12.7±1.5
B1–8	137–147	12.7±1.7	0.752±0.120	17.0±3.1

Table 10.5 G Block: AMS radiocarbon dates on bone

Sample	13C/12C ratio	Conven-tional age	2 sigma calibrated age	Lab no.
B2–1	−19.1‰	40±50 BP	265–215 Cal BP	Beta–136815
B2–2	−18.1‰	100.4±0.6% modern	140–25 Cal BP	Beta–136816*

*Contained an average C14 content greater than modern standard, includes atmospheric 'bomb carbon' generated in the past 40 years.

Table 10.4 G Block: alpha, beta, gamma and cosmic dose rate measurements. Dose rates are given in Grays per millennium (gy/ka)

Sample	Alpha dose rate (gy/ka)	Beta dose rate (gy/ka)	Gamma dose rate (gy/ka)	Cosmic dose rate (gy/ka)
B2–7	0.151	0.129	0.787	0.180
B2–7	0.009	0.008	0.786	0.180
B2–8	0.002	0.008	0.389	0.170
B2–8	0.073	0.081	0.390	0.170
B1–8	0.002	0.003	0.588	0.160

lake system filled the Kafue basin and extended as far north as Twin Rivers (appendix 7). The shallow lake and its margins would have enabled the residents of the hill to live in the area during glacial stages and stadials.

Artefacts

The lithic assemblages from all areas of excavation were analysed using the same attributes and classification scheme as applied to the Mumbwa Caves sequence. Manuports, including potential pigments, are discussed first, followed by core and flake debitage and then utilised and retouched pieces. The artefacts from A and F Block are each treated as single assemblages. The assemblage from G Block is not included in the analysis because of the mixed deposits, but for comparative purposes some illustrations are included of retouched artefacts from B2 that can be linked to the TL date of 101±16 ka BP. Where appropriate, comparisons are made with data from the previous excavation of Twin Rivers (1954–6). J D Clark and K S Brown kindly made this data available in advance of its pending publication. Differences in the excavation strategies and recovery methods between the excavations make direct quantitative comparisons potentially misleading, but general patterns can be discussed.

the formation of the grike. Its long channel concentrated the Middle Stone Age occupation debris and presumably caused slumping of the deposit inwards with some mixing. There is no visible stratigraphic separation in the brown sandy sediments with the exception of a dark brown humic surface layer 5–10 cm thick. This top 15 cm of deposit contains both Later Stone Age and Iron Age artefacts and has been AMS radiocarbon dated to the present (table 10.5).

The dating effort overall has confirmed the Middle Pleistocene attribution of A and F Blocks and constrained the time range of the deposits further. An age range of 266–170 ka BP is suggested for the combined deposits with A Block having the potential of being more than 400 ka BP. Deposition in the passages ceased about 140–170 ka BP and the cave roofs may have collapsed at this time. The central platform of the hill was occupied at intervals during the Late Pleistocene and Holocene. The presence of people at 60 ka (Stage 4) and 17 ka BP (Stage 2) is of particular interest because these periods are not represented in the Mumbwa Caves sequence. Twin Rivers lies far enough to the east of Mumbwa and near a permanent source of water (Kafue River) to have remained a habitable site during arid phases. In the Middle Pleistocene before 200 ka BP, a large arid phase

Manuports

A BLOCK

Of the 186 objects transported to A Block and classified as manuports, five are quartz cobbles, one is a piece of schist and the remaining 180 are interpreted as potential pigments. These include specularite, hematite, limonite, ferruginous sandstone and manganese dioxide. The percentage frequencies of each are shown in table 10.6 and illustrated in figure 10.16

The re-excavation of A Block had, in part, been undertaken with the aim of recovering more possible

Table 10.6 Frequencies and percentages of non-quartz manuports in A Block

Raw material

	Frequency	Per cent	Cumulative per cent
Hematite	48	26.7	26.7
Specularite	110	61.1	87.8
Manganese dioxide	1	0.6	88.3
Red sandstone	8	4.4	92.8
Limonite	13	7.2	100.0
Total	180	100.0	

pigment after the discovery of three pieces of specularite/hematite in the section in 1996 (Barham 1998). A survey of the hillsides in 1999 did not locate any sources of iron minerals with the exception of thin (2 mm) bands of hematite in quartz veins found at the base of the hill. Geochemical analyses of the breccia in A Block (appendix 5) show that the cave deposits are rich in manganese and poor in iron and are an unlikely source of the iron minerals found in the site. Local sources of hematite and limonite were found in outcrops of laterite that occur within 2 km of the hill. The specularite derives from a different lithology, having formed in quartz veins and as small crystals in schist. Thick (5–8 cm) veins of specularite were located 22 km to the west, but thinner specularite veins and specularite cobbles were found along the margins of the Lusaka dolomite plateau 5 km to the north and west of the cave. The occupants of A Block would have had relatively easy access to these iron minerals assuming the landscape has changed little. Sandstone also outcrops locally in the surrounding hills. A source of manganese dioxide was not located, but is presumed to be local in origin.

The specularite tends to be harder than the lateritic hematite and its primary identifying feature is the colour and content of its streak. Specularite produces a darker, more purple shade of red (Munsell 10R 4–3/3–3) containing crystal inclusions that sparkle. Hematite by comparison produces a strong red streak (10R 5/8–4/8) with no additional reflective properties. The local limonite is soft and gives a yellow to greenish yellow streak (2.5Y 8/8). A similar colour can be extracted from the weathered rind of dolerite and the potential for confusion exists in distinguishing between the intentional introduction of iron hydroxide (limonite) to the site and the *in situ* degradation of an igneous material that was used for purposes other than as a pigment. On specimens where the distinction was ambiguous, an edge would be broken and the interior examined. Red sandstone may have been used as a pigment given the similarity in streak colour to hematite, or the sandstone was unintentionally reddened by exposure to heat. As with the Mumbwa Caves manuports, red sandstone is treated as a possible pigment. No yellow sandstone was found in the site.

Among the non-quartz assemblage, only specimens of specularite exhibit visible signs of alteration from use or from preparation. Seven pieces of specularite, or 3.9 per

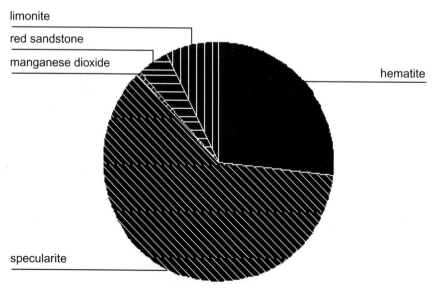

raw material

Figure 10.16 Pie chart illustrating the predominance of specularite in the non-quartz manuport assemblage in A Block.

cent of the pigment sample, are modified and of these six show wear facets as recognised by abrupt changes in surface texture (fig. 10.17a, b, c) and by shallow striations probably caused by rubbing against a coarse surface (fig. 10.17d). Striations and a change in texture are also visible on the internal concave surface of the largest specimen (fig. 10.18). This piece appears to have been shaped by rubbing on all surfaces (fig. 10.17c) with the concave surface created by rubbing against a rounded object. One small broken fragment of specularite (fig. 10.17e) has two surfaces scarred with fine V-shaped

(c)

(a)

(d)

(b)

(e)

Figure 10.17 Modified pigment specimens from A Block: (a, b, c) show wear facets from rubbing, (d) has shallow striations from contact with a coarse surface and (e) has incised surfaces (scale in millimetres).

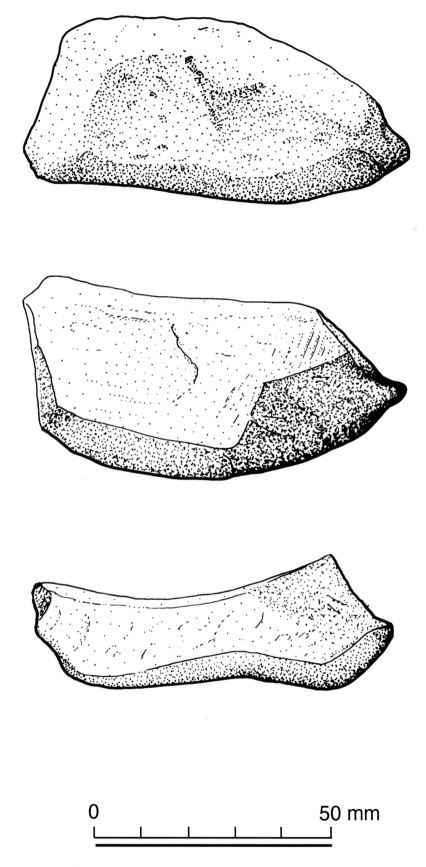

Figure 10.18 Illustration of specimen 10.17c showing concave profile created by rubbing.

striations that run parallel to its length and are truncated by the break. The striations could be caused by rubbing against a fine-grained sandstone or quartzite.

These marks of intentional modification of specularite are interpreted as evidence for the production of a coloured powder. The lack of visibly modified hematite specimens can be explained by the relatively soft texture of the material. Hematite from the local lateritic sources crumbled into fragments when rubbed and was easily ground into a powder. The size and weight distribution of the two iron oxides reflects the differing physical properties (table 10.7). Specimens of specularite are larger in all dimensions and significantly heavier (15.35 g mean weight) than those of hematite (1.63 g). Of the 48 hematite pieces recovered, only 19 (40 per cent) weighed more than 1 g in contrast to the 81 pieces of specularite (74 per cent) in a sample of 110.

The evidence for the processing of specularite by the inhabitants of A Block is supported by the geochemical analysis of an oblong cobble of quartzite excavated from A Block in 1954. The cobble measures 74 mm in length, 57 mm wide and has a maximum thickness of 40 mm (fig. 10.19). Both ends are pockmarked from use and all surfaces are stained yellow or contain yellow sediment trapped in the interstices between quartz grains. Geochemical analyses were undertaken to determine the probable source of the staining by profiling its chemical signature and by comparing it to the hematite, limonite and specularite found at Twin Rivers in 1996. The results are presented in appendix 5. The nearest match is specularite rather than the expected limonite. The staining occurred as a result of the processing of an iron mineral, either by grinding or pounding, which was transported to the site.

Table 10.7 Raw material frequencies and mean length, width, thickness in millimetres and weight in grams of non-quartz manuports, A Block. Pieces weighing less than 1 gram are entered as 0

Descriptive statistics

Raw material		N	Minimum	Maximum	Mean	Std deviation
Hematite	Number	48	1	1	1.00	0.00
	Length	10	11	22	15.90	4.36
	Width	10	7	28	12.60	5.93
	Thickness	10	3	13	7.80	3.46
	Weight	18	0	6	1.67	1.33
	Valid N	10				
Specularite	Number	110	1	1	1.00	0.00
	Length	73	10	90	22.67	15.06
	Width	73	6	53	16.26	9.36
	Thickness	72	3	49	9.92	7.88
	Weight	83	0	368	14.98	49.32
	Valid N	72				
Manganese dioxide	Number	1	1	1	1.00	.
	Length	1	4	4	4.00	.
	Width	1	2	2	2.00	.
	Thickness	1	1	1	1.00	.
	Weight	1	0	0	0.00	.
	Valid N	1				
Red sandstone	Number	8	1	1	1.00	0.00
	Length	6	11	28	16.50	6.95
	Width	6	8	25	13.67	6.02
	Thickness	6	4	13	8.17	3.66
	Weight	8	0	4	1.50	1.60
	Valid N	6				
Limonite	Number	13	1	1	1.00	0.00
	Length	11	10	64	20.00	15.08
	Width	11	8	39	13.55	8.56
	Thickness	11	4	40	9.64	10.39
	Weight	13	0	102	9.00	27.96
	Valid N	11				

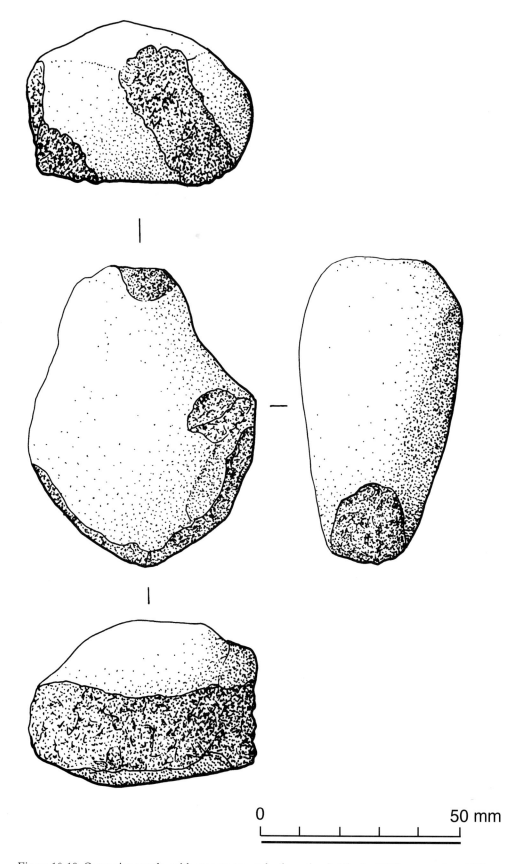

Figure 10.19 Quartzite pestle with use wear at both ends, A Block, 1954 excavation. Yellow sediment, identified as iron oxide, adheres to the worn surfaces.

The combined physical and geochemical evidence for the processing of iron minerals lends support to the hypothesis that later Middle Pleistocene hominids were capable of using pigments in socially defined contexts that involved syntactic language (Barham 1998). This argument is developed further in the final chapter. At the very least, the relatively high frequency of pigments found is indicative of systematic use of mineral colourants. Approximately 4–5 m³ of deposit were excavated from A Block in 1954 (Clark and Brown in press) and assuming a similar frequency of pigments across the cave as found in 1999 (n=180, weight=1404 g), then the original totals can be estimated. The number of pieces would have been 8–9 times greater (n=1440–1620) as would have been the total weight (11.2–12.6 kg). Pigments were recovered from the 1954 excavations, but the necessity of using dynamite to remove the breccia meant that much of the iron mineral content was retained within the breccia as small lumps or accidentally destroyed. Pieces of specularite and hematite are visible in the surviving breccia. The bulk analysis of the small flaking debris (<10 mm) recovered in 1999 (see appendix 6) increases the absolute numbers by an estimated 762 pieces in A Block and 130 pieces in F Block. The pigment sample excavated in 1999 from A and F Blocks combined is currently the largest reported collection from a Middle Pleistocene context (Barham in press).

F BLOCK

Among the total of 127 manuports in F Block, three are quartz cobbles, one is schist, one is grey sandstone and the remaining 122 are interpreted as potential sources of pigment. Table 10.8 outlines the frequencies by raw material and the metrical attributes of the specimens. The frequencies of hematite and specularite are roughly equal but the two differ in size and weight with specularite consistently the larger and heavier specimens. The differing properties of the raw materials have been discussed for A Block and the correlation between hardness and fragmentation and specimen size holds

Table 10.8 Raw material frequencies (a) and mean length, width, thickness in millimetres and weight in grams, F Block (b). Pieces weighing less than one gram are entered as 0

Raw material

	Frequency	Per cent	Cumulative per cent
Hematite	50	41.0	41.0
Specularite	59	48.4	89.3
Manganese dioxide	1	0.8	90.2
Sandstone	8	6.6	96.7
Limonite	4	3.3	100.0
Total	122	100.0	

Descriptive statistics

Raw material		N	Minimum	Maximum	Mean	Std deviation
Hematite	Length	4	13	21	16.00	3.56
	Width	4	8	20	11.50	5.69
	Thickness	4	3	13	6.50	4.43
	Weight	8	0	8	1.88	2.64
Specularite	Length	31	10	37	19.26	7.56
	Width	31	8	33	14.90	6.41
	Thickness	31	3	18	9.29	3.73
	Weight	36	1	36	4.94	7.21
Manganese dioxide	Length	1	17	17	17.00	.
	Width	1	13	13	13.00	.
	Thickness	1	5	5	5.00	.
	Weight	1	1	1	1.00	.
Sandstone	Length	1	47	47	47.00	.
	Width	1	30	30	30.00	.
	Thickness	1	14	14	14.00	.
	Weight	3	0	14	5.00	7.81
Limonite	Length	3	12	22	16.33	5.13
	Width	3	10	12	11.33	1.15
	Thickness	3	3	9	6.00	3.00
	Weight	4	0	2	1.00	0.82

true for F Block. All specimens, regardless of raw material, are smaller than those in A Block and this can be attributed to the filtering effect of the narrow passage leading to J23/K23.

Of the sample of 122 potential pigments, three (2.45 per cent) have been modified by rubbing and this includes two pieces of specularite and one of hematite (fig. 10.20). The hematite is noteworthy in that it represents the only faceted piece of this material found in 1999 in either block. Hematite was processed by rubbing as was specularite. The amount of pigment that may have existed in F Block can be estimated by using the volume of material excavated in 1956 (120 m^3, based on Clark 1971:fig. 3) and comparing this to the weight of pigment and volume of deposit recovered in 1999. The result is 29,792 pieces weighing 56.7 kg (n=112, weight=213 g, sediment volume=0.45 $m^3 \times 266$). The highly fragmented state of the pigment in J23/K23 is likely to produce an overestimate of actual numbers, but the quantity by weight can be considered a more reliable guide. These estimates should be treated as guidelines to the potential use of pigment at Twin Rivers and as indicators of the importance of iron minerals in the lives of the occupants. The cognitive and social implications of systematic pigment use so early in the Middle Pleistocene are discussed in chapter 13.

Pigments, including pieces with use facets, also occur throughout the G Block levels from the Late Pleistocene to the historic present. The mixing that has occurred in the grike makes attribution of the pigments to the Middle Stone Age less certain, but pigment use is well documented for the Late Pleistocene at Mumbwa Caves and can be assumed to have been part of the behavioural repertoire at Twin Rivers. The G Block pigment data will be published separately.

Cores

A BLOCK

Table 10.9 and figure 10.21 display the frequency and percentage of cores by type. The bipolar technique is the most common approach to flaking (19.4 per cent), followed by angular chunks used as cores. The two techniques involve no preparation of the raw material and represent an informal reduction strategy with little planning except for the collection of cobbles. Cobbles are accessible in the landscape today in the bed of the Casavera stream that flows to the north and west of the hill. Vein quartz that is relatively free of flaws is available at the base of the hill. The distance to this source is only 200 m, but the effort involved in bringing blocks up to the cave may account for the frequent use of chunks and for the prevalence of flakes used as cores (8.8 per cent), including topknot flakes. Informal reduction techniques are also evident in the relatively high frequencies of single and multiple platform cores (13.1 per cent and

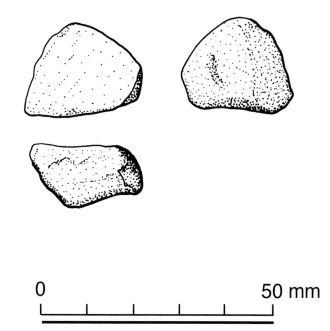

0   50 mm

Figure 10.20 Hematite with wear facets, F Block.

Table 10.9 Frequencies and percentages of cores by type, A Block

Type	Frequency	Per cent	Cumulative per cent
Two platforms-right	6	3.8	3.8
Radial	13	8.1	11.9
Single platform	21	13.1	25.0
Multiple platforms	18	11.3	36.3
Prepared core	10	6.3	42.5
Blade	5	3.1	45.6
Bladelet	3	1.9	47.5
Bipolar	31	19.4	66.9
Chunk core	28	17.5	84.4
Flake as core	14	8.8	93.1
Core fragment	2	1.3	94.4
Split radial core	1	0.6	95.0
Opposed platforms	6	3.8	98.8
Disc	2	1.3	100.0
Total	160	100.0	

11.3 per cent respectively). The controlled production of flakes of predetermined size, shape and thickness is evident in the percentages of blade, radial, disc and prepared cores.

The blade cores (fig. 10.22) merit further description given the age of the deposit and unexpectedly early use of this reduction technique. The cores are flat faced rather than pyramidal and with opposed platforms. They resemble blade cores found in the Mid-Late Pleistocene

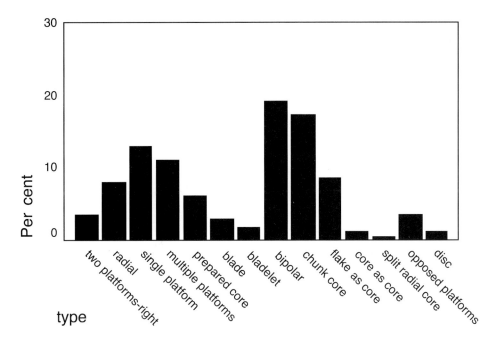

Figure 10.21 Percentage frequencies of core by type, A Block.

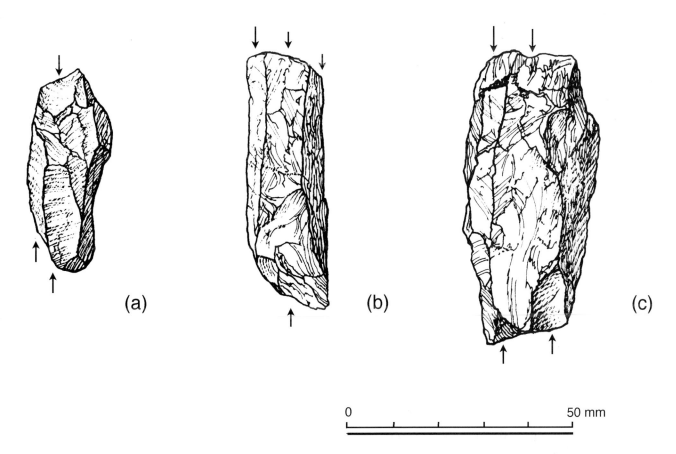

Figure 10.22 Opposed platform blade cores from Twin Rivers, A Block, all vein quartz: (a) E5/F5–2; (b) E5/G4–2; (c) A Block 1996.

sequence at Mumbwa Caves (units XII–V) (fig. 8.8). The platform angles approach 90° on some specimens and others were discarded because of hinge fractures or similar impediments to further blade removal. The frequency of blade cores is low, as it is at Mumbwa, but the end-products are typologically significant when retouched.

Centripetal flaking techniques are represented by radial and disc cores and technically by prepared cores. Small radial and prepared cores (<30 mm) (fig. 10.23), some made on topknot flakes, are a feature that has parallels with the assemblage in unit VII at Mumbwa Caves (fig. 8.9). Small triangular flakes are evidently a part of the range of blanks produced in the Mid-Later

Pleistocene along with larger triangular flakes. As a group, centripetally flaked cores account for 16.3 per cent (n=26) of the assemblage which represents a low but not insignificant proportion. In the assemblage excavated in 1954 (n=101), the frequency of discoidal cores exceeds 40 per cent and biconical and proto-biconical (equivalent of radial cores) contribute approximately 20 per cent to the total. Single and multiple platform and bipolar cores account for much of the remainder with prepared cores making a neglible contribution. Centripetal flaking is well established in this assemblage.

Differences in the mean dimensions of core types (fig. 10.24) follow a pattern that in part reflects the origin of

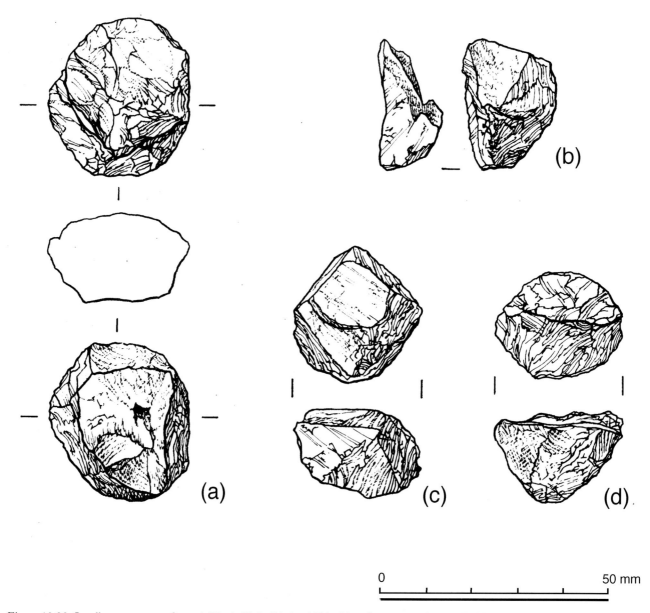

Figure 10.23 Small quartz cores from A Block, Twin Rivers 1999: (a) a flat prepared core (E5/F5–1); (b) opposed platform flake and bladelet core (E5/F5–1); (c) centripetally flaked topknot flake (E5/F5–1); (d) prepared core (E5/F5–1).

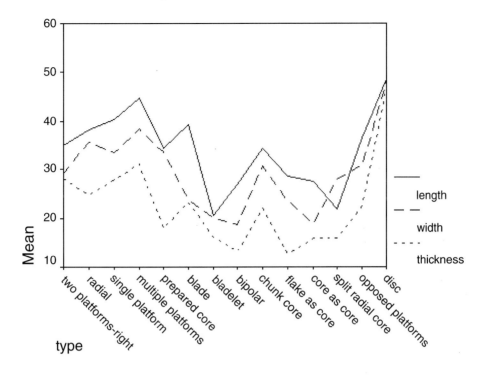

Figure 10.24 Mean length, width and thickness (millimetres) of cores by type, A Block.

the raw material and the reduction sequence. Bipolar and bladelet cores are made on cobbles which limits the potential size range of these artefacts. Flakes as cores and cores as cores are smaller because they represent a late stage in the reduction sequence. Disc cores are the largest form followed by the multiple platform cores with both types made on blocks of vein quartz. Vein quartz was the raw material of choice for all techniques of flaking (table 10.10).

F BLOCK

The small assemblage of cores from F Block (n=59) resembles that of A Block in the predominance of bipolar and informal flaking methods and in the low but persistent frequencies of more controlled flaking techniques (table 10.11; fig. 10.25).

Single platform, bipolar and chunk cores account for more than 50 per cent of the assemblage. Quartz cobbles, as in A Block, were transported to the site from a nearby stream or river and the remainder of the assemblage is made from vein quartz or shades of coloured quartz of presumed vein origin (table 10.12). The use of coloured quartz has a parallel in the Last Interglacial occupation (unit VII) at Mumbwa Caves.

Frequencies of blade, prepared and radial cores are low and similar to those in A Block. Among the large sample excavated in 1956 (n=404 in total), a similar pattern emerges as seen in A Block. Discoidal cores

Table 10.10 Raw material frequencies for A Block cores

Raw material

	Frequency	Per cent	Cumulative per cent
Crystal	11	6.9	6.9
Vein quartz	146	91.3	98.1
Granular quartz	2	1.3	99.4
Limonite	1	0.6	100.0
Total	160	100.0	

Table 10.11 Frequencies and percentages of cores by type, F Block

Type

	Frequency	Per cent	Cumulative per cent
Two platforms-right	5	8.5	8.5
Radial	4	6.8	15.3
Single platform	13	22.0	37.3
Multiple platforms	2	3.4	40.7
Prepared core	3	5.1	45.8
Blade	3	5.1	50.8
Bipolar	10	16.9	67.8
Chunk core	8	13.6	81.4
Flake as core	6	10.2	91.5
Core fragment	1	1.7	93.2
Opposed platforms	4	6.8	100.0
Total	59	100.0	

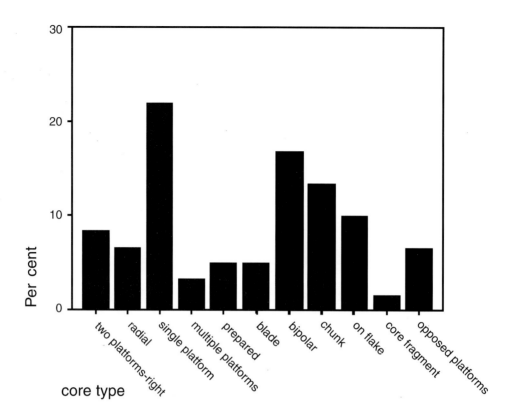

Figure 10.25 Percentage frequencies of cores by type, F Block.

Table 10.12 Raw material frequencies and percentages for cores, F Block

Raw material

	Frequency	Per cent	Cumulative per cent
Crystal	3	5.1	5.1
Vein quartz	53	89.8	94.9
Blue quartz	1	1.7	96.6
Granular quartz	1	1.7	98.3
Green quartz	1	1.7	100.0
Total	59	100.0	

account for nearly 40 per cent of the combined total of the upper (F1) and lower (F2, F3) excavation levels. Multiple platform cores are the next most numerous type followed by proto-biconical and bipolar forms. Prepared cores occur in low frequencies and comprise less than 5 per cent of the assemblage.

The size distribution of cores reflects the same raw material source bias as seen in A Block: bipolar cores are the smallest (fig. 10.26). The size distribution of cores is in part controlled by the topography of this part of F Block. A rise in the floor leading to overhang in J23/K23 appears to have acted as a filter that prevented large artefacts from entering this passage. The cores are generally smaller than those in A Block and smaller than those found in F Block in 1956.

Core by-products

The sample of discarded and broken cores and core rejuvenation flakes is small for A Block (n=70) (table 10.13) and even smaller for F Block (n=12), but informative about reduction strategies nonetheless. Top-knot flakes are the most frequent form of waste (35.7 per cent) and these specialised core rejuvenation flakes are indicators of radial flaking and the extension of the working life of radial cores. There are more topknot flakes (n=25) than radial cores (n=11) and split radial cores (n=11) combined. The imbalance can be interpreted as evidence of the extensive use of the cores to minimise the collection and transport of vein quartz back to the site. The prevalence of split bipolar cores (segments) in the assemblage (24.3 per cent) corresponds relatively closely to the percentage of bipolar cores (19 per cent). The reduction of cobbles accounted for a significant proportion of the flaking strategy. Broken blade cores (n=9,12.9 per cent) are more abundant than discarded whole blade cores (n=3). The propensity of quartz to shatter may explain the dis-

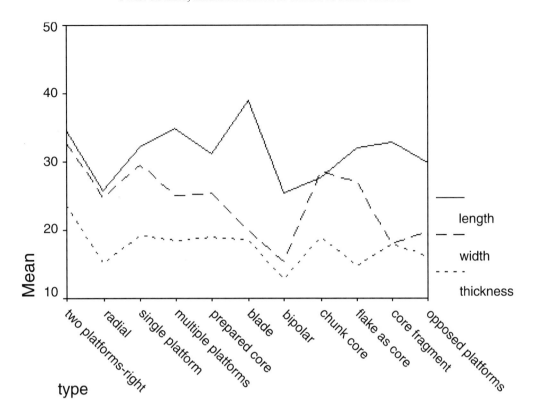

Figure 10.26 Mean length, width and thickness (millimetres) of cores by type, F Block.

Table 10.13 Raw material frequencies (a) and type frequencies (b) of core by-products from A Block

Raw material

	Frequency	Per cent	Cumulative per cent
Crystal	6	8.6	8.6
Vein quartz	63	90.0	98.6
Quartzite	1	1.4	100.0
Total	70	100.0	

(a)

Type

	Frequency	Per cent	Cumulative per cent
Bipolar segment	17	24.3	24.3
Core rejuvenation flake	1	1.4	25.7
Topknot flake	25	35.7	61.4
Split radial	11	15.7	77.1
Split prepared core	2	2.9	80.0
Blade core fragment	9	12.9	92.9
Split disc core	2	2.9	95.7
Core fragments	3	4.3	100.0
Total	70	100.0	

(b)

crepancy, and this is reflected in the raw material frequencies for the category as a whole.

The F Block sample is too small for viable statistical comparison but it does contain elements in common with the A Block assemblage and indicative of radial, bipolar and blade flaking techniques (table 10.14).

Whole flakes

A BLOCK

A total of 367 whole flakes was analysed for evidence of techniques of production, raw material selection and use damage. The attributes applied and type codes are outlined in appendices 3–4.

The presence/absence of cortex provides an indicator of the stage in the reduction sequence (cortex=early) and for the sources of raw material used. Cobble exteriors are indicative of fluvial sources. Approximately 26 per cent of flakes in the assemblage (n=93) have more than 50 per cent of the dorsal surface covered in cortex (table 10.15) and of these only three can be attributed to cobbles (3.2 per cent). The remaining majority are from vein sources.

The pattern of dorsal surface scarring is used as an indicator of the form of the core and technique of

Table 10.14 Raw material frequencies (a) and type frequencies (b) of core by-products from F Block

Raw material

	Frequency	Per cent	Cumulative per cent
Crystal	2	16.7	16.7
Vein quartz	9	75.0	91.7
Limonite	1	8.3	100.0
Total	12	100.0	

(a)

Type

	Frequency	Per cent	Cumulative per cent
Bipolar segment	3	25.0	25.0
Core rejuvenation flake	2	16.7	41.7
Topknot flake	6	50.0	91.7
Blade core fragment	1	8.3	100.0
Total	12	100.0	

(b)

Table 10.15 Frequency and percentage of whole flakes with cortex, A Block

Cortex

	Frequency	Per cent	Valid per cent	Cumulative per cent
Absent	269	73.3	74.3	74.3
Present	93	25.3	25.7	100.0
Total	362	98.6	100.0	
Missing	5	1.4		
Total	367	100.0		

Table 10.16 Dorsal surface scar pattern frequencies and percentages on whole flakes, A Block

Dorsal scars

	Frequency	Per cent	Valid per cent	Cumulative per cent
Cortex	33	9.0	9.1	9.1
Parallel	86	23,4	23.6	32.7
Convergent	33	9.0	9.1	41.8
Irregular	27	7.4	7.4	49.2
Opposed to butt	1	0.3	0.3	49.5
Opposed	47	12.8	12.9	62.4
Radial	104	28.3	28.6	90.9
Irregular 2D	32	8.7	8.8	99.7
Convergent 2D	1	0.3	0.3	100.0
Total	364	99.2	100.0	
Missing	3	0.8		
Total	367	100.0		

and radial cores (~40 per cent). Parallel flake scars are also common (23 per cent) and the percentage agrees closely with that for single platform cores (22 per cent).

The percentage of flakes with opposed scars (12.8 per cent) is twice that of opposed platform flake cores, and may also reflect the quantity of flakes produced by the technique. The frequency of flakes with irregular scars from two or more directions (8 per cent) roughly matches the percentage of multiple platform cores (11 per cent). A single flake with convergent scars from two directions (and with a faceted butt) appears to have been made from a prepared core. The occurrence of a single flake in contrast to the higher percentage of prepared cores (6.3 per cent) resembles the prepared flake:core ratio at Mumbwa. The latter was interpreted as evidence for the use and discard of the flakes away from the site.

The frequency of faceted butts is an additional indicator of the use of centripetal and prepared core flaking techniques (table 10.17). Simple facets are the product of radial and disc cores, also occasionally from multiple platform cores, and in A Block they account for 44 per cent of the assemblage. Multifaceted flakes comprise an additional 6.8 per cent of the assemblage. Taken together, these two types show the importance of centripetal flaking as the primary means of creating blanks. Flakes with plain butts are the next most common type and reflect the use of a variety of other flaking techniques, in particular single and opposed platform cores.

Vein quartz is the most commonly knapped raw material (81 per cent) with other forms of quartz, including coloured varieties, contributing an additional

flaking. Centripetal flaking techniques are reflected in radial and convergent scars, single platform cores are indicated by scars parallel to the flaking axis and originating from the distal end. Two platform and opposed platform cores are represented by scars opposed to the butt or distal end and by irregular scarring from one direction. Multiple platforms are correlated with irregular scarring from two or more directions (irregular–2D), depending on the stage of reduction. Prepared core techniques are equated with convergent scarring approaching from two or more directions. The results in table 10.16 show that centripetal techniques are best represented among the complete flakes. Radial and convergent scars when combined account for 38 per cent of the assemblage, which is surprisingly high given the relatively low percentage of radial cores (6 per cent) in A Block. Radial flaking is a productive approach to reducing a mass of material and this may account for the discrepancy between core and flake frequencies. The prevalence of radial scarring does correspond closely to the core data from 1954 with its high frequencies of disc

Table 10.17 Frequencies and percentages of butt types on whole flakes, A Block

Butt type

	Frequency	Per cent	Valid per cent	Cumulative per cent
Plain	108	29.4	30.5	30.5
Simple facet	156	42.5	44.1	74.6
Shattered	41	11.2	11.6	86.2
Multifaceted	24	6.5	6.8	92.9
Cortex	15	4.1	4.2	97.2
Point	10	2.7	2.8	100.0
Total	354	96.5	100.0	
Missing	13	3.5		
Total	367	100.0		

Table 10.18 Raw material frequencies and percentages among whole flakes, A Block

Raw material

	Frequency	Per cent	Valid per cent	Cumulative per cent
Quartz crystal	34	9.3	9.3	9.3
Vein quartz	296	80.7	80.9	90.2
Blue quartz	1	0.3	0.3	90.4
Granular quartz	9	2.5	2.5	92.9
Green quartz	2	0.5	0.5	93.4
Quartzite	12	3.3	3.3	96.7
Chert	4	1.1	1.1	97.8
Hematite	1	0.3	0.3	98.1
Sandstone	1	0.3	0.3	98.4
Dolerite	4	1.1	1.1	99.5
Limonite	1	0.3	0.3	99.7
Other	1	0.3	0.3	100.0
Total	366	99.7	100.0	
Missing	1	0.3		
Total	367	100.0		

12.6 per cent of the total (table 10.18). A fine-grained brown quartzite is a rarely used material as is chert and dolerite. The latter two materials occur locally within a 5 km radius of the site, but the source of the quartzite has not been located. A siliceous form of limonite is represented by a single flake and by a single core. This form of limonite produces flakes with cutting edges that are not as sharp as quartz but they may be more durable and they impart a characteristic yellow streak. All the dolerite in the assemblage has degraded and formed a soft cortex that obscures most flaking features. The final indicator of preferred flaking techniques comes from the distribution of flake types (appendix 4) (table 10.19) as defined by overall morphology and combining butt preparation data.

Quadrilateral flakes with plain butts and irregular flakes with plain butts together account for 55 per cent of the assemblage. As with the Later Pleistocene and Holocene samples at Mumbwa Caves, these two types are the basic forms produced by informal flaking. More informative variation occurs in the percentage of five-sided flakes; a form indicative of centripetal techniques. Pentagonal flakes with simple faceted butts represent 14 per cent of the sample. Multifaceted convergent flakes (fig. 10.27) are a small but distinctive sample (4.9 per cent). The flakes are wide in relation to length and relatively thin and there are some morphological characteristics of classic Levallois flakes (van Peer 1992). Blades as a component of the assemblage comprise only 2.7 per cent of flakes and bladelets 2.3 per cent, but they represent the intentional production of long flakes to complement the generally broad and squat centripetal forms. Two crested blades were found in the assemblages and are indicative of the initial stages of blade debitage. A small number (n=7) of burin blow spalls were recovered (fig. 10.35e) and can be related to the making of burins and awls (becs) as described below.

The dimensions of the continuous variables of flake length, width, thickness and butt width and thickness

Table 10.19 Flake type code frequencies and percentages, A Block

Type code

	Frequency	Per cent	Cumulative per cent
Missing	2	0.4	0.4
01400	2	0.4	0.8
01410	104	21.4	22.3
01412	8	1.6	23.9
01416	1	0.2	24.1
01420	164	33.8	57.9
01421	2	0.4	58.4
01422	9	1.9	60.2
01430	7	1.4	61.6
01440	27	5.6	67.2
01460	13	2.7	69.9
01461	4	0.8	70.7
01462	1	0.2	70.9
01470	11	2.3	73.2
01471	3	0.6	73.8
01472	2	0.4	74.2
01480	72	14.8	89.1
01486	3	0.6	89.7
01490	7	1.4	91.1
01910	1	0.2	91.3
02220	2	0.4	91.8
02311	11	2.3	94.0
02312	14	2.9	96.9
02313	1	0.2	97.1
02314	7	1.4	98.6
02315	1	0.2	98.8
02316	2	0.4	99.2
02317	1	0.2	99.4
02319	1	0.2	99.6
02337	2	0.4	100.0
Total	485	100.0	

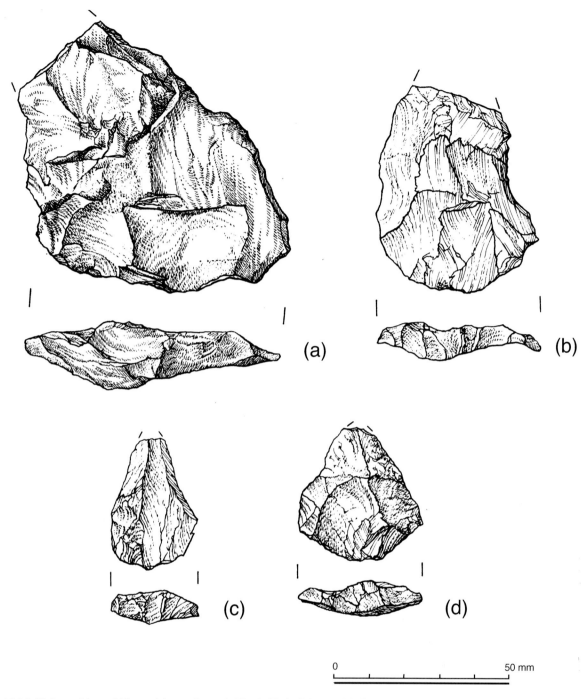

Figure 10.27 Flakes with multifaceted butts from A Block, Twin Rivers: (a) fine-grained quartzite (E5/E6–3); (b) vein quartz (E5/E6–2); (c) vein quartz covergent form (E5/E6–2); (d) vein quartz, convergent form (E5/E6–2). Flakes c and d were produced on prepared cores.

(table 10.20) provide the final indicator of flaking methods. As discussed in the analysis of the Mumbwa assemblage, a knapper exercises control over flake dimensions by manipulating variables of the core surface, platform and by the type and weight of force applied. Figure 10.28 illustrates the effect of dorsal surface preparation on flake size and indirectly shows the correl-

ation between reduction technique and the morphology of the blank. Convergent flakes with faceted butts are nearly as wide as they are long and relatively thin for their large size. Core preparation and faceting are the variables that govern the morphology of these flakes. Radial flakes are also relatively wide in comparison to length. Flakes with opposed and parallel scars are the

Table 10.20 Mean flake length, width, thickness, butt width, butt thickness (millimetres) and weight (grams), A Block

Descriptive statistics

	N	*Minimum*	*Maximum*	*Sum*	*Mean*	*Std deviation*
Length	366	9	73	10702	29.24	9.14
Width	367	5	79	9100	24.80	9.78
Thickness	365	2	87	3404	9.33	6.99
Butt width	330	2	287	5510	16.70	17.53
Butt thickness	324	1	21	2122	6.55	3.80
Weight (g)	365	1	114	2146	8.62	11.64

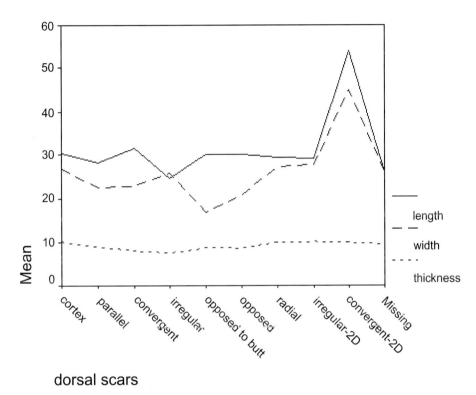

Figure 10.28 Mean flake length, width and thickness (millimetres) by type of dorsal surface scar pattern, A Block.

narrowest in relation to length and are indicative of the production of blades or long flakes.

The effect of butt preparation on flake dimensions can be seen among pentagonal and convergent flakes with faceted platforms. Pentagonal flakes as a rule have simple facets with 2–3 scars and convergent flakes are mulifaceted. Among the sample of pentagonal flakes from both A and F Blocks, mean butt width and thickness are significantly correlated with mean flake length, width and thickness (table 10.21). Unlike convergent flakes, the butt is not generally the widest part of the flake, which means these two variables are independent and the relationship is more likely to be causal. Butt attributes are also independent of flake length which suggests a controlling effect.

Among convergent flakes with two directional scarring and with faceted platforms, butt width is correlated with flake width and not length and thickness (table 10.22). Butt thickness is significantly correlated with both width and thickness as might be expected as the two are dependent variables. The butt is usually the widest and thickest portion of convergent flakes. Flake length, width and thickness are correlated with each other. At an intuitive level, the correlation between flake length and thickness and the correlation between butt thickness and flake thickness suggests that butt thickness does affect flake length. The latter correlation existed in the Mumbwa Caves convergent flake sample.

The correlation data as a whole suggests that the knappers at Twin Rivers appreciated the causal links between flaking technique and flake size and shape. The reduction strategies of centripetal flaking and core preparation both involve an understanding of the complex links between core geometry and desired

Table 10.21 Pearson bivariate correlations of butt width and thickness with flake length, width and thickness (millimetres). Sample restricted to pentagonal flakes with simple faceted butts, A Block

Correlation

		Length	Width	Thickness	Butt width	Butt thickness
Length	Pearson correlation	1.000	0.658★★	0.589★★	0.317★★	0.393★★
	Sig. (2-tailed)	.	0.000	0.000	0.009	0.001
	N	72	72	72	67	66
Width	Pearson correlation	0.658★★	1.000	0.626★★	0.581★★	0.509★★
	Sig. (2-tailed)	0.000	.	0.000	0.000	0.000
	N	72	72	72	67	66
Thickness	Pearson correlation	0.589★★	0.626★★	1.000	0.333★★	0.524★★
	Sig. (2-tailed)	0.000	0.000	.	0.006	0.000
	N	72	72	72	67	66
Butt width	Pearson correlation	0.317★★	0.581★★	0.333★★	1.000	0.522★★
	Sig. (2-tailed)	0.009	0.000	0.006	.	0.000
	N	67	67	67	67	66
Butt thickness	Pearson correlation	0.393★★	0.509★★	0.524★★	0.522★★	1.000
	Sig. (2-tailed)	0.001	0.000	0.000	0.000	.
	N	66	66	66	66	66

Table 10.22 Pearson bivariate correlations of butt width and thickness with flake length, width and thickness (millimetres). Sample restricted to convergent flakes with multifaceted butts, A Block

Correlation

		Length	Width	Thickness	Butt width	Butt thickness
Length	Pearson correlation	1.000	0.508★★	0.605★★	−0.092	0.191
	Sig. (2-tailed)	.	0.007	0.001	0.654	0.350
	N	27	27	27	26	26
Width	Pearson correlation	0.508★★	1.000	0.742★★	0.637★★	0.637★★
	Sig. (2-tailed)	0.007	.	0.000	0.000	0.000
	N	27	27	27	26	26
Thickness	Pearson correlation	0.605★★	0.742★★	1.000	0.229	0.772★★
	Sig. (2-tailed)	0.001	0.000	.	0.260	0.000
	N	27	27	27	26	26
Butt width	Pearson correlation	−0.092	0.637★★	0.229	1.000	0.539★★
	Sig. (2-tailed)	0.654	0.000	0.260	.	0.004
	N	26	26	26	26	26
Butt thickness	Pearson correlation	0.191	0.637★★	0.772★★	0.539★★	1.000
	Sig. (2-tailed)	0.350	0.000	0.000	0.004	.
	N	26	26	26	26	26

★★ Correlation is significant at the 0.01 level (2-tailed).

outcomes. This level of cognitive awareness or 'operational intelligence' had developed by *c* 270 ka BP in the case of Twin Rivers and had its roots in the complex spatial geometry of late Acheulian biface production (Wynn 1989).

F BLOCK

The smaller and taphonomically biased F Block sample resembles the A Block flake assemblage in the percentage of flakes with cortex (table 10.23). Cortex is found on approximately 20 per cent of flakes and indicates that the early stages in the reduction sequence were taking place on site.

The pattern of dorsal scar distribution (table 10.24) shows a higher percentage frequency of radial flaking (31 per cent) compared with A Block. Parallel (23 per cent) and opposed scars are relatively common (12 per cent) and represent the reduction of single and opposed platform cores. Irregular flakes with scars originating from two or more directions are also numerous (14 per

Table 10.23 Frequency and percentage of whole flakes with
>50 per cent cortex, F Block

Cortex

	Frequency	Per cent	Cumulative per cent
Absent	94	79.7	79.7
Present	24	20.3	100.0
Total	118	100.0	

Table 10.24 Dorsal scar pattern frequencies and percentages
for whole flakes, F Block

Dorsal scars

Type	Frequency	Per cent	Cumulative per cent
Cortex	10	8.5	8.5
Parallel	27	22.9	31.4
Convergent	9	7.6	39.0
Irregular	2	1.7	40.7
Opposed to butt	2	1.7	42.4
Opposed	14	11.9	54.2
Radial	37	31.4	85.6
Irregular-2D	17	14.4	100.0
Total	118	100.0	

Table 10.25 Butt type frequencies and percentages for whole
flakes, F Block

Butt prep

Type	Frequency	Per cent	Cumulative per cent
Plain	37	31.4	31.4
Simple facet	41	34.7	66.1
Shattered	15	12.7	78.8
Multifaceted	10	8.5	87.3
Cortex	9	7.6	94.9
Point	6	5.1	100.0
Total	118	100.0	

Table 10.26 F Block, flake type frequencies by code number

Type code

Type	Frequency	Per cent	Cumulative per cent
01400	1	0.8	0.8
01410	28	23.7	24.6
01412	2	1.7	26.3
01420	43	36.4	62.7
01430	4	3.4	66.1
01440	9	7.6	73.7
01460	3	2.5	76.3
01462	1	0.8	77.1
01480	22	18.6	95.8
01490	1	0.8	96.6
02311	1	0.8	97.5
02312	2	1.7	99.2
02313	1	0.8	100.0
Total	118	100.0	

cent) and are the likely products of multiple platform
cores as well as radial flaking. Convergent scars account
for 7.6 per cent of the assemblage which compares
closely with the percentage of flakes with multifaceted
butts (8.5 per cent) (table 10.25)

Flakes with simple facets dominate the assemblage
(34.7 per cent) followed by plain platforms (31.4 per
cent). The prevalence of these two types reflects two
differing reduction strategies, one centripetal flaking and
the other the removal of flakes from single or opposed
platform cores. The outcomes differ in shape (table
10.26).

Quadrilateral and irregular plan forms with plain
butts are the two most common flake types (table 10.26)
and are equated with single, opposed and multiple platform cores. The moderately high percentage of pentagonal forms (18.6 per cent) is linked to radial flaking,
but the higher frequency of radial dorsal scars (31.4 per
cent) suggests that some convergent flakes are also the
result of centripetal flaking. Adding both convergent
forms to the pentagonal total gives an overall percentage
of 29.6 per cent.

The size distribution of flakes is smaller than that in A
Block with the largest flakes (fig. 10.29) having a length
of 35 mm as compared with 55 mm in A Block. The
filtering effect of the raised platform outside the F Block
passage is evident. Only smaller flakes have been
deposited in the slurry that filled J23/K23, with larger,
heavier flakes having settled in the deepest portion of the
cave and nearer the entrance. Flakes from the 1956
excavation are indeed larger and some exceed 100 mm
in length (Clark & Brown in press).

As shown in figure 10.29, the majority of flakes from
the 1999 excavation are relatively wide in relation to
length with the exception of those with parallel scars.
The latter type is linked to single and opposed platform
cores and to blade production. The thinnest flakes have
convergent scarring which suggests that some have been
struck from prepared cores. Levallois core reduction
techniques generate thin flakes (van Peer 1992) as a
predetermined outcome.

Raw material selection in F Block (table 10.27) also
resembles that in A Block with vein quartz being the
primary material used. A fine-grained brown quartzite,
similar to that found in A Block, was used to a limited
degree.

Broken flakes
The artefacts in this category are classified by size
range (20–30 mm, 30–40 mm, 40–50 mm, 50–60 mm,

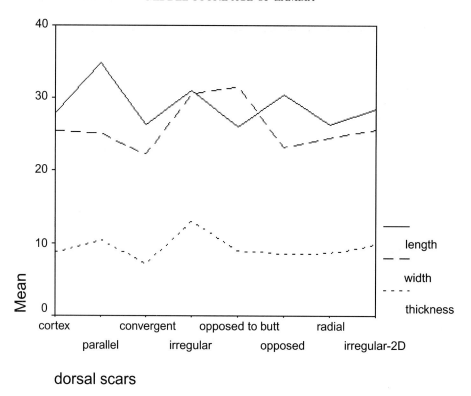

Figure 10.29 Mean flake length, width and thickness (mm) by dorsal surface pattern, F Block.

Table 10.27 Raw material frequencies and percentages for whole flakes, F Block

Raw material

Type	Frequency	Per cent	Cumulative per cent
Quartz crystal	5	4.2	4.2
Vein quartz	106	89.8	94.1
Granular quartz	2	1.7	95.8
Quartzite	4	3.4	99.2
Limonite	1	0.8	100.0
Total	118	100.0	

>60 mm) and by raw material. Both the quantity and volume of debris provide additional indicators of the intensity of stone working that took place near the cave entrances. Both assemblages have been transported in slurry flows and in the case of F Block the topography of the passage will have winnowed out the largest flakes as was the case in the whole flake category.

The A Block assemblage contains 1348 flakes weighing a total of 5276 grams. The sample is all quartz with the exception of eight pieces of dolerite (0.6 per cent), seven pieces of quartzite (0.5 per cent), three pieces of chert (0.2 per cent) and one flake of limonite (0.07 per cent). The highest frequency and weight of broken flakes (fig. 10.30) occurs in the 20–30 mm size range and declines markedly between 30 and 60 mm.

In F Block, the total of 396 broken flakes weighs 1239 grams. The raw material frequency is almost all quartz with the minor exceptions of four flakes of dolerite (1.0 per cent), three flakes of quartzite (0.75 per cent), two flakes of diorite (0.5 per cent) and one flake of sandstone (0.25 per cent). The distribution by size and weight (fig. 10.31) resembles that in A Block with the bulk of the sample falling in the 20–30 mm range. F Block does differ slightly in its lack of flakes >60 mm which may reflect the winnowing effect of the passage entrance.

The predominance of small flaking debris in both blocks provides evidence for active flaking having taken place around the cave entrances. The incidence of rolled or battered edges is low (not quantified) in the whole and broken flake categories which is in keeping with the gentle mode of deposition. Clark & Brown (in press) note that the majority of the F Block assemblage is slightly abraded (~60 per cent) and among the remainder about 25 per cent are fresh in appearance and roughly 15 per cent are abraded.

Chunks
This category includes angular blocks of material (>20 mm) that are the by-products of flaking. In A

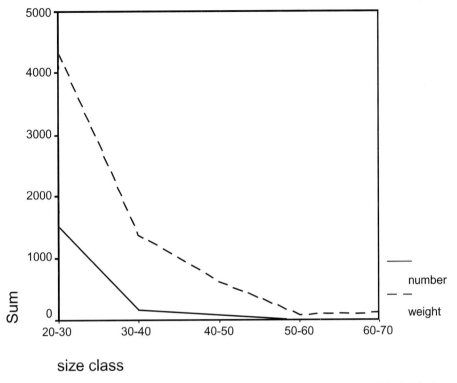

Figure 10.30 Distribution of broken flakes by size class (mm) and weight (g), A Block.

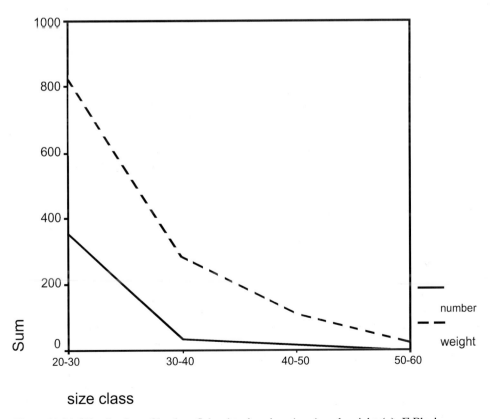

Figure 10.31 Distribution of broken flakes by size class (mm) and weight (g), F Block.

Block, a total of 4003 chunks weighed 5141 grams. Quartz was by far the most common material (n=3909, 97.7 per cent). Other materials include quartzite (n=47, 1.2 per cent, 47 g), chert (n=21, 0.3 per cent, 24 g), dolerite (n=14, 0.35 per cent, 25 g), sandstone (n=10, 0.25 per cent, 21 g) and schist (n=1, 0.02 per cent, 1 g).

In F Block, the total of 2635 chunks weighs 3331 grams. Quartz accounts for 98.2 per cent of the sample (n=2588) and 98.5 per cent of the total weight (3280 g). The remaining chunks include quartzite (n=18, 0.7 per cent, 8 g), diorite (n=13, 0.5 per cent, 20 g), chert (n=4, 0.15 per cent, 4 g) and dolerite (n=3, 0.1 per cent, 3 g).

The ratio of chunks to weight is similar in both blocks (A=.78, F=.79), which suggests that sorting by size has not affected this particular artefact class in F Block.

Small flaking debris (<10 mm)
By far the most numerous artefacts at Twin Rivers are the fragments of flakes, chunks and angular shatter less than 10 mm in maximum dimension. These were recovered in quantity as a result of the use of a fine-meshed sieve (0.5 mm). This material is produced during flaking and constitutes primary evidence for knapping in the vicinity of the cave entrances. Included in this sample are other raw materials, including hematite and specularite, as well as bone fragments. The sheer quantity of material from both excavation blocks meant that the analysis in the field could not proceed in the normal sequence of sorting, counting and weighing individual pieces. Bulk analysis was introduced to expedite processing. From each 10 cm excavation unit, a 100 g unselected sample was used to estimate the frequencies of raw materials and weight of bone for each unit as a whole. All pieces in each test sample were counted and sorted by raw material and then multiplied by a factor of 10 to give the quantities per one kilogram. The 1 kg figure was multiplied by the actual weight of material excavated. The results per unit are presented in appendix 6. The combined numbers by excavation block are as follows:

A Block:
  Quartz: n=106,466
  Pigment: n= 762

F Block:
  Quartz: n=220,270
  Pigment: n= 130

The quantity of material from F Block is particularly large given that the total volume of sediment excavated is less than that of A Block. Small, light debitage may have been preferentially rafted into the passage by debris flows. The inclusion of small flaking debris in the artefact total for each block would overwhelm the frequencies of all other artefacts in any reduction category. The percentage frequencies of utilised and retouched tools would be particularly disadvantaged given the low numbers of these artefacts.

The frequency of pigments by weight of deposit is potentially an underestimate because of the preferential selection of these minerals during artefact sorting. The pieces that were found had been missed on first inspection. An unselected sample would yield a higher figure.

Edge damaged and utilised flakes
Of the whole flake assemblage, 8.2 per cent (n=40) are classified as edge damaged (table 10.19). The majority (55 per cent, n=25) are flakes with irregular or quadrilateral plan forms with some degree of damage to one or more cutting edge. The frequency of damage mirrors the frequency of the two flake types in the assemblage. No secure behavioural information can be gleaned from this sample. The F Block sample (n=4, 3.4 per cent) is too small to consider.

Among the small sample of natural pieces modified by use (n=6) from both blocks, the artefacts from A Block include three grindstones (fig. 10.32), one spheroid (fig. 10.33) and an octagonal piece with facets worn smooth by abrasion (fig. 10.34). All of these were quartzite as was the yellow stained hammerstone found in A Block in 1954 (see manuports above). A sandstone abrader was the only modified object in F Block. Grindstones were recorded in the 1956 excavation of F Block (Clark 1971). The variety of modified objects known from the site is a further indicator of its use as a living site where a range of activities took place in addition to the knapping of quartz.

Retouched tools
One hundred and twenty retouched objects were found in A Block (table 10.28) and 24 in F Block (table 10.29). Quartz accounts for 98.3 per cent of the assemblage in A Block and 100 per cent of the F Block assemblage. A Block contains a variety of types that can be condensed in classes of artefacts for ease of description. Awls are the most common type (n=38, 31.6.8 per cent) with backed artefacts as a combined group accounting for a similar percentage (n=27, 22.5 per cent). Scrapers (n=22, 18.3 per cent) are the next most numerous. These three classes of artefacts taken together comprise more than two-thirds (72.4 per cent) of the retouched tools.

Awls as a type are sub-divided into two forms that are distinguished by the techniques used to form the working edge. The majority (type 03420) have a tip formed by the intersection of two flake scars (fig. 10.35a,c). A finer, thinner cutting edge is created by

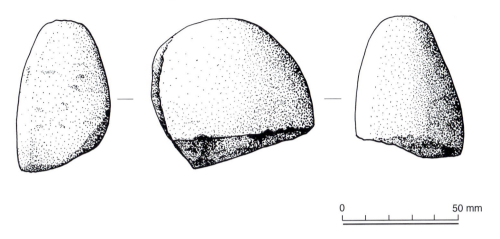

Figure 10.32 Quartzite grinding stone, A Block (E5/E6–1).

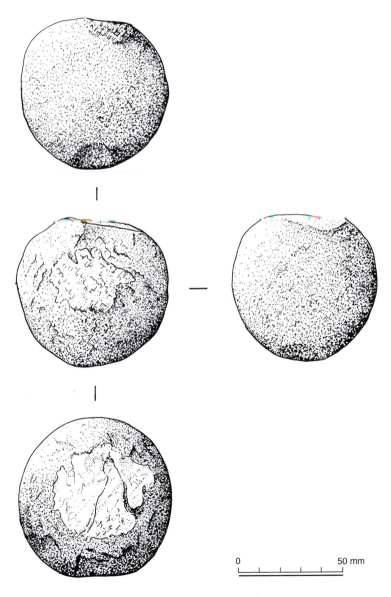

Figure 10.33 Quartzite spheroid, A Block (1996).

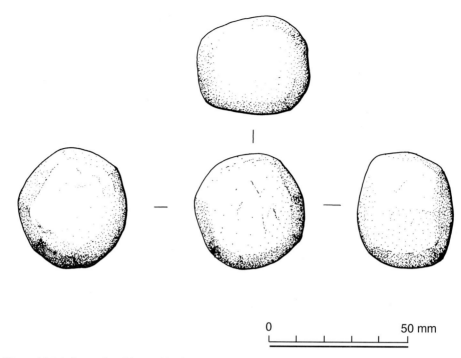

Figure 10.34 Quartzite object with eight faceted surfaces, A Block (1996 collection).

Table 10.28 Frequencies and percentages of retouched tools by type code, A Block

Type	Frequency	Per cent	Cumulative per cent	Type (continued)	Frequency	Per cent	Cumulative per cent
03111	8	6.7	6.7	03320	1	0.8	42.5
03112	4	3.3	10.0	03321	1	0.8	43.3
03115	2	1.7	11.7	03420	31	25.8	69.2
03116	3	2.5	14.2	03426	1	0.8	70.0
03120	1	0.8	15.0	03430	1	0.8	70.8
03121	2	1.7	16.7	03440	2	1.7	72.5
03122	1	0.8	17.5	03460	7	5.8	78.3
03125	1	0.8	18.3	03511	2	1.7	80.0
03211	2	1.7	20.0	03513	2	1.7	81.7
03213	4	3.3	23.3	03520	1	0.8	82.5
03214	1	0.8	24.2	03521	1	0.8	83.3
03216	2	1.7	25.8	03600	6	5.0	88.3
03217	1	0.8	26.7	03700	3	2.5	90.8
03221	1	0.8	27.5	03710	4	3.3	94.2
03222	2	1.7	29.2	03720	3	2.5	96.7
03223	10	8.3	37.5	03810	1	0.8	97.5
03225	1	0.8	38.3	03820	1	0.8	98.3
03226	2	1.7	40.0	03900	2	1.7	100.0
03230	1	0.8	40.8				
03312	1	0.8	41.7	Total	120	100.0	

striking a burin blow opposite a flake scar (fig. 10.35d) (type 03460). Burins as a distinct type (03600) (fig. 10.35b) account for 5.0 per cent of the retouched assemblage (n=6) and are basic dihedral forms made on two intersecting burin scars. The separation of burins

from awls in the classification scheme may be an unnecessary splitting of tools with very similar working edges, though produced by slightly different techniques. All have robust tips suitable for scraping, planing, drilling and engraving. The burin tip differs in being

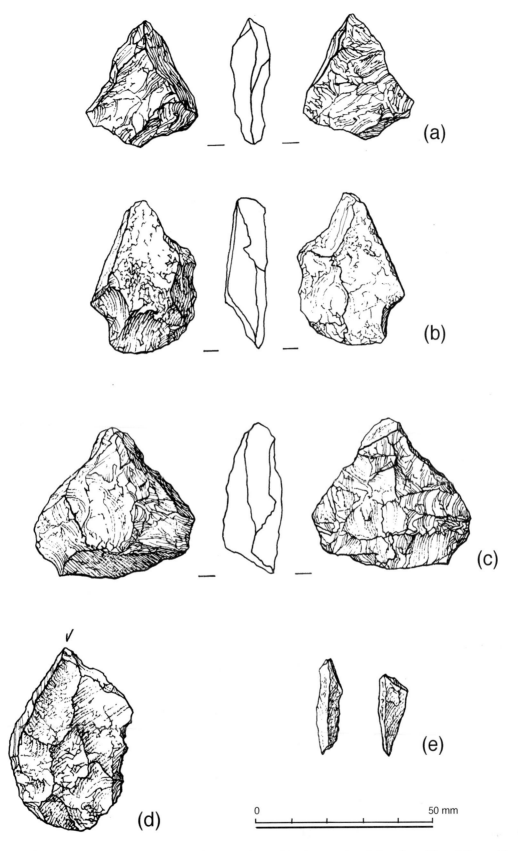

Figure 10.35 Awls and burins from A Block: (a) and (c) awls formed by intersecting flake scars; (d) awl formed by burin blow opposite flake scar; (b) burin; (e) burin spalls. All vein quartz.

more chisel-like, and this can be produced on awls as a result of rejuvenating the working edge. Burin spalls occur in the assemblage (fig. 10.35e) and add to the impression that awls/burins, and the activities associated with their use, were essential elements of life at Twin Rivers.

The broad class of backed tools encompasses 11 different tool types. Transverse cutting edges, formed by the backing and snapping of flakes, are the most common form (9.1 per cent) and are classified as *tranchets* or trapezes (>25 mm, n=1)) and *petits tranchets* (<25 mm, n=10). Quartz flakes were transformed into triangles with broad sharp cutting edges (fig. 10.36a,b,c) supported by laterals blunted by deliberate breakage or by retouch. The brittle quality of quartz favours the use of blunting by snapping with retouch used to accentuate the triangular form (fig. 10.36c). The base opposite the cutting edge is sometimes thinned as if designed for hafting (fig. 10.36a). The cutting edges tend to be damaged.

The remaining types of backed tools occur in small number and are often represented by just one or two specimens. Obliquely truncated blades (n=4) are common by comparison (fig. 10.36d,e). The truncations create a pointed rhomboidal shape with one cutting edge. Backed flakes (n=3) are less regular in plan (fig. 10.36f,j,k) with one or more cutting edges. An unusual artefact form, of which two were found in A Block, is a bladelet with a series of notches removed along one edge (fig. 10.36n). The small size makes it likely that this was a hafted insert.

Segments or flakes with convex backing opposite a cutting edge (fig. 10.36l) are rare (n=2), but their presence is significant because they represent a form of composite tool insert not thought to be a component of sub-Saharan assemblages at this early date. Segments are described from unit VII at Mumbwa Caves in association with Last Interglacial dates (chapter 8), but south of the Limpopo they fall within a later time range of 80–59 ka BP (Thackeray 1992; Miller et al 1999). North of the Zambezi, in central Africa, presumed Late Pleistocene deposits with segments have not been securely dated (Van Noten 1982). The segments at Twin Rivers, and the associated evidence for other forms of small backed tools, represent the earliest known occurrence of this technology. Clark and Brown (in press) record a low frequency of backed flakes, blades and segments recovered during the main excavations at Twin Rivers in the 1950s. The wider regional significance of this component of the retouched assemblage is discussed in chapter 13.

Large segments were also found in 1999 in the basal deposits of G Block (areas B1 and B2) (fig. 10.36,g-i,m). These might be associated with the TL date of 101±16 ka BP from this deposit as well as the later date

of 57±8 ka BP from the overlying level in which a large segment was found (fig. 10.36i). The distinction between large (>25 mm) and small (<25 mm) is significant in attempting to disentangle the G Block sequence. Small segments are only found in the upper 20 cm with equally small scrapers and are dated to the historic present. At Mumbwa Caves (units I–III), small segments are restricted in time to the Holocene–Late Glacial, and by extension the large segments in G Block are presumably Late Pleistocene in age. Other components of the lower deposits support an early age for much of this material (see below).

In F Block, the sample of retouched tools is too small (n=23) for reliable statistical analysis. This caveat aside, the assemblage does have a predominance of backed tools (n=9), in particular *petit tranchets* (n=3) (fig. 10.36b,c) and segments (n=3). Awls (n=3) are represented, as are scrapers (n=6).

In both blocks, scrapers vary widely in form, size and in the types of blanks chosen. Nosed, end, side and concave forms occur (fig. 10.37a,b,c,e), all larger than 20mm and made on flakes, cobbles (fig. 10.37d) and on cores (fig. 10.37f). This variety and apparent informality contrasts with the limited size and forms made in the Late Glacial–Holocene deposits at Mumbwa Caves and in the upper deposits in G Block. A range of scraper forms is also reported from the 1950s excavations in A and F Blocks (Clark and Brown in press).

Other types of retouched tools found in both blocks, include bifacially flaked pieces including points and a core axe. A point with a notched base was found in A Block (fig. 10.38a) as was a bifacially flaked object, badly damaged, with what appears to be a basal tang (fig. 10.38b). A tanged bifacial point was also found near the base of G Block (B1/7) (fig. 10.38c). The identification of tangs presupposes the use of hafting.

A range of broken bifaces is illustrated in figure 10.40 and includes points (a, b, c), the mid-section of a large biface or lanceolate (d) and the tip of a pick that is diamond-shaped in section (e). Complete forms were recovered in A and F Blocks in Clark's excavations in the 1950s (Clark 1971; Clark & Brown in press). A bifacial point appears to have been re-used as a burin (fig. 10.39d) with facets forming a straight edge and the body of the piece retaining the basic biface form. No unifacial points were found in either A or F Block, but they are reported, in low frequencies, from the 1956 excavation of F Block. Unifacial and bifacial points occur in the lower levels of G Block (fig. 10.39a,b,c).

Three retouched tools from A Block with steep, and damaged, cutting edges (fig. 10.41) deserve a brief mention. The largest of the three (fig. 10.41b) (60× 50×25 mm) has a broadly symmetrical plan and was made on a flake struck from a prepared platform as

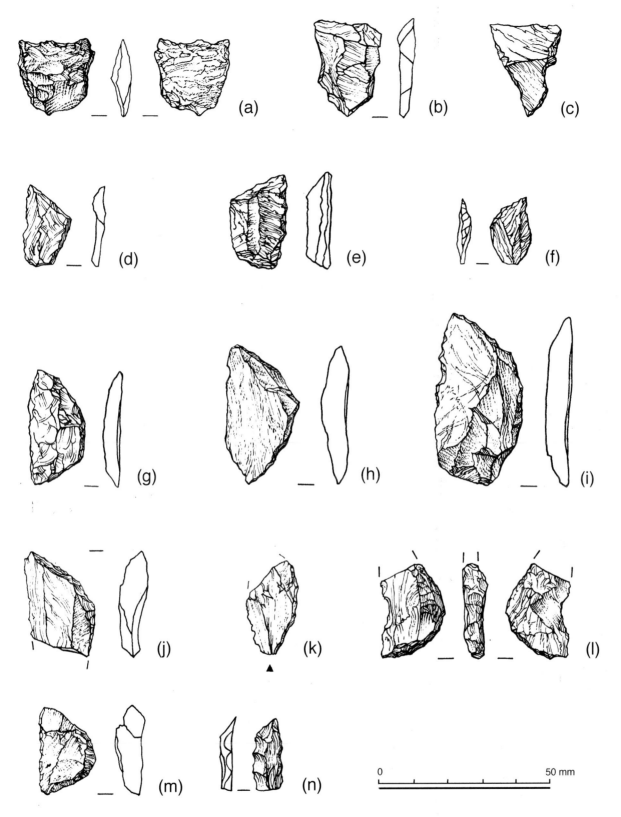

Figure 10.36 Backed and truncated quartz artefacts, A, F and G Blocks: (a) (E5/E6–2), (b) (K23–1) and (c) (J23–3) are trapezes or *tranchets*; (d) (E7), (e) (K23–2) are backed and obliquely truncated blades; (f) (J23–2) is an obliquely backed flake; (g) (B2–5); (h) (B1–8) and (i) (B1–7) are segments from G Block; (j) broken obliquely backed piece (B2/8); (k) broken backed flake, A Block (E5/E6–3); (l) segment, A Block (E5/E6–2); (m) segment, G Block (B1–8); (n) denticulated bladelet, F Block (K23/2).

Table 10.29 Frequencies and percentages of retouched tools by type code, F Block

Type

	Frequency	Per cent	Cumulative per cent
03111	2	8.7	8.7
03112	2	8.7	17.4
03115	1	4.3	21.7
03122	1	4.3	26.1
03213	1	4.3	30.4
03214	3	13.0	43.5
03217	1	4.3	47.8
03221	3	13.0	60.9
03226	1	4.3	65.2
03330	1	4.3	69.6
03420	2	8.7	78.3
03430	1	4.3	82.6
03460	1	4.3	87.0
03520	2	8.7	95.7
03700	1	4.3	100.0

indicated by the intersecting dorsal scars that have been amplified by retouch. The butt is multifaceted and the steep working edge forms a convex flange and has been retouched. A patch of breccia adheres to the lower right lateral. An almost identical artefact from Zambia is illustrated in the British Museum publication (1956) *Flint Implements* (plate III). A less formal piece, but similar in plan and with a steep working edge (fig. 10.41a), is effectively a large notched tool. The third example (fig. 10.41c) shows the basic symmetry and steep working edge that characterises this little group. For lack of a better term, they are classified as chisels (after Clark & Kleindienst 1974).

OVERVIEW AND INTERPRETATION

The human occupation of Twin Rivers took place in cave entrances and later on the open central platform of the hilltop. The now unroofed caves acted as sediment traps that filled with occupation debris which in time

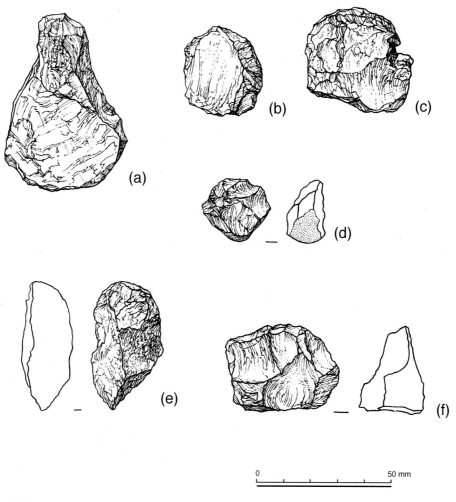

Figure 10.37 Vein quartz scrapers from A and F Blocks, Twin Rivers: (a) nosed form on flake (E5/E6–1); (b) side retouch on flake (E5/E6–1); (c) end and side retouch on flake (E5/E6–1); (d) on split cobble (E7); (e) end scraper on flake/blade (E4/F4–1); (f) side retouch on exhausted prepared core (K23–2).

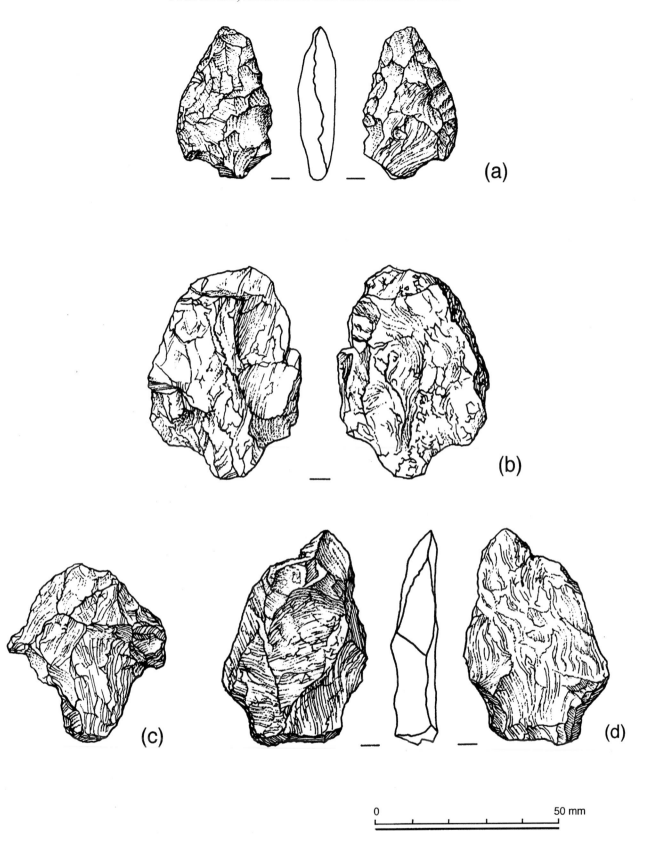

0   50 mm

Figure 10.38 Bifacially flaked and tanged pieces, Twin Rivers: (a) bifacial point or knife with notched base, A Block (E5/E6–1); (b) tanged piece with heavy edge and tip damage (E5/E6–3); (c) tanged and shouldered piece, G Block (B1–7); (d) flake with notched base, A Block (E5/F5–1). All vein quartz.

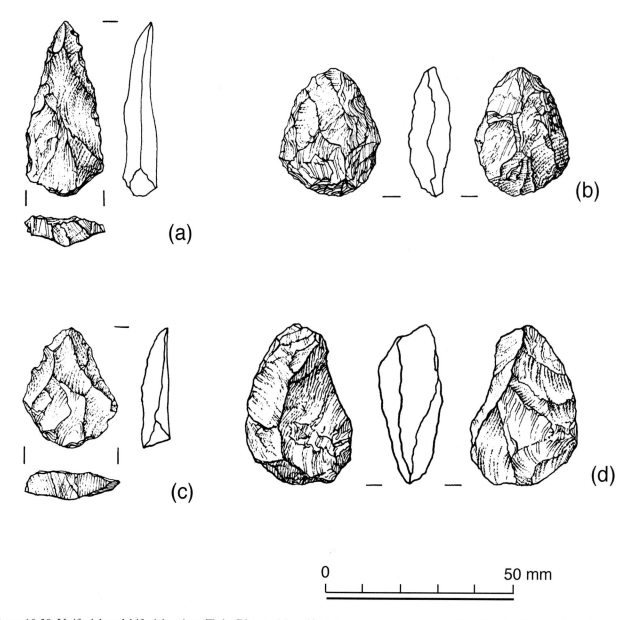

0   50 mm

Figure 10.39 Unifacial and bifacial points, Twin Rivers: (a) unifacial point on quartz crystal, G Block (B1–7); (b) vein quartz bifacial point (B2–8); (c) vein quartz unifacial point (B2–5); (d) vein quartz bifacial piece with burin blow on break, A Block (E5/E6–1).

became cemented into the breccia that preseved bone as well as stone artefacts. Lenses of speleothem deposited in the former caves have been dated by uranium-series to the Middle Pleistocene. The earlier of the two caves – A Block – contains breccia and sediments that may range in age from >400 ka BP at the base to 170 ka BP near the top. A more cautious reading of the dates places the archaeological deposits in the period 270–170 ka BP. The cave represented by F Block was filled with deposits between 140 and 200 ka BP. The two openings may have been partially contemporaneous in the later phases of occupation. The topography of the cave floor in F Block acted as a sediment filter that prevented larger pieces of stone and bone from entering the narrow passage that was excavated in 1999. No stratigraphic separation was made of the deposits in either block and no attempt was made to discern spatial patterning given the small areas available for excavation. After both caves had either filled or collapsed, the area of occupation shifted to the open hilltop in the Late Pleistocene. Excavation in G Block produced a partially mixed archaeological sequence dated by TL on burnt quartz to three periods in the Late Pleistocene (~100 ka, 56 ka and 17–13 ka BP) and by radiocarbon dating to the historic present.

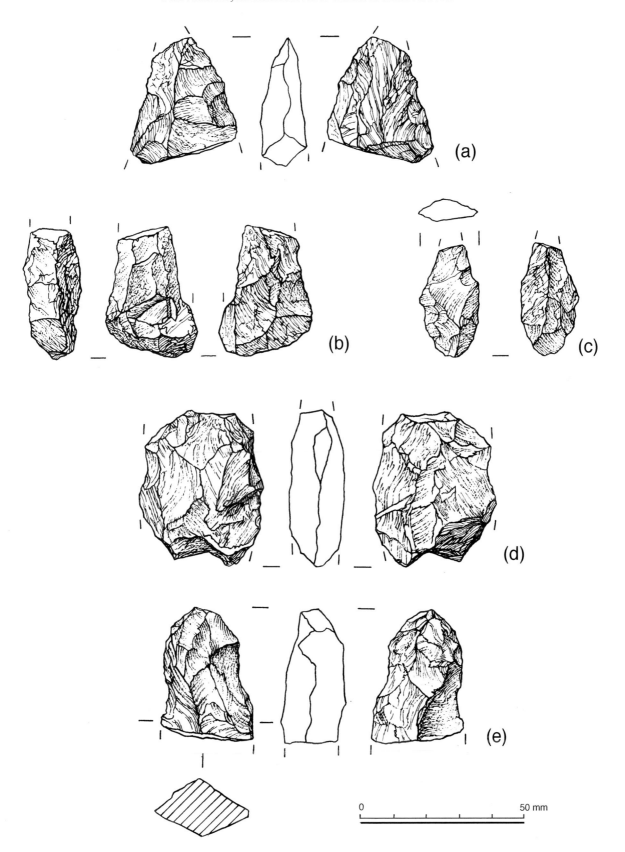

Figure 10.40 Broken bifacially flaked pieces, all vein quartz, Twin Rivers: (a) snapped and fractured point, A Block (E4/F4–1); (b) snapped tip; (c) basal thinning, A Block (E4/F4–1); (d) mid-section of lanceolate, A Block (E5/E6–4); (e) tip or distal end of a pick, F Block (K23–1).

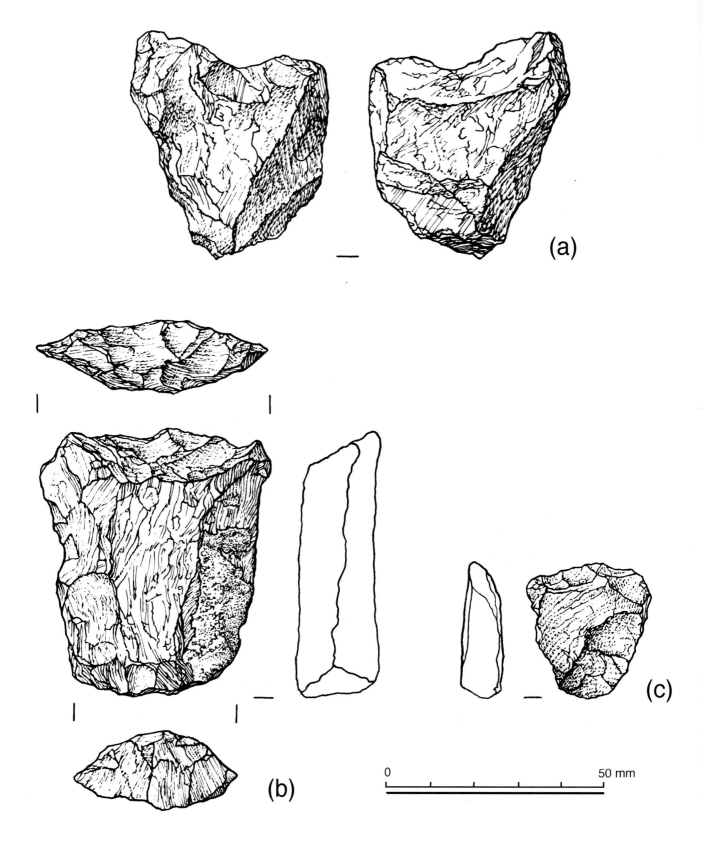

Figure 10.41 Chisel-edged artefacts with steep flanges, A Block, Twin Rivers: (a) vein quartz chunk with one steeply retouched side (E5/E6–3); (b) clear crystal with preformed laterals and multifaceted butt indicative of prepared core origin (breccia adheres to lower right-hand edge); (c) E4/F4–1.

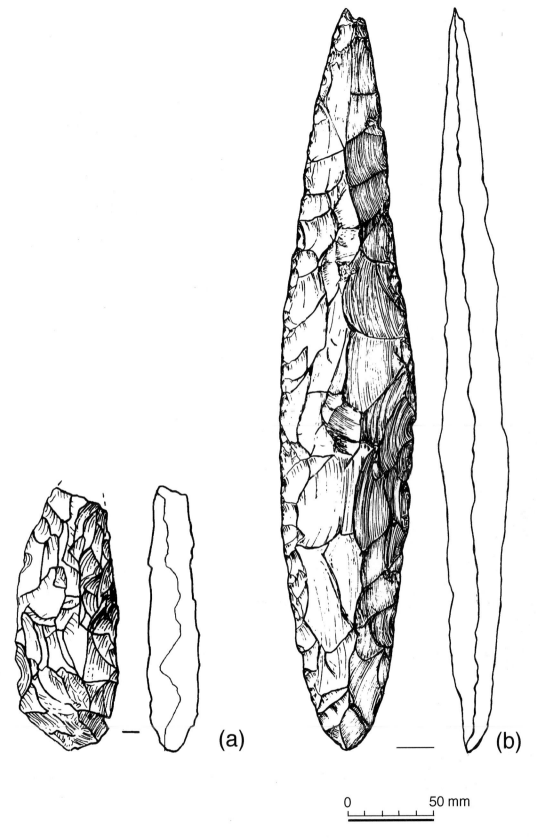

Figure 10.42 A comparison of Lupemban lanceolates from Twin Rivers: (a) F Block, quartz, after Clark (1971) and northeastern Angola (b) chert, after Clark (1966), showing the effect of raw material on size and thickness.

The A and F Block assemblages were made almost exclusively on quartz from local veins and river cobbles. The cores, core by-products and the range of flake debitage taken together show an equal mix of informal and planned flaking techniques. Cobbles were flaked using an anvil technique (bipolar) and the angular vein quartz was reduced by approaches that used existing platforms (chunk, single and multiple platform cores). Wide triangular flakes were made by alternate flaking around the circumference of a core (radial, disc) or by shaping the dorsal surface to remove particularly thin flakes (prepared). Longer, narrower flakes were made from opposed platform and blade cores. None of these techniques alone is indicative of a particular technological tradition, but as an assemblage they can be attributed to the Middle Stone Age. As conventionally used, the term refers to flake-based technologies that also involve the making of hafted or composite tools (Clark 1992). The contrast with earlier technologies lies in the emphasis in the Middle Stone Age on the making of a variety of flake tools – many hafted – and the use of few or no core tools. The retouched tools among the A Block assemblage confirm a Middle Stone Age attribution. The backed tools are too small to be used independently and are interpreted as inserts in composite tools as are the bifacial points, in particular the notched and tanged pieces. The lanceolate mid-section is of particular interest as one typological indicator of an early phase of the Lupemban Industrial Complex (Clark 1982) of the central African Middle Stone Age. Lower Lupemban assemblages are recognised by a combination of a variety of small retouched tools with large cutting tools and picks and core axes. The later or Upper Lupemban consists of small retouched tools, but with more numerous and more carefully made bifacial lanceolates and the replacement of large picks with regularly shaped core axes. An increased use of prepared core technology and the addition of tranchet and tanged tools identify the final phase or Lupembo–Tshitolian Industry. Bifacial lanceolates continued to be made.

Clark and Brown (in press) conclude that the Twin Rivers assemblage as a whole most closely matches the Lower Lupemban in technology and typology. The low incidence of Levallois cores, the presence of large picks, few core axes and the relatively large and thick lanceolates most closely resemble early Lupemban assemblages from undated sequences in northeastern Angola (Clark 1966) and at Kalambo Falls (Clark 1969, 1974). Similarities are also drawn with the undated sequence at Redcliff, Zimbabwe (Cooke 1978) and these are discussed further in chapter 13. The relative thickness of the Twin Rivers lanceolates (fig. 10.42) may reflect the inherent limitations of vein quartz. Large thin blanks are difficult to make on quartz in contrast to the fine-grained silicates that were used by makers of the Lupemban in Angola and at Kalambo Falls. The knappers at Twin Rivers were skilled workers of a less tractable raw material.

The 1999 excavations confirm that Lupemban elements exist in A Block and perhaps in F Block, but the variety and types of retouched pieces recovered from both areas do not accord with the accepted industrial sequence, unless the deposits are mixed. Tranchet tools as an indicator of the later Lupemban are present at Twin Rivers as are tanged or notched points in A Block. It is possible that early and later phases became mixed in the course of deposition and excavation. The breccias contain material from more than 100,000 years of human occupation of the caves. The Lupemban as an industry ceased to be made at Twin Rivers by the Last Interglacial, if not before, by 170 ka BP, but the making of bifacial points and small backed tools continued into the Late Pleistocene. Continuity in the use of local pigments also characterises the Twin Rivers assemblages from the Middle Pleistocene to the late Holocene.

11 Fauna from Twin Rivers

LC Bishop and SC Reynolds

Here we present results of an analysis of faunal remains from Twin Rivers, Zambia recovered during the 1999 field season under the direction of Larry Barham. Animal remains from the locality were divided into three provenance groups – A Block, F Block and G Block – and examined for taxonomic and taphonomic information. This information is used to discuss the palaeoecology and site formation of these assemblages. This contribution examines the faunal remains from each assemblage in chronological order of the deposits. The identifications and characteristics of the bones from each recovered group of remains are described. The inferences about human behaviour and palaeoenvironment are discussed.

A BLOCK

Description and skeletal part representation

The oldest assemblage at the Twin Rivers site is that recovered from the remnants of A Block (see previous chapter). The assemblage consisted of 3624 bone and tooth fragments, and the entire collection weighed 3.11 kg, giving a mean weight of 0.86 grams per specimen. This assemblage was extremely comminuted. Some very small fragments preserved sufficient anatomical landmarks to be identifiable to skeletal part (233 or 6.4 per cent), but these were relatively few. The high level of breakage in the Twin Rivers faunal assemblages rendered the use of most standard zooarchaeological techniques impossible (eg, Klein and Cruz-Uribe 1984). In order to expand the descriptive and analytical possibilities of the assemblage, we considered skeletal portion, ie, long bone/appendicular, axial, or cranial/dental regions, rather than the more precise assignment to anatomical part. Using this method, 24.6 per cent (891 specimens) could be assigned to a skeletal portion. When considered as regions of the skeleton, the identifiable comminuted bone was almost equally divided between the appendicular skeleton (473 or 53 per cent of the bone fragments identifiable to skeletal region) and craniodental (378 or 43 per cent) remains, with relatively few axial bones represented (40, or 4 per cent).

Damage

The bones and teeth in the A Block assemblage were extremely fragmentary. Approximately 39 per cent (n=1418) of the bones from the assemblage showed some form of damage or chemical alteration beyond simple breakage (fig. 11.1). The cortical surfaces and broken edges were in most cases of fresh appearance, except in 160 (4.4 per cent) of the assemblage which had rolled or abraded edges and surfaces. Chemical alteration affected numerous specimens, with 1188 (32.8 per cent) classified as leached/burnt and 68 (1.9 per cent) classified as leached/decalcified. This analysis could not determine the cause of these alterations. In the case of the bones of burnt appearance, a chemical change other than burning could not be ruled out. Although close inspection was carried out, no agent of damage was apparent. There were neither percussion marks nor cut marks on the bones. There were no indications of carnivore punctures or tooth scratches, but two bones showed evidence of gnawing by porcupines. Although bone-collecting carnivores can be partially ruled out as a main agent of accumulation because their remains are uncharacteristically rare in this assemblage, it is difficult to identify conclusively any other agent of breakage, including hominid activity.

Taxonomic identification

Of the 3624 specimens recovered from A Block, only 153 (4.22 per cent) were identifiable to the family level and many of these were fragmentary teeth. Despite this rather unpromising representation, A Block has the most diverse mammalian fauna of the stratigraphic units at Twin Rivers (table 11.1). Artiodactyls are particularly well represented, with four tribes of antelope (Antilopini, Bovini, Tragelaphini and two size classes of Alcelaphini) and two species of pig (*Potamochoerus porcus* and *Phacochoerus aethiopicus*) represented. There were three carnivore families, Felidae, Hyaenidae and Canidae, recovered. Numerous equid and rhinocerotid fragments represent the Perissodactyls. Several specimens attributable to the porcupine have also been identified. Bovids are most numerous, with rhinocerotids atypically frequent. Even a sliver of rhinoceros enamel is easily identified to family while similar fragments of other animal teeth might not be so readily classified. Pigs and equids are present in equal numbers. Warthog and bushpig are both easily identified from the fragmentary dental remains preserved in the assemblage since they have very different permanent dentitions. The relatively

A Block - Bone Damage Categories

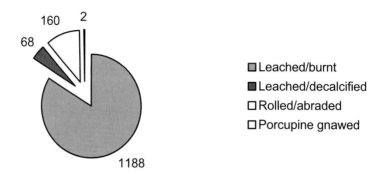

F Block - Bone Damage Categories

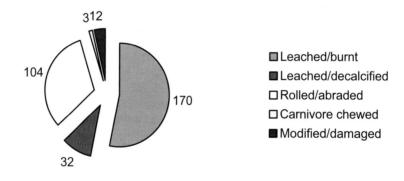

G Block - Bone Damage Categories

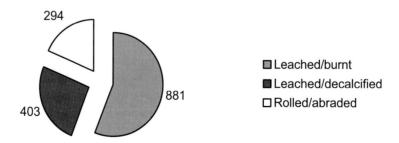

Figure 11.1 Summary of the damage categories exhibited by the faunal remains from Twin Rivers, by stratigraphic unit. Note that in all cases, damaged bone accounts for between 30 and 40 per cent of the entire assemblage. No attempt was made to quantify breakage, since the assemblage was so fragmentary that the vast majority of remains were broken. Only a tiny proportion could be considered 'complete'.

Table 11.1 Faunal list for A Block

Taxon	NISP
Reptilia	1
Mammalia	
Rodentia	
Hystricidae	
Hystrix sp.	4
Carnivora	
Felidae indet.	1
Hyaenidae indet.	1
Canidae	
Canis sp.	1
Perissodactyla	
Rhinocerotidae	33
Equidae	
Equus sp.	22
Artiodactyla	
Suidae indet.	1
Phacochoerus aethiopicus	20
Potamochoerus porcus	1
Bovidae indet.	40
Alcelaphini size 2	1
Alcelaphini size 3	5
Antilopini	4
Tragelaphini	1
Bovini	1

high NISP (numbers of identifiable specimens) of the warthog *Phacochoerus* is attributable to the fact that broken fragments of enamel are identifiable since they are often isolated pillars from the extremely hypsodont third molars of that species.

Differing ease of identification for some taxa is reflected in relatively high NISPs given in table 11.1. A relatively high NISP for each MNI (minimum number of individuals) can indicate how well represented (or how broken up) any individual is in an assemblage, or how identifiable even small fragments of a particular taxon might be. Twenty fragments of warthog tooth could easily come from one individual, or even one tooth. Despite high NISPs, the MNI for each named A Block taxon is one except for the Equidae. In this case one fragment of a deciduous premolar indicates the presence of at least a second, juvenile individual in the assemblage.

Palaeoecological indications

Since it is impossible to attribute either deposition or damage of the faunal remains to the activities of the Twin Rivers hominids, it is preferable to view the palaeoecological indications of the faunal assemblage as representing the local environment rather than the foraging preferences of the hominids. Since only 4.3 per cent of the assemblage are identifiable to taxon, there is much scope for error in any reconstruction due to poor or unrepresentative sampling. The identified remains from the A Block fauna present a different palaeoecological profile than that shown in the other stratigraphic units. The diversity of the A Block antelopes suggests that in the region of the site there were habitats which harboured antelopes which preferred both bushland and grassland habitats. The dominance of alcelaphines and antilopines, which are both more numerous and more diverse (a minimum of three species) in the fauna, would tend to suggest that grasslands and more open environments dominated the region around the site (Vrba 1980). The numerous equid remains also suggest this. However, the presence of tragelaphine and bovine antelopes requires that bushland habitats were also available nearby. This conclusion is also indicated by the presence of bushpig, which is highly dependant on water and on more bushland or riverine/lakeside vegetation. Neither tragelaphines, bovines nor *Potamochoerus* are known from the subsequent stratigraphic units of Blocks F and G which suggests that the environments surrounding the site were at their wettest phase during the deposition of A Block. This result conforms with the history of the nearby palaeolake system (appendix 7).

F BLOCK

Description and skeletal part representation

The fauna from F Block was the smallest of the three assemblages examined. F Block is the middle one in the chronological sequence of the site; its deposition occurred between that of A Block and G Block. There was a total of 1012 specimens recovered from this stratigraphic unit. The faunal remains weighed 954 grams, with a mean weight of 0.94 grams per specimen being the largest of the three units. This still represents a highly comminuted assemblage, only a small proportion of which was identifiable. Skeletal part was determinable for 159 (or 15.7 per cent) of the F Block assemblage. More specimens could be assigned to a skeletal portion since 274 (27.1 per cent) of the assemblage possessed this level of detail. Of these, nearly equal proportions were attributable to the appendicular region (120, 44 per cent) and to the craniodental region (131, 48 per cent). This is similar to the case for A Block, but the relative frequencies are reversed with craniodental remains more common in F Block. As was the case previously, axial region remains are relatively infrequent (23, 8 per cent).

Damage

As was the case for A Block, the F Block fauna exhibits a high degree of breakage. Few elements are complete or even identifiable to skeletal part, and breakage characterises the entire faunal collection. The surfaces and edges appear fresh for the most part, but 321 (31 per cent) of the assemblage show signs of chemical alteration and damage beyond simple breakage (fig. 11.1). The proportion of rolled/abraded bones is higher in this unit, with 104 (10.3 per cent) bones showing this form of damage. Rolled/abraded bones are thus found twice as frequently as in the A Block assemblage. Chemical causes for the 'burnt' appearance of 170 (16.7 per cent) of the assemblage could not be ruled out, so these bones were described as 'leached/burnt'. Some bones (32 or 3.2 per cent of the assemblage) were decalcified. This assemblage showed some slight indication of carnivore damage, with three bones having carnivore tooth marks upon their surfaces. A further 12 bones appeared to be modified, with burnished or chipped edges, but the agents of this type of damage could be human, carnivore or trampling by other animals. Once again it is difficult to suggest what the main agents of accumulation might be here, but there is a suggestion that carnivores were involved, and the possibility that humans caused some of the damage found on the bone fragments.

Taxonomic identification

Fragments of bird (3) and reptile (5) bones were recovered from F Block, along with 35 other bones which were identifiable at least to the family level (3.5 per cent of the assemblage in total) (table 11.2). The assemblage includes a fragment of a hominid humerus (see Pearson's appendix 8). One of the bones was identifiable as a phalanx of the aardvark, *Orycteropus afer*. This species is only rarely recovered in fossil assemblages. Some bovid fossils were not identifiable beyond the family level, but some were attributable to Antilopini. The warthog and indeterminate other suid fossils were recovered. Equids and rhinocerotids were also present in the assemblage. A single felid specimen documents the

Table 11.2 Faunal list for F Block

Taxon	NISP
Aves	3
Reptilia	5
Mammalia	
Primates	
Hominidae	
Homo sp.	1
Carnivora	
Felidae indet.	1
Tubulidentata	
Orycteropodidae	
Orycteropus afer	1
Perissodactyla	
Rhinocerotidae	2
Equidae	
Equus sp.	6
Artiodactyla	
Suidae indet.	1
Phacochoerus aethiopicus	1
Bovidae indet.	19
Antilopini	3

presence of carnivores in the assemblage; their activity left a mark on some (3) bone specimens. Although this faunal list is fairly impoverished, this is hardly surprising given that only 34 mammalian fossils were identifiable to taxon.

Palaeoecological indications

The relative poverty of this faunal list gives very few grounds for any palaeoecological reconstruction. The absence of the bushland preferring species which were locally present during A Block deposition could be significant. It might indicate that the local environment had lost standing water and concomitantly lost more bushland vegetation. All the taxa identified from F Block are found in open, grassland environments. Only Antilopini and none of the more bushland preferring antelope tribes were identified. Since only 3.4 per cent of the assemblage contributed to the formation of this faunal list, the remaining unidentifiable 96.6 per cent might well contain the anonymous remains of other species which preferred more bushland habitats. Further, the indications of carnivore or potentially even human damage in the assemblage leave open the possibility that the collecting agent(s) might have biased the collection of bones to reflect habitat preference rather than strict local habitat availability.

G BLOCK

Description and skeletal part representation

The fauna from G Block, the most recently formed of the deposits, is the most damaged assemblage from Twin Rivers. The assemblage consisted of 4924 specimens and weighed 2.6 kg, yielding an average weight of 0.53 grams per specimen. This is the lowest mean weight of the Twin Rivers assemblages and accurately reflects the level of breakage in the assemblage. Only 397 specimens (8.1 per cent) were identifiable to skeletal part, but the level of damage was so high that only 759 specimens (or 15.4 per cent of the assemblage) were identifiable to skeletal portion. Of these, the appendicular skeleton (374, 49.3 per cent) and craniodental remains (344, 45.3 per cent) had approximately equal representation, while axial bones accounted for only a small proportion (5.4 per cent or 41 specimens). These results more closely resemble those from A Block than the intervening F Block assemblage.

Damage

Like the other faunal assemblages, the G Block bones exhibit a high degree of damage beyond simple breakage. More than 32 per cent (1578) of the bones showed some form of damage. Although neither porcupine gnaw marks, carnivore tooth scratches nor other modifications were visible on the bones, the other categories of damage found in the A Block and F Block assemblages were present (fig. 11.1). Of these, the 'leached/burnt' appearance was most common, with 881 specimens (17.9 per cent) showing this damage. Leached, demineralised bones were most common in the G Block assemblage, with 8.2 per cent (403) of the bones having this characteristic appearance. Rolled, abraded bones were also relatively common, with almost 6 per cent (294) of the G Block bones showing worn, abraded breakage edges and bone surfaces. The proportions of damage categories are slightly different in this assemblage, but this might be due to differences in depositional history (see previous chapter).

Taxonomic identification

A high level of breakage in the G Block assemblage contributed to the difficulty in making taxonomic identifications. The breakage is most extreme in this stratigraphic unit. Only 76 specimens (1.5 per cent of the collection), the smallest proportion of any of the Blocks, were identifiable to the family level (table 11.3). The faunal list is thus a brief one, and the level of breakage only rarely allowed for identification below the family level. Only a single antilopine antelope tooth was identified to tribe. Other fragmentary teeth and post-crania demonstrate the presence of two other antelope size classes. The presence of the warthog *Phacochoerus* is documented, but the high number of specimens may represent a single individual. Both rhinoceros and equids are present in the assemblage. The sole carnivore is a canid. The collection also included some few reptile bone fragments and the sole gastropod shell fragment recovered during the 1999 season.

Palaeoecological indications

The small faunal list and poor representation of the faunal sample from this Block preclude any far-ranging conclusions about the palaeoenvironmental circumstances under which this stratigraphic unit was formed. It seems possible to say that the faunal elements which are most indicative of bushland habitats are absent here, as they were in the F Block assemblage. The few identifiable specimens represent taxa that prefer an open grassland habitat. However, the relatively small proportion of faunal remains that are taxonomically identifiable demands caution in this interpretation.

SUMMARY AND CONCLUSIONS

Some general observations can be made about the entire assemblage. Taken as a whole, the entire faunal collection is extremely comminuted. Nearly the entire collection from Twin Rivers consisted of bone or tooth fragments that were under 2 cm in maximum length. Mean weight for each specimen was less than one gram throughout the entire site, although G Block had even smaller (on

Table 11.3 Faunal list for G Block

Taxon	NISP
Gastropoda	1
Reptilia	4
Mammalia	
Carnivora	
Canidae	1
Perissodactyla	
Rhinocerotidae	7
Equidae	
Equus sp.	16
Artiodactyla	
Suidae indet.	7
Phacochoerus aethiopicus	11
Bovidae indet.	33
size 1	2
size 2	1
Alcelaphini	1

average) specimens. This meant that even a thorough taphonomic investigation turned up little besides frequent indications of breakage, and these were not attributable to any particular cause. Carnivore damage was infrequently, but definitely, documented in some instances. The absence of a high proportion of carnivore remains suggests that they were not a main agent of accumulation and damage for the bones recovered (Brain 1981).

In the case of such highly damaged bone, the significance of the equal representation of craniodental and appendicular remains could have several interpretations. First, it could imply that bones from these two skeletal regions were transported by whatever vector or vectors to the cave in equal frequencies. Second, it could mean that, although brought to the cave in different proportions, breakage favoured one over the other, resulting in equal numbers due to their survivorship in this taphonomic environment. Third, biases in identifiability could favour one portion over the other. For example, broken teeth are highly identifiable as teeth, whereas in the absence of a particular anatomical landmark, a fragment of long bone must at least contain some portion of the radius of shaft curvature or an epiphysis in order to be identified as belonging to the appendicular skeleton. It is difficult to say whether, given the degree of breakage, the identifications would be biased in favour of craniodental elements or at their expense but it is important to bear this potential bias in mind when examining these results. Once again, in all the assemblages it is only a relatively small proportion that can be identified to skeletal portion; the majority of the skeletal remains were non-identifiable fragments.

In assemblages from Twin Rivers, human activity is suggested but not proven. Chemical analyses of the bones with a burnt appearance might reveal whether or not fire was the agent of chemical alteration. The documented presence of fire at the site would certainly suggest human agency in the creation of the assemblages and their damage. However, in the absence of conclusive proof of fire, there is some damage to bones in F Block that might suggest interaction of human and fauna. Large numbers of stone artefacts and the debitage associated with their production amply document human activity in the area (see previous chapter). The fragment of a single human bone was recovered from F Block (see appendix 8). It is the causal association and relationship between the fauna and the humans which is difficult to characterise here and thus must be viewed with caution. This is especially true given that local topography effectively rules out the possibility that some of the taxa were living very close to the Twin Rivers site. In this case, agents of transport and accumulation are particularly important to document. A complete taphonomic study of the deposits would be of potential use here.

Faunal identifications were very difficult to make, and were often possible only to the family level. The fauna identifiable to species (or even tribe in the case of the Bovidae) constitutes such a small proportion of the entire assemblage that any palaeoecological observations must be viewed as suggestions rather than solid conclusions. In the case of this poor representation of the macromammals, microfauna may be more able to provide an accurate and representational picture of the local palaeoenvironment and its changes through time (Avery, in prep.). Here we can only conclude that the evidence suggests that some standing water and dense vegetation was present during the A Block phase, supporting some fauna which preferred bushland habitats which were locally available near Twin Rivers (see appendix 7). These taxa which preferred more closed habitats disappear from the later stratigraphic units (Blocks F and G) and are replaced by the dominant grassland-preferring taxa. This suggests that environments during the formation of these units were quite open and dry. The faunal evidence from Twin Rivers documents a shift from a time when more wooded, intermediate habitats were locally available to a time when open habitats completely dominated the surrounding area.

ACKNOWLEDGEMENTS

We would like to thank Larry Barham for inviting us to examine the assemblage from Twin Rivers and for his patience in awaiting the result. The staff of the National Museums of Kenya kindly provided access to comparative faunal material from their collections. Liverpool John Moores University and The Nuffield Foundation provided financial support for this investigation.

12 The palaeobiogeography of central Africa

L Barham

INTRODUCTION

The popular image of central Africa as a landscape of impenetrable rainforest grossly oversimplifies a diverse biogeographical region as well as creating a false sense of timeless stability. Humid lowland equatorial forests grade into deciduous dry woodland on the plateau that rings the Congo River basin. Rainforest and woodland savanna alike have contracted and expanded repeatedly in concert with long-term changes in rainfall patterns throughout the Late Pleistocene. Recent palaeoecological studies of marine and terrestrial deposits across central Africa reveal a broad pattern of vegetation shifts with the distribution of forest and woodland savannas contracting during cool dry phases and expanding to their modern extent under interglacial conditions. The pulse of climatic change, as driven largely by orbital forcing, is assumed to have affected the biogeography of central and south central Africa throughout the Middle Pleistocene in much the same ways seen during the past 130 ka years. This assumption provides the basis for modelling potential human responses to changing plant and animal distributions and for interpreting the spatial distribution of archaeological sites in a region that includes Zambia. The palaeoecological data generated by the recent excavations at Mumbwa Caves and Twin Rivers are integrated into the wider regional framework in this chapter.

Well-dated, stratified sites with palaeoecological data are rare in central Africa. As a consequence, the environmental contexts in which behaviourally and anatomically modern humans developed can only be approximated at present. Climate change undoubtedly played a role in the evolutionary process and acted as a stimulus for demographic and behavioural changes. Cyclical changes in the availability of animal, and to a lesser extent plant foods, are identified as potential stimuli for significant shifts in the archaeological record of central Africa. The transition from the late Acheulian to the Middle Stone Age may mark a primary cognitive development that underlies the development of modern humans (Foley and Lahr 1997). In central Africa, the first regionally distinct industry, the Lupemban, emerges as a post-Acheulian phenomenon and then disappears by 170 ka BP. The replacement of the large cutting tools of the Acheulian (handaxes and cleavers) by more specialised large cutting tools (picks and core axes) in association with a variety of new flake and blade tool forms is linked to the development of composite tool technology (Klein 2000). This departure from the Acheulian technological pattern is recognised in central Africa as the Sangoan–Lupemban Industrial Complex (Clark 1982). The two terms are often joined (Clark 1988) in recognition of the technological continuity of heavy-duty tool types and the gradual development of a bifacial lanceolate form that is distinctive of the Lupemban. The Sangoan is the earlier development as based on the few stratified deposits excavated from the region (McBrearty 1988). Technological continuity characterises the late Acheulian to Sangoan transition with cores, scrapers, and other tool types providing the link, but a behavioural change took place as indicated by innovations in tool design, the systematic use of pigments and by differences in the geographical distribution of the complexes (chapter 13). The first inhabitants of the equatorial rainforest were makers of Sangoan–Lupemban tools (Lanfranchi 1997) (fig. 12.1). Lupemban assemblages, unlike the Sangoan, are restricted to central and south-central Africa (fig. 12.2) and as such represent the first regionally specific archaeological complex south of the Sahara.

These behaviours evolved in the context of repeated shifts in the biogeography of central Africa. The absence of the Acheulian from the equatorial forest belt reflects a genuine inability, both technological and social, to exploit the limited food resources offered by closed canopy environments. Sangoan–Lupemban foragers overcame these limitations with an expanded repertoire of tools and perhaps by more co-operative behaviours. The Lupemban, as distinguished from the Sangoan, is restricted in its distribution to the current woodland savanna and equatorial forest belt of central Africa and reflects the emergence of a woodland adaptation by 270 ka BP. Repeated contractions of the central African woodlands during glacials and stadials would be directly linked to the spread of the Mega Kalahari northwards and eastwards into the Congo basin. Arid and semi-arid grasslands would expand at the expense of woodland areas. The makers of the Lupemban tradition may have moved with the retreating woodland savanna and

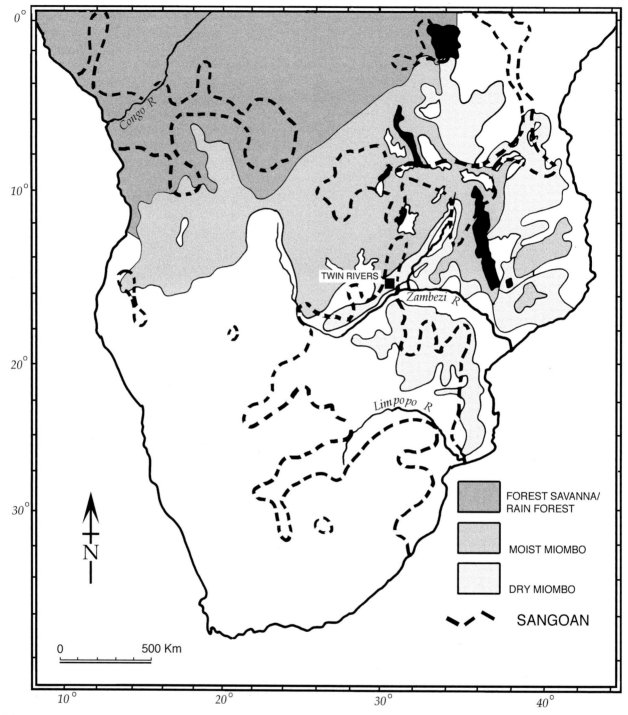

Figure 12.1 The geographical distribution of Sangoan sites in central and southern Africa (after Clark 1967) in the context of the modern distribution of Zambezian (miombo) and Guineo–Congolian vegetation (after F White 1983).

abandoned much of the dry interior. In Zambia, where direct dates are now available for the Middle Pleistocene archaeological record (Mumbwa and Twin Rivers), the Lupemban does not persist far into Stage 6 (186–127 ka BP). Before the end of the Middle Pleistocene, the distinctive large cutting tools and lanceolate points of the Lupemban are no longer made. A more informal Middle Stone Age characterised by fewer standardised tool types follows and shows continuity in the techniques of flake and blade production and in the use of pigments.

The Lupemban with its distinctive tools, pigments and limited geographical and temporal range is interpreted as early evidence for the emergence of identity-conscious social groups united by language and a

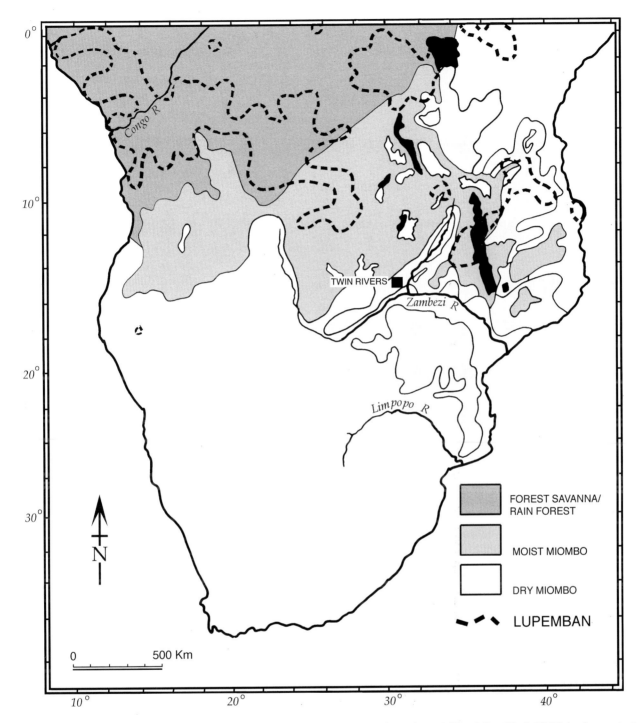

Figure 12.2 The geographical distribution of Lupemban sites in central and southern Africa (after Clark 1967) in the context of the modern distribution of Zambezian (miombo) and Guineo–Congolian woodland (after F White 1983).

common habitat. These behavioural themes are developed further in chapter 13 and are based on the palaeoecological framework developed below.

BIOGEOGRAPHY PRESENT

Among extant African foragers seasonal (and longer term) variability in the distribution of plants, animals and especially of surface water affects directly the structuring of subsistence strategies as well ancillary behaviours relating to the maintenance and reproduction of the social group (Winterhalder and Smith 1981; Lee and Daly 1999). Any diachronic analysis of the evolution of human behaviour must consider the effects of climatic variability on water and food sources, population densities, intra and intergroup competition and the consequences for natural selection (Potts 1996). In the case of central Africa, there is no direct regional record of climatic change for the Middle Pleistocene. Reconstructions of changes to the region's biogeography and the resulting opportunities and stresses for foragers must be based on more recent data. As a guide to interglacial and interstadial conditions, the historic distribution of plants and animals is used in this analysis with the awareness that anthropogenic forces, farming and pastoralism in particular, have altered the region's biogeography (Bourlière 1983). Holocene sources of palaeoecological data are also considered. Measures of habitat variability during glacial and stadial conditions are derived from late Pleistocene terrestrial and marine deposits.

The boundaries of central Africa are defined by the watersheds of the Congo (Zaire) river (~4°N) to the north and of the Zambezi river (~17°S) to the south and include the interlacustrine highland region of western Kenya, Uganda, Burundi, Rwanda and Tanzania. These boundaries encompass the two main physiographic zones of central Africa: the Congo river basin and the high plateau to the south and east. Drainage from the plateau feeds the major river systems with the south-central plateau forming the watershed of the Congo and the Zambezi. The highland plateau maintains an average height of 1000 m and rises above 2600 m in Angola and in southern Tanzania. Within this roughly oval-shaped region, rainfall gradients and the availability of soil nutrients largely govern the distribution of plants and animals (Bell 1982; East 1984) and are the limiting factors controlling the density of human occupation today (Barnes and Lahm 1997). This last observation underlies the model developed below which assumes that the close links between rainfall, soil quality and human population levels operated in the past as they do today. Estimates of Middle Pleistocene periodicities in rainfall can be constructed from the coastal and terrestrial records of central and southern Africa (eg, Gingele et al 1998; Partridge et al 1997). These preserve indirect signals of orbital forcing of climate, operating over the past 200 ka BP. Changes in soil quality are estimated in relation to changes in rainfall and potential leaching of nutrients.

RAINFALL, VEGETATION, SOILS AND HERBIVORES

These four variables are inextricably linked in determining the amount of available energy for omnivorous, mobile human foragers in central Africa. Rainfall combined with the underlying geology governs the leaching of nutrients from soils which affects plant growth and the available browse and graze for mammalian herbivores. The high rainfall of the equatorial belt (1600–

2400 mm per year) reflects the twice yearly movement of the meteorological equator (Intertropical Convergence Zone, ITCZ) from south to north (16°S-15–24°N) (Jolly et al 1998). The two wet seasons promote the leaching of soil nutrients in a region where soils are already poor because of the geological substrate. As a consequence, the plant biomass of the Guineo–Congolian evergreen forest (F White 1983) offers low quality forage for mammalian herbivores and for humans. Plant biomass is typically high, but largely inaccessible to mammal herbivores because of physical and chemical defences (Coley et al 1985) and the low carbohydrate content of leaves. The energy inherent in the ecosystem bypasses the mammals and is consumed by invertebrate herbivores (Barnes & Lahm 1997: 254–245). A closed canopy primary forest also impedes the growth of a grass layer (Menaut 1983:126), which further limits the available grazing.

For humans living in this high rainfall zone, the controlling factor on population densities is the availability of animal protein (Barnes and Lahm 1997:257). Large-bodied mammals such as the forest elephant (*Loxodonta africana cyclotis*) and primates can tolerate the poor quality forage and dominate the animal biomass. In the lowland rainforest of southwest Gabon, elephant account for 52 per cent of herbivores and primates for 25 per cent (Prins & Reitsma 1989). Buffalo (*Syncerus caffer*) and hippopotamus (*Hippopotamus amphibius*) are the other widespread forest grazers (East 1984). These large mammals are slow to reproduce, which reduces the available protein for human consumption, further limiting the carrying capacity of tropical forests. Primates as largely arboreal mammals pose additional problems for humans as terrestrial hunters. Extant foragers of the forest region (Aka and Mbuti) employ a range of technological (eg, bow and poisoned arrow, spears, nets) and social solutions (eg, cooperative and specialised hunting, trade with agriculturalists) to the challenge of extracting protein and energy from the environment (Bahuchet 1988; Ichikawa 1996). Small antelopes (duikers), invertebrates and honey are additional sources of energy. Areas of human-derived secondary forest are of particular importance today (Ichikawa 1996) because they offer extra light to food trees and naturalised crops.

From the perspective of Middle Pleistocene and later foragers who lacked much of the technological repertoire of modern foragers, not to mention external sources of domesticated foods, the primary forest of the equatorial belt would always have been a demanding environment. Doubts have been raised on the viability (and antiquity) of foraging in tropical forests in the absence of economic links with food producing communities (Bailey et al 1989). As discussed below, the earliest human settlement of the central African rainforest coincides with the development of composite tool technology in the Middle Pleistocene (~300 ka) and perhaps with more complex forms of social relations. A flexible technology with a mixture of lightweight and heavy-duty tools seems to have been the physical key to unlocking the limited resources of the rainforest. The social key may have been the development of alliance networks and cooperative group behaviours.

VARIATIONS ON A THEME

The simplified equation of rainfall with soil fertility and herbivore biomass masks variations in the underlying geology and of local topography which create areas of greater ecological productivity (Fritz & Duncan 1994) with more accessible foods for humans. The volcanic highlands of the eastern margins of central Africa offer nutrient rich (eutrophic) soils and these, combined with high rainfall, form a productive environment for plants and animals (Bell 1982). Rift valley soils derived from sedimentary parent material are intermediate in quality (mesotrophic) but still productive with increasing rainfall to more than 1000 mm (East 1984:246). The Cameroon–Gabon highlands on the western fringe of the Congo basin also support mesotrophic soils. The poorest soils (dystrophic) are developed on basement rock and on Kalahari sands (East 1984; Barnes and Lahm 1997) and these underlie much of central and south central Africa.

South of the Guineo–Congolian block of closed canopy forest lies a floristically rich area, the Zambezian domain (Menaut 1983) (fig. 12.3). The transition from forest to Zambezian open woodland is marked by a mosaic of secondary grassland and woodland that contains elements of both regions (E White 1983:172). Beyond the transition zone, the high plateau from 3°S to 17°S receives between 650 and 1400 mm of monsoonal summer rainfall with a prolonged winter dry season and supports an open wooded C_4 grassland. Legumes dominate among the woody species of which the most widespread are known as 'miombo' (*Brachystegia* with *Julbernardia* or *Isoberlinia*) woodlands (Walter 1971). The Zambezian woodland savannas are fire and drought tolerant biomes in which trees produce thick protective bark layers, seedlings produce deep roots, and the perennial grasses and geophytes flower after burning (Menaut 1983:120). Miombo woodlands are frost sensitive and occur across a broad spread (2500 km long) of interior plateau from Angola to southern Tanzania and northern Mozambique (Huntley 1982:106).

A subtle but ecologically significant distinction is made between wetter and drier miombo (fig. 12.1) (F White 1983:93). Wetter miombo grows in areas that receive more than 1000 mm of rain annually and are widespread north of the Zambezi valley. Drier miombo grows in areas that receive less than 1000 mm of rainfall yearly and is found on the southern margins of central

Africa and south across the Zimbabwe plateau. To the southwest, around the margins of the Kalahari, the drier miombo grades into arid woodland dominated by acacias and mopane (*Colophosperman mopane*). This region receives on average less than 650 mm of rainfall per year.

The apparently fine distinctions drawn between wetter, drier and arid woodlands are important in relation to the leaching of soil nutrients and the resulting quality of vegetation and density of mammal biomass. The Zambezian region supports the greatest diversity and density of large mammal species in southern Africa (Klein 1984b). Within this broad region, zonal variations exist in the nutrient quality of the soil which in turn govern the quality of the vegetation as food for mammals. Grasses of the wetter/dystrophic woodland are low in nutrients (sugars and proteins) and high in structural materials (lignins, cellulose) (Huntley 1982: 111–115). Wetter miombo grows in highly leached soils and the resulting poor quality vegetation supports a low density of large mammals compared to the less leached soils of the drier miombo and the mesotrophic soils of the arid woodlands. East (1984:249) observes that arid savanna herbivores reach a peak biomass on poor soils at an annual rainfall of <820 mm and moist savanna species reach a peak biomass on similarly poor soils at >1000 mm. The two faunal communities differ in response to rainfall, in feeding strategies but more importantly they differ in overall biomass. Productive zones along the hot, dry and deeply incised valleys of the Cubango, Zambezi and Luangwa rivers interrupt the broad span of wetter miombo across the southern plateau. Dry valley vegetation in the form of acacias and mopane trees coupled with nutritious grazing supports dense concentrations of otherwise dispersed species of large mammals including elephant, buffalo, wildebeest and zebra (ibid:113). The Luangwa valley, in particular, forms a corridor for the exchange of the dry woodland fauna of south central Africa with that of the dry woodlands of southeastern Africa (Tanzania) (ibid:fig. 1). The valleys would also have been a source of colonising vegetation in the past when annual rainfall fell below the tolerance levels of drier miombo which is about 850 mm.

Away from the major rivers, surface water is seasonally scarce in the Zambezian region. The six-month-long dry winter season is a stressful period for large herbivores and humans alike as surface water is in short supply on the plateaux. During the summer rainy season, water is trapped in the shallow, flat, closed depressions ('dambos' or 'mbugas') that are common on the gently undulating plateaux (Mäckel 1974). These temporary summer lakes and swamps attract game as well as humans. In the winter months, the shallow depressions revert to open grassland or remain lightly

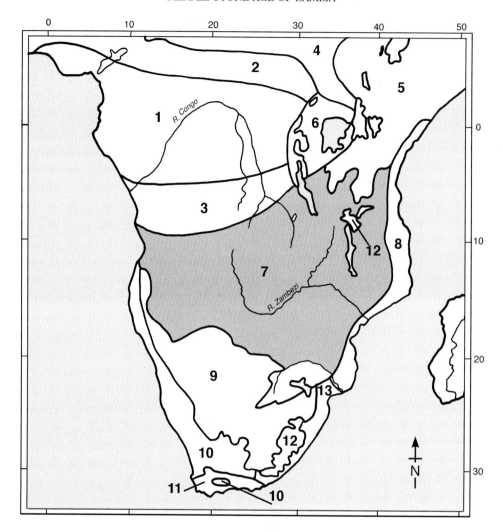

Figure 12.3 The main vegetation zones of central and southern Africa (after White 1983). The Zambezian zone (7) is shaded.

wooded. Along the eastern margins of central Africa a series of large permanent rift valley lakes (Tanganyika, Bangwelu, Mweru, Cheshi) extends into the moist woodland savanna zone. These lakes and swamps could have played an important role as focal points for human settlement during the drier phases of the Pleistocene.

To summarise the current biogeography of central Africa from the perspective of unspecialised foragers, a gradient of *increasing* energy availability follows declining annual rainfall gradients from north to south. With increasing aridity the productivity of the mammal biomass increases in direct relation to the nutrient value of the soil. The high rainfall closed canopy equatorial forest is vegetatively productive, but offers the least accessible energy to humans. Forest dwellers depend on a mix of strategies, technological and social, to extract energy from the tree canopy as well as from the forest floor. The open woodlands of the Zambezian region have more accessible energy for humans and within this

region the drier miombo and arid woodland savanna are the most productive. For human foragers living in interglacial conditions with similar distributions of rainfall, soils and vegetation to today, the dry southern fringes and the eastern highlands of central Africa offer the most accessible sources of protein and carbohydrates. If this simple equation held true in the past then the archaeological record should reflect a greater density of human habitation in these regions compared with the Congo basin.

Predicting human settlement preferences during glacials and stadials, holding technology constant, depends on estimates of the past potential of central African landscapes based on reduced rainfall regimes. In this study the soil nutrient level of the region is assumed to have remained low given an unchanging underlying geology, but to be higher than at present as a result of lower rainfall and reduced leaching. A proxy measure of ecological productivity to be used is the current rainfall gradient of 1000 mm which marks the division between moist and dry woodland across the Zambezian zone. An expansion of drier to arid woodland savannas (<1000 mm) is assumed to have increased the plant and animal biomass available to human foragers. A generalised distribution map of dry woodlands for a typical cool/dry phase is produced in the next section and used to define areas most favourable for human occupation. The estimated effects of climate change on the distribution of food resources will be used to model potential demographic, technological and social responses.

BIOGEOGRAPHY PAST

Rainfall is a dominant factor in determining the productivity of central African landscapes today and presumably was so in the past. As a generalisation, across the low latitudes the terrestrial response to glacial conditions in the high latitudes is aridity coupled with a reduction in temperatures of 2–5°C (Gingele et al 1998; Tyson 1999). Fifty per cent of the low latitude landmass is estimated to have been desert during the Last Glacial Maximum (21–18 ka BP) with the drying of continental interiors brought about by complex ocean-atmosphere interactions (Sarnthein 1978).

In the northern hemisphere, a lowering of North Atlantic sea surface temperatures linked to the expansion of ice sheets resulted in reduced evaporation and a decrease in available moisture to monsoonal systems coupled with increased trade winds as the polar-meridional temperature gradient increased (de Menocal et al 1993). The source of drier conditions across much of southern and central Africa was similar and dominated by the equatorwards expansion of the polar Benguela current into the southeastern Atlantic. Lowered tropical sea surface temperatures on the western coast of sub-equatorial Africa meant a reduction in available water vapour from evaporation. As a consequence, the monsoonal westerlies were starved of moisture and the interior became drier (Gasse 2000). Reduced vegetation cover combined with increased trade winds provided the conditions for the expansion of the Kalahari desert into central Africa from the south.

The alternation of arid and humid phases during the Late Pleistocene was largely driven by long-term periodicities in the earth's orbit around the sun (Milankovitch cycles) with the added variability of abrupt millennial (sub-Milankovitch) events (Leuschner and Sirocko 2000). Indirect evidence for the orbital forcing of southern hemisphere climates in the Middle Pleistocene comes from the Vostok ice core, Antarctica (Petit et al 1999), with more direct evidence available from central Africa in the form of continuous marine and terrestrial sequences. The Vostok core spans 420 ka of climate and atmospheric history and records long-term oscillations between glacials and interglacials as

well as millennial variability. A rhythm emerges of a dominant ~100 ka climate cycle that corresponds with the earth's orbital eccentricity within which there are shorter cycles of 41 ka and 23 ka that reflect changes in axial tilt and orbital precession respectively. These global cycles have a bearing on the central African record in that they provide a chronology for modelling changes in rainfall and biogeography. The 100 and 40 ka periodicities are linked with global cooling and as a consequence with drier conditions for central Africa (Prell and Kutzbach 1987). The shorter rhythms of precession govern the season during which the earth passes closest to the sun and hemispheric exposure to summer insolation. Maximum summer insolation in the northern hemisphere is linked with enhanced monsoonal rainfall in the tropics (Street-Perrott 1994) and minimum summer insolation with a weakening of the monsoonal system. Imprinted onto the periodicities of the glacial cycle are a succession of short-lived climate oscillations associated with interstadials (Dansgaard-Oeschger cycles) and stadials (Heinrich Events) in the northern hemisphere). Direct evidence is lacking for these millennial events in Africa, but Heinrich events may be linked to increased aridity in the tropics (Leuschner & Sirocko 2000). High resolution and well-dated records are needed from central Africa, in particular, given the consequences of the expansion of the Mega Kalahari on the biogeography of the region (see below).

Glacial terminations in the Vostok core are recorded at roughly 100 ka intervals of ~324 ka, 238 ka, 128 ka and 14ka. The full climate cycles follow a sawtooth pattern of stable warm interglacial periods of ~4 ka followed by rapid cooling then more gradual cooling reaching a maximum cold period just before a rapid warming to the next interglacial stage. Within this general framework there are variations in the duration of interglacials and the intensity of the glacials. Interglacial Stage 7.5 was shorter (7 ka) than preceding and following stages and glacial stage 10 was colder than stages 8 and 6.

The Vostok chronology and evidence for varying amplitudes within and between climate cycles forms the framework for reconstructing biogeographic cycles for central Africa. Palaeoclimatic data from the region itself extends to only 200 ka with the bulk of the data available from Late Pleistocene and Holocene contexts. The proxies used to gauge cycles of aridity–humidity include terrestrial, lacustrine and marine sediments and a variety of biological markers. For this study, the most informative sources for reconstructing broad patterns of rainfall change are two long, continuous sedimentary sequences, one from the submerged fan of the Congo (Zaire) river (Gingele et al 1998) and the other from the Pretoria Saltpan (Tswaing Crater), South Africa (Partridge et al 1997). Both sequences span approximately 200 ka and provide data specifically from the equatorial region and from the summer rainfall zone on the margins of the Zambezian biome. A third source of indirect rainfall data comes from the extensive relict dune fields of the Mega Kalahari that reach northwards from the Kalahari basin to the equator (Thomas & Goudie 1984). The presence of fossil linear dunes in areas that are today woodland savanna and evergreen forest is the clearest indicator available for earlier arid phases (Deacon & Lancaster 1988) and a direct chronology is now available for the waxing and waning of the Mega Kalahari during the Late Pleistocene (Stokes et al 1998).

RAINFOREST REFUGES

The Congo fan deposits provide a record of changes in rainfall over 200 ka as reflected in the clay minerals deposited by the river. Mineralogical and chemical evidence for increased freshwater discharges show a 100 ka periodicity that matches interglacial stages 1, 5 and 7 (Gingele et al 1998:23). Shorter peaks of rainfall are recorded at 10–5, 130–125, 196, 81, 103, 175, 145 and 29 ka BP (ibid) and these correspond with precessional periodicities (23–19 ka BP) of increased northern hemisphere insolation. Low river flows combined with the introduction of aeolian sediments are interpreted as indicators of glacial aridity and increased trade winds during isotope stages 2, 4 and 6. Pollen profiles from other Congo fan cores provide direct evidence of changes in vegetation during the Late Pleistocene and these can be linked to shifts in monsoonal rainfall (Marret et al 1999). Dry conditions prevailed between 27 and 14 ka BP as indicated by widespread grassland in the Congo basin. The appearance of rainforest vegetation between 14 and 13 ka reflects increased humidity in the Late Glacial with rainforest continuing into the Holocene. Pollen data collected from offshore sites in equatorial west Africa confirm the Congo fan pattern of rainforest expansion during interglacial Stages 1 and 5 and contraction during the cooler and drier conditions of Stages 3 and 4. Open grassland mosaics and dry forests predominated during dry glacial stages with two rainforest refuges persisting, one in the highlands of southwest Guinea and the other on the coastal lowlands of the Gulf of Guinea (Dupont et al 2000). Corresponding shifts from dry to humid conditions occur on the eastern margins of the equatorial belt as seen in pollen profiles from the interlacustrine highlands (Jolly et al 1997) and phytolith sequences from the Ituri Forest, Democratic Republic of Congo (Mercader et al 2000). Eighteen thousand years ago, grassland and ericaceous scrub dominated a highland interlacustrine landscape that is now montane forest. The shift to more modern conditions began just before the Holocene boundary. Stable carbon isotope analyses of plant material from lacustrine deposits in west central Africa and from the eastern highlands provide additional evidence for the expansion of C_4 grasslands at the expense of C_3 forest during dry phases (Street-Perrott 1994).

The pattern of alternation of grassland and forest in concert with changes from dry to wet conditions has a direct bearing on the potential productivity of the region for foragers. A global cooling of 5°C across the tropics at the Last Glacial Maximum may have restricted the distribution of lowland rainforest to altitudes below 200 m in areas such as the Amazon basin in contrast to the current distribution of rainforest up to 1000 m (Guilderson et al 1994). In central Africa the contraction of rainforest in response to glacial aridity is thought to have created two large forest refuges, one in the west (Cameroon/Gabon) and the second in the east (eastern Democratic Republic of Congo), both bordering on highlands and surrounded by savanna woodlands (Maley 1996). Past refuges have been identified by the mapping of the modern distribution and diversity of bird and primate species (eg, Chapman 1983; Prigogine 1988) with concentrations of endemic species thought to mark centres of past isolation and speciation. Apparent species level differences have been found recently between the mitochondrial and nuclear DNA of the central African forest elephant (*Loxodonta africana cyclotis*) and the woodland savanna elephant (*Loxodonta africana*) (Day 2000). These differences, if confirmed, support the theory of past isolation of forest and woodland savanna biomes. The extent of fragmentation and persistence of forest refuges has, however, been questioned on the basis of palynological and geomorphological data. In the area of the putative eastern Congo (former Zaire) refuge, pollen profiles (Jolly et al 1997) and slope sediments (Runge 1996) indicate drier conditions and more open vegetation cover on the highland margins than predicted by the refuge model. Low lake levels in equatorial east Africa (Gasse 2000) provide additional evidence for significantly reduced rainfall between 23 and 18 ka BP. Phytolith data from the Ituri region shows a much reduced but persistent forest cover during the Last Glacial Maximum (Mercader et al 2000). A rainforest refuge, if it did exist, was not as widespread as once thought. An alternative and reduced 'fluvial refuge' has been proposed for the central Congo River basin (Colyn et al 1991).

Also in question is the structure of a glacial phase equatorial rainforest. Reduced rainfall levels in general may have produced drier, more seasonal semi-evergreen forests as recorded in the pollen record for the Last Glacial Maximum of the Bateke plateau, Congo (Elenga et al 1994). A semi-evergreen forest could, in theory, be a more productive environment for human foragers than rainforest because of reduced levels of soil nutrient leaching which in turn could support more nutritious grazing for large herbivores. The highland margins of the

Congo basin as a whole supported a complex mosaic of grassland and forest (eg, Brook et al 1990) that would have offered foragers a range of opportunities for which no modern analogue exists. Ongoing excavations of upland caves and rockshelters are providing new palaeo-ecological data for the Late Pleistocene (eg, Mercader et al 2000) which will be the basis for more detailed biogeographic models. In the interim, attempts at reconstructing the vegetation history of the region for the Pleistocene (eg, Maley 1996) inevitably suffer from a lack of detailed and well-dated information from the Congo basin itself. For the purposes of this review, it will be assumed that some element of closed canopy forest remained intact along the equator and these areas would have remained poor sources of energy and protein for foragers lacking specialised technology. The reduction of forest and spread of grassland and open woodland during dry phases would have increased the available energy to foragers, and, in theory, central African populations would have benefited for much of the Middle and Late Pleistocene. Interglacials, conversely and somewhat unexpectedly, would have been periods of greater ecological stress for equatorial populations.

THE TSWAING CRATER (PRETORIA SALTPAN) AND THE MEGA KALAHARI

From southern Africa on the margins of the Zambezian zone of decidous woodland comes further support for dramatic shifts in monsoonal rainfall linked to orbital forcing of climate. The Pretoria Saltpan is a closed lake basin that formed 220 ka BP as a result of a meteor impact (Tswaing Crater) (Partridge et al 1997). Ninety metres of lacustrine sediments fill the basin and record alternating wet and dry conditions from the late Middle Pleistocene through the Holocene. The rainfall proxy data show dry conditions at 150–130 ka (Stage 6) and at ~21 ka (Stage 2) with rainfall estimated to be between 25 and 50 per cent below the modern average (ibid: 1131). The dominant rainfall cycle is that of the 23 ka precession tuned to maximum summer insolation in the southern hemisphere. The influence of orbital forcing on rainfall diminishes between 50 and 10 ka in the Tswaing record, perhaps reflecting the greater sub-Milankovitch variability recorded for this period worldwide (Leuschner & Sirocko 2000).

Both hemispheres record increased rainfall with maximum summer insolation, but the climatic responses are predictably 180° out of phase north and south of the equator (Tyson 1999:336). South of the equator, the occurrence of maximum summer insolation at perihelion creates a pronounced temperature gradient between the land and ocean and between the meridional equator and the South Pole. The result is an enhanced monsoonal system (Tyson 1999) and the current interglacial pattern of summer rainfall. The temperature gradient is reduced

when summer insolation occurs when the earth is furthest from the sun (aphelion) with the consequence that the monsoonal system is weakened and drier conditions prevail across the tropics. A full precessional cycle from perihelion to aphelion takes 23 ka.

During the Last Glacial Maximum in the southern tropics, atmospheric circulation was dominated by the westerlies which carried dry air into central Africa. The disparity between summer and winter rainfall patterns was reduced but not inverted (Tyson 1999:337). By the early Holocene, the atmospheric circulation pattern was dominated by tropical easterlies and the monsoonal pattern of summer rainfall/winter drought was established. This pattern of alternating arid–humid phases linked to orbitally tuned periodicities can be detected in the waxing and waning of the Mega Kalahari.

Kalahari sands form the largest continuous sand sheet on earth (Thomas & Shaw 1991) and extend 3500 km from the equator to 29°S and cover an area of 2.5 million km^2 (Thomas & Goudie 1984) or roughly about 50 per cent of central Africa as defined here (fig. 12.4). Long linear dunes, now heavily vegetated and degraded, underlie the Congo basin and attest to past aridity. The advent and application of optically stimulated lumin-escence dating to linear dunes has produced a chrono-logy of dune expansion that provides a strong indicator of past rainfall patterns. Assuming a ready supply of sand, dunes can become active under semi-arid condi-tions with annual rainfall of ~200mm (O'Connor and Thomas 1999). South of the Zambezi, the luminescence dating of linear dunes shows several active phases during the last glacial cycle: 115–95, 46–41, 26–20 and 16–9 ka (Stokes 1997; Stokes et al 1998). A possible stage 6 date (~160 ka) was also recorded but with a large error range (Stokes et al 1998:316). The later phases after 50 ka correspond to periodic and short-lived decreases in the sea surface temperature in the southeastern Atlantic which may be linked to northern hemisphere (Heinrich) stadials (ibid:318). Stable isotopes from a stalagmite sequence in Botswana record a series of brief dry periods at 46, 43, 26, 24, and 22 ka (Holmgren et al 1995) that closely match the dune sequence and Heinrich events.

In southwestern Zambia the phasing differs with no record of activity before 32 ka followed by dune activity from 32–27, 16–13, 10–8 ka, and in the mid-Holocene between 5–4 ka (O'Connor and Thomas 1999). The link between lowered sea surface temperatures and aridity is less clear in this sequence and may reflect the precession of summer insolation in the southern hemisphere (ibid:54). Further complexity is added to the phasing of arid episodes in the Late Pleistocene with the dating of dune formation in northern Namibia to 121–48 ka BP (Thomas et al 2000). The apparent record of continuous dune activity throughout this period contrasts with the evidence cited above for punctuated aridity to the north and south. The aeolian processes that led to linear dune formation may have masked intervening humid episodes in this area.

Disparities aside, the current assemblage of dated dune sequences does correlate with the global 100 ka climate cycle and to a lesser extent to periodicities of 40 and 23 ka. Like the Tswaing crater sediments, the dune sequences record more variability after 50 ka BP than before, and this may be linked to sub-Milankovitch events in the southern hemisphere.

The importance of the dune data is twofold. First, the large area of central Africa formerly covered by active dunes would have been a marginal environment for foragers in terms of the availability of energy and water. This simple correlation between sand and stress reduces the area of habitable landscape by up to 50 per cent during glacials and stadials. Second, the extent of the Mega Kalahari has profound implications for rainfall estimates and for reconstructions of vegetation patterns across the region as a whole. The spread of Mega Kalahari sands as far north as the equator must reflect past periods of significantly reduced rainfall. A sense of the magnitude of climate change from interglacial to glacial rainfall patterns can be gleaned from the relict dune fields of western Zambia. The average annual rainfall in the region today is 1400 mm, the dunes are vegetated and are dormant. To reactivate the dunes would require a reduction in rainfall to semi-arid levels of 200 mm^{-1}yr combined with increased winds (O'Connor and Thomas 1999). The spread of linear dunes along the Zambezi during the Last Glacial Maximum reflects a ~85 per cent drop in effective rainfall from current levels. Equally dramatic reductions in rainfall (64–82 per cent) are estimated to have occurred in the monsoonal region north of the equator (Dong et al 1996). Rainfall estimates from the Tswaing Crater for glacial Stages 6 and 2 show reductions of at least 40–50 per cent compared to modern conditions. These proxy records of climate change confirm that the tropics of central Africa were subjected to dramatic cyclical changes in effective rainfall during the Late Pleistocene. A similar pattern of glacial/stadial dry phases is assumed to have affected the region throughout the Middle Pleistocene.

BUILDING A MODEL

Current models of changes in the biogeography of tropical and equatorial Africa during the Late Pleistocene are based largely on proxy rainfall records derived from lake basins and pollen profiles (eg, Jolly et al 1998; Gasse 2000). Models that integrate the various continuous and discrete geomorphological indicators for climate and habitat change (eg, the Mega Kalahari) are badly needed. At present, the impact of glacial phase aridity on the landscape – from the tropics to the equator – is underestimated (see Thomas 1999). The palaeoenvironmental database for much of the region is poor, with the Congo basin particularly underrepresented (Gasse 2000:206). The availability of energy, protein and water to foragers during a cool dry phase can at this stage only be estimated at a qualitative level.

The current rainfall requirements of Guineo–Congolian and Zambezian vegetation could be used as a guide to past vegetation distribution with the simple equation of lowered rainfall with the spread of Zambezian woodland northwards at the expense of closed canopy forest. In such a correlation, the expansion of open woodland and grassland during glacial phases would increase the productivity of tropical and equatorial environments for humans. Interglacials, by contrast, would be periods of relatively reduced availability of energy and protein especially in rainforest regions. The intuitive appeal of this model comes at the expense of neglecting the added complexity of lowered temperature on effective evaporation. Jolly et al (1998) have incorporated temperature as a variable in a quantitative model of African vegetation at 21, 11 and 6 ka BP. The simulation is based on an atmospheric general circulation model (AGCM) combined with the physiological constraints that govern the distribution of modern African vegetation zones, in particular extremes of temperature and soil moisture.

The simulation predicts relatively little change in the distribution of tropical rainforest because of minimal change in effective precipitation across the equatorial zone. Cooler conditions (a reduction of 4–5°C) compensated for the estimated slight reduction in rainfall (0–200mm yr^{-1}) along the equator (ibid:636). The simulation data also predict a contraction of the southern margin of Zambezian woodlands between 5 and 15° S as a result of lowered temperatures limiting the distribution of frost sensitive species (ibid:636, 643). Semi-desert species of succulents and shrub spread northwards as far as northern Lake Malawi (9°S) and across to Angola. A modern analogue would be the xerophytic vegetation found today in the Karoo region of South Africa, an area which receives less than 250 mm of rainfall per year (F White 1983:136). Zambezian vegetation could not tolerate such dry conditions or the danger of frost. The simulated reduction of Zambezian woodland is accompanied by the creation of an arid corridor between lakes Tanganyika and Malawi (Jolly et al 1998:643).

Sediment and microfossil data from Lake Cheshi, northern Zambia, show drier conditions about 15 ka (Stager 1988), but pollen data from Lake Malawi (De Busk 1998) show cooler but not drier conditions at the Last Glacial Maximum. The apparently contradictory data from the eastern margins of central Africa reflects the diversity in topography and the influence of the Indian Ocean on climate. Palaeoclimatic indicators in southern Africa record an east–west gradient in rainfall during the Last Glacial Maximum (Tyson 1999:fig. 6) with the Kalahari basin receving less than 40 per cent of the current average and the eastern highlands more than 60 per cent. The simulation model underestimates the extent of drier conditions across central Africa when compared against the geomorphological and palynological records. In the equatorial region, the Congo fan sediment sequence and pollen profile show dry conditions (Gingele et al 1998) and widespread grassland between 21 and 14 ka BP (Marret et al 1999). Semi-

evergreen forest on the Bateke Plateau (Congo) at this time shows that closed canopy rainforest had retreated northwards (Elenga et al 1994). The presence of Mega Kalahari sands at the equator also attests to past aridity greatly exceeding the simulation data, though a Last Glacial Maximum date cannot be assigned to these sands with certainty.

If the extent of the Mega Kalahari is added to the model and the Congo fan evidence for drier conditions along the equator is considered then a dramatically altered glacial phase pattern of vegetation emerges

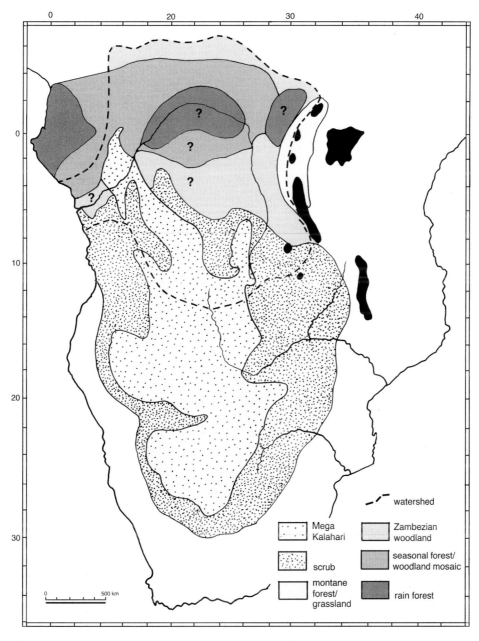

Figure 12.4 A hypothetical reconstruction of the distribution of vegetation zones in central and southern Africa during a glacial maximum. The Mega Kalahari spreads into the Congo basin replacing deciduous and evergreen woodlands (see text).

(fig. 12.4). Figure 12.4 incorporates the simulated expansion of semi-desert vegetation northwards as far as 5–10°S but places it around an expanded Mega Kalahari that reaches into the Congo basin. Seasonal semi-evergreen forest vegetation is found on highlands fringing the Congo basin. Patches of closed canopy evergreen forest persist along the river margins and perhaps in refuges to the west and east though these are smaller than previously estimated. The infilling area is open woodland and grassland. The prevailing image is of a fractured distribution of vegetation split by the Mega Kalahari. Dry (eutrophic) woodland spread into the Congo basin and eastwards to the highland margins. Evidence for a more northerly extension of Zambezian woodland during dry phases comes from the current flora of the Guinea–Congolia/Zambezia transitional zone. This zone stretches from the Atlantic coast in the west to the highlands of Lake Tanganyika in the east and spans latitudes 4–9°S (F White 1983:170). Kalahari sands cover the western two-thirds of the plateau with closed forest penetrating southwards along the tributaries of the Congo river. Zambezian flora predominates on the heavily leached Kalahari sand cover and as secondary wooded grasslands. The presence of Zambezian species on the plateau interfluves is attributed to edaphically controlled refuges during past dry conditions (ibid:174). Based on modern Zambezian floral and faunal assemblages, glacial phase dry savanna woodlands would be relatively productive environments for large herbivores and for humans compared with closed canopy forest. The expected expansion of Zambezian woodland into the Congo basin would have shifted the distribution of these favourable habitats to the north and east of the Mega Kalahari during periods of maximum aridity. The archaeological record for the Middle Pleistocene should reflect the climatically driven shifts in the distribution of woodland savanna as the preferred zone of human occupation in central Africa.

THE ARCHAEOLOGICAL EVIDENCE

The Acheulian tradition of flake tools and large biface manufacture has a restricted distribution across central Africa with no occurrences reported from the equatorial belt (Clark 1967; van Noten 1982). The absence of this long-lived and distinctive archaeological entity from the closed canopy forest region is significant on two accounts. As argued above, the equatorial forest is an interglacial phenomenon and one that poses severe dietary challenges to unspecialised foragers. Closed canopy forests offer limited sources of protein and carbohydrates and these often require specialised hunting and gathering tactics and technologies to extract the available nutrition from terrestrial and arboreal contexts. Acheulian foragers apparently lacked either the social flexibility or technological skills to colonise the

equatorial region during interglacials. This argument is supported by the absence of Acheulian foragers from the region during what may have been more favourable conditions during glacial phases. The complex mosaic of desert, semi-desert, dry woodland, seasonal forest and evergreen forest that was the glacial pattern in central Africa also challenged these early foragers. The availability of surface water may have been a limiting factor. HJ Deacon (1998) and Deacon & Wurz (in press) observe a correlation between the distribution of Acheulian sites in southern Africa and the distribution of streams, springs and lakes. In central Africa, a similar pattern holds true. Acheulian sites are relatively rare, but the few known occurrences are found near rivers; in particular the southern Congo river (Cahen 1976; van Noten 1982), the Luembe river of northeastern Angola (Clark 1966) and along the Kalambo River, northern Zambia (Clark 1969, 1974). The absence of Acheulian material from the Congo basin itself is distinctive and reflects a genuine lacuna rather than limited archaeological research in the region (DW Phillipson 1993:36). If glacial phase environments in the Congo basin supported a mosaic of dry woodlands, grasslands and seasonal forests these should have been desirable habitats for mobile foragers. The missing Acheulian is curious in this context and suggests that other limiting factors were at work, in particular seasonal shortages of surface water. The central basin itself would have remained closed canopy forest and impenetrable to generalist foragers.

The Acheulian presence in central Africa is assumed to be late in the context of the 1.5 million year history of biface technology, but no unequivocal absolute dates are available. Radiocarbon determinations for the Acheulian at Kalambo Falls are considered to be open dates and an amino acid racemisation date of 110 ka on wood from an Acheulian context should also be considered a minimal date (Sheppard & Kleindienst 1996). Post-Acheulian assemblages have now been dated to between 200 and 300 ka BP in south-central and east Africa (Barham & Smart 1996; Barham 1999; McBrearty et al 1996; McBrearty 1999). The central African Acheulian is probably a Middle Pleistocene entity and the shift in technology that marks its end is also a Middle Pleistocene phenomenon. The timing of this shift may be explicable in terms of increased amplitude in orbital forcing of climate, in particular the emergence of the dominant 100 ka glacial cycle after 600 ka BP. Stage 11 (423–362 ka BP) was an unusually long interglacial (60 ka) and preceded by the most severe climatic transition (12/11) in the past 500 ka (Howard 1997).

The change from Acheulian to Middle Stone Age technologies is recognised in the term Sangoan–Lupemban, which denotes the appearance of assemblages lacking large cutting bifaces (handaxes and cleavers) but having a greater range of flake tool types, including small bifacial points, and a distinctive heavy-duty tool element. The points in particular show that composite tool technology had developed by the second half of the Middle Pleistocene. Triangular picks and core axes are features of the heavy-duty element of the Sangoan and have their origin in the Acheulian (McBrearty 1988:389). The Lupemban is distinguished by elongated lanceolate-shaped bifacial points which have no Acheulian precursor. Continuity across the Acheulian/Sangoan–Lupemban divide is seen in the persistence of large tools including picks, choppers, core-scrapers and spheroids, in the variety of scrapers and in flaking strategies. Centripetal flaking, as demonstrated by radial and discoidal cores, occurs in late Acheulian and post-Acheulian industries.

Stratified deposits that contain the succession from late Acheulian to Middle Stone Age technologies are rare and none is adequately dated. The Sangoan was named after surface finds made on the western shore of Lake Victoria around Sango Bay (Wayland & Smith 1923). The Lupemban was named after the Lupemba stream terraces in Kasai province, former Zaire, where mining had revealed deposits containing blades and lanceolate points (Breuil 1944). Neither type site provided the secure contexts on which to define an industry and for some researchers the composite term Sangoan–Lupemban is preferred (Isaac 1982; McBrearty 1988) in recognition of the continuing poor stratigraphic resolution and loose typological definition of the two industries. The site of Kalambo Falls is a notable exception in central Africa in offering a clear stratigraphic succession of late Acheulian and post-Acheulian assemblages that are well defined and published (Clark 1969, 1974). Here, the Sangoan overlies the Acheulian and the Lupemban is stratified above the Sangoan and is succeeded by Middle and Later Stone Age assemblages. Gaps in the sequence make the concept of a gradual transition difficult to support or reject (Sheppard & Kleindienst 1996:172). Waterlogged conditions in the late Acheulian deposits have preserved evidence of woodworking and the availability of fruits at this riverside location. The survival of these organic remains reminds us that a large part of the behavioural repertoire of hominids in the woodlands of central Africa has not survived.

On the southern rim of the Congo basin, a typological sequence from the late Acheulian through Lupemban has been excavated in the sand mantle near Kinshasa at the open site of Gombe Point (Cahen 1976). The sequence is typical of sites in the Mega Kalahari sands in that artefacts cluster towards the base of the section. Vertical movement has affected the integrity of the industrial sequence with artefacts and charcoal moving distances of up to one metre (Cahen & Moeyersons 1977). No bone survives in these heavily leached sands.

Despite the taphonomic processes affecting the deposits, a technological sequence is discernible with Sangoan and Lupemban artefacts near the base and overlain by later Lupemban material. The radiocarbon dates associated with these post-Acheulian assemblages give infinite ages (ibid:813).

The deposits at Twin Rivers, Zambia, contain Lupemban assemblages (Clark & Brown in press) that have been dated to 170–270 ka BP by uranium–thorium analyses on speleothem (chapter 10). These are the only direct dates available for the Lupemban and, assuming contemporaneity across central Africa, the industry is a Middle Pleistocene development and the Sangoan must be earlier. The limited palaeoecological data available from Twin Rivers (chapter 11), shows that the earlier part of the Lupemban (~270–200 ka BP) occupation (A Block) was associated with wet interglacial-like conditions and a nearby source of standing water. A large shallow lake system, Lake Patrick, filled the Kafue River basin and extended across an estimated 17,000 km^2 (appendix 7). Twin Rivers would have been a promontory that overlooked the vast expanse of water. The lake ceased to exist about 200 ka BP as dated by uraniun–thorium analyses of tufa that cap the sequence (table 10.1). Drier conditions are indicated by the fauna associated with the later Lupemban occupation at Twin Rivers (F Block) dated to ~170–200 ka BP. The onset of Stage 6 may be recorded at Twin Rivers and may mark the end of this technological tradition.

On the eastern margins of central Africa, Sangoan asssemblages overlie the Acheulian at the open site of Nsongezi, Uganda (Cole 1967). At Muguruk, western Kenya, the Acheulian is absent but the succession follows from Sangoan, to Lupemban which is overlain by a Middle Stone Age industry that lacks a heavy tool component (McBrearty 1988). These sequences are undated but by extrapolation from Twin Rivers they must be Middle Pleistocene in age and probably older than 170 ka BP.

WOODLAND ADAPTATIONS?

The Sangoan and Lupemban have long been considered to be expressions of early woodland adapted cultures (Clark 1970). This interpretation is based on the assumed function of the heavy-duty tools and on the spatial distribution of the two industries.

Core axes and picks have been interpreted as wood-working tools (Clark 1963) and preliminary replication experiments have shown them to be effective at bark stripping and as planes (Miller 1988). Controlled use-wear analyses have yet to be done and in their absence the wood working function of these tools should be considered speculative (Cormack 1994). The geographical distribution of the Sangoan coincides in part with the modern distribution of Zambezian and Guinea-

Congolia/Zambezia woodland (fig. 12.1), but it also extends further south and east into the open landscapes of the Kalahari–Highveld zone (Sampson 1974) and of East Africa (McBrearty 1987). Sangoan-like artefacts (picks, scrapers and discoidal cores) have been found in stone lines in the equatorial Congo (1–2°N, 15–16°E) and are the earliest evidence for a human presence in this region (Lanfranchi 1997). The area is rainforest today and lies in the hypothetical western forest refuge of glacial phase central Africa.

In the context of the model of glacial/interglacial habitat change proposed above, the distribution of the Sangoan accords with an interglacial occupation of central Africa and may be correlated with Stage 9 (303–342 ka BP). The Mega Kalahari at its maximum extent would have spread into the southern Congo basin, an area that contains a concentration of Sangoan sites (fig. 12.1). The Sangoan occupation of a desert or semi-desert marginal environment seems less likely than the use of the region under conditions similar to those of today. The limited palaeoenvironmental record of the region indicates greater aridity during the Last Glacial Maximum, but not enough is known of less extreme dry phases to model more typical glacial cycle patterns of vegetation. South of the Congo basin, the bulk of Sangoan sites occur in what is today Zambezian woodland and notably in the drier and more productive zones of the Zambezian faunal domain (Clark 1967). According to the simulation model of Jolly et al (1998) this region would have been semi-desert during the Last Glacial Maximum. The extension of the Mega Kalahari into the southern monsoonal zone belt further limits the potential zone of human occupation. On balance, the eastern highland margins of central and south central Africa would have provided the most favourable mix of plant and animal resources during dry phases. Glacial phase demographic pressures may have been a stimulus for cultural change on the eastern fringes of the region.

The distribution of the Lupemban most closely matches that of the current interglacial distribution of woodland and closed canopy forest across central and south central Africa (fig. 12.2). The technological innovations that characterise the Lupemban at Twin Rivers, in particular backed flakes and blades, are arguably designed to maximise the available food resources from woodland landscapes (see chapter 13). The chronology of the Lupemban at Twin Rivers provides an indirect date for the settlement of the forests of central Africa by technologically specialised Middle Stone Age foragers. Lupemban sites have been reported from Equatorial Guinea (Mercader & Marti 1999b) in a region that would have remained forested during glacial

as well as interglacial phases (Dupont et al 2000). If these sites are contemporaries of Twin Rivers, then the initial colonisation of the Congo basin could have taken place during Stage 7 or just before. As discussed above, the trophic structure of closed canopy forests limits the accessibility of carbohydrates and animal proteins for human consumption. Lupemban foragers apparently overcame these obstacles. The development of new forms of composite tools would have enabled foragers to extract the latent energy stored in woodlands. Social innovations many have been equally important in the settlement of the Congo basin. Extant hunter-gatherers in stressful environments can minimise their exposure to risk by maintaining long-distance exchange networks between dispersed communities (Yellen 1986). In the context of the Lupemban settlement of central Africa, the exchange of goods and marriage partners would insure against starvation and reproductive isolation. The distinctive tools of the Lupemban may reflect not just a technological adaptation to woodland habitats, but also the emergence of a socially maintained index of inter-action between widespread communities that shared similar problems. Mineral pigments may have played a role as gift items between exchange partners as they do today in parts of the Kalahari (eg, Cashdan 1985). Speculation aside, the Lupemban represents the earliest clearly Middle Stone Age technology in central Africa and its distinctive technology and restricted geographical distribution reflect a set of behaviours not seen previously.

The onset of Stage 6 appears to coincide with the end of the Lupemban at Twin Rivers. The expansion of desert and semi-desert habitats into Zambezian woodlands may have pushed Lupemban populations eastwards and northwards where the technological tradition continued, or was altered as a response to differing biogeographical and demographic pressures. The archaeological record of the region is too poorly dated to test this proposition. At Mumbwa Caves, there are limited traces of human occupation at 170 ka BP with no clear evidence for the Lupemban. This woodland tradition appears to have ended and been replaced by a more generalised and flexible technology that retained some of the backed tool element of its predecessor. The less specialised stone tool technology of the Late Pleistocene is accompanied by the emergence of bone tool working as a component of the Middle Stone Age repertoire. The new mixture of technologies presumably included wooden tools and, as a package, the potential variety of tools would have enabled foragers to cope with the periodicities of changing resources during the Late Pleistocene.

13 A speculative summary

L Barham

Recent excavations in Zambia have provided new data with which to build a chrono-stratigraphic framework for south central and central Africa. The deposits at Mumbwa Caves and Twin Rivers have also contributed to the development of a regional terrestrial record of cyclical climatic changes and corresponding shifts in biogeography. These data are knitted together in this final chapter and interwoven with the behavioural record from Zambia to create a fabric of changing human adaptations – social and technological – to environmental stimuli. Comparisons are made with regional sequences in southern and eastern Africa and these reinforce the position of central Africa as an early centre of innovation. Finally, the behavioural and fossil data from Zambia are used to address the question posed at the outset: what is the relation between behavioural and anatomical modernity? The answer has a direct bearing on the Out of Africa debate.

Before reviewing the behavioural record, a working concept of behavioural modernity is needed for comparative analysis. Mithen (1994, 1996a, b) has drawn clear distinctions between modern and pre-modern forms of cognition and he has outlined the respective archaeological signatures. The distinctions are based on the (controversial) concept that the human mind is modular in its operation with domain-specific intelligences that evolved to cope with distinct evolutionary challenges. Mithen recognises four primary domains: technological, social, linguistic and an environmental or a natural history domain. Modern humans possess a unique form of cognition in which the various domains interact fully in problem solving. This cognitive fluidity is expressed archaeologically by the appearance of new forms of tool types designed for specific tasks. Artefacts made by modern minds also operate simultaneously in social and symbolic contexts and these considerations may be included in tool design and use. Pre-modern cognition retains domain specific barriers to problem solving with the consequence that tool design follows conservative cultural traditions. Technical competences may be high in pre-modern humans, but the capacity to innovate is low. The limited range of tool types found in the Early and Middle Pleistocene of Europe (and Africa) is indicative of limited cognitive fluidity. The greater variety of tool types associated with the Upper Palaeolithic is cited as evidence of the modern mind integrating technical competence with the demands of the biogeography of glacial Europe (Mithen 1996b: 211).

Mithen also draws attention to the social and environmental contexts in which tools are made and used. Among modern humans, social learning (tradition) and individual learning (adaptation) are balanced as the sources of information on which the individual knapper draws when making decisions. The tools of modern humans are embedded in multiple domains including symbolic communication. As a consequence, the archaeologist faces a near impossible task in attempting to untangle the various inputs involved in creating a specific tool form (Sackett 1982). Among pre-moderns, tradition overrides individual learning with general-purpose tools an indicator of the weight of tradition. Traditions are slow to change especially if multiple intelligences remain separated in the process of problem solving. The relative uniformity of the shape of Acheulian handaxes across time and space is a case in point (Wynn & Tierson 1990). Handaxes show a high degree of spatial competence (Wynn 1989) in their construction, but little variability over time and between regions by comparison with rates of change in the later periods. The design of the biface appears to be governed largely by function (Gowlett 1996) and raw material availability (White 1998; McPherron 2000). The expertise needed to make some highly symmetrical and thin bifaces could be learned by both imitation and instructed tuition. Mithen argues (1996a:218) that large group size promotes uniformity in tool design because of the strength of cultural tradition in the context of greater peer observation and increased opportunities for imitation and instruction. In small social units, the individual has more freedom to experiment and innovate because of the lessened effects of tradition and of more limited social interaction. The predicted archaeological signature of the small group is an assemblage characterised by a variety of informally made tools and a greater influence of raw material variation on tool forms in the absence of strong cultural traditions governing design (ibid:218).

A causal link is drawn between biogeography and group size as derived from non-human primate models and this is then extended to Middle Pleistocene hominids in a European context. Large social groups (>130 individuals) are an adaptive response to open environments in which food resources are unevenly distributed as large parcels of meat, and predators are an ever-present risk. Safety in numbers also fosters greater social interaction and the transmission of technical knowledge by cultural tradition. Closed or wooded landscapes offer more dispersed mixes of resources in smaller quantities and with fewer predators. Woodlands favour smaller social groups and as a consequence the opportunities for social interaction are reduced and cultural traditions are less dominant in the process of learning technical skills (ibid:220–1). The level of cognitive fluidity appears to be an independent variable in the transmission of technical knowledge.

Mithen applied this ecological model of group size and social learning to the industrial variability found in the Lower Palaeolithic of Britain (Acheulian and Clactonian). He predicted that the glacial/interglacial sequence of open and closed landscapes should be reflected in the technological sequence of the Middle Pleistocene. Small groups would make informal tools in wooded landscapes (flakes and scrapers) during interglacials and members of large social groups would make bifaces in open landscapes during glacial phases. The chronological and environmental distinctions made by the model have since been challenged (McNabb & Ashton 1995; Wenban-Smith 1998), but the basic theoretical framework provides a useful scheme for assessing the cognitive abilities and social organisation of foragers in south central Africa. The general correlation of glacial phases with drier conditions and more open landscapes and interglacials with more wooded habitats (chapter 12) mirrors the broad European environmental sequence. Habitat based variability in predator and prey chains is also roughly comparable to the European Pleistocene, but with notable differences that affect the predictions of Mithen's model. Across sub-Saharan Africa, the highest levels of ungulate biomass are associated with mixed woodland savanna in areas that receive between 750–1000 mm of mean annual rainfall and where mean annual temperatures range from 19–22°C (Thackeray 1995). Closed forests and semi-arid to desert regions (<250mm of mean annual rainfall) are the least supportive of ungulates and people, as described in chapter 12. The location of mixed woodland savanna during glacial and interglacial phases is a key factor in predicting where foragers are most likely to have lived and in the greatest numbers. As suggested in the previous chapter, the eastern fringes of central Africa were the likely preferred habitats for foragers during dry periods and the southeastern margins of the Zambezian zone would have supported the greatest density of foragers during interglacials. Mithen's model would predict that group size was smallest in the closed

canopied forests of central Africa during interglacials and the technology should be informal and less patterned than that found in more open environments to the south and east. The spread of more open woodland into the Guineo-Congolian zone during cool phases (Mercader et al 2000) would have increased the available ungulate biomass and made the area more attractive to larger numbers of foragers. Regardless of the climatic phase, mixed savanna woodland would have been the zone that retained the potential for relatively large social groups to form. The model would predict that as social interaction increased so would the potential for socially determined standards of tool making. Cultural tradition acquired by social learning would express itself in the archaeological record in the form of standardised and generalised tools. The development of a more modern form of integrated cognition along with a balance of individual and social learning would be reflected in a combination of technological innovations with other domains of intelligence.

VARIABILITY IN THE MIDDLE PLEISTOCENE

As discussed in chapter 12, makers of late Acheulian tools largely avoided the closed canopied forests of central Africa. Biface assemblages are found in river terraces of the southern Congo basin but not further north (van Noten 1982). Early *Homo heidelbergensis* (or *Homo rhodesiensis*) apparently lacked the technological, social and cognitive flexibility needed to extract the limited available nutrients from interglacial forests. In Mithen's terms, these hominids were unable to integrate their domain specific intelligences and apply them towards the subsistence challenges posed by forested landscapes. The inference could also be made that cultural tradition governed the technical domain, but late Acheulian assemblages do exhibit greater technological variability than earlier Acheulian occurrences.

At Kalambo Falls, a variety of flaking strategies is used in the late Acheulian, including centripetal and blade making techniques (Clark pers comm), that become the mainstay of Middle Stone Age technologies. A large cutting tool component coexists with smaller, informal flake tools and this basic dichotomy persists into the Sangoan and Lupemban. Both industries are characterised by new types of large and small tools, including hafted forms in the Lupemban, but technological continuity underlies the conventional typological threshold used to separate the two industrial complexes. An unexpectedly high degree of variability characterises the late Acheulian in east Africa (McBrearty et al 1996; McBrearty 1999) and in south Africa (Deacon & Wurz in press) with blade and prepared flake cores found in both regions. The period between 400 and 300 ka BP encompasses both technological continuity and variability that cannot be attributed to raw material differences alone. At the risk of circular reasoning, the changes evident in the late Acheulian reflect a lessening of social learning (tradition) and an increase in individual learning as part of shifting adaptive strategies. The question of why such shifts took place at this time and across sub-Saharan Africa is too large an issue to be addressed with the current limited archaeological and palaeoenvironmental database. The broad geographical scale of the changes points to climate change as a likely stimulus.

Among the glacial cycles of the past half million years, the most pronounced change in climate took place at the abrupt Stage 12/11 transition (Howard 1997). The glacial maximum of Stage 12 (~440 ka) was one of the coldest and was followed by the longest interglacial stage (423–362 ka BP). The 12/11 transition would have triggered profound changes in the biogeography of sub-Saharan Africa with predictable consequences for the distribution of human populations. The social and technological responses to changes in habitat (open to closed) and population density (large to small groups) can be modelled at a very crude level. The return of interglacial conditions can be equated with a weakening of cultural tradition as smaller social groups formed in the expanding woodlands. If the model holds true, the archaeological record of interglacials should show greater variability in central Africa as a consequence of reduced social interaction and a greater impact of individual learning on technological patterning. Conversely, the more open habitats of dry phases should be reflected in the standardised, general purpose tools such as handaxes that are the product of tradition. The temporal and spatial resolution of the archaeological record of the late Acheulian is too coarse-grained for this model to be tested, but it draws attention to the interaction of habitat change, group size, and learning patterns as variables that affect assemblage variability.

The end of the Stage 11 interglacial may have been an alternative climatic trigger for technological change in the late Acheulian. Stage 10 was short-lived (362–343 ka BP), but would have disrupted long established patterns of adaptation to an interglacial distribution of water and food resources. Later glacial/interglacial transitions (eg, stage 9/8) could also be cited as possible forcing events. Dating controls on the late Acheulian and early Middle Stone Age (Sangoan-Lupemban) are poor and attempts to link the transition to specific phases of a glacial cycle are premature. The suggested link between Stage 9 and the wide spatial distribution of the Sangoan industry is simply speculation. That said, climate change and its effects on biogeography must be factored into any model of behavioural change at this general level of abstraction.

COGNITION, CONTINUITY AND CHANGE

The standard archaeological yardstick for recognising a modern form of cognitive fluidity is the Upper Palaeo-lithic of Europe. For example, the variety of standardised stone and bone tool types reflects the integration of technical knowledge of raw materials with an under-standing of the behaviours of specific game animals in specific contexts (Mithen 1996a:211). The incontrovert-ible evidence for visual symbolic expression (art) is further proof of a generalised intelligence that integrates all domains; social, natural and technical. Other aspects of the Upper Palaeolithic that are commonly cited as modern forms of behaviour include relatively rapid innovation, long distance exchange, the structured use of space in settlements, stone-lined hearths, specialised hunting strategies and deliberate burial with grave goods (Stringer & Gamble 1993; Mellars 1996; Gamble 1999). This list of behaviours should be viewed in its European context as the product of cognitively and anatomically modern hunter-gatherers living in the northern hemisphere during the last glacial cycle. Extant hunter-gatherers in near arctic climates by necessity produce a greater range of standardised tools and other aids to survival than contemporary foragers in the tropics (Hayden 1981; Wobst 1990). The criteria developed for distinguishing pre-modern from modern behaviours in Europe cannot be applied directly to the tropics. In sub-Saharan Africa, population replacement is not an issue; anatomically modern humans evolved from indigenous pre-modern populations (see chapter 9). Biological and behavioural continuity are features of the palaeo-anthropological record of the subcontinent with the consequence that the shifts from pre-modern to modern forms will be blurred with no clear thresholds.

With these caveats in mind, how can the cognitive development of Middle Stone Age hominids be assessed? Cognitive ability is expressed as behaviours applied to solving specific problems and meeting general needs. In southern Africa, the behaviours of extant and historic foragers have been used as guidelines for gauging the cognitive modernity of Middle and Late Pleistocene populations in the region (Deacon & Deacon 1999: 102). The criteria used include the presence of hearths with associated domestic debris, the structured use of the landscape away from immediate sources of water, the formation of exchange networks, the active hunting of game and manipulation of plant foods, and the use of symbolic communication. Deliberate burial is a Holocene phenomenon in southern Africa (Walker 1994) and the absence of this behaviour from earlier periods is not a reliable guide to modernity. These criteria can be used in southern Africa where direct historical continuity exists with living hunter-gatherers, where organic preservation is often good and decades of sustained research have produced an unparalleled archaeological record. The comparative poverty of the database from central and south central Africa makes direct comparisons proble-matic. Poor preservation of bone in the tropics (eg, Twin

Rivers) largely excludes economic criteria from the list of cognitive indicators. Geomorphological processes have probably obscured the spatial distribution of surface sites across much of the high plateau of south central Africa based on the evidence from Mumbwa Caves. Recent research on the margins of the Congo basin (Lanfranchi 1997; Mercader & Marti 1999a, b) promises to redress the balance but these sites remain undated. The lack of spatial data also impinges on the detection of past networks of reciprocal exchange. The remaining criteria of the structuring of domestic space and the use of symbols can be applied to the archaeological record of Zambia.

THE LUPEMBAN AND THE EMERGENCE OF A REGIONAL IDENTITY

The attribution of the Twin Rivers assemblage to the Lupemban industry of central Africa (Clark & Brown in press) allows a time frame to be extended across the region. In the absence of reliable dates for the Lupemban, the industry has been assumed on typological grounds to date to about 200 ka (Clark 1988). The uranium series dating of A and F Blocks confirms the Middle Pleistocene attribution and extends the age range. In F Block, the deposits are bracketed by dates of 170–200 ka BP and in A Block the deposits are directly associated with a date of 270 ka BP within a wider range from 170–>400 ka BP. A conservative interpretation of the dates from the site places the Lupemban in the period from 170–270 ka BP which corresponds roughly with the time span of interglacial stage 7 (180–248 ka BP). If all of the material originally excavated from A Block is attributable to the Lupemban, as demonstrated by Clark and Brown (in press), then the industry is potentially 400 ka old. A potassium-argon date was reported of c 400 ka BP for a 'Pseudo-Stillbay' assemblage from the Kinangop plateau in Kenya (Evernden & Curtis 1965). The attribution of this material to the Middle Stone Age may be misleading (Clark 1988), but the presence of an atypical assemblage for the Middle Pleistocene is indicative of the great variability in technology at this time across sub-Saharan Africa.

If the age range of the Lupemban was consistent across central and south central Africa, then the earliest occupation of the Guineo-Congolian forest zone took place in the Middle Pleistocene and probably during an interglacial. The presence of foragers in closed canopy forests represents a behavioural and cognitive development that distinguishes Middle Stone Age hominids from their predecessors. The variety of backed tools found in the Lupemban at Twin Rivers may represent technological innovations designed to exploit forest resources, particularly large game and high canopy sources of protein. An armoury of hafted composite tools could be envisaged that incorporated spears of differing weights with tranchets, backed blades and bifacial points as cutting edges. Similarly shaped metal spearheads are used today by hunters in the riverine forests of the southern Congo plateau region (Miller 1988). Among the Mbuti of the Ituri forest spears are used primarily for killing large terrestrial game including elephant, hippo, okapi, bongo, chimpanzees, buffalo and lesser game such as pangolins, pythons and monitor lizards (Harako 1981). Spear hunting is dangerous and as a consequence is most effective as a co-operative venture that involves pairs or groups of experienced men. Large packages of meat are the reward for a successful hunt. Poison-tipped arrows are used for hunting arboreal prey and iron-tipped arrows for smaller terrestrial game. The bow and arrow allows individual hunters of varying experience to work alone and is a particularly effective technology for harvesting arboreal primates. The bulk of protein acquired in the Ituri forest is caught by a combination of bow and arrow and communal net hunting. In the context of Lupemban technology, the lanceolates could be equated with the spearheads used for hunting large terrestrial game and tranchets and backed blades with light-weight spears for hunting arboreal and small terrestrial game. The advent of the bow and arrow would have made the spear redundant for arboreal hunting. Nets constructed from root or bark fibres may also have been an essential innovation for life in the forest. Concave scrapers and chisels may have been useful tools for working these organic materials. These suggested functions for Lupemban tools also carry implicit assumptions about social organisation (individual, group and communal hunting), including divisions of labour.

The designing of tools for specific tasks is a mark of cognitive integration as argued for the Upper Palaeolithic (Mithen 1996a, b) and this argument can be applied to the Lupemban. Twin Rivers is not unique in its technological variety. *Petits tranchets* have been found in Lupemban assemblages in the Kalahari sand deposits at Gombe Point, Kinshasa (Cahen 1976). The vertical movement of artefacts through the sands has been demonstrated by refitting experiments (Cahen & Moeyersons 1977). Taphonomic processes may explain the association of small backed pieces with the Lupemban in the Congo basin, but the association is genuine at Twin Rivers. Truncated flakes and blades occur in the later Lupemban ('Siszya Industry') at Kalambo Falls (Clark 1974:table 10) in association with unifacial and bifacial points, awls, burins, scrapers and lanceolates. Backed tools have also been found in an early Middle Stone Age assemblage at the site of Redcliff Cave, Zimbabwe (Cooke 1978). The Redcliff sequence is undated, but the assemblage in Lens 4 is typologically similar to that at Twin Rivers with its backed blades and anvils (Clark & Brown in press) though it lacks the large lanceolates of the Lupemban. The Zimbabwean Middle Stone Age sequence is discussed in greater detail below.

The vegetation of the Zimbabwean plateau is an extension of the Zambezian dry miombo woodland (see chapter 12) and presumably would have been so in previous interglacials. The distribution of the Lupemban across central, south central and the interlacustrine region of east Africa coincides with the modern distribution of forest and woodland biomes. Assuming that this spatial pattern is not an artefact of the history of archaeological research in these areas, then the Lupemban can be considered to be a woodland adaptation. Woodworking as an activity crosscuts ecological zones and is not necessarily an indicator of cultural identity (Inskeep 1967:572), but in the case of the Lupemban the *choice* of tools and reduction strategies is specific to a woodland biome. As a working hypothesis, the Lupemban is linked here to interglacial Stage 7. Reliable dates from other sites are needed to constrain the age range more closely and the proposed woodland association is amenable to testing by microwear analyses of Lupemban tools and by the recovery of palaeo-environmental data from undisturbed contexts. The Lupemban is not the earliest post-Acheulian entity in the culture-stratigraphic sequence of central and east Africa; that position is occupied by the Sangoan industry (Clark 1988; McBrearty 1988). The Sangoan must therefore be older than 270 ka BP and possibly older than 400 ka BP. No direct dates are available for the Sangoan in central Africa. In east Africa, Sangoan assemblages have been reported from the Kapthurin Formation, Kenya (McBrearty pers comm) in tuff deposits dated to approximately 300 ka BP. If confirmed, the latter date would support a Stage 9 attribution.

The restricted spatial distribution of the Lupemban combined with its diagnostic artefacts (lanceolate bifaces and backed tools) is evidence for the earliest regionally distinct industry in sub-Saharan Africa. The distribution of the Sangoan is irregular (fig.12.1) by comparison and does not neatly fit a particular biome (McBrearty 1987). A regional identity and one centred on woodland marks a clear departure from the Acheulian pattern of generalised tools and restricted habitat use. The tools of the Lupemban appear to be functionally diverse and stylistically varied. The large lanceolate is emblematic of the industry and can be considered as an index of tool making standards of the community (Wynn 1993:402). Indices as such are the unintended consequences of a community's accepted range of technological solutions to a particular problem. They equate with the concept of cultural tradition as applied above to the Acheulian biface. The Lupemban lanceolate differs from the handaxe in that the former is an index of a regionally constrained tradition. The lanceolate could perhaps be a latent signal of a woodland association when viewed by outsiders.

The woodland context is also important from the perspective of Mithen's model of group size, social learning, technological complexity and cognition. According to the model Lupemban tool forms should be largely governed by raw material constraints and informal in design because of the greater influence of individual decision making in small groups. These are the patterns expected of a pre-modern mind in a woodland landscape. The variety and mix of specialised and informal tools in the Lupemban reflects both the social and individual learning that typifies an integrated modern intelligence.

The use of symbols in the form of language and image making is a universal feature of modern humans and a criterion that is used to distinguish modern from pre-modern behaviour in the archaeological record of Europe and Africa. The presence of painted, engraved or incised images is an unambiguous indicator of symbolic expression. Items of personal adornment reflect a sense of self and are considered forms of symbolic communication (White 1989). In sub-Saharan Africa, the earliest painted images are found on stone slabs from a late Middle Stone Age context at Apollo 11 Cave, Namibia (Wendt 1976). The slabs are associated with radiocarbon dates of approximately 27 ka BP. The discovery of an incised geometric design on a piece of ochre (hematite) found in Middle Stone Age (Stillbay) deposits at Blombos Cave, South Africa, has extended the capacity for symbol making – in the minds of some archaeologists – to the Last Interglacial (127–115 ka BP). The archaeological record of the Late Pleistocene in southern Africa is notable for the consistency and continuity of iron oxide use from the Middle through the Later Stone Age. Archaeological, ethnographic and experimental data have been marshalled in extended arguments, not repeated here, in favour of early pigment use in symbolic contexts in the Late Pleistocene (Knight et al 1995; Power & Watts 1996; Power & Aiello 1997; Volman n.d.). Sporadic evidence of iron oxide use has been reported from seven Middle Pleistocene contexts in southern Africa (Knight et al 1995) and in each case the number of pieces is small, often just a single specimen. From south central and central Africa, pigment is recorded from the probable Sangoan at Broken Hill (Kabwe) in Zambia (Clark et al 1947) and from later Lupemban assemblages at Kalambo Falls (Clark 1974:table 10) and Burundi (van Noten 1982). In the case of the Lupemban occurrences, they are associated with grinding stones. The systematic collection and processing of pigments – and by implication symbol use – appears to be a Late Pleistocene phenomenon with roots in the Middle Pleistocene. The recovery of 302 pieces of pigment from the limited intact deposits at Twin Rivers combined with evidence for systematic processing (eg, use facets, specularite-stained pestle) extends the capacity for symbol use, and syntactic language, to Middle Pleistocene hominids. Makers of the first regionally distinct tool making tradition, the Lupemban, were using that capacity for symbolic communication.

If these people were behaviourally modern in their use of technology and symbols, then other aspects of the archaeological record of central Africa should reflect this level of cognitive development. The colonisation of closed canopied forests is one such indicator but other forms of spatial and social data are missing from the region because of the lack of suitable sites and an interrupted history of research.

CONTINUITY AND CHANGE IN THE LATE PLEISTOCENE

The Lupemban as an industrial package with its distinctive lanceolates is not found at Mumbwa Caves nor does it occur in the Late Pleistocene surface deposits on the central platform at Twin Rivers. The package apparently ceased to be made by 170 ka BP. A few finite radiocarbon dates have been reported for the Lupemban in the southern Congo basin (van Noten 1982) and from Kalambo Falls (Clark 1974) and should be treated with caution. The absence of the Lupemban from Mumbwa Caves is puzzling given the trace of an Acheulian occupation at the site and the overlapping of dates (>170ka BP) with F Block at Twin Rivers. The estimated maximum age of 250 ka BP for unit XIV as based on the microfauna adds to the conundrum. The basal deposit may contain a palimpsest of debitage from the Middle Pleistocene. Some flaking methods associated with the Lupemban at Twin Rivers continue into the Mumbwa Caves sequence, in particular blades. Backed blades, large segments and rare *petits tranchets* are a small component of the Last Interglacial assemblage, but they represent continuity with the Lupemban as does the use of pigments. The presence of small hearths in the Middle Pleistocene deposits at Mumbwa Caves suggests that these features may be found in earlier assemblages given adequate preservation.

The archaeological sequence at Mumbwa Caves retains a record of occupation punctuated by intervals of minimal or no human presence. The episodes of abandonment coincide with regional increases in aridity linked to larger scale climatic events. Most notable of these is the long hiatus in occupation between 130–170 ka BP that corresponds with glacial Stage 6. The proximity of the Mega Kalahari to the west of Mumbwa Caves (120–90 km) means the site and its environs would have been more readily affected by drought than regions further to the east and north. The decision to avoid the caves at times of increased aridity was made by Middle and Late Pleistocene occupants as well as by the mid-Holocene inhabitants. Developments in anatomy, technology and behaviour could not compensate for the

loss or unpredictability of such a basic resource. The archaeological sequence at Border Cave, South Africa, (Grün & Beaumont in press) contains a remarkably similar sequence of use and abandonment in concert with glacial cyles and sub-cycles. Greater continuity of occupation should be found in the wetter eastern margins of central and south central Africa along major watercourses. In Zambia, the floodplain of the Kafue River was occupied by foragers in the mid-Holocene at a time when Mumbwa Caves had been abandoned. A similar pattern of tethered occupation around water sources can be expected during earlier dry intervals. Lake Patrick formed under semi-arid conditions in the Middle Pleistocene and would have been a source of water and food for the occupants of Twin Rivers.

The structured use of space within living sites is a feature of extant foragers in the Kalahari (Yellen 1976) and of the mid-Holocene occupants of the Kafue flats (Fagan & van Noten 1971). This aspect of modern behaviour is found in the Late Pleistocene sequence at Mumbwa Caves. Large hearths (60–150 cm) with stone surrounds were built near the entrance of the main cave and toward the back where the outline of at least one windbreak was preserved in the Last Interglacial unit VII. Small hearths (30 cm) without stone surrounds are Holocene and Middle Pleistocene features. The size of the Late Pleistocene hearths and the use of stone reflect more extended periods of occupation and efforts to protect living areas from windblown ash. Windbreaks served as barriers to the prevailing winter wind that enters the cave system to the east and gathers force along the main passages. The Middle Stone Age occupants demonstrated an ability to modify their immediate surroundings in ways that are recognisably modern and that may be culturally specific. In an overview of cave and rockshelter use among extant foragers in the tropics, Galanidou (2000) demonstrates that the structuring of space in these bounded areas mirrors the use of space in open sites. The placement of hearths, location of sleeping areas, construction of windbreaks and size of hearths are culturally defined and may serve as territorial markers in areas where competition exists for caves or shelters. At Mumbwa Caves, the large stone lined hearths characteristic of the Late Pleistocene units are not found in the Holocene. A functional argument has been put forward that explains the differences in size and permanence of hearths as a response to differing climatic conditions. Cultural differences may also play a role, but without comparable data from contemporary sites in the region this hypothesis cannot be developed further.

In South Africa, rare examples of spatial patterning within caves have been reported from Middle and Later Stone Age contexts. Variability exists in patterning between regions and in time. Small circular hearths associated with food remains are a feature of the Last

Interglacial and later deposits at Klasies River (Henderson 1992) and Boomplaas Cave (Deacon 1979). At both sites, the Middle and Later Stone Age hearths are identical in size and form and the argument is made that this reflects behavioural continuity through the Late Pleistocene (Deacon 1989, 1995). Differences between Middle and Later Stone Age use of space do exist at Rose Cottage Cave. The Later Stone Age occupants apparently adhered to rules governing spatial patterning of activities that remained essentially unchanged from the Late Glacial through the Holocene (Wadley 1996). No clear patterning is evident in the underlying deposits dated to 20 ka and earlier (Harper 1998). In contrast, in deposits dated to 29–26 ka BP from Strathalan Cave B in the north eastern Cape (Opperman 1990), clear divisions in the use of space are preserved. The Middle Stone Age occupants placed grass bedding along the walls and located their hearths and food processing near the mouth of the cave. A similar segregation of sleeping and food areas is evident in the Holocene occupation of Strathalan A (Opperman 1996).

Little evidence exists for the organisation of sleeping areas in earlier Late Pleistocene contexts. Possible sleeping hollows have been reported from Border Cave (Volman 1984) and in a late Acheulian level at Wonderwerk Cave, northern Cape, where bedding material has survived (Beaumont 1990). The windbreak at the back of Mumbwa Caves was presumably a sleeping area as based on analogies with contemporary foragers (Yellen 1976; Galanidou 2000). No windbreaks have been reported from confirmed Middle Stone Age contexts in sub-Saharan Africa apart from Mumbwa Caves. Evidence for the restructuring of a living area has been found at Katanda 9, northeastern Democratic Republic of Congo, where a stone surface or pavement was laid across the slopes of a river terrace (Yellen 1996). The dating of Katanda 9 to approximately 90 ka BP (Brooks et al 1995) and the taphonomic integrity of the terrace deposits continue to cause controversy (Feathers 1996:33), but they are accepted here as intact Late Pleistocene sites.

Intentionally shaped bone tools are relatively common elements in Late Glacial and Holocene assemblages in southern Africa (Deacon 1984). Earlier occurrences in Middle Stone Age contexts have, until recently, been rare (eg, Klasies River Mouth, Border Cave, Apollo 11) to the extent of being considered intrusive. The discovery of shaped bone tools from Last Interglacial deposits at Blombos Cave, southern Cape (Henshilwood & Sealy 1997) in association with bifacial points of the Stillbay industry has altered perceptions about the capacity of Middle Stone Age humans to work bone. The discovery of bone harpoons from two sites at Katanda (Yellen 1998) provides dramatic, if controversial, support for the antiquity of composite tool technology that incorporates

bone. In the context of growing evidence for early bone tool use, the identification of a likely bone point from the Last Interglacial deposits in Area I at Mumbwa Caves is less remarkable than might have been the case a few years ago.

Limited but significant evidence of the long distance transport of raw materials comes from the Last Interglacial occupation at Mumbwa. A single Levallois flake of Luapula porphyry was found in the debris concentration that formed the outline of the windbreak. The source of the stone is either 450 km to the northeast or 200 km to the southeast of the caves depending on the specific lithology of the porphyry. Both sources are considerable distances from the site and the acquisition of the raw material could have taken place in the course of annual shifts in settlement or by indirect means such as trade and exchange alliances. The latter possibility has parallels in the social lives of extant hunter-gatherers of the northern Kalahari (Cashdan 1985). Reciprocal exchange of gifts (hxaro) takes place between friends and distant relatives over a radius of 100 km and creates and maintains a network of mutual obligations across landscapes. Arrows are among the gifts exchanged between males today and the convergent flake from Mumbwa Caves could be interpreted as an example of a valued gift item. Alternatively, someone who had previously lived near the source of stone could have brought the flake to the site as a curated object. No evidence for the knapping of porphyry was found in the deposits indicating that the flake was brought to the cave as a finished object.

The stone tool sequence at Mumbwa Caves is currently the only dated sequence available from central Africa and north of the Limpopo River that spans the Middle to Late Pleistocene. The importance of the sequence should not be exaggerated because of the inherent risks in using a single site as a template for a regional culture-stratigraphic sequence. The gaps in the Mumbwa sequence suggest that the site may be representative of the western or more arid parts of Zambia (eg, Phillipson 1977) rather than for the country and region as a whole. Humans were present at Twin Rivers at 60 ka BP (central platform), but absent from Mumbwa Caves, and present in eastern Zambia at Kalemba Rockshelter around 25 ka BP (Phillipson 1976) when they were again absent from Mumbwa Caves. With these limitations in mind, Mumbwa Caves can be used as a skeletal framework on which to build a regional sequence.

The Late Pleistocene sequence at Mumbwa Caves is best represented in deposits dated between 130 and 105 ka BP. A smaller sample dated to 40 ka BP marks the latest Middle Stone Age occupation which is followed by a gap in occupation until the Late Glacial 15–12 ka BP by which time the artefacts are typologically Later Stone

Age. Similar reduction strategies are used in the two Late Pleistocene occupation phases. Centripetal methods of flaking are common and are used to make relatively short triangular and pentagonal flakes. Less formal methods of flaking from multiple platform and irregular cores produce longer flakes as does the production of blades. Blade making is a feature of the Middle Pleistocene deposits as well and represents a long strand of continuity throughout the combined Mumbwa and Twin Rivers sequences. A trend toward smaller flakes and blades is evident in the Late Pleistocene sequence with some bladelets and bladelet cores occurring at 40 ka BP. The trend culminates with the consistent production of bladelets by the Late Glacial and Holocene occupants.

The types and frequencies of retouched tools also show continuity throughout the sequence. Awls, borers and medium to large (>30 mm) scrapers are the most common forms in the Middle Stone Age phases and are replaced by backed flakes and blades and small scrapers as the dominant forms in the Late Glacial and Holocene units. A variety of backed tools accounts for a small percentage of the Middle Stone Age assemblages, but these represent a link with the Lupemban at Twin Rivers and the Later Stone Age as known from central and eastern Zambia (Miller 1969; Phillipson 1976; Savage 1983; Musonda 1984). The large segments found in the Last Interglacial occupation are notable in that they occurred at roughly the same depth (190–210 cm) and probably represent an individual lens in the larger aggregate unit. The percentage frequency of backed tools is lower than at Twin Rivers, but the variety is similar. The differences between the sites may reflect differing activity levels involving hafted tools. Bifacial and unifacial points are present at Twin Rivers and in the Late Pleistocene sequence at Mumbwa Caves including the dambo excavation. Points cease to be made by the Late Glacial, if not by the Last Glacial Maximum, as seen elsewhere in Zambia (eg, Leopard's Hill Cave; Miller 1969).

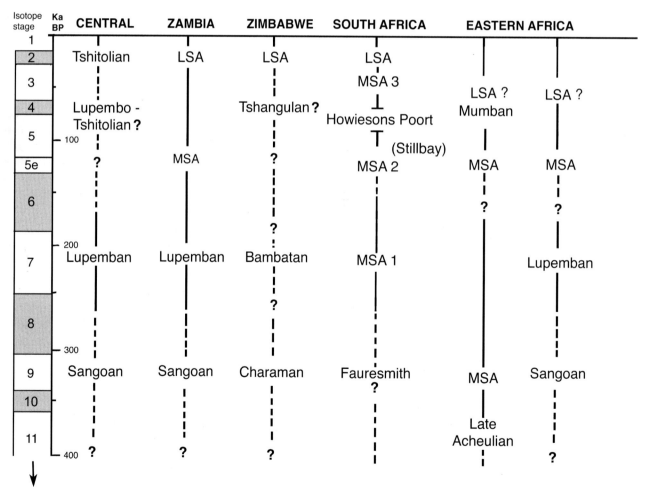

Figure 13.1 A comparison of the culture-stratigraphic sequences of sub-Saharan Africa and estimated correlations with oxygen isotope stages (see text). Solid lines represent dated sequences and broken lines are undated or uncertain chronologies.

The general culture-stratigraphic sequence for Zambia from the earliest Middle Stone Age to its latest expression can be summarised as starting with the Lupemban, or perhaps the Sangoan if the latter is not considered an expression of the late Acheulian (eg, Cormack 1994). The Lupemban is tentatively placed in Stage 7, though it may be significantly earlier (fig.13.1). The assemblage at Twin Rivers is notable for the relatively high frequency of backed tools at such an early date. No industrial name can as yet be applied to the assemblages in the lower deposits (units IX–XII) at Mumbwa Caves, but they do overlap in time with the Lupemban at Twin Rivers and may represent this industry. The period 170–130 ka BP coincides with the coldest part of Stage 8 during which Mumbwa Caves was unoccupied. No other deposits of this age are known from Zambia, but they may exist in caves to the east of Mumbwa or to the northeast at Kalambo Falls. The Last Interglacial and its sub-stages from 130–105 ka BP are known only from Mumbwa Caves. This period should be represented across the country but surface sites will be blanketed beneath sands of the Mega Kalahari in the west and beneath colluvium across the plateau. The sand scarps flanking the Zambezi River at Victoria Falls contain Middle Stone Age deposits with backed blades and bladelets including large segments and trapezes (Clark 1990). These undated assemblages could be Last Interglacial in age based on comparisons with the Mumbwa Caves sequence or they could be as early as the Lupemban at Twin Rivers with its backed tool component. No industrial name is applied to the Mumbwa assemblage and naming should be resisted until other assemblages of this age are known. Large segments made on blades are a minor element, but are a continuation of the tradition of backed tools seen in the Lupemban at Twin Rivers. The period between 105 and 40 ka BP is poorly represented in Zambia with two dates (101 ka BP and 60 ka BP) available from the surface of Twin Rivers and both are associated with bifacial points and large segments. Increased aridity during Stage 4 (76–60 ka BP) may have led to the abandonment of the western half of the country. The Middle Stone Age occupation of Mumbwa Caves at 40 ka BP is the latest at this site and is associated with flaking strategies typical of the Last Interglacial, but with a reduction of centripetal flaking techniques in favour of a broader mix of flake and blade forms. The assemblage is too small and isolated to warrant an industrial attribution, and should perhaps be linked to an assemblage from Kalemba Rockshelter (horizon G; radiocarbon dated to >37 ka BP, bone apatite) in which scrapers and points are the only retouched tools (Phillipson 1976). Kalemba is also a source of radiocarbon dates for the latest Middle Stone Age in Zambia at about 25 ka BP. Scrapers and points are again the only retouched tools. At Leopard's Hill Cave, 60 km northeast of Twin Rivers, the basal assemblage interpreted as 'proto-Late Stone Age' (Clark

1970:241) contains bifacial points (4 per cent) and backed flakes (13 per cent) among a retouched tool sample dominated by scrapers (76 per cent). The Leopard's Hill deposit is radiocarbon dated to 24–22 ka BP. Kalemba and Leopard's Hill together document a shift towards an increased use of backed hafted elements. Retouched points disappear altogether in assemblages after 20 ka BP and these are characterised by specialised production of backed flakes and scrapers and attributed to the Nachikufan I industry of the Later Stone Age (Miller 1971).

The Lupemban aside, no distinct industries can as yet be recognised in the Zambian Middle Stone Age sequence. Continuity in reduction strategies and in the types of retouched tools made is the overriding theme from the Middle Pleistocene onwards. A gradual drift towards smaller flakes and blades takes place in the Late Pleistocene along with a general reduction in the size of retouched tools. The loss of bifacial points and increased frequencies of backed flakes and bladelets marks the appearance of the Later Stone Age. Searching for clearcut divisions in this 300 ka long sequence is an exercise in the imposition of arbitary classificatory criteria that emphasises differences and obscures an underlying unity.

REGIONAL COMPARISONS

Miombo woodland extends southwards across the Zimbabwean plateau and in theory the archaeological sequence from this near neighbour should resemble that of Zambia. In reality, the evidence is insufficient and often confusing. No sequences have been dated using techniques appropriate for deposits that are likely to be beyond the age range of the radiocarbon method. Many existing radiocarbon dates are probably infinite dates. The earlier archaeological record of Zimbabwe has been largely neglected in recent decades as research interests have shifted towards later periods (Walker 1995). As a consequence, comparisons with the newly dated Zambian record are highly tentative. Inconsistencies in the use of terminology have also led to confusion about the content and culture-stratigraphic position of the later phases of the Middle Stone Age sequence (Volman 1984; Larsson 1996). These limitations aside, the Zimbabwean archaeological record is of particular importance because of its physical continuity with Zambia, but also because of its intermediate position between behavioural developments in central and southern Africa.

Archaeological research in Zimbabwe has been largely concentrated in the southwestern part of the country with the result that the terminology applied to the Stone Age derives from work in the Matopos and Bulawayo (Walker 1990). A tripartite industrial division of the post-Acheulian record has been applied since the 1960s: Charama, Bambata and Tshangula. A Sangoan equivalent or Charama industry (formerly 'Proto-Stillbay') (Cooke 1966) was recognised in the basal units at Bambata and Pomongwe caves in the Motopos region. Charama open site assemblages have also been found in the region with a notable stratified sample excavated at Khami Waterworks (Cooke 1957). A developmental sequence appears to take place in the open site assemblages with upper sequences containing fewer large tools (picks) and higher percentages of retouched points than earlier phases of the Charama. Comparisons have been made with sites in Zambia (Volman 1984:185), in particular the basal assemblage excavated by Dart and Del Grande at Mumbwa main cave, a selected sample of Sangoan artefacts found with the Broken Hill (Kabwe) hominid remains and the Twin Rivers assemblage excavated in the 1950s. The Mumbwa assemblage should no longer be considered a possible example of a Sangoan-like entity and the Twin Rivers assemblage is now assigned to the Lupemban (Clark & Brown in press). The closest equivalent to the Charama in Zambia comes from Kalambo Falls where Sangoan artefacts occur in channel deposits and are assigned to a local industrial variant (Clark 1974). The broad uniformity of the Sangoan complex across south central and parts of eastern Africa (Clark 1988) reflects its roots in the Acheulian. The Charama is effectively undated, but should be at least 270 ka BP, if not older than 400 ka BP, by extrapolation from the uranium-series dates at Twin Rivers.

The Charama is succeeded by a sequence of Middle Stone Age assemblages grouped within the Bambata industry (formerly Stillbay) (Cooke 1969, 1971). The type site material from Bambata Cave (Armstrong 1931) was a selected sample (Volman 1984), but excavations in the 1960s at Zombepata Cave (Cooke 1971) in the north and at Redcliff Cave (Cooke 1978) in central Zimbabwe have provided a less biased sample. A sequence of six phases of the Bambatan has been identified at Redcliff with the final phase attributed to a partially microlithic industry, the Tshangulan (ibid). Armstrong (1931) in his excavations at Bambata Cave noted that assemblages with backed blades were intercalated within the sequence of otherwise flake tool assemblages. Cooke (1971, 1978) reported similar lenses at Zombepata and Redcliff. The presence of large segments is of particular importance in making comparisons with the Mumbwa Caves sequence. The Bambatan industry has a minimum radiocarbon age of 35–40 ka BP (Cooke 1971), but is effectively undated. If a firm link could be drawn between assemblages with large segments and the Mumbwa Caves main Middle Stone Age occupation (Last Interglacial) then the Bambatan sequence could be anchored in time. This is not possible at present without the application of new dating methods combined with the recovery of additional palaeoenvironmental data. Lens 4 of the Redcliff

sequence, with its blades – some backed – and unifacial points, is compared by Clark and Brown (in press) to the Lupemban at Twin Rivers. If the two assemblages are indeed coeval, then the Bambatan has Middle Pleistocene roots. Comparisons have also been made with the Howiesons Poort industry known from south of the Limpopo and the large segments found in the Bambatan/Tshangulan (eg, Larsson 1996). This linkage, if correct, would place part of the Bambatan sequence in the period between 56 and 80 ka BP. Outside Zimbabwe, a Bambatan assemblage from the open site of ≠ Gi in Botswana has been dated to 70–80 ka BP by amino acid racemisation on ostrich eggshell (Brooks et al 1990).

The varying interpretations of the chronology of the Bambatan reflect the intermediate position of the industry, because it lies at the midpoint between cultural influences originating north of the Zambezi and those from south of the Limpopo. These influences are evident in the composition of Later Stone Age microlithic industries, with those from northern Zimbabwe more closely resembling Zambian forms (Walker 1995). Differences in the biogeography of the country presumably played a role in structuring assemblage variation. Dry miombo woodland extends across the central plateau with short grass savanna found in southern Zimbabwe. Climate change adds a significant complicating factor with northwestern Zimbabwe experiencing active dune formation during dry phases of the Late Pleistocene (Stokes et al 1999). The highlands of eastern Zimbabwe may have been a refuge at such times. Gaps in the occupation of sites like Redcliff and Zombepata could be expected given their relative proximity to the drier parts of the country.

The final phase of the Middle Stone Age sequence is conventionally labelled the Tshangulan industry (Cooke 1978), but considerable uncertainty exists about its typology, chronology and stratigraphic integrity (Volman 1984; Walker 1980, 1990, 1995; Larsson 1996). The industry has been described as a transitional form (Cooke 1969, 1971) with overall artefact size decreasing and backed blades and segments becoming more frequent at the expense of retouched points and other more conventional Middle Stone Age tools. Bone tools and ostrich eggshell beads appear for the first time in the sequence. The Tshangulan may span more than 30 ka with radiocarbon dates ranging from 42 to 13 ka BP, but the current consensus favours an end of the Middle Stone Age by 20 ka BP (Volman 1984; Walker 1995). The Middle to Later Stone Age transition was underway in northern Botswana well before 30 ka BP (Robbins 1999).

Comparisons have been made between the Bambata-Tshangula sequence and the Middle Stone Age sequences at Mumbwa Caves and Kalemba rockshelter (Volman 1984:211). The basal assemblage at Leopard's

Hill could be added to this list. The late Zambian sequences (25–22 ka BP) show a similar gradual decrease in artefact size and increasing frequencies of backed tools made on flakes and blades. This appears to be a widespread trend, and the similarity between the regions can be extended back in time. Both the Bambatan at Redcliff (Cooke 1978:50) and the Middle Stone Age at Mumbwa Caves contain blades and blade cores throughout their respective sequences. At Mumbwa, blades occur in the Middle Pleistocene and perhaps this is the case at Redcliff. The discovery of other similarities awaits the full publication of the Redcliff excavations. The recent renewal of active Middle Stone Age research in Zimbabwe (Larsson 1996) promises to address the many outstanding issues raised above.

South of the Limpopo, the Middle Stone Age sequence is the most comprehensively studied and dated in sub-Saharan Africa (see Thackeray 1992 for summary). A basic culture-stratigraphic framework for the region was developed from the deeply stratified cave and associated deposits at Klasies River on the Tsitsikama coast (Singer & Wymer 1984). The main cave deposits provided the database on which five chronostratigraphic phases were originally defined: MSA I, MSA II, Howiesons Poort, MSA III and MSA IV. The sequence emphasised subtle changes in flake morphology and frequencies of specific classes of retouched tools. In brief, MSA I assemblages are characterised by the production of long thin flake-blades as blanks for retouching and as tools in their own right. At Klasies River they are associated with Last Interglacial deposits (127–115ka BP). MSA II assemblages have higher frequencies of convergent forms of flake-blades and retouched points and date from c 100–80 ka BP. The Howiesons Poort represents a typological break in the sequence. Flake-blades are smaller but the main difference lies in the retouched tools among which are found backed pieces (blades and flakes) designed for hafting, including large and small segments, trapezoids and truncated forms. The backed element is typically made on fine-grained raw materials as are the unifacial and bifacial points associated with the industry. Howiesons Poort assemblages range in age from about 80–60 ka BP across southern Africa and attribution has been extended to Tshangulan assemblages in Zimbabwe (J Deacon 1995). At some multicomponent sites the Howiesons Poort is the middle or penultimate phase of the Middle Stone Age and is overlain by MSA III and MSA IV assemblages. The MSA III is characterised by large flake-blades and unifacial points with little use of fine-grained raw materials. The MSA IV is recognised by smaller convergent flake-blades. These two facies post-date 60 ka BP and extend to about 20 ka BP at a few sites, but not Klasies River (J Deacon 1995). There is further variation in the southern African sequence

with some sites having no Howiesons Poort phase (eg, Die Kelders) and others with no Middle Stone Age succeeding the Howiesons Poort (eg, Cave of Hearths, Nelson Bay Cave). Not all sites with post-Howiesons Poort assemblages conform to the sequence of MSA III–IV phases (eg, Blombos Cave) (Thackeray 1992, 2000). The long tradition of making flake-blades and triangular flakes changes gradually and between 32 and 22 ka BP late Middle Stone Age assemblages undergo a shift towards small flakes and bladelets as the predominant blank forms. By 20 ka BP fully microlithic technologies had become the norm across most of southern Africa (Wadley 1997).

Underlying the variability in the southern African sequence is a unity in the basic preferred reduction strategies, in particular the production of flake-blades as blanks. Variations in blank size and in tool types are not highly standardised with the exception of the Howiesons Poort blades and backed pieces (Wurz 1999). Finely made bifacial points attributed to the Stillbay (or Still Bay) industry have been found at Blombos Cave (Henshilwood & Sealy 1997) in association with bone points and hematite above an MSA II layer (c 100–80 ka BP). The Howiesons Poort and Stillbay highlight the spatial and temporal variation in composite tool technology that exists within the context of a generalised flake-blade technology.

The basic trends denoted by the five phases at Klasies River have since been independently corroborated (Thackeray 1989) and the scheme is often used as an informal framework for analysis and comparison of sites in the southern Cape and further afield (eg, Thackeray 2000). A variant of the scheme has been proposed (Volman 1984) that extends the classification of Middle Stone Age assemblages into the Middle Pleistocene and across the whole of southern Africa. In Volman's version, MSA 1 incorporates assemblages characterised by large flake-blades that pre-date the Last Interglacial. His MSA 2a and 2b includes Wymer's MSA I and II, and following the Howiesons Poort is MSA 3, which subsumes MSA III and IV. The two schemes coexist and are distinguished by the respective use of Arabic and Roman numerals.

The preferred form of blank production that underlies the Zambian Middle Stone Age sequence differs from that south of the Limpopo, with triangular flakes dominant and blades a consistent but minor component. The Zambian record also differs in its earliest manifestation. No equivalent to the Lupemban has been found in southern Africa. The transition from the late Acheulian to the Middle Stone Age is marked by increased variability in flaking techniques (Deacon & Wurz in press). Small bifaces and flakes made from prepared cores are associated with the late Acheulian Fauresmith industry (Volman 1984), which has a minimum age of >200 ka BP. No regionally distinctive Middle Stone Age industry appears to develop from the Fauresmith in contrast to the Lupemban. Backed tools including large segments occur from the start of the Zambian sequence at least 270 ka BP and continue to be made at intervals through the Late Pleistocene. A small and typologically informal assemblage from the basal spring deposits at Florisbad, South Africa, has been attributed to the Middle Stone Age and is dated to 279 ± 47 ka BP by optically stimulated luminescence on sediment (Kuman et al 1999). The attribution and dating, if sustained, makes the early Middle Stone Age of southern Africa the temporal equivalent to that of Zambia. The Fauresmith, by implication, must be at least 300,000 years old (fig. 13.1).

The Howiesons Poort as a time-specific florescence has no counterpart in Zambia. Wymer and Singer (1982) speculated that the Howiesons Poort was an intrusive technology introduced by an incoming population. The backing of blades and flakes had no clear precursors in the MSA II. Such diffusionist models have long fallen from favour, but south central Africa could be considered the technological reservoir from which the concept of backed composite tools was initially drawn. The periodic depopulation of the interior of the subcontinent during arid phases and the subsequent repopulation during interglacials and interstadials could be the mechanism by which people and ideas travelled. Zimbabwe is the geographical bridge between central and southern African technological traditions. The radiometric dating of Bambatan sequences should be a research priority. The shift from Middle to Later Stone Age techniques of flaking is esssentially contemporaneous between the regions. The social and physical mechanisms by which microlithic technology developed and spread deserve closer attention as they may have roots in Middle Stone Age patterns of behaviour.

The archaeological record of central Africa, like that of Zimbabwe, suffers from a lack of well-dated sites beyond the age limit of the radiocarbon technique. In addition, organic preservation in the tropics tends to be poor, caves and shelters are a rarity in the Congo basin, and deposits in the sands of the Mega Kalahari have been subjected to vertical mixing (Cahen & Moeyersons 1977). The latter can create false associations between charcoal based radiocarbon dates and archaeological assemblages (Brooks & Robertshaw 1990). The relative poverty of the known archaeological record has been exacerbated by long running civil wars in several countries including the largest in the region, the Democratic Republic of Congo (ex-Zaire). As a consequence, research involving the application of new radiometric techniques has been limited (eg, Brooks et al 1995). In a promising development, research has recently resumed in the Democratic Republic of Congo (Mercader 1997; Mercader et al

2000). In the tropical forest belt on the fringes of the Congo basin, active research on the Middle Stone Age is underway in Congo (Lanfranchi 1997), Equatorial Guinea (Mercader & Marti 1999b), and southwestern Cameroon (Mercader & Marti 1999b). The discovery of numerous new rockshelters in the latter two countries should contribute valuable palaeoecological and behavioural data.

The most complete post-Acheulian succession comes from the southern Congo basin, in particular from the open site of Gombe Point, near Kinshasa (Cahen 1976). The Gombe Point sequence is contained in sands of the Mega Kalahari with the archaeological assemblages concentrated towards the base of the deposits. The industrial succession is as follows: Sangoan/Lower Lupemban, Upper Lupemban or Lupemban/Tshitolian, Lower Tshitolian and Upper Tshitolian (Cahen & Moeyersons 1977). A similar succession was recorded from open sites in northeastern Angola (Clark 1971). The Tshitolian is the central Africa expression of the Later Stone Age and contains technological elements that show continuity with the Lupemban industry. *Petits tranchets* made on blades are a feature of the Tshitolian, as are long thin finely flaked bifacial points or lanceolates and a tanged bifacial point (Miller 1988). The recent excavations at Twin Rivers show a long ancestry for the transverse cutting edge of the tranchet form and for the making of tanged tools. Radiocarbon dates from the sands of Gombe and from northeastern Angola place the transition from the Lupemban to the Tshitolian in the Late Glacial between 14 and 9 ka BP (van Noten 1982). The upper and lower Lupemban combined as a single entity ranges in age from 9 ka BP to effectively infinite dates of >40 ka BP. The basal Sangoan is also beyond the range of radiocarbon dating. The disparity in dates for the Lupemban at Twin Rivers (~270–170 ka BP) and in the southern Congo Basin reflects the limited time range of the radiocarbon method and the taphonomic processes that affect the sand deposits at Gombe and elsewhere in the region (Cahen & Moeyersons 1977). Vertical movement at Gombe, sometimes exceeding 1m, means that the dated charcoal samples have "no direct relation with the archaeological material" (ibid:815). The culture-stratigraphic value of the industrial sequence is also undermined.

In the absence of cave deposits from the Congo basin, the archaeological sequence from Zambia offers a provisional framework that can be extended northwards for the Lupemban and later periods. If the Lupemban ends about 170 ka BP, as seems to be the case in Zambia, then a long gaps exists in the industrial sequence or the Tshitolian is much older than expected. These possibilities can only be tested by the discovery and excavation of sealed, datable deposits closer to the Congo basin. At Katanda, in the Rift Valley of the

Democratic Republic of Congo, typologically non-descript quartz and quartzite assemblages are associated with discoidal cores, grindstones, uniserial harpoons and an economy based largely on fishing (Brooks et al 1995; Yellen et al 1995). The averaged date of 90 ka BP for the Katanda sites places them in part of the long gap between the Lupemban and Tshitolian, but the Rift Valley location is no nearer the Congo Basin than the Zambian plateau. Central Africa is of particular importance for modelling the development of modern behaviours because of the unexpectedly early occupation of tropical forests by Lupemban foragers. The Middle Pleistocene date for the Lupemban at Twin Rivers may not be representative of the age of the industry further north, but without further research in the tropics it stands as a provocative benchmark.

The final comparison to be made is with east Africa. The archaeological record for the late Acheulian and early Middle Stone Age resembles that of Zambia with considerable technological variation present in the Middle Pleistocene. Deposits of the Kapthurin Formation west of Lake Baringo, in the eastern Rift Valley of Kenya, preserve assemblages left by 'archaic' *Homo sapiens* (eg, *Homo helmei?*) who lived on the shores of an alkaline lake. A volcanic marker tuff (K4) near the top of the sequence has been isotopically dated to >240 ka BP (McBrearty 1999) and is probably closer to 300 ka BP (McBrearty pers comm). Blades and blade cores occur in association with Acheulian bifaces at a depth of 3–4 m below the tuff. Blade making is also an element of the late Acheulian at Kalambo Falls (Clark pers comm) and the Cave of Hearths (Beds 1–3), South Africa (Quinney pers comm). In other parts of the Kapthurin Formation, contemporary assemblages based on small basalt cobbles contain no bifaces (McBrearty 1999). Middle Stone Age assemblages, including the Sangoan, with few retouched tools occur just beneath and in the K4 tuff. Pigments and grinding stones are a feature of these assemblages as well (McBrearty 1999). Small bifaces, leaf shaped retouched points and small Levallois cores are found in roughly contemporaneous assemblages in the Formation. In comparison with the Lupemban at Twin Rivers, the Kapthurin Middle Stone Age assemblages are similar in age, in techniques of flaking and in the use of pigments. They differ in not having the distinctive lanceolates and backed tools. The small bifaces of the early Middle Stone Age at Kapthurin and those from the Ethiopian Rift Valley (Clark 1992) resemble the late Acheulian Fauresmith bifaces of South Africa. The replacement of large cutting tools in both regions appears to have been gradual. In south central Africa and in parts of east Africa, the Sangoan marks the process of transformation to post-Acheulian technologies. The transition can now be roughly bracketed in time between 400–300 ka BP based on dates from Twin Rivers and the K4 tuff.

Middle Pleistocene dates from 235–170 ka BP are associated with Middle Stone Age assemblages elsewhere in east Africa including Ethiopia, Tanzania and Kenya (summary in Clark 1988). Sangoan-Lupemban assemblages occur in open sites around the Lake Victoria basin (McBrearty 1988) and by correlation with the K4 tuff and Twin Rivers they are in the 170 ka to 300 ka age range. The period between 170–130 ka BP is poorly represented and may reflect demographic changes linked to climatic changes experienced during stage 6. This is also the time that Mumbwa Caves and Border Cave were abandoned (see above).

A long sequence of assemblages dated to the Late Pleistocene is known from Mumba Rockshelter, central Tanzania (not to be confused with Mumbwa Caves). A Last Interglacial assemblage (Bed VI) associated with uranium-series dates of 131–109 ka BP contains prepared flakes and cores, leaf shaped retouched points (bifacial and unifacial), a variety of scraper forms, borers, burins and backed flakes (Mehlman 1989). The backed flake component is notable because the overlying Bed V assemblage (66–24 ka BP, U-series dates on shell and bone plus radiocarbon dates) contains large segments that resemble those of the penecontemporaneous Howiesons Poort of southern Africa. The tradition of backing tools to create inserts for composite tools has Last Interglacial roots at Mumba. The Bed V assemblage or 'Mumba Industry' also contains backed flakes or knives, finely flaked bifacial points, small scrapers and ostrich eggshell beads. The Mumba sequence and that from other rockshelters in northern Tanzania shows that transition from Middle to Later Stone Age technologies took place between 50 and 30 ka BP (Brooks & Robertshaw 1991). In Kenya, the transition may have been complete by 50 ka BP. At Enkapune ya Muto rockshelter in the central Rift Valley of Kenya, the Middle to Later Stone Age transition appears to have taken place by 50 ka BP (Ambrose 1998a). A lithic industry ('Sakutiek') made on obsidian and dominated by thumbnail scrapers and *outils écaillés* is interpreted as an early example of Later Stone Age technology. Radiocarbon dates for the assemblage (charcoal and ostrich eggshell) vary from 16–40 ka BP with temperature adjusted obsidian hydration dates supporting an age of 35 ka BP. The industry also contains low frequencies of backed flakes and blades with Middle Stone Age elements including discoidal cores, faceted flakes and partially bifacial knives. Like the Mumba Industry, the Sakutiek contains ostrich eggshell beads. Underlying the Sakutiek is an assemblage containing large backed blades and geometric microliths that lacks centripetal cores or faceted flakes. The assemblage ('Nasmpolai Industry') is attributed to the Later Stone Age because of the predominance of blades. No radiometric dates are available but a temperature adjusted date of 46 ka BP accords with its stratigraphic position. An underlying flake based Middle Stone Age assemblage is associated with a minimum radiocarbon date of 41 ka BP and a temperature adjusted obsidian hydration date of 32 ka BP. The latter date is considered inaccurate and is rejected (Ambrose 1998a: 384). The Middle to Later Stone Age transition is argued to have taken place by 50 ka BP based on estimated sedimentation rates.

The dating of these transitional assemblages at Enkapune ya Muto and at Mumba remains problematical with persistent inconsistencies within and between techniques. These problems aside, considerable technological variation exists in the archaeological record of east Africa between 50 and 30 ka BP. The use of backed inserts in composite tools becomes increasingly common in this interval and the distinction between Middle and Later Stone Age is blurred. The standard classificatory terminology becomes a hindrance rather than an analytical tool in the context of increasing variability. The Nasmpolai Industry, for example, with its large blades could be considered an activity variant of the Middle Stone Age rather than an early marker of the Later Stone Age. Without a larger sample of contemporaneous assemblages, the extent and behavioural significance of this variability cannot be properly studied or fully appreciated.

In east Africa, the shift away from the Middle Stone Age pattern of flaking strategies appears to take place 10–30 ka before that in south central and southern Africa. The apparently precocious development of microlithic technology in Kenya has been attributed to demographic shifts spurred by climatic changes during Stage 4 (76–60 ka BP) (Ambrose 1998b). The sample of well dated sites for this transitional period in east Africa is small and the chronological resolution is poor. The end of the Middle Stone Age here and elsewhere across sub-Saharan Africa involves more than technological and demographic changes though these are intimately linked. Social models such as that adapted from a European context (eg, Mithen 1996; Gamble 1998) and used above are a starting point for the development of more inclusive hypotheses that humanise the archaeological record of the Mid-Late Pleistocene. The use of pigments from the start of the Middle Stone Age in south central and east Africa suggests that some forms of modern behaviours had developed by 300,000 BP. Questions of social organisation and ideology that are asked of later periods in which symbol use plays an integral role in social relations (eg, Mitchell 1997) are now appropriate for the Middle Stone Age, if applied with caution.

At the outset of this study the question of the relation of biological to anatomical change was posed. Early modern or 'near modern' *Homo sapiens* (Klein 1999) had evolved by 130–100 ka BP in sub-Saharan Africa

and the Near East from more robust Middle Pleistocene forms (eg, Kabwe and KNM-ER 999) (Bräuer et al 1997) that have been attributed to *Homo heidelbergensis* or to the not yet formally defined taxon *Homo helmei* (Stringer 1996). Taxonomic uncertainties aside, the Middle Pleistocene hominids at Twin Rivers and Mumbwa Caves behaved in ways that were recognisably modern: they made systematic use of pigments for communication and new kinds of tools to solve specific problems unique to central Africa. The initial settlement of the Congo basin was as a consequence of innovations by Middle Pleistocene hominids. These behaviours reflect a cognitively integrated species and possibly one that used syntactic language in the creation of the first regionally distinct industry, the Lupemban. The full suite of modern behaviours outlined at the outset of this chapter does not appear with the Lupemban. Evidence is lacking for structured use of space and the long distance transport of raw materials. These absences may simply reflect the limitations of the archaeological record of the region rather than the behavioural capacities of the hominids. At Mumbwa Caves, small hearths occur in the Middle Pleistocene deposits and where horizontal excavation was possible, the structured use of living areas was a feature of the Middle Stone Age from the Last Interglacial. Evidence for the long distance transport (>200 km) of stone also occurs in the Last Interglacial at Mumbwa Caves and may have earlier roots.

Regardless of what future research will reveal about the Lupemban in particular, the existing record shows long threads of behavioural continuity in central Africa that link the Middle Pleistocene with the Holocene. The composite tool technology of the Middle Stone Age emerged from a background of technological variability in the late Acheulian. The standardised backed tools and scrapers of the Later Stone Age are elaborations on a Middle Stone Age theme of hafted technology. There is also no apparent difference over time in the demographic response to climatically driven changes in the distribution of plants and animals. Mumbwa Caves was abandoned during dry phases in the Middle and Late Pleistocene as well as during the mid-Holocene. *Homo sapiens* reacted to adversity in much the same way as *Homo rhodesiensis* (or *Homo heidelbergensis*). The technological and demographic continuity seen in Zambia is strong evidence for the potential emergence of most if not all aspects of behavioural modernity in the Middle Pleistocene. Anatomical modernity (*Homo sapiens sensu stricto*) developed as a mosaic of features over time and these appear to follow a behavioural lead in the case of central Africa. Proponents of a recent African origin of modern humans now have a new set of data with which to amplify or refine their models.

Appendix 1
Mumbwa Caves stratigraphic groupings

L Barham

Late Holocene – Iron Age/LSA:
unit I (0–34 cm below datum)

D11–1–1, D11–1–2, D11–2–1, D11–3–1, D11–4–1, D11–5–1, D11–5–2, D12–1–1, D12–1–2, D12–1–3, D12–2–1

(no mid-Holocene)

Early Holocene – LSA: unit II (34–75 cm)

D11–5–3, D11–5–4, D11–5–5, D11–6–1, D11–6–2, D11–6–3, D11–6–4, D11–6–5, C11–1–1, C11–1–2, C11–1–3, D12–2–2, D12–2–3, D12–2–4, D12–2–5, D12–2–6, D12–2–7, D12–2–8, D12–2–9, D10–1–1, D10–1–2, D10–2–1, D10–2–2, D10–2–3, D11–6–1/C11–1–1, D11–6–2/C11–6–2, D11–6–3/C11–1–3

Late Glacial – LSA: unit III (75–86 cm)

D12–2–10, D12–2–11, D11–6–6, D11–6–7, D11–6–8, C12–1–1, D10–2–4, D10–2–5

LSA/MSA interface – unit IV (86–91 cm)

D11–7–1, D12–2–12, C12–1–2, D10–2–6

Stage 3? – upper MSA – unit V (91–103/116 cm)

D11–8–1, D12–2–13, D12–2–14, D12–2–15, C12–1–3, C12–1–4, D10–2–7

Hiatus?

C12–1–5, D12–2–16

Stage 5 – main MSA occupation – unit VII (103–250 cm)

D10–2–8, D10–2–9, D10–2–10, D10–2–11, D10–2–12, D10–2–13, D10–2–14, D10–2–15, D10–2–16, D10–2–17, D10–2–18, D10–2–19, D10–3–1, D10–3–2, D10–3–3, D10–4–1, D10–4–2, D10–4–3, D10–4–4, D10–4–5, D10–4–6, D10–4–7, D10–5–1, D10–5–2, D10–5–3, D10–5–4, D10–5–5, D10–5–6, D10–5–7, D9–1–1a, D9–1–1, D9–1–1b, D9–1–2, D9–1–3, D9–1–4, D9–1–5, D9–2–1, D9–2–2, D9–2–3, D9–3–1, D9–3–2, D9–4–1, D9–4–2, D9–4–3, D9–4–4, D9–4–5, D9–4–6, D9–4–7, D9–4–8, D9–4–9, D9–5–1, D9–6–1, D9–7–1, D9–7–2, D9–7–3, D9–7–4, D9–7–5, D9–7–6, D8–2–2, D8–2–3, D8–2–4, D8–2–5, D8–2–6, D8–2–7, D8–2–8, D8–3–1, D8–2–5/E8–51–4, E8–1–2, E8–1–3, E8–1–4, E8–1–5, E8–1–6, E8–1–7/E8–2, E8–51–1, E8–51–2, E8–51–3, E8–51–4, E8–51–5, E8–51–6, E8–51–7, E8–51–8, E9–1–2, E9–1–3, E9–1–3, E9–1–4, E9–1–5, E9–1–6, E9–1–7, E9–1–8, E9–1–9, E9–1–10, E9–1–11, E9–1–12, E9–1–13, E9–1–14, E9–1–15, E9–1–16, E9–1–17, E9–1–18, E9–1–19, E9–2–1, E9–2–2, E9–2–3–, E9–2–4, E9–3–1, E9–3–2, E9–3–3, E9–3–4, E9–3–5, E10–1–0, E10–1–1, E10–1–2, E10–1–3, E10–1–4, E10–1–5, E10–1–6, E10–1–7, E10–1–8, H7–2–1, H7–2–2, H7–2–3, H7–2–4, H7–2–5, H7–2–6, H7–2–7, H7–2–8, H7–2–9, H7–2–10, H7–2–11, H7–2–12, H7–2–13, H7–3–1, H7–3–2, H7–4–1, H7–5–1, H7–6–1, H7–7–1, H7–7–2, H7–7–3, H7–8–1, H7–9–1, H8–2–1, H8–2–1a, H8–2–1b, H8–2–2, H8–2–3, H8–2–4, H8–2–5, H8–2–6, H8–2–7, H8–2–8, H8–2–9, H8–2–10, H8–3–1, H8–3–2, H8–3–3, H8–4–1, H8–4–2, H8–4–3, H8–4–4, H8–5–1, H8–6–1, H8–7–1, H8–8–1, H9–2–1, H9–2–2, H9–2–3, H9–2–4, H9–2–5, H9–2–6, H9–2–7, H9–2–8, H9–2–9, H9–2–10, H9–2–11, H9–3–1, H9–3–2, H9–4–1, H9–4–2, H9–4–3, H9–5–1, G7–2–1, G7–2–2, G7–2–3, G7–2–4, G7–2–5, G7–2–6, G7–2–7, G7–2–8, G7–2–9, G7–2–10, G7–2–11, G7–6–1, G7–7–1, G7–7–2, G7–7–3, G8–2–1, G8–2–2, G8–2–3, G8–2–4, G8–2–5, G8–2–6, G8–2–7, G8–2–8, G8–2–9, G8–2–10, G8–2–11, G8–3–1, G8–3–2, G8–3–3, G8–4–1, G8–4–2, G8–4–3, G8–6–1, G8–6–2, G8–7–1, G8–7–2, G8–8–1, G8–9–1, G8–10–1, G9–1–1, G9–1–2, G9–2–1, G9–2–2, H7/G7/5–1, H7/G7/5–2, H7/G7/5–3, H7/G7/5–4, G7/H7/H8/5–1, G7/H7/H8/5–2, G7/H7/H8/5–3, G7/H7/H8/5–4, G7/H7/H8/5–5

Stage 6 – colluvium: unit VIII (230/250–360 cm)

H8–9–1, H8–9–2, G8–11–1, G9–3–1, G9–3–2, G9–3–3, G9–3–4, D9–7–7, D9–7–8, D9–7–9, D9–7–10, D9–7–11, D9–7–12, D9–7–13, D9–7–14, D9–7–15, D9–7–16, D9–7–17, D9–7–18, D10–5–8, D10–5–9, D10–5–10, D10–5–11, D10–5–12, D10–5–13, D10–5–14, D10–5–15, D10–5–16, D10–5–17, D10–5–18, D10–5–19, E10–1–9, E10–1–10, E10–1–11, E10–1–12, E10–1–13, E10–1–14, E10–1–15, E10–1–16, E10–1–17, E10–1–18, E10–1–19, E9–3–7

Stage 6/7 interface: unit IX (360–380cm below datum)

E10–1–19, E10–2–1, E10–2–2, D10–6–1, D10–7–1, D9–7–19, D9–7–20, D9–8–1, D9–8–2, E9–3–17

Stage 7: unit X – dark reddish brown with grit (380–460 cm)

D9–9–1, D9–9–2–, D9–9–3, D9–9–4, D9–9–5, D9–9–6, D9–9–7, D9–9–8, D9–9–9, D10–7–1, D10–7–2, D10–7–3, D10–7–4, D10–7–5, E10–2–2, E10–2–3, E10–2–4, E10–2–5, E10–2–6, E10–2–7, E10–2–8, E10–2–9, E10–2–10, H6–1–3, H6–1–4, G4–1–4, G4–1–5, E9–3–18, E9–3–19, E9–3–20, E9–3–21

Stage 7: unit XI – dark reddish brown with clay, grit and manganese concretions (460–580 cm)

D9–10–1, D9–10–2, D9–10–3, D9–10–4, D9–10–5, D9–10–6, D9–10–7, D9–10–8, D9–10–9, D9–10–10, D9–10–11, D9–11–1, E10–3–1, E10–4–1, E10–4–2, E10–4–3, H6–1–4, H6–1–5, H6–1–6, H6–1–7, H6–1–8, G4–1–6, G4–1–7, G4–1–8, G4–1–9, G4–1–9, G4–1–10, G4–1–11, G4–1–12, E9–3–22, E9–3–23, E9–3–24

Stage 7?: unit XII – dark brown with manganese concretions (580–650 cm)

D9–11–2, D9–11–3, D9–11–4, D9–11–5, D9–11–6, D9–11–7, E9–5–1, E9–5–2, E9–5–3, E9–5–4, H6–1–9, H6–1–10, H6–1–11, D10–8–1, E9–3–24, E9–4–1, E9–4–2, E9–4–3, E9–4–4

Stage ?: unit XIII – basal stratum – strong brown (650–750 cm)

D9–12–1, D9–12–2, D9–12–3, D9–12–4, D9–12–5, E9–6–1, E9–6–2, E9–6–3

Stage ?: unit XIV – weathered bedrock -dark yellowish red (750–790 cm)

D9–13–1, D913–2, H6–12

Appendix 2
Analysis of sediments from Mumbwa Caves

S Stokes and A Goudie

INTRODUCTION

During a site visit in June 1994 which was primarily intended for the collection of samples for optical dating, a sequence of sediment samples was collected for sedimentological analysis. The objective of this exercise was to establish whether subtle details of the apparently homogeneous deposits or unconformities could be identified via evaluation of quantitative and qualitative laboratory techniques which explored aspects of sediment chemistry, mineralogy, bulk texture and grain surface texture. This brief report summarises our findings.

SAMPLE COLLECTION AND PREPARATION

Samples of between 150 and 200 g of material were collected from two related vertical excavated sections (H6, H8) near the rear of the cave (figs 2.10 and 2.18). Sampling intervals of either 5 or 10 cm were used throughout the *c* 6 m of section exposed at that time. Each sample consisted of a grab sample typically chiselled or trowelled from a freshly cleaned face and was placed immediately into labelled sealed plastic bags. Upon return to Oxford, the samples were dried at 40°C and split for the various procedures employed.

For determination of carbonate content, approximately, 5 g samples were crushed, precisely weighted (4 d.p.) and then placed in a 1 M HCl solution for 48 hours. The remaining sample was then rinsed onto a pre-weighed filter paper and the carbonate content was estimated by loss of mass. In addition to the carbonate analysis, organic carbon and nitrogen abundance were estimated by combustion of 20 mg finely ground samples in a Carlo-Erba CHN analyser.

Approximately 20 g samples were separated for mineral magnetic analysis. These were then crushed using a mortal and pestle and placed within purpose-specific plastic containers. The containers were sealed and placed within a Bartington Magnetic susceptibility meter; the susceptibility being measured in both high (10 MHz) and low (1 MHz) frequency magnetic fields. The frequency dependent susceptibility (expressed as a percentage) was also estimated as the difference between high and low field susceptibilities relative to the low field susceptibility.

Approximately 100 g samples for grain size analysis were first dried (at 40°C), weighed and then wet sieved at 4 phi. The coarse fraction was dried and reweighed in order to establish the percentage abundance of the sand fraction and then sieved at quarter phi intervals. The weight distribution of sand-sized material was evaluated using graphical statistical methods (for details see Folk (1968) and Gale and Hoare (1991)). The fine (>4 phi) fraction was analysed via a Cilas Laser Granulometer which provides quantitative estimates of grain sizes down to 0.7 μm. These data were combined to estimate sediment population summary parameters discussed below.

Four samples from the upper levels of section 1 were observed under the SEM. For each sample, an aggregate was broken open to reveal a clean sediment surface to be analysed. These were mounted onto 1 cm diameter aluminium stubs for analysis. The clay-rich poorly-sorted nature of the sediment, meant that grain surface characteristics were generally obscured by coatings of fine sediment and heavy cementation. This limited the amount of information available, particularly in the lower samples tested, where clasts were more or less completely obscured by cement substances. These relatively negative observations prohibited a more systematic investigation.

RESULTS

Generally, our analyses confirm the field observations that the sediments are essentially a succession of poorly sorted, fine-dominated sands, silts and clays (table A2.1). Mean grain sizes for samples examined varied relatively little around a mean grain size of 5 phi. The samples are however relatively well sorted, exhibit generally negative skewness values and a kurtosis of around 1.0, the latter two indexes exhibiting considerable variability down-section (fig. A2.1). The lower half of the section is generally more sandy than the upper portions, while clay is least dominant in the upper 100 cm (fig. A2.2).

Magnetic susceptibility measurements are low throughout the profile, with particularly low concentrations (and possibly increases of autocthonous sediment input via

Table A2.1 Chemical, mineral magnetic and sedimentological data for Locality 1

Sample	Locality	Selection depth (cm)	Total depth (cm)	Dry colour	Wet colour	Calcimetry (% inorganic carbon)	%N	%C (% organic carbon)	Magnetic low freq.	Susceptibility high freq.	Frequency-dependent susceptiblity	Graphic mean	Graphic st. dev.	Graphic skewness (incl.)	Graphic kurtosis	Sand/ silt	Silt/ clay
1	1	0–5		7.5 yr 4/6	7.5 yr 2.5/3	4.8	0.14	0.60	55.62	48.43	12.93	5.83	2.75	−0.09	1.04	0.44	2.56
2	1	5–10		7.5 yr 4/6	7.5 yr 3/4	0.0	0.13	0.62	74.09	65.97	10.96	6.17	2.81	−0.22	1.20	0.41	2.31
3	1	10–15		7.5 yr 4/6	7.5 yr 3/4	0.0	0.11	0.46	53.13	47.66	10.30	5.75	2.50	−0.02	1.04	0.38	3.50
4	1	15–20		5 yr 4/4	5 yr 3/3	0.0	0.12	0.50	51.80	45.76	11.66	5.75	2.73	−0.09	0.87	0.49	2.91
5	1	20–25		5 yr 4/4	5 yr 3/4	0.0	0.11	0.44	56.78	49.91	12.10	5.92	2.60	−0.05	1.07	0.39	3.18
6	1	25–30		5 yr 5/4	2.5 yr 3/4	3.2	0.11	0.57	59.47	54.20	8.86	6.42	2.91	−0.37	1.23	0.39	1.66
7	1	30–35		5 yr 3/4	5 yr 3/3	1.6	0.11	0.54	59.14	52.00	12.07	5.50	2.60	−0.19	1.00	0.44	4.16
8	1	35–40		5 yr 4/4	5 yr 3/3	1.1	0.10	0.48	56.89	48.94	13.97	7.08	2.14	−0.23	1.02	0.24	1.67
9	1	50–55		5 yr 4/4	5 yr 3/3	16.6	0.11	0.35	53.44	46.03	13.87	6.17	2.40	−0.06	1.09	0.27	3.00
10	1	60–65		5 yr 3/4	7.5 yr 3/4	16.1	0.11	0.36	54.97	47.52	13.55	5.50	1.97	0.30	1.32	0.27	6.88
11	1	65–70		5 yr 3/4	5 yr 3/4	3.8	0.10	0.37	8.42	7.82	7.13	6.58	2.36	−0.02	0.98	0.24	2.36
12	1	70–75		5 yr 3/4	7.5 yr 3/4	0.0	0.09	0.16	6.22	5.71	8.20	4.83	3.33	−0.11	1.02	0.60	3.22
13	1	75–80		5 yr 4/3	5 yr 4/3	0.0	0.10	0.34	7.21	6.71	6.93	5.00	2.85	−0.01	1.45	0.53	4.33
14	1	80–85		7.5 yr 6/2	7.5 yr 4/2	0.0	0.10	0.18	5.53	5.25	5.06	4.25	3.48	−0.08	0.84	0.78	3.52
15	1	90–95		7.5 yr 5/3	7.5 yr 3/4	0.0	0.09	0.21	25.28	23.19	8.27	4.83	3.10	−0.05	1.23	0.61	3.70
16	1	95–100		7.5 yr 6/3	7.5 yr 4/3	0.0	0.09	0.22	8.78	8.26	5.92	4.83	3.10	−0.05	1.07	0.60	3.78
17	1	100–110		5 yr 5/4	5 yr 4/4	0.0	0.09	0.22	8.72	8.30	4.82	5.00	3.19	−0.35	0.97	0.44	4.52
18	1	110–120		2.5 yr 4/4	2.5 yr 4/3	0.0	0.10	0.28	27.03	23.40	13.43	5.25	3.04	−0.12	1.00	0.54	3.37
19	1	120–130		5 yr 4/3	2.5 yr 3/4	13.9	0.10	0.31	48.79	42.37	13.16	5.42	2.79	−0.09	1.33	0.40	3.99
20	1	130–140		5 yr 4/4	2.5 yr 4/4	0.0	0.09	0.09	50.66	44.45	12.26	5.92	2.60	−0.05	1.16	0.33	3.30
21	3	0–10	140–150	7.5 yr 4/6	5 yr 3/4	–	–	–	45.13	39.04	13.49	6.58	2.58	−0.12	1.37	0.21	2.58
22	3	10–20	150–160	7.5 yr 4/4	5 yr 3/4	–	–	–	50.82	44.36	12.71	6.58	2.41	−0.17	1.07	0.23	2.36
23	3	20–30	160–170	5 yr 4/4	5 yr 3/3	0.0	0.09	0.23	56.33	48.53	13.85	6.42	2.48	−0.11	1.07	0.30	2.47
24	3	30–40	170–180	5 yr 4/4	5 yr 3/3	–	–	–	56.78	49.48	12.86	6.58	2.41	−0.17	1.07	0.26	2.33
25	3	40–50	180–190	5 yr 4/4	5 yr 3/4	–	–	–	61.20	53.14	13.17	7.00	2.54	−0.36	1.07	0.33	1.28
26	3	50–60	190–200	5 yr 4/6	5 yr 3/4	–	–	–	58.24	50.08	14.01	7.00	2.54	−0.36	1.07	0.34	1.20
27	3	60–70	210–220	7.5yr 4/6	5 yr 4/6	0.0	0.09	0.11	58.44	50.78	13.11	6.33	2.77	−0.20	1.26	0.34	2.39
28	3	70–80	220–230	5 yr 4/6	5 yr 3/4	–	–	–	60.49	52.06	13.94	6.42	2.83	−0.17	1.17	0.37	1.95
29	3	80–90	230–240	7.5 yr 5/4	7.5 yr 3/4	–	–	–	21.51	18.69	13.11	4.92	3.70	−0.29	1.17	0.35	2.42
30	3	90–100	240–250	7.5 yr 5/6	5 yr 4/6	15.5	0.09	0.07	42.75	36.92	13.64	6.33	2.95	−0.28	1.09	0.40	2.02
31	3	100–110	250–260	7.5 yr 4/6	5 yr 3/4	2.1	0.10	0.26	57.11	50.45	11.66	6.50	2.49	−0.33	1.05	0.35	1.12
32	3	110–120	260–270	7.5 yr 4/6	5 yr 4/6	1.1	0.10	0.22	94.83	81.35	14.21	5.67	2.61	−0.21	1.05	0.30	2.79
33	3	120–130	270–280	5 yr 4/4	5 yr 3/3	4.3	0.09	0.13	73.21	62.74	14.30	6.50	1.91	0.08	0.82	0.29	2.79

#	3	Depth 1	Depth 2	Munsell 1	Munsell 2												
34	3	130–140	280–290	5 yr 4/4	5 yr 3/4	2.1	0.09	0.21	65.41	55.91	14.52	6.67	2.82	−0.38	1.64	0.22	1.38
35	3	140–150	290–300	5 yr 4/6	2.5 yr 3/6	–	–	–	73.86	65.30	11.59	3.50	4.32	−0.19	0.76	1.05	2.30
36	3	150–160	310–320	5 yr 3/4	2.5 yr 3/4	–	–	–	110.00	95.52	13.16	5.67	3.22	−0.36	1.23	0.54	1.31
37	3	160–170	320–330	5 yr 4/6	2.5 yr 3/6	–	–	–	62.30	51.96	16.60	4.83	3.57	−0.27	1.41	0.27	2.87
38	3	170–180	330–340	5 yr 3/4	5 yr 3/3	–	–	–	60.74	52.69	13.25	4.83	3.22	−0.06	0.96	0.65	2.58
39	3	180–190	340–350	5 yr 4/6	2.5 yr 4/6	1.6	0.09	0.27	44.06	38.49	12.64	5.00	3.69	−0.23	1.41	0.30	2.56
40	3	190–200	350–360	5 yr 4/6	2.5 yr 4/6	0.0	0.09	0.31	57.18	48.99	14.32	5.33	3.42	−0.28	0.82	0.76	1.35
41	3	200–210	360–370	5 yr 4/6	2.5 yr 4/6	0.0	0.09	0.21	45.04	39.71	11.83	4.67	3.69	−0.29	0.82	0.65	2.28
42	3	210–220	370–380	5 yr 4/4	5 yr 3/3	0.0	0.08	0.06	35.10	30.74	12.42	6.83	2.79	−0.28	1.50	0.31	1.35
43	3	220–230	380–390	5 yr 4/6	5 yr 3/4	0.0			45.17	38.62	14.50	5.17	3.57	−0.20	1.09	0.53	2.25
44	3	230–240	390–400	5 yr 4/3	5 yr 3/2	–			54.14	46.40	14.30	4.50	3.69	−0.18	−0.98	0.73	2.29
45	3	240–250	400–410	5 yr 4/6	2.5 yr 3/6	–			39.33	33.83	13.98	5.17	3.27	−0.12	1.17	0.47	2.30
46	3	250–260	410–420	5 yr 3/4	2.5 yr 3/4	–			80.18	69.08	13.84	4.00	3.94	−0.13	0.82	1.12	2.15
47	3	270–280	420–430	5 yr 4/6	2.5 yr 3/6	–			58.54	49.41	15.60	5.17	3.39	−0.27	1.02	0.51	2.27
48	3	280–290	430–440	5 yr 3/3	2.5 yr 2.5/3	–			42.79	37.06	13.39	2.67	4.12	0.14	0.79	1.63	2.36
49	3	290–300	440–450	5 yr 3/3	2.5 yr 2.5/3	–			40.29	34.85	13.50	3.50	3.74	0.02	0.79	1.40	2.54
50	3	300–310	450–460	5 yr 4/4	5 yr 3/4	–			57.95	50.56	12.75	4.50	3.34	0.02	0.86	0.95	2.42
51	3	310–320	460–470	5 yr 3/2	5 yr 3/1	0.0	0.38	0.08	43.93	38.94	11.36	4.17	3.06	0.12	0.87	1.08	2.79
52	3	320–330	470–480	2.5 yr 3/4	2.5 yr 2.5/4	0.0	0.39	0.06	52.18	46.79	10.33	4.33	3.09	0.10	1.08	1.22	2.98
53	3	330–340	480–490	2.5 yr 4/6	2.5 yr 3/4	0.0	0.38	0.10	47.58	41.62	12.53	5.17	2.74	0.10	0.92	0.74	2.49
54	3	350–360	490–500	5 yr 3/4	5 yr 3/2	0.0	0.38	0.08	58.68	50.84	13.36	4.50	3.19	0.08	0.78	1.01	2.22
55	3	360–370	500–510	2.5 yr 3/4	5 yr 4/2	0.0	0.09	0.07	61.73	57.43	6.97	2.83	3.62	0.32	0.86	2.35	2.42
56	3	370–380	510–520	2.5 yr 4/6	2.5 yr 3/6	–	–		55.46	47.78	13.85	5.50	3.22	−0.23	0.96	0.67	1.44
57	3	380–390	520–530	2.5 yr 3/4	5 yr 3/4	2.7	0.09	0.15	37.64	33.20	11.80	5.17	2.66	0.13	0.87	0.74	2.51
58	3	390–400	530–540	5 yr 4/6	2.5 yr 3/1	5.9	0.08	0.03	25.81	22.63	12.32	5.17	2.74	0.10	0.92	0.70	2.69
59	3	400–410	540–550	5 yr 4/6	2.5 yr 4/6	0.0	0.08	0.08	7.14	6.29	11.90	4.50	2.74	0.26	0.92	1.07	3.02
60	3	410–420	550–560	2.5 yr 4/1	5 yr 4/2	3.8	0.08	0.08	11.31	9.90	12.47	3.67	3.29	0.04	1.13	1.87	2.84
61	3	430–440	560–570	10 yr 3/2	10 yr 3/3	0.0	0.08	0.13	3.22	2.83	12.11	4.33	3.02	0.13	1.02	1.11	3.15
62	3	440–450	570–580	5 yr 4/6	7.5 yr 3/2	0.0	0.08	0.03	2.53	2.32	8.30	5.50	2.61	0.00	1.05	0.37	2.76
63	3	450–460	580–590	7.5 yr 3/2	10 yr 3/2	0.0	0.09	0.03	3.03	2.73	9.90	5.17	3.09	−0.15	1.23	0.51	2.58
64	3	460–470	590–600	7.5 yr 3/2	10 yr 3/2	0.0	0.10	0.08	7.56	6.59	12.83	5.00	3.09	−0.02	1.08	0.63	2.77
65	3	470–480	600–610	10 yr 3/1	7.5 yr N2/1	5.4	0.15	0.58	4.36	3.82	12.39	3.17	2.74	0.16	1.23	2.89	2.77
66	3	480–490	610–620	10 yr 3/1	7.5 yr N2/1	0.0	0.16	0.61	5.50	4.82	12.36	2.83	2.86	0.19	1.05	2.78	3.55
67	3	490–500	620–630	7.5 yr 3/1	5 yr 3/3	0.0	–	–	12.32	10.76	12.66	–	–	–	–	–	–
Mean						1.6	0.1	0.2	45.7	39.7	12.8	5.1	3.1	−0.1	1.0	0.8	2.3
St Dev						3.3	0.0	0.2	24.6	21.2	1.6	1.2	0.5	0.2	0.4	0.6	0.6
Median						0.0	0.1	0.1	50.8	44.4	13.1	5.2	3.1	−0.1	1.1	0.6	2.4
Maximum						15.5	0.2	0.6	110.0	95.5	16.6	7.0	4.3	0.3	1.6	2.9	3.5
Minimum						0.0	0.1	0.0	2.5	2.3	7.0	2.7	1.9	−0.4	−1.0	0.2	1.1

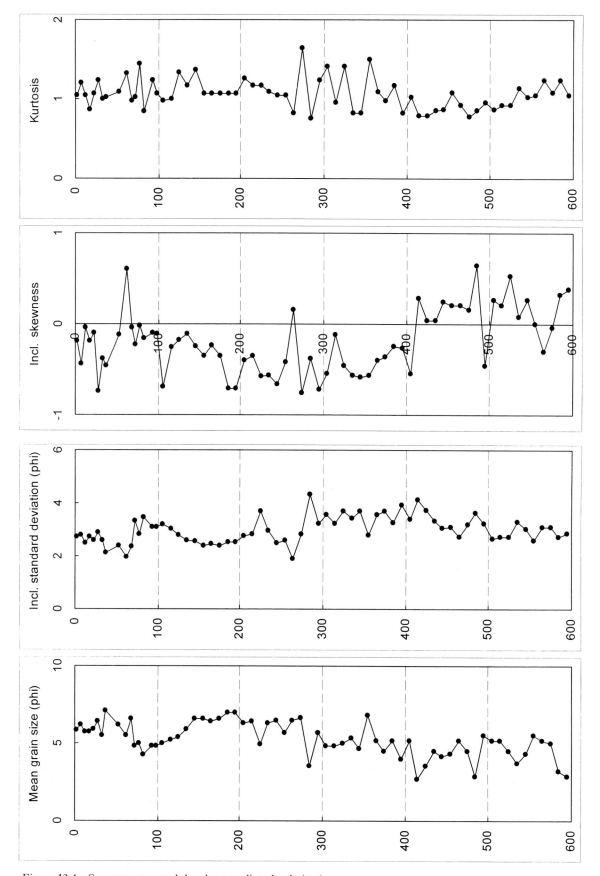

Figure A2.1   Summary textural data by sampling depth (cm).

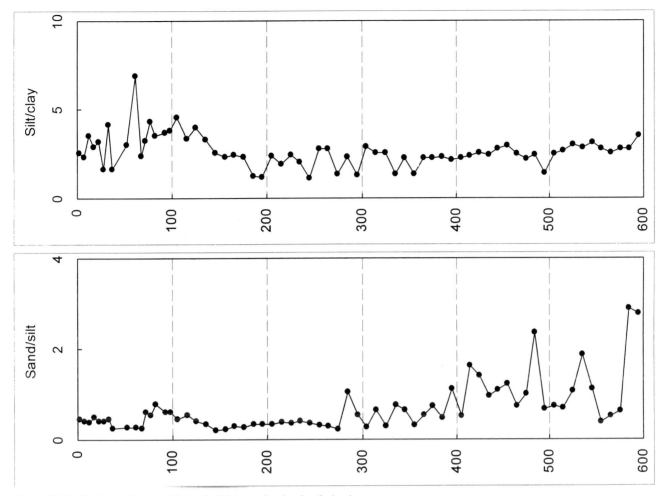

Figure A2.2 Variations in sand/silt and silt/clay ratios by depth (cm).

cave spall and erosion processes) from 80–100 cm and 520–600 cm (fig. A2.3). The frequency-dependent susceptibility exhibits relatively little variability down core with the exception of an excursion at 80–120 cm which may be an artefact of the extremely low magnetic susceptibility values at that level.

Carbonate content variations down the section are complex. Infrequent 'spikes' of carbonate occur at the top (0–230 cm) and bottom (500–600 cm) of the section where carbonate contents reach up to 17 and 5 per cent respectively. These sporadic occurrences may relate to the presence of bone fragments, though this observation is not strongly supported by the nitrogen profile which exhibits a virtually constant low value of 0.1 per cent throughout most of the section. Organic carbon values are similarly low, ranging from <0.1 to 0.5 per cent.

If an attempt is made to estimate where stratigraphic boundaries might be present, the combined variations in magnetic susceptibility, mean grain size and carbonate content are suggestive of a contact at around 100 cm. The shifts noted in sand/silt ratios, and increases in variability down section of that ratio, coupled with changes in the silt/clay ratio are suggestive of a potentially important stratigraphic boundary at *c* 300 cm. Significant reductions in magnetic susceptibility below 500 cm imply an increasingly important contribution from the quartz-rich cave spall material which is devoid of magnetic minerals.

The lack of sorting of the material, the lack of classic bedding structures, and the similarity of the material to the regolith on neighbouring bedrock slopes, suggests that most of the material is a locally-derived colluvium that has accumulated by the transport of material from adjacent bedrock slopes into the cavity. It may in part have been trapped by rockfall debris but in any event deposition would be expected to occur on the low angle slope at the margin of the dambo.

Colluvium is defined as a sediment composed of poorly sorted mixtures of clay, silt, sand and gravel particles. It accumulates on lower hill slopes and may be contrasted with material that is deposited by rivers (alluvium) and with *in situ* weathered material (eluvium). Colluvium is derived from bedrock weathered on upper hill slopes, the product of which has been stripped off by mass movement processes and now mantles adjacent

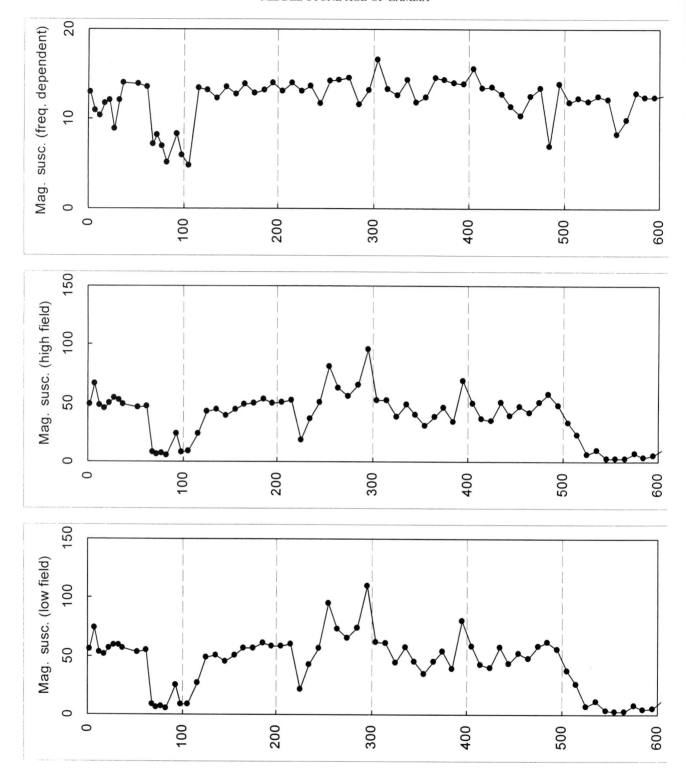

Figure A2.3   Variations in mineral magnetic properties by depth (cm).

pediments and chokes former drainage lines. Colluvium is widespread in southern and central Africa in bedrock areas of diverse lithologies, including granite, sandstone and clay (Watson et al 1984; Botha et al 1994). The conditions of climate and vegetation under which it is thought that these deposits can accumulate, 'involve highly seasonal rainfall regimes with an open vegetation cover. Sufficient rainfall to cause runoff must be combined with sediment yields from slopes high enough to avoid channel cutting and trenching of the slope'

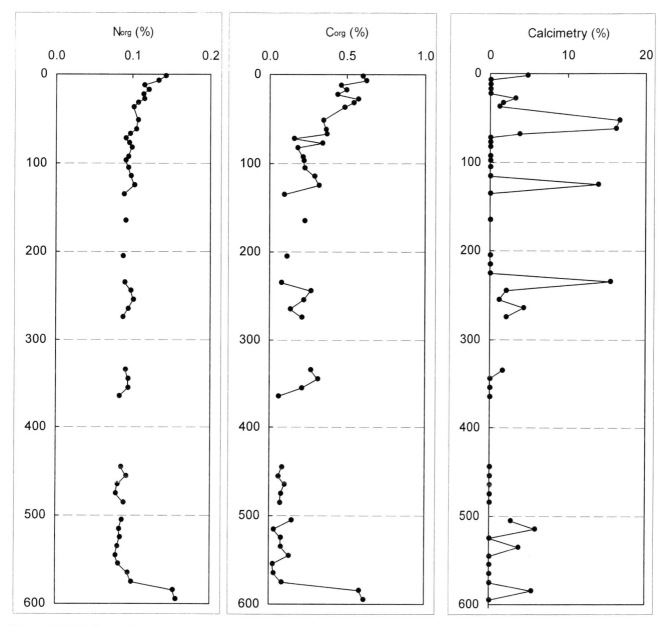

Figure A2.4 Variations in carbonate content and organic carbon and nitrogen by depth (cm).

(Thomas 1994:242). The material can either be deposited by seasonal transfers of thin layers of sediment or as a more torrential mudflow deposit.

In climatic terms, the colluvia of southern Africa have been interpreted as the result of an acceleration of the operation of such slope processes and as a result of a reduction in vegetation cover brought about by a reduction in rainfall during more arid phases (Watson et al 1984).

Appendix 3
Artefact attribute list

L Barham

All measurements of dimensions are to the nearest millimetre and of weights to the nearest gram.

Length: the shortest rectangle into which the artefact can be fitted. Flakes are oriented with butt on base line.

Width: the maximum breadth of an artefact within the rectangle.

Thickness: maximum dimension at right angles to the planes of length and width.

A   FLAKE ATTRIBUTES

1 Length
2 Width
3 Thickness
4 Cortex: presence/absence
5 Butt width
6 Butt thickness
7 Dorsal surface scar pattern:

one direction	*two or more directions*
10 – cortex, if >50 per cent	21 – opposed
11 – parallel	22 – radial
12 – convergent	23 – irregular
13 – irregular	24 – convergent
14 – opposed to butt	(Levallois)

8 Platform preparation:

01 – plain	04 – multifaceted
02 – simple/peaked facet	05 – cortical, if >50
03 – shattered	per cent
	06 – point

9 Raw material code:

00 – amethyst	16 – sandstone
01 – quartz crystal	18 – dolerite
02 – milky or vein quartz	20 – diorite
03 – blue quartz	21 – granite
04 – yellow granular quartz	22 – shale/mudstone
05 – chalcedony/agate	23 – talc
06 – green quartz	24 – galena
11 – quartzite	25 – phyllite
12 – chert	26 – dolomite
13 – hematite	27 – limonite
15 – ferric/magnetite	28 – other, specify

10 Artefact type number – see Appendix 4
11 Weight

B   CORE ATTRIBUTES

1 Length
2 Width
3 Thickness or height
4 Raw material
5 Type code: can be multiple types
6 Weight

C   CORE BY-PRODUCT ATTRIBUTES

1 Length
2 Width
3 Thickness
4 Raw material
5 Type code
6 Weight

D   SMALL DEBITAGE ATTRIBUTES

In size classes of <10 mm and 10–20 mm maximum dimension
1 Number, by raw material
2 Weight, by raw material

E   FLAKE FRAGMENT ATTRIBUTES

Grouped by 10 mm size classes: 20–30 mm, 30–40 mm, 40–50 mm, 50–60 mm, >60 mm
1 Number, size class, raw material
2 Weight, size class, raw material

F   EDGE DAMAGED/USED ATTRIBUTES

Flake attributes apply as above, for other forms:
1 Length
2 Width
3 Thickness
4 Raw material
5 Type code
6 Weight

G   RETOUCHED ARTEFACT ATTRIBUTES

1 Length
2 Width
3 Thickness
4 Raw material
5 Type code
6 Weight

H MANUPORT ATTRIBUTES

(unmodified materials transported to the site)

1 Length
2 Width
3 Thickness
4 Raw material
5 Weight

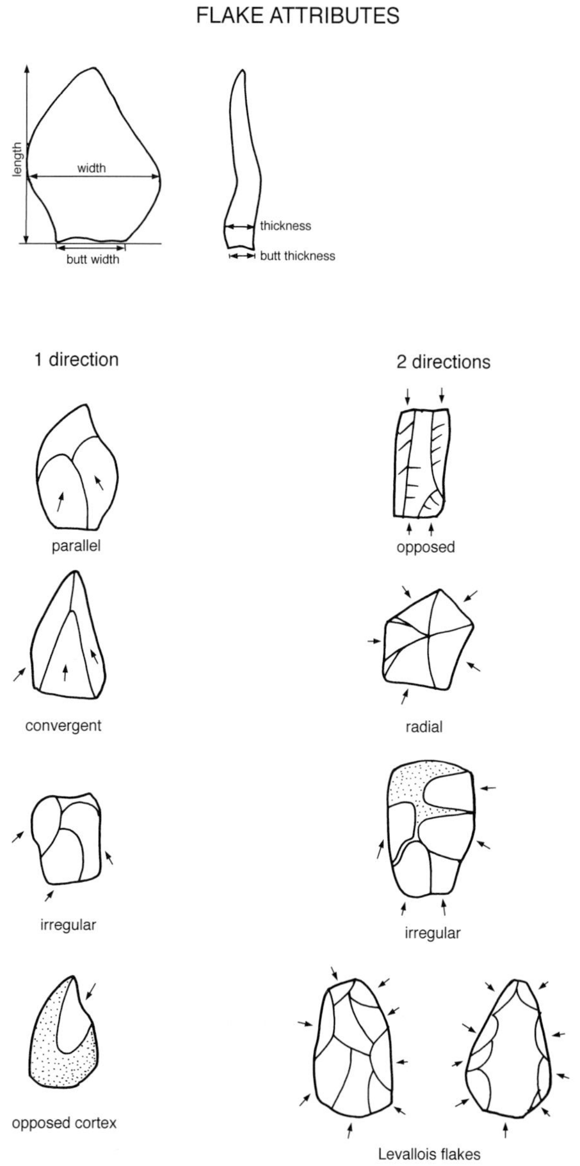
FLAKE ATTRIBUTES
length
width
butt width
thickness
butt thickness
1 direction
2 directions
parallel
opposed
convergent
radial
irregular
irregular
opposed cortex
Levallois flakes

Figure A3.1

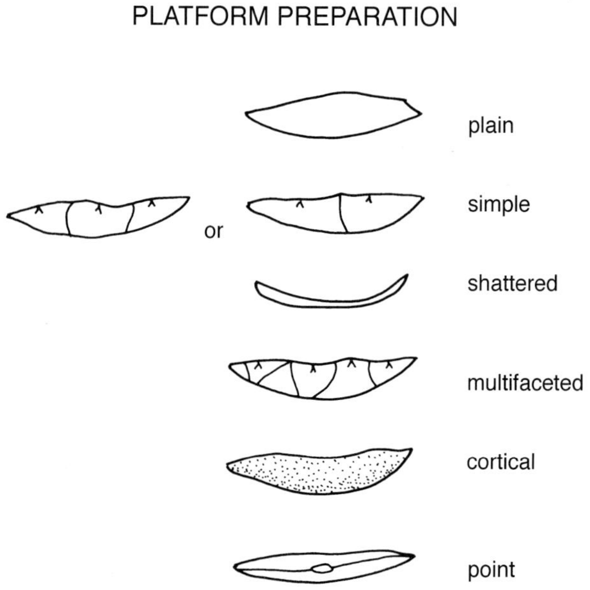
PLATFORM PREPARATION
plain
or
simple
shattered
multifaceted
cortical
point

Figure A3.2

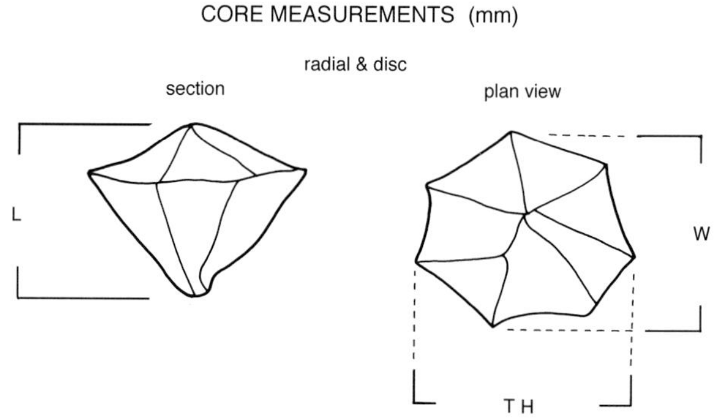
CORE MEASUREMENTS (mm)
radial & disc
section
plan view
L
W
T H

Figure A3.3

Appendix 4
Lithic classification scheme code sheet based on J Deacon 1982

L Barham

DEBITAGE

01–100	Cores	Informal coding
01–110	chunks with one or two flake scars	08
01–120	two platforms at right angles	00
01–121	radial core	01
01–122	single platform	02
01–123	multiple platforms (3 or more), irregular	03
01–124	prepared core (Levallois)	04
01–125	blade core	05
01–126	bladelet core	06
01–127	bipolar core	07
01–129	flake as core	09
01–130	core as core (change of form)	10
01–131	opposed platform	16
01–132	disc core	17

01–200	Core by-products	
01–210	exhausted bipolar	07
01–211	bipolar split segment	08
01–212	core rejuvenation flake	09
01–213	topknot flake	10
01–214	split radial core	11
01–215	split prepared core	12
01–216	blade core fragment	13
01–217	split disc core	14
01–218	core fragment	15

01–300	Debitage <10mm
01–310	Debitage 10–20mm
01–320	Chunks >20mm
01–330	Flake fragments >20 (by size class and raw material)
01–330	20–30mm
01–340	30–40mm
01–350	40–50mm
01–350	50–60mm
01–360	>60mm

01–400	Unretouched complete flakes with no edge damage
01–410	irregular
01–412	bipolar
01–420	quadrilateral
01–422	bipolar
01–430	convergent, plain butt
01–440	convergent, faceted butt
01–450	convergent, no butt
01–460	blade
01–462	bipolar
01–470	bladelet
01–472	non-functional
01–480	pentagonal
01–481	faceted butt
01–490	burin spall

EDGE DAMAGED/UTILISED

02–100	Natural pieces modified by use
02–110	anvil
02–120	hammerstone
02–130	lower grindstone
02–140	upper grindstone
02–150	combination hammerstone/upper grindstone
02–160	milled edge pebble
02–170	'palette'
02–180	spheroid
02–190	abrader

02–200	Cores/chunks with use damage
02–210	heavy edge flaked piece
02–220	scaled piece – as distinct from exhausted bipolar core
02–230	chunk with used margins

02–300	Flakes with use/edge damage
02–310	damage to cutting edge
02–311	irregular
02–312	quadrilateral
02–313	convergent, plain butt
02–314	convergent, faceted butt
02–315	convergent, no butt
02–316	blade
02–316	bladelet
02–318	pentagonal flake, plain butt
02–319	pentagonal flake, faceted butt
02–320	bipolar flake
02–320–327	steep damage
02–330–337	notched edges

FORMAL TOOLS BASED ON FLAKES

03–100   Scraper
    03–110   large scraper, maximum dimension
              >30 mm
    03–111   end
    03–112   side
    03–113   circular
    03–114   backed
    03–115   concave
    03–116   carinate/nosed
    03–120   medium scraper, 20–30 mm maximum
              dimensions
      03–121   sub-types as above
    03–130   small scraper, <20 mm maximum
              dimension
      03–131   sub-types as above
03–200   Backed/truncated tool
    03–210   backed blade, length >25mm
      03–211   segment
      03–212   straight backed blade
      03–213   obliquely truncated blade
      03–214   tranchet/trapeze
      03–215   irregular backed piece
      03–216   backed flake, length >25 mm
      03–217   obliquely truncated flake
      03–218   segment on flake
    03–220   backed/truncated, maximum dimension
              < 25 mm
      03–221   segment
      03–222   backed bladelet
      03–223   petit tranchet/trapeze
      03–224   irregular backed piece
      03–225   broken backed piece
      03–226   denticulated bladelet
    03–230   naturally backed knife
03–300   Step-flaked tool
    03–310   adze
      03–311   pebble adze

03–312   one side retouched
03–313   both sides retouched
03–320   Spokeshave (notched)
    03–321   one notch
    03–322   two notches
    03–323   more than two notches
03–330   Denticulate – three or more notches
03–400   Pointed tools
    03–410   reamer
    03–420   awl/bec
      03–460   awl/burin blow opposite
    03–430   borer
    03–440   pick
    03–450   core-axe
03–500   Point
    03–510   unifacial
      03–511   retouch along one lateral
      03–512   retouch along two laterals
      03–513   with basal tang
      03–514   with notched laterals
    03–520   bifacially flaked
      03–521   fully bifacial
      03–522   partly bifacial, <50 per cent
      03–523   with basal tang
      03–524   with notched laterals
03–600   Burin (see also 03–460)
03–700   Miscellaneous retouched piece (includes
        broken pieces)
    03–710   flat invasive retouch
    03–720   steep retouch
    03–730   notched retouch
    03–740   'normal' retouch
03–800   Tranchet edge
    03–810   on flake
      03–811   thinned base
    03–820   on chunk
03–900   Chisel

Appendix 5
Geological analysis of ferruginous materials from Twin Rivers

T Young

SUMMARY

Four submitted samples of lump iron ore, previously identified as hematite and limonite and tentatively interpreted as laterite were examined petrographically and geochemically. Only one of these specimens was confirmed as being laterite, with two being hematitic iron ores with a replacement texture, and the fourth a specularite.

Ochre impregnation from a supposed hammerstone was sampled and analysed geochemically. Although there was no complete correspondence between the ochre and any of the lump samples, the overall chemical composition made a derivation from the laterite unlikely, with the similarity with the specularite being strongest.

Further investigation of the possible origin of the ochreous material was made through examination of the matrix and of a clast from the breccia. The carbonate clast proved not to be likely source material for ochre, and the matrix proved to be very highly phosphatic, rather than ferruginous.

INTRODUCTION

A variety of samples from the Twin Rivers site was examined for evidence concerning the origin of the ferruginous materials. Sampling included one specimen identified in the field as 'limonite' (TR96 Block F limonite: TR1) and three specimens identified as laterite (laterites 2–4: TR2–4). Ochre was collected from the surface of a probable hammerstone (TR5) and ochreous-appearing material from the matrix of a breccia specimen (TR6). A sample was also taken from a clast within the breccia (TR8) for examination as a polished block.

Analyses and investigations taken are listed below:

Sample	XRF: major elements	ICP-MS: trace elements	Polished block for SEM
TR1	X	X	X
TR2	X	X	X
TR3	X	X	X
TR4	X	X	X
TR5		X	
TR6	X	X	X
TR8			X

The iron ore specimens were texturally divisible into laterite (TR1), replacement iron ores (TR2, TR4) and specularite (TR3).

Analytical studies were made using the Cambridge Instruments (LEO) S360 scanning electron microscope, with a Link Analytical Ltd (now Oxford Instruments) AN10000 energy dispersive X-ray analysis system, a Philips PW 1400 X-ray fluorescence (XRF) spectrometer and the Perkin-Elmer Elan 5000A inductively coupled plasma-mass spectrometer (ICP-MS) of the Department of Earth Sciences, Cardiff University.

DESCRIPTION OF THE IRON ORE LUMP SPECIMENS

TR1 (labelled: TR96 Block F limonite)

This sample comprises a brown pebble approximately 4 cm in diameter, which is partly coated in a dark brown ferruginous rind, resembling desert varnish. The rock appears to comprise well-lithified, ferruginous particles 1–2 cm across, with softer, more silty areas between.

The polished block shows that the rock contains silt- and sand-grade grains (20–1000 μm) of quartz, feldspar and mica (fig. A5.1a,b), in a fine-grained matrix dominated by iron oxides. The micas show little evidence of penetrative alteration, but have a sharp contact with the enclosing iron oxides (fig. A5.1a,c). The iron rich groundmass shows a variable backscatter coefficient, with amorphous areas (20–80 μm across) of greater electron density probably representing areas of anhydrous hematite in an otherwise dominantly hydrated (goethite?) material (fig. A5.1c,d). Some of the hematitic patches show small (sub-micron) grains of cerium-rich phosphate (monazite?; fig. A5.1d). There are some examples of ferruginous coated grains of up to 200 μm (fig. A5.1e), but these are uncommon. The brown coating on the pebble was apparently clay-rich (fig. A5.1f).

TR2 (labelled: Twin Rivers 96, east wall solution cavity)

This sub-angular pebble, 6 cm maximum diameter, is dominantly hard and very dark. It is traversed by a vein and a tubular structure, containing saccharoidal quartz.

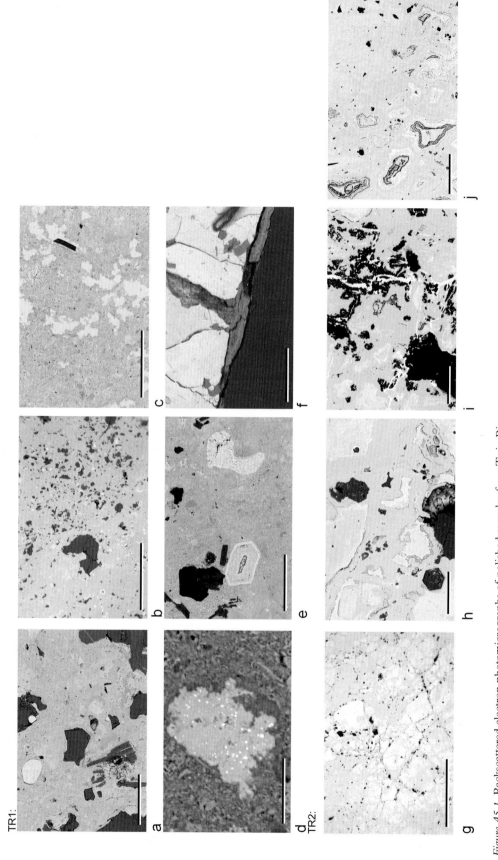

Figure A5.1 Backscattered electron photomicrographs of polished samples from Twin Rivers.

a–f. TR1

a–b. Areas rich in surviving detrital minerals. Grains are dominantly quartz (dark grey), but K-feldspar (lower right (a)), mica (eg. biotite lower left of centre (a)), spinels and phosphates also occur. Scale bar in (a) is 200 μm and in (b) is 2.00 mm.

c. Area poor in detrital grains, apart from mica (right centre). Matrix shows patchy distribution of material with differing backscatter coefficients. Scale bar 200 μm.

d. Detail of area to lower left of mica in (c) with high backscatter coefficient, showing very small monazite grains in hematite. Scale bar 20 μm.

e. Coated ferruginous grains (bright, laminated), alongside quartz and mica (both black) in ferruginous matrix. Scale bar 200 μm.

f. Detail of superficial coating on pebble (pale grey), showing penetration into cracks in pebble (bright). Dark grey in lower part of image is mounting medium. Scale bar 200 μm.

g–j. TR2

g. Low magnification view showing polygonal network marked by small quartz grains (dark) representing grain boundaries of replaced texture. Scale bar 2.00 mm.

h. neomorphic euhedral quartz (grey) with intergrown hematite (bright). Scale bar 100 μm.

i. Detail showing variable development of hematite (white) and quartz (black) on former grain boundaries. Scale bar 200 μm.

j. Internal structure of some replaced grains defined by concentric voids (picked out in this image through the influence of secondary electrons). Scale bar 200 μm.

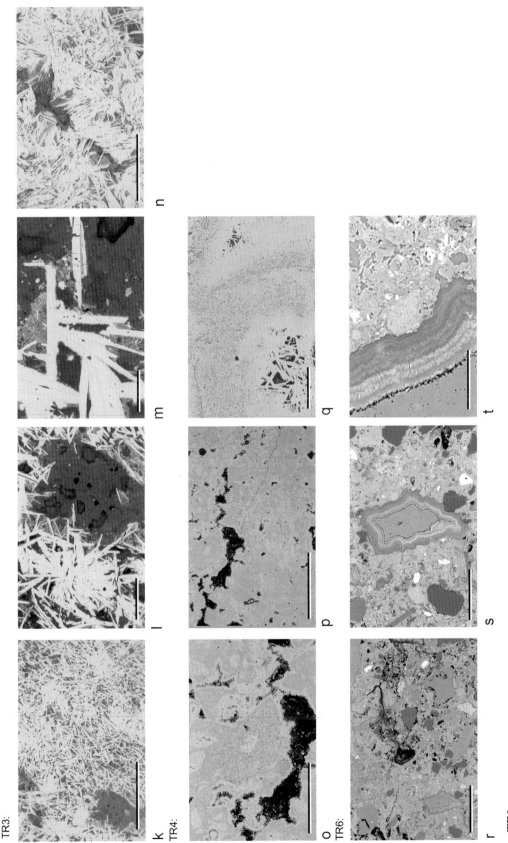

k–n. TR3

k. Low magnification view of specularite texture. Scale bar 2.00 mm.

l. Detail of area at bottom left of (k) showing porosity filled by alumina minerals and kaolinite (both dark grey). Scale bar 500 µm.

m. Detail of area in centre of (l) showing specularite (white) overgrown by a second generation normal to platelet surfaces, in turn overlain by a Mn, Al-bearing mineral, possibly galaxite (mid grey). Dark grey areas include various aluminosilicates and alumina minerals (very dark). Scale bar 100 µm.

n. Region of specularite showing a coarser scale structure in platelet orientation. Scale bar 2.00 mm.

o–q. TR4

o–p. Low magnification views showing void space, angular grains replaced by hematite (picked out by differing density of crystallites). Scale bar in (o) 1.00 mm, in (p) 2.00 mm.

q. Specularite occurrence in centre of replaced grain. Scale bar 100 µm.

r–t. TR6

r. Low magnification view showing poorly sorted sediment and porespace occluded by cement. Scale bar 500 µm.

s. Pore with phosphate (zoned) and calcite cements. Sediment shows well-rounded grains of quartz, K-feldspar, apatite, ilmenite, which may show some corrosion, set in a matrix which is heavily phosphatised. Scale bar 200 µm.

t. Detail of area in (s) showing phosphate fringing cements, overlain by calcite and overlying the sediment. Scale bar 50 µm.

267

One end of the pebble presents a delicate mesh-like structure suggesting dissolution of an originally abutting mineral phase (possibly carbonate or sulphide).

The polished section shows this sample bears a network of quartz (fig. A5.1g), apparently marking the boundaries of a former grain texture, with the original grains 50–1000 μm in diameter. The grain boundaries may be marked by discontinuous rims of quartz (fig. 5.1g–i), discontinuous rims of hematite (fig. A5.1i), or discrete neomorphic quartz grains (which may show intergrown hematite; fig. A5.1h). In some areas of the section, variation in the hematite produces a concentrically laminated structure (fig. A5.1h,j).

TR3 (labelled: Twin Rivers 96, east wall solution cavity, hematite)

This sample is a rounded pebble, 6 cm maximum diameter, with a brown, polished surface coating resembling desert varnish. This is a specimen of coarse specularite, with substantial porosity, some of which is occluded by a fine-grained white material.

The main generation of hematite crystals range up to 1000 μm in length, and 25 μm in width (fig. A5.1k–n). These are coated by a second generation, oriented approximately normal to the surface of the first, and just a few microns in length (fig. A5.1m). The main generation of crystals are arranged randomly, or in sheaves of crystals up to 1000mm across (fig. A5.1n). In some areas these sheaves are arranged in a crudely radial arrangement.

The whole structure is highly porous, but large pores up to 1000 μm across may be largely occluded by aluminous material, including kaolinite, alumina and iron aluminium silicates (fig. A5.1l). Adjacent to these pores the hematite may be overgrown by a very fine-grained mineral containing Mn and Al, locally with some Ti (eg, fig. A5.1m, lower left). This phase is too fine-grained to obtain a meaningful microanalysis, but the composition would be compatible with the Mn-Al spinel galaxite.

TR4 (labelled: Twin Rivers 96, east wall solution cavity)

This specimen is a sub-rounded pebble 4 cm across, with an irregular surface corresponding to significant internal porosity. The cut specimen shows pale crystals within the dominant hematite, and these are almost certainly quartz, but unfortunately none appeared within the examined section.

This specimen shows a relict texture preserved by varying density and size of hematite crystallites. The chemical analysis shows this specimen to be almost pure hematite. The relict grains are angular, show a well defined rim overgrown by radially oriented hematite (fig. A5.1o,p). Inside, the grains show a slightly more porous fine-grained hematite. The centres of the grains may be formed of the less porous hematite, like the overgrowths, sometimes with preserved void space at the centre of the original grain. In some cases the fill occluding this pore space is a specularite with crystals of hematite up to 100 μm in length (fig. A5.1q).

DESCRIPTION OF THE MATRIX OF THE BRECCIA

The breccia has a fine-grained matrix which has a brownish colour; this led to its investigation within the examination of the ferruginous materials. However, the colour does not reflect a high iron content, but rather this material is highly phosphatic.

The polished block (fig. A5.1r,s) shows that the clastic component of the sediment includes subrounded to well rounded quartz and feldspar grains of up to 500 μm (more usually 150 μm). Iron oxides and ilmenite are also abundant, but mainly at a finer grain size. The sediment also includes abundant irregular and rounded particles of an apatite, which has a high backscatter coefficient. Voids within the sediment bear botryoidal fringing phosphatic cements with a fibrous microstructure (fig. A5.1t), followed by calcite.

Geochemistry

The major element analyses by XRF (table A5.1) show a reasonably good approach to a 100 per cent total. The exception (TR4) is just a little high, which is due to calibration problems when Fe_2O_3 is at such extreme values. TR1 shows a high loss on ignition (LOI) of 14.6 per cent, indicating that the iron minerals are hydrated, and that water is contained elsewhere in the material (if the Fe_2O_3 were all goethite and lepidocrocite the expected LOI would be 7.3 per cent). It is possible therefore that the specimen includes some hydrated gel material. The LOI for TR2 indicates that this specimen is a mixture of hydrous and anhydrous iron oxides. The LOI is very low for TR3 and TR4 suggesting they are relatively pure hematite.

TR1 shows a moderate concentration of elements other than iron, consistent with the detrital materials observed petrographically. TR2 shows a high SiO_2 content, corresponding to the observed abundance of quartz. TR3 and TR4 are both relatively pure hematite, and therefore show very high iron contents, extremely low phosphate, very low loss on ignition and low silica and alumina. They differ in TR3 being more aluminous, corresponding to the significant quantities of alumina and kaolinite observed in the pore spaces. TR6 shows elevated phosphate and calcium contents, corresponding to a francolite content of approximately 55 per cent.

Concentrations of trace elements (table A5.2) are typically rather low in the iron ores, and the lack of correlation between the various samples reinforces the disparate nature of their petrology.

Table A5.1 Major element chemistry in wt% determined by XRF (values for TR5 based on ICP-MS analysis). nd=not determined, <=below detection

	SiO_2	Al_2O_3	Fe_2O_3	MnO	MgO	CaO	Na_2O	K_2O	TiO_2	P_2O_5	LOI	$Total$
TR1	9.31	3.22	72.58	0.38	0.34	0.19	<	0.24	0.36	0.68	14.60	*101.91*
TR2	10.01	0.67	83.21	0.09	0.14	0.54	<	0.08	0.23	0.39	5.55	*100.90*
TR3	1.64	1.83	94.85	0.40	0.01	0.12	<	0.02	0.04	0.04	1.70	*100.65*
TR4	2.80	0.48	99.08	0.01	<	0.05	<	0.06	<	0.03	0.89	*103.41*
TR5	nd	nd	nd.	0.03	0.12	0.28	nd	nd	0.11	0.24	nd	nd
TR6	20.38	3.91	2.72	0.57	0.69	32.07	0.16	1.00	0.25	19.33	17.96	*99.05*

Table A5.2 Trace element chemistry in ppm, determined by ICP–MS (elements also determined by XRF excluded). <=below detection

	Li	Be	Sc	V	Cr	Cu	Zn	Ga	Ge	As	Rb	Sr
TR1	10.41	15.67	17.08	316.51	123.98	22.43	119.71	13.46	1.62	127.80	4.95	14.26
TR2	1.86	0.37	1.50	477.15	22.09	404.27	158.52	2.82	2.07	59.12	4.27	6.75
TR3	15.86	0.34	0.55	20.58	4.70	58.63	17.60	1.85	1.21	2.62	2.58	9.13
TR4	1.51	4.10	5.81	30.42	2.22	5.50	4.80	3.00	37.97	11.22	7.36	10.13
TR5	<	<	<	23.08	28.02	81.52	129.66	2.33	1.21	<	10.24	8.48
TR6	14.94	1.01	4.55	38.75	37.32	32.87	122.47	5.87	0.59	<	45.14	136.76

	Y	Zr	Nb	Mo	Cd	Cs	Ba	Tl	Pb	Bi	Th	U
TR1	44.08	95.07	8.83	11.31	0.26	0.12	188.96	0.15	5.06	0.87	3.93	4.18
TR2	6.22	33.74	4.08	1.96	<	0.11	87.57	<	178.59	0.91	1.32	0.68
TR3	3.02	5.96	1.30	4.87	<	0.18	295.29	0.21	28.23	0.85	0.65	2.20
TR4	5.68	6.40	0.53	8.77	<	0.70	32.66	<	13.26	0.70	0.42	9.17
TR5	1.59	33.07	1.84	<	<	0.51	54.96	<	13.39	<	1.40	0.50
TR6	11.26	49.10	5.00	0.57	<	1.10	65.37	0.23	7.83	0.23	4.21	1.55

	La	Ce	Pr	Nd	Sm	Eu	Gd	Tb	Dy	Ho	Er	Tm	Tb	Lu
TR1	20.74	55.74	3.39	12.50	3.21	0.96	4.03	0.74	5.50	1.37	4.98	0.89	6.59	1.18
TR2	5.16	5.60	1.29	5.12	1.06	0.25	1.09	0.18	1.03	0.21	0.56	0.09	0.5	0.07
TR3	4.35	62.91	0.91	3.21	0.62	0.27	0.95	0.11	0.62	0.09	0.26	0.04	0.18	0.03
TR4	14.31	12.39	3.92	12.88	2.72	0.54	2.27	0.34	1.85	0.26	0.74	0.11	0.88	0.12
TR5	3.39	10.03	0.72	<	<	<	<	0.07	<	<	0.14	<	<	*(0.06)*
TR6	17.00	31.59	3.77	13.91	2.68	0.71	2.61	0.38	2.16	0.40	1.12	0.16	0.97	0.15

Figure A5.2 shows the upper crust-normalised REE profiles (Taylor & McLennan 1981) for the iron ore specimens. The dissimilarity between the specimens is again apparent:

TR1 shows elevated heavy REE (HREE) contents, with progressive relative depletion towards the light REE (LREE) (Lu_N=3.69, Pr_N=0.48). The sample shows a very slight positive Ce anomaly of $Ce/Ce\star$ equal to 1.52 ($Ce/Ce\star=Ce_N/[La_N^{0.5} \star Pr_N^{0.5}]$, where E_N denotes an element normalised against average upper crustal abundance using the normalising factors of Taylor & McLennan 1981).

TR2 shows low REE contents, with the HREE present at a steady value of approximately 0.26 of average upper crust levels. The LREE show progressive depletion below this level down to La (La_N=0.17), with a marked negative Ce anomaly ($Ce/Ce\star$=0.49).

TR3 shows REE contents generally around 0.1–0.2 of average upper crustal levels, with a somewhat humped profile, with Eu_N reaching 0.3 (although this may be somewhat raised by interference with the significant Ba content of this sample). The LREE have normalised values of approximately 0.13–0.14, upon which is superimposed a large positive Ce anomaly ($Ce/Ce\star$=7.20).

TR4 shows a somewhat similar profile to TR2, with slightly higher REE contents (range 0.32 – 0.61 of UC average for elements other than Ce), and a slight relative depletion of the HREE. The negative Ce anomaly is more marked than that of TR2 ($Ce/Ce\star$=0.38).

TR5 shows very low REE contents, and many elements fall below the detection limits. The LREE show a small positive Ce anomaly ($Ce/Ce\star$=1.47). The few heavier REE detectable show a relative depletion towards the REE. The overall profile is probably closest to TR3.

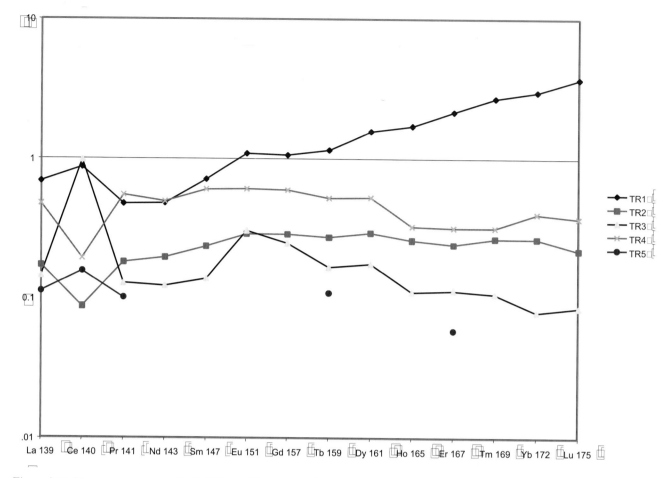

Figure A5.2 Upper crust normalised REE profiles (normalisation factors after Taylor & McLennan 1981) for the iron ore specimens.

The upper crust-normalised REE profile for TR6 (figure A5.3) is only very slightly humped, and is therefore typical of fine-grained sediment. The profile suggests that the sediment source is a primary source, and the sediment has not been recycled through lateritic deposits.

Conclusions

The iron ores recovered from the site include material derived from both laterites and probable vein mineral-isation. It is safe to say that only one of the four is a typical laterite – the other three are probably derived from other, older, geological sources. However, the variability present does not permit determination of whether they derive from a single variable source, or (more likely the case) that they derive from several distinct sources.

Two of the iron ore specimens (TR1, TR3) bore a brown ferruginous crust, and the other two (TR2, TR4) had very dark, smoothed outer surfaces. This suggests that the materials were derived pebbles, and not materials obtained fresh at outcrop.

The two replacement ores are texturally dissimilar. TR2 shows relict polygonal grain boundaries, picked out by discontinuous rims of quartz, discontinuous rims of dense hematite, euhedral neomorphic quartz crystals (with intergrown hematite) and by cracking. In contrast TR4 shows angular replaced grains with a low-density of hematite crystals, overgrown with more dense hematite crystals which become specularite in voids. The two samples share some similarities in their chemical compositions, including their upper crust-normalised REE profiles, but TR2 has elevated levels of most trace elements compared with TR4 (except for U, Mo, Sr, Ge).

The specularite sample (TR3) is marked by an open texture of large hematite crystals. Some of the void space is filled by aluminous material, including kaolinite, an alumina mineral (?bauxite), fine-grained Al, Si, Fe bearing clay and a fine-grained Mn, Al mineral possibly a spinel. The upper crust-normalised REE profile differs from all the other specimens, with a large positive cerium anomaly.

Determination of the nature of the ochreous residue on the hammerstone (TR5) was one of the main aims of the

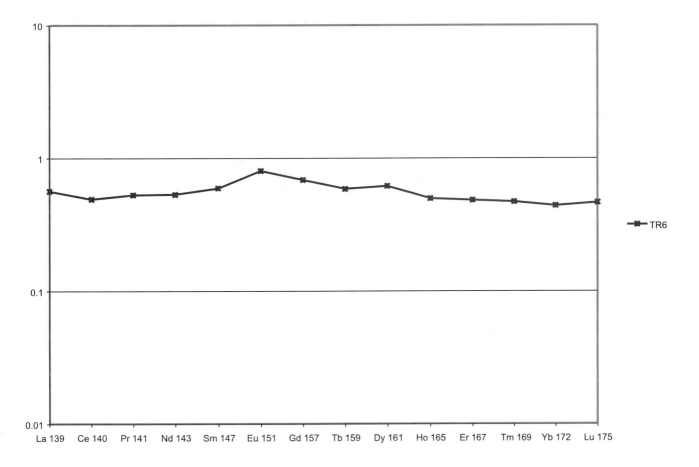

Figure A5.3 Upper crust normalised REE profiles (normalisation factors after Taylor & McLennan 1981) for the matrix of the breccia (TR6).

work. Sampling of the ochre will inevitably have involved some contamination from the hammerstone itself. This leads to uncertainty in the interpretation, given that the ochre does not have a very close chemical resemblance to any of the lump ore types. The ochre was present in only a very small quantity, so major element analysis was not possible. The REE profile hints at a similarity to that of the specularite (TR3), but low concentrations of the REE precludes detailed comparison of the profile. Some of the other elements (eg, Th being present in significantly greater quantities than U) suggest comparison with the quartz-rich replacement ore (TR2). Other elements again (particularly the metals V, Cu, As, Pb) are present in much higher concentrations in TR2 than in the ochre. There are no suggestions in the chemical analyses that the ochre was derived from the laterite. Until some evidence for the spectrum of possible sources of replacement ores/ specularites becomes available (and for the compositional range within each source) it will not be possible to refine the provenancing of the ochre any more closely, than to say that it is unlikely to have been produced from laterite alone.

The matrix of the breccia (TR6) proved to contain little iron (despite its colour). The material proved to be dominated by phosphate minerals, probably representing material reworked from animal droppings and/or bone.

The examination of a clast from the breccia (TR8) to examine whether the carbonate rocks contained any fine-grained iron oxides which might be the source of the ochre demonstrated that, in this clast at least, there was no included iron oxide material which could be liberated on weathering.

Zambian geology includes numerous distinct occurrences of specularite of different ages and host stratigraphic horizon. Detailed consideration of the solid geology close to the site may reveal potential sources, and any future attempt to refine the provenancing of the samples would require collection of comparative material. Given the possibility that the materials are derived pebbles, then the ultimate geological source may not necessarily be the immediate provenance, but rather they may derive from secondary deposits.

Appendix 6
Small flaking debris bulk analysis data

L Barham

Level	Number	Wt/100g	RM	Total wt g	Estimate g	Estimate N
E7	221	28	quartz		1709	**13490**
		56	bone		3418	
	1	1	pigment		61	61
		14	other		855	
totals		99		6104	6043	
G5	210	36	quartz		729	**4255**
		57	bone		1155	
	6	2	pigment		41	122
		5	other		101	
totals		100		2026	2026	
E4/F4/1	196	30	quartz		980	**6405**
		42	bone		1373	
	2	0	pigment		0	65
		28	other		915	
totals		100		3268	3268	
E4/F4/2	108	20	quartz		573	**3093**
		26	bone		745	
	2	1	pigment		29	57
		53	other		1518	
totals		100		2864	2865	
E4/F4/3	166	22			657	**4960**
		36			1076	
	0	0			0	
		42			1255	
totals		100		2988	2988	
E5/F5/1	304	30	quartz		819	**8299**
		48	bone		1310	
	6	2	pigment		55	164
		20	other		546	
totals		100		2730	2730	
E5/F5/2	448	28	quartz		800	**12795**
		58	bone		1656	
	2	1	pigment		29	57
		12	other		343	
totals		99		2856	2828	
E5/E6/1	350	28	quartz		939	**11739**
		54	bone		1811	
	3	1	pigment		34	101
		16	other		537	
totals		99		3354	3321	
E5/E6/2	240	32	quartz		650	**4877**
		42	bone		852	
	3	2	pigment		41	61
		24	other		488	
totals		100		2032	2031	

Level	Number	Wt/100g	RM	Total wt g	Estimate g	Estimate N
E5/E6/3	201	50	quartz		1839	**7393**
		23	bone		846	
	1	0	pigment		0	37
		27	other		993	
totals		100		3678	3678	
E5/E6/4	283	40	quartz		1421	**10052**
		24	bone		852	
	0	0	pigment		0	
		36	other		1279	
totals		100		3552	3552	
E5/E6/5	219	45	quartz		1079	**5252**
		12	bone		288	
		0	pigment		0	
		43	other		1031	
totals		100		2398	2398	
E5/E6/6	424	29	quartz		948	**13856**
		20	bone		654	
	0	0	pigment		0	
		50	other		1634	
totals		99		3268	3236	
TOTAL QUARTZ						**106466**
TOTAL PIGMENT						762

Level	Number	Wt/100g	RM	Total wt g	Estimate g	Estimate N
K23/1	334	30	quartz		4216	**46934**
		14	bone		1967	
	0	0	pigment		0	
		56	other		7869	
totals		100		14052	14052	
K23/2	166	32	quartz		4056	**21042**
		14	bone		1775	
	0	0	pigment		0	
		54	other		6845	
totals		100		12676	12676	
K23/3	446	19	quartz		1449	**34021**
		8	bone		610	
	0	0	pigment		0	
		72	other		5492	
totals		99		7628	7551	
J23/1	524	25	quartz		2255	**47254**
		8	bone		721	
	1	0	pigment		0	90
		67	other		6042	
totals		100		9018	9018	
J23/2	463	18	quartz		731	**18798**
		15	bone		609	
	1	0	pigment		0	40
		67	other		2720	
totals		100		4060	4060	
J23/3	333	19	quartz		2980	**52221**
		52	bone		8155	
		0	pigment		0	
		29	other		4548	
		100			15683	
TOTAL QUARTZ						**220270**
TOTAL PIGMENT						130

Appendix 7

(a) PRELIMINARY REPORT ON THE SEDIMENTS OF LAKE PATRICK

MJ Simms

Description

Extensive exposures of lacustrine carbonates with interbedded palaeosols are exposed along the course of the, normally dry, Casavera Stream to the north and west of Twin Rivers kopje. A series of low ridges and scarps located to the southwest, west, north and northeast of the Twin Rivers kopje define a small basin, a few km² in area. This circle of hills is broken only at one point, to the westsouthwest of Twin Rivers kopje, where the course of the Casavera Stream extends out onto the western edge of the Kafue Flats. Lacustrine carbonates were exposed extensively around the southern end of the kopje into this area, indicating that the lake must at one time have extended right across the Kafue Flats and covered an area of several thousand km². This ancient lake has been named Lake Patrick, after Patrick Roberts on whose farm the deposits were first discovered.

The overall succession, described below and depicted in figure A7.1, was logged in July 1999. It is a composite section, based on three main sites along the Casavera Stream to the north and northeast of Twin Rivers kopje. The basic sedimentary sequence comprises five lacustrine carbonate units separated by clastic-dominated units, which range in thickness from only 1 or 2 cm to just over one metre. No petrographic, isotopic or clay mineral analyses of the sediments have yet been undertaken and hence reference to particular grain size (eg, clay, silt), and the palaeoenvironmental interpretations, are based largely on field observations and must be considered only preliminary.

14   *c* 1.20 m – (seen below fairly thin modern soil cover). Soft, chalky, greyish-white limestone with abundant small gastropods. Rather more indurated and with abundant irregular tubular cavities towards the top.

13   0.30 m – Slightly brownish-grey blocky clay with numerous gastropod shell fragments. Unlaminated but with numerous small stress cutans (pedogenic slickensides). Passes down into:

12   0.20 m – Orange-brown clays with abundant small carbonate pellets.

11   *c* 0.70 m – Soft, chalky, greyish-white limestone with fairly abundant root traces. Slightly more indurated towards the top. Large (1 cm+) colour-banded gastropods (*Achatina tavaresiense*) common with smaller gastropods abundant.

10   0.02 m – Grey clay parting with carbonate pellets.

9   0.45 m – Soft, chalky, creamy-white limestone with abundant root traces. Basal 0.05 m almost a distinct unit with a diffuse to sharp top and containing numerous small (5×15 mm) tubes with closely-spaced menisci and abundant gastropod debris in upper part.

8   0.08 m – Brown clay with very abundant carbonate pellets.

7   0.45 m – Pale, chalky, creamy-brown limestone with abundant root traces and small gastropods. Large gastropods (*Achatina tavaresiense*) also fairly common. Extensively bioturbated with reddish silt piped up into base along small burrows. Rather irregular base and crudely laminated in lowest few cm.

6   0.50 m – Orange-brown silty clay, becoming more reddish towards top, with scattered carbonate pellets up to a few cm across and a few indistinct stress cutans (pedogenic slickensides). Numerous dark root traces decreasing in abundance downwards and sharply truncated at top. Also numerous elongate subvertical burrows <1 cm wide and filled with reddish silt.

5   0.20 m – Orange-brown silty clay with abundant angular quartz fragments, concentrated particularly towards the top, and occasional blocks of marble and fragments of schist. Includes possible artefacts (definite examples of Middle Stone Age types found loose in stream). Passes down into:

4   0.15 m – Orange-brown silty clay with scattered carbonate pellets and small quartz fragments. Passes down into:

3   0.20 m (seen) – Orange-brown silty clay with abundant carbonate pellets and scattered large (several cm) angular quartz fragments.

2   0.40 m – Hard, pale-brown, well-cemented micritic limestone with abundant ramifying subvertical tubular cavities (?root traces). Gastropods common as small, subspherical, crystal-lined cavities.

1   1.80 m (seen) – Fairly densely packed, creamy-yellow, carbonate pellets in a matrix of brown clay. Pellets range in size from a few mm to 1 cm or so. The top 0.1 m has a higher proportion of larger clasts and appears to have a rather irregular contact with the overlying unit.

Bed no.

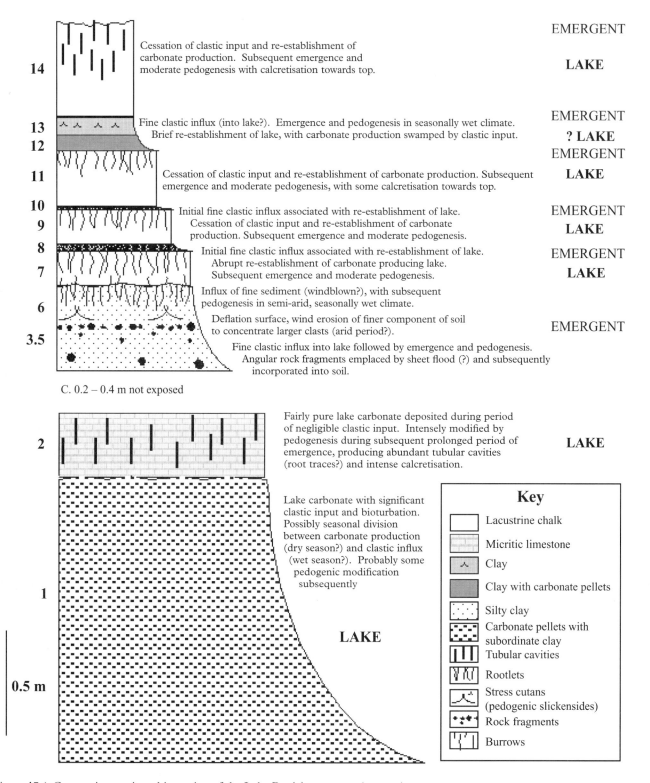

14 — Cessation of clastic input and re-establishment of carbonate production. Subsequent emergence and moderate pedogenesis with calcretisation towards top.

EMERGENT

LAKE

13 — Fine clastic influx (into lake?). Emergence and pedogenesis in seasonally wet climate. Brief re-establishment of lake, with carbonate production swamped by clastic input.

EMERGENT

? LAKE

12

EMERGENT

11 — Cessation of clastic input and re-establishment of carbonate production. Subsequent emergence and moderate pedogenesis, with some calcretisation towards top.

LAKE

10 — Initial fine clastic influx associated with re-establishment of lake.

9 — Cessation of clastic input and re-establishment of carbonate production. Subsequent emergence and moderate pedogenesis.

EMERGENT

LAKE

8 — Initial fine clastic influx associated with re-establishment of lake.

7 — Abrupt re-establishment of carbonate producing lake. Subsequent emergence and moderate pedogenesis.

EMERGENT

LAKE

6 — Influx of fine sediment (windblown?), with subsequent pedogenesis in semi-arid, seasonally wet climate.

Deflation surface, wind erosion of finer component of soil to concentrate larger clasts (arid period?).

EMERGENT

3.5 — Fine clastic influx into lake followed by emergence and pedogenesis. Angular rock fragments emplaced by sheet flood (?) and subsequently incorporated into soil.

C. 0.2 – 0.4 m not exposed

2 — Fairly pure lake carbonate deposited during period of negligible clastic input. Intensely modified by pedogenesis during subsequent prolonged period of emergence, producing abundant tubular cavities (root traces?) and intense calcretisation.

LAKE

Lake carbonate with significant clastic input and bioturbation. Possibly seasonal division between carbonate production (dry season?) and clastic influx (wet season?). Probably some pedogenic modification subsequently

1

LAKE

0.5 m

Key

☐	Lacustrine chalk
▦	Micritic limestone
⌃	Clay
▨	Clay with carbonate pellets
∴	Silty clay
▪	Carbonate pellets with subordinate clay
‖‖	Tubular cavities
Ψ	Rootlets
⌄	Stress cutans (pedogenic slickensides)
•∗•	Rock fragments
⊔	Burrows

Figure A7.1 Composite stratigraphic section of the Lake Patrick sequence (see text).

In the less deeply incised upper reaches of the Casavera Stream, on a bearing of 070° from Twin Rivers kopje, *in situ* schist and marble is commonly exposed in the stream bed. The actual contact between these basement rocks and the lacustrine sequence above has not been seen but field relationships indicate that at least the lowest unit, bed 1, is absent and suggest that there is a progressive onlapping of higher lacustrine units onto an irregular surface of the underlying bedrock as the margins of this small basin are approached.

Interpretation

Field evidence indicates that the carbonates were originally chalky and poorly cemented. They were probably deposited as inorganically precipitated lacustrine chalks (Kelts and Hsu 1978), with the carbonate perhaps originating from springs issuing from the marble outcrops around the lake margins. The lack of clastic contamination within the carbonate units suggests some mechanism for exclusion of terrigenous material and perhaps indicates the presence of extensive shoreline marshes acting as baffles for siliciclastic input (Freytet and Plaziat 1982). Any fall in lake level would cause the lakeward expansion of this marsh zone and may well account for the abundant rootlet traces in the carbonate units. Oolitic carbonates are a well documented feature of some other large east African lakes, such as Lake Tanganyika (Cohen and Thuoin 1987), and might be anticipated in Lake Patrick. Their apparent absence from the logged succession may reflect the small size of this sub-basin and proximity to shoreline marshes. However, they should be looked for during any future work in the main lake basin.

The interbedded clastic units appear to represent palaeosols or at least have been pedogenically modified, with the possible exception of bed 10. The lowest clastic interval, comprising beds 3–6, clearly represents a substantial period of soil development which has caused extensive secondary cementation of the underlying carbonate unit, bed 2, which is now a hard, brownish-grey micrite. Together with the underlying clay and pelletal carbonate unit, bed 1, this has the characteristics of a fairly mature calcrete profile. However, subspherical cavities, often with vestiges of a columella, represent well-preserved gastropod shells and indicate that bed 2 is a pedogenically altered lacustrine carbonate. The underlying pellety carbonate and clay unit of bed 1 may represent a period of lacustrine deposition in which fine clastic influxes were still a significant component of sedimentation. The presence of stress cutans (pedogenic slickensides) in several of the clastic units indicates a semi-arid climate with seasonal wetting and drying cycles, as do the carbonate units themselves (Cecil 1990).

Beds 3–6 represent a complex palaeosol profile which

will require further lab work to fully interpret. The carbonate pellets in a clay matrix in bed 3 and 4 might suggest a return of significant clastic input to the lake, but the angular quartz fragments suggest a much more competent flow than would be anticipated within a lake. A more realistic scenario is that the carbonate pellets are actually fragments of the underlying carbonate unit reworked by stream floods, which also transported the quartz fragments from the adjacent basement outcrops. The angular nature of the quartz is clear evidence of little transportation, although in this area the role of human working of quartz cobbles cannot be dismissed as a source of angular quartz fragments. There is a clear upward-fining sequence from bed 3 into beds 4 and 5, indicated by more scattered carbonate pellets and smaller size of the quartz fragments in bed 4. There is a marked concentration of angular quartz fragments towards the top, together with occasional subangular blocks of marble and fragments of schist. The general succession is characteristic of fluvial deposition by at least two waning flow events, perhaps each representing a major flood. The concentration of quartz clasts towards the top of bed 5 indicates lower energy winnowing of fine particles, either by fluvial action or wind deflation. Bed 6 is a very clearly defined palaeosol. The truncation of many of the root traces at the boundary with the overlying carbonate unit indicates erosive removal of the top O (organic) horizon, as is common in many palaeosols (Tucker and Wright 1990). The reddish silt-filled burrows may post-date the overlying carbonate unit since some of them cross the boundary between beds 5 and 6. The presence of indistinct pedogenic stress cutans in bed 6 indicates some wet/dry seasonality of climate.

Beds 7 and 9 contain abundant aquatic, non-marine, gastropods and are unquestionably lacustrine carbonates. However, the presence of abundant root traces in each of these indicates minor pedogenic modification during regressive episodes, which followed carbonate deposition. The clay and carbonate pellet unit of bed 8 may represent another rather short-lived clastic influx to the lake. Field evidence does not indicate obvious pedogenic modification, though the presence of root traces in the underlying carbonate unit suggests that some pedogenesis or bioturbation has occurred. The succeeding thin grey clay unit with carbonate pellets, bed 10, can perhaps be interpreted as a short-lived period of clastic influx diluting carbonate production, with bioturbation or subsequent pedogenesis causing the formation of carbonate pellets.

Bed 11 is clearly another lacustrine carbonate, which, with the exception of minor calcretisation towards the top, has experienced very little post-depositional alteration. The large colour-banded gastropods are actually a terrestrial species (*Achatina tavaresiense*) and suggest proximity to the lake shore or, more probably, widespread drifting of empty shells. Their exceptional preservation may enable some oxygen isotope data to be obtained from them, providing a potential source of information on seasonal temperatures. Beds 12 and 13 are interpreted as a more prolonged clastic influx, which, in bed 13, more or less swamped carbonate production. The presence of fairly abundant gastropod shell fragments indicates a lacustrine clay, but the occurrence of numerous small stress cutans (pedogenic slickensides) indicate a brief period (10^2–10^3 years) of vertisol development in a climate of alternating wet and dry periods.

Bed 14 is also lacustrine carbonate, as indicated by the abundant small gastropods. The calcretisation towards the top may be a fairly recent phenomenon associated with surface exposure in the present climatic regime. This was the highest carbonate unit seen at any of the sections and in the lower reaches of the stream the higher parts of the succession have been removed by surface lowering. In many places the stream has incised to a depth of several metres through the softer units to the more heavily indurated carbonate of bed 2.

Age and duration of lacustrine and pedogenic events

The presence in several of the lacustrine carbonates of the gastropod *Achatina tavaresiense*, a species still extant in this region, suggests a Pleistocene age for the succession. The possible anthropogenically worked quartz fragments in bed 5 are, unfortunately, not diagnostic of a particular age. However, loose implements found in the stream a short distance downstream of exposures of this unit are of Middle Stone Age type (L Barham pers comm; see fig. A7.2) and may possibly be derived from bed 5 since none was found in the Casavera Stream upstream of this point.

Only approximate estimates of the duration of particular sedimentary units can be made at this stage in the investigation. Beds 3–6 represent the most prolonged period of pedogenesis in the sequence and, although it is difficult to estimate its duration, it probably was of the order of 10^3–10^4 years. It was during this episode that the lacustrine carbonate of bed 2 experienced intense calcretisation. Without knowing general rates of carbonate precipitation in tropical lakes it is impossible at this stage to estimate the time interval represented by each of the carbonate units. Drawing an analogy with temperate lacustrine marl deposits in Ireland (Coxon 1994; Coxon and Coxon 1994), each carbonate unit may represent no more than a few thousand years. None of the clastic intervals above bed 6 have experienced much pedogenesis. The incipient vertisol structure of bed 13 could form in as short a time as a few decades and is unlikely to represent much more than one or two centuries at most, while the good preservation of gastropod shell fragments also suggests a relatively short period of pedogenesis.

Piecing together these various lines of evidence, the total duration of the succession as preserved (beds 1–14) may have been of the order of no more than a few tens of thousands of years. However, extensive dissection and denudation of the lacustrine sequence may well have destroyed higher units and, at this stage, it is impossible to estimate the full duration of this lake phase. However, the extent of dissection of these lake deposits, and subsequent events represented by features associated with the Casavera Stream, suggest that the lake did not persist into the late Pleistocene.

Post-lake events in the Casavera Stream basin

In its upper reaches the course of the Casavera Stream is a broad V-shape, little more than about three metres deep, with steeper cliffs sometimes eroded on the outside of bends. The bed of the stream is developed on basement rocks in the higher reaches and on gravel-covered lake carbonates further downstream. Over a fairly extensive stretch it appears to be floored by the highly indurated carbonate of bed 2. This has been breached at a prominent knick-point, downstream of which the stream course is more steeply incised into the pellety carbonate unit of bed 1. Above bed 2 the stream cross-section at this point has more gently sloping banks similar to those upstream of the knick point. A section through the lake sediments exposed further downstream on the Casavera Stream (southwest of Twin Rivers kopje, several hundred metres downstream of the road between Twin Rivers Farm and Hilltop Farm) appears to correlate well with beds 1–7 exposed in the upper reaches, as described in this account. It is possible that they represent lithologically similar units at a stratigraphically lower level, although if they actually represent the same units then it indicates that there may have been some tectonic movement in this region since the sediments were deposited.

A conspicuous tufa cascade is developed across the Casavera Stream where bed 2 forms a knick-point just upstream from a conspicuous fire-break orientated at 195°. It is more than a metre wide and high, and stretches the full width of the stream channel, which here has temporarily broadened to about eight metres or more. It is completely inactive and has been eroded and partly broken up by fluvial erosion, with subangular blocks incorporated into the coarse consolidated gravels exposed in the banks just downstream. In places are found elongate tubular cavities up to 2–3 cm in diameter, representing enclosed plant stems. Much of the tufa is fairly porous, with a texture reminiscent of deposition over a cover of moss. The outer surface of the tufa locally may be more compact, with a series of paler and darker layers discernible, each a few millimetres thick. Several other degraded tufa cascades and barriers are present along the course of the river from a little up-

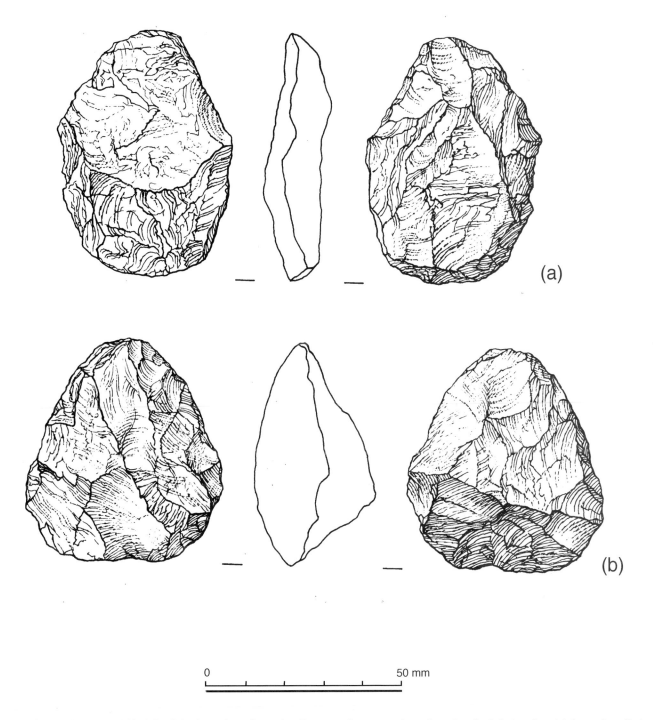

(a)

(b)

0   50 mm

Figure A7.2 Vein quartz bifacially flaked artefacts from the Casavera Stream and attributed to bed 5. Artefact (a) has a bevelled cutting edge and (b) is a reworked fragment of a core or a biface.

stream of this one to several hundred metres downstream of the road between Twin Rivers Farm and Hilltop Farm. They clearly post-date most of the incision of the Casavera Stream but obviously relate to a very different hydrological regime. Flow may have still been seasonal but must have been significantly slower, more constant and less flashy than at present, with the water having sufficient time to become saturated with calcium carbonate derived from the marble or, more probably, from the lacustrine carbonates. CO_2 degassing at knickpoints or riffles led to precipitation of calcite, often over moss or stranded plant debris, to form the tufa cascades and barriers. It is difficult to ascertain the duration of active tufa deposition but it is probably of the order of several thousand years at least. Uranium-series dating of a compact piece of tufa from near the top of this cascade has given a date of 200 ka BP (see chapter 10).

This date for the tufa cascade is surprisingly old and has significant implications both for the age of the lake sediments, which necessarily must be older, and for 'post-lake' events in this region. It would appear that much of the incision of the Casavera Stream occurred prior to tufa deposition and that subsequent incision rates have been remarkably low, less than half a metre per hundred thousand years. If average incision rates have remained constant since the lake was drained, then the depth of incision of the Casavera Stream suggests that the youngest lake sediments may be half a million years old or more. However, on the evidence available at present this can be considered no more than speculation.

A substantial accumulation of coarse gravel, made up largely of blocks of calcretised lake carbonate, tufa, quartz fragments and minor quantities of marble and schist, forms a wedge-like body immediately downstream of the main tufa cascade, discussed above. This clearly formed as a current-shadow deposit, which subsequently has been incised by the present stream. The deposit, of mostly rather angular blocks, is very poorly-sorted and lacks any obvious stratification, suggesting that it may have been deposited in a single major flood event.

Conclusions

A more than four metre thick succession of carbonates with interbedded siliciclastic units, exposed in the incised channel of the Casavera Stream near Twin Rivers kopje, represents a series of pedogenically modified lacustrine carbonates and clay-rich palaeosols. These indicate a semi-arid environment in which lake level fluctuated, exposing the lake sediments to pedogenic processes. The distribution of these sediments provides evidence for the existence of a major lake, Lake Patrick, extending across the Kafue Flats during early to mid-Pleistocene times. Uranium-series dating of a tufa cascade within the stream channel indicates that much of the incision of the Casavera Stream occurred prior to

200 ka ago and demonstrates that the lake was already drained prior to the start of the late Pleistocene. A great deal more research needs to be undertaken to elucidate the palaeoenvironments represented by this stratigraphic sequence, to ascertain the full extent of the lake, to obtain more precise age constraints for the sequence, and to establish how the lake related to the occupation site on Twin Rivers kopje.

(b) PRELIMINARY REPORT ON THE MOLLUSCAN FAUNA FROM LAKE PATRICK

P Davies

The following analysis is based on samples collected from lake exposures in the Casavera Stream. Most identifications are to family level only. Family ecologies are usually fairly clear, but the particular species involved here are poorly known in terms of specific ecologies. The report follows stratigraphic units as described above.

Unit 14 (marl) – Mollusca abundant, with fauna dominated by Planorbidae and Succineidae. The former family are of broad freshwater ecology, but the latter (with very few exceptions) are firmly wetland to amphibious and commonly found on emergent vegetation. The presence of *Vertigo* sp. also supports an interpretation of emergent vegetation within the shallow waters of the littoral zone.

Units 13 and 8 (carbonate clay – clastic inwash). Each sample had only one individual Planorbidae (see ecology above). This poor preservation would support the view that these units underwent pedogenic alteration.

Unit 11 (marl) – Very abundant Mollusca, particularly Lymnaedae, Planorbidae, Succineidae and *Vertigo* sp. Again, an emergent vegetation zone. Also very low numbers of Euconulidae, Subulinidae and Achatinidae, all terrestrial, probably inwash from the lake margins.

Units 12, 9 and 7 – No Mollusca, again supporting Simms' view that these were all pedogenically altered.

A rough calculation has been made of the former extent of Lake Patrick based on the 1:250,000 map 'Flooded areas: Kafue flats, Zambia' published by the Kafue Basin Research Project in conjunction with the Survey Department, Lusaka, Zambia 1985. The estimate comes out at about 17,000 square kilometres. Such a lake would today rank as the seventeenth largest in the world and the fourth largest in Africa after Nyanza (Victoria), Tanganyika and Nyassa.

Acknowledgement: Mary Seddon of the National Museum of Wales helped identify specimens.

Appendix 8
Human remains from Twin Rivers

Osbjorn Pearson

Laura Bishop identified a fragment of bone (fig A8.1) from the Twin Rivers fauna as a probable hominin bone and sent it to Osbjorn Pearson. He studied the bone and showed it to Debra Komar for a second opinion. She identified the fragment as probably part of the dorsal side of a left humeral shaft near midshaft. The fragment likely derives from a hominin upper limb bone because of its general size, curvature, lack of strongly modelled crests or grooves on its external surface, and the round cross-section of its medullary cavity.

Additional comparisons between the fragment and recent human humeri by Valerie Prilop and O Pearson indicated that the fragment most likely came from one of two positions on a human humerus and could be from either the left or right side depending upon its point of origin (figure 8.1a). The proximal and distal directions on the fragment are the same in both cases, but medial and lateral are different. The description below is simplified by assuming that the fragment comes from a left humerus.

The fragment is a dark ochre-yellow colour with spots of darker, brownish-grey stains. The broken edges of the bone have the same patina as the endosteal and periosteal cortex except for a small area around the margin of the endosteal surface at the level of the distal end of the bone in which the cortical bone has been worn away to reveal yellowish-white cortical bone. The antero-medial edge of the fragment forms a compact, nearly straight-edged surface whereas the cortical bone of posterior edge of the fragment evidently underwent some weathering and presents a series of ragged, parallel lamallae. The periosteal surface also bears a series of fine, longitudinal fracture lines due to weathering. The endosteal surface shows no signs of weathering.

The fragment measures 64.1 mm in length and tapers from a width of 16.4 mm distally to 7.8 mm just above the proximal end. The cortical bone of the fragment reaches an impressive thickness of 6.5 mm at the antero-medial edge of the proximal end and 7.1 mm in the same direction 11 mm from the distal end (the most distal place at which the cortical thickness may be measured). At the distal end of the fragment, the medullary cavity measures only 6.0 mm in width. The endosteal surface at this level constitutes close to half of the medullary cavity and the diameter of the intact medullary cavity would probably have measured less than 7.0 mm in width.

The distal end of the fragment bears a very shallow groove that measures 4.3 mm in width at the distal end of the fragment. The lateral side of the periosteal surface forms a distinct angle with the grooved surface, forming a blunt crest of bone that follows the groove inferiorly and laterally for 38 mm until it disappears in the antero-lateral edge of the fragment. The groove corresponds to a slight depression between the surfaces for the anterior and posterior compartments of the arm.

The external surface of the bone bears four short (6 – 3 mm long and about 0.8 mm wide), blunt impressions that may be tooth marks or scratch marks. Each mark runs medio-laterally across the crest on the lateral side and onto the posterior side. These marks were likely made before fossilisation because they have been split by weathering cracks.

The diameter of the original shaft was estimated by tracing the outline of the remaining part of the proximal fragment, completing a circular shape based on the curvature of the preserved part, and measuring the result. This produced an anterior-posterior (AP) diameter of roughly 20 mm. The cortical bone of the fragment is strikingly thick relative to recent humans but similar to the thick-walled long bones of other Pleistocene hominins. More detailed comparisons and analysis of the humeral fragment will be published elsewhere.

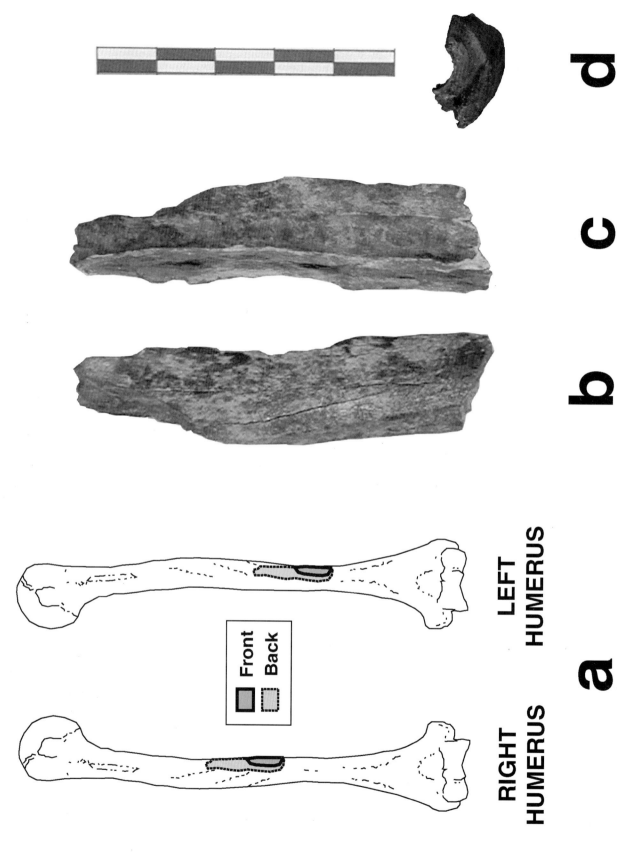

Figure A8.1 The Twin Rivers hominin humeral fragment: (a) possible locations of the fragment; (b) external view; (c) internal view; (d) the end that has the more abrupt break (corresponding to the bottom of the bone in (b) and (c). Figures b and d are the same scale (see 5 cm scale).

Appendix 9
Whole flake frequencies by type (Mumbwa Caves)

L Barham

Unit I

		Frequency	Per cent	Cumulative per cent
Valid	01410	48	30.8	30.8
	01411	1	0.6	31.4
	01412	1	0.6	32.1
	01420	54	34.6	66.7
	01421	1	0.6	67.3
	01422	2	1.3	68.6
	01430	8	5.1	73.7
	01431	1	0.6	74.4
	01460	10	6.4	80.8
	01461	4	2.6	83.3
	01470	5	3.2	86.5
	01471	11	7.1	93.6
	01472	1	0.6	94.2
	02311	1	0.6	94.9
	02312	6	3.8	98.7
	02313	2	1.3	100.0
	Total	156	100.0	

Unit II

		Frequency	Per cent	Cumulative per cent
Valid	01410	103	32.9	33.0
	01411	5	1.6	34.6
	01420	108	34.5	69.2
	01421	6	1.9	71.2
	01422	1	0.3	71.5
	01430	23	7.3	78.8
	01431	1	0.3	79.2
	01440	1	0.3	79.5
	01460	25	8.0	87.5
	01461	9	2.9	90.4
	01470	1	0.3	90.7
	01471	12	3.8	94.6
	02210	1	0.3	94.9
	02230	1	0.3	95.2
	02311	7	2.2	97.4
	02312	5	1.6	99.0
	02312337	1	0.3	99.4
	02314	1	0.3	99.7
	02512	1	0.3	100.0
	Total	312	99.7	
Missing		1	0.3	
Total		313	100.0	

Unit III

		Frequency	Per cent	Cumulative per cent
Valid	01410	20	36.4	36.4
	01411	1	1.8	38.2
	01420	18	32.7	70.9
	01421	2	3.6	74.5
	01430	6	10.9	85.5
	01440	1	1.8	87.3
	01460	3	5.5	92.7
	01461	1	1.8	94.5
	02311	1	1.8	96.4
	02312	1	1.8	98.2
	02316	1	1.8	100.0
	Total	55	100.0	

Unit IV

		Frequency	Per cent	Cumulative per cent
Valid	01410	10	31.3	31.3
	01411	1	3.1	34.4
	01420	9	28.1	62.5
	01430	5	15.6	78.1
	01461	2	6.3	84.4
	01471	2	6.3	90.6
	02310327	1	3.1	93.8
	02311	2	6.3	100.0
	Total	32	100.0	

Unit V

		Frequency	Per cent	Cumulative per cent
Valid	01410	11	35.5	35.5
	01420	11	35.5	71.0
	01421	1	3.2	74.2
	01430	4	12.9	87.1
	01431	1	3.2	90.3
	02310337	1	3.2	93.5
	02311	1	3.2	96.8
	02316	1	3.2	100.0
	Total	31	100.0	

Unit VII

		Frequency	Per cent	Cumulative per cent
Valid	01410	166	17.7	17.8
	01411	14	1.5	19.3
	01412	1	0.1	19.4
	01420	300	32.0	51.4
	01421	61	6.5	58.0
	01422	5	0.5	58.5
	01430	104	11.1	69.6
	01431	34	3.6	73.3
	01440	12	1.3	74.5
	01441	2	0.2	74.8
	01450	3	0.3	75.1
	01460	30	3.2	78.3
	01461	11	1.2	79.5
	01470	6	0.6	80.1
	01471	2	0.2	80.3
	01480	82	8.7	89.1
	01481	3	0.3	89.4
	02310327	1	0.1	89.5
	02310337	4	0.4	89.9
	0231037	1	0.1	90.1
	02311	8	0.9	90.9
	02311327	1	0.1	91.0
	02311337	5	0.5	91.6
	02312	40	4.3	95.8
	02312327	3	0.3	96.1
	02312337	8	0.9	97.0
	02313	3	0.3	97.3
	02314	8	0.9	98.2
	02315	3	0.3	98.5
	02316	5	0.5	99.0
	02317	1	0.1	99.1
	02319	1	0.1	99.3
	02322	1	0.1	99.4
	0232337	1	0.1	99.5
	02332	1	0.1	99.6
	02336	1	0.1	99.7
	02420	1	0.1	99.8
	02514	1	0.1	99.9
	02812	1	0.1	100.0
	Total	935	99.7	
Missing		3	0.3	
Total		938	100.0	

Unit XII (*a composite of units XIII–XIV*)

		Frequency	Per cent	Cumulative per cent
Valid	01410	3	25.0	25.0
	01420	1	8.3	33.3
	01422	1	8.3	41.7
	01460	5	41.7	83.3
	02312	2	16.7	100.0
	Total	12	100.0	

Bibliography

Aitken, MJ, 1998. *Science based dating in archaeology* (2nd edn). London: Longman.

Albert, RM, Lavi, O, Estroff, L, Weiner, S, Tsatskin, A, Ronen, A, & Lev-Yadun, S, 1999. Mode of occupation of Tabun Cave, Mt Carmel, Israel, during the Mousterian period: a study of the sediments and phytoliths. *Journal of Archaeological Science* 26:1249–1260.

Alexandre, A, Colin, F, & Meunier, JD, 1994. Les phytolithes, indcateur du cycle biogéchimique du silicium en forêt équatorial. *C R Académie des Sciences, Paris*, tome 319, série II:453–458.

Ambrose, SL, 1998a. Chronology of the Later Stone Age and food production in East Africa. *Journal of Archaeological Science* 25:377–392.

Ambrose, SL, 1998b. Late Pleistocene human population bottlenecks, volcanic winter, and differentiation of modern humans. *Journal of Human Evolution* 34:623–651.

Ambrose, SL, & Lorenz, KG, 1990. Social and ecological models for the Middle Stone Age in southern Africa. In Mellars, P, (ed) *The emergence of modern humans*; 3–33. Edinburgh: University of Edinburgh Press.

Andrews, P, 1990. *Owls, caves and fossils*. London: Natural History Museum.

Andrews, P, 1997. What taphonomy can and cannot tell us. *Cuadernos de Geología Ibérica* 23:53–72.

Ansell, WFH, 1978. *The mammals of Zambia*. Chilanga, Zambia: National Parks and Wildlife Service of Zambia.

Armstrong, AL, 1931. Rhodesian archaeological expedition (1929): excavations in Bambata Cave and researches on prehistoric sites in southern Rhodesia. *Journal of the Royal Anthropological Institute* 61:239–276.

Avery, DM, 1987. Holocene natural vegetation in the Magaliesberg, Transvaal, and the introduction of farming: micromammalian evidence. *South African Journal of Science* 83:221–225.

Avery, DM, 1996a. Late Quaternary micromammals from Mumbwa Caves, Zambia. *Journal of African Zoology* 110:221–234.

Avery, DM, 1996b. Late Quaternary environmental change at Mumbwa Caves, Zambia. In Pwiti, G, & Soper, R, (eds) *Aspects of African Archaeology*; 63–70. Harare: University of Zimbabwe Publications.

Avery, DM, 1997. Micromammals and the Holocene environment of Rose Cottage Cave, *South African Journal of Science* 93:445–448.

Avery, DM, submitted. The Plio-Pleistocene vegetation and climate of Sterkfontein and Swartkrans, South Africa, based on micromammals. *Journal of Human Evolution*.

Armstrong, AL, 1931. Excavations at Bambata Cave and researches on prehistoric sites in Southern Rhodesia. *Journal of the Royal Anthropological Institute* 61.

Bahuchet, S, 1988. Food supply uncertainty among the Aka Pygmies. In deGarine, I, & Harrison, G, (eds), *Coping with uncertainty in food supply*; 118–149. Oxford: Clarendon Press.

Bailey, RC, Head, G, Jenke, M, Owen, B, Rechtman, R, & Zechenter, E, 1989. Hunting and gathering in tropical rain forest: is it possible? *American Anthropologist* 91: 59–82.

Barham, LS, 1987. The bipolar technique in southern Africa: a replication experiment. *South African Archaeological Bulletin* 42:45–50.

Barham, LS, 1993. Preliminary results from Mumbwa Caves, central Zambia. *Southern African Field Archaeology* 2: 108–110.

Barham, LS, 1995. Making the most of radial core: the topknot flake. *Lithics* 14:9–14.

Barham, LS, 1996. Recent research on the Middle Stone Age at Mumbwa Caves, central Zambia. In Pwiti, G, & Soper, R, (eds) *Aspects of African prehistory*; 191–200. Harare: University of Zimbabwe Publications.

Barham, LS, 1998. Possible early pigment use in south-central Africa. *Current Anthropology* 39(5):703–710.

Barham, LS, in press. Systematic pigment used in the Middle Pleistocene of central Africa. *Current Anthropology*.

Barham, LS & Smart, PL, 1996. An early date for the Middle Stone Age of central Zambia. *Journal of Human Evolution* 30:287–290.

Barker, P, 1993. (3rd ed) *Techniques of archaeological excavation*. London: Routledge.

Barnes, RFW, & Lahm, SA, 1997. An ecological perspective on human densities in the central African forests. *Journal of Applied Ecology* 34:245–260.

Bartram, LE, & Marean, CW, 1999. Explaining the 'Klasies pattern': Kua ethnoarchaeology, the Die Kelders Middle Stone Age archaeofauna, long bone fragmentation and carnivore ravaging. *Journal of Archaeological Science* 26:9–20.

Beaumont, PB & Morris, D, 1990. *Guide to archaeological sites in the Northern Cape*. Kimberly: McGregor Museum.

Beaumont, PB, & Vogel, JC, 1972. On a new radiocarbon chronology for Africa south of the equator. *African Studies* 31:65–89, 155–182.

Bell, RHV, 1982. The effect of soil nutrient availability on the community structure in African ecosystems. In Huntley, BJ, & Walker, BH, (eds) *Ecology of tropical savannas*; 193–216. Berlin: Springer-Verlag.

Binford, LR, 1965. Archaeological systematics and the study of cultural process. *American Antiquity* 31:203–210.

Binford, LR, 1981. *Bones: ancient men and modern myths*. New York: Academic Press.

Binford, LR, 1984. *Faunal remains from Klasies River Mouth*. Orlando: Academic Press.

Bishop, WW & Clark, JD, (eds) 1967. *Background to evolution in Africa*. Chicago: University of Chicago Press.

Botha, GA, Wintle, AG, & Vogel, JC, 1994. Episodic late Quaternary palaeogully erosion in northern Kwa-Zulu-Natal, South Africa. *Catena* 23:327–340.

Boule, M, (1911–1913). L'Homme fossil de la Chapelle-aux-Saints. *Annales de Paléontologie* 6:111–172, 7:3–192, 8:1–67.

Boule, M, & Vallois, HV, 1957. *Fossil men*. London: Thames & Hudson.

Bourlière, F, (ed) 1983. *Ecosystems of the world 13: tropical savannas*. New York: Elsevier.

Bradbury, AP, & Carr, PJ, 1995. Flake typologies and alternative approaches: an experimental assessment. *Lithic Technology* 20:100–115.

Brain, CK 1981. *The hunters or the hunted? An introduction to African cave taphonomy*. Chicago: University of Chicago Press.

Bräuer, G, 1984. A craniological approach to the origin of anatomically modern *Homo sapiens* in Africa and implications for the appearance of modern Europeans. In Smith, FH, & Spencer, F, *The origins of modern humans: a world survey of the fossil evidence*; 327–410. New York: Alan R Liss.

Bräuer, G, & Mehlman, MJ, 1988. Hominid molars from a Middle Stone Age level at Mumba Rock Shelter, Tanzania. *American Journal of Physical Anthropology* 75:69–76.

Bräuer, G, Yokoyama, Y, Falguères, C, & Mbua, E, 1997. Modern human origins backdated. *Nature* 386:337–338.

Breuil, H, 1944. La paléolithique au Congo Belge d'après les recherches du Docteur Cabu. *Transactions Royal Society of South Africa* 30:143–160.

Brook, G, Burney, D, & Cowart, J, 1990. Paleoenvironmental data for Ituri, Zaire, from sediments in Matupi Cave, Mount Hoyo. In Boaz, N, (ed) *Evolution of environments and Hominidae in the African western Rift Valley*; 49–70. Martinsville: Virginia Museum of Natural History.

Brooks, AS, Hare, PE, Kokis, JE, Miller, GH, Ernst, RD, & Wendorf, F, 1990. Dating Pleistocene archaeological sites by protein diagenesis in ostrich eggshell. *Science* 248:60–64.

Brooks, AS, Helgren, DM, Cramer, JS, Franklin, A, Hornyat, M, Keating, JM, Klein, RG, Rink, WJ, Schwarcz, H, Smith, JNL, Stewart, K, Todd, N, Verniers, J, & Yellen, J, 1995. Dating and context of three Middle Stone Age sites with bone points in the Upper Semliki Valley, Zaire. *Science* 268:548–553.

Brooks, AS, & Robertshaw, P, 1990. The glacial maximum in tropical Africa: 22000–12000 BP. In Gamble, C, & Soffer, O, (eds) *The world at 18000 BP, vol 2, low latitudes*; 121–169. London: Unwin Hyman.

Butzer, KW, Beaumont, PB, & Vogel, JC, 1978. Lithostratigraphy of Border Cave, KwaZulu, South Africa: a Middle Stone Age sequence beginning c. 195,000 B.P. *Journal of Archaeological Science* 5:317–341.

Cahen, D, 1976. Nouvelles fouilles a la pointe de la Gombe (ex-pointe de Kalina), Kinshasa, Zaire. *L'Anthropologie* 80(4):573–602.

Cahen, D, & Moeyersons, J, 1977. Subsurface movements of stone artefacts and their implications for the prehistory of Central Africa. *Nature* 266:812–815.

Cahen, D, & Mortelmans, G, 1973. *Un site Tshitolien sur le plateau des Bateke*. Tervuren: Musée Royale de l'Afrique Centrale.

Calsteren, P, van & Schwieters, JB, 1995. Performance of a thermal ionisation mass spectrometer with a deceleration lens system and post-deceleration detector selection. *International Journal of Mass Spectrometry Ionisation Processes* 146/147:119–129.

Cann, RLM, Stoneking, M, & Wilson, AC, 1987. Mitochondrial DNA and human evolution. *Nature* 325:31–36.

Carretero, JM, Lorenzo, C, & Arsuaga, JL, 1999. Axial and appendicular skeleton of *Homo antecessor*. *Journal of Human Evolution* 37:459–499.

Cashdan, E, 1985. Coping with risk: reciprocity among the Basarwa of northern Botswana. *Man* 20:454–474.

Cecil, CB, 1990. Palaeoclimate controls on stratigraphic representation of chemical and siliciclastic rocks. *Geology* 18:533–536.

Chagula, WK, 1960. The cusps on the mandibular molars of East Africans. *American Journal of Physical Anthropology* 18:83–90.

Chapman, C, 1983. Speciation of tropical rainforest primates of Africa: insular biogeography. *African Journal of Ecology* 21:297–308.

Churchill, SE, Pearson, OM, Grine, FE, Trinkaus, E, & Holliday, TW, 1996. Morphological affinities of the proximal ulna from Klasies River Mouth main site: archaic or modern? *Journal of Human Evolution* 31:213–237.

Cikin, M, & Drysdall, AR, 1971. *The geology of the country north-west of Mumbwa (The Big Concession)*. Lusaka: The Government Printer.

Clapham, C, 1996. *Africa and the international system*. Cambridge: Cambridge University Press.

Clark, AMB, 1997. The MSA/LSA transition in southern Africa: new technological evidence. *South African Archaeological Bulletin* 52:113–121.

Clark, AMB, 1999. Late Pleistocene technology at Rose Cottage Cave: a search for modern behavior in an MSA context. *African Archaeological Review* 16(2):93–120.

Clark, JD, 1942. Further excavations (1939) at the Mumbwa Caves, Northern Rhodesia. *Transactions of the Royal Society of South Africa* 29:133–201.

Clark, JD, 1950. *The Stone Age cultures of Northern Rhodesia*. Claremont: South African Archaeological Society.

Clark, JD, 1959. *The prehistory of southern Africa*. Harmondsworth: Penguin.

Clark, JD, 1963. *Prehistoric cultures of northeast Angola and their significance in tropical Africa*. Lisbon: Museo do Dundo.

Clark, JD, 1966. *The distribution of prehistoric cultures in Angola*. Lisbon: Companhia de Diamantes de Angola.

Clark, JD, 1967. *Atlas of African prehistory*. Chicago: University of Chicago Press.

Clark, JD, 1969. *Kalambo Falls prehistoric site*. Vol 1. Cambridge: Cambridge University Press.

Clark, JD, 1970. *The prehistory of Africa*. London: Thames & Hudson.

Clark, JD, 1971. Human behavioral differences in southern Africa during the later Pleistocene. *American Anthropologist* 73:1211–1236.

Clark, JD, 1974. *Kalambo Falls prehistoric site*. Vol II. Cambridge: Cambridge University Press.

Clark, JD, 1975. Africa: peripheral or paramount? *Man* 10:175–198.

Clark, JD, (ed) 1982. *The Cambridge history of Africa I: from the earliest times to c.500 B.C.* Cambridge: Cambridge University Press.

Clark, JD, 1988. The Middle Stone Age of East Africa and the beginnings of regional identity. *Journal of World Prehistory* 2(3):235–303.

Clark, JD, 1989. The origins and spread of modern human: a broad perspective on the African evidence. In Mellars, P, & Stringer, C, (eds) *The human revolution*; 565–588. Edinburgh: Edinburgh University Press.

Clark, JD, 1990a. A personal memoir. In Robertshaw, P, (ed) *A history of African Archaeology*; 189–204. London: James Curry Ltd.

Clark, JD, 1990b. Stone Age man at the Victoria Falls. In Phillipson, DW, (ed) *Mosi-oa-Tunya: a handbook to the Victoria Falls region*; 32–50. Harare: Longman Zimbabwe.

Clark, JD, 1992. African and Asian perspectives on the origins of modern humans. *Philosophical Transactions of the Royal Society of London* Series B 337 (1280): 201–215.

Clark, JD, 1994. Digging on: a personal record and appraisal of archaeological research in Africa and elsewhere. *Annual review of anthropology* 23:1–23.

Clark, JD, & Brown, K, in press. The Middle Pleistocene site of Twin Rivers Kopje, Zambia. *Journal of Archaeological Science*.

Clark, JD, & Cole, S (eds), 1957. *Third Pan-African Congress on Prehistory, Livingstone 1955*. London: Chatto and Windus.

Clark, JD, & Haynes, CV, 1970. An elephant butchery site at Mwangandas village, Karonga, Malawi, and its relevance for Palaeolithic archaeology. *World Archaeology* I(3):390–411.

Clark, JD, Cole, GH, Isaac, GL, & Kleindienst, MR, 1966. Precision and definition in African archaeology. *South African Archaeological Bulletin* 21:114–121.

Clark, JD, & Kleindienst, M, 1974. Chapter 4. The Stone Age cultural sequence: terminology, typology and raw material. In Clark, JD, *Kalambo Falls prehistoric site, volume 3*; 71–106.

Clark, JD, Wells, L, Oakley, K, & McClelland, J, 1947. New studies on Rhodesian Man. *Journal of the Royal Anthropological Society* 77:7–32.

Cohen, AS, & Thouin, C, 1987. Nearshore carbonate deposits in Lake Tanganyika. *Geology* 15:414–418.

Cole, GH, 1967. The Later Acheulian and Sangoan of southern Uganda. In Bishop, WW, & Clark, JD, (eds) *Background to evolution in Africa*; 481–528. Chicago: University of Chicago Press.

Colette, J, 1935. Complexes et convergences en préhistoire. *Bulletin de la Société Royale Belge d'Anthropologie et de Préhistoire* 50:49–192.

Coley, PD, Bryant, JP, & Chapin, FS, III, 1985. Resource availability and plant anti-herbivore defense. *Science* 230:895–899.

Colyn, M, Gautier-Hion, A, & Verheyen, W, 1991. A re-appraisal of palaeoenvironmental history of central Africa: evidence for a major fluvial refuge in the Zaire Basin. *Journal of Biogeography* 18:403–407.

Cooke, CK, 1957. The waterworks site at Khami, Southern Rhodesia. Stone Age and proto-historic. *Occasional Papers National Museum Southern Rhodesia* 21A.

Cooke, CK, 1969. A re-examination of the 'Middle Stone Age' industries of Rhodesia. *Arnoldia Rhodesia* 4(7):1–20.

Cooke, CK, 1971. Excavation in Zombepata Cave, Sipolilo District, Mashonaland, Rhodesia. *The Southern African Archaeological Bulletin* 26:104–127.

Cooke, CK, 1978. The Redcliff Stone Age cave site: Rhodesia. *Occasional Papers of the National Museums and Monuments of Rhodesia A Human Sciences* 4(2):45–73.

Cooke, HBS, 1950. Quaternary fossils from northern Rhodesia. In Clark, JD, (ed) *The Stone Age cultures of Northern Rhodesia*; 137–142. Claremont: South African Archaeological Society.

Cooke, HBS, 1952. Quaternary events in South Africa. In Leakey, LSB, & Cole, S, (eds) *Proceedings of the Pan-African Congress on Prehistory, Nairobi 1947*; 26–35. Oxford: Basil Blackwell.

Cooke, HBS, Malan, BD, & Wells, LH, 1945. Fossil man in the Lebombo Mountains, South Africa: the 'Border Cave', Ingwavuma District, Zululand. *Man* 45:6–13.

Cormack, JL, 1994. *Early Stone Age heavy duty implements of Africa.* Unpublished PhD thesis, Liverpool University.

Coxon, CE, 1994. Carbonate deposition in turloughs on the western limestone lowlands of Ireland I: present day processes. *Irish Geography* 27:14–27.

Coxon, CE, & Coxon, P, 1994. Carbonate deposition in turloughs on the western limestone lowlands of Ireland II: the sedimentary record. *Irish Geography* 27:28–35.

Crabtree, D, 1972. *An introduction to flintworking.* Pocatello, Idaho: Occasional Papers of the Idaho State University Museum, number 28.

Crader, D, 1984. Faunal remains from Chencherere II rock shelter, Malawi. *South African Archaeological Bulletin* 39:7–16.

Dart, RA, & Del Grande, N, 1931. The ancient iron-smelting cavern at Mumbwa. *Transactions of the Royal Society of South Africa* 19:379–427.

Day, M, 2000. Jumbo discovery: Africa is home to not one but two species of elephant. *New Scientist* 166(2232):15.

Day, MH, 1971. Postcranial remains of *Homo erectus* from Bed IV, Olduvai Gorge, Tanzania. *Nature* 232:383–387.

Day, MH, & Leakey, REF, 1974. New evidence from the Genus *Homo* from East Rudolf, Kenya (III). *American Journal of Physical Anthropology* 41:367–380.

Day, MH, & Stringer, CB, 1991. Les restes crâniens d'Omo-Kibish et leur classification à l'intérieur du genre *Homo. L'Anthropologie* 95:573–594.

Day, MH, Twist, MHC, & Ward, S, 1991. Les vestiges post-crâniens d'Omo I (Kibish). *L'Anthropologie* 95:595–610.

Deacon, HJ, 1979. Excavations at Boomplaas Cave: a sequence through the Upper Pleistocene and Holocene in South Africa. *World Archaeology* 10:241–257.

Deacon, HJ, 1989. Late Pleistocene palaeoecology and archaeology in the southern Cape, South Africa. In Mellars, PA, & Stringer, C, (eds), *The human revolution*; 547–564.

Deacon, HJ, 1992. Southern Africa and modern human origins. In Aitken, MJ, Stringer, CB, & Mellars, P, (eds) The origin of modern humans and the impact of chronometric dating; 177–183. *Philosophical Transactions of the Royal Society of London* Series B 337(1280).

Deacon, HJ, 1995. Two late Pleistocene-Holocene archaeological depositories from the Southern Cape, south Africa. *South African Archaeological Bulletin* 50:121–131.

Deacon, HJ, 1998. Elandsfontein and Klasies River revisited. In Ashton, N, Healy, F & Pettitt, P, (eds) *Stone Age archaeology: essays in honour of John Wymer*; 23–28. Oxford: Oxbow Monograph 102.

Deacon, HJ, & Deacon, J, 1999. *Human beginnings in South Africa.* Cape Town: David Phillip.

Deacon, HJ, & Thackeray, JF, 1984. Late Pleistocene environmental changes and implications for the archaeological record in southern Africa. In Vogel, JC, (ed) *Late Cainozoic palaeoclimates of the southern hemisphere*; 375–390. Rotterdam: AA Balkema.

Deacon, HJ, & Wurz, S, in press. In Barham, L, & Robson-Brown, K, (eds) *Human roots: Africa and Asia in the Middle Pleistocene.* Bristol: Western Academic and Specialist Press.

Deacon, J, 1982. The Later Stone Age in the southern Cape, South Africa, Unpublished PhD thesis, University of Cape Town.

Deacon, J, 1984. Later Stone Age people and their descendants in southern Africa. In Klein, RG, (ed) *Southern African prehistory and paleoenvironments*; 221–328. Rotterdam: AA Balkema.

Deacon, J, 1990. Weaving the fabric of Stone Age research in southern Africa. In Robertshaw, P, (ed) *A History of African archaeology*; 39–58. London: James Curry Ltd.

Deacon, J, 1995. An unsolved mystery at the Howieson's Poort name site. *South African Archaeological Bulletin* 50:110–120.

Deacon, J, & Lancaster, N, 1988. *Late Quaternary palaeoenvironments of southern Africa.* Oxford: Oxford University Press.

De Busk, GH, Jr, 1998. A 37,500–year pollen record from Lake Malawi and implications for the biogeography of afromontane forests. *Journal of Biogeography* 25:479–500.

De Maret, P, 1990. Phases and facies in the archaeology of Central Africa. In Robertshaw, P. (ed.) *A history of African archaeology*: 109–134. London: James Curry Ltd.

De Menocal, PB, Ruddiman, WF, Pokras, EM, 1993. Influences of high-and-low latitude processes on African terrestrial climate: Pleistocene eolian records from equatorial Atlantic drilling program site 663. *Paleoceanography* 8(2):209–242.

De Vos, A, 1975. *Africa, the devastated continent?* The Hague: Dr W Junk.

Dibble, H, 1997. Platform variability and flake morphology: a comparison of experimental and archaeological data and implications for interpreting prehistoric lithic technological strategies. *Lithic Technology* 22:155–170.

Dibble, H, & Lenoir, M, (eds), 1995. *The Middle Paleolithic site of Combe Capelle Bas (France).* Philadelphia: University Museum Press.

Dibble, H, & Whittaker, JC, 1981. New experimental evidence on the relation between percussion flaking and flake variation. *Journal of Archaeological Science* 6:283–296.

Dong, B, Valdes, PJ, & Hall, NMJ, 1996. The changes of monsoonal climates due to Earth's orbital perturbations and Ice Age boundary conditions. *Palaeoclimates* 1:203–240.

Dupont, LM, Jahns, S, Marret, F, & Ning, S, 2000. Vegetation changes in equatorial West Africa: time-slices for the last 150 ka. *Palaeogeography, Palaeoclimatology, Palaeoecology* 155:95–122.

Edwards, LR, Chen, JH, & Wasserburg, GJ, 1986. 238U-234U-230Th-232Th systematics and the precise measurement of time over the past 500 000 years. *Earth and Planetary Science Letters* 81: 175–192.

Elenga, H, Schwartz, D, & Vincens, A, 1994. Pollen evidence of Late Quaternary vegetation and inferred climate changes in Congo. *Palaeogeography, Palaeoclimatology, Palaeoecology* 109: 345–356.

East, R, 1984. Rainfall, soil nutrient status and biomass of large African savanna mammals. *African Journal of Ecology* 22:245–270.

Evernden, JF, & Curtis, GH, 1965. Potassium-argon dating of Late Cainozoic rocks in East Africa and Italy. *Current Anthropology* 6:343–385.

Fagan, BM & Van Noten, FL, 1971. *The hunter-gatherers of Gwisho.* Tervuren: Musée Royale de l'Afrique Centrale.

Feathers, JK, 1996. Luminescence dating and modern human origins. *Evoultionary Anthropology* 5(1):25–36.

Flohn, H, 1984. Climatic evolution in the southern hemisphere and the equatorial region during the Late Cenozoic. In Vogel, JC, (ed) *Late Cainozoic palaeoclimates of the southern hemisphere* 5–20. Rotterdam: AA Balkema.

Foley, R, & Lahr, M, 1997. Mode 3 technologies and the evolution of modern humans. *Cambridge Archaeological Journal* 7(1):3–36.

Folk, RL, 1968. *The petrology of sedimentary rocks.* Austin: Hemphill's.

Fredlund, GG, & Tieszen, LT, 1994. Modern phytolith assemblages from the North American Great Plains. *Journal of Biogeography* 21:321–335.

Freytet, P, & Plaziat, JC, 1982. Continental carbonate sedimentation and pedogenesis – Late Cretaceous and Early Tertiary of southern France. *Contributions to Sedimentology* 12.

Fritz, H & Duncan, P, 1994. On the carrying capacity for large ungulates of African savanna ecosystems. *Proceedings of the Royal Society of London* Series B; 77–82.

Gabel, C, 1963. Further human remains from the Central African Late Stone Age. *Man* 44:38–43.

Gabel, C. 1965. *Stone Age hunters of the Kafue: the Gwisho A site.* Boston: Boston University Press.

Galanidou, N, 2000. Patterns in caves: foragers, horticulturists, and the use of space. *Journal of Anthropological Archaeology* 19(3):243–275.

Gale, SJ, & Hoare, PG, 1991. *Quaternary sediments.* New York: Belhaven-Halstead.

Gamble, C, 1998. Palaeolithic society and the release from proximity: a network approach to intimate relations. *World Archaeology* 29(3):426–449.

Gamble, C, 1999. *The Palaeolithic societies of Europe.* Cambridge: Cambridge University Press.

Gasse, F, 2000. Hydrological changes in the African tropics since the last Glacial Maximum. *Quaternary Science Reviews* 19; 189–211.

Gingele, FX, Müller, PM, & Schneider, RR, 1998. Orbital forcing of freshwater input in the Zaire Fan area – clay mineral evidence from the last 200kyr. *Palaeogeography, Palaeoclimatology, Palaeoecology* 138:17–26.

Goodenough, WH, 1990. Evolution of the human capacity for beliefs. *American Anthropologist* 92:597–612.

Goodwin, AJH, & van Riet Lowe, C. 1929. The Stone Age cultures of South Africa. *Annals of the South African Museum* 27:1–289.

Gowlett, JAJ, 1990. Archaeological studies of human origins and early prehistory in Africa. In Robertshaw, P, (ed) *A history of African archaeology*; 3–12. London: James Curry Ltd.

Gowlett, JAJ, 1996. Mental abilities of early Homo: elements of constraint and choice in rule systems. In Mellers, PA, & Gibson, KR, (eds), *Modelling the early human mind*; 191–215. Cambridge: McDonald Institute Monograph.

Grine, FE, 1981. Occlusal morphology of the mandibular permanent molars of the South African Negro and the Kalahari San (bushman). *Annals of the South African Museum* 86:157–215.

Grine, FE, 2000. Middle Stone Age human fossils from Die Kelders Cave 1, Western Cape Province, South Africa. *Journal of Human Evolution* 38:129–145.

Grine, FE, Jungers, WL, Tobias, PV, & Pearson, OM, 1995. Fossil Homo femur from Berg Aukas, northern Namibia. *American Journal of Physical Anthropology* 97:151–185.

Grine, FE, & Klein, RG, 1985. Pleistocene and Holocene human remains from Equus Cave, South Africa. *Anthropology* 8:55–98.

Grine, FE, Klein, RG, & Volman, TP, 1991. Dating, archaeology and human fossils from the Middle Stone Age levels of Die Kelders, South Africa. *Journal of Human Evolution* 21:363–395.

Grün, R, & Beaumont, PB (in press) Border Cave revisited: revised ESR chronology and an update on hominids from BC1 to BC8. *Journal of Human Evolution.*

Guilderson, TP, Fairbanks, RG, & Rubenstone, JL, 1994. Tropical temperature variations since 20,000 years ago: modelling inter-hemispheric climate change. *Science* 263:663–665.

Hall, M, 1987. *The changing past: farmers, kings and traders in southern Africa:* 200–1860. Cape Town: David Philip.

Hall, M, 1990. 'Hidden history': Iron Age archaeology in southern Africa. In Robertshaw, P, (ed) *A history of African archaeology*; 59–77. London: James Curry.

Handreck, EB, & Jones, LBH, 1968. Studies of silica in the oat plant IV. Silica content of plant parts in relation to stage of growth, supply of silica, and transpiration. *Plant and Soil* 29:449–459.

Harako, R, 1981. The cultural ecology of hunting behaviour among Mbuti Pygmies in the Ituri forest, Zaire. In Harding, RSO, & Teleki, G, (eds) *Omnivorous primates: gathering and hunting in human evolution*; 499–555. New York: Columbia University Press.

Harper, PT, 1998. The Middle Stone Age sequences at Rose Cottage Cave: a search for continuity and discontinuity. *South African Journal of Science* 93:470–475.

Hayden, B, 1981. Subsistence and ecological adaptations of modern hunter-gatherers. In Harding, RSO, & Teleki, G, (eds) *Omnivorous primates: gathering and hunting in human evolution*; 344–421. New York: Columbia University Press.

Hayden, B, Franco, N, & Spafford, J, 1996. Evaluating lithic strategies and design criteria. In Odell, GH, (ed), *Stone tools: theoretical insights into human prehistory*; 9–45. New York: Plenum.

De Heinzelin, J, 1963. Observations on the absolute chronology of the Upper Pleistocene. In Howell, FC, & Bourlière, F, (eds) *African Ecology and Human Evolution*; 285–303. New York: Wenner-Gren Foundation.

Henderson, Z, 1992. The context of some Middle Stone Age hearths at Klasies River Mouth Cave. *Southern African Field Archaeology* 1:14–26.

Henshilwood, C, & Sealy, JC, 1997. Bone artefacts from the Middle Stone Age at Blombos Cave, Southern Cape, South Africa. *Current Anthropology* 38:890–895.

Hodder, I, 1990. Style as historical quality. In Conkey, M, & Hastorf, C, (eds) *The uses of style in archaeology*; 44–51. Cambridge: Cambridge University Press.

Hole, F, 1959. A critical analysis of the Magosian. *South African Archaeological Bulletin* 14:126–134.

Holliday, TW, 1997a. Body proportions in Late Pleistocene Europe and modern human origins. *Journal of Human Evolution* 32:423–447.

Holliday, TW, 1997b. Postcranial evidence of cold adaptation in European Neandertals. *American Journal of Physical Anthropology* 104:245–258.

Holmgren, K, Karlén, W, & Shaw, P, 1995. Paleoclimatic significance of the stable isotopic composition and petrology of a late Pleistocene stalagmite from Botswana. *Quaternary Research* 43(3):320–328.

Howard, WR, 1997. A warm future in the past. *Nature* 388:418–419.

Howell, FC, & Bourlière, F, (eds) 1963. *African ecology and human evolution.* New York: Wenner-Gren Foundation.

Howell, FC, & Clark, JD, 1963. Acheulian hunter-gatherers of sub-Saharan Africa. In Howell, FC, & Bourlière, F, (eds) *African ecology and human evolution*; 458–533. New York: Wenner-Gren Foundation.

Huckaby, JD, 1989. Man and disappearance of Zambezian dry evergreen forest. In Kadomura, H, (ed) *Savannization processes in tropical Africa* I; 89–108. Zambia Geographical Association: Occasional Study No.17.

Huntley, BJ, & Walker, BH, (eds) *Ecology of tropical savannas.* Heidelberg: Springer Verlag Berlin.

Huntley, BJ, 1982. *Southern African savannas* In Huntley, BJ, & Walker, BH, (eds), *Ecology of tropical savannas*; 101–119. Heidelberg: Springer Verlag Berlin.

Hutton, JT, & Norrish, K, 1994. Silicon content of wheat husks in relation to water transpired. *Journal of Agricultural Research* 25:203–212.

Ichikawa, M, 1996. The co-existence of man and nature in the central African rain forest. In Ellen, RF, & Fukui, K, (eds) *Redefining nature*; 467–492: Oxford: Berg.

Inizan, M-L, Racher, H, & Tixier, J, 1992. *Technology of knapped stone.* Meudon: CREP.

Isaac, GLI, 1982. The earliest archaeological traces. In Clark, JD, (ed), *The Cambridge History of Africa, volume 1: from the earliest times to 500 B.C.*; 157–247. Cambridge: Cambridge University Press.

Inskeep, RR, 1967. The Late Stone Age in southern Africa. In Clark, JD, & Bishop, WW, (eds) *Background to evolution in Africa*; 557–582. Chicago: University of Chicago Press.

Irish, JD, 1997. Characteristic high- and low-frequency dental traits in sub-Saharan African populations. *American Journal of Physical Anthropology* 102:455–467.

Isaac, G, Ll, 1972. Chronology and tempo of cultural change during the Pleistocene. In Bishop, WW, & Miller, JA (eds) *Calibration of hominoid evolution*; 381–430. Edinburgh: Scottish Academic Press.

Isaac, GW, 1977. *Olorgesailie.* Chicago: University of Chicago Press.

Jacobson, A, 1982. *The Dentition of the South African Negro.* Anniston, Alabama: Higginbotham.

Jahns, S, Huls, M, & Sarnthein, M, 1998. Vegetation and climate history of west equatorial Africa based on marine pollen record off Liberia (site GIK 16776) covering the last 400,000 years. *Review of Palaeobotany and Palynology* 102:277–288.

Jolly, D, Harrison, SP, Damnati, B, & Bonnefille, R, 1998. Simulated climate and biomes of Africa during the late quaternary: comparison with pollen and lake status data. *Quaternary Science Reviews* 17:629–657.

Jolly, D, Taylor, D, Marchant, R, Hamilton A, Bonnefille, R, Buchet, G, & Riollet, G, 1997. Vegetation dynamics in central Africa since 18000yrBP:pollen records from the interlacustrine highlands of Burundi, Rwanda and western Uganda. *Journal of Biogeography* 24:495–512.

Jones, TR, 1940. Human skeletal remains from the Mumbwa Cave, North Rhodesia. *South African Journal of Science* 37:313–319.

Josens, G, 1983. The soil fauna of tropical savannas. III. The termites. In Bourlière, F, (ed) *Ecosystems of the world 13: tropical savannas*:505–524. Amsterdam: Elsevier.

Kadomura, H, (ed) 1989. *Savannization processes in tropical Africa.* Occasional study No.17 Zambia Geographical Association.

Kaiser, TM, Seiffert, C, & Truluck, T, 1998. The speleological potential of limestone karst in Zambia (Central Africa) – a reconnaissance survey. *Cave and Karst Science* 25(1):23–28.

Kaufmann, H, 1941. Recherches de morphologie humaine comparative: le squelette dupied chez les Boschimans, les Hottentots, et les Griquas. *Archives Suisses d'Anthropologie Générale* 9:195–301.

Keeley, L, 1980. *Experimental determination of stone tool uses.* Chicago: University of Chicago Press.

Kennedy, GE, 1984. The emergence of *Homo sapiens*: the post cranial evidence. *Man* 19:94–110.

Kelts, K, & Hsu, KJ, 1978. Freshwater carbonate sedimentation. In Lermon, A, (ed) *Lakes: chemistry, geology, physics*. New York: Springer-Verlag.

Kittles, R, & Keita, OY, 1999. Interpreting African genetic diversity. *African Archaeological Review* 16(2):87–91.

Klein, RG, 1980a. Environmental and ecological implications of large mammals from Upper Pleistocene and Holocene sites in southern Africa. *Annals of the South African Museum* 81:223–283.

Klein, RG, 1980b. The interpretation of mammalian faunas from stone age archaeological sites, with special reference to sites in the southern Cape Province, South Africa. In Behrensmeyer, AK, & Hill, A, (eds) *Fossils in the making; 223–246*. Chicago: University of Chicago Press.

Klein, RG, 1984a. Later Stone Age faunal samples from Heuningsneskrans Shelter (Transvaal) and Leopard's Hill Cave (Zambia). *South African Archaeological Bulletin* 39:109–116.

Klein, RG, 1984b. The large mammals of southern Africa: Late Pliocene to Recent. In Klein, RG, (ed) *Southern African prehistory and Paleoenvironments*; 107–146. Rotterdam: AA Balkema.

Klein, RG, 1992. The archaeology of modern human origins. *Evolutionary Anthropology* 1(1):5–14.

Klein, RG, 1999. *The Human Career*. Second edition. Chicago: University of Chicago Press.

Klein, RG, 2000. Archaeology and the evolution of human behavior. *Evolutionary Anthropology* 9(1):17–36.

Klein, RG, & Cruz-Uribe, K. 1984. *The analysis of animal bones from archaeological sites*. Chicago: University of Chicago Press.

Klein, RG, & Cruz-Uribe, K, & Beaumont, PB, 1991. Environmental, ecological, and palaeoanthropological implications of the late Pleistocene mammalian fauna from Equus Cave, northern Cape Province, South Africa. *Quaternary Research* 36:94–110.

Kleindienst, MR, 1967. Questions of terminology in regard to the study of Stone Age Industries in eastern Africa: 'cultural stratigraphic unit'. In Bishop, WW, & Clark, JD, (eds) *Background to evolution in Africa*; 821–860. Chicago: University of Chicago Press.

Knight, C, 1991. *Blood relations: menstruation and the origins of culture*. London: Yale University Press.

Knight, C, Power, C, & Watts, I, 1995. The human symbolic revolution: a Darwinian account. *Cambridge Archaeological Journal* 5(1):75–114.

Knight, J, 1991. Vein quartz. *Lithics* 12:37–56.

Kuman, K, Inbar, M, & Clarke, RJ, 1999. Palaeoenvironments and cultural sequence of the Florisbad Middle Stone Age hominid site, South Africa. *Journal of Archaeological Science* 26:1409–1425.

Lanfranchi, F, 1986. *Les industries préhistoriques congolaises dans le context du quaternaire récent*. INQUA Dakar symposium. Changements globaux en Afrique: 247–249.

Lanfranchi, R, 1997. Une industrie MSA de stone-line en forêt dense: le site de Mokeko (Congo). In Pwiti, G, Soper, R, (eds) *Aspects of African Archaeology*: 165–175. Harare: University of Zimbabwe Publications.

Larsson, L, 1996. The Middle Stone Age of Zimbabwe: some aspects of former research. In Pwiti, G, and Soper, R, (eds) *Aspects of African Archaeology*; 201–206. Harare: University of Zimbabwe Publications.

Leakey, MD, 1971. *Olduvai Gorge, volume 3, excavations in Beds I and II, 1960–1963*. Cambridge: Cambridge University Press.

Lee, RB, 1979. *The !Kung San: men, women and work in a foraging society*. Cambridge: Cambridge University Press.

Lee, RB, & Daly, R, 1999. *The Cambridge encyclopedia of hunters and gatherers*. Cambridge: Cambridge University Press.

Leuschner, DC, & Sirocko, F, 2000. The low-latitude monsoon climate during Dansgaard-Oeschger cycles and Heinrich events. *Quaternary Science Reviews* 19:243–254.

Levi-Scala, I, 1996. *A study of macroscopic polish on flint implements*. Oxford: British Archaeological Reports International Series 629.

Lieberman, DE 1993. The rise and fall of seasonal mobility among hunter-gatherers: the case of the southern Levant. *Current Anthropology* 34:599–631.

Lieberman, DE, 1998. Neandertal and early modern human mobility patterns: Comparing archaeological and anatomical evidence. In Akazawa, T, Aoki, K & Bar-Yosef, O, (eds) *Neandertals and modern humans in Western Asia*; 263–275. New York: Plenum.

Lieberman, DE, & Shea, JJ 1994. Behavioral differences between archaic and modern humans in the Levantine Mousterian. *American Anthropologist* 96:300–332.

Livingstone, DA, 1971. A 22,000-year pollen record from the plateau of Zambia. *Limnology and Oceanography* 16(2):349–356.

Mäckel, R, 1974. Dambos: a study in morphodynamic activity on the plateau regions of Zambia. *Catena* 1:327–366.

Macrae, FB, 1926. The Stone Age in Northern Rhodesia. *NADA* 1(4).

Madella, M, 2000. Morphological analysis of phytoliths: a botanical tools for the interpretation of archaeological and geological sediments from Eurasia. Unpublished PhD thesis: University of Cambridge.

Madella, M, Powers-Jones, A, & Jones, MK, 1998. A simple method of extraction of opal phytoliths from sediments using a non-toxic heavy liquid. *Journal of Archaeological Science* 25:801–803.

Madella, M, Hovers, E, Jones, M, Goldberg, P, & Goren, Y, (submitted). Plant exploitation in Amud Cave (Israel): a case for Middle Palaeolithic broad spectrum economy. *Journal of Archaeological Science*.

Maley, J, 1996. The African rainforest – main characteristics of changes in vegetation and climate from the Upper Cretaceous to the Quaternary. In Alexander, IJ, Swaine, MD, & Watlings, R, (eds) Essays on the ecology of the Guinea-Congo rain forest. *Proceedings Royal Society of Edinburgh* 104B:31–73.

Maley, J, & Brenac, P, 1998. Vegetation dynamics, palaeoenvironments and climatic changes in the forests of western Cameroon during the last 28,000 years B.P. *Review of Paleobotany and Palynology* 1998:157–187. De Maret, P, 1990. Phases and facies in the archaeology of Central Africa. In Robertshaw, P, (ed) *A History of African Archaeology*; 109–134. London: James Curry.

Marret, F, Scourse, J, Jansen, JHF & Schneider, R, 1999. Climate and palaeoceano-graphic changes in west Central Africa during the last deglaciation: palynological investigation. *Comptes rendus de l'academie des sciences serie II fascicule A-sciences de la terre et des planetes* 329(10):721–726.

Martinson, DG, Pisias, NG, Hays, JD, Imbrie, J, Moore, TC & Shackleton, NJ, 1987. Age dating and the orbital theory of the Ice Ages: development of a high resolution 0 to 300,000–year chronostratigraphy. *Quaternary Research* 27:1–29.

McBrearty, S, 1987. Une evaluation du Sangoen: son âge, son environment et son rapport avec l'origine de l'Homme sapiens. *L'Anthropologie* 91;127–140.

McBrearty, S, 1988. The Sangoan-Lupemban and Middle Stone Age sequence at the Muguruk site, western Kenya. *World Archaeology* 19(3):388–420.

McBrearty, S, 1999. The archaeology of the Kapthurin formation. In Andrews, P & Banham, P, (eds) *Late cenozoic environments and hominid evolution: a tribute to Bill Bishop*; 143–156. London: Geological Society.

McBrearty, S, in press. The Middle Pleistocene of East Africa. In Barham, L, & Robson-Brown, K, (eds) *Human roots: Africa and Asia in the Middle Pleistocene*. Bristol: Western Academic and Specialist Press.

McBrearty, S, Bishop, LC, & Kingston, JD, 1996. Variability in traces of Middle Pleistocene hominid behaviour in the Kapthurian Formation, Baringo, Kenya. *Journal of Human Evolution* 30: 563–580.

McBrearty, S, & Brooks, AS, 2000. The revolution that wasn't: a new interpretation of the origin of modern human behavior. *Journal of Human Evolution* 39:453–563.

McCown, TD & Keith, A, 1939. *The Stone Age of Mount Carmel II: The fossil human remains from the Levalloiso-Mousterian*. Oxford: Clarendon Press.

McCrossin, ML, 1992. Human molars from later Pleistocene deposits of Witkrans Cave, Gaap Escarpment, Kalahari margin. *Human Evolution* 7:1–10.

McNabb, J, & Ashton, N, 1995. Thoughtful flakers. *Cambridge Archaeological Journal* 5:289–301.

McPherron, SP, 2000. Handaxes as a measure of the mental capabilities of early hominids. *Journal of Archaeological Science* 27:655–663.

Mehlman, M, 1989. *Later Quaternary archaeological sequences in northern Tanzania*. PhD thesis, University of Illinois, Urbana. Ann Arbor: University Microfilms International.

Mellars, P, 1996. *The Neanderthal legacy*. Princeton: Princeton University Press.

Menaut, J-C, 1983. The vegetation of African savannas. In Bourlière, F, (ed) *Ecosystems of the world 13: tropical savannas*; 109–149. New York: Elsevier.

Mercader, J & Marti, R, 1999a. Archaeology in the tropical forest of Banyang-Mbo, southwest Cameroon. *Nyame Akuma* 52:17–24.

Mercader, J, & Marti, R, 1999b. Middle Stone Age sites in the tropical forests of Equatorial Guinea. *Nyame Akuma* 51:14–21.

Mercader, J, Runge, F, Vrydaghs, L, Doutrelepont, H, & Ewange, CEN, & Juan-Tressaras, J, 2000. Phytoliths from archaeological sites in the tropical forest of Ituri, Democratic Republic of Congo. *Quaternary Research* 54:102–112.

Miller, GH, & Beaumont, PB, 1989. Dating the Middle Stone Age at Border Cave, South Africa by the epimerization of isoleucine in ostrich egg shell. *Geological Society of America, Abstracts with Programs* 21, A235.

Miller, GH, Beaumont, PB, Brooks, AS, Deacon, HJ, Hare, PE, & Jull, AJT, 1999. *Quaternary Science Review* 18:1537–1548.

Miller, SF, 1969. *The Nachikufan industries of the Later Stone Age in Zambia*. University of California, Berkeley, PhD. Ann Arbor: University Microfilms International.

Miller, SF, 1971. The age of Nachikufan industries in Zambia. *The South African Archaeological Bulletin* 26:143–146.

Miller, SF, 1988. Patterns of environment utilization by late prehistoric cultures in the southern Congo basin. In Bower, J, & Lubell, D, (eds) *Prehistoric cultures and environments in the Late Quaternary of Africa*; 127–144. Oxford: BAR International Series 405.

Milo, R, 1998. Evidence for hominid predation at Klasies River Mouth, South Africa, and its implications for the behaviour of early modern humans. *Journal of Archaeological Science* 25:99–133.

Mitchell, PJ, 1994. Understanding the MSA/LSA transition: the pre-20000BP assemblages from new excavations at Sehonghong rock shelter, Lesotho. *Southern African Field Archaeology* 3(1):15–25.

Mitchell, PJ, 1997. Holocene Later Stone Age hunter-gatherers south of the Limpopo river, Ca. 10,000–2000BP. *Journal of World Prehistory* 11(4):359–424.

Mithen, S, 1990. *Thoughtful foragers, a study of prehistoric decision making*. Cambridge: Cambridge University Press.

Mithen, S, 1994. Technology and society during the Middle Pleistocene: hominid group size, social learning and industrial variability. *Cambridge Archaeological Journal* 4:3–32.

Mithen, S, 1996. Social learning and cultural tradition: interpreting early Palaeolithic technology. In Steele, J, & Shennan, S, (eds) *The archaeology of human ancestry: power, sex and tradition*; 207–229. London: Routledge.

Mithen, S, 1996a. Social learning and cultural tradition: interpreting early Palaeolithic technology. In Steele, J, & Shennan, S, (eds) *The archaeology of human ancestry: power, sex and tradition*; 207–229. London: Routledge.

Mithen, S, 1996b. *The prehistory of the mind*. London: Thames & Hudson.

Musonda, FB, 1984. Late Pleistocene and Holocene microlithic industries from the Lunsemfwa Basin, Zambia. *South African Archaeological Bulletin* 39:24–36.

Musonda, FB, 1987. The significance of pottery in Zambian Later Stone Age contexts. *African Archaeological Review* Vol 5:147–158.

Nelson, MC, 1991. The study of technological organization. In Schiffer, M, (ed), *Archaeological Method and Theory*; 57–100. Tucson:University of Arizona Press.

Newcomer, MH, 1974. Study and replication of bone tools from Ksar Akil (Lebanon) *World Archaeology* 6(2):138–153.

Noten, F, van 1982. *The archaeology of central Africa*. Graz: Akademische, Druck und Verlagsantatt.

O'Connor, PW, & Thomas, DSG, 1999. The timing and environmental significance of Late Quaternary linear dune development in western Zambia. *Quaternary Research* 52:44–55.

Olsen, SL, 1984. Analytical approaches to the manufacture and use of bone artifacts in prehistory. PhD Thesis, Institute of Archaeology, University of London.

Opperman, H, 1990. A 22,000 year-old Middle Stone Age camp site with plant food remains from the north-eastern Cape. *South African Archaeological Bulletin* 45:93–99.

Opperman, H, 1996. Excavation of a Later Stone Age deposit in Strathalan Cave A, Maclear District, northeastern Cape, South Africa. In Pwiti, G, & Soper, R, (eds); 335–342. Harare: University of Zimbabwe Press.

Partridge, TC, Demenocol, PB, Lorentz, SA, Paiker, MJ & Vogel, JC, 1997. Orbital forcing of climate over South Africa: a 200,000 year rainfall record from the Pretoria Saltpan. *Quaternary Science Review* 16:1125–1133.

Pearsall, DM, 2000. *Paleoethnobotany – a handbook of procedures* (2nd ed). San Diego: Academic Press.

Pearson, OM, 1997. *Postcranial morphology and the origin of modern humans*. PhD thesis, State University of New York at Stony Brook.

Pearson, OM, 2000. Activity, climate, and postcranial robusticity: Implications for modern human origins and scenarios of adaptive change. *Current Anthropology* 41:569–607.

Pearson, OM, & Grine, FE, 1996. Morphology of the Border Cave hominid ulna and humerus. *South African Journal of Science* 92:231–236.

Pearson, OM & Grine, FE, 1997. Re-analysis of the hominid radii from Cave of Hearths and Klasies River Mouth, South Africa. *Journal of Human Evolution* 32:577–592.

Peer, P, van 1992. *The Levallois reduction strategy*. Madison, Wisconsin: Prehistory Press.

Péringuey, L, 1911. Stone Ages of South Africa. *Annals of the South African Museum* 3:1–211.

Petit, JR, Jouzel, J, Raynaud, D, Barkov, NI, Barnola, J-M, Basile, I, Benders, M, Chappellaz, J, Davis, M, Delaygue, G, Delmotte, M, Kotlyakov, VM, Legrand, M, Lipenkov, VY, Lorius, C, Pépin, L, Ritz, C, Saltzman, E, & Stievenard, M, 1999. Climate and atmospheric history of the past 420,000 years from the Vostok ice core, Antarctica. *Nature* 399:429–436.

Phillipson, DW, 1976. *The prehistory of eastern Zambia*. Nairobi: British Institute in Eastern Africa.

Phillipson, DW, 1993. *African archaeology* 2nd ed. Cambridge: Cambridge University Press.

Phillipson, L, 1978. *The Stone-Age archaeology of the Upper Zambezi Valley*. Memoir no.7 of the British Institute in Eastern Africa, Nairobi.

Piperno, DR, 1998. Paleoethnobotany in the neotropics form the macrofossils: New insights into ancient plant use and agricultural origins in the tropical forest. *Journal of World Prehistory* 12:393–449.

Plug, I, 1985. The faunal remains from two Iron Age sites, Rooikrans and Rhenosterkloof, central Transvaal. *Annals of the Cape Provincial Museums* (Human Sciences) 1:201–210.

Potts, R, 1996. Evolution and climate variability. *Science* 273:922–923.

Potts, R, in press. In Barham, L, & Robson-Brown, K, (eds) *Human roots: Africa and Asia in the Middle Pleistocene*. Bristol: Western Academic and Specialist Press.

Potts, R, 1998. Environmental hypotheses of hominin evolution. *Yearbook of Physical Anthropology* 41:93–136.

Potts, R, & Shipman, P, 1981. Cutmarks made by stone tools on bones from Olduvai Gorge, Tanzania. *Nature* 291:577–580.

Power, C, & Aiello, L, 1997. Female proto-symbolic strategies. In Hager, LD, (ed) *Women in Human Evolution*; 153–171.

Power, C, & Watts, I, 1996. Female strategies and collective behaviour: the archaeology of earliest Homo sapiens. In Steele, J, & Shennan, S, (eds) *The archaeology of human ancestry: power, sex and tradition*; 306–330. London: Routledge.

Prell, WL, & Kutzbach, JE, 1987. Monsoon variability over the past 150,000 years. *Journal of Geophysical Research* 92:8411–8425.

Prigogine, A, 1988. Speciation pattern of birds in the Central African forest refugia and their relationship with other refugia. *Acta XIX Congressus Internationalis Ornithologici*, vol II:144–157. Ottawa: University of Ottawa Press.

Prins, HHT, and Reitsma, JM, 1989. Mammalian biomass in an African equatorial rain forest. *Journal of African Ecology* 58:851–861.

Pycraft, WP, Smith, GE, Yearsley, M, Carter, JT, Smith, RA, Hopwood, T, Bate, DMA & Swinton, WE, 1928. *Rhodesian man and associated remains*. London: The British Museum.

Retallack, GJ, 1990. *Soils of the past: an introduction to paleopedology.* Boston: Unwin Hyman.

Rightmire, GP, 1984. *Homo sapiens* in Sub-Saharan Africa. In Smith, FH & Spencer, F, (eds) *The origins of modern humans: a world survey of the fossil evidence;* 295–325. New York: Alan R Liss.

Rightmire, GP, 1996. The human cranium from Bodo, Ethopia: evidence for speciation in the Middle Pleistocene? *Journal of Human Evolution* 31:21–39.

Rightmire, GP & Deacon, HJ, 1991. Comparative studies of late Pleistocene human remains from Klasies River Mouth, South Africa. *Journal of Human Evolution* 20: 131–156.

Robbins, LH, 1999. Direct dating of worked ostrich eggshell in the Kalahari. *Nyame Akuma* 52:11–16.

Robertshaw, P, 1990. A history of African archaeology: an introduction. In Robertshaw, P, (ed) *A history of African archaeology;* 3–12. London: James Curry.

Ruff, CB, 1987. Sexual dimorphism in human lower limb bone structure: relationship to subsistence strategy and sexual division of labor. *Journal of Human Evolution* 16:391–416.

Ruff, CB, 1994. Morphological adaptation to climate in modern and fossil hominids. *Yearbook of Physical Anthropology* 37:65–107.

Ruff, CB, 1995. Biomechanics of the hip and birth in early *Homo. American Journal of Physical Anthropology* 98:527–574.

Ruff, CB, Trinkaus, E, Walker, A, & Larsen, CS, 1993. Postcranial robusticity in *Homo I: Temporal trends and mechanical interpretation.* American Journal of Physical Anthropology 91:21–53.

Runge, F, 1995. Potential of opal phytoliths for use in paleoecological reconstruction in the humid tropics of Africa. *Zeitschrift für geomorphologie, NF,* supplement-bd 99:53–63.

Runge, F, 1996. Opal phytoliths in Pflanzen aus dem humiden und semi-ariden Osten Afrikas und ihre Bedeutung für die Klima-und Vegetationgeschicte. *Botanishce Jarbücher für Systematik, Pflanzen geschicte un Pflanzengeographie* 118 (3):303–363.

Runge, F, & Runge, J, 1997. Opal phytoliths in East African plants and soils. In Pinilla, A, Juan-Tresseras, J, & Machado, JM, (eds) *Estados actual de los estudios de los fitolitos en suelos y plantas;* 71–82. Madrid: Consejo Superior de Investigationes Cientifica, Monografias 4.

Sackett, JR, 1982. Approaches to style in lithic archaeology. *Journal of Anthropological Archaeology* 1:59–112.

Sackett, JR, 1990. Style and ethnicity in archaeology: the case for isochrestism. In Conkey, M, & Hastorf, C, (eds), *The uses of style in archaeology;* 32–43. Cambridge: Cambridge University Press.

Sampson CG, 1968. *The Middle Stone Age industries of the Orange river scheme area.* National Museum, Bloemfontein memoir no. 4.

Sampson, CG, 1974. *The Stone Age archaeology of southern Africa.* New York: Academic Press.

Sarnthein, M, 1978. Sand deserts during glacial maximum and climatic optima. *Nature* 272:43–46.

Savage, CD, 1983. *Identifying industries in south central Africa: the Zambian Wilton example.* Unpublished PhD dissertation, University of California, Berkeley.

Schwarcz, H, in press. Chronometric dating of the Middle Pleistocene. In Barham, L, & Robson-Brown, K, (eds), *Human roots: Africa and Asia in the Middle Pleistocene.* Bristol: Western Academic and Specialist Press.

Scott, GR, & Turner, CG II, 1997. *The anthropology of modern human teeth.* Cambridge: Cambridge University Press.

Shackelton, NJ, 1982. Stratigraphy and chronology of the KRM deposits: oxygen isotope evidence. In Singer, R, & Wymer, J, *The Middle Stone Age at Klasies River Mouth in South Africa;* 194–199. Chicago: University of Chicago Press.

Sheppard, PJ, & Kleindienst, MR, 1996. Technological change in the Earlier and Middle Stone Age of KalamboFalls (Zambia). *African Archaeological Review* 13(3): 171–196.

Silberbauer, GB, 1981. *Hunter and habitat in the central Kalahari desert.* Cambridge: Cambridge University Press.

Sillen, A, & Morris, AG, 1996. Diagenesis of bone from Border Cave: implications for the age of the Border Cave hominids. *Journal of Human Evolution* 31:499–506.

Simms, MJ, 1994. Emplacement and preservation of vertebrates in caves and fissures. *Zoological Journal of the Linnean Society* 112:261–283.

Singer, R, & Wymer, J, 1982. *The Middle Stone Age at Klasies River Mouth in South Africa.* Chicago: University of Chicago Press.

Skinner, JH, & Smithers, RHN, 1990. *The mammals of the southern African subregion.* 2nd edn. Pretoria: University of Pretoria.

Smith, BH, 1991. Standard of human tooth formation and dental age assessment. In Kelly, MA, & Larsen, CS, (eds) *Advances in dental anthropology;* 143–168. New York: Wiley-Liss.

Smithers, RHN, 1966. *The mammals of Rhodesia, Zambia and Malawi.* London: Collins.

Stager, JC, 1988. Environmental changes at Lake Cheshi, Zambia since 40,000 years BP. *Quaternary Research* 29:54–65.

Stokes, S, 1993. Optical dating of sediment samples from Bir Tarfawi and Bir Sahara East: an initial report. In Wendorf, F, Schild, R, & Close, AE *Egypt during the Last Interglacial: the Middle Palaeolithic of Bir Tarfawi and Bir Sahara East;* 229–233. New York: Plenum.

Stokes, S, Haynes, G, Thomas, DSG, Horrocks, JL, Higginson, M, Malita, M, 1998. Punctuated aridity in southern Africa during the last glacial cycle: the chronology of linear dune construction in the northeastern Kalahari. *Palaeogeography, Palaeoclimatology, Palaeoecology* 137:305–332.

Street-Perrot, FA, 1994. Palaeo-perspectives: changes in terrestrial ecosystems. *Ambio* 23(1):37–43.

Stringer, CB, 1986. An archaic character in the Broken Hill innominate E719. *American Journal of Physical Anthropology* 71:115–120.

Stringer, CB, 1994. Out of Africa – a personal history. In Nitecki, MH, & Nitecki, DV, *Origins of anatomically modern humans;* 149–172. New York: Plenum.

Stringer, CB, 1996. Current issues in modern human origins. In Meikle, WE, Howell, FC, & Jablonski, NG, (eds), *Contemporary issues in human evolution;* 115–134. San Francisco: California Academy of Sciences.

Stringer, CB, Barton, RNE, Currant, AP, Finlayson, JC, Goldberg, P, Macphail, R, & Pettitt, PB, 1999. Gibraltar Palaeolithic revisited: new excavations at Gorham's and Vanguard Caves. In Davies, W, & Charles, R, (eds), *Dorothy Garrod and the progress of the Palaeolithic;* 84–96. Oxford: Oxbow Books.

Stringer, CB, Hublin, J-J, & Vandermeersch, B, 1984. The origin of anatomically modern humans in Western Europe. In Smith, FH, & Spencer, F, (eds) *The origins of modern humans: a world survey of the fossil evidence;* 51–135. New York: Alan R Liss.

Stringer, CB, & Andrews, P, 1988. Genetic and fossil evidence for the origin of modern humans. *Science* 239:1263–1268.

Stringer, C, & Gamble, C, 1993. *In search of the Neanderthals.* London: Thames & Hudson.

Surveyor-General 1998. *Republic of Zambia: vegetation and climate.* Scale 1: 250,000. Lusaka: Government of the Republic of Zambia.

Talbot, M, & Johannessen, T, 1992. A high resolution palaeoclimatic record for the last 27,500 years in tropical West Africa from the carbon and nitrogen isotopic composition of lacustrine organic matter. *Earth and Planetary Science Letters* 110:23–37.

Talma, AS, & Vogel, JC, 1993. A simplified approach to calibrating C14 dates. *Radiocarbon* 35(2):317–322.

Templeton, AR, 1992. Human origins and analysis of mitochondrial DNA sequences. *Science* 255:737.

Thackeray, AI, 1989. Changing fashions in the Middle Stone Age: the stone artefact sequence from Klasies River Mouth main site, South Africa. *The African Archaeological Review* 7:33–58.

Thackeray, AI, 1992. The Middle Stone Age south of the Limpopo. *Journal of World Prehistory* 6:385–440.

Thackeray, AI, 2000. Middle Stone Age artefacts from the 1993 and 1995 excavations of Die Kelders Cave 1, South Africa. *Journal of Human Evolution* 38(1)147–168.

Thackeray, AI, & Kelly, AJ, 1988. A technological and typological analysis of Middle Stone Age assemblages antecedent to the Howieson's Poort at Klasies River main site. *South African Archaeological Bulletin* 43:15–26.

Thackeray, JF, 1995. Exploring ungulate diversity, biomass, and climate in modern and past environments. In Vrba, ES, & Partridge, TC, (eds) *Paleoclimate and evolution, with emphasis on human origins;* 479–482. London: Yale University Press.

Thieme, JG, & Johnson, RL, 1981. *Geological map, Republic of Zambia 1:1.000.000.* Lusaka: Geological Survey Department, Zambia Ordnance Survey.

Thomas, DSG, & Goudie, AS, 1984. Ancient ergs of the southern hemisphere. In Vogel, JC, (ed) *Late Cainozoic palaeoclimates of the southern hemisphere*; 407–418. Rotterdam: AA Balkema.

Thomas, DSG, O'Connor, PW, Bateman, MD, Shaw, PA, Stokes, S, Nash, DJ, 2000. Dune activity as a record of Late Quaternary aridity in the northern Kalahari: new evidence from northern Namibia interpreted in the context of regional arid and humid chronologies. *Palaeogeography, Palaeoclimatology, and Palaeoecology* 156:243–259.

Thomas, MF, 1994. *Geomorphology in the tropics.* Chichester: Wiley.

Thomas, MF, 1999. Evidence for high energy landforming events on the central African plateau: eastern province, Zambia. *Zeitschrift für geomorphologie* 43(3):273–297.

Tobias, PV, 1971. Human skeletal remains from the Cave of Hearths, Makapansgat, Northern Transvaal. *American Journal of Physical Anthropology* 34:335–368.

Torrence, R, 1989. *Time, energy and stone tools.* Cambridge: Cambridge University Press.

Trapnell, CG, & Clothier, JN, 1996. *The soils, vegetation and traditional agriculture. Vol 1 central and western Zambia (ecological survey 1932–1936).* Bristol: Redcliffe Press Ltd.

Trigger, BG, 1990. A history of African archaeology in world perspective. In Robertshaw, P, (ed) *A history of African archaeology*; 309–319. London: James Curry.

Trigger, BG, 1994. *A history of archaeological thought.* Cambridge: Cambridge University Press.

Trinkaus, E, 1976. The evolution of the hominid femoral diaphysis during the Upper Pleistocene in Europe and the Near East. *Zeitschrift für Morphologie und Anthropologie* 67:291–319.

Trinkaus, E, 1981. Neandertal limb proportions and cold adaptation. In Stringer, CB, (ed) *Aspects of Human Evolution*; 187–224. London: Taylor and Francis.

Trinkaus, E, 1983. *The Shanidar Neandertals.* New York: Academic Press.

Trinkaus, E, 1993. A note on the KNM-ER 999 hominid femur. *Journal of Human Evolution* 24:493–504.

Trinkaus E, & Churchill, SE, 1988. Neandertal radial tuberosity orientation. *American Journal of Physical Anthropology* 75:15–21.

Trinkaus E, & Hilton, CE, 1996. Neandertal pedal proximity phalanges: diaphyseal loading patterns. *Journal of Human Evolution* 30:399–425.

Trinkaus, E, & Ruff, CB, 1999. Diaphyseal cross-sectional geometry of Near Eastern Middle Paleolithic humans: the femur. *Journal of Archaeological Science* 26:409–424.

Trinkaus, E, 1992. Morphological contrasts between the Near Eastern Qafzeh-Skhul and late archaic human samples: grounds for a behavioral difference? In Akazawa, T, Aoki, K, & Kimura, T, (eds) *The evolution and dispersal of modern humans in Asia*; 277–294. Tokyo: Hokusen-sha Publishing Co.

Trinkaus, E, Ruff, CB, Churchill, SE, & Vandermeersch, B, 1998. Locomotion and body proportions of the Saint-Césaire 1 Châtelperronian Neandertal. *Proceedings of the National Academy of Science* (USA) 95:5636–5840.

Trinkaus, E, Churchill, SE, Ruff, CB, & Vandermeersch, B, 1999. Long bone shaft robusticity and body proportions of the Saint-Césaire 1 Châtelperronian Neanderthal. *Journal of Archaeological Science* 26:753–773.

Tucker, ME, & Wright, VP, 1990. *Carbonate sedimentology.* Oxford: Blackwell Scientific Publications.

Twiss, PC, 1992. Predicted world distribution of C_3 and C_4 grass phytoliths. In Rapp, G, Jr, & Mulholland, SC (eds) *Phytolith systematics – emerging issues*; 113–128. New York: Plenum.

Tyson, PD, 1999. Late-Quaternary and Holocene palaeoclimates of southern Africa: a synthesis. *South African Journal of Geology* 102(4):335–349.

Valladas, H, 1992. Thermoluminescence dating of flint. *Quaternary Science Reviews* 11:1–5.

Vandermeersch, B, 1981. *Les hommes fossiles de Qafzeh (Israël).* Paris: CNRS.

Vermeersch, PM, Paulissen, E, Stokes, S, Charlier, C, Van Peer, P, Stringer, C, & Lindsay, W, 1998. A Middle Palaeolithic burial of a modern human at Taramsa Hill, Egypt. *Antiquity* 72:475–484.

Voigt, EA, 1973. Faunal remains from the Iron Age sites of Matope Court, Namichumbe and Chikuma, southern Malawi. *Malawi Government Department of Antiquities Publication* 13:135–167.

Voigt, EA, 1983. Mapungubwe: an archaeozoological interpretation of an Iron Age Community. *Transvaal Museum Monograph* 11: 1–203.

Volman, TP, 1984. Early prehistory of southern Africa. In Klein, RG, (ed) *Southern African prehistory and paleoenvironments*; 169–220. Rotterdam: AA Balkema.

Volman, TP, nd. A study in scarlet: red ochre and economy in the Stone Age. Unpublished manuscript.

Vrba, ES, 1980. The significance of bovid remains as an indicator of environment and predation patterns. In Behrensmeyer, AK, & Hill, AP, (eds) *Fossils in the making*; 247–272. Chicago: University of Chicago Press.

Wadley, L, 1993. The Pleistocene Later Stone Age south of the Limpopo River. *Journal of World Prehistory* 7:243–296.

Wadley, L, 1996. The Robberg industry of Rose Cottage Cave, eastern Free State: the technology, spatial patterns and environment. *South African Archaeological Bulletin* 51:64–74.

Walker, NJ, 1980. Later Stone Age research in the Matopos. *South African Archaeological Bulletin* 35:19–24.

Walker, NJ, 1990. Zimbabwe at 18 000 BP. In Gamble, C, & Soffer, O, (eds), *The world at 18 000 BP, volume two, low latitudes*; 206–213. London: Unwin Hyman.

Walker, N, 1994. Later Stone Age funerary practice in the Matopos, Zimbabwe: a contribution to understanding prehistoric death rites in southern Africa. *Southern African Field Archaeology* 3(2): 94–102.

Walker, NJ, 1995. *Late Pleistocene and Holocene hunter-gatherers of the Matopos.* Uppsala: Societas Archaeologia Upsaliensis, Studies in African Archaeology 10.

Walter, H, 1971. *Ecology of tropical and subtropical vegetation.* Edinburgh: Oliver & Boyd.

Walter, H, 1973. *Vegetation of the earth: in relation to climate and eco-physiological conditions.* London: English Universities Press Ltd.

Wandsnides, LA, 1997. The roasted and the boiled: food consumption and heat treatment with special emphasis on pit-hearth cooking. *Journal of Anthropological Archaeology* 16(1):1–48.

Watson, A, Price Williams, D, & Goudie, AS, 1984. The palaeo-environmental interpretation of colluvial sediments and paleosols of the late Pleistocene hypothermal in southern Africa. *Palaeogeography, Palaeoclimatology, Palaeoecology* 45:225–249.

Wayland, EJ, 1929. African pluvial periods. *Nature* 123:31–33.

Wayland, EJ, & Smith, R, 1923. Some primitive stone tools from Uganda. *Geological Survey of Uganda, Entebbe, Occasional Paper no. 1.*

Weidenreich, F, 1941. The extremity bones of *Sinanthropus pekinensis. Paleontologia Sinica*, new series D 5:1–150.

Weissner, P, 1985. Style or isochrestic variation? A reply to Sackett. *American Antiquity* 50(1): 160–166.

Wenban-Smith, FF, 1998. Clactonian and Acheulian industries in Britain: their chronology and significance reconsidered. In Ashton, N, Healy, F, Pettit, P, (eds) *Stone Age archaeology: essays in honour of John Wymer*; 90–97. Oxford: Oxbow Monograph 102.

Werger, MJA, (ed) 1978. *Biogeography and ecology of southern Africa.* The Hague: Dr W Junk bv Publishers.

White, F, 1983. *The vegetation of Africa.* Paris: UNESCO.

Wendorf, F, Laury, L, Albritton, CC, Schild, R, Haynes, CV, Damon, PE, Shafquillah, M, & Scarborough, R, 1975. Dates for the Middle Stone Age in East Africa. *Science* 187:740–742.

Wendt, WE, 1976. Art mobilier from the Apollo 11 Cave, South West Africa: Africa's oldest dated works of art. *South African Archaeological Bulletin* 31:5–11.

Werger, MJA, (ed) 1978. *Biogeography and ecology of southern Africa.* The Hague: Dr W Junk bv Publishers.

White, JP, 1968. Fabricators, outils écailles or scalar cores? *Mankind* 6:658–666.

White, MJ, 1998. On the significance of Acheulean biface variability in southern Britain. *Proceedings of the Prehistoric Society* 64:15–44.

White, R, 1989. Production complexity and standardization in early Aurignacian bead and pendant manufacture: evolutionary implication. In Mellars, PA, & Stringer, C, (eds), *The human revolution*; 360–399. Edinburgh: Edinburgh University Press.

White, TD, 1987. Cannibals at Klasies? *Sagittarius* 2:6–9.

Willoughby, P, 1985. Spheroids and battered stones in the African Early Stone Age. *World Archaeology* 17(1):44–60.

Willoughby, PR, 1993. The Middle Stone Age in East Africa and modern human origins. *African Archaeological Review* 11: 3–21.Weidenreich, F, 1941. The extremity bones of *Sinanthropus pekinensis*. *Paleontologia Sinica*, new series D 5:1–150.

Winterhalder, B, & Smith, EA, (eds) 1981. *Hunter-gatherer foraging strategies: ethnographic and archaeological analyses*. Chicago: University of Chicago Press.

Wobst, HM, 1990. Afterword: minitime and megaspace in the Palaeolithic at 18k and otherwise. In Soffer, O, & Gamble, C, (eds) *The world at 18000BP, volume 1, high latitudes*; 331–343. London: Unwin Hyman.

Wurz, S, 1999. The Howiesons Poort backed artefacts from Klasies River: an argument for symbolic behaviour. *South African Archaeological Bulletin* 64:38–50.

Wynn, T, 1989. *The evolution of spatial competence*. Urbana: University of Illinois Press.

Wynn, T, 1993. Layers of thinking in tool behaviour. In Gibson, KR, & Ingold, T, (eds) *Tools, language and cognition in human evolution*; 389–406. Cambridge: Cambridge University Press.

Wynn, T, & Tierson, F, 1990. Regional comparison of the shapes of later Acheulian handaxes. *American Anthropologist* 92:73–84.

Yellen, JE, 1976. Settlement patterns of the !kung. In Lee, RB, & De Vore I, (eds) *Kalahari hunter-gatherers: studies of the !kung San and their neighbours*; 47–72. London: Harvard University Press.

Yellen, JE, 1986, Optimization and risk in human foraging strategies. *Journal of Human Evolution* 15:733–750.

Yellen, JE, Brooks, AS, Corneilsen, E, Mehlman, M, & Stewart, K, 1995. A Middle Stone Age worked bone industry from Katanda, Upper Semliki Valley, Zaire. *Science* 268:553–556.

Yellen, JE, 1996. Behavioural and taphonomic patterning at Katanda 9: a Middle Stone Age site, Kivu Province, Zaire. *Journal of Archaeological Science* 6:915–932.

Yellen, JE, 1998. Barbed bone points: tradition and continuity in Saharan and sub-Saharan Africa. *African Archaeological Review* 15(3):173–198.

Index